NUTRITION, OBESITY & EATING DISORDERS

Handbook & Resource Guide

FIRST EDITION

NUTRITION, OBESITY & EATING DISORDERS

Handbook & Resource Guide

GREY HOUSE PUBLISHING

Grey House Health & Wellness Guides

PUBLISHER: Leslie Mackenzie
EDITORIAL DIRECTOR: Laura Mars
MANAGING EDITOR & COMPOSITION: Stuart Paterson
PRODUCTION MANAGER: Kristen Hayes
MARKETING DIRECTOR: Jessica Moody
EDITORIAL ASSISTANT: Kathlyn Del Castillo

Grey House Publishing, Inc.
4919 Route 22
Amenia, NY 12501
518.789.8700
Fax: 845.373.6390
www.greyhouse.com
books@greyhouse.com

First edition published 2021

Publisher's Cataloging-In-Publication Data
(Prepared by The Donohue Group, Inc.)

Title: Nutrition, obesity & eating disorders handbook & resource guide.
Other Titles: Nutrition, obesity and eating disorders handbook and resource guide
Description: First edition. | Amenia, NY : Grey House Publishing, 2021. | Series: Grey House health & wellness guides ; [5] | Includes indexes.
Identifiers: ISBN 9781637000632
Subjects: LCSH: Nutrition—Handbooks, manuals, etc. | Obesity—Handbooks, manuals, etc. | Eating disorders—Handbooks, manuals, etc. | LCGFT: Reference works. | Handbooks and manuals.
Classification: LCC RA784 .N88 2021 | DDC 613.2—dc23

Table of Contents

Section One: Studies & Statistics About Nutrition, Obesity & Eating Disorders

Section Two: Conditions Directly Related to Nutrition

Section Three: Conditions Indirectly Related to Nutrition

Section Four: Appendix & Indexes

Publisher's Note

Grey House Publishing is pleased to announce *Nutrition, Obesity & Eating Disorders Handbook & Resource Guide*—the fourth volume in a health series that supports our long-standing consumer health titles on such topics as mental health, older Americans, chronic illness, pediatric disorders, and people with disabilities. This title follows *Dementia Handbook & Resource Guide* and *Cardiovascular Disease Handbook & Resource Guide* and *Autoimmune Diseases Handbook & Resource Guide*.

This work covers 11 conditions that are either directly caused, or affected, by the food that we eat, from allergies to ulcerative colitis, and seven conditions that are affected to varying degrees by our diet, like cancer, mental illness, and sleep disorders.

Nutrition, Obesity & Eating Disorders combines valuable, easy-to-understand educational information for consumers, and patients and their families, with official guidelines about good nutrition, healthy life styles and how to prevent and treatment related conditions. This new volume is arranged in the following sections:

Section One: Studies & Statistics About Nutrition, Obesity, & Eating Disorders

This robust, colorful section of 315 pages includes detailed reports, fact sheets, graphs and statistics from a number of sources, including the Centers for Disease Control and the National Institutes of Health. It begins with a detailed report on dietary guidelines, followed by various diet plans that are known to prevent or manage specific conditions and support a healthy lifestyle.

Following this general information are helpful facts and treatment plans about specific conditions related to nutrition issues that are covered in Section Two, including food allergies, type 2 diabetes, eating disorders, kidney disease, bone health, and obesity.

Section Two: Conditions Directly Related to Nutrition

This section includes 11 chapters, each covering a specific condition that has a direct relation to the foods that we eat from allergies to ulcerative colitis. Each chapter starts with a clear, concise description of the condition, followed by a variety of resources for patients, families, and caregivers, including Agencies & Associations, Libraries & Resource Centers, Foundations & Research Centers, Support Groups & Hotlines, Journals, and Digital Resources.

Section Three: Conditions Indirectly Related to Nutrition

This section includes seven conditions that have a nutritional element to them, although not as significant as is thought for the conditions in Section Two. These chapters do include a description of the condition and how nutrition plays a role, followed by resources — national associations and websites — so users know where to go for further information. A General Resources section is also included for easy reference.

Following that, users will find the following pieces of backmatter:

- **Glossary of Terms** lists major terms and concepts related to nutrition and eating disorders.
- **Entry Index** lists all directory entries alphabetically.
- **Geographic Index** organizes listings alphabetically by state.

The *Nutrition, Obesity & Eating Disorders Handbook & Resource Guide* is a necessary reference for public and academic libraries, as well as health care and senior center collections, providing information crucial to sufferers of conditions that are related to nutrition, their broader support network, caseworkers, social workers, and other health care providers.

Introduction

Healthy nutrition is critical to health and development at all ages, leading to improved overall health, stronger immune systems, safer pregnancy and childbirth, a lower risk of non-communicable diseases, and increased longevity, according to the World Health Organization. Healthy children learn better, adults are more productive, healthy nutrition prevents and improves certain disease, therefore decreasing the burden on the health system, and often promotes a feeling of well-being.

The goal of good nutrition is to consume a variety of healthy foods that support health. Knowing the food groups often learned in elementary school, reading about healthy diets, and talking with your doctor about prevention and management of health risks through diet is a good start. While malnutrition is often thought to be a condition found only outside the United States, it exists in all countries in a variety of forms. Undernutrition fosters being underweight and having deficiencies in sufficient vitamins and minerals, as often seen in individuals living in poverty. Eating too much of the wrong foods can cause obesity, and may be the result of not knowing, or not having access to, healthy food choices leading to poor nutrition. Diseases such as diabetes and wasting are all diet-related. Learning the role of food and making healthy choices contributes to a healthier life and may prevent or heal disease.

So much of today's social interaction revolves around eating, whether at home, at family or friends, or at a restaurant. When cooking at home, consider baking, sauteing or grilling, and adapting favorite recipes to be more health-friendly. Ask for help in selecting healthy menus and determining the best shopping strategies. Resources are readily available online, in the library, and from community health providers and organizations. When you shop for groceries, make a list and stick to it. Avoid the snack, cookie and candy aisles, and focus instead on fresh produce where available. When choosing a restaurant, look at menus to determine if offerings fit within your healthy eating plan.

If your diet is adequate in nutrition, nutritional supplements are usually not needed. In today's busy world, however, it's likely that you need to complement your diet with supplements, or choose fortified foods, to meet required nutritional needs. Vitamins will supplement nutrients that are lacking in your diet, or are necessary due to a medical condition. Talk to your healthcare provider before beginning any supplement regimen.

Adequate nutrition, appropriate physical activity and a healthy body weight are essential to good health and can also, according to the U.S. Department of Health and Human Services (HHS), help decrease your risk of developing serious health conditions. The scientific connection between food and health is well documented. Many conditions and diseases that are diagnosed in adults—such as heart disease, hypertension, stroke, high cholesterol, diabetes, and cancer—include nutrition, activity, and a healthy weight as important strategies in managing the conditions. Many Americans do not eat a healthy diet for a variety of reasons including lack of knowledge, economic factors, and accessibility to healthy choices. The vegetable and fruit intakes of average Americans do not meet government recommendations. Nearly 80 percent of Americans don't get the recommended amount of physical activity resulting in high rates of obesity—more than a third of U.S. adults are considered obese. Heart disease, stroke, and type 2 diabetes, which all have an obesity-related component, are responsible for increasing medical costs and are a leading cause of death in the U.S. Following a healthy eating plan, participating in regular activity and achieving and maintaining a healthy body weight is essential to good health.

The Dietary Guidelines for Americans are revised every five years by the U.S. Department of Health and Human Services (HHS) and the U.S. Department of Agriculture (USDA); they are available online, and on page 3 of this work. The dietary guidelines are aimed at helping all Americans, from policy makers to community members, consume a healthy, nutritionally adequate diet, as well as being the basis for Federal nutrition programs education materials. Physicians and registered clinical dieticians use these guidelines in determining a healthy eating plan for both healthy individuals and for those with various health conditions. Treatment of many chronic diseases will often include healthy eating or a specific eating plan to prevent or manage disease. Adopting the Dietary Guidelines for Americans as a basis for both personal interventions and prescribed interventions contributes to better health and management of chronic health conditions.

There are four guidelines that encourage healthy eating in each life stage:

- Follow a healthy eating plan during infancy, toddlerhood, childhood, adolescence, adulthood, pregnancy and lactation, and older adulthood. A well-balanced eating plan throughout the life span may prevent or reduce the potential for chronic illness.
- Choose a diet plan with nutrient-dense foods and beverages that takes into consideration personal preferences, cultural traditions and budget.
- Stay within calorie limits designed to maintain or achieve a healthy weight by focusing on vegetables, fruits, grains, dairy, protein foods, and oils (all nutrient dense foods).
- Limit food and beverages high in added sugars, saturated fat, sodium, and limiting alcoholic beverages.

Regardless of age or health status, achieving a healthy eating plan will require education, support, and often changes in how one eats. The guidelines present overall guidance, but asking for help from healthcare providers or community resources is recommended, and helpful.

Choosing and sticking to a healthy diet plan from infancy through old age is a good way to help achieve and maintain good health and reduce the risk of chronic diseases. Regardless of when you start, however, making changes in diet, activity, and achieving a healthy weight is important to making life-style improvements. This text provides invaluable information related to managing your health, preventing certain diseases, and managing both chronic and acute diseases you may have. It is always recommended to talk with your physician and a registered clinical dietician regarding your individual nutritional needs and plan.

SECTION ONE: STUDIES & STATISTICS ABOUT NUTRITION, OBESITY & EATING DISORDERS

This first section of *Nutrition, Obesity & Eating Disorders* includes the most current research on how nutrition relates to the featured health conditions, with data, nutritional information, and eating plans from the the U.S. Department of Agriculture and U.S. Department of Health and Human Services, The National Institutes of Health, The National Heart, Lung and Blood Institute, the Centers for Disease Control and Prevention, and more. Totaling more than 300 pages, Studies & Statistics comprises 12 detailed reports and summaries with easy to understand graphics. Colorful photos, graphs, charts, and maps help to visualize the data.

The large reports start with a detailed table of contents to help you maneuver through the information that each contains.

DGA | Dietary Guidelines for Americans

2020 - 2025

Make Every Bite Count With the *Dietary Guidelines*

DietaryGuidelines.gov

This publication may be viewed and downloaded from the internet at **DietaryGuidelines.gov.**

Suggested citation: U.S. Department of Agriculture and U.S. Department of Health and Human Services. *Dietary Guidelines for Americans, 2020-2025.* 9th Edition. December 2020. Available at **DietaryGuidelines.gov**.

December 2020

2020 - 2025

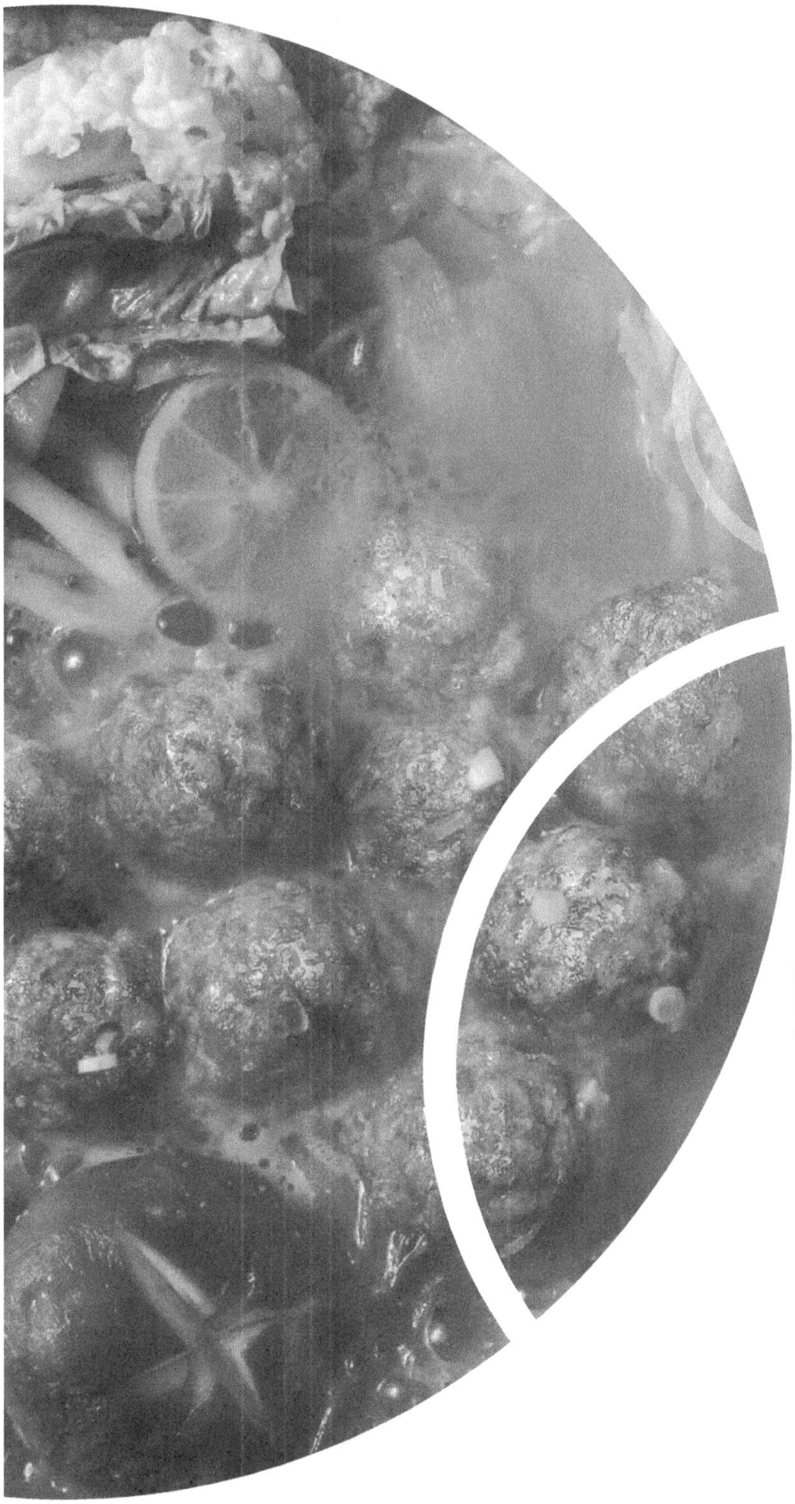

Make Every Bite Count With the *Dietary Guidelines*

Ninth Edition • DietaryGuidelines.gov

Table of Contents

List of Tables

List of Figures

Message From the Secretaries

We are pleased to present the *Dietary Guidelines for Americans, 2020-2025*. This edition marks the first time the Guidelines provide recommendations by life stage, from birth through older adulthood.

Each stage of life is distinct and has unique needs that affect health and disease risk. Early food preferences influence food and beverage choices later. And the science has evolved to focus on the importance of a healthy dietary pattern over time. The science also shows it's never too late to start and maintain a healthy dietary pattern, which can yield health benefits in the short term and cumulatively over years. This new edition of the *Dietary Guidelines* includes specific recommendations for all life stages, now including infants and toddlers, and pregnant and lactating women. We are excited this is the first edition to provide guidance for every life stage.

This edition of the *Dietary Guidelines* is grounded in robust scientific reviews of the current body of evidence on key nutrition and health topics for each life stage. We thank the 20 distinguished scientists on the 2020 Dietary Guidelines Advisory Committee for their expertise and dedication in conducting an independent scientific review that was characterized by more transparency and public participation throughout the process than ever before. The Committee's work culminated in a comprehensive scientific report on the current state of nutrition science and provided advice to the Departments for our development of this 9th edition of the *Dietary Guidelines*. The Committee also included important considerations for future research, such as a need to reconsider the Dietary Reference Intakes. The U.S. and Canadian Dietary Reference Intake Steering Committees are currently developing plans to re-examine energy, protein, fat, and carbohydrate–the timeline for these macronutrient reviews has not been established. USDA and HHS are looking forward to jointly funding the work to help guide our Departments' research agendas in the coming years.

With the science must come practice—that is, making food and beverage choices that align with the *Dietary Guidelines*. Using the new edition of the *Dietary Guidelines*, we hope Americans can find ways to "Start Simple" and incorporate modest changes each day that push Americans closer to meeting the recommendations. It's more important than ever to make healthy eating a priority in the United States. With the release of the *Dietary Guidelines for Americans, 2020-2025*, we have an important call to action for you as health professionals and policymakers. We are asking you to help the public "make every bite count with the *Dietary Guidelines for Americans*." Help people make food and beverage choices that are rich in nutrition—individual choices that can become a healthy routine over time, choices they can enjoy in good health for many years to come.

Thank you for all you do to help Americans make strides toward aligning closer to the *Dietary Guidelines* as we all work together to help the public lead healthier lives.

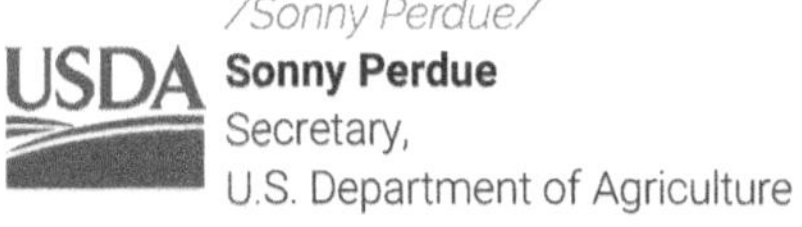

/Sonny Perdue/
Sonny Perdue
Secretary,
U.S. Department of Agriculture

/Alex M. Azar II/
Alex M. Azar II
Secretary,
U.S. Department of Health and Human Services

Acknowledgments

The U.S. Department of Agriculture and U.S. Department of Health and Human Services acknowledge the work of the 2020 Dietary Guidelines Advisory Committee whose recommendations informed the development of this edition of the *Dietary Guidelines for Americans*.

Dietary Guidelines Advisory Committee Members

Barbara Schneeman, PhD; Ronald Kleinman, MD; Jamy Ard, MD; Regan Bailey, PhD, MPH, RD; Lydia Bazzano, MD, PhD; Carol Boushey, PhD, MPH, RD; Teresa Davis, PhD; Kathryn Dewey, PhD; Sharon Donovan, PhD, RD; Steven Heymsfield, MD; Heather Leidy, PhD; Richard Mattes, PhD, MPH, RD; Elizabeth Mayer-Davis, PhD, RD; Timothy Naimi, MD, MPH; Rachel Novotny, PhD, RDN, LD; Joan Sabaté, MD, DrPH; Linda Snetselaar, PhD, RDN; Jamie Stang, PhD, MPH, RD; Elsie Taveras, MD, MPH; Linda Van Horn, PhD, RDN, LD.

The Departments also acknowledge the work of the scientists, staff, and policy officials responsible for the production of this document.

Policy Officials

USDA: Secretary Sonny Perdue, DVM; Brandon Lipps; Pamilyn Miller; Jackie Haven, MS, RD.

HHS: Secretary Alex M. Azar II, JD; Brett P. Giroir, MD; Paul Reed, MD; Don Wright, MD, MPH (through March 2020).

Dietary Guidelines Writing Team

USDA: Eve E. Stoody, PhD; Julie Obbagy, PhD, RD; TusaRebecca Pannucci, PhD, MPH, RD; Stephenie L. Fu; Elizabeth Rahavi, RD; Jean Altman, MS; Meghan Adler, MS, RDN; Clarissa (Claire) Brown, MS, MPH, RDN; Kelley S. Scanlon, PhD, RD.

HHS: Janet de Jesus, MS, RD; Richard Olson, MD, MPH; Cria Perrine, PhD; Julia Quam, MSPH, RDN; Katrina Piercy, PhD, RD; Ashley Vargas, PhD, MPH, RDN; Jennifer Lerman, MPH, RD; Dana DeSilva, PhD, RD; Dennis Anderson-Villaluz, MBA, RD, LDN.

Editorial Support: Anne Brown Rodgers; Jane Fleming.

Reviewers

The Departments acknowledge the contributions of numerous other internal departmental scientists and external peer reviewers who provided consultation and review during the production of this document.

Finally, the Departments would like to acknowledge the important role of the Federal staff who supported the development of this edition of the *Dietary Guidelines*, and of those who provided public comments throughout the process.

Executive Summary

The foods and beverages that people consume have a profound impact on their health. The scientific connection between food and health has been well documented for many decades, with substantial and increasingly robust evidence showing that a healthy lifestyle—including following a healthy dietary pattern—can help people achieve and maintain good health and reduce the risk of chronic diseases throughout all stages of the lifespan: infancy and toddlerhood, childhood and adolescence, adulthood, pregnancy and lactation, and older adulthood. The core elements of a healthy dietary pattern are remarkably consistent across the lifespan and across health outcomes.

Since the first edition was published in 1980, the *Dietary Guidelines for Americans* have provided science-based advice on what to eat and drink to promote health, reduce risk of chronic disease, and meet nutrient needs. Publication of the *Dietary Guidelines* is required under the 1990 National Nutrition Monitoring and Related Research Act, which states that at least every 5 years, the U.S. Departments of Agriculture (USDA) and of Health and Human Services (HHS) must jointly publish a report containing nutritional and dietary information and guidelines for the general public. The statute (Public Law 101-445, 7 United States Code 5341 et seq.) requires that the *Dietary Guidelines* be based on the preponderance of current scientific and medical knowledge. The 2020-2025 edition of the *Dietary Guidelines* builds from the 2015 edition, with revisions grounded in the *Scientific Report of the 2020 Dietary Guidelines Advisory Committee* and consideration of Federal agency and public comments.

The *Dietary Guidelines* is designed for policymakers and nutrition and health professionals to help all individuals and their families consume a healthy, nutritionally adequate diet. The information in the *Dietary Guidelines* is used to develop, implement, and evaluate Federal food, nutrition, and health policies and programs. It also is the basis for Federal nutrition education materials designed for the public and for the nutrition education components of USDA and HHS nutrition programs. State and local governments, schools, the food industry, other businesses, community groups, and media also use *Dietary Guidelines* information to develop programs, policies, and communication for the general public.

The aim of the *Dietary Guidelines* is to promote health and prevent disease. Because of this public health orientation, the *Dietary Guidelines* is not intended to contain clinical guidelines for treating chronic diseases. Chronic diseases result from a complex mix of genetic, biological, behavioral, socioeconomic, and environmental factors, and people with these conditions have unique health care requirements that require careful oversight by a health professional. The body of scientific evidence on diet and health reviewed to inform the *Dietary Guidelines* is representative of the U.S. population—it includes people who are healthy, people at risk for diet-related chronic conditions and diseases, such as cardiovascular disease, type 2 diabetes, and obesity, and some people who are living with one or more of these diet-related chronic illnesses. At the same time, it is essential that Federal agencies, medical organizations, and health professionals adapt the *Dietary Guidelines* to meet the specific needs of their patients as part of an individual, multifaceted treatment plan for the specific chronic disease.

Consistent and Evolving

Although many recommendations have remained relatively consistent over time, the *Dietary Guidelines* also has built upon previous editions and evolved as scientific knowledge has grown. The *Dietary Guidelines for Americans, 2020-2025* reflects this in three important ways:

The first is its recognition that diet-related chronic diseases, such as cardiovascular disease, type 2 diabetes, obesity, and some types of cancer, are very prevalent among Americans and pose a major public health problem. Today, more than half of adults have one or more diet-related chronic diseases. As a result, recent editions of the *Dietary Guidelines* have focused on healthy individuals, as well as those with overweight or obesity and those who are at risk of chronic disease. A fundamental premise of the *2020-2025 Dietary Guidelines* is that just about everyone, no matter their health status, can benefit from shifting food and beverage choices to better support healthy dietary patterns.

The second is its focus on dietary patterns. Researchers and public health experts, including registered dietitians, understand that nutrients and foods are not consumed in isolation. Rather, people consume them in various combinations over time—a dietary pattern—and these foods and beverages act synergistically to affect health. The *Dietary Guidelines for Americans, 2015-2020* puts this understanding into action by focusing its recommendations on consuming a healthy dietary pattern. The *2020-2025 Dietary Guidelines* carries forward this emphasis on the importance of a healthy dietary pattern as a whole—rather than on individual nutrients, foods, or food groups in isolation.

The third is its focus on a lifespan approach. This edition of the *Dietary Guidelines* highlights the importance of encouraging healthy dietary patterns at every life stage from infancy through older adulthood. It provides recommendations for healthy dietary patterns by life stage, identifying needs specific to each life stage and considering healthy dietary pattern characteristics that should be carried forward into the next stage of life. For the first time since the 1985 edition, the *2020-2025 Dietary Guidelines* includes recommendations for healthy dietary patterns for infants and toddlers.

The Guidelines

The *2020-2025 Dietary Guidelines* provides four overarching Guidelines that encourage healthy eating patterns at each stage of life and recognize that individuals will need to make shifts in their food and beverage choices to achieve a healthy pattern. The Guidelines also explicitly emphasize that a healthy dietary pattern is not a rigid prescription. Rather, the Guidelines are a customizable framework of core elements within which individuals make tailored and affordable choices that meet their personal, cultural, and traditional preferences. Several examples of healthy dietary patterns that translate and integrate the recommendations in overall healthy ways to eat are provided. The Guidelines are supported by Key Recommendations that provide further guidance on healthy eating across the lifespan.

The Guidelines

Make every bite count with the *Dietary Guidelines for Americans*. Here's how:

1 **Follow a healthy dietary pattern at every life stage.**

At every life stage—infancy, toddlerhood, childhood, adolescence, adulthood, pregnancy, lactation, and older adulthood—it is never too early or too late to eat healthfully.

- **For about the first 6 months of life,** exclusively feed infants human milk. Continue to feed infants human milk through at least the first year of life, and longer if desired. Feed infants iron-fortified infant formula during the first year of life when human milk is unavailable. Provide infants with supplemental vitamin D beginning soon after birth.
- **At about 6 months,** introduce infants to nutrient-dense complementary foods. Introduce infants to potentially allergenic foods along with other complementary foods. Encourage infants and toddlers to consume a variety of foods from all food groups. Include foods rich in iron and zinc, particularly for infants fed human milk.
- **From 12 months through older adulthood,** follow a healthy dietary pattern across the lifespan to meet nutrient needs, help achieve a healthy body weight, and reduce the risk of chronic disease.

2 **Customize and enjoy nutrient-dense food and beverage choices to reflect personal preferences, cultural traditions, and budgetary considerations.**

A healthy dietary pattern can benefit all individuals regardless of age, race, or ethnicity, or current health status. The *Dietary Guidelines* provides a framework intended to be customized to individual needs and preferences, as well as the foodways of the diverse cultures in the United States.

3 **Focus on meeting food group needs with nutrient-dense foods and beverages, and stay within calorie limits.**

An underlying premise of the *Dietary Guidelines* is that nutritional needs should be met primarily from foods and beverages—specifically, nutrient-dense foods and beverages. Nutrient-dense foods provide vitamins, minerals, and other health-promoting components and have no or little added sugars, saturated fat, and sodium. A healthy dietary pattern consists of nutrient-dense forms of foods and beverages across all food groups, in recommended amounts, and within calorie limits.

The core elements that make up a healthy dietary pattern include:

- **Vegetables of all types**—dark green; red and orange; beans, peas, and lentils; starchy; and other vegetables
- **Fruits,** especially whole fruit
- **Grains,** at least half of which are whole grain
- **Dairy,** including fat-free or low-fat milk, yogurt, and cheese, and/or lactose-free versions and fortified soy beverages and yogurt as alternatives
- **Protein foods,** including lean meats, poultry, and eggs; seafood; beans, peas, and lentils; and nuts, seeds, and soy products
- **Oils,** including vegetable oils and oils in food, such as seafood and nuts

4 Limit foods and beverages higher in added sugars, saturated fat, and sodium, and limit alcoholic beverages.

At every life stage, meeting food group recommendations—even with nutrient-dense choices—requires most of a person's daily calorie needs and sodium limits. A healthy dietary pattern doesn't have much room for extra added sugars, saturated fat, or sodium—or for alcoholic beverages. A small amount of added sugars, saturated fat, or sodium can be added to nutrient-dense foods and beverages to help meet food group recommendations, but foods and beverages high in these components should be limited. Limits are:

- **Added sugars**—Less than 10 percent of calories per day starting at age 2. Avoid foods and beverages with added sugars for those younger than age 2.
- **Saturated fat**—Less than 10 percent of calories per day starting at age 2.
- **Sodium**—Less than 2,300 milligrams per day—and even less for children younger than age 14.
- **Alcoholic beverages**—Adults of legal drinking age can choose not to drink, or to drink in moderation by limiting intake to 2 drinks or less in a day for men and 1 drink or less in a day for women, when alcohol is consumed. Drinking less is better for health than drinking more. There are some adults who should not drink alcohol, such as women who are pregnant.

Terms to Know

Several terms are used throughout the *Dietary Guidelines* and are essential to understanding the Guidelines and putting them into action. These terms are defined here:

- **Dietary pattern:** It is the combination of foods and beverages that constitutes an individual's complete dietary intake over time. This may be a description of a customary way of eating or a description of a combination of foods recommended for consumption.

- **Nutrient dense:** Nutrient-dense foods and beverages provide vitamins, minerals, and other health-promoting components and have little added sugars, saturated fat, and sodium. Vegetables, fruits, whole grains, seafood, eggs, beans, peas, and lentils, unsalted nuts and seeds, fat-free and low-fat dairy products, and lean meats and poultry—when prepared with no or little added sugars, saturated fat, and sodium—are nutrient-dense foods.

For most individuals, no matter their age or health status, achieving a healthy dietary pattern will require changes in food and beverage choices. Some of these changes can be accomplished by making simple substitutions, while others will require greater effort to accomplish. This edition of the *Dietary Guidelines* presents overall guidance on choosing nutrient-dense foods and beverages in place of less healthy choices and also discusses special nutrition considerations for individuals at each life stage—infants and toddlers, children and adolescents, adults, women who are pregnant or lactating, and older adults.

Although individuals ultimately decide what and how much to consume, their personal relationships; the settings in which they live, learn, work, play, and gather; and other contextual factors—including their ability to consistently access healthy and affordable food—strongly influence their choices. Health professionals, communities, businesses and industries, organizations, government, and other segments of society all have a role to play in supporting individuals and families in making choices that align with the *Dietary Guidelines* and ensuring that all people have access to a healthy and affordable food supply. Resources, including Federal programs that support households, regardless of size and make-up, in choosing a healthy diet and improving access to healthy food, are highlighted throughout this edition of the *Dietary Guidelines for Americans*.

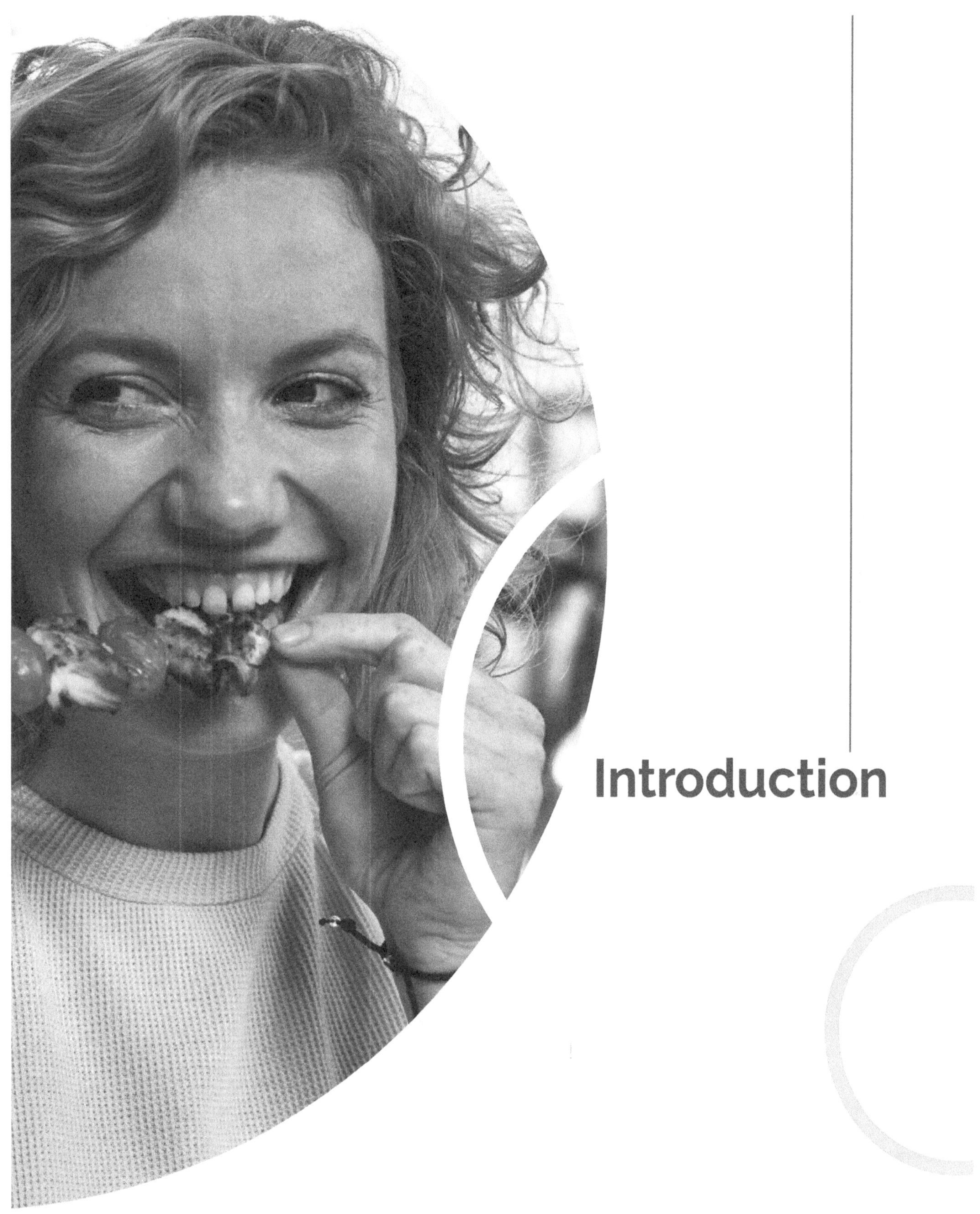

Introduction

Setting the Stage

The foods and beverages that people consume have a profound impact on their health. The scientific connection between food and health has been well documented for many decades, with substantial evidence showing that healthy dietary patterns can help people achieve and maintain good health and reduce the risk of chronic diseases throughout all stages of the lifespan. Yet, Federal data show that from the first edition of the *Dietary Guidelines for Americans* in 1980 through today, Americans have fallen far short of meeting its recommendations, and diet-related chronic disease rates have risen to pervasive levels and continue to be a major public health concern.

The *Dietary Guidelines* is an important part of a complex, multifaceted approach to promote health and reduce chronic disease risk. The *Dietary Guidelines* provides science-based advice on what to eat and drink to promote health, help reduce risk of chronic disease, and meet nutrient needs. The *Dietary Guidelines* is the foundation of Federal food, nutrition, and health policies and programs. An important audience is health professionals and nutrition program administrators who work with the general public to help them consume a healthy and nutritionally adequate diet and establish policies and services to support these efforts. Comprehensive, coordinated strategies built on the science-based foundation of the *Dietary Guidelines*—and a commitment to drive these strategies over time across sectors and settings—can help all Americans consume healthy dietary patterns, achieve and maintain good health, and reduce the risk of chronic diseases.

Grounded in Science and Focused on Public Health

The U.S. Departments of Agriculture (USDA) and of Health and Human Services (HHS) update the *Dietary Guidelines* at least every 5 years, based on the current science. A fundamental premise of the *Dietary Guidelines* is that everyone, no matter their age, race, or ethnicity, economic circumstances, or health status, can benefit from shifting food and beverage choices to better support healthy dietary patterns.

To make sure that the dietary advice provided in the *Dietary Guidelines* is aimed at improving public health, the science used to inform the Guidelines has examined diet through a lens of health promotion and disease prevention and considered various segments of the United States population, including ethnic populations who have disproportionately and/or historically been affected by diet-related disparities. This means that priority has been placed on scientific studies that examine the relationship between diet and health across all life stages, in men, women, and children from diverse racial and ethnic backgrounds, who are healthy or at risk of chronic disease.

Over time, eating patterns in the United States have remained far below *Dietary Guidelines* recommendations (**Figure I-1**). Concurrently, it has become increasingly clear that diet-related chronic diseases, such as cardiovascular disease, type 2 diabetes, obesity, liver disease, some types of cancer, and dental caries, pose a major public health problem for Americans. Today, 60 percent of adults have one or more diet-related chronic diseases (**Table I-1**). Given its aim to prevent further disease incidence by promoting health and reducing chronic disease risk, the *Dietary Guidelines* focuses on the general public, including healthy individuals, as well as those with overweight or obesity and those who are at risk of chronic disease. The importance of following the *Dietary Guidelines* across all life stages has been brought into focus even more with the emergence of COVID-19, as people living with diet-related chronic conditions and diseases are at an increased risk of severe illness from the novel coronavirus.

Grounded in the current body of scientific evidence on diet and health that is relevant to all Americans, the *Dietary Guidelines* is a critically important tool for health professionals, policymakers, and many other professionals. It is designed to help people make food and beverage choices all through life that are enjoyable and affordable and that also promote health and help prevent chronic disease.

Figure I-1

Adherence of the U.S. Population to the *Dietary Guidelines* Over Time, as Measured by the Average Total Healthy Eating Index-2015 Scores

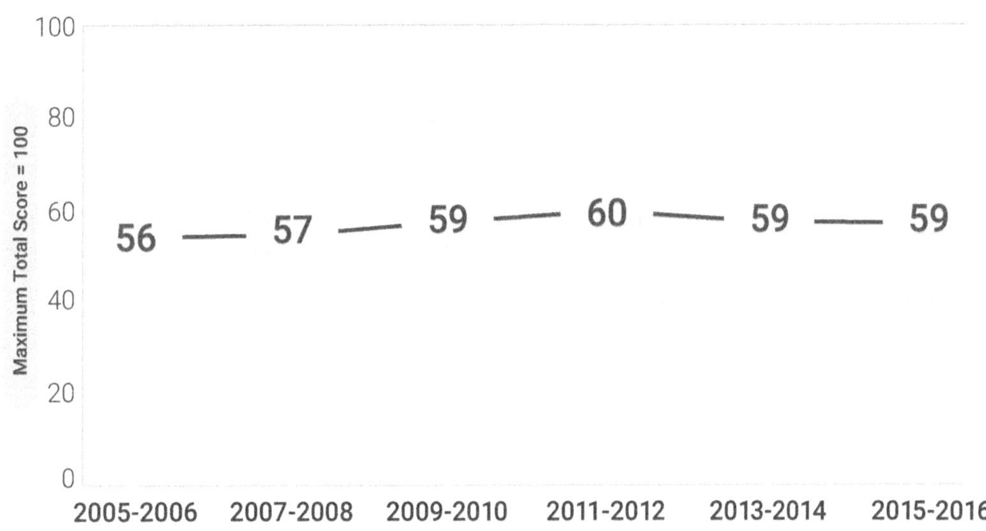

NOTE: HEI-2015 total scores are out of 100 possible points. A score of 100 indicates that recommendations on average were met or exceeded. A higher total score indicates a higher quality diet.

Data Source: Analysis of What We Eat in America, National Health and Nutrition Examination Survey (NHANES) data from 2005-2006 through 2015-2016, ages 2 and older, day 1 dietary intake data, weighted.

Table I-1

Facts About Nutrition-Related Health Conditions in the United States

HEALTH CONDITIONS	STATISTICS
Overweight and Obesity	• About 74% of adults are overweight or have obesity. • Adults ages 40 to 59 have the highest rate of obesity (43%) of any age group with adults 60 years and older having a 41% rate of obesity. • About 40% of children and adolescents are overweight or have obesity; the rate of obesity increases throughout childhood and teen years.
Cardiovascular Disease (CVD) and Risk Factors: • Coronary artery disease • Hypertension • High LDL and total blood cholesterol • Stroke	• Heart disease is the leading cause of death. • About 18.2 million adults have coronary artery disease, the most common type of heart disease. • Stroke is the fifth leading cause of death. • Hypertension, high LDL cholesterol, and high total cholesterol are major risk factors in heart disease and stroke. • Rates of hypertension and high total cholesterol are higher in adults with obesity than those who are at a healthy weight. • About 45% of adults have hypertension.[a] • More Black adults (54%) than White adults (46%) have hypertension. • More adults ages 60 and older (75%) than adults ages 40 to 59 (55%) have hypertension. • Nearly 4% of adolescents have hypertension.[b] • More than 11% of adults have high total cholesterol, ≥240 mg/dL. • More women (12%) than men (10%) have high total cholesterol, ≥240 mg/dL. • 7% of children and adolescents have high total cholesterol, ≥200 mg/dL.
Diabetes	• Almost 11% of Americans have type 1 or type 2 diabetes. • Almost 35% of American adults have prediabetes, and people 65 years and older have the highest rate (48%) compared to other age groups. • Almost 90% of adults with diabetes also are overweight or have obesity. • About 210,000 children and adolescents have diabetes, including 187,000 with type 1 diabetes. • About 6-9% of pregnant women develop gestational diabetes.
Cancer[c] • Breast Cancer • Colorectal Cancer	• Colorectal cancer in men and breast cancer in women are among the most common types of cancer. • About 250,520 women will be diagnosed with breast cancer this year. • Close to 5% of men and women will be diagnosed with colorectal cancer at some point during their lifetime. • More than 1.3 million people are living with colorectal cancer. • The incidence and mortality rates are highest among those ages 65 and older for every cancer type.
Bone Health and Muscle Strength	• More women (17%) than men (5%) have osteoporosis. • 20% of older adults have reduced muscle strength. • Adults over 80 years, non-Hispanic Asians, and women are at the highest risk for reduced bone mass and muscle strength.

[a] For adults, hypertension is defined as systolic blood pressure (SBP) >130 mm Hg and/or a diastolic blood pressure (DBP) >90 mm Hg.

[b] For children, hypertension was defined using the 2017 American Academy of Pediatrics (AAP) Clinical Practice Guideline.

[c] The types of cancer included here are not a complete list of all diet- and physical activity-related cancers.

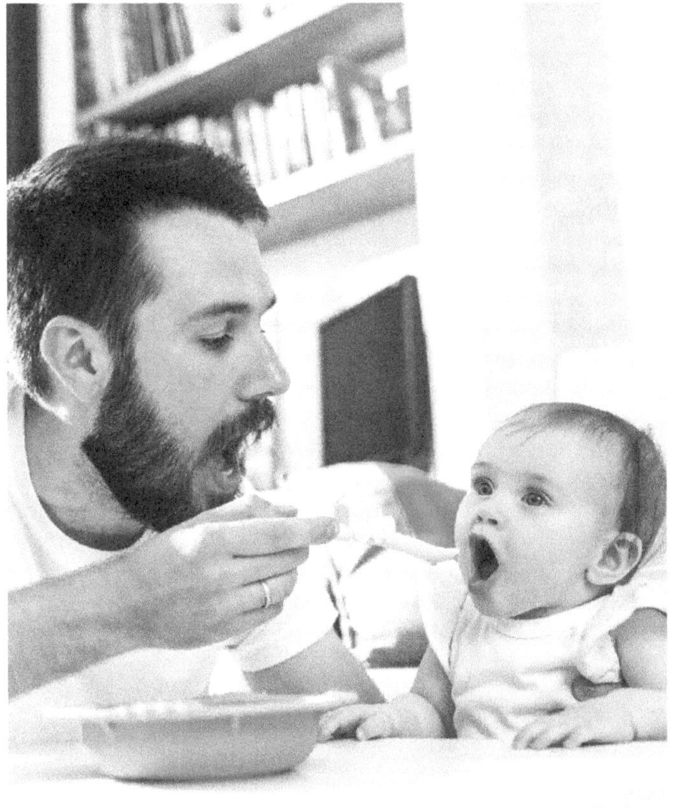

A Spotlight on Dietary Patterns

Although many of its recommendations have remained relatively consistent over time, the *Dietary Guidelines* has evolved as scientific knowledge has grown. Early *Dietary Guidelines* editions used evidence that examined the relationships between individual nutrients, foods, and food groups and health outcomes. In recent years, researchers, public health experts, and registered dietitians have acknowledged that nutrients and foods are not consumed in isolation. Rather, people consume them in various combinations over time—a dietary pattern—and these foods and beverages act synergistically to affect health.

The *2015-2020 Dietary Guidelines* put this understanding into action by focusing its recommendations on consuming a healthy dietary pattern. The *2020-2025 Dietary Guidelines* carries forward this emphasis on the importance of a healthy dietary pattern as a whole—rather than on individual nutrients or foods in isolation.

Serving as a framework, the Guidelines' dietary patterns approach enables policymakers, programs, and health professionals to help people personalize their food and beverage choices to accommodate their wants and needs, food preferences, cultural traditions and customs, and budgetary considerations.

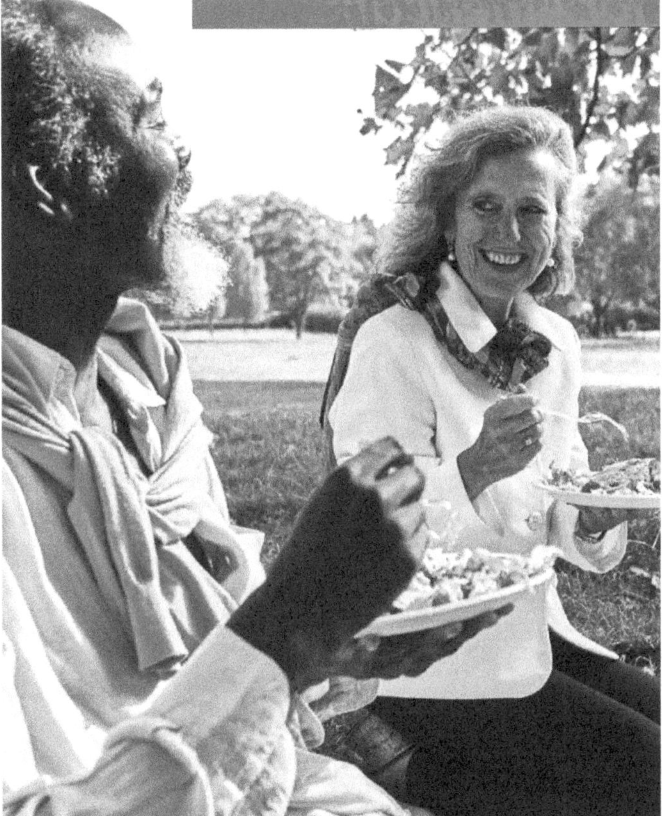

Healthy Dietary Patterns at Every Life Stage

The *2020-2025 Dietary Guidelines* takes the dietary patterns approach one step further by focusing on the importance of encouraging healthy dietary patterns at every stage of life, from birth to older adulthood. It provides recommendations for healthy dietary patterns by life stage, identifying needs specific to each life stage and considering healthy dietary pattern characteristics that should be carried forward into the next stage of life. And, for the first time since the 1985 edition, this edition of the *Dietary Guidelines* includes recommendations for infants and toddlers as well as continuing the emphasis on healthy dietary patterns during pregnancy and lactation.

This approach recognizes that each life stage is distinct—nutrient needs vary over the lifespan and each life stage has unique implications for food and beverage choices and disease risk. At the same time, it recognizes an important continuity. Because early food preferences influence later food choices, establishing a healthy dietary pattern early in life may have a beneficial impact on health promotion and disease prevention over the course of decades.

Dietary Guidelines for Americans: What It Is, What It Is Not

The *Dietary Guidelines* translates the current science on diet and health into guidance to help people choose foods and beverages that comprise a healthy and enjoyable dietary pattern—the "what" and "how much" of foods and beverages to consume to achieve good health, reduce risk of diet-related chronic diseases, and meet nutrient needs. The *Dietary Guidelines* is just one piece of the nutrition guidance landscape, however. Other guidance is designed to address requirements for the specific nutrients contained in foods and beverages or to address treatments for individuals who have a chronic disease. The following section describes the role of the *Dietary Guidelines* within this larger nutrition guidance landscape.

Quantitative Guidance on Foods, Not Nutrient Requirements

Nutrient requirements are established and updated by the National Academies of Sciences, Engineering, and Medicine. At the request of the U.S. and Canadian Federal Governments, the Academies set the quantitative requirements or limits—known as Dietary Reference Intakes (DRI)—on nutrients, which include macronutrients (i.e., protein, carbohydrates, and fats), vitamins and minerals (e.g., vitamin C, iron, and sodium), and food components (e.g., dietary fiber).

Because foods provide an array of nutrients and other components that have benefits for health, nutritional needs should be met primarily through foods. Thus, the *Dietary Guidelines* translates the Academies' nutrient requirements into food and beverage recommendations. The *Dietary Guidelines* recognizes, though, that in some cases, fortified foods and dietary supplements are useful when it is not possible otherwise to meet needs for one or more nutrients (e.g., during specific life stages such as pregnancy).

Health Promotion, Not Disease Treatment

At its core, the *Dietary Guidelines* has a public health mission—that is, health promotion and disease prevention. Medical and nutrition professionals may use or adapt the *Dietary Guidelines* to encourage their patients or clients to follow a healthy dietary pattern. The body of current scientific evidence on diet and health reviewed to inform the *Dietary Guidelines* included study participants who represent the U.S. population, including healthy individuals and people at risk of diet-related chronic conditions and diseases, such as cardiovascular disease, type 2 diabetes, or obesity, and some people who are living with a diet-related chronic illness.

Because of this public health orientation, the *Dietary Guidelines* is not intended to be a clinical guideline for treating chronic diseases. However, the *Dietary Guidelines* often has served as a reference for Federal, medical, voluntary, and patient care organizations as they develop clinical nutrition guidance tailored for people living with a specific medical condition. Chronic diseases result from a complex mix of genetic, biological, behavioral, socioeconomic, and environmental factors, and people with these conditions have unique health care requirements that require careful oversight by a health professional. Health professionals can adapt the *Dietary Guidelines* to meet the specific needs of their patients with chronic diseases, as part of a multi-faceted treatment plan.

Developing the *Dietary Guidelines for Americans*

The process to develop the *Dietary Guidelines* has evolved over time, in step with developments in nutrition science, public health, and best practices in scientific review and guidance development. USDA and HHS work together to determine the approach for each edition.

As stipulated by law, USDA and HHS must update the *Dietary Guidelines* at least every 5 years. The Guidelines must be grounded in the body of scientific and medical knowledge available at that time, not in individual studies or individual expert opinion. In establishing the process for the *2020-2025 Dietary Guidelines*, USDA and HHS considered and integrated recommendations from a comprehensive 2017 National Academies' study, *Review of the Process to Update the Dietary Guidelines*. Greater transparency figured prominently in the Academies' recommendations. As a result, in developing the 2020-2025 process, USDA and HHS made significant changes to increase transparency and public participation while maintaining the core element of scientific integrity.

One of these changes was the addition of a new stage at the beginning of the process. Thus, the 2020-2025 process consisted of four stages: (1) identify the topics

and supporting scientific questions to be examined; (2) appoint a Dietary Guidelines Advisory Committee to review current scientific evidence; (3) develop the new edition of the *Dietary Guidelines*; and (4) implement the *Dietary Guidelines* through Federal programs. The following information provides an overview of the 4-stage process. More details are available at **DietaryGuidelines.gov**.

Stage 1: Identify Topics and Supporting Scientific Questions

The Departments added a new step of identifying topics and scientific questions to begin the process of developing the next *Dietary Guidelines*. This was done to promote a deliberate and transparent process, better define the expertise needed on the Committee, and ensure the scientific review conducted by the Committee would address Federal nutrition policy and program needs and help manage resources.

In consultation with agencies across the Federal Government, USDA and HHS identified potential topics and supporting scientific questions that were of greatest importance and relevance to Federal nutrition programs, policies, and consumer education priorities. Compared to all previous *Dietary Guidelines* processes, the topic areas for 2020-2025 expanded due to the added focus on infants and toddlers from birth through age 23 months, as well as women who are pregnant. The Agricultural Act of 2014 mandated that, beginning with the 2020-2025 edition, the *Dietary Guidelines* should expand to include dietary guidance for these populations. Thus, the topics and questions—and areas of expertise needed on the Committee—reflected this change.

The Departments posted the topics and questions publicly on **DietaryGuidelines.gov**, allowing the public and Federal agencies 30 days to view and provide comments. Following review of the comments, USDA and HHS posted the final topics and questions, along with the public call for nominations to the 2020 Committee. Having topics and questions identified upfront helped inform the public's nominations by defining which areas of nutrition expertise were needed on the Committee.

Stage 2: Appoint a Dietary Guidelines Advisory Committee To Review Current Scientific Evidence

In the second stage, the Secretaries of USDA and HHS appointed the Committee with the single, time-limited task of reviewing the *2015-2020 Dietary Guidelines*, examining the evidence on the selected nutrition and public health topics and scientific questions, and providing independent, science-based advice and recommendations to USDA and HHS. The 20 nationally recognized scientific experts appointed to the Committee represented a mix of practitioners, epidemiologists, scientists, clinical trialists, and others from every region of the United States.

The use of a Federal advisory committee is a commonly used best practice to ensure the Federal Government seeks sound, external scientific advice to inform decisions. The Committee's work concluded with its scientific report submitted to the Secretaries of USDA and HHS in June 2020.[1] This report was not a draft of the *Dietary Guidelines*; it was a scientific document that detailed the Committee's evidence review and provided advice to USDA and HHS.

The Committee was divided into six subcommittees to conduct its work: Dietary Patterns, Pregnancy and Lactation, Birth to Age 24 Months, Beverages and Added Sugars, Dietary Fats and Seafood, and Frequency

[1] Dietary Guidelines Advisory Committee. 2020. *Scientific Report of the 2020 Dietary Guidelines Advisory Committee: Advisory Report to the Secretary of Agriculture and the Secretary of Health and Human Services*. U.S. Department of Agriculture, Agricultural Research Service, Washington, DC.

of Eating. The Committee also formed one cross-cutting working group—Data Analysis and Food Pattern Modeling—to support work across the subcommittees.

The Committee's work had three defining characteristics: the use of three approaches to examine the evidence, the creation of transparent protocols before the evidence review began, and the development of scientific review conclusion statements for the scientific reviews conducted.

THREE APPROACHES TO EXAMINE THE EVIDENCE

The 2020 Committee used three state-of-the-art approaches to conduct its robust and rigorous reviews:

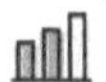

Data analysis: Using Federal, nationally representative data, this approach provided insights into current eating habits of the U.S. population and current diet-related chronic disease rates in the United States. These data helped make the *Dietary Guidelines* practical, relevant, and achievable.

The Committee used data analysis to address scientific questions that looked at current dietary patterns and beverage consumption, current intakes of food groups and nutrients, dietary components of public health concern, prevalence of nutrition-related chronic health conditions, and relationships between eating habits and achieving nutrient and food group recommendations.

Nutrition Evidence Systematic Review (NESR): Systematic reviews are research projects that follow meticulously defined protocols (i.e., plans) to answer clearly formulated scientific questions by searching for, evaluating, and synthesizing all relevant, peer-reviewed studies. Systematic reviews are considered a gold standard method to inform development of evidence-based guidelines by ensuring consideration of the strongest, most appropriate body of evidence available on a topic. USDA's Nutrition Evidence Systematic Review is a team of scientists who specializes in conducting systematic reviews focused on nutrition and disease prevention and evaluating scientific evidence on nutrition topics relevant to Federal policy and programs. NESR used its rigorous, protocol-driven methodology to support the Committee in conducting its systematic reviews. New to the 2020 process, USDA and HHS added a step for peer review of the systematic reviews by Federal scientists.

Food pattern modeling: This type of analysis illustrates how changes to the amounts or types of foods and beverages in a dietary pattern might affect meeting nutrient needs across the U.S. population.

The Committee used this method to assess potential changes to the USDA Dietary Patterns, which help meet the DRIs set by the National Academies, while taking into consideration current consumption in the United States and the conclusions from its systematic reviews. As with all food pattern modeling for the *Dietary Guidelines*, the results of the Committee's food pattern modeling tests were interpreted in light of two key assumptions. First, the modeling tests were based on nutrient profiles of nutrient-dense foods in the U.S. food supply and U.S. population-based dietary data. Population-based patterns articulate the evidence on the relationships between diet and health in ways that might be adopted by the U.S. public as a whole. Second, modeling tests assumed population-wide compliance with all food intake recommendations. As with other types of modeling, the food pattern modeling is hypothetical and does not predict the behaviors of individuals.

Each of these approaches had its own rigorous, protocol-driven methodology, and each had a unique, complementary role in examining the science. Additional detailed information is available at **DietaryGuidelines.gov** and **NESR.usda.gov**.

TRANSPARENT PROTOCOLS FIRST, THEN REVIEW

To answer each scientific question, the Committee first created a protocol that described how the Committee would apply one of the three approaches to examine the evidence related to that specific question. The Committee created each protocol before examining any evidence, and, for the first time, the protocols were posted online for the public as they were being developed. This enabled the public to understand how a specific scientific question would be answered and to have the opportunity to submit public comments before the Committee completed the protocols and conducted its reviews of the scientific evidence. Detailed information on the Committee's review is documented in its scientific report, which is available on **DietaryGuidelines.gov**.

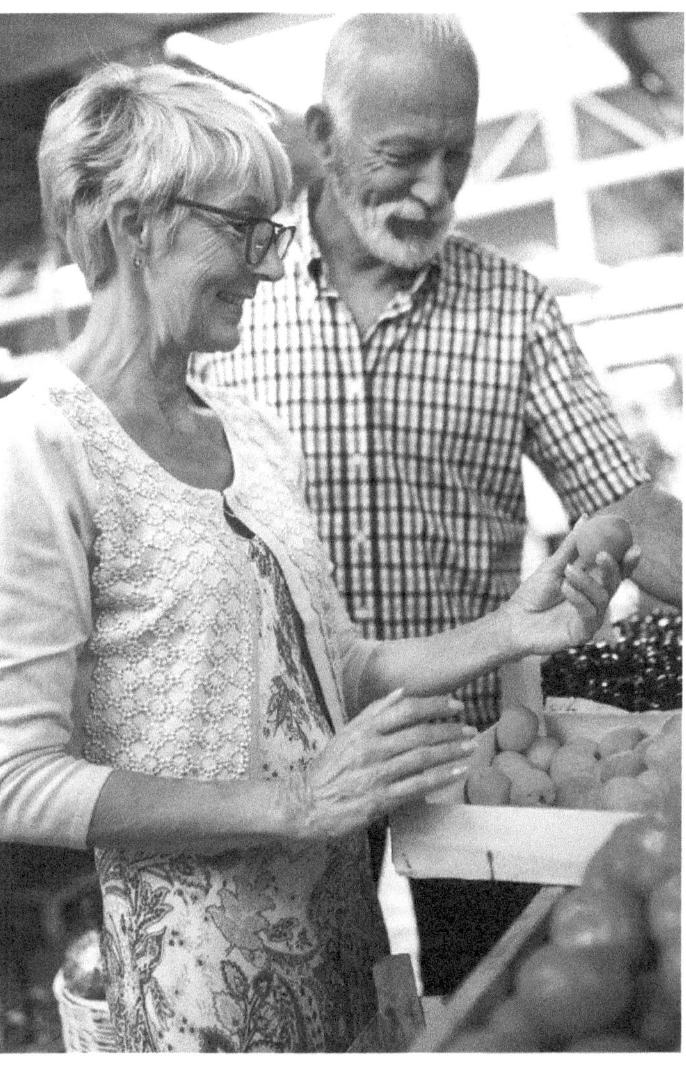

Health Status of Participants in Studies Included in Nutrition Evidence Systematic Reviews

To ensure that the *Dietary Guidelines* promotes the health of and reduce risk of disease among all Americans, the evidence base that informs the *Dietary Guidelines* must comprise studies conducted with people who are representative of the general public and must examine diet through a health promotion and disease prevention lens.

As outlined in the Committee's systematic review protocols, the Committee's reviews included studies with participants who were healthy and/or who were at risk of a chronic disease, including participants with obesity, as well as studies that enrolled *some* participants with a disease. Because the *Dietary Guidelines* is not intended to be a clinical guideline for treating chronic diseases, the Committee excluded studies that enrolled *only* patients with a disease with the intention to treat those individuals.

In general, the majority of the reviews conducted to inform the *Dietary Guidelines* included trials that exclusively enrolled participants with overweight or obesity, or who were at high risk of cardiovascular disease or type 2 diabetes, and observational studies that enrolled participants from a wide range of health and weight status, including those with healthy weight, overweight, or obesity. The reviews included few studies that enrolled only healthy participants.

Thus, the *Dietary Guidelines* are applicable to the overall U.S. population, including healthy individuals and people at risk of diet-related chronic conditions and diseases, such as cardiovascular disease, type 2 diabetes, and obesity. In addition, people living with a diet-related chronic illness can benefit from a healthy dietary pattern. The *Dietary Guidelines* can serve as a reference for Federal, medical, voluntary, and patient care organizations as they develop nutrition guidance tailored for people living with a specific medical condition. Health professionals can adapt the *Dietary Guidelines* to meet the specific needs of their patients with chronic diseases, as part of a multifaceted treatment plan.

CONCLUSION STATEMENTS FOR THE SCIENTIFIC REVIEWS CONDUCTED

For all topics and questions, regardless of the approach used to identify and evaluate the scientific evidence, the Committee developed conclusion statements. Each conclusion statement provided a succinct answer to the specific question posed. The Committee took the strengths and limitations of the evidence base into consideration when formulating conclusion statements.

For questions answered using NESR systematic reviews, the conclusion statements included a grade to indicate the strength of the evidence supporting the conclusion statement. The grades were Strong, Moderate, Limited, or Grade Not Assignable.

Grading the strength of the evidence applied only to questions answered using NESR systematic reviews; it did not apply to questions answered using data analysis or food pattern modeling. Therefore, data analysis and food pattern modeling conclusion statements were not graded.

As it completed its work, the Committee looked across all of the conclusion statements to develop overarching advice for USDA and HHS to consider as the Departments developed the next edition of the *Dietary Guidelines*.

Using these three approaches, the Committee worked collaboratively for 16 months and deliberated on the scientific reviews in six meetings, all of which were open to the public. Two of the six meetings included an opportunity for the public to provide oral comments to the Committee. An ongoing period for written public comments to the Committee spanned 15 months of its work. And, for the first time, a final public meeting was included for the Committee to discuss its draft scientific report 1 month before the final report was posted for public comment.

In addition to documenting its rigorous review of the evidence to answer the scientific questions from USDA and HHS and providing advice for the Departments' development of the next *Dietary Guidelines* edition, the Committee provided recommendations for future research. These research recommendations reflected an acknowledgment that science in nutrition, diet, and health associations continues to evolve, and that new findings build on and enhance existing evidence.

Upon submitting its final scientific report to the USDA and HHS Secretaries, the Committee disbanded. The Departments then posted the scientific report and asked the public for comments. The Departments received written comments on the report over a 30-day period and also held an online meeting to hear oral comments.

Stage 3: Develop the *Dietary Guidelines*

Each edition of the *Dietary Guidelines* builds on the preceding edition, with the scientific justification for revisions informed by the Committee's scientific report and consideration of public and Federal agency comments. As with previous editions, development of the *2020-2025 Dietary Guidelines* involved a step-by-step process of writing, review, and revision conducted by a writing team of Federal staff from USDA and HHS.

The writing team included Federal nutrition scientists with expertise in the *Dietary Guidelines* and related research and programs as well as specialists with expertise in communicating nutrition information.

Key tenets of writing the *Dietary Guidelines* are that it must:

- Represent the totality of the evidence examined
- Address the needs of Federal programs
- Reduce unintended consequences
- Follow best practices for developing guidelines
- Use plain language

The draft *Dietary Guidelines* went through internal and external review. Ultimately, the document was reviewed by all Agencies with nutrition policies and programs across USDA and HHS, such as USDA's Food and Nutrition Service and its Food Safety and Inspection Service, and HHS' National Institutes of Health, Food and Drug Administration, and Centers for Disease Control and Prevention. The draft *Dietary Guidelines* also went through an external expert peer review to ensure that it accurately reflected the body of evidence documented in the Committee's scientific report.

This process culminated with approval by the Secretaries of USDA and HHS. After approval by the Secretaries, the Departments released the *Dietary Guidelines* to Federal agencies and the public for implementation across programs and through educational activities.

Stage 4: Implement the *Dietary Guidelines*

The U.S. Government uses the *Dietary Guidelines* as the basis of its food assistance and meal programs, nutrition education efforts, and decisions about national health objectives. For example, the National School Lunch Program and the Older Americans Act Nutrition Program incorporate the *Dietary Guidelines* in menu planning; the Special Supplemental Nutrition Program for Women, Infants, and Children applies the *Dietary Guidelines* in its program and educational materials; and the Healthy People objectives for the Nation include objectives based on the *Dietary Guidelines*.

The *Dietary Guidelines* also provides a critical structure for State and local public health promotion and disease prevention initiatives. In addition, it provides foundational, evidence-based nutrition guidance for use by individuals and those who serve them in public and private settings, including health professionals, public health and social service agencies, health care and educational institutions, researchers, agricultural producers, food and beverage manufacturers, and more.

Implementation of the *Dietary Guidelines* Through MyPlate

Using MyPlate as a Guide To Support Healthy Dietary Patterns

The *Dietary Guidelines for Americans* is developed and written for a professional audience. Therefore, its translation into actionable consumer messages and resources is crucial to help individuals, families, and communities achieve healthy dietary patterns.

MyPlate is one example of consumer translation. Created to be used in various settings and adaptable to meeting personal preferences, cultural foodways, traditions, and budget needs, MyPlate is used by professionals across sectors to help people become more aware of and informed about making healthy food and beverage choices over time. More information is available at **MyPlate.gov**.

Following a healthy dietary pattern from birth through older adulthood can have a profound impact on a person's lifelong health. The *Dietary Guidelines* provides the framework for following such a pattern. However, broad and multisector collaboration is needed to help people achieve that goal. Action on many fronts is needed to ensure that healthy dietary choices at home, school, work, and play are the affordable, accessible norm. Everyone has a role to play in helping all Americans shift to a healthy dietary pattern and achieve better health.

Try the MyPlate Plan

A healthy eating routine is important at every stage of life and can have positive effects that add up over time. It's important to eat a variety of fruits, vegetables, grains, dairy or fortified soy alternatives, and protein foods. When deciding what to eat or drink, choose options that are full of nutrients. Make every bite count.

Think about how the following recommendations can come together over the course of your day or week to help you create a healthy eating routine:

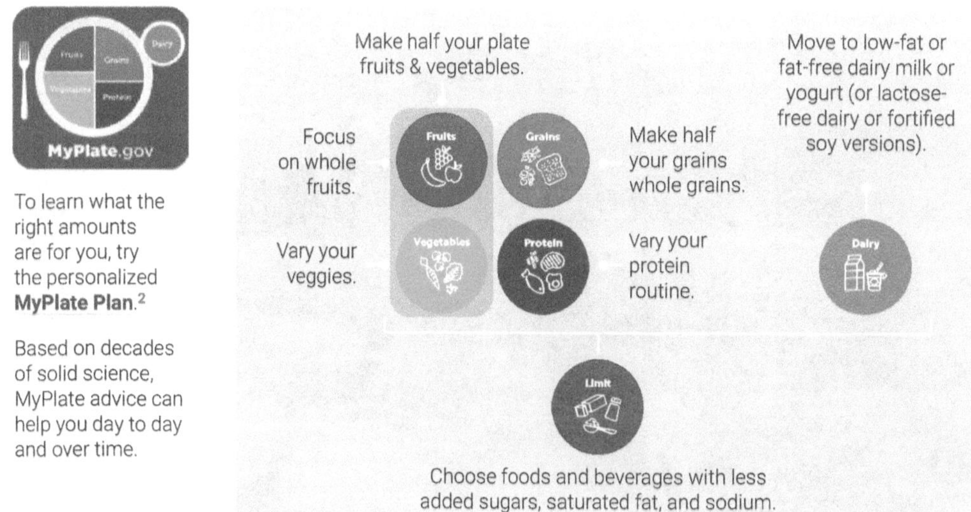

The benefits of healthy eating add up over time, bite by bite. Small changes matter. **Start Simple with MyPlate.**

[2] Available at: **MyPlate.gov/myplate-plan**

A Roadmap to the *Dietary Guidelines for Americans, 2020-2025*

Reflecting the accumulating body of evidence about the relationships between diet and health outcomes, the *2020-2025 Dietary Guidelines* presents its recommendations with a primary emphasis on encouraging the consumption of a healthy overall dietary pattern at every stage of life, from birth through older adulthood. This edition of the *Dietary Guidelines* consists of an Executive Summary, this Introduction, six chapters, and three appendixes.

- Chapter 1: **Nutrition and Health Across the Lifespan: The Guidelines and Key Recommendations** discusses the health benefits of lifelong healthy dietary choices and explains the four Guidelines and supporting Key Recommendations. This chapter is the basis for all the succeeding chapters. Chapters 2 through 6 should be read in tandem with Chapter 1.

- Chapter 2: **Infants and Toddlers** is the first of five chapters that focus on healthy dietary patterns for a specific life stage. This edition of the *Dietary Guidelines* is the first since the 1985 edition to provide guidance for infants and toddlers (birth through age 23 months). The chapter provides specific key recommendations for this age group, along with guidance on how to put these recommendations into action. The chapter closes with a Healthy Dietary Pattern during the second year of life and a look toward the next life stage—Children and Adolescents.

- Chapter 3: **Children and Adolescents** first sets the stage by describing nutrition issues specific to children and adolescents ages 2 through 18. It then presents the recommended Healthy Dietary Patterns for this age group, explains how current intakes compare to recommendations, and discusses special dietary guidance considerations for this life stage. The chapter concludes with a discussion of ways to support healthy dietary patterns among children and adolescents and a look toward the next life stage—Adults.

- Chapter 4: **Adults** opens with a discussion of selected nutrition issues that characterize the adult life stage (ages 19 through 59). It then presents the recommended Healthy Dietary Patterns for this age group, explains how current intakes compare to recommendations, and discusses special dietary guidance considerations for adults. The chapter concludes with suggestions for how to support healthy dietary patterns among adults and a look toward two important adult life stages—Women Who Are Pregnant or Lactating and Older Adults.

- Chapter 5: **Women Who Are Pregnant or Lactating** opens with a discussion of selected nutrition issues important to this stage of adult life. It then presents the recommended Healthy Dietary Patterns for this life stage, explains how current intakes compare to recommendations, and discusses special dietary guidance considerations for women who are pregnant or lactating. The chapter concludes with suggestions for how to support healthy dietary patterns among this population group.

- Chapter 6: **Older Adults** opens with a discussion of selected nutrition issues that are important for older adults, ages 60 and older. It then presents the recommended Healthy Dietary Patterns for this life stage, explains how current intakes compare to recommendations, and discusses special dietary guidance considerations for this age group. The chapter concludes with suggestions for how to support healthy dietary patterns among older adults.

- **Appendixes** include a table summarizing nutritional goals for age-sex groups, estimated calorie needs for all ages and at three physical activity levels, and the USDA Dietary Patterns.

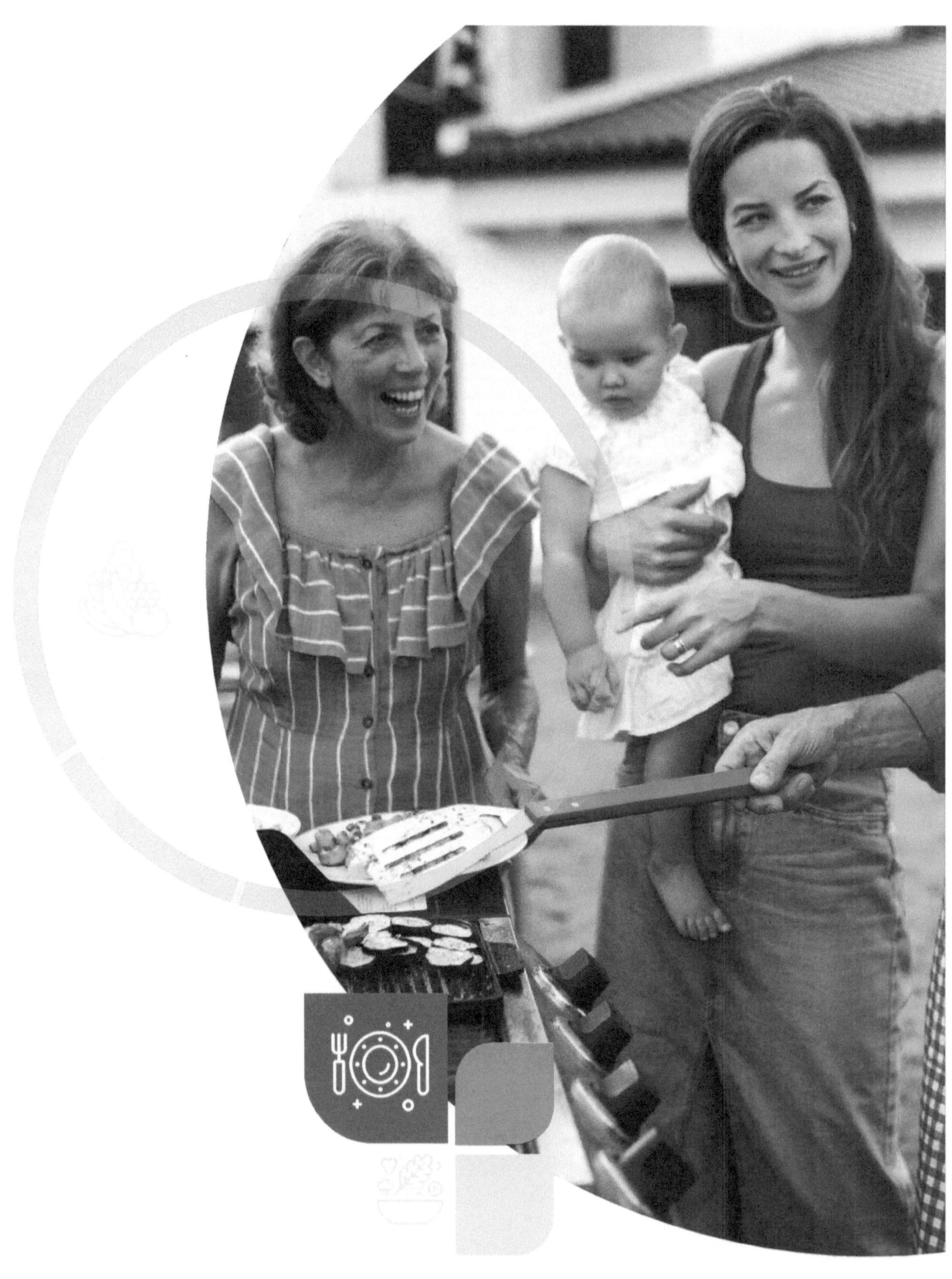

CHAPTER 1

Nutrition and Health Across the Lifespan:

The Guidelines and Key Recommendations

The Guidelines

Make every bite count with the *Dietary Guidelines for Americans*. Here's how:

Follow a healthy dietary pattern at every life stage.

1

Customize and enjoy nutrient-dense food and beverage choices to reflect personal preferences, cultural traditions, and budgetary considerations.

2

4

Limit foods and beverages higher in added sugars, saturated fat, and sodium, and limit alcoholic beverages.

Focus on meeting food group needs with nutrient-dense foods and beverages, and stay within calorie limits.

Key Recommendations

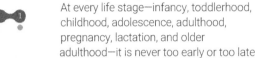

Guideline

Follow a healthy dietary pattern at every life stage.

At every life stage—infancy, toddlerhood, childhood, adolescence, adulthood, pregnancy, lactation, and older adulthood—it is never too early or too late to eat healthfully.

- **For about the first 6 months of life**, exclusively feed infants human milk. Continue to feed infants human milk through at least the first year of life, and longer if desired. Feed infants iron-fortified infant formula during the first year of life when human milk is unavailable. Provide infants with supplemental vitamin D beginning soon after birth.
- **At about 6 months**, introduce infants to nutrient-dense complementary foods. Introduce infants to potentially allergenic foods along with other complementary foods. Encourage infants and toddlers to consume a variety of foods from all food groups. Include foods rich in iron and zinc, particularly for infants fed human milk.
- **From 12 months through older adulthood**, follow a healthy dietary pattern across the lifespan to meet nutrient needs, help achieve a healthy body weight, and reduce the risk of chronic disease.

Guideline

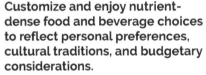

Customize and enjoy nutrient-dense food and beverage choices to reflect personal preferences, cultural traditions, and budgetary considerations.

A healthy dietary pattern can benefit all individuals regardless of age, race, or ethnicity, or current health status. The *Dietary Guidelines* provides a framework intended to be customized to individual needs and preferences, as well as the foodways of the diverse cultures in the United States.

Guideline

Focus on meeting food group needs with nutrient-dense foods and beverages, and stay within calorie limits.

An underlying premise of the *Dietary Guidelines* is that nutritional needs should be met primarily from foods and beverages—specifically, nutrient-dense foods and beverages. Nutrient-dense foods provide vitamins, minerals, and other health-promoting components and have no or little added sugars, saturated fat, and sodium. A healthy dietary pattern consists of nutrient-dense forms of foods and beverages across all food groups, in recommended amounts, and within calorie limits.

The core elements that make up a healthy dietary pattern include:

- Vegetables of all types—dark green; red and orange; beans, peas, and lentils; starchy; and other vegetables
- Fruits, especially whole fruit
- Grains, at least half of which are whole grain
- Dairy, including fat-free or low-fat milk, yogurt, and cheese, and/or lactose-free versions and fortified soy beverages and yogurt as alternatives
- Protein foods, including lean meats, poultry, and eggs; seafood; beans, peas, and lentils; and nuts, seeds, and soy products
- Oils, including vegetable oils and oils in food, such as seafood and nuts

Guideline

Limit foods and beverages higher in added sugars, saturated fat, and sodium, and limit alcoholic beverages.

At every life stage, meeting food group recommendations—even with nutrient-dense choices—requires most of a person's daily calorie needs and sodium limits. A healthy dietary pattern doesn't have much room for extra added sugars, saturated fat, or sodium—or for alcoholic beverages. A small amount of added sugars, saturated fat, or sodium can be added to nutrient-dense foods and beverages to help meet food group recommendations, but foods and beverages high in these components should be limited. **Limits are:**

- **Added sugars**—Less than 10 percent of calories per day starting at age 2. Avoid foods and beverages with added sugars for those younger than age 2.
- **Saturated fat**—Less than 10 percent of calories per day starting at age 2.
- **Sodium**—Less than 2,300 milligrams per day—and even less for children younger than age 14.
- **Alcoholic beverages**—Adults of legal drinking age can choose not to drink or to drink in moderation by limiting intake to 2 drinks or less in a day for men and 1 drink or less in a day for women, when alcohol is consumed. Drinking less is better for health than drinking more. There are some adults who should not drink alcohol, such as women who are pregnant.

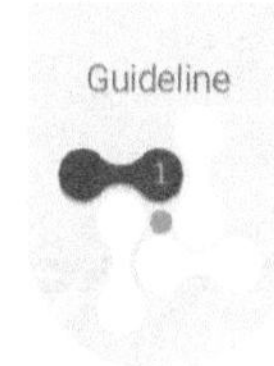

Guideline 1

Follow a Healthy Dietary Pattern at Every Life Stage

A fundamental premise of the *Dietary Guidelines* is that almost everyone, no matter an individual's age, race, or ethnicity, or health status, can benefit from shifting food and beverage choices to better support healthy dietary patterns.

Healthy eating starts at birth with the exclusive consumption of human milk, if possible, for about the first 6 months. If human milk is unavailable, infants should be fed an iron-fortified commercial infant formula (i.e., labeled "with iron") regulated by the U.S. Food and Drug Administration (FDA), which are based on standards that ensure nutrient content and safety. Healthy eating continues with the introduction of complementary foods and beverages at about 6 months of age. By 12 months, infants should maintain their healthy eating as they transition to developmentally appropriate foods and beverages. Healthy eating continues in each life stage thereafter. Even though nutrient needs vary across life stages, the foods and beverages that individuals should eat over the lifespan are remarkably consistent.

This chapter provides foundational guidance about maintaining a healthy dietary pattern across each life stage—infancy, toddlerhood, childhood, adolescence, adulthood, pregnancy, lactation, and older adulthood. Because the nutritional needs and transition of infants and toddlers are unique, ***Chapter 2*** provides a focused discussion on this age group. ***Chapters 3***, ***4***, ***5***, and **6** then provide tailored nutrition information specific to children and adolescents, adults, women who are pregnant or lactating, and older adults, respectively.

What Is a Dietary Pattern?

Over the course of any given day, week, or year, individuals consume foods and beverages[1] in combination—a dietary pattern. A dietary pattern represents the totality of what individuals habitually eat and drink, and the parts of the pattern act synergistically to affect health. As a result, the dietary pattern may better predict overall health status and disease risk than individual foods or nutrients.

A healthy dietary pattern consists of nutrient-dense forms of foods and beverages across all food groups, in recommended amounts, and within calorie limits. Achieving a healthy dietary pattern at each life stage not only supports health at that point in time, but also supports health in the next life stage and possibly for future generations. If healthy dietary patterns can be established early in life and sustained thereafter, the impact on health could be significant. Establishing and maintaining a healthy dietary pattern can help minimize diet-related chronic disease risk. Conversely, consuming foods and beverages that are not nutrient-dense may lead to disease expression in later years. High intakes of such foods (i.e., an unhealthy dietary pattern) throughout the lifespan can increase the risk of developing chronic diseases.

The good news is that at any stage of life, individuals can make efforts to adopt a healthy dietary pattern and improve their health. The Healthy U.S.-Style Dietary Pattern, USDA's primary Dietary Pattern, provides a framework for healthy eating that all Americans can follow. It is based on the types and proportions of foods Americans of all ages, genders, races, and ethnicities typically consume, but in nutrient-dense forms and appropriate amounts.

The Healthy U.S.-Style Dietary Pattern is carried forward from the *2015-2020 Dietary Guidelines for Americans*. The 2,000-calorie level of the pattern is shown in **Table 1-1**. The Healthy Mediterranean-Style Dietary Pattern and the Healthy Vegetarian Dietary Pattern—also carried forward from the *2015-2020 Dietary Guidelines for Americans*—are variations of the Healthy U.S.-Style Dietary Pattern that have the same core elements. The USDA Dietary Patterns are described in ***Appendix 3. USDA Dietary Patterns*** and are meant to be tailored to meet cultural and personal preferences and used as guides to plan and serve meals for individuals, households, and in a variety of institutions and other settings. The Dietary Approaches to Stop Hypertension (DASH) dietary pattern is an example of a healthy dietary pattern and has many of the same characteristics as the Healthy U.S.-Style Dietary Pattern. Additional details on DASH are available at **nhlbi.nih.gov/health-topics/dash-eating-plan**.

[1] If not specified explicitly, references to "foods" refer to "foods and beverages."

Guideline

Table 1-1

Healthy U.S.-Style Dietary Pattern at the 2,000-Calorie Level, With Daily or Weekly Amounts From Food Groups, Subgroups, and Components

FOOD GROUP OR SUBGROUP[a]	**Daily Amount[b] of Food From Each Group** (Vegetable and protein foods subgroup amounts are per week.)
Vegetables (cup eq/day)	**2 ½**
	Vegetable Subgroups in Weekly Amounts
Dark-Green Vegetables (cup eq/wk)	1 ½
Red and Orange Vegetables (cup eq/wk)	5 ½
Beans, Peas, Lentils (cup eq/wk)	1 ½
Starchy Vegetables (cup eq/wk)	5
Other Vegetables (cup eq/wk)	4
Fruits (cup eq/day)	**2**
Grains (ounce eq/day)	**6**
Whole Grains (ounce eq/day)	≥ 3
Refined Grains (ounce eq/day)	< 3
Dairy (cup eq/day)	**3**
Protein Foods (ounce eq/day)	**5 ½**
	Protein Foods Subgroups in Weekly Amounts
Meats, Poultry, Eggs (ounce eq/wk)	26
Seafood (ounce eq/wk)	8
Nuts, Seeds, Soy Products (ounce eq/wk)	5
Oils (grams/day)	**27**
Limit on Calories for Other Uses (kcal/day)[c]	**240**
Limit on Calories for Other Uses (%/day)	12%

[a] Definitions for each food group and subgroup are provided throughout the chapter and are compiled in ***Appendix 3***.

[b] Food group amounts shown in cup or ounce equivalents (eq). Oils are shown in grams. Quantity equivalents for each food group are defined in ***Appendix 3***. Amounts will vary for those who need <2,000 or >2,000 calories per day.

[c] Foods are assumed to be in nutrient-dense forms, lean or low-fat and prepared with minimal added sugars, refined starches, saturated fat, or sodium. If all food choices to meet food group recommendations are in nutrient-dense forms, a small number of calories remain within the overall limit of the pattern (i.e., limit on calories for other uses). The amount of calories depends on the total calorie level of the pattern and the amounts of food from each food group required to meet nutritional goals. Calories up to the specified limit can be used for added sugars, saturated fat, and/or alcohol, or to eat more than the recommended amount of food in a food group.

NOTE: The total dietary pattern should not exceed *Dietary Guidelines* limits for added sugars, saturated fat, and alcohol; be within the Acceptable Macronutrient Distribution Ranges for protein, carbohydrate, and total fats; and stay within calorie limits. Values are rounded. See ***Appendix 3*** for all calorie levels of the pattern.

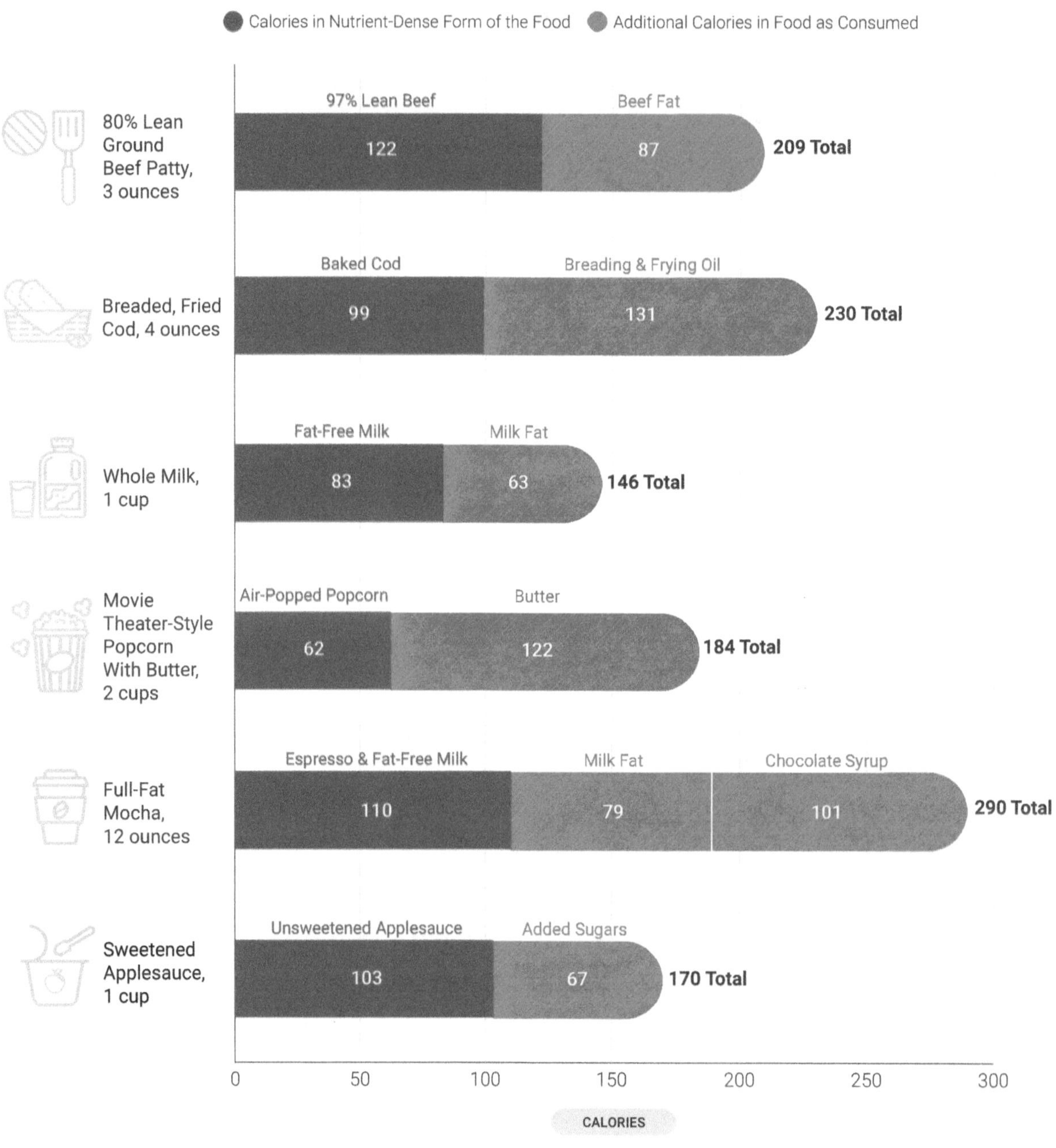

Data Source: U.S. Department of Agriculture, Agricultural Research Service. FoodData Central, 2019. **fdc.nal.usda.gov**.

Guideline

Figure 1-2

Making Nutrient-Dense Choices: One Food or Beverage At a Time

Every food and beverage choice is an opportunity to move toward a healthy dietary pattern. Small changes in single choices add up and can make a big difference. These are a few examples of realistic, small changes to nutrient-dense choices that can help people adopt healthy dietary patterns.

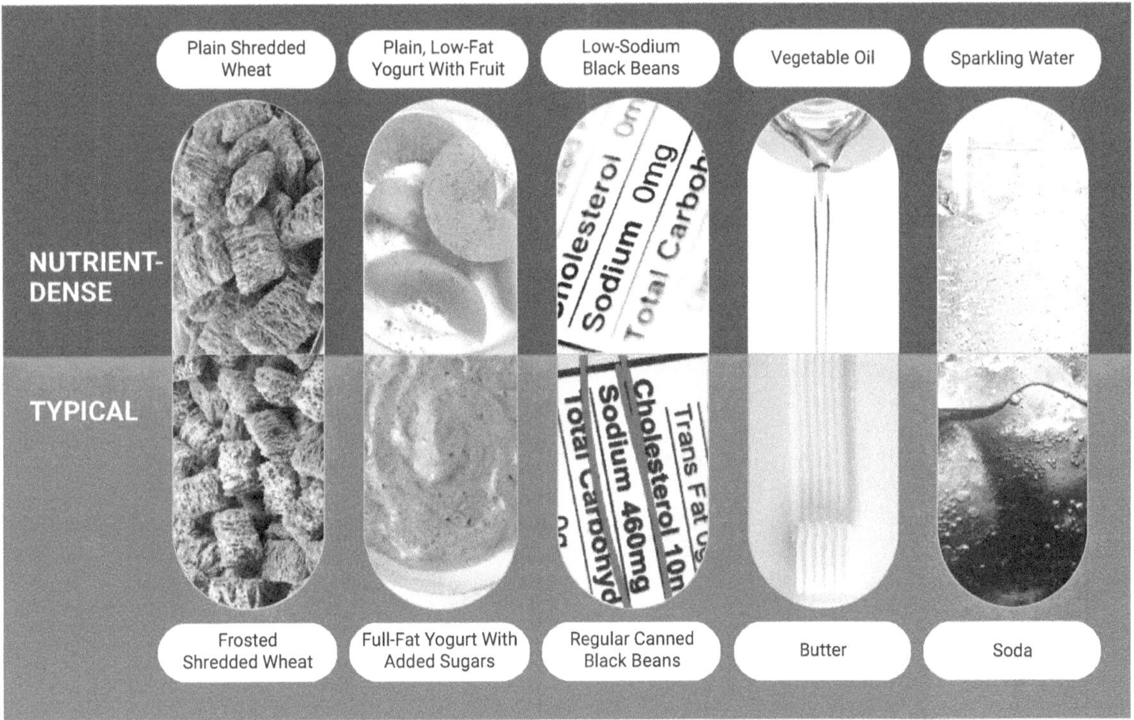

Guideline 1

The Health Benefits of a Healthy Dietary Pattern

Science is the foundation of the *Dietary Guidelines* recommendations on what Americans should eat and drink to promote health, reduce risk of chronic disease, and meet nutrient needs. The science shows that consuming a healthy dietary pattern, meeting food group and nutrient needs with nutrient-dense foods and beverages, and limiting intake of foods and beverages that are not nutrient-dense is related to many health benefits. Science also supports the idea that every life stage provides an opportunity to make food choices that promote health and well-being, achieve and maintain appropriate weight status, and reduce risk of diet-related chronic disease.

The science supporting the *Dietary Guidelines* is extensively documented in the *Scientific Report of the 2020 Dietary Guidelines Advisory Committee*, which describes the state of the science on key topics related to diet and health. Outcomes with Strong or Moderate evidence are provided in **Figure 1-3**. The report is available at **DietaryGuidelines.gov**.

Evidence on the association between dietary patterns and reduced risk of diet-related chronic diseases has expanded in recent years and supports the use of dietary patterns as a foundation for the recommendations in the *Dietary Guidelines for Americans, 2020-2025*. Consistent evidence demonstrates that a healthy dietary pattern is associated with beneficial outcomes for all-cause mortality, cardiovascular disease, overweight and obesity, type 2 diabetes, bone health, and certain types of cancer (breast and colorectal).

Common characteristics of dietary patterns associated with positive health outcomes include relatively higher intake of vegetables, fruits, legumes, whole grains, low- or non-fat dairy, lean meats and poultry, seafood, nuts, and unsaturated vegetable oils, and relatively lower consumption of red and processed meats, sugar-sweetened foods and beverages, and refined grains. The evidence examined showed broad representation across a number of populations and demographic groups. This suggests a consistent association no matter the region or cultural context in which a healthy dietary pattern is consumed. In addition, dietary patterns characterized by higher intake of red and processed meats, sugar-sweetened foods and beverages, and refined grains are, in and of themselves, associated with detrimental health outcomes. These findings are consistent with—and build on—the evidence base that informed the *2015-2020 Dietary Guidelines*.

A Healthy Dietary Pattern Supports Appropriate Calorie Levels

The total number of calories a person needs each day varies depending on a number of factors, namely the person's age, sex, height, weight, level of physical activity, and pregnancy or lactation status. Due to reductions in basal metabolic rate that occur with aging, calorie needs generally decrease for adults as they age. In addition, a need to lose, maintain, or gain weight affects how many calories should be consumed. Estimated amounts of calories needed based on age, sex, and level of physical activity are provided in ***Appendix 2. Estimated Calorie Needs***, and estimated calorie needs relevant for different ages are provided in each life stage chapter. These estimates are based on the Estimated Energy Requirement (EER) equations established by the National Academies of Sciences, Engineering, and Medicine (National Academies) using reference heights (average) and reference weights (healthy) for each age-sex group. These amounts are estimates. **The best way to evaluate calorie intake, in comparison to calorie needs, is by measuring body weight status.**

Rather than focus on weight status at any one point in life, **the *Dietary Guidelines* supports healthy weight trajectories at each stage of life—appropriate weight gain during pregnancy and postpartum weight loss, healthy growth and development from infancy through adolescence, weight stability during mid-life, and healthy body composition late in life. Meeting the *Dietary Guidelines* recommendations within calorie needs can help prevent excess weight gain at every life stage and support overall good health.**

Guideline

Figure 1-3

The Science Underlying the *Dietary Guidelines* Demonstrates That Healthy Eating Across the Lifespan Can Promote Health and Reduce Risk of Chronic Disease

Birth Through 23 Months

- Lower risk of overweight and obesity
- Lower risk of type 1 diabetes
- Adequate iron status and lower risk of iron deficiency
- Lower risk of peanut allergy
- Lower risk of asthma

Children and Adolescents

- Lower adiposity
- Lower total and low-density lipoprotein (LDL) cholesterol

Women Who Are Pregnant or Lactating

- Favorable cognitive development in the child
- Favorable folate status in women during pregnancy and lactation

Adults, Including Older Adults

- Lower risk of all-cause mortality
- Lower risk of cardiovascular disease
- Lower risk of cardiovascular disease mortality
- Lower total and LDL cholesterol
- Lower blood pressure
- Lower risk of obesity
- Lower body mass index, waist circumference, and body fat
- Lower risk of type 2 diabetes
- Lower risk of cancers of the breast, colon, and rectum
- Favorable bone health, including lower risk of hip fracture

NOTE: The 2020 Dietary Guidelines Advisory Committee examined the evidence on diet and health across the lifespan. Evidence is not available for all combinations of exposures and outcomes for the population subgroups presented in this figure. The Committee rated the evidence on diet and health as Strong, Moderate, Limited, or Grade Not Assignable. Only outcomes with Strong or Moderate evidence are included in this table. See the **Committee's Report** for specific graded conclusion statements.

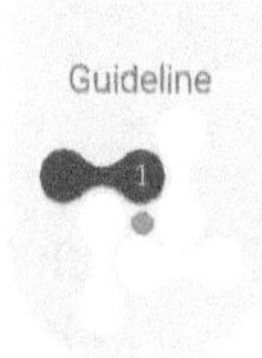

Key Dietary Principles

To help people meet the Guidelines and Key Recommendations, the following are important principles when making decisions about nutrient-dense food and beverage choices to achieve a healthy dietary pattern.

MEET NUTRITIONAL NEEDS PRIMARILY FROM FOODS AND BEVERAGES

The *Dietary Guidelines* are designed to meet the Recommended Dietary Allowances and Adequate Intakes for essential nutrients, as well as Acceptable Macronutrient Distribution Ranges, all set by the National Academies. An underlying premise of the *Dietary Guidelines* is that nutritional needs should be met primarily from foods and beverages—specifically, nutrient-dense foods and beverages. In some cases, when meeting nutrient needs is not otherwise possible, fortified foods and nutrient-containing dietary supplements are useful. It is important to note that the nutrient density and healthfulness of what people eat and drink often is determined ultimately by how a food item, dish, or meal is prepared, at home and away from home or produced by a manufacturer. Based on the U.S. food supply and marketplace, the examples of healthy dietary patterns in this edition are achievable through thoughtful, informed choices one decision, one meal, one day at a time—and consistently over time.

CHOOSE A VARIETY OF OPTIONS FROM EACH FOOD GROUP

Enjoy different foods and beverages within each food group. This can help meet nutrient needs—and also allows for flexibility so that the *Dietary Guidelines* can be tailored to meet cultural and personal preferences. All forms of foods, including fresh, canned, dried, frozen, and 100% juices, in nutrient-dense forms, can be included in healthy dietary patterns.

PAY ATTENTION TO PORTION SIZE

Portion size is a term often used to describe the amount of a food or beverage served or consumed in one eating occasion. It is important to pay attention to portion size when making food and beverage choices, particularly for foods and beverages that are not nutrient-dense. A concept that can help people choose appropriate portions is ***serving size***. This term is included on the Nutrition Facts label and refers to the amount of a food or beverage that is customarily consumed—it is not a recommendation of how much to eat or drink. Consuming less than the stated serving size results in consuming fewer calories and other nutrients or food components. Some products may have multiple servings per package.

Most Americans Do Not Follow a Healthy Dietary Pattern

The typical dietary patterns currently consumed by many in the United States do not align with the *Dietary Guidelines* (**Figure 1-4**). The Healthy Eating Index (HEI) is a measure of diet quality that can be used to assess compliance with the *Dietary Guidelines*. For Americans ages 2 and older, HEI-2015 scores indicate that intakes are not consistent with recommendations for a healthy dietary pattern. Average diet quality has slightly improved in the past 10 years, but the average score of 59 (on a scale from 0 to 100) indicates that people have much room for improvement. Differences in overall HEI scores are seen across age, sex, race-ethnic, and income subgroups and by pregnancy and lactation status, though poor diet quality is observed across all groups. With each step closer to a diet that aligns with the core elements of a healthy dietary pattern, HEI scores will increase and risk for chronic disease will decrease.

Figure 1-4

Adherence of the U.S. Population to the *Dietary Guidelines* Across Life Stages, as Measured by Average Total Healthy Eating Index-2015 Scores

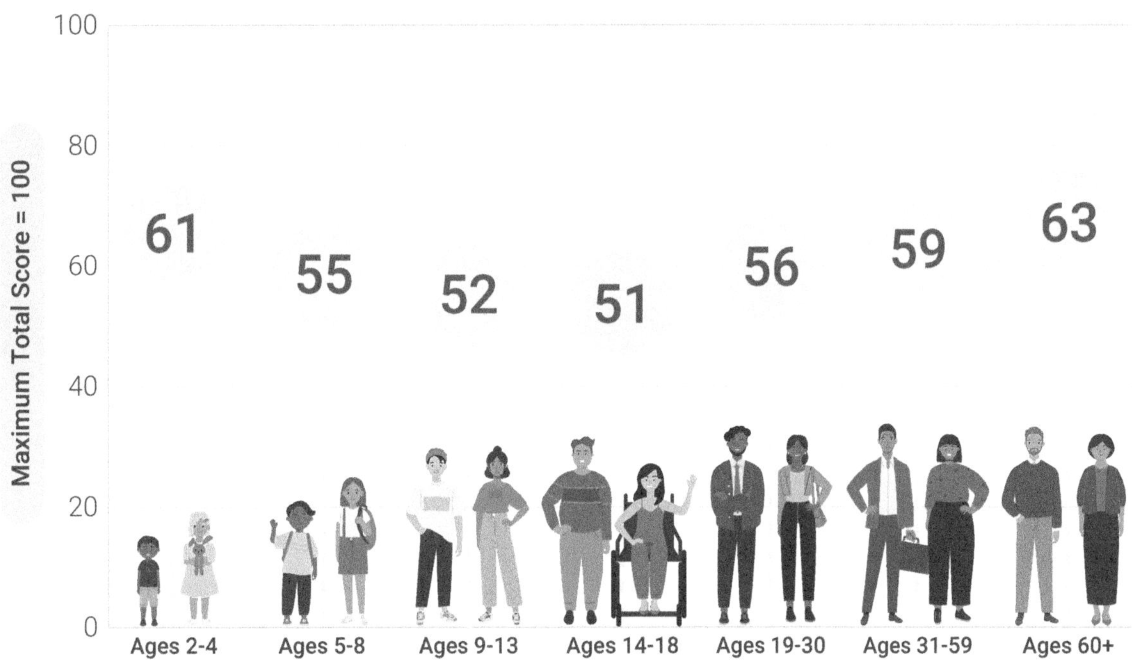

NOTE: HEI-2015 total scores are out of 100 possible points. A score of 100 indicates that recommendations on average were met or exceeded. A higher total score indicates a higher quality diet.

Data Source: Analysis of What We Eat in America, NHANES 2015-2016, ages 2 and older, day 1 dietary intake data, weighted.

In addition, the high percentage of the population with overweight or obesity suggests that many people in the United States consume foods and beverages that contribute to a calorie imbalance, a situation more likely to occur with low physical activity. As shown in the ***Introduction,* Table I-1**, 74 percent of all adults and 40 percent of all children and youth in the United States have either overweight or obesity.

Even from the youngest ages, almost all Americans should shift to healthier food and beverage choices and consume smaller portions to achieve a healthy dietary pattern within an appropriate number of calories. It is never too early or too late to improve intake and establish a healthy dietary pattern.

Guideline

Guideline 2

Customize and Enjoy Food and Beverage Choices to Reflect Personal Preferences, Cultural Traditions, and Budgetary Considerations

Eating should be enjoyed, and a healthy dietary pattern can be enjoyable, from early life to older adulthood. The science reviewed to inform the *Dietary Guidelines* represents the diversity of Americans, including all ages and life stages, different racial and ethnic backgrounds, and a range of socioeconomic statuses. A healthy dietary pattern can benefit all individuals regardless of age, race or ethnicity, or current health status.

The *Dietary Guidelines* provides a framework intended to be customized to fit individual, household, and Federal program participants' preferences, as well as the foodways of the diverse cultures in the United States. The U.S. population is diverse in myriad ways. The *Dietary Guidelines* framework purposely provides recommendations by food groups and subgroups—not specific foods and beverages—to avoid being prescriptive. This framework approach ensures that people can "make it their own" by selecting healthy foods, beverages, meals, and snacks specific to their needs and preferences.

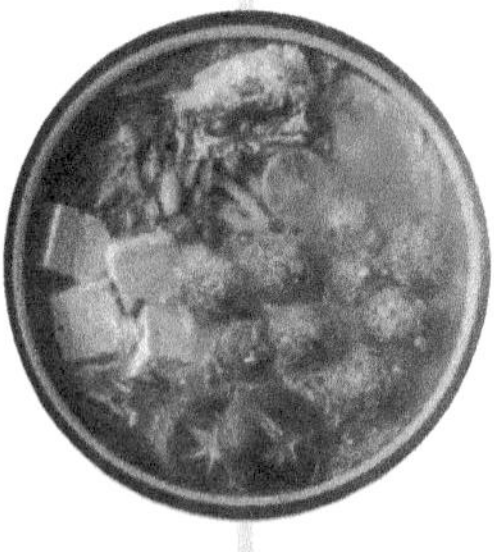

The food groups include a broad variety of nutrient-dense food and beverage choices. In every setting, across all cultures, and at any age or budget, there are foods and beverages that can fit within the *Dietary Guidelines* framework.

Start with Personal Preferences

Exposure to different types of food is important early in life to better develop a child's interest and willingness to eat and enjoy a variety of foods. Through each life stage that follows, a key starting point for establishing and maintaining a healthy dietary pattern is to ensure that individual and/or family preferences—in nutrient-dense forms—are built into day-to-day choices.

Incorporate Cultural Traditions

Cultural background can have significant influence on food and beverage choices. Customizing the *Dietary Guidelines* framework to reflect specific cultures and traditions is an important strategy to help communities across the country eat and enjoy a healthy dietary pattern. Nutrient-dense culturally relevant foods and beverages are part of all of the food groups. Spices and herbs can help flavor foods when reducing added sugars, saturated fat, and sodium, and they also can add to the enjoyment of nutrient-dense foods, dishes, and meals that reflect specific cultures. Relying on the expertise of professionals in nutrition and in specific cultural foodways can help people prepare foods healthfully while retaining heritage.

Consider Budget

Despite a common perception that eating healthfully is expensive, a healthy dietary pattern can be affordable and fit within budgetary constraints. There are a range of strategies that can be used to help individuals and families follow a healthy dietary pattern including advanced planning; considering regional and seasonal food availability; and incorporating a variety of fresh, frozen, dried, and canned options. **The USDA Food Plans—Thrifty, Low-Cost, Moderate-Cost, and Liberal-Cost food plans**—each represent a nutritious diet at a different cost level. These plans are scheduled to be revised, with an updated Thrifty Food Plan published by the end of 2022 to reflect this edition of the *Dietary Guidelines* and updated food availability and food cost data.

Guideline

Figure 1-5

Customizing the *Dietary Guidelines* Framework

The *Dietary Guidelines* approach of providing a framework–not prescriptive details–ensures that its recommendations can "meet people where they are," from personal preferences to cultural foodways, and including budgetary considerations. The examples below are a sample of the range of options in each food group—to be eaten in nutrient-dense forms. Additional examples are listed under **Table A3-2** in ***Appendix 3***.

Vegetables

- **Dark-Green Vegetables:** All fresh, frozen, and canned dark-green leafy vegetables and broccoli, cooked or raw: for example, amaranth leaves, bok choy, broccoli, chamnamul, chard, collards, kale, mustard greens, poke greens, romaine lettuce, spinach, taro leaves, turnip greens, and watercress.
- **Red and Orange Vegetables:** All fresh, frozen, and canned red and orange vegetables or juice, cooked or raw: for example, calabaza, carrots, red or orange bell peppers, sweet potatoes, tomatoes, 100% tomato juice, and winter squash.
- **Beans, Peas, Lentils:** All cooked from dry or canned beans, peas, chickpeas, and lentils: for example, black beans, black-eyed peas, bayo beans, chickpeas (garbanzo beans), edamame, kidney beans, lentils, lima beans, mung beans, pigeon peas, pinto beans, and split peas. Does not include green beans or green peas.
- **Starchy Vegetables:** All fresh, frozen, and canned starchy vegetables: for example, breadfruit, burdock root, cassava, corn, jicama, lotus root, lima beans, plantains, white potatoes, salsify, taro root (dasheen or yautia), water chestnuts, yam, and yucca.
- **Other Vegetables:** All other fresh, frozen, and canned vegetables, cooked or raw: for example, asparagus, avocado, bamboo shoots, beets, bitter melon, Brussels sprouts, cabbage (green, red, napa, savoy), cactus pads (nopales), cauliflower, celery, chayote (mirliton), cucumber, eggplant, green beans, kohlrabi, luffa, mushrooms, okra, onions, radish, rutabaga, seaweed, snow peas, summer squash, tomatillos, and turnips.

Fruits

Fruits

- All fresh, frozen, canned, and dried fruits and 100% fruit juices: for example, apples, Asian pears, bananas, berries (e.g., blackberries, blueberries, currants, huckleberries, kiwifruit, mulberries, raspberries, and strawberries); citrus fruit (e.g., calamondin, grapefruit, lemons, limes, oranges, and pomelos); cherries, dates, figs, grapes, guava, jackfruit, lychee, mangoes, melons (e.g., cantaloupe, casaba, honeydew, and watermelon); nectarines, papaya, peaches, pears, persimmons, pineapple, plums, pomegranates, raisins, rhubarb, sapote, and soursop.

Figure 1-5 **Customizing the *Dietary Guidelines* Framework (continued)**

Grains

- **Whole grains:** All whole-grain products and whole grains used as ingredients: for example, amaranth, barley (not pearled), brown rice, buckwheat, bulgur, millet, oats, popcorn, quinoa, dark rye, whole-grain cornmeal, whole-wheat bread, whole-wheat chapati, whole-grain cereals and crackers, and wild rice.
- **Refined grains:** All refined-grain products and refined grains used as ingredients: for example, white breads, refined-grain cereals and crackers, corn grits, cream of rice, cream of wheat, barley (pearled), masa, pasta, and white rice. Refined-grain choices should be enriched.

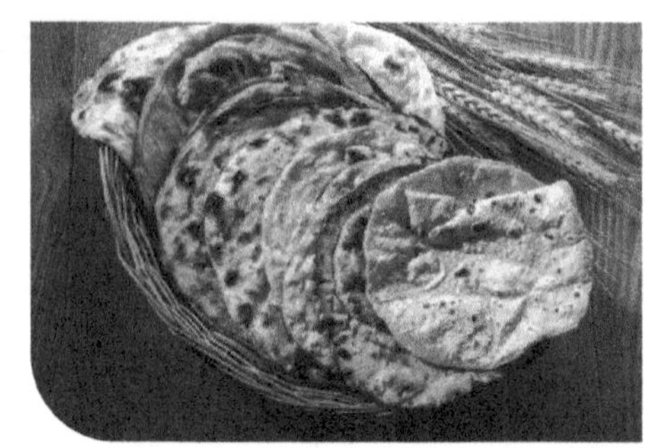

Dairy and Fortified Soy Alternatives

- All fluid, dry, or evaporated milk, including lactose-free and lactose-reduced products and fortified soy beverages (soy milk), buttermilk, yogurt, kefir, frozen yogurt, dairy desserts, and cheeses. Most choices should be fat-free or low-fat. Cream, sour cream, and cream cheese are not included due to their low calcium content.

Protein Foods

- **Meats, Poultry, Eggs:** Meats include beef, goat, lamb, pork, and game meat (e.g., bison, moose, elk, deer). Poultry includes chicken, Cornish hens, duck, game birds (e.g., ostrich, pheasant, and quail), goose, and turkey. Organ meats include chitterlings, giblets, gizzard, liver, sweetbreads, tongue, and tripe. Eggs include chicken eggs and other birds' eggs. Meats and poultry should be lean or low-fat.
- **Seafood:** Seafood examples that are lower in methylmercury include: anchovy, black sea bass, catfish, clams, cod, crab, crawfish, flounder, haddock, hake, herring, lobster, mullet, oyster, perch, pollock, salmon, sardine, scallop, shrimp, sole, squid, tilapia, freshwater trout, light tuna, and whiting.
- **Nuts, Seeds, Soy Products:** Nuts and seeds include all nuts (tree nuts and peanuts), nut butters, seeds (e.g., chia, flax, pumpkin, sesame, and sunflower), and seed butters (e.g., sesame or tahini and sunflower). Soy includes tofu, tempeh, and products made from soy flour, soy protein isolate, and soy concentrate. Nuts should be unsalted.

Guideline

Guideline 3

Focus on Meeting Food Group Needs With Nutrient-Dense Foods and Beverages, and Stay Within Calorie Limits

The *Dietary Guidelines* include recommendations for food groups—vegetables, fruits, grains, dairy, and protein foods—eaten at an appropriate calorie level and in forms with limited amounts of added sugars, saturated fat, and sodium. Science shows that these same core elements of a healthy dietary pattern are consistent across each life stage.

However, as shown in **Figure 1-6**, when compared to the Healthy U.S.-Style Dietary Pattern, most Americans have substantial room for improvement:

- More than 80 percent have dietary patterns that are low in vegetables, fruits, and dairy.
- More than half of the population is meeting or exceeding total grain and total protein foods recommendations, but are not meeting the recommendations for the subgroups within each of these food groups.

Figure 1-6

Dietary Intakes Compared to Recommendations: Percent of the U.S. Population Ages 1 and Older Who Are Below and At or Above Each Dietary Goal

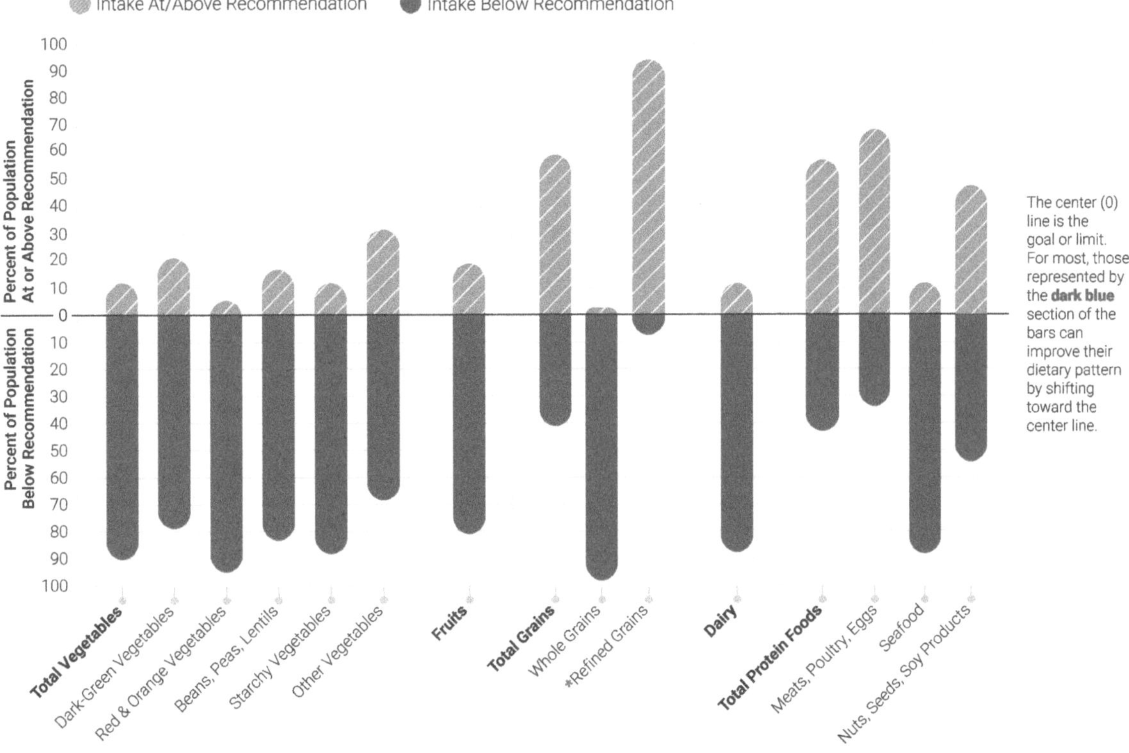

***NOTE:** Recommended daily intake of whole grains is to be at least half of total grain consumption, and the limit for refined grains is to be no more than half of total grain consumption.

Data Source: Analysis of What We Eat in America, NHANES 2013-2016, ages 1 and older, 2 days dietary intake data, weighted. *Recommended Intake Ranges*: Healthy U.S.-Style Dietary Patterns (see ***Appendix 3***).

Learn More:
Table A3-2 in *Appendix 3* provides the food group-based Healthy U.S.-Style Dietary Pattern as a sample framework. Information on what counts as a cup- or ounce-equivalent is also provided under this table in **footnote c**.

About Beans, Peas, and Lentils

"Beans, peas, and lentils" is a new name for the vegetable subgroup formerly called "legumes (beans and peas)." Beans, peas, and lentils, which also are known as pulses, include the dried edible seeds of legumes. The foods in this vegetable subgroup have not changed. However, the new name of the subgroup more accurately reflects the category of foods included. Beans include varieties such as kidney beans, pinto beans, white beans, black beans, lima beans, and fava beans. Also included are dried peas (e.g., chickpeas, black-eyed peas, pigeon peas, and split peas) and lentils. Edamame, which is the soybean in the pod, is counted in the beans, peas, and lentils subgroup even though it is eaten fresh and not dried.

Because beans, peas, and lentils have a similar nutrient profile to foods in both the vegetable group and the protein foods group, they may be thought of as either a vegetable or a protein food when aiming to meet recommended intakes.

Green peas and green (string) beans are not counted in the beans, peas, and lentils subgroup because the nutrient content of these vegetables is more similar to vegetables in other subgroups. Green peas, which are not dried before consumption, are grouped with starchy vegetables and green beans are in the other vegetables subgroup, which includes onions, iceberg lettuce, celery, and cabbage. Generally, foods made from processed soybeans are a part of the nuts, seeds and soy products protein foods subgroup.

The following sections use the Healthy U.S.-Style Dietary Pattern to show how people can make shifts in their choices to achieve a healthy dietary pattern. Information on the amounts to consume—in cup and ounce equivalents—for each life stage is discussed in the subsequent life stage chapters and ***Appendix 3. USDA Dietary Patterns***.

Eating an appropriate mix of foods from the food groups and subgroups—within an appropriate calorie level—is important to promote health at each life stage. Each of the food groups and their subgroups provides an array of nutrients, and the amounts recommended reflect eating patterns that have been associated with positive health outcomes. Foods from all of the food groups should be eaten in nutrient-dense forms. The following sections describe special considerations related to each food group.

Vegetables

Healthy dietary patterns include a variety of vegetables from all five vegetable subgroups—dark green; red and orange; beans, peas, and lentils; starchy; and other. These include all fresh, frozen, canned, and dried options in cooked or raw forms, including 100% vegetable juices. Vegetables in their nutrient-dense forms have limited additions such as salt, butter, or creamy sauces. Examples of vegetables in each of the subgroups are available in ***Appendix 3***.

Almost 90 percent of the U.S. population does not meet the recommendation for vegetables. In addition, with few exceptions, the U.S. population does not meet intake recommendations for any of the vegetable subgroups. About 45 percent of all vegetables are eaten as a separate food item; about 40 percent as part of a mixed dish; and the remainder are mostly consumed as snack foods and condiments. Vegetables, when consumed on their own, are generally consumed in forms with additional sodium either from salt added in cooking or added sauces such as soy sauce or bottled stir-fry sauces. Many vegetables are consumed as part of mixed dishes like sandwiches, pasta with a tomato-based sauce, or casseroles that may have other ingredients that are sources of saturated fat and/or sodium.

For most individuals, following a healthy eating pattern will require an increase in total vegetable intake and from all vegetable subgroups, shifting to nutrient-dense forms, and an increase in the variety of different vegetables consumed over time. Vegetables can be part of many types of mixed dishes, from burgers, sandwiches, and tacos, to pizza, stews, pasta dishes, grain-based casseroles, and soups. Strategies to increase vegetable intake include increasing the vegetable content of mixed dishes or eating less of a main dish to allow for more vegetables as side dishes—keeping these nutrient dense.

Fruits

The fruit food group includes whole fruits and 100% fruit juice. Whole fruits include fresh, canned, frozen, and dried forms. Whole fruits can be eaten in various forms, such as cut, sliced, diced, or cubed. At least half of the recommended amount of fruit should come from whole fruit, rather than 100% juice. When juices are consumed, they should be 100% juice and always pasteurized or 100% juice diluted with water (without added sugars). Also, when selecting canned fruit, choose options that are canned with 100% juice or options lowest in added sugars.

About 80 percent of the U.S. population does not meet fruit recommendations. Over 60 percent of all fruit intake comes from whole forms—fresh, canned, frozen, or dried—or 100% juice. Fruit is generally consumed in nutrient-dense forms such as plain bananas, apples, oranges, or grapes. However, some fruit is consumed as part of foods that may not be nutrient-dense, such as fruit pie or similar desserts.

Most people would benefit from increasing their intake of fruit, mostly as whole fruits in nutrient-dense forms. A wide variety of fruits are available in the U.S. marketplace, some year-round and others seasonally. Strategies to help achieve this shift include choosing more whole fruits as snacks and including them in meals.

Grains

Healthy dietary patterns include whole grains and limit the intake of refined grains. At least half of total grains should be whole grains. Individuals who eat refined grains should choose enriched grains. Individuals who consume all of their grains as whole grains should include some that have been fortified with folic acid. Grain-based foods in nutrient-dense forms limit the additions of added sugars, saturated fat, and sodium.

A food is a 100% whole-grain food if the only grains it contains are whole grains. A 1 ounce-equivalent of 100% whole grains has 16 grams of whole grains. The recommendation to consume at least half of total grains as whole grains can be met in a number of ways.

- Choose 100% whole-grain foods for at least half of all grains consumed. The relative amount of whole grain in the food can be inferred by the placement of the grain in the ingredient list. The whole grain should be the first ingredient—or the second ingredient after water. For foods with multiple whole-grain ingredients, they should appear near the beginning of the ingredient list.

- Choose products with at least 50 percent of the total weight as whole-grain ingredients. If a food has at least 8 grams of whole grains per ounce-equivalent then half of the grains are whole-grain ingredients.

Most Americans meet recommendations for total grain intakes, although 98 percent fall below recommendations for whole grains and 74 percent exceed limits for refined grains. Almost half of all intake of refined grains is from mixed dishes, such as sandwiches, burgers, tacos, pizza, macaroni and cheese, and spaghetti with meatballs. About 20 percent of intake of refined grains comes from snacks and sweets, including crackers, pretzels, cakes, cookies, and other grain desserts. The remaining refined grains are generally eaten as separate food items, such as pancakes, cereals, breads, tortillas, pasta, or rice. About 60 percent of whole-grain intake in the United States is from individual food items, mostly cereals and crackers, rather than mixed dishes. Grains are generally consumed in forms with higher amounts of sodium (e.g., breads, tortillas, crackers) and added sugars (e.g., grain-based desserts, many ready-to-eat breakfast cereals) rather than the nutrient-dense forms. Further, grains are often consumed as part of mixed dishes, such as pasta dishes, casseroles, and sandwiches that may have other ingredients that are not in nutrient-dense forms.

Shifting from refined to whole-grain versions of commonly consumed foods—such as from white to 100% whole-wheat breads, and white to brown rice where culturally appropriate—would increase whole-grain intakes and lower refined grain intakes to help meet recommendations. Additionally, shifting to more nutrient-dense forms of grains, such as ready-to-eat breakfast cereals with less sugar, will help meet healthy dietary patterns. With careful planning, limited amounts of salt, butter, or sources of added sugars can be used to make

some grain-based foods more palatable while staying within calorie and nutrient limits, but most grains should be eaten in their most nutrient-dense forms. Reducing intakes of cakes, cookies, and other grain desserts will also support reducing refined grain intakes and staying within calorie needs.

Dairy and Fortified Soy Alternatives

Healthy dietary patterns feature dairy, including fat-free and low-fat (1%) milk, yogurt, and cheese. Individuals who are lactose intolerant can choose low-lactose and lactose-free dairy products. For individuals who choose dairy alternatives, fortified soy beverages (commonly known as "soy milk") and soy yogurt—which are fortified with calcium, vitamin A, and vitamin D—are included as part of the dairy group because they are similar to milk and yogurt based on nutrient composition and in their use in meals.

Other products sold as "milks" but made from plants (e.g., almond, rice, coconut, oat, and hemp "milks") may contain calcium and be consumed as a source of calcium, but they are not included as part of the dairy group because their overall nutritional content is not similar to dairy milk and fortified soy beverages. Therefore, consuming these beverages does not contribute to meeting the dairy group recommendation.

About 90 percent of the U.S. population does not meet dairy recommendations. The percent of Americans who drink milk as a beverage on a given day is 65 percent among young children, 34 percent in adolescents, and about 20 percent for adults. Dairy is generally consumed in forms with higher amounts of sodium (e.g., cheeses as part of mixed dishes such as sandwiches, pizza, and pasta dishes) and saturated fat (e.g., higher fat milks and yogurts) and can be a source of added sugars such as flavored milk, ice cream, and sweetened yogurts.

Most individuals would benefit by increasing intake of dairy in fat-free or low-fat forms, whether from milk (including lactose-free milk), yogurt, and cheese, or from fortified soy beverages or soy yogurt. Strategies to increase dairy intake include drinking fat-free or low-fat milk or a fortified soy beverage with meals or incorporating unsweetened fat-free or low-fat yogurt into breakfast or snacks.

Protein Foods

Healthy dietary patterns include a variety of protein foods in nutrient-dense forms. The protein foods group comprises a broad group of foods from both animal and plant sources, and includes several subgroups: meats, poultry, and eggs; seafood; and nuts, seeds, and soy products. As noted previously, beans, peas, and lentils may be considered a part of the protein foods group as well as the vegetable group. Protein also is found in some foods from other food groups, such as dairy. Meats and poultry vary in fat content and include both fresh and processed forms. Most intake of meats and poultry should be from fresh, frozen, or canned, and in lean forms (e.g., chicken breast or ground turkey) versus processed meats (e.g., hot dogs, sausages, ham, luncheon meats).

A healthy vegetarian dietary pattern can be achieved by incorporating protein foods from plants. Compared with the Healthy U.S.-Style Dietary Pattern, the Healthy Vegetarian Dietary Pattern is higher in soy products (particularly tofu and other processed soy products); beans, peas, and lentils; nuts and seeds; and whole grains. Inclusion of dairy and eggs make this an example of a lacto-ovo vegetarian pattern. Meats, poultry, and seafood are not included.

Seafood, which includes fish and shellfish, is a protein foods subgroup that provides beneficial fatty acids (e.g., eicosapentaenoic acid [EPA] and docosahexaenoic acid [DHA]). In addition, mercury, in the form of methylmercury, is found in seafood in varying levels. The U.S. Food and Drug Administration (FDA) and the U.S. Environmental Protection Agency (EPA) provide joint advice regarding seafood consumption to limit methylmercury exposure for women who might become or are pregnant or lactating and young children.[2] Seafood choices higher in EPA and DHA and lower in methylmercury are encouraged. Seafood varieties commonly consumed in the United States that are higher in EPA and DHA and lower in methylmercury include salmon, anchovies, sardines, Pacific oysters, and trout. Tilapia, shrimp, catfish, crab, and flounder are commonly consumed varieties that also are lower in methylmercury.

Intakes of protein foods are close to the target amounts, but many Americans do not meet recommendations for specific protein subgroups. About three-quarters of Americans meet or exceed the recommendation for meats, poultry, and eggs. However, almost 90 percent do not meet the recommendation for seafood and more than half do not meet the recommendation for nuts, seeds, and soy products. Slightly less than half (43%) of all protein foods are consumed as a separate food item, such as a chicken breast, a steak, an egg, a fish filet, or peanuts. About the same proportion are consumed as part of a mixed dish (48%), with the largest amount from sandwiches including burgers and tacos. Protein foods are generally consumed in forms with higher amounts of saturated fat or sodium and often part of mixed dishes (e.g., sandwiches, casseroles, pasta dishes) that include other ingredients that are not in nutrient-dense forms.

Shifts are needed within the protein foods group to add variety to subgroup intakes. Selecting from the seafood subgroup or the beans, peas, and lentils subgroup more often could help meet recommendations while still ensuring adequate protein consumption. Replacing processed or high-fat meats (e.g., hot dogs, sausages, bacon) with seafood could help lower intake of saturated fat and sodium, nutrients that are often consumed in excess of recommended limits. Replacing processed or high-fat meats with beans, peas, and lentils would have similar benefits, as well as increasing dietary fiber, a dietary component of public health concern.

[2] Available at **FDA.gov/fishadvice** and **EPA.gov/fishadvice**.

Follow Food Safety Recommendations

An important part of healthy eating is keeping food safe. Individuals in their own homes can help keep food safe by following safe food handling practices. Four basic food safety principles work together to reduce the risk of foodborne illness—Clean, Separate, Cook, and Chill.

1: Clean	**2: Separate**	**3: Cook**	**4: Chill**
Wash hands and surfaces often.	Separate raw meats from other foods.	Cook food to safe internal temperatures.	Refrigerate foods promptly.

Some eating behaviors, such as consuming raw, undercooked, or unpasteurized food products, increase the risk of contracting a foodborne illness. Populations at increased risk of foodborne illness, or those preparing food for them, should use extra caution. These include women who are pregnant, young children, and older adults. Specific guidance for these life stages is discussed in subsequent chapters. Individuals with weakened immune systems are also at increased risk for foodborne illness. More information about food safety is available at:

- Your Gateway to Food Safety: **foodsafety.gov**
- USDA Food Safety Education campaigns: **fsis.usda.gov/wps/portal/fsis/topics/food-safety-education/teach-others/fsis-educational-campaigns**
- Fight BAC!®: **fightbac.org** and for Babies and Toddlers: **fightbac.org/kids/**
- CDC 4 Steps to Food Safety: **cdc.gov/foodsafety**
- FDA: Buy, Store & Serve Safe Food at **fda.gov/food/consumers/buy-store-serve-safe-food**

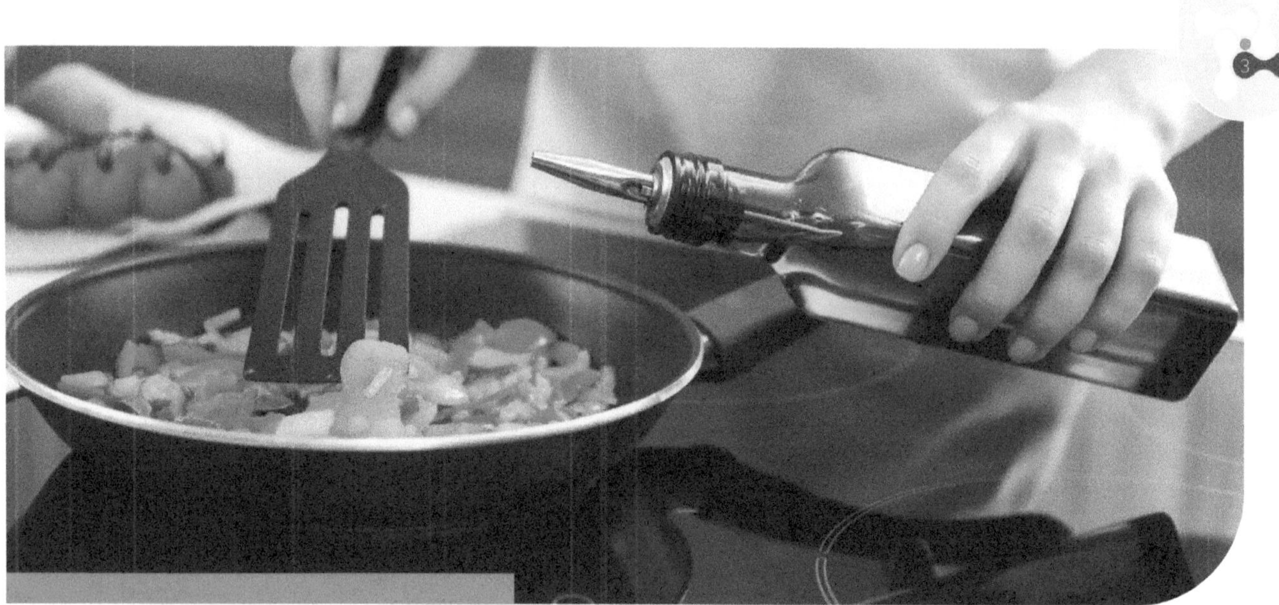

Oils

Oils are important to consider as part of a healthy dietary pattern as they provide essential fatty acids. Commonly consumed oils include canola, corn, olive, peanut, safflower, soybean, and sunflower oils. Oils also are naturally present in nuts, seeds, seafood, olives, and avocados. The fat in some tropical plants, such as coconut oil, palm kernel oil, and palm oil, are not included in the oils category because they contain a higher percentage of saturated fat than do other oils.

Strategies to shift intake include cooking with vegetable oil in place of fats high in saturated fat, including butter, shortening, lard, or coconut oil. However, some foods, such as desserts and sweet snacks, that are prepared with oils instead of fats high in saturated fat are still high in added sugars, and are thus not a nutrient-dense food choice.

Beverages

When choosing beverages in a healthy dietary pattern, both the calories and nutrients that they provide are important considerations. Beverages that are calorie-free—especially water—or that contribute beneficial nutrients, such as fat-free and low-fat milk and 100% juice, should be the primary beverages consumed. Coffee, tea, and flavored waters also are options, but the most nutrient-dense options for these beverages include little, if any, sweeteners or cream. For discussion on sugar-sweetened beverages or alcohol, see "**Added Sugars**" and "**Alcoholic Beverages**," respectively.

CAFFEINE

Caffeine is a dietary component that functions in the body as a stimulant. Most intake of caffeine in the United States comes from coffee, tea, and soda. Caffeine is a substance that is Generally Recognized as Safe (GRAS) in cola-type beverages by the Food and Drug Administration (FDA). For healthy adults, the FDA has cited 400 milligrams per day of caffeine as an amount not generally associated with dangerous, negative effects. Additional information related to caffeine is provided in subsequent life stage chapters.

Beverages and Added Sugars

Examples of beverages that often have added sugars are regular soda (i.e., not sugar-free), fruit drinks, sports drinks, energy drinks, sweetened waters, and coffee and tea beverages with added sugars. Coffee and tea beverages from restaurants can contain many extra calories because of the addition of cream or milk and sugar. See below for examples of 12-ounce beverages showing the added sugars and total calories.

Drink (12-ounce serving)	Total Calories	Added Sugars (Grams)	Added Sugars (Teaspoons)
Plain Water	0	0	0
Unsweetened Tea	0	0	0
Sports Drinks	97	20	5
Cafe Mocha	290	21	5
Chai Tea Latte	180	23	5 ½
Sweetened Tea	115	29	7
Regular Soda	156	37	9
Lemonade	171	43	10
Fruit Drinks	238	59	14

Data Source: U.S. Department of Agriculture, Agricultural Research Service. 2020. *USDA Food and Nutrient Database for Dietary Studies and USDA Food Patterns Equivalents Database 2017-2018.* Food Surveys Research Group Home Page, **ars.usda.gov/nea/bhnrc/fsrg**.

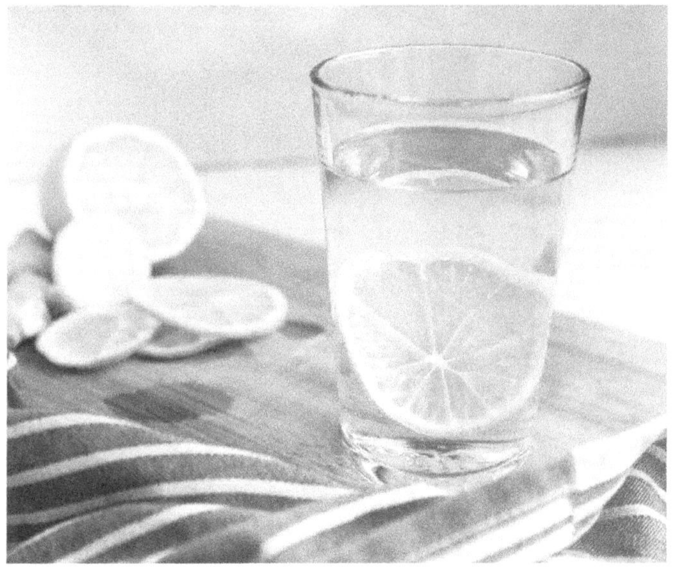

Dietary Components of Public Health Concern for Underconsumption

Current inadequate intake of nutrient-dense foods and beverages across food groups has resulted in underconsumption of some nutrients and dietary components. Calcium, potassium, dietary fiber, and vitamin D are considered dietary components of public health concern for the general U.S. population because low intakes are associated with health concerns. Additional dietary components that are underconsumed during specific life stages are highlighted in subsequent chapters.

If a healthy dietary pattern is consumed, amounts of calcium, potassium, and dietary fiber can meet recommendations. Individuals should be encouraged to make shifts to increase the intake of vegetables, fruits, beans, whole grains, and dairy to move intakes of these underconsumed dietary components closer to recommendations. In some cases, fortified foods and dietary supplements may be useful in providing one or more nutrients that otherwise may be consumed in less than recommended amounts. Vitamin D recommendations are harder to achieve through natural sources from diet alone and would require consuming foods and beverages fortified with vitamin D. In many cases, taking a vitamin D supplement may be appropriate especially when sunlight exposure is limited due to climate or the use of sunscreen. Lists of dietary sources of calcium, potassium, dietary fiber, and vitamin D are available at **DietaryGuidelines.gov**.

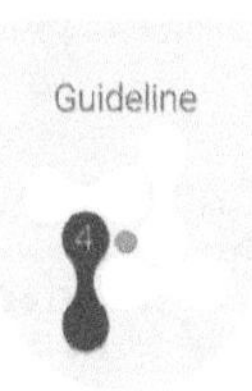

Guideline 4

Limit Foods and Beverages Higher in Added Sugars, Saturated Fat, and Sodium, and Limit Alcoholic Beverages

A healthy dietary pattern is designed to meet food group and nutrient recommendations while staying within calorie needs. Additionally, a healthy dietary pattern is designed to not exceed the Tolerable Upper Intake Level (UL) or Chronic Disease Risk Reduction (CDRR) level for nutrients. To achieve these goals, the pattern is based on consuming foods and beverages in their nutrient-dense forms—forms with the least amounts of added sugars, saturated fat, and sodium.

Most of the calories a person needs to eat each day—around 85 percent—are needed to meet food group recommendations healthfully, in nutrient-dense forms. The remaining calories—around 15 percent—are calories available for other uses, including for added sugars or saturated fat beyond the small amounts found in nutrient-dense forms of foods and beverages within the pattern, to consume more than the recommended amount of a food group, or for alcoholic beverages. This equates to 250 to 350 remaining calories for calorie patterns appropriate for most Americans.

Figure 1-7

The 85-15 Guide: Percentage of Calories Needed To Meet Food Group Needs With Nutrient-Dense Choices and Percentage Left for Other Uses

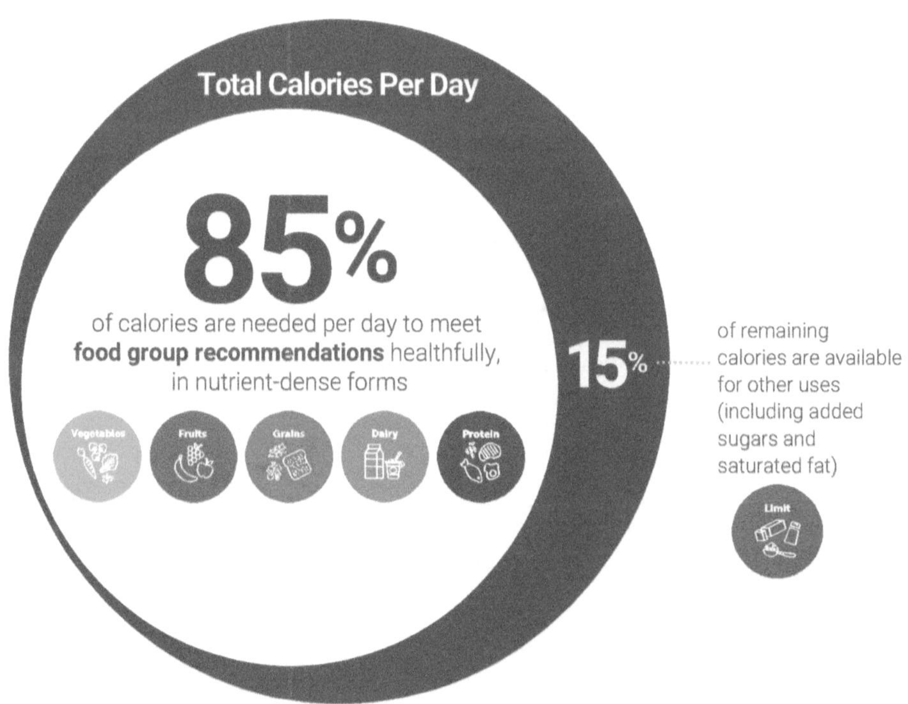

Guideline

Figure 1-8

Making Nutrient-Dense Choices: One Meal At a Time

Slight changes to individual parts of a meal can make a big difference. This meal shows examples of small shifts to more nutrient-dense choices that significantly improve the nutritional profile of the meal overall while delivering on taste and satisfaction.

Typical Burrito Bowl Total Calories = 1,120	Nutrient-Dense Burrito Bowl Total Calories = 715
White rice (1½ cups)	Brown rice (1 cup) + Romaine lettuce (½ cup)
Black beans (⅓ cup)	Black beans, reduced sodium (⅓ cup)
Chicken cooked with sauce (2 ounces)	Grilled chicken with spice rub (2 ounces)
No grilled vegetables	Added grilled vegetables (⅓ cup)
Guacamole (½ cup)	Sliced avocado (5 slices)
Jarred salsa (¼ cup)	Fresh salsa/pico de gallo (¼ cup)
Sour cream (¼ cup)	No sour cream
Cheese (⅓ cup)	Reduced-fat cheese (⅓ cup)
Jalapeño (5 slices)	Jalapeño (5 slices)
Iced tea with sugar (16 ounces)	Iced tea, no sugar (16 ounces)

Guideline

Figure 1-9

Making Healthy Choices: One Day At a Time

Small changes to more nutrient-dense, single food and beverage choices that, when combined, become a nutrient-dense meal, can lead to a whole day made up of nutrient-dense meals and snacks. The following example, which comes in under 2,000 calories, shows how people can make thoughtful choices that meet their food group needs, stay within limits, and, importantly, that they can enjoy.

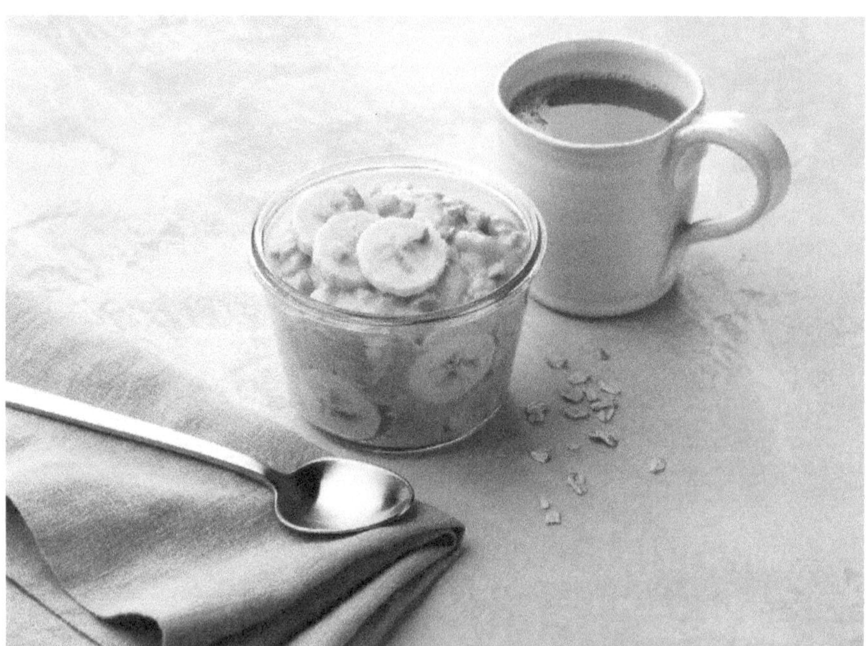

BREAKFAST

Total calories: 375

- **Banana-Walnut Overnight Oats (350 calories):**
  - » Oats (½ cup raw)
  - » Low-fat, plain Greek yogurt (¼ cup)
  - » Fat-free milk (¼ cup)
  - » Banana (½ banana)
  - » Walnuts (4 nuts)
  - » Honey (1 tsp)
- **Coffee (25 calories):**
  - » Coffee (1 cup)
  - » Fat-free milk (¼ cup)

LUNCH

Total calories: 715

- **Chicken Burrito Bowl (710 calories)**
  - » Brown rice (1 cup)
  - » Romaine lettuce (½ cup)
  - » Black beans, low sodium (⅓ cup)
  - » Grilled chicken with spice rub (2 ounces)
  - » Grilled vegetables (⅓ cup)
  - » Sliced avocado (5 slices)
  - » Fresh salsa/pico de gallo (¼ cup)
  - » Reduced-fat cheese (⅓ cup)
  - » Jalapeño (5 slices)
- **Iced Tea, No Sugar (16 ounces) (5 calories)**

Guideline

The nutrient density and healthfulness of what people eat and drink often is determined ultimately by how a food item, dish or meal is prepared, at home and away from home, or produced by a manufacturer. Based on the U.S. food supply and marketplace, the examples of healthy dietary patterns in this edition are achievable through thoughtful, informed choices one decision, one meal, one day at a time—and consistently over time.

DINNER

Total calories: 585

- **Oven-Roasted Tilapia and Vegetables With Pasta (510 calories)**
  - » Tilapia (4 ounces)
  - » Broccoli (½ cup)
  - » Carrots (⅓ cup)
  - » Summer squash (⅓ cup)
  - » Pasta (¾ cup cooked)
  - » Garlic-herb oil (1 Tbsp)
- **Orange (1 medium) (75 calories)**
- **Sparkling Water (8 ounces) (0 calories)**

SNACKS

Total calories: 300

- **Air-Popped Popcorn (2 cups) (60 calories)**
- **Yogurt and Peaches (240 calories)**
  - » Plain, low-fat Greek yogurt (1 cup yogurt)
  - » Canned peaches packed in 100% juice (½ cup)

TOTAL CALORIES FOR THE DAY: 2,000

As such, a nutrient-dense diet, where most nutritional needs are met by 85% of the calories consumed, offers a small amount of leeway to add minimal amounts of added sugars or saturated fat to the diet. For example, one way to use remaining calories is to add small amounts of added sugars or saturated fat to *some* nutrient-dense foods to help make some foods more palatable while working towards meeting food group recommendations—for example, oatmeal with a small amount of brown sugar or vegetables prepared with small amounts of butter. However, to achieve a healthy dietary pattern, all (or mostly all) food group recommendations should be met with foods and beverages that are in nutrient-dense forms.

A healthy dietary pattern has little room available for foods and beverages high in added sugars, saturated fat, and/or sodium. Intakes of foods and beverages high in these components should be limited. These foods and beverages should be occasional choices—consumed in small portions.

While intakes of added sugars, saturated fat, and sodium should be limited, the guidance below is intended to allow programs and individuals to have some flexibility to choose a healthy dietary pattern within calorie limits that fits personal preferences and cultural traditions—and allows day-to-day flexibility to support a healthy dietary pattern over time. Additionally, if alcoholic beverages are consumed, intakes should be within the limits described in this chapter, and calories should be accounted for to keep total calorie intake at an appropriate level.

Added Sugars

A healthy dietary pattern limits added sugars to less than 10 percent of calories per day. Added sugars can help with preservation; contribute to functional attributes such as viscosity, texture, body, color, and browning capability, and/or help improve the palatability of some nutrient-dense foods. In fact, the nutrient-dense choices included in the Healthy U.S.-Style Dietary Pattern are based on availability in the U.S. food supply and include 17-50 calories from added sugars, or 1.5-2 percent of total calories.

Foods and beverages high in calories from added sugars should be limited to help achieve healthy dietary patterns within calorie limits. When added sugars in foods and beverages exceed 10 percent of calories, a healthy dietary pattern within calories limits is very difficult to achieve. Most Americans have less than 8 percent of calories available for added sugars, including the added sugars inherent to a healthy dietary pattern. The limit for added sugars is based on the following assumptions:

- Most calorie levels have less than 15 percent of calories remaining after meeting food group recommendations through nutrient-dense choices.

- Approximately half of remaining calories are consumed as saturated fat and half consumed as added sugars.

- Total saturated fat intakes meet the recommendation for less than 10 percent of total calorie intake.

- No alcoholic beverages are consumed.

- Overall calorie intake does not exceed intake needs to maintain or achieve a healthy weight.

Based on the assumptions above, an individual who needs 2,000 calories per day (based on age, sex, and physical activity level) has less than 7 percent of calories available for added sugars. Individuals who need 2,800 calories per day or less have less than 8 percent of calories available for added sugars. Individuals who need more than 3,000 calories may have a total of 9 to 10 percent of calories available for added sugars. In this portion of the population that requires high calorie intake, an upper limit of 10 percent of calories from added sugars may be consumed while still meeting food group recommendations in nutrient-dense forms. The 10 percent added sugar limit allows for flexibility in food choices over time but also requires careful planning. For example, if one chooses to eat less than the allotted amount of calories for saturated fat, 10 percent of added sugars may fit in a healthy dietary pattern.

Added sugars account on average for almost 270 calories—or more than 13 percent of total calories—per day in the U.S. population. As shown in **Figure 1-10,** the major sources of added sugars in typical U.S. diets are sugar-sweetened beverages, desserts and sweet snacks, sweetened coffee and tea, and candy. Together, these food categories make up more than half of the intake of all added sugars while contributing very little to food group recommendations.

Individuals have many potential options for reducing the intake of added sugars, including reducing the intake of major sources of added sugars. Strategies include reducing portions, consuming these items less often, and selecting options low in added sugars. For those with a weight loss goal, limiting intake of foods and beverages high in added sugars is a strategy to help reduce calorie intake.

It should be noted that replacing added sugars with low- and no-calorie sweeteners may reduce calorie intake in the short-term and aid in weight management, yet questions remain about their effectiveness as a long-term weight management strategy. For additional information about high-intensity sweeteners permitted for use in food in the United States, see **fda.gov/food/food-additives-petitions/high-intensity-sweeteners**.

Guideline

Figure 1-10

Top Sources and Average Intakes of Added Sugars: U.S. Population Ages 1 and Older

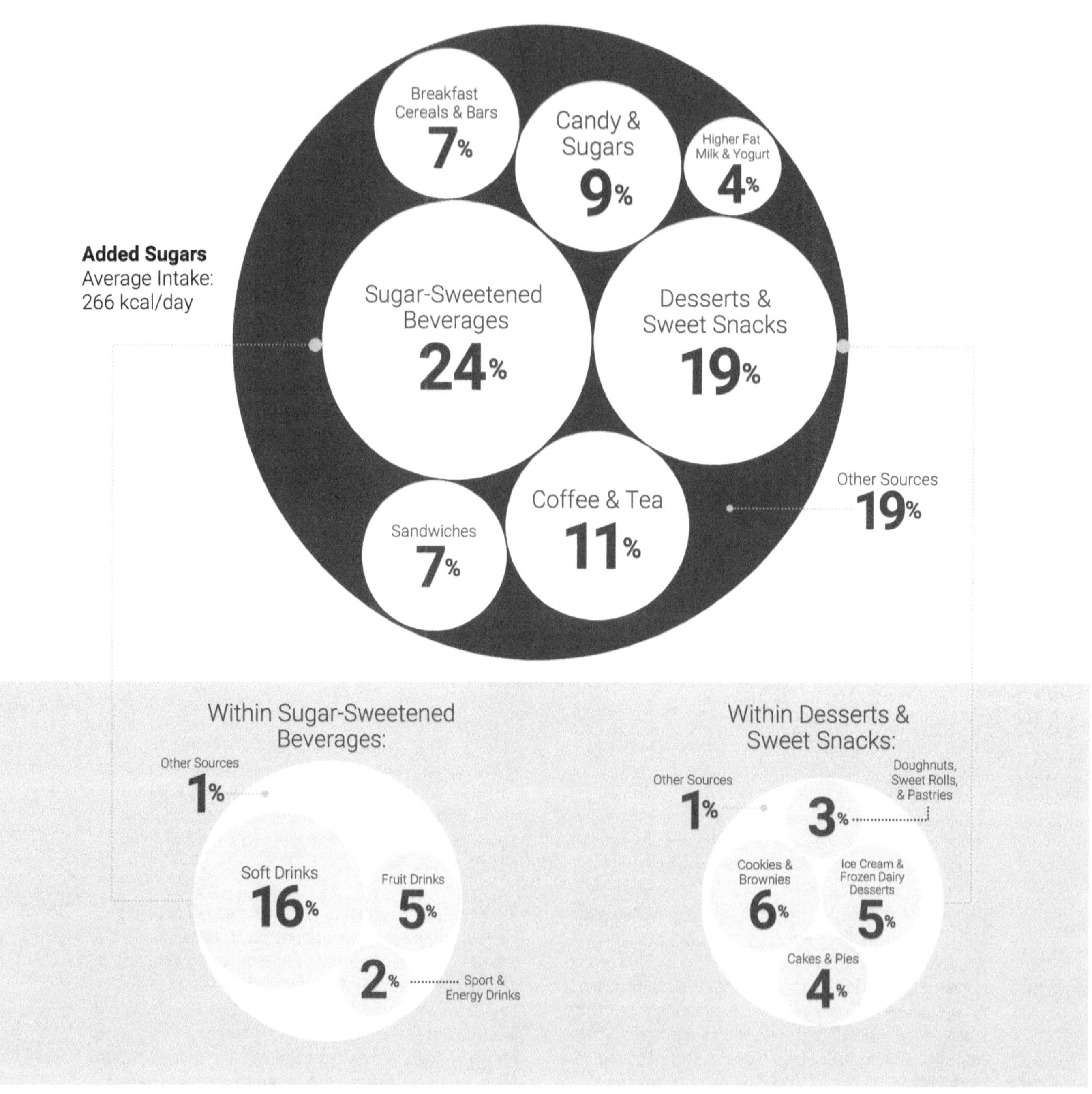

Data Source: Analysis of What We Eat in America, NHANES, 2013-2016, ages 1 and older, 2 days dietary intake data, weighted.

Saturated Fat

For those 2 years and older, intake of saturated fat should be limited to less than 10 percent of calories per day by replacing them with unsaturated fats, particularly polyunsaturated fats. Although some saturated fat is inherent in foods (e.g., high-fat meat), some sources are added (e.g., butter on toast). Similar to added sugars, some of the nutrient-dense choices included in the Healthy U.S.-Style Dietary Pattern include saturated fat. Approximately 5 percent of total calories inherent to the nutrient-dense foods in the Healthy U.S.-Style Dietary Pattern are from saturated fat from sources such as lean meat, poultry, and eggs; nuts and seeds; grains; and saturated fatty acids in oils. As such, there is little room to include additional saturated fat in a healthy dietary pattern while staying within limits for saturated fat and total calories.

Current average intakes of saturated fat are 11 percent of calories. Only 23 percent of individuals consume amounts of saturated fat consistent with the limit of less than 10 percent of calories. The main sources of saturated fat in the U.S. diet include sandwiches, including burgers, tacos, and burritos; desserts and sweet snacks; and rice, pasta, and other grain-based mixed dishes (**Figure 1-11**). Saturated fat is commonly found in higher amounts in high-fat meat, full-fat dairy products (e.g., whole milk, ice cream, cheese), butter, coconut oil, and palm kernel and palm oil.

Strategies to lower saturated fat intake include reducing intakes of dessert and sweet snacks by consuming smaller portion sizes and eating these foods less often. Additional strategies include reading food labels to choose packaged foods lower in saturated fats and choosing lower fat forms of foods and beverages (e.g., fat-free or low-fat milk instead of 2 percent or whole milk; lean rather than fatty cuts of meat). When cooking and purchasing meals, select lean meat and lower fat cheese in place of high-fat meats and regular cheese—or replace them with ingredients with oils, such as nuts, seeds, or avocado. Cook and purchase products made with oils higher in polyunsaturated and monounsaturated fat (e.g., canola, corn, olive, peanut, safflower, soybean, and sunflower) rather than butter, shortening, or coconut or palm oils.

A note on *trans* fats and dietary cholesterol: The National Academies recommends that *trans* fat and dietary cholesterol consumption to be as low as possible without compromising the nutritional adequacy of the diet. The USDA Dietary Patterns are limited in *trans* fats and low in dietary cholesterol. Cholesterol and a small amount of *trans* fat occur naturally in some animal source foods. As of June 2018, partially hydrogenated oils (PHOs), the major source of artificial *trans* fat in the food supply, are no longer Generally Recognized as Safe (GRAS). Therefore, PHOs are no longer added to foods.

Guideline 1

Figure 1-11

Top Sources and Average Intakes of Saturated Fat: U.S. Population Ages 1 and Older

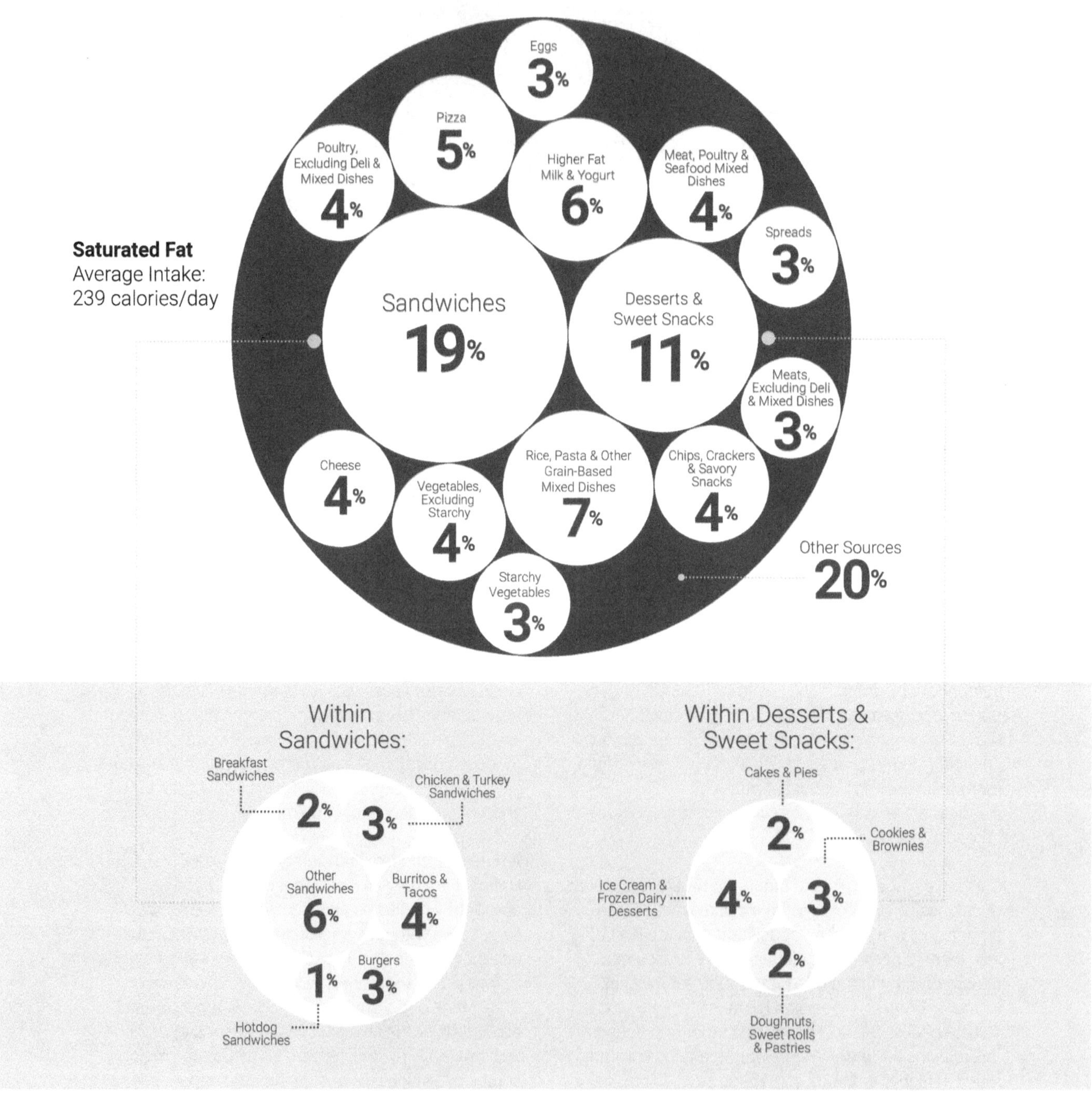

Data Source: Analysis of What We Eat in America, NHANES, 2013-2016, ages 1 and older, 2 days dietary intake data, weighted.

Sodium

Sodium is an essential nutrient primarily consumed as salt (sodium chloride). Healthy eating patterns limit sodium to the Chronic Disease Risk Reduction (CDRR) levels defined by the National Academies—1,200 mg/day for ages 1 through 3; 1,500 mg/day for ages 4 through 8; 1,800 mg/day for ages 9 through 13; and 2,300 mg/day for all other age groups. The CDRR for sodium was established using evidence of the benefit of reducing sodium intake on cardiovascular risk and hypertension risk.

As a food ingredient, sodium is used in multiple ways, including curing meat, baking, as a thickening agent, as a flavor enhancer, as a preservative, and to retain moisture. The nutrient-dense choices in the Healthy U.S.-Style Dietary Pattern provide approximately 60-100 percent of the age-specific CDRR for sodium across calorie levels with amounts ranging from about 1,000 to 2,200 mg. For most calorie levels and at most ages, there is very little room for food choices that are high in sodium.

Average intakes of sodium are high across the U.S. population compared to the CDRRs. Average intakes for those ages 1 and older is 3,393 milligrams per day, with a range of about 2,000 to 5,000 mg per day. Only a small proportion of total sodium intake is from sodium inherent in foods or from salt added in home cooking or at the table. Most sodium consumed in the United States comes from salt added during commercial food processing and preparation, including foods prepared at restaurants.

Sodium is found in foods from almost all food categories across the food supply (**Figure 1-12**), including mixed dishes such as sandwiches, burgers, and tacos; rice, pasta, and grain dishes; pizza; meat, poultry, and seafood dishes; and soups. Calorie intake is highly associated with sodium intake (i.e., the more foods and beverages people consume, the more sodium they tend to consume).

Because sodium is found in so many foods, multiple strategies should be implemented to reduce sodium intake to the recommended limits. Careful choices are needed in all food groups to reduce intake. Strategies to lower sodium intake include cooking at home more often; using the Nutrition Facts label to choose products with less sodium, reduced sodium, or no-salt-added, etc.; and flavoring foods with herbs and spices instead of salt based on personal and cultural foodways.

Figure 1-12

Top Sources and Average Intakes of Sodium: U.S. Population Ages 1 and Older

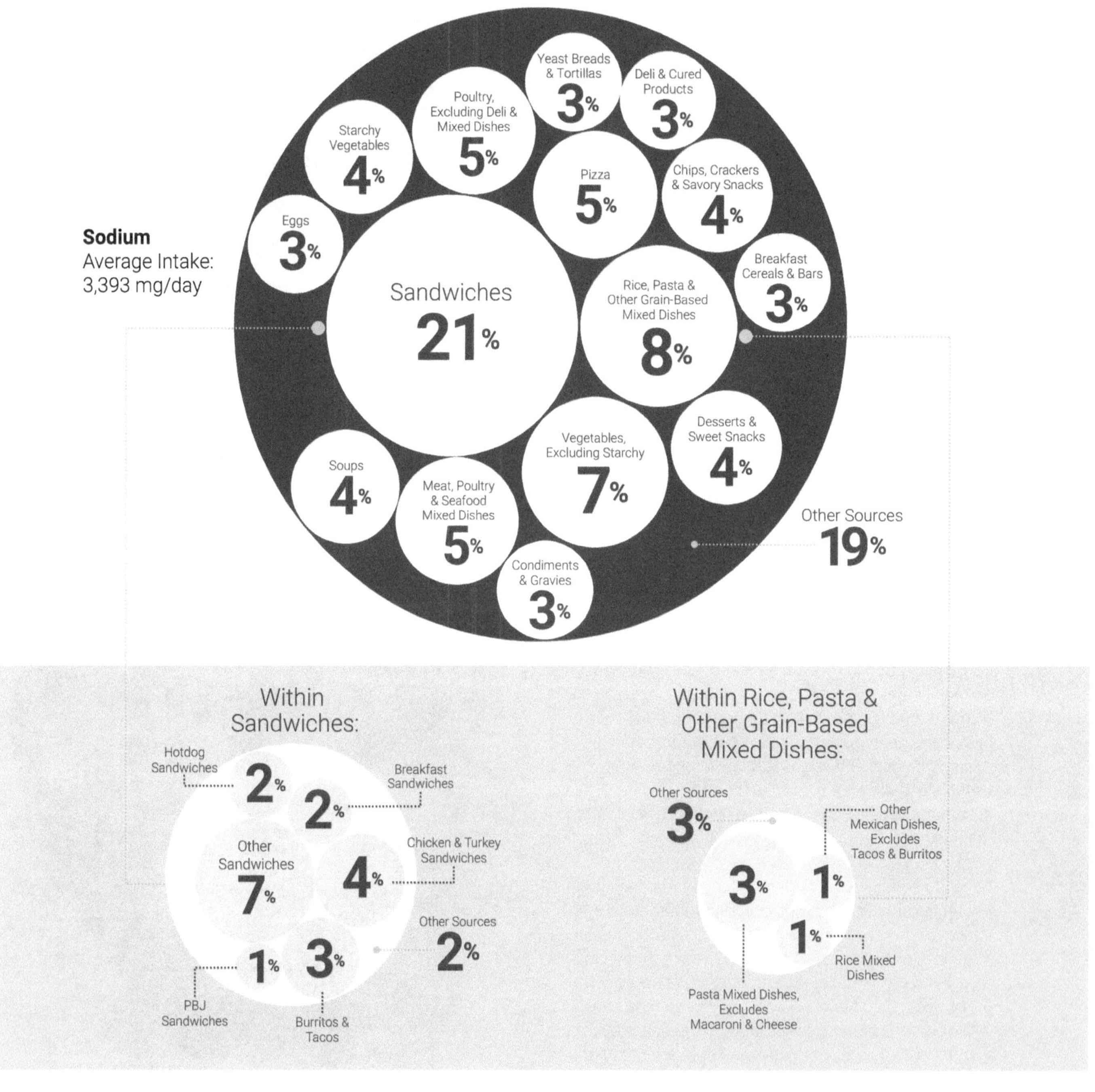

Data Source: Analysis of What We Eat in America, NHANES, 2013-2016, ages 1 and older, 2 days dietary intake data, weighted.

Guideline

Nutrition Facts Label

The Nutrition Facts label on packaged foods and beverages is a tool for making informed and healthy food choices. For the first time in more than 20 years, the U.S. Food and Drug Administration (FDA) has updated the Nutrition Facts label. There are a number of key changes to the label including:

Nutrition Facts

8 servings per container

Serving size 2/3 cup (55g)

Amount per serving

Calories 230

	% Daily Value*
Total Fat 8g	**10%**
Saturated Fat 1g	**5%**
Trans Fat 0g	
Cholesterol 0mg	**0%**
Sodium 160mg	**7%**
Total Carbohydrate 37g	**13%**
Dietary Fiber 4g	**14%**
Total Sugars 12g	
Includes 10g Added Sugars	**20%**
Protein 3g	
Vitamin D 2mcg	10%
Calcium 260mg	20%
Iron 8mg	45%
Potassium 235mg	6%

* The % Daily Value (DV) tells you how much a nutrient in a serving of food contributes to a daily diet. 2,000 calories a day is used for general nutrition advice.

The serving size information is now in large, bold font and has been updated to better reflect the amount that people typically eat and drink.

Calories are displayed in larger, bolder font.

Some Daily Values have been updated. The percent Daily Value (%DV) shows how much a nutrient in a serving of food contributes to a total daily diet. Five percent or less is low; 20 percent or more is high.

Added sugars, vitamin D, and potassium are now listed.

Along with the updated design, the Nutrition Facts label helps support healthy dietary patterns by providing information on nutrients of public health concern—dietary fiber, vitamin D, calcium, iron, and potassium—and on dietary components to limit, such as added sugars, saturated fat, and sodium.

More information on the Nutrition Facts label is available at: **fda.gov/NewNutritionFactsLabel**.

Menu Nutrition Labeling

Americans eat and drink about one-third of their calories from foods prepared away from home. Usually, these foods provide more calories, saturated fat, and sodium than meals prepared at home. To help individuals make informed and healthy decisions, many food establishments and chain restaurants list calories in foods or beverages on menus or menu boards and additional nutrition information is available upon request. More information is available at **fda.gov/CaloriesOnTheMenu**.

Alcoholic Beverages

The *Dietary Guidelines* does not recommend that individuals who do not drink alcohol start drinking for any reason. There are also some people who should not drink at all, such as if they are pregnant or might be pregnant; under the legal age for drinking; if they have certain medical conditions or are taking certain medications that can interact with alcohol; and if they are recovering from an alcohol use disorder or if they are unable to control the amount they drink. If adults age 21 years and older choose to drink alcoholic beverages, drinking less is better for health than drinking more.

Evidence indicates that, among those who drink, higher average alcohol consumption is associated with an increased risk of death from all causes compared with lower average alcohol consumption. Alcohol misuse or consuming alcohol in excess of recommendations increases risk of several other conditions such as liver disease, cardiovascular disease, injuries, and alcohol use disorders.

For the purposes of evaluating amounts of alcohol that may be consumed, the *Dietary Guidelines* defines drink equivalents. One alcoholic drink equivalent is defined as containing 14 grams (0.6 fl oz) of pure alcohol. The following count as one alcoholic drink equivalent: 12 fluid ounces of regular beer (5% alcohol), 5 fluid ounces of wine (12% alcohol), or 1.5 fluid ounces of 80 proof distilled spirits (40% alcohol). To help Americans move toward a healthy dietary pattern and minimize risks associated with drinking, adults of legal drinking age can choose not to drink or to drink in moderation by limiting intakes to 2 drinks or less in a day for men and 1 drink or less in a day for women, on days when alcohol is consumed. This is not intended as an average over several days, but rather the amount consumed on any single day. Binge drinking,[3] defined as 5 or more drinks for the typical adult male or 4 or more drinks for the typical adult female in about 2 hours, should be avoided. Emerging evidence suggests that even drinking within the recommended limits may increase the overall risk of death from various causes, such as from several types of cancer and some forms of cardiovascular disease. Alcohol has been found to increase risk for cancer, and for some types of cancer, the risk increases even at low levels of alcohol consumption (less than 1 drink in a day). Caution, therefore, is recommended.

Alcoholic beverages are not a component of the USDA Dietary Patterns. The amount of alcohol and calories in beverages varies and should be accounted for within the limits of healthy dietary patterns, so that calorie limits are not exceeded (see "**Calories in Alcoholic Beverages**").

Approximately 60 percent of adults report alcoholic beverage consumption in the past month. Of those, approximately 30 percent binge drink, sometimes multiple times per month. During days when men and women consume alcohol, their consumption typically exceeds current guidance. Among adults, including those who do not drink, alcoholic beverages contribute approximately 5 percent of calorie intake (3 to 4% of calories for women and 5 to 7% for men); this translates into approximately 9 percent of calories among those who drink. As such, among those who drink, alcoholic beverages, alone, account for most of the calories that remain after meeting food group recommendations in nutrient-dense forms—leaving very few calories for added sugars or saturated fat.

Adults who choose to drink, and are not among the individuals listed above who should not drink, are encouraged to limit daily intakes to align with the *Dietary Guidelines*—and to consider calories from alcoholic beverages so as not to exceed daily calorie limits.

[3] More information is available at **niaaa.nih.gov/alcohol-health/overview-alcohol-consumption/moderate-binge-drinking**.

Calories in Alcoholic Beverages

Alcoholic beverages supply calories but few nutrients, and calories from alcoholic beverages should be accounted for to keep total calorie intake at an appropriate level. Alcoholic beverages may contain calories from both alcohol and other ingredients, such as soda, juice, and added sugars. It is important to consider ingredients and portion size. The range of calories in cocktails varies widely depending on serving size and ingredients. Examples of calories contained in alcoholic beverages include:

12 fluid ounces of regular beer (5% alcohol): about 150 calories	**5 fluid ounces of wine (12% alcohol):** about 120 calories
1.5 fluid ounces of 80 proof distilled spirits (40% alcohol): about 100 calories	**7 fluid ounces of a rum (40% alcohol) and cola:** about 190 calories

More information on calories in alcoholic beverages is available at **rethinkingdrinking.niaaa.nih.gov/Tools/Calculators/calorie-calculator.aspx**.

Support Healthy Dietary Patterns for All Americans

Everyone has a role to play to support access to healthy foods and beverages in multiple settings nationwide where people live, learn, work, play, and gather. Having access to healthy, safe, and affordable food is crucial for an individual to achieve a healthy dietary pattern. Concerted efforts within communities, businesses and industries, organizations, government, and other segments of society are needed to support individuals and families in making lifestyle choices that align with the *Dietary Guidelines*.

Food manufacturers and retail establishments can support Americans in achieving a healthy dietary pattern by providing healthy options in all the places where foods and beverages are purchased. During the past few decades, food products and menus have evolved substantially in response to consumer demand and public health concerns. Food reformulation and menu and retail modification opportunities include offering more vegetables, fruits, whole grains, low-fat and fat-free dairy, and a greater variety of protein foods that are nutrient dense, while also reducing sodium and added sugars, reducing saturated fat and replacing it with unsaturated fats, and reducing added refined starches. Portion sizes also can be reduced to help individuals make choices that better fit within their calorie needs. Food manufacturers are encouraged to consider the entire composition of the food or beverage, and not just individual nutrients or ingredients when developing or reformulating products.

Similarly, when developing or modifying menus, establishments can consider the range of offerings both within and across food groups and other dietary components to determine whether the healthy options offered reflect the proportions in healthy dietary patterns. In taking these actions, care should be taken to assess any potential unintended consequences so that as changes are made to better align with the *Dietary Guidelines*, undesirable changes are not introduced. For example, a change made to reduce the amount of added sugars in a product should not come at the expense of increasing the amount of saturated fat or sodium.

Food access is influenced by diverse factors, such as proximity to food retail outlets (e.g., the number and types of stores in an area), ability to prepare one's own meals or eat independently, and the availability of personal or public transportation. The underlying socioeconomic characteristics of a neighborhood also may influence an individual's ability to access foods to support healthy eating patterns.

In 2019, 10.5 percent of households were food insecure at least some time during the year. Food insecurity occurs when access to nutritionally adequate and safe food is limited or uncertain. Food insecurity can be temporary or persist over time, preventing individuals and families from following a healthy dietary pattern that aligns with the *Dietary Guidelines*. The prevalence of food insecurity typically rises during times of economic downturn as households experience greater hardship. Government and nongovernment nutrition assistance programs help alleviate food insecurity and play an essential role by providing food, meals, and educational resources so that participants can make healthy food choices within their budget. ***Chapters 2***, ***3***, ***4***, ***5***, and ***6*** highlight examples of these resources at each life stage.

As discussed in subsequent chapters, everyone has an important role in leading disease prevention efforts within their organizations and communities to make healthy eating an organizational and societal norm. Changes at multiple levels of society are needed, and these changes, in combination and over time, can have a meaningful impact on the health of current and future generations.

Looking Toward the Life Stages

This chapter has provided guidance about the fundamentals of a healthy dietary pattern. These fundamentals are remarkably consistent across life stages, even though each stage also has its own specific nutrition considerations. The following chapters build on this chapter and take a closer look at each of the life stages: ***Chapter 2*** provides a focused discussion of the unique nutritional needs of infants and toddlers. ***Chapters 3***, ***4***, ***5***, and ***6*** present recommended dietary patterns, describe current nutrition intakes, and provide tailored nutrition information specific to children and adolescents, adults, women who are pregnant or lactating, and older adults, respectively.

BIRTH THROUGH 23 MONTHS

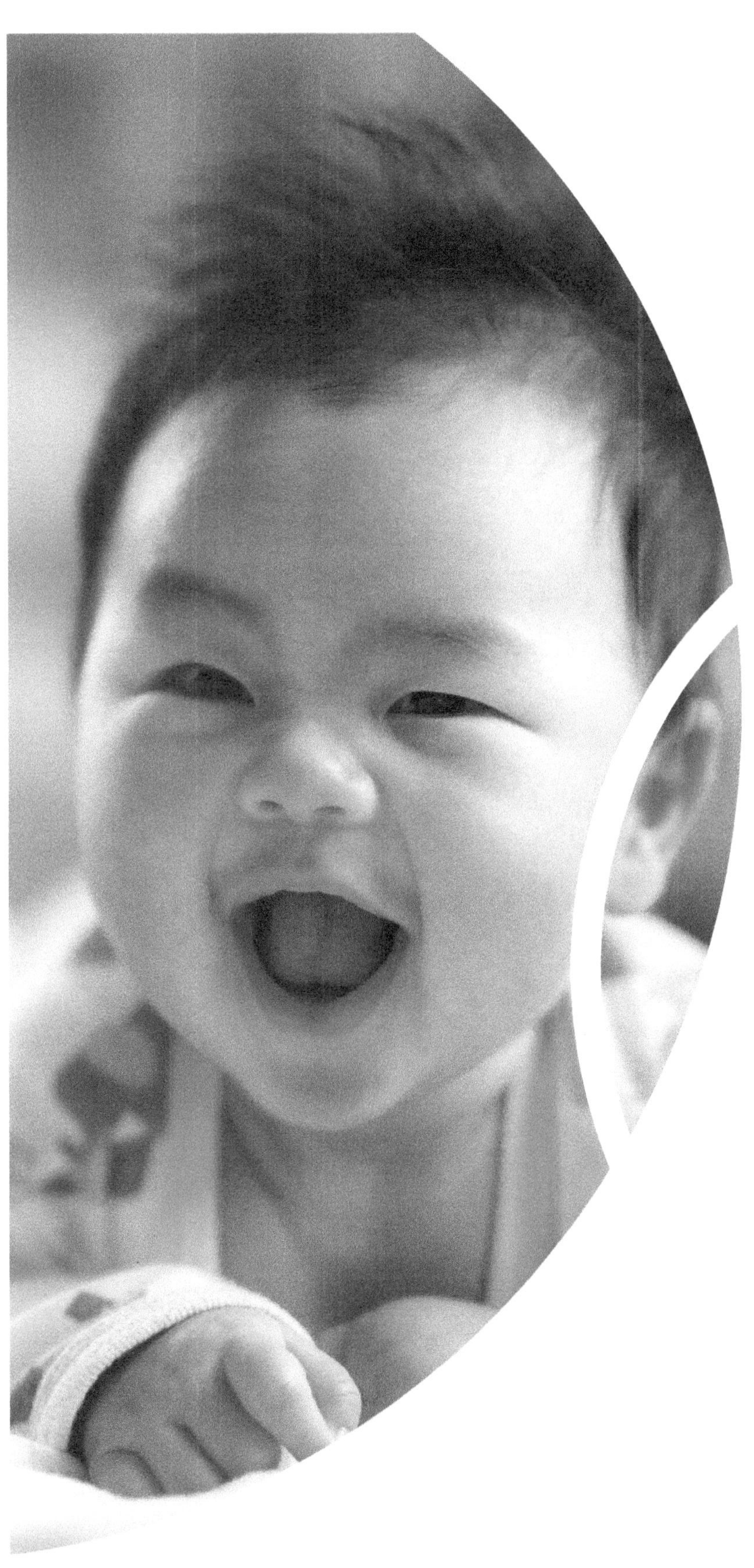

CHAPTER 2

Infants and Toddlers

BIRTH THROUGH 23 MONTHS

Introduction

The time from birth until a child's second birthday is a critically important period for proper growth and development. It also is key for establishing healthy dietary patterns that may influence the trajectory of eating behaviors and health throughout the life course. During this period, nutrients critical for brain development and growth must be provided in adequate amounts. **Children in this age group consume small quantities of foods, so it's important to make every bite count!**

Key Recommendations

- **For about the first 6 months of life,** exclusively feed infants human milk. Continue to feed infants human milk through at least the first year of life, and longer if desired. Feed infants iron-fortified infant formula during the first year of life when human milk is unavailable.
- Provide infants with supplemental vitamin D beginning soon after birth.
- **At about 6 months,** introduce infants to nutrient-dense complementary foods.
- Introduce infants to potentially allergenic foods along with other complementary foods.
- Encourage infants and toddlers to consume a variety of foods from all food groups. Include foods rich in iron and zinc, particularly for infants fed human milk.
- Avoid foods and beverages with added sugars.
- Limit foods and beverages higher in sodium.
- As infants wean from human milk or infant formula, transition to a healthy dietary pattern.

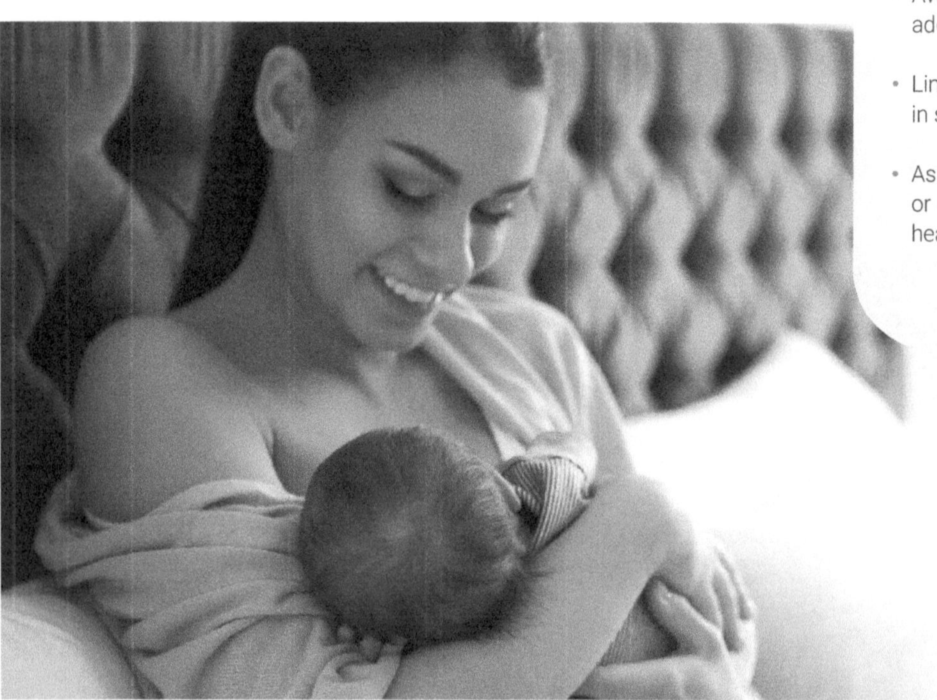

Human milk feeding alone is the ideal form of nutrition from birth through about age 6 months. Human milk provides necessary nutrients, protective factors against disease, and other unique immunological benefits. If human milk is unavailable, infants should be fed an iron-fortified commercial infant formula. Once an infant is developmentally ready, foods and beverages should be introduced to complement human milk feeding. These complementary foods and beverages are essential to meet the nutrient requirements of infants starting at about age 6 months and should be selected carefully to help meet these needs. As an infant becomes a toddler, and learns to eat a variety of foods, flavors, and textures, the goal of complementary feeding becomes establishing a healthy dietary pattern and transitioning to a healthy family diet by age 2.

Putting the Key Recommendations Into Action

Feed Infants Human Milk for the First 6 Months, If Possible

Exclusive human milk feeding is one of the best ways to start an infant off on the path of lifelong healthy nutrition. Exclusive human milk feeding, commonly referred to as exclusive breastfeeding, refers to an infant consuming only human milk, and not in combination with infant formula and/or complementary foods or beverages (including water), except for medications or vitamin and mineral supplementation.

Human milk can support an infant's nutrient needs for about the first 6 months of life, with the exception of vitamin D and potentially iron. In addition to nutrients, human milk includes bioactive substances and

immunologic properties that support infant health and growth and development.

U.S. data show that about 84 percent of infants born in 2017 were ever fed human milk, with only 25 percent fed human milk exclusively through age 6 months, and 35 percent continuing to be fed any human milk at age 12 months. Nearly one-quarter of infants were fed some human milk beyond age 12 months, with about 15 percent of toddlers being fed human milk at age 18 months.

Families may have a number of reasons for not having human milk for their infant. For example, a family may choose not to breastfeed, a child may be adopted, or the mother may be unable to produce a full milk supply or may be unable to pump and store milk safely due to family or workplace pressures. If human milk is unavailable, infants should be fed an iron-fortified commercial infant formula (i.e., labeled "with iron") regulated by the U.S. Food and Drug Administration (FDA), which is based on standards that ensure nutrient content and safety. Infant formulas are designed to meet the nutritional needs of infants and are not needed beyond age 12 months. It is important to take precautions to ensure that expressed human milk and prepared infant formula are handled and stored safely (see "**Proper Handling and Storage of Human Milk and Infant Formula**").

Donor Human Milk

If families do not have sufficient human milk for their infant but want to feed their infant human milk, they may look for alternative ways to obtain it. It is important for the family to obtain pasteurized donor human milk from a source, such as an accredited human milk bank, that has screened its donors and taken appropriate safety precautions. When human milk is obtained directly from individuals or through the internet, the donor is unlikely to have been screened for infectious diseases, and it is unknown whether the human milk has been collected or stored in a way to reduce possible safety risks to the baby. More information is available at **fda.gov/science-research/pediatrics/use-donor-human-milk**.

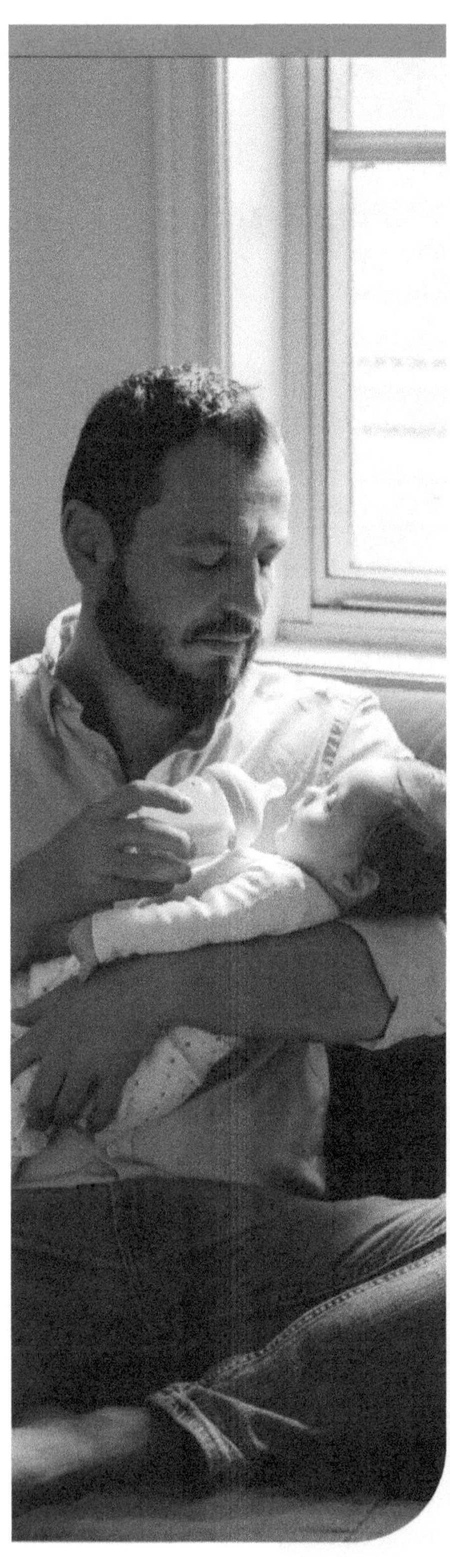

Proper Handling and Storage of Human Milk and Infant Formula

- Wash hands thoroughly before expressing human milk or preparing to feed human milk or infant formula.
- If expressing human milk, ensure pump parts are thoroughly cleaned before use.
- If preparing powdered infant formula, use a safe water source and follow instructions on the label.
- Refrigerate freshly expressed human milk within 4 hours for up to 4 days. Previously frozen and thawed human milk should be used within 24 hours. Thawed human milk should never be refrozen. Refrigerate prepared infant formula for up to 24 hours.
- Do not use a microwave to warm human milk or infant formula. Warm safely by placing the sealed container of human milk or infant formula in a bowl of warm water or under warm, running tap water.
- Once it has been offered to the infant, use or discard leftovers quickly (within 2 hours for human milk or 1 hour for infant formula).
- Thoroughly wash all infant feeding items, such as bottles and nipples. Consider sanitizing feeding items for infants younger than 3 months of age, infants born prematurely, or infants with a compromised immune system.

More information on storing and handling human milk is available at **cdc.gov/breastfeeding/recommendations/handling_breastmilk.htm**. More information on storing and preparing powdered infant formula is available at **cdc.gov/nutrition/downloads/prepare-store-powered-infant-formula-508.pdf**.

Additional information on how to clean, sanitize, and store infant feeding items is available at **cdc.gov/healthywater/hygiene/healthychildcare/infantfeeding/cleansanitize.html**.

Homemade infant formulas and those that are improperly and illegally imported into the United States without mandated FDA review and supervision should not be used. Toddler milks or toddler formulas should not be fed to infants, as they are not designed to meet the nutritional needs of infants.

Provide Infants Supplemental Vitamin D Beginning Soon After Birth

All infants who are fed human milk exclusively or who receive both human milk and infant formula (mixed fed) will need a vitamin D supplement of 400 IU per day beginning soon after birth. Infant formula is fortified with vitamin D, thus, when an infant is receiving full feeds of infant formula, vitamin D supplementation is not needed. Families who do not wish to provide a supplement directly to their infant should discuss with a healthcare provider the risks and benefits of maternal high dose supplementation options. Even when consuming a varied diet, achieving adequate vitamin D from foods and beverages (natural sources) alone is challenging, suggesting that young children may need to continue taking a vitamin D supplement after age 12 months. Parents, caregivers, and guardians should consult with a healthcare provider to determine how long supplementation is necessary.

Introduce Infants To Nutrient-Dense Complementary Foods at About 6 Months Old

At about age 6 months, infants should be introduced to nutrient-dense, developmentally appropriate foods to complement human milk or infant formula feedings. Some infants may show developmental signs of readiness before age 6 months (see "**Developmental Readiness for Beginning to Eat Solid Foods**"), but introducing complementary foods before age 4 months is not recommended. Waiting until after age 6 months to introduce foods also is not recommended. Starting around that time, complementary foods are necessary to ensure adequate nutrition and exposure to flavors, textures, and different types of foods. Infants should be given age- and developmentally appropriate foods to help prevent choking. It is important to introduce potentially allergenic foods along with other complementary foods. For infants fed human milk, it is particularly important to include complementary foods that are rich in iron and zinc when starting complementary foods (see ***Appendix 1: Nutritional Goals for Age-Sex Groups***).

About one-third (32%) of infants in the United States are introduced to complementary foods and beverages before age 4 months, highlighting the importance of providing guidance and support to parents, guardians, and caregivers on the timing of introduction to complementary foods. Early introduction of complementary foods and beverages is higher among infants receiving infant formula (42%) or a combination of infant formula and human milk (32%) than among infants exclusively fed human milk (19%).

Supplemental Vitamin B_{12}

Human milk has sufficient vitamin B_{12} to meet infant needs unless the mother's vitamin B_{12} status is inadequate. This can occur for different reasons, including when the mother eats a strictly vegan diet without any animal source foods. When the mother is at risk of vitamin B_{12} deficiency, human milk may not provide sufficient vitamin B_{12}. In these cases, the mother and/or infant fed human milk may require a vitamin B_{12} supplement. Parents, caregivers, and guardians should consult with a healthcare provider to determine whether supplementation is necessary.

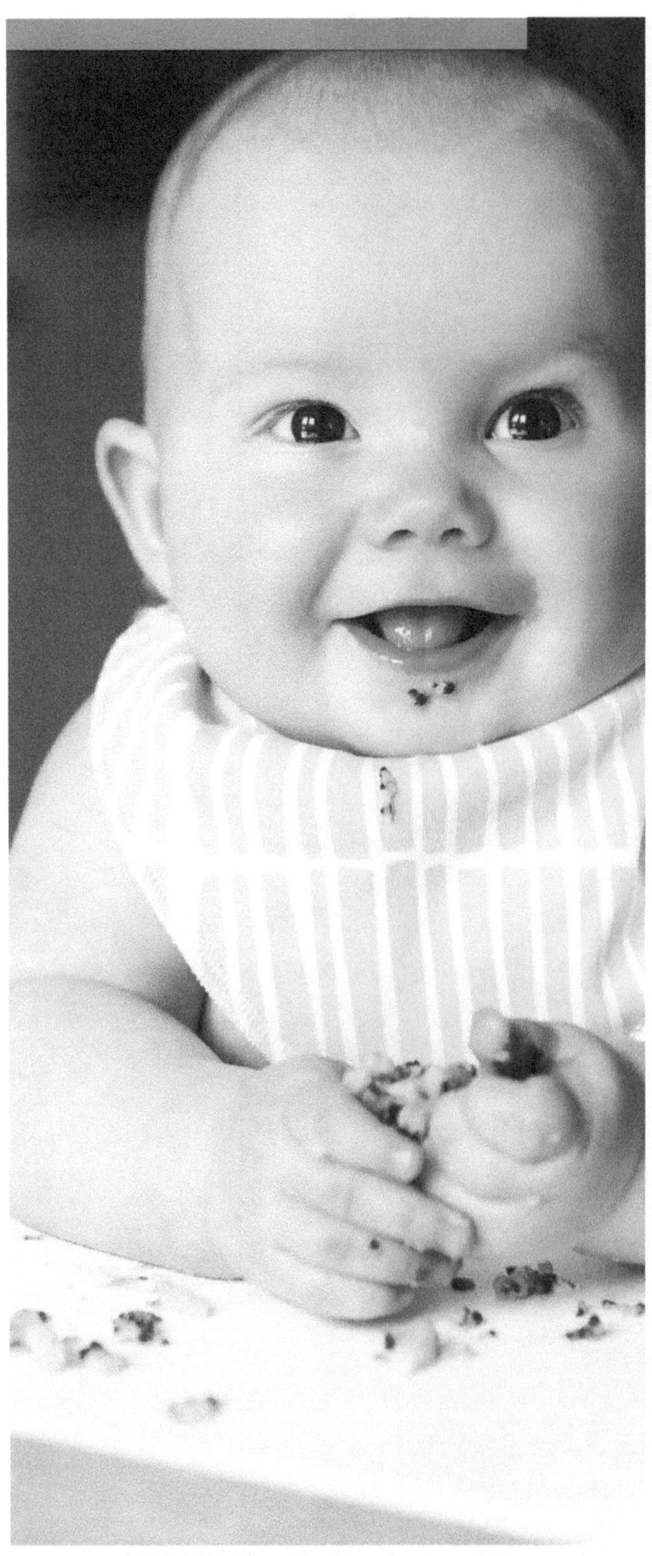

Developmental Readiness for Beginning To Eat Solid Foods

The age at which infants reach different developmental stages will vary. Typically between age 4 and 6 months, infants develop the gross motor, oral, and fine motor skills necessary to begin to eat complementary foods. As an infant's oral skills develop, the thickness and texture of foods can gradually be varied. Signs that an infant is ready for complementary foods include:

- Being able to control head and neck.
- Sitting up alone or with support.
- Bringing objects to the mouth.
- Trying to grasp small objects, such as toys or food.
- Swallowing food rather than pushing it back out onto the chin.

Infants and young children should be given age- and developmentally appropriate foods to help prevent choking. Foods such as hot dogs, candy, nuts and seeds, raw carrots, grapes, popcorn, and chunks of peanut butter are some of the foods that can be a choking risk for young children. Parents, guardians, and caregivers are encouraged to take steps to decrease choking risks, including:

- Offering foods in the appropriate size, consistency, and shape that will allow an infant or young child to eat and swallow easily.
- Making sure the infant or young child is sitting up in a high chair or other safe, supervised place.
- Ensuring an adult is supervising feeding during mealtimes.
- Not putting infant cereal or other solid foods in an infant's bottle. This could increase the risk of choking and will not make the infant sleep longer.

More information on foods that can present choking hazards is available from USDA at **wicworks.fns.usda.gov/resources/reducing-risk-choking-young-children-mealtimes**.

Introduce Infants to Potentially Allergenic Foods Along With Other Complementary Foods

Potentially allergenic foods (e.g., peanuts, egg, cow milk products, tree nuts, wheat, crustacean shellfish, fish, and soy) should be introduced when other complementary foods are introduced to an infant's diet. Introducing peanut-containing foods in the first year reduces the risk that an infant will develop a food allergy to peanuts. Cow milk, as a beverage, should be introduced at age 12 months or later (see "**Establish a Healthy Beverage Pattern**"). There is no evidence that delaying introduction of allergenic foods, beyond when other complementary foods are introduced, helps to prevent food allergy. For more information, see "**For Infants at High Risk of Peanut Allergy, Introduce Peanut-Containing Foods at Age 4 to 6 Months.**"

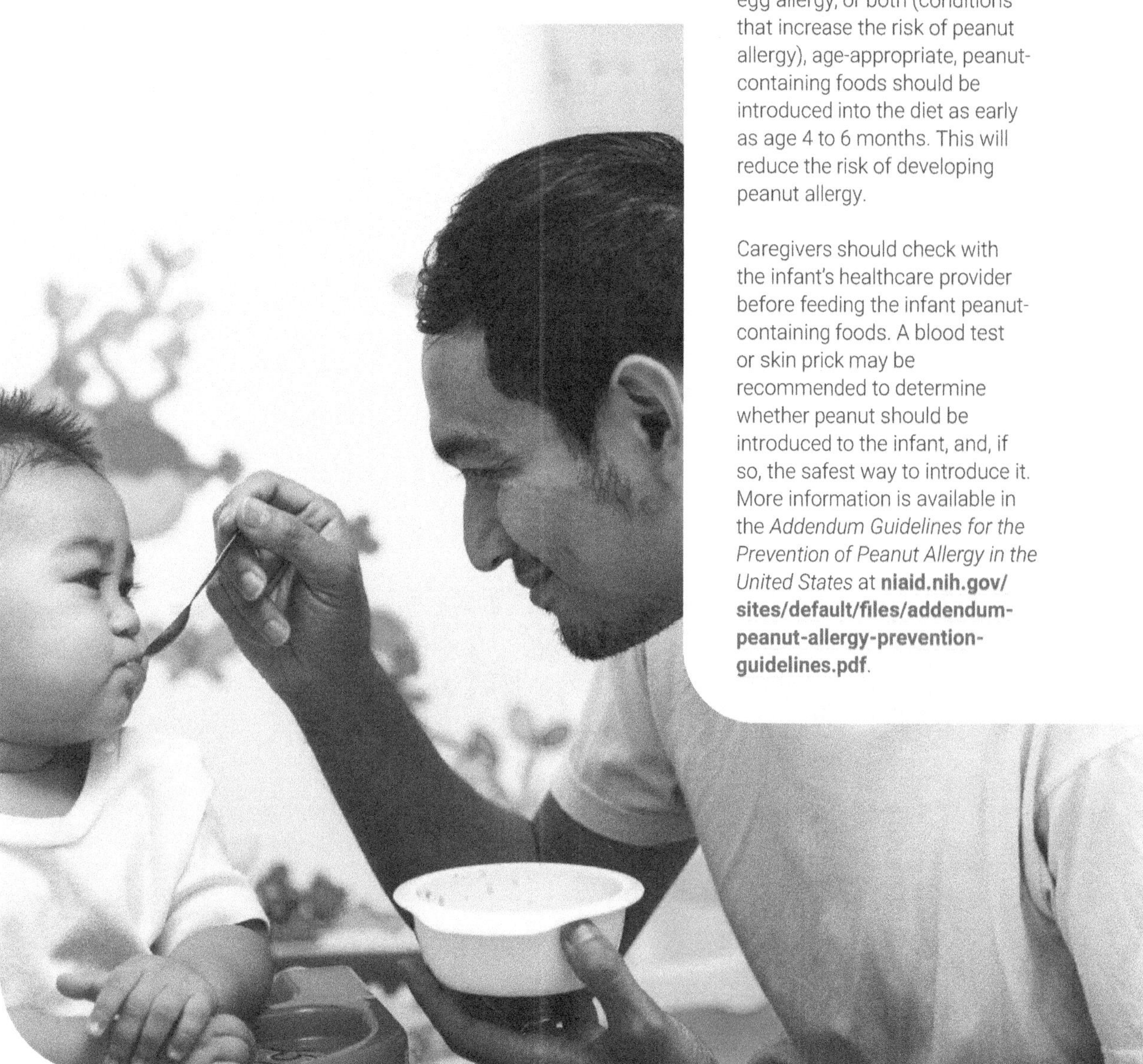

For Infants at High Risk of Peanut Allergy, Introduce Peanut-Containing Foods at Age 4 to 6 Months

If an infant has severe eczema, egg allergy, or both (conditions that increase the risk of peanut allergy), age-appropriate, peanut-containing foods should be introduced into the diet as early as age 4 to 6 months. This will reduce the risk of developing peanut allergy.

Caregivers should check with the infant's healthcare provider before feeding the infant peanut-containing foods. A blood test or skin prick may be recommended to determine whether peanut should be introduced to the infant, and, if so, the safest way to introduce it. More information is available in the *Addendum Guidelines for the Prevention of Peanut Allergy in the United States* at **niaid.nih.gov/sites/default/files/addendum-peanut-allergy-prevention-guidelines.pdf**.

Encourage Infants and Toddlers To Consume a Variety of Complementary Foods and Beverages To Meet Energy and Nutrient Needs

Parents, caregivers, and guardians are encouraged to introduce foods across all the food groups—as described below and carrying forward the principles in ***Chapter 1***—including items that fit within a family's preferences, cultural traditions, and budget. Complementary foods and beverages should be rich in nutrients, meet calorie and nutrient requirements during this critical period of growth and development, and stay within limits of dietary components such as added sugars and sodium. Although the *Dietary Guidelines* does not provide a recommended dietary pattern for infants ages 6 through 11 months, infants should be on the path to a healthy dietary pattern that is recommended for those ages 12 through 23 months (see ***Appendix 3: USDA Dietary Patterns***).

In the United States, some dietary components are of public health concern for infants and toddlers. Iron is a dietary component of public health concern for underconsumption among older infants ages 6 through 11 months who are fed primarily human milk and consume inadequate iron from complementary foods. Older infants who are fed primarily human milk also underconsume zinc and protein from complementary foods, and vitamin D, choline, and potassium are notably underconsumed by all older infants. During the second year of life, the dietary components of public health concern for underconsumption are vitamin D, calcium, dietary fiber, and potassium and for overconsumption are added sugars and sodium. Lists of dietary sources of iron, calcium, potassium, dietary fiber, and vitamin D are available at **DietaryGuidelines.gov**.

INTRODUCE IRON-RICH FOODS TO INFANTS STARTING AT ABOUT 6 MONTHS OLD

Iron-rich foods (e.g., meats and seafood rich in heme iron and iron-fortified infant cereals) are important components of the infant's diet from age 6 through 11 months to maintain adequate iron status, which supports neurologic development and immune function. Infants are typically born with body stores of iron adequate for about the first 6 months of life, depending on gestational age, maternal iron status, and timing of umbilical cord clamping. By age 6 months, however, infants require an external source of iron apart from human milk.

Caregivers of infants exclusively fed human milk should talk with their pediatric care provider about whether there may be a need for infants supplementation with iron before age 6 months. A complementary food source of iron beginning at about 6 months is particularly important for infants fed human milk because the iron content of human milk is low and maternal iron intake during lactation does not increase its content. In the United States, an estimated 77 percent of infants fed human milk have inadequate iron intake during the second half of infancy, highlighting the importance of introducing iron-rich foods starting at age 6 months.

Infants receiving most of their milk feeds as iron-fortified infant formula are likely to need less iron from complementary foods beginning at 6 months of age. After

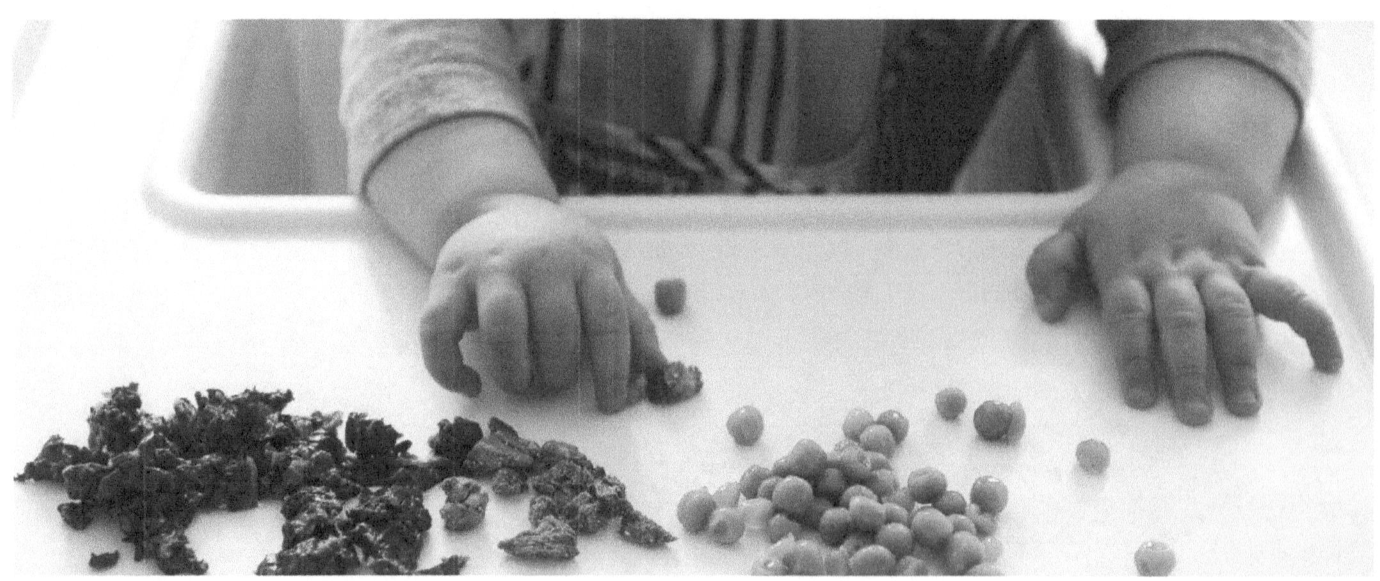

age 12 months, children have a lower iron requirement, but good food sources of iron are still needed to maintain adequate iron status and prevent deficiency.

INTRODUCE ZINC-RICH FOODS TO INFANTS STARTING AT ABOUT 6 MONTHS OLD

Zinc-rich complementary foods (e.g., meats, beans, zinc-fortified infant cereals) are important from age 6 months onwards to support adequate zinc status, which supports growth and immune function. Although the zinc content of human milk is initially high and efficiently absorbed, the concentration declines over the first 6 months of lactation and is not affected by maternal zinc intake. During the second half of infancy, approximately half (54%) of U.S. infants fed human milk have inadequate zinc intake. Prioritizing zinc-rich foods starting at 6 months of age to complement human milk feedings will help infants meet their requirement for zinc.

ENCOURAGE A VARIETY OF FOODS FROM ALL FOOD GROUPS TO INFANTS STARTING AT ABOUT 6 MONTHS OLD

To support nutrient adequacy, foster acceptance of healthy foods, and set intakes on a path toward a healthy pattern, it is important to encourage foods from all food groups. Because very young children are being exposed to new textures and flavors for the first time, it may take up to 8 to 10 exposures for an infant to accept a new type of food. Repeated offering of foods such as fruits and vegetables increases the likelihood of an infant accepting them. A nutrient-dense, diverse diet from age 6 through 23 months of life includes a variety of food sources from each food group.

- Protein foods, including meats, poultry, eggs, seafood, nuts, seeds, and soy products, are important sources of iron, zinc, protein, choline, and long chain polyunsaturated fatty acids. The long-chain polyunsaturated fatty acids, specifically the essential omega-3 and omega-6 fatty acids supplied through seafood, nuts, seeds, and oils, influence the infant's fatty acid status and are among the key nutrients needed for the rapid brain development that occurs through the infant's first 2 years of life. Some types of fish such as salmon and trout are also natural sources of vitamin D. To limit exposure to methylmercury from seafood, the U.S. Food and Drug Administration and the U.S. Environmental Protection Agency issued joint guidance regarding the types of seafood to choose.[1]

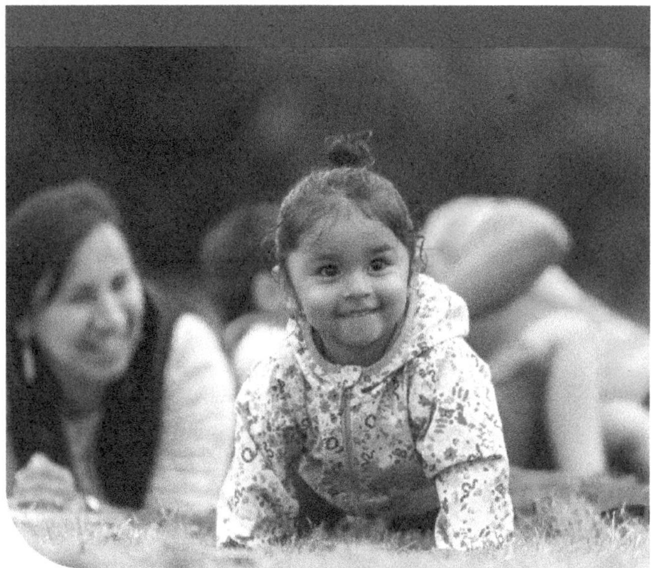

- Vegetables and fruits, especially those rich in potassium, vitamin A, and vitamin C, should be offered to infants and toddlers age 6 through 23 months. The vegetable subgroup of beans, peas, and lentils also provides a good source of protein and dietary fiber.

- For dairy, families can introduce yogurt and cheese, including soy-based yogurt, before 12 months. However, infants should not consume cow milk, as a beverage, or fortified soy beverage, before age 12 months as a replacement for human milk or infant formula (see "**Cow Milk and Fortified Soy Beverages**"). In the second year of life, when calcium requirements increase, dairy products, including milk, yogurt, cheese, and fortified soy beverages and soy yogurt provide a good source of calcium. Vitamin D-fortified milk and soy beverages also provide a good source of vitamin D. For those younger than the age of 2, offer dairy products without added sugar (see "**Avoid Added Sugars**").

- Grains, including iron-fortified infant cereal, play an important role in meeting nutrient needs during this life stage. Infant cereals fortified with iron include oat, barley, multigrain, and rice cereals. Rice cereal fortified with iron is a good source of nutrients for infants, but rice cereal shouldn't be the only type of cereal given to infants. Offering young children whole grains more often than refined grains will increase dietary fiber as well as potassium intake during the second year of life and help young children establish healthy dietary practices.

[1] U.S. Food and Drug Administration and U.S. Environmental Protection Agency. Advice About Eating Fish. Available at **FDA.gov/fishadvice**; **EPA.gov/fishadvice**.

BIRTH THROUGH 23 MONTHS

DIETARY COMPONENTS TO LIMIT

While encouraging intake from each food group, some dietary components should be limited.

Avoid Added Sugars

Infants and young children have virtually no room in their diet for added sugars. This is because the nutrient requirements for infants and young children are quite high relative to their size, but the amount of complementary foods they consume is small. Complementary foods need to be nutrient-dense and not contain additional calories from added sugars. In addition, low- and no-calorie sweeteners, which can also be called high-intensity sweeteners, are not recommended for children younger than age 2. Taste preferences are being formed during this time period, and infants and young children may develop preferences for overly sweet foods if introduced to very sweet foods during this timeframe. For more information on added sugars, see ***Chapter 1.***

Avoid Foods Higher in Sodium

Sodium is found in a number of foods, including some salty snacks, commercial toddler foods, and processed meats. In addition to keeping sodium intake within limits for toddlers (see ***Appendix 1***), another reason to avoid high-sodium foods is that taste preferences for salty food may be established early in life. Choose fresh or low-sodium frozen foods, when available, and low-sodium canned foods to minimize sodium content. For more information on sodium, see ***Chapter 1***.

Avoid Honey and Unpasteurized Foods and Beverages

Infants should not be given any foods containing raw or cooked honey. Honey can contain the *Clostridium botulinum* organism that could cause serious illness or death among infants. Infants and young children also should not be given any unpasteurized foods or beverages, such as unpasteurized juices, milk, yogurt, or cheeses, as they could contain harmful bacteria.

Establish a Healthy Beverage Pattern

An important part of establishing an overall healthy dietary pattern is careful consideration of beverages. Guidance for different beverage categories is provided below.

WATER

For healthy infants with adequate intake of human milk or infant formula, supplemental water is typically not needed in the first 6 months. Small amounts (up to 4 to 8 ounces per day) of plain, fluoridated drinking water can be given to infants with the introduction of complementary foods. Plain, fluoridated drinking water intake can slowly be increased after age 1 to meet hydration and fluoride needs.

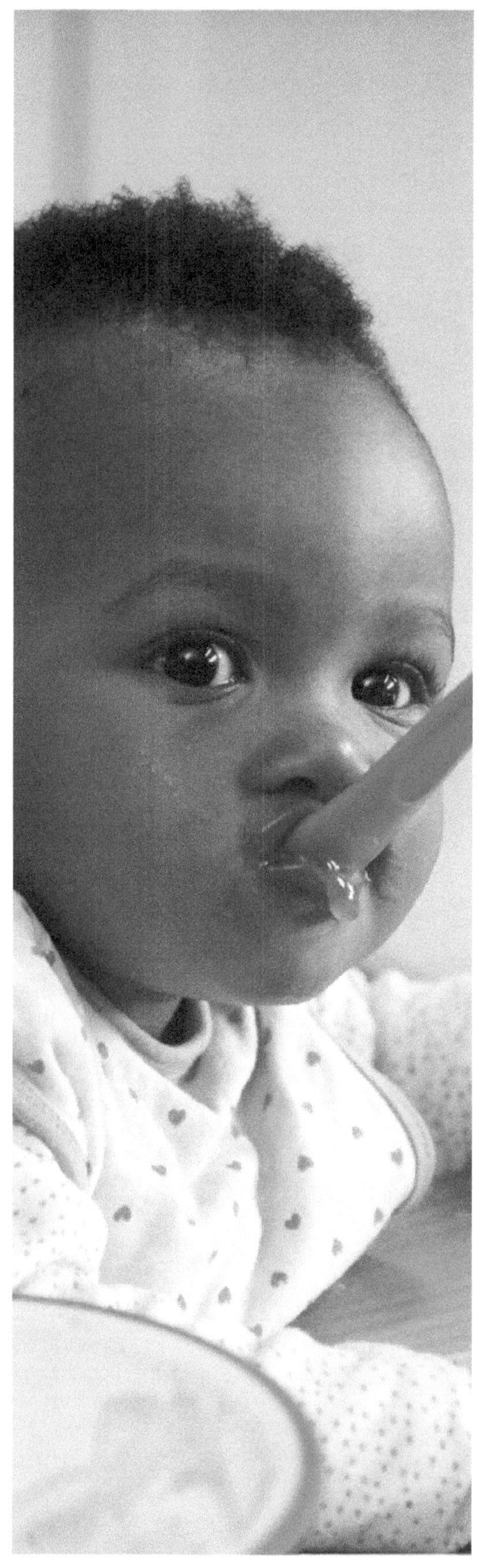

COW MILK AND FORTIFIED SOY BEVERAGES

Infants should not consume cow milk or fortified soy beverages before age 12 months to replace human milk or infant formula. Cow milk does not have the correct amount of nutrients for infants, and its higher protein and mineral content are hard for an infant's kidneys and digestive system to process. Plain cow milk (whole milk) or fortified unsweetened soy beverage can be offered beginning around 12 months of age to help meet calcium, potassium, vitamin D, and protein needs. Flavored milks for children age 12 through 23 months should be avoided because they contain added sugars.

PLANT-BASED MILK ALTERNATIVES

Plant-based milk alternatives, which are sometimes referred to as milk alternatives, include beverages made from plants, such as soy, oat, rice, coconut, and almond. These beverages should not be used in the first year of life to replace human milk or infant formula. They may come in different flavors and some forms have added sugars. Unsweetened versions of these beverages may be accommodated in small amounts in the diet during the second year of life, but most have significantly less protein than cow milk and are not always fortified with calcium and vitamin D. Among plant-based milk alternatives, only fortified soy beverage is currently considered a dairy equivalent. Thus, consuming other plant-based beverages does not contribute to meeting dairy recommendations.

100% FRUIT JUICE

Before age 12 months, 100% fruit or vegetable juices should not be given to infants. In the second year of life, fruit juice is not necessary, and most fruit intake should come from eating whole fruit. If 100% fruit juice is provided, up to 4 ounces per day can fit in a healthy dietary pattern. Juices that contain added sugars should be avoided.

TODDLER MILK AND TODDLER DRINKS

There are no clear needs for toddler milks or drinks. Needed nutrients can be obtained from cow milk or fortified soy beverage and appropriate solid foods. Toddler milks and toddler drinks are drinks supplemented with nutrients, and typically contain added sugars. A variety of nutrient-dense complementary foods and beverages without added sugars should be emphasized for achieving nutrient recommendations.

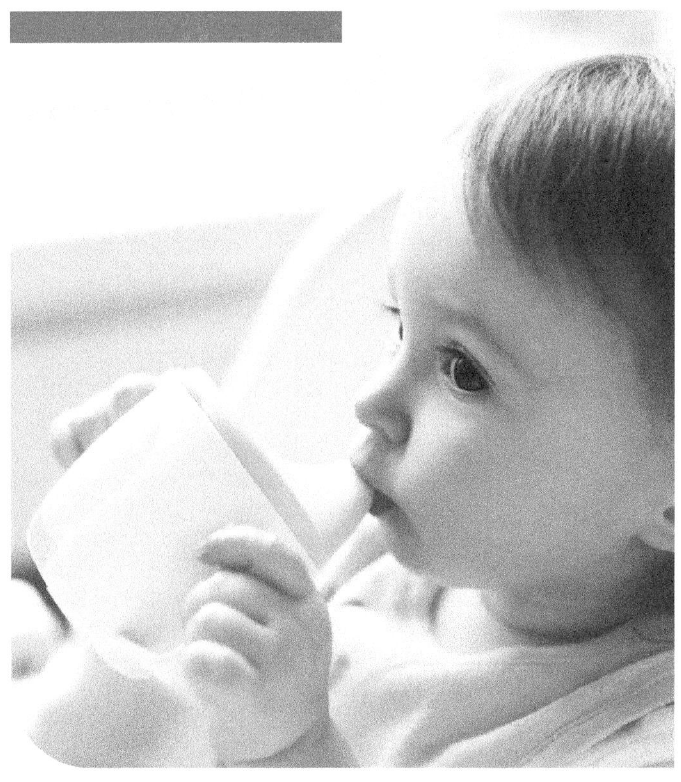

SUGAR-SWEETENED BEVERAGES

Sugar-sweetened beverages (e.g., regular soda, juice drinks [not 100% fruit juice], sports drinks, and flavored water with sugar) should not be given to children younger than age 2. Drinks labeled as fruit drinks or fruit-flavored drinks are not the same as 100% fruit juice and contain added sugars. These beverages displace nutrient-dense beverages and foods in the diet of young children. Infants and toddlers do not have room in their diets for the additional calories from added sugars found in these beverages. In addition, sugar-sweetened beverage intake in infancy and early childhood may predispose children to consume more of these beverages later in life.

CAFFEINATED BEVERAGES

Concerns exist about potential negative health effects of caffeine for young children, and no safe limits of caffeine have been established for this age group. Caffeine is a stimulant that can occur naturally in foods and beverages or as an additive. Major sources of caffeine for Americans include beverages such as soft drinks, tea, coffee, and sports drinks. Beverages containing caffeine should be avoided for children younger than age 2.

BIRTH THROUGH 23 MONTHS

Healthy Dietary Pattern During a Toddler's Second Year of Life

In the second year of life, toddlers consume less human milk, and infant formula is not recommended. Calories and nutrients should predominantly be met from a healthy dietary pattern of age-appropriate foods and beverages. The Healthy U.S.-Style Dietary Pattern presented here is intended for toddlers ages 12 through 23 months who no longer consume human milk or infant formula. The pattern represents the types and amounts of foods needed to meet energy and nutrition requirements for this period (**Table 2-1**). For toddlers who are still consuming human milk (approximately one-third at 12 months and 15 percent at 18 months), a healthy dietary pattern should include a similar combination of nutrient-dense complementary foods and beverages.

Table 2-1 displays the Healthy U.S.-Style Dietary Pattern to illustrate the specific amounts and limits for food groups and other dietary components that make up healthy dietary patterns. The pattern is provided at calorie levels ranging from 700 to 1,000 calories per day, which are appropriate for most toddlers ages 12 through 23 months (see ***Appendix 2. Estimated Calorie Needs***). A healthy dietary pattern includes a variety of nutrient-dense fruits, vegetables, grains, protein foods (including lean meats, poultry, eggs, seafood, nuts, and seeds), dairy (including milk, yogurt, and cheese), and oils. Based on FDA and EPA's joint "Advice About Eating Fish," young children should eat seafood lowest in methylmercury, and certain species of seafood should be avoided.[2] If young children are lower in body weight, they should eat less seafood than the amounts in the Healthy U.S.-Style Dietary Pattern. More information is available on the FDA or EPA websites at **FDA.gov/fishadvice** and **EPA.gov/fishadvice**.

After food group and subgroup recommendations are met, a small number of calories are allocated to oils. The recommendation to limit saturated fat to less than 10 percent of calories per day does not apply to those younger than age 2, and the inclusion of higher fat versions of dairy is a notable difference in the pattern for toddlers ages 12 through 23 months compared to patterns for ages 2 and older. However, no calories remain in the pattern for additional saturated fat or for added sugars. To illustrate the concept of nutrient density, **Figure 2-1** shows examples of foods and beverages appropriate for this life stage in forms that are not in nutrient-dense forms compared to those that are in nutrient-dense forms. This dietary pattern requires careful choices of foods and beverages but does not require inclusion of fortified products specifically formulated for infants or toddlers to meet nutrient recommendations.

Figure 2-1

Make Healthy Shifts To Empower Toddlers To Eat Nutrient-Dense Foods in Dietary Patterns

Science shows that early food preferences influence later food choices. Make the first choice the healthiest choices that set the toddlers on a path of making nutrient-dense choices in the years to come. Examples of shifts in common choices to healthier, more nutrient-dense food choices include:

[2]**If consuming up to 2 ounces of seafood per week**, children should only be fed cooked varieties from the "Best Choices" list in the FDA/EPA joint "Advice About Eating Fish," available at **FDA.gov/fishadvice** and **EPA.gov/fishadvice**. **If consuming up to 3 ounces of seafood per week**, children should only be fed cooked varieties from the "Best Choices" list that contain even lower methylmercury: flatfish (e.g., flounder), salmon, tilapia, shrimp, catfish, crab, trout, haddock, oysters, sardines, squid, pollock, anchovies, crawfish, mullet, scallops, whiting, clams, shad, and Atlantic mackerel. If consuming up to 3 ounces of seafood per week, many commonly consumed varieties of seafood should be avoided because they cannot be consumed at 3 ounces per week by children without the potential of exceeding safe methylmercury limits; examples that should not be consumed include: canned light tuna or white (albacore) tuna, cod, perch, black sea bass. For a complete list please see: **FDA.gov/fishadvice** and **EPA.gov/fishadvice**.

Table 2-1

Healthy U.S.-Style Dietary Pattern for Toddlers Ages 12 Through 23 Months Who Are No Longer Receiving Human Milk or Infant Formula, With Daily or Weekly Amounts From Food Groups, Subgroups, and Components

CALORIE LEVEL OF PATTERN[a]	700	800	900	1,000
FOOD GROUP OR SUBGROUP[b,c]	**Daily Amount of Food From Each Group[d]** (Vegetable and protein foods subgroup amounts are per week.)			
Vegetables (cup eq/day)	**⅔**	**¾**	**1**	**1**
	Vegetable Subgroups in Weekly Amounts			
Dark-Green Vegetables (cup eq/wk)	1	⅓	½	½
Red and Orange Vegetables (cup eq/wk)	1	1 ¾	2 ½	2 ½
Beans, Peas, Lentils (cup eq/wk)	¾	⅓	½	½
Starchy Vegetables (cup eq/wk)	1	1 ½	2	2
Other Vegetables (cup eq/wk)	¾	1 ¼	1 ½	1 ½
Fruits (cup eq/day)	**½**	**¾**	**1**	**1**
Grains (ounce eq/day)	**1 ¾**	**2 ¼**	**2 ½**	**3**
Whole Grains (ounce eq/day)	1 ½	2	2	2
Refined Grains (ounce eq/day)	¼	¼	½	1
Dairy (cup eq/day)	**1 ⅔**	**1 ¾**	**2**	**2**
Protein Foods (ounce eq/day)	**2**	**2**	**2**	**2**
	Protein Foods Subgroups in Weekly Amounts			
Meats, Poultry (ounce eq/wk)	8 ¾	7	7	7 ¾
Eggs (ounce eq/wk)	2	2 ¾	2 ½	2 ½
Seafood (ounce eq/wk)[e]	2-3	2-3	2-3	2-3
Nuts, Seeds, Soy Products (ounce eq/wk)	1	1	1 ¼	1 ¼
Oils (grams/day)	**9**	**9**	**8**	**13**

[a] Calorie level ranges: Energy levels are calculated based on median length and body weight reference individuals. Calorie needs vary based on many factors. The DRI Calculator for Healthcare Professionals, available at **usda.gov/fnic/dri-calculator**, can be used to estimate calorie needs based on age, sex, and weight.

[b] Definitions for each food group and subgroup and quantity (i.e., cup or ounce equivalents) are provided in ***Chapter 1*** and are compiled in ***Appendix 3***.

[c] All foods are assumed to be in nutrient-dense forms and prepared with minimal added sugars, refined starches, or sodium. Foods are also lean or in low-fat forms with the exception of dairy, which includes whole-fat fluid milk, reduced-fat plain yogurts, and reduced-fat cheese. There are no calories available for additional added sugars, saturated fat, or to eat more than the recommended amount of food in a food group.

[d] In some cases, food subgroup amounts are greatest at the lower calorie levels to help achieve nutrient adequacy when relatively small number of calories are required.

[e] **If consuming up to 2 ounces of seafood per week**, children should only be fed cooked varieties from the "Best Choices" list in the FDA/EPA joint "Advice About Eating Fish," available at **FDA.gov/fishadvice** and **EPA.gov/fishadvice**. **If consuming up to 3 ounces of seafood per week**, children should only be fed cooked varieties from the "Best Choices" list that contain even lower methylmercury: flatfish (e.g., flounder), salmon, tilapia, shrimp, catfish, crab, trout, haddock, oysters, sardines, squid, pollock, anchovies, crawfish, mullet, scallops, whiting, clams, shad, and Atlantic mackerel. If consuming up to 3 ounces of seafood per week, many commonly consumed varieties of seafood should be avoided because they cannot be consumed at 3 ounces per week by children without the potential of exceeding safe methylmercury limits; examples that should not be consumed include: canned light tuna or white (albacore) tuna, cod, perch, black sea bass. For a complete list please see: **FDA.gov/fishadvice** and **EPA.gov/fishadvice**.

BIRTH THROUGH 23 MONTHS

Current Intakes

Figure 2-2 and **2-3** highlight the dietary intakes of toddlers during the second year of life. Average intakes of the food groups are compared to the range of recommended intakes at the calorie levels most relevant to males and females in this age group **(Figure 2-2)**. Additionally, the average intakes and range of intakes of added sugars, saturated fat, and sodium are displayed. Average intakes compared to recommended intake ranges of the subgroups for grains are represented in daily amounts; subgroups for vegetables and protein foods are represented in weekly amounts (**Figure 2-3**).

Figure 2-2

Current Intakes: Ages 12 Through 23 Months

Average Daily Food Group Intakes Compared to Recommended Intake Ranges

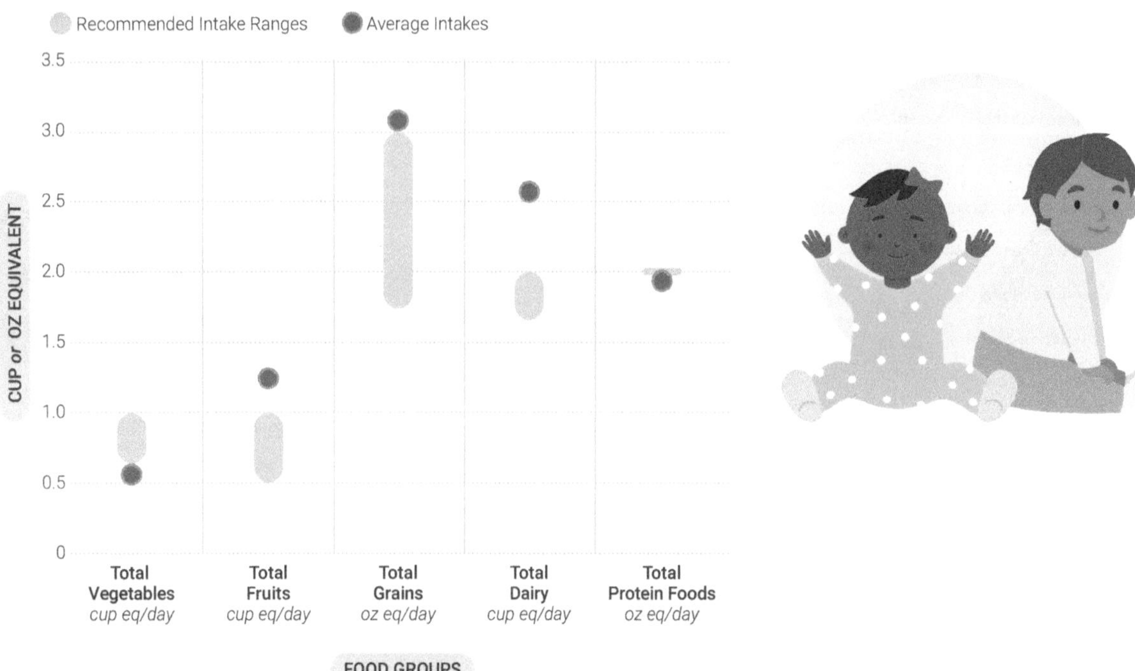

Average Intakes of Added Sugars, Saturated Fat, and Sodium

Added Sugars	Saturated Fat	Sodium
Limit: **Avoid**	Limit: **N/A**	Limit: **1,200 mg**
Average Intakes	Average Intakes	Average Intakes
104 kcals	**167 kcals**	**1,586 mg**

Data Sources: *Average Intakes:* Analysis of What We Eat in America, NHANES 2007-2016, day 1 dietary intake data, weighted. *Recommended Intake Ranges:* Healthy U.S.-Style Dietary Patterns (see ***Appendix 3***).

Figure 2-3
Average Intakes of Subgroups Compared to Recommended Intake Ranges: Ages 12 Through 23 Months

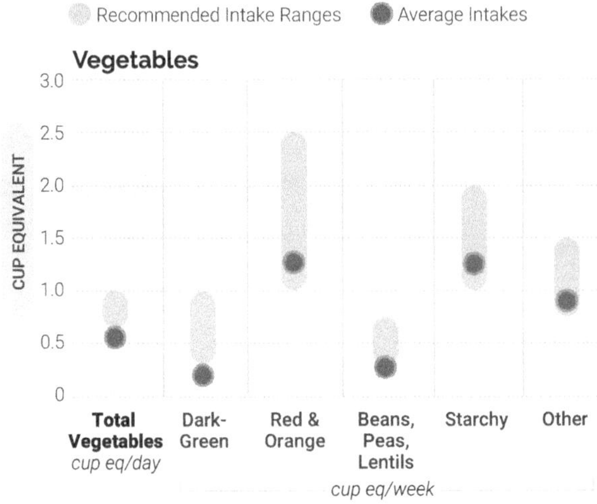

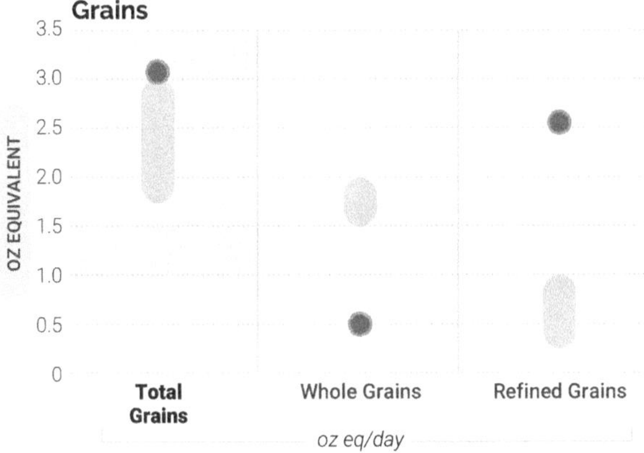

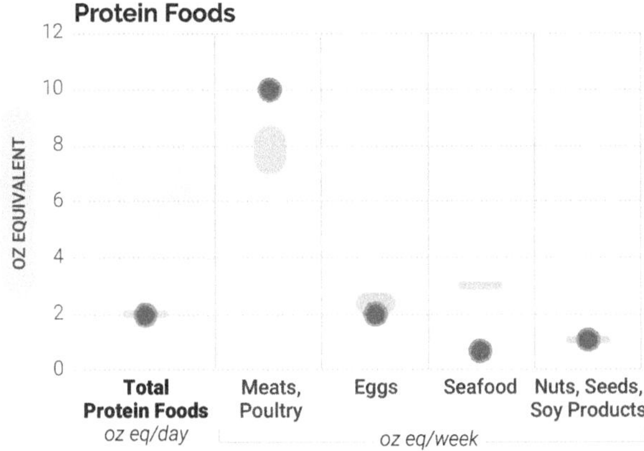

Data Sources: *Average Intakes:* Analysis of What We Eat in America, NHANES 2007-2016, day 1 dietary intake data, weighted. *Recommended Intake Ranges:* Healthy U.S.-Style Dietary Patterns (see **Appendix 3**).

Approximately 60 percent of toddlers meet or exceed recommended intakes for fruit. A majority of fruit is consumed as whole fruit (fresh, canned, puréed, frozen) or as 100% fruit juice. Average intake of total vegetables is below the range of recommended amounts, with nearly 90 percent of toddlers falling short of recommendations. About one-half of vegetables are consumed on their own, one-quarter are consumed as part of a mixed dish, and nearly 5 percent are consumed as savory snacks (e.g., potato chips).

Total grains, particularly refined grains, are consumed in amounts that exceed recommendations. Conversely, intakes of whole grains fall short of recommended amounts for more than 95 percent of toddlers. A majority of grains are consumed through breads, rolls, tortillas, or other bread products or as part of a mixed dish. Ten percent of grains come from sweet bakery products and approximately 15 percent come from crackers and savory snacks. Many of these categories are top sources of sodium or added sugars in this age group.

Average intakes of dairy foods, most of which is consumed as milk, generally exceed recommended amounts in this age group. Intakes of yogurt and cheese account for about 10 percent of dairy intakes. Plant-based beverages and flavored milks each make up about 2 percent of dairy intakes among toddlers.

Protein foods intakes fall within recommended range, on average. Intakes of meats, poultry, and eggs make up a majority of protein foods intakes, however seafood intakes in this age group is low. Children in this age group can reduce sodium intake by eating less cured or processed meats including hot dogs, deli meats, and sausages.

Due to the relatively high nutrient needs of toddlers, a healthy dietary pattern has virtually no room for added sugars. Toddlers consume an average of more than 100 calories from added sugars each day, ranging from 40 to 250 calories a day (about 2.5 to 16 teaspoons). Sugar-sweetened beverages, particularly fruit drinks, contribute more than 25 percent of total added sugars intakes and sweet bakery products contribute about 15 percent. Other food category sources contribute a smaller proportion of total added sugars on their own, but the wide variety of sources, which include yogurts, ready-to-eat cereals, candy, fruits, flavored milk, milk substitutes, baby food products, and breads, points to the need to make careful choices across all foods.

Vegetarian Dietary Pattern During the Second Year of Life

A Healthy Vegetarian Dietary Pattern for young children ages 12 through 23 months who are not fed human milk or infant formula is included in ***Appendix 3***. This pattern describes a lacto-ovo vegetarian diet that includes regular consumption of eggs, dairy products, soy products, and nuts or seeds, in addition to vegetables including beans, peas, and lentils, fruits, grains, and oils. Iron may be of particular concern because plant source foods contain only non-heme iron, which is less bioavailable than is heme iron. Food source lists for both heme and non-heme iron are available at **DietaryGuidelines.gov**. Vitamin B_{12} also may be of concern because it is present only in animal source foods. When feeding infants and toddlers a lacto-ovo vegetarian diet, parents, caregivers, and guardians should consult with a healthcare provider to determine whether supplementation of iron, vitamin B_{12}, and/or other nutrients is necessary and if so, appropriate levels to meet their unique needs.

Supporting Healthy Eating

Parents, guardians, and caregivers play an important role in nutrition during this life stage because infants and toddlers are fully reliant on them for their needs. In addition to "what" to feed children, "how" to feed young children also is critical. As noted above, repeated exposure to foods can increase acceptance of new foods. Another important concept is responsive feeding, a feeding style that emphasizes recognizing and responding to the hunger or fullness cues of an infant or young child (see "**Responsive Feeding**").

Responsive Feeding

Responsive feeding is a term used to describe a feeding style that emphasizes recognizing and responding to the hunger or fullness cues of an infant or young child. Responsive feeding helps young children learn how to self-regulate their intake.

See **Table 2-2** for some examples of signs a child may show for hunger and fullness when he or she is a newborn through age 5 months, and signs a child may start to show between age 6 through 23 months.

Table 2-2
Signs a Child is Hungry or Full

Birth Through Age 5 Months	
A child may be **hungry** if he or she: • Puts hands to mouth. • Turns head toward breast or bottle. • Puckers, smacks, or licks lips. • Has clenched hands.	A child may be **full** if he or she: • Closes mouth. • Turns head away from breast or bottle. • Relaxes hands.
Age 6 Through 23 Months	
A child may be **hungry** if he or she: • Reaches for or points to food. • Opens his or her mouth when offered a spoon or food. • Gets excited when he or she sees food. • Uses hand motions or makes sounds to let you know he or she is still hungry.	A child may be **full** if he or she: • Pushes food away. • Closes his or her mouth when food is offered. • Turns his or her head away from food. • Uses hand motions or makes sounds to let you know he or she is still full.

It is important to listen to the child's hunger and fullness cues to build healthy eating habits during this critical age. If parents, guardians, or caregivers have questions or concerns, a conversation with a healthcare provider will be helpful.

For more information on signs a child is hungry or full, see: **cdc.gov/nutritioninfantandtoddlernutrition/mealtime/signs-your-child-is-hungry-or-full.html**. More information on infant development skills, hunger and satiety cues, and typical daily portion sizes is available at **wicworks.fns.usda.gov/sites/default/files/media/document/Infant_Nutrition_and_Feeding_Guide.pdf**.

Accessing a Healthy Dietary Pattern

Many resources exist to support healthy growth and development during infancy and toddlerhood. These include the following Government programs that aim to support a healthy dietary pattern for infants and toddlers living in households with limited incomes:

- The **Special Supplemental Nutrition Program for Women, Infants, and Children (WIC)** supports infant and early childhood nutrition through supplementing the diets of women who are pregnant or lactating and by providing breastfeeding support and iron-fortified infant formula when human milk is unavailable or fed only partially. WIC accommodates the transition to solid foods by providing nutrient-dense foods in the supplemental food packages offered to older infants and toddlers. Nutrition education and counseling and referrals to healthcare and social services are other important resources offered to income-eligible WIC participants.

- The **Child and Adult Care Food Program (CACFP)** provides reimbursement for nutrient-dense meals and snacks served to infants and toddlers in participating child care centers, including at **Head Start** programs, and day care homes where infants and toddlers also have access to health screenings and families can be connected to health services to support their overall well-being.

- The **Supplemental Nutrition Assistance Program (SNAP)** is the largest food assistance program in the United States. SNAP helps meet the nutritional needs of infants and toddlers living in low-income households by providing temporary monthly benefits that can be used to access a healthy dietary pattern.

These Government nutrition programs are especially important for the 14 percent[3] of families with children who experience food insecurity and may struggle to access the foods needed to support a healthy dietary pattern. Professionals can use these, and additional Government and non-Government resources that exist within communities, to support healthy eating during infancy and toddlerhood.

Looking Toward Chapter 3: Children and Adolescents

This chapter focused on nutrition issues important to infants and toddlers—exclusive human milk feeding, if possible; introducing nutrient-dense complementary foods at about age 6 months; and encouraging infants and toddlers to sample and consume a variety of nutrient-dense foods and beverages to meet their needs. As toddlers grow and their dietary patterns become more integrated with the family's food patterns, new issues arise. These issues, and how to accommodate them within a lifelong healthy dietary pattern, are discussed in the next chapter, which focuses on children and adolescents.

[3] More information on food insecurity is available at **ers.usda.gov/data-products/ag-and-food-statistics-charting-the-essentials/food-security-and-nutrition-assistance**.

AGES 2-18

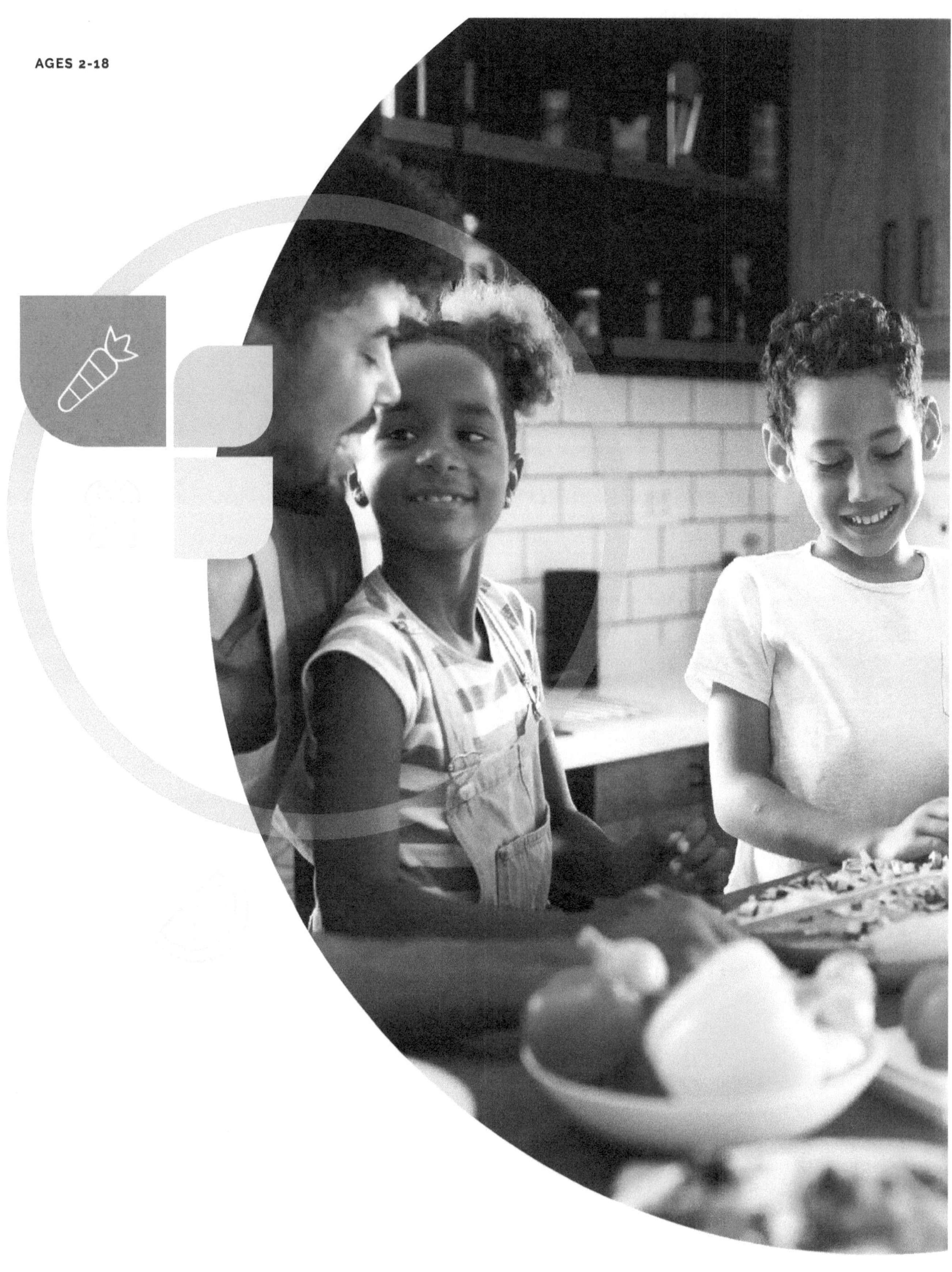

CHAPTER 3 Children and Adolescents

AGES 2-18

Introduction

Children and adolescents include individuals ages 2 through 18—a life stage characterized by transitions and the formation of dietary patterns. Suboptimal current intake patterns among children and adolescents and inadequate physical activity contribute to overweight and obesity in this life stage and risk of chronic disease (e.g., type 2 diabetes, cardiovascular disease) later in life. Changing this trajectory is crucial because dietary patterns established during this life stage tend to continue into adult years.

Healthy eating throughout this life stage involves the child or adolescent, families and caregivers, and institutions and settings where food is provided and consumed. Young children are fully reliant on others to provide their meals and snacks. As children transition to school-age and through adolescence, they are exposed to new food choices and begin to have more autonomy in the foods that are selected. New influences on eating behavior also emerge, such as peer pressure, which can create opportunities or challenges for establishing dietary patterns consistent with health and longevity. Adolescents acquire ever-greater independence in their food choices as they mature, with more time spent on their own with peers and more foods and beverages frequently consumed in social settings. Other factors that influence eating behavior include social supports, exposure to food marketing and promotion, and policies that determine community design.

Youth have diverse calorie and nutrient needs based on age and patterns of growth, development, and physical activity. Current intake data of young children show some components of a healthy dietary pattern that continue from the infant and toddler life stages. Before these components of a healthy dietary pattern are established, however, diet quality worsens through childhood and into adolescence and intake patterns drift further from recommendations in the *Dietary Guidelines*. Active community support is needed to help youth meet food group and nutrient goals with nutrient-dense foods and beverages.

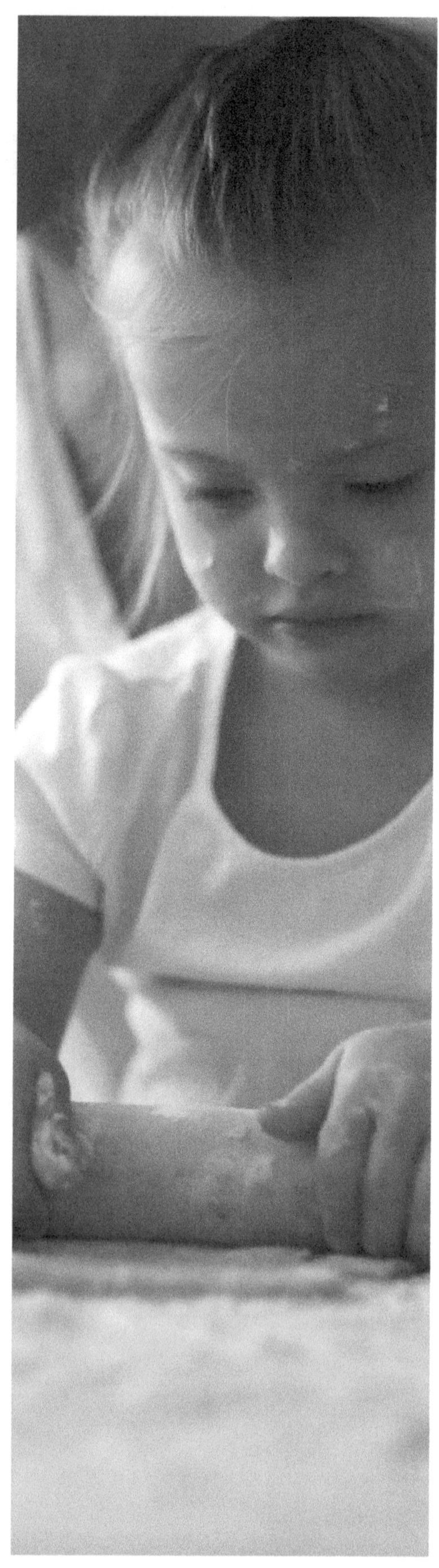

Childhood Overweight and Obesity

In the United States, 41 percent of children and adolescents are overweight or have obesity, and the prevalence is higher among Hispanic and non-Hispanic Black children and adolescents as compared to non-Hispanic Asians and Whites. Overweight and obesity put youth at high risk of serious health concerns. Youth with obesity are more likely to have immediate health risks, including high blood pressure, high cholesterol, and impaired glucose tolerance. They also are at increased risk of cardiovascular disease and type 2 diabetes beginning as soon as the teenage years and into adulthood. Psychological (e.g., anxiety, depression) and social concerns (e.g., bullying, stigma) also are more likely in children and adolescents with overweight or obesity.

The causes of childhood obesity are complex and interconnected. Behaviors (e.g., eating habits, level of physical activity, sedentary time) and the community in which a child or adolescent resides can influence risk of obesity. Genetics and the fetal environment also play a role in the development of obesity. However, many opportunities exist to help prevent or manage overweight and obesity as children transition through these life stages. The goal for children and adolescents with overweight or obesity is to reduce the rate of weight gain while allowing normal growth and development. This can primarily be done by emphasizing nutrient-dense food and beverage choices, minimizing calories from sources that do not contribute to a healthy dietary pattern, and encouraging regular physical activity.

Healthy Dietary Patterns

Children and adolescents are encouraged to follow the recommendations on the types of foods and beverages that make up a healthy dietary pattern described in ***Chapter 1. Nutrition and Health Across the Lifespan: The Guidelines and Key Recommendations***. **Tables 3-1** to **3-3** display the Healthy U.S.-Style Dietary Pattern to illustrate the specific amounts and limits for food groups and other dietary components that make up healthy dietary patterns at the calorie levels appropriate for most children and adolescents across four age ranges: one table combining patterns relevant for ages 2 through 4 and ages 5 through 8, and single tables for ages 9 through 13 and for ages 14 through 18. **Tables 3-1** to **3-3** also show the calories remaining for other uses—about 10-15 percent of the total available—after meeting food group and nutrient goals through the selection of nutrient-dense foods and beverages.

Calorie needs generally increase throughout this life stage to support growth and development. Child and adolescent females generally have lower calorie needs than do males, with variations based on size and level of physical activity. During adolescence, the range of calorie intakes widens to support diverse growth trajectories. More information on the calorie estimates is provided in **Tables 3-1** to **3-3** (see **footnote a**) and in ***Appendix 2. Estimated Calorie Needs***.

The USDA Dietary Patterns, including the Healthy U.S.-Style Dietary Pattern, provide a framework to help children and adolescents follow a healthy dietary pattern and meet the Guidelines and their Key Recommendations. The USDA Foods Patterns can be customized based on dietary needs, personal preferences, and budgetary constraints. A variety of nutrient-dense foods and beverages can be selected across the food group and subgroups as part of an overall healthy dietary pattern. For more information about the USDA Food Patterns, see ***Chapter 1*** and ***Appendix 3. USDA Dietary Patterns***. For this age group, as for all the others, a figure comparing current intakes to recommendations is presented. See "**Current Intakes**" for more information.

AGES 2-18

Children Ages 2 Through 8

In early childhood (ages 2 through 4), females require about 1,000 to 1,400 calories per day and males require about 1,000 to 1,600 calories per day. With the transition to school-age (ages 5 through 8), females require about 1,200 to 1,800 calories per day and males require about 1,200 to 2,000 calories per day.

Physical Activity

Childhood and adolescence is a critical period for developing movement skills, learning healthy habits, and establishing a firm foundation for lifelong health and well-being. For youth, regular physical activity can improve bone health, cardiorespiratory and muscular fitness, and cognition (including academic achievement), and reduce the symptoms of depression.

Preschool-aged children should be active throughout the day to enhance growth and development. Adults caring for children during this age should encourage active play that includes a variety of activity types (light, moderate, or vigorous intensity) and aim for at least 3 hours per day.

School-aged children and adolescents need at least 60 minutes of moderate-to-vigorous activity daily to attain the most health benefits from physical activity. Most activity can be aerobic, like walking, running, or anything that makes their heart beat faster. They also need muscle-strengthening and bone-strengthening activities that make their muscles and bones strong, like climbing on playground equipment, playing basketball, and jumping rope.

The U.S. Department of Health and Human Service's ***Physical Activity Guidelines for Americans*** and related Move Your Way® resources have more information about the benefits of physical activity and tips on how to get started. Available at **health.gov/paguidelines**.

Nutrient-Dense Foods and Beverages

Nutrient-dense foods and beverages provide vitamins, minerals, and other health-promoting components and have little added sugars, saturated fat, and sodium. Vegetables, fruits, whole grains, seafood, eggs, beans, peas, and lentils, unsalted nuts and seeds, fat-free and low-fat dairy products, and lean meats and poultry—when prepared with no or little added sugars, saturated fat, and sodium—are nutrient-dense foods.

Table 3-1

Healthy U.S.-Style Dietary Pattern for Children Ages 2 Through 8, With Daily or Weekly Amounts From Food Groups, Subgroups, and Components

CALORIE LEVEL OF PATTERN[a]	1,000	1,200	1,400	1,600	1,800	2,000
FOOD GROUP OR SUBGROUP[b]	Daily Amount of Food From Each Group (Vegetable and protein foods subgroup amounts are per week.)					
Vegetables (cup eq/day)	**1**	**1 ½**	**1 ½**	**2**	**2 ½**	**2 ½**
	Vegetable Subgroups in Weekly Amounts					
Dark-Green Vegetables (cup eq/wk)	½	1	1	1 ½	1 ½	1 ½
Red and Orange Vegetables (cup eq/wk)	2 ½	3	3	4	5 ½	5 ½
Beans, Peas, Lentils (cup eq/wk)	½	½	½	1	1 ½	1 ½
Starchy Vegetables (cup eq/wk)	2	3 ½	3 ½	4	5	5
Other Vegetables (cup eq/wk)	1 ½	2 ½	2 ½	3 ½	4	4
Fruits (cup eq/day)	**1**	**1**	**1 ½**	**1 ½**	**1 ½**	**2**
Grains (ounce eq/day)	**3**	**4**	**5**	**5**	**6**	**6**
Whole Grains (ounce eq/day)	1 ½	2	2 ½	3	3	3
Refined Grains (ounce eq/day)	1 ½	2	2 ½	2	3	3
Dairy (cup eq/day)	**2**	**2 ½**	**2 ½**	**2 ½**	**2 ½**	**2 ½**
Protein Foods (ounce eq/day)	**2**	**3**	**4**	**5**	**5**	**5 ½**
	Protein Foods Subgroups in Weekly Amounts					
Meats, Poultry, Eggs (ounce eq/wk)	10	14	19	23	23	26
Seafood (ounce eq/wk)[c]	2-3[d]	4	6	8	8	8
Nuts, Seeds, Soy Products (ounce eq/wk)	2	2	3	4	4	5
Oils (grams/day)	**15**	**17**	**17**	**22**	**22**	**24**
Limit on Calories for Other Uses (kcal/day)[e]	**130**	**80**	**90**	**150**	**190**	**280**
Limit on Calories for Other Uses (%/day)	13%	7%	6%	9%	10%	14%

[a] Calorie level ranges: Ages 2 through 4, Females: 1,000-1,400 calories; Males: 1,000-1,600 calories. Ages 5 through 8, Females: 1,200-1,800 calories; Males: 1,200-2,000 calories. Energy levels are calculated based on reference height (median) and reference weight (healthy) corresponding with a healthy body mass index (BMI). Calorie needs vary based on many factors. The DRI Calculator for Healthcare Professionals, available at **nal.usda.gov/fnic/dri-calculator**, can be used to estimate calorie needs based on age, sex, height, weight, and activity level.

[b] Definitions for each food group and subgroup and quantity (i.e., cup or ounce equivalents) are provided in ***Chapter 1*** and are compiled in ***Appendix 3***.

[c] The U.S. Food and Drug Administration (FDA) and the U.S. Environmental Protection Agency (EPA) provide joint advice regarding seafood consumption to limit methylmercury exposure for children. Depending on body weight, some children should choose seafood lowest in methylmercury or eat less seafood than the amounts in the Healthy US-Style Dietary Pattern. More information is available on the FDA and EPA websites at **FDA.gov/fishadvice** and **EPA.gov/fishadvice**.

[d] **If consuming up to 2 ounces of seafood per week**, children should only be fed cooked varieties from the "Best Choices" list in the FDA/EPA joint "Advice About Eating Fish," available at **FDA.gov/fishadvice** and **EPA.gov/fishadvice**. **If consuming up to 3 ounces of seafood per week**, children should only be fed cooked varieties from the "Best Choices" list that contain even lower methylmercury: flatfish (e.g., flounder), salmon, tilapia, shrimp, catfish, crab, trout, haddock, oysters, sardines, squid, pollock, anchovies, crawfish, mullet, scallops, whiting, clams, shad, and Atlantic mackerel. If consuming up to 3 ounces of seafood per week, many commonly consumed varieties of seafood should be avoided because they cannot be consumed at 3 ounces per week by children without the potential of exceeding safe methylmercury limits; examples that should not be consumed include: canned light tuna or white (albacore) tuna, cod, perch, black sea bass. For a complete list please see: **FDA.gov/fishadvice** and **EPA.gov/fishadvice**.

[e] Foods are assumed to be in nutrient-dense forms; lean or low-fat; and prepared with minimal added sugars, refined starches, saturated fat, or sodium. If all food choices to meet food group recommendations are in nutrient-dense forms, a small number of calories remain within the overall limit of the pattern (i.e., limit on calories for other uses). The number of calories depends on the total calorie level of the pattern and the amounts of food from each food group required to meet nutritional goals. Calories up to the specified limit can be used for added sugars and/or saturated fat, or to eat more than the recommended amount of food in a food group.

NOTE: The total dietary pattern should not exceed *Dietary Guidelines* limits for added sugars and saturated fat; be within the Acceptable Macronutrient Distribution Ranges for protein, carbohydrate, and total fats; and stay within calorie limits. Values are rounded. See ***Appendix 3*** for all calorie levels of the pattern.

AGES 2-18

Current Intakes

Figures 3-2 to **3-9** highlight the dietary intakes of children and adolescents, including the Healthy Eating Index-2015 score, which is an overall measure of how intakes align with the *Dietary Guidelines*, as well as information on the components of a healthy diet—specifically, the food groups. **Figures 3-1**, **3-3**, **3-5**, and **3-7** display the average intakes of the food groups compared to the range of recommended intakes at the calorie levels most relevant to males and females in these age groups. Additionally, the percent of children and adolescents exceeding the recommended limits for added sugars, saturated fat, and sodium are shown, along with average intakes of these components. Average intakes compared to recommended intake ranges of the subgroups for grains are represented in daily amounts; subgroups for vegetables and protein foods are represented in weekly amounts (see **Figures 3-2**, **3-4**, **3-6**, and **3-8**).

Current intakes show that from an early age, dietary patterns are not aligned with the *Dietary Guidelines*. The Healthy Eating Index score of 61 out of 100 for children ages 2 through 4 indicates that overall diet quality is poor. Notably, HEI Scores decline throughout childhood and adolescence, with scores for adolescents approximately 10 points lower than those for young children (**Figure 3-1**).

Among children ages 2 through 4, consumption of total fruit is generally adequate for about 60 percent of children. Compared to other age groups, a higher percentage of young children also have intakes of total vegetables at or above recommended levels. The difference between recommended and actual intakes of total fruit and total vegetables emerges and expands as children age. By late adolescence, average fruit and vegetable consumption is about half of the recommended range of intake. Throughout youth, starchy vegetables (e.g., white potatoes, corn)—often in forms that are fried or prepared with additions such as butter and salt—are more frequently consumed than the red and orange; dark green; or beans, peas, and lentils vegetable subgroups. For fruit, about 70 percent of intake comes from whole forms—fresh, canned, frozen, or dried—and 100% juice, which are often nutrient-dense forms. Some fruit is consumed through sources that are not nutrient-dense; for example, fruit as part of a baked dessert or juice drink.

Figure 3-1

Healthy Eating Index Scores Across Childhood and Adolescence

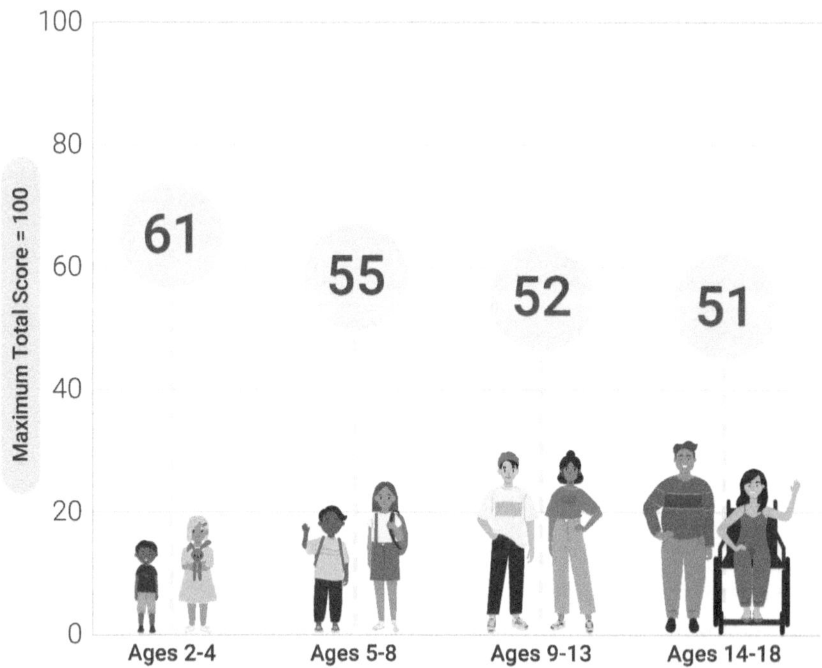

Data Source: Analysis of What We Eat in America, NHANES 2015-2016, ages 2 through 18, day 1 dietary intake, weighted.

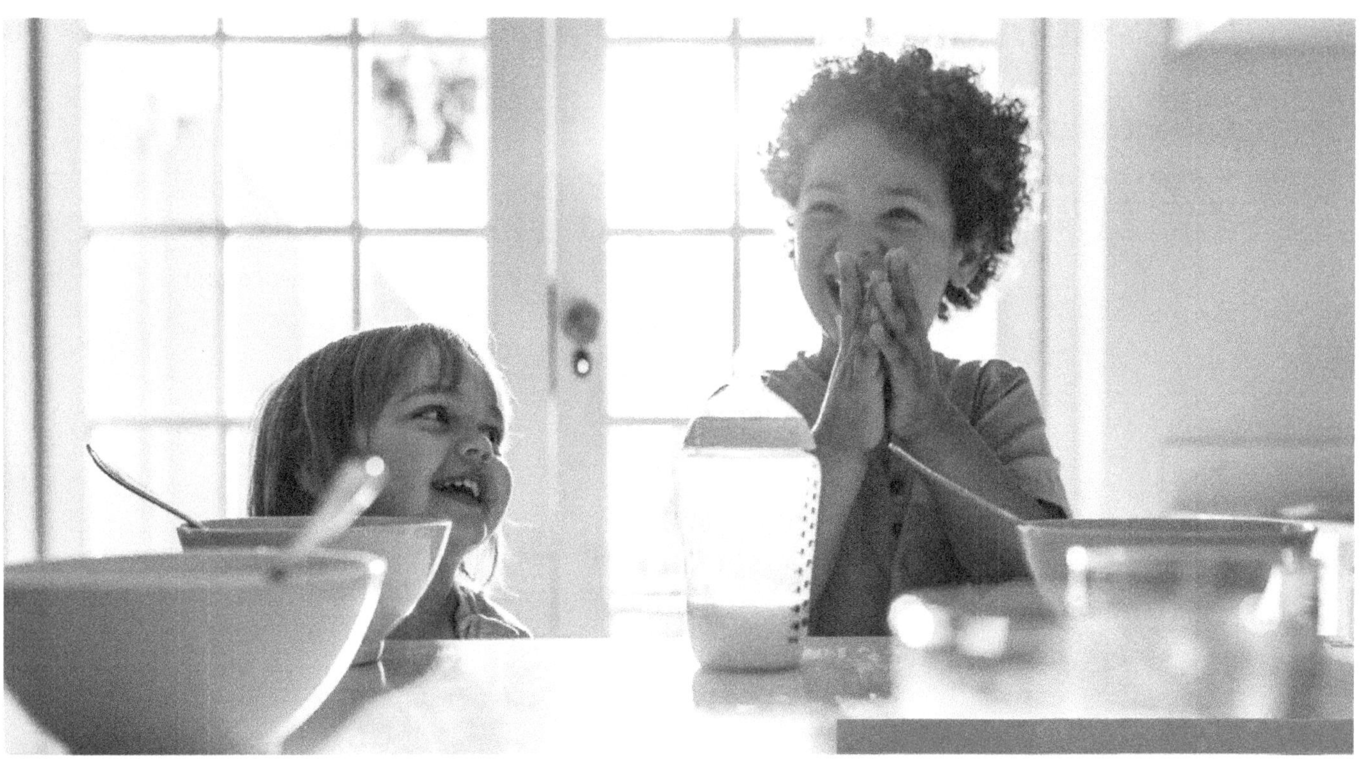

The amount of dairy foods consumed by children and adolescents is relatively stable across age groups. Beginning at age 9 the amount of dairy foods in a healthy dietary pattern increases from 2 ½ to 3 cup equivalents per day to support an increase in calcium intake that is needed during these life stages. As a result, average intake of dairy foods is close to or at recommended levels for children younger than age 9 while consumption among adolescents is typically below recommended intake levels.

Although the gaps between recommended and current intakes widen throughout these life stages for some dietary components, others, principally whole grains and seafood, are infrequently consumed by any youth. Whole grains are consumed below recommended levels even by young children. As the difference between recommended and current intakes widens across age groups, the types of refined and whole-grain foods consumed remains consistent. Mixed dishes, such as pizza, pasta, sandwiches, burgers, and tacos, contribute about 50 percent of total grains intake, and snacks and sweets, such as chips, crackers, and cookies, about 20 percent. Breakfast cereals and bars, including ready-to-eat and cooked varieties, are the top contributor to whole-grains intake during these life stages. Despite the underconsumption of whole grains, intakes of total grains trend toward overconsumption due to the contribution of refined grains.

Total protein intake generally meets targets except for adolescent females ages 14 through 18. Youth typically meet or exceed recommendations for meats, poultry, and eggs. Seafood, a protein subgroup that can support intakes of beneficial fatty acids, is consumed at levels far below the lower end of the recommended intakes range. When seafood is consumed, it is typically as part of a mixed dish rather than as an individual food item.

Children and adolescents can improve intake patterns by maintaining the components of a healthy diet that are evident in early childhood, particularly total fruit and dairy foods, while increasing consumption of food groups that are underconsumed across all age groups, specifically total vegetables and vegetable subgroups, whole grains, and seafood. Reducing intakes of added sugars, saturated fat, and sodium—components of a dietary pattern that are often consumed above recommended limits beginning at an early age—also will support youth in achieving a healthy dietary pattern, particularly when considering the very limited amount of calories available outside of those needed for meeting food group and nutrient goals.

AGES 2-18

Current Intakes

Figure 3-2

Current Intakes: Ages 2 Through 4

Average Daily Food Group Intakes Compared to Recommended Intake Ranges

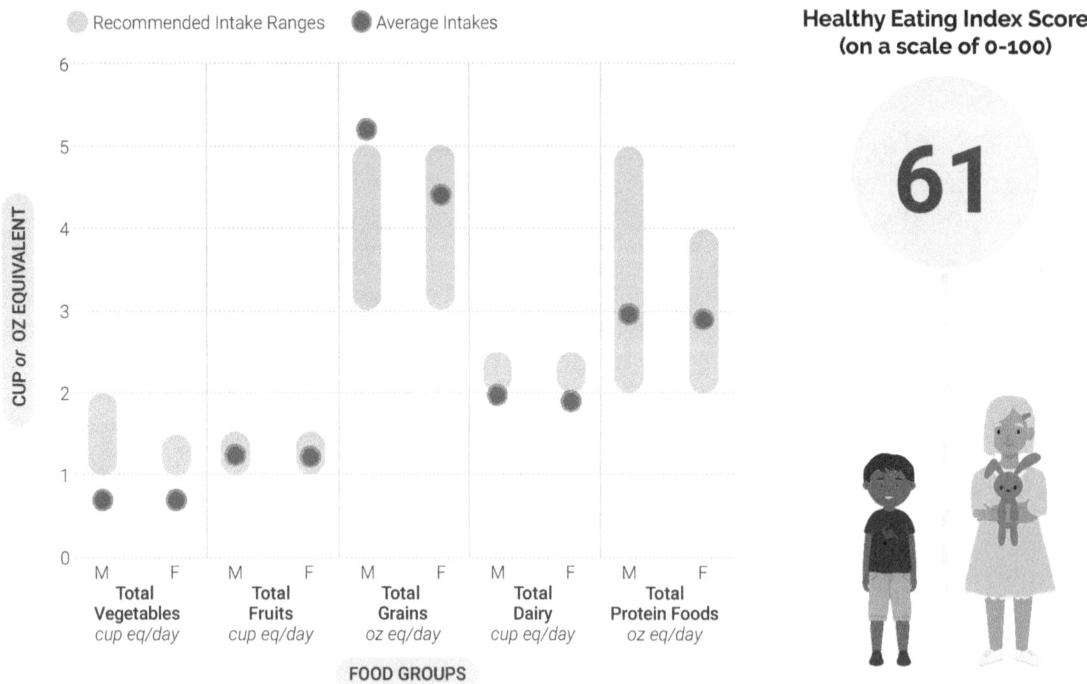

Percent Exceeding Limits of Added Sugars, Saturated Fat, and Sodium

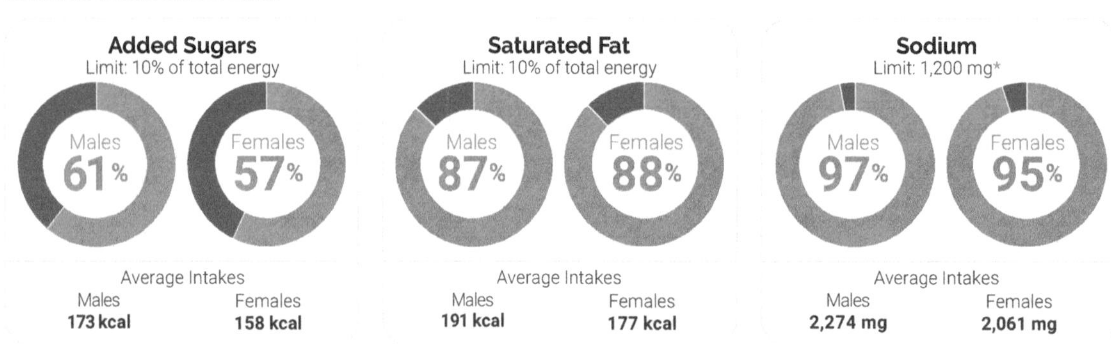

***NOTE:** Children ages 2 through 3 should reduce sodium intake if above 1,200 mg/d and those age 4 should reduce intake if above 1,500 mg/d.

Data Sources: *Average Intakes and HEI-2015 Scores:* Analysis of What We Eat in America, NHANES 2015-2016, day 1 dietary intake data, weighted. *Recommended Intake Ranges:* Healthy U.S.-Style Dietary Patterns (see ***Appendix 3***). *Percent Exceeding Limits:* What We Eat in America, NHANES 2013-2016, 2 days dietary intake data, weighted.

Figure 3-3

Average Intakes of Subgroups Compared to Recommended Intake Ranges: Ages 2 Through 4

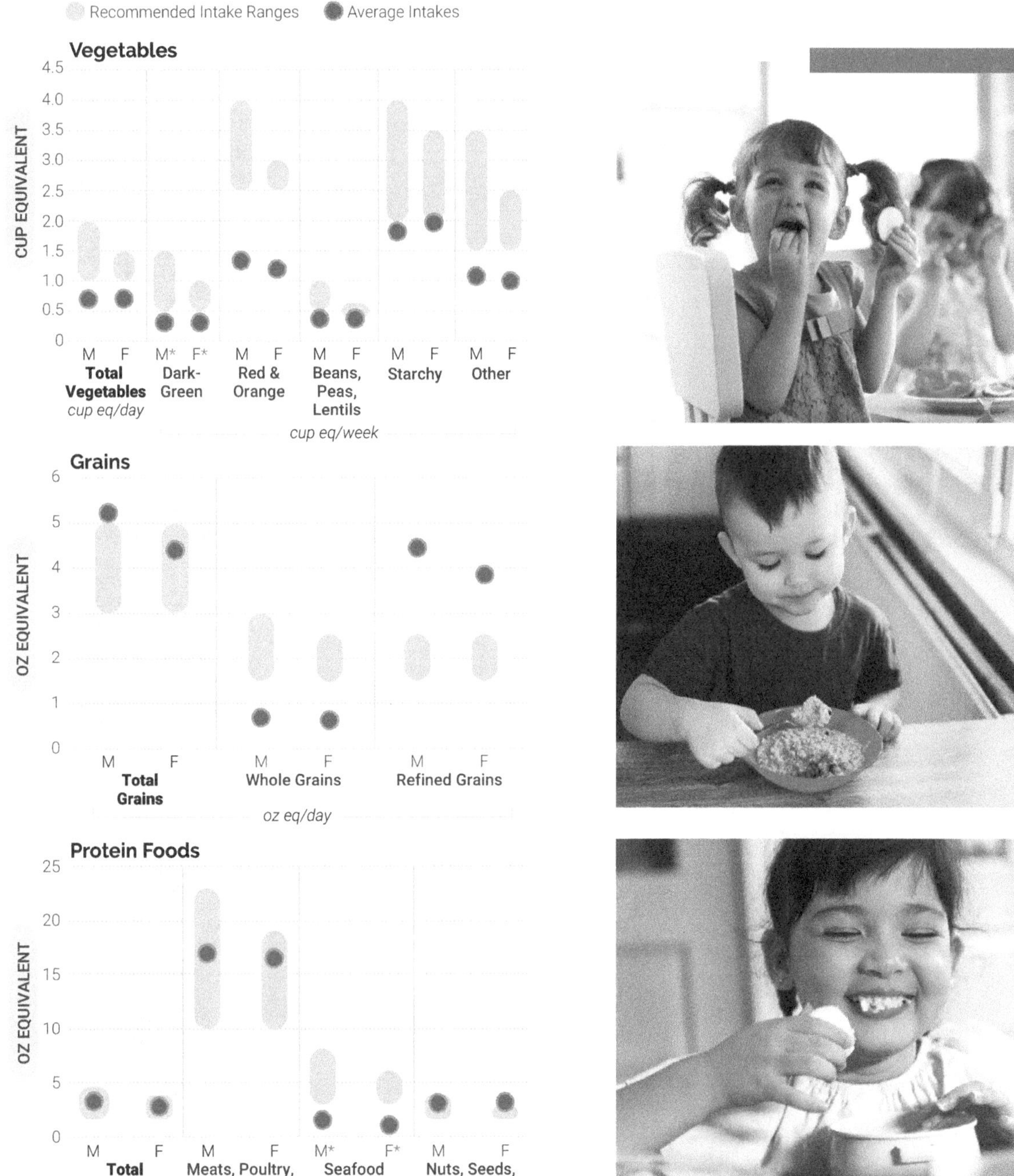

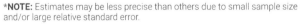

***NOTE:** Estimates may be less precise than others due to small sample size and/or large relative standard error.

Data Sources: *Average Intakes:* Analysis of What We Eat in America, NHANES 2015-2016, day 1 dietary intake data, weighted. *Recommended Intake Ranges:* Healthy U.S.-Style Dietary Patterns (see ***Appendix 3***).

AGES 2-18

Current Intakes

Figure 3-4

Current Intakes: Ages 5 Through 8

Average Daily Food Group Intakes Compared to Recommended Intake Ranges

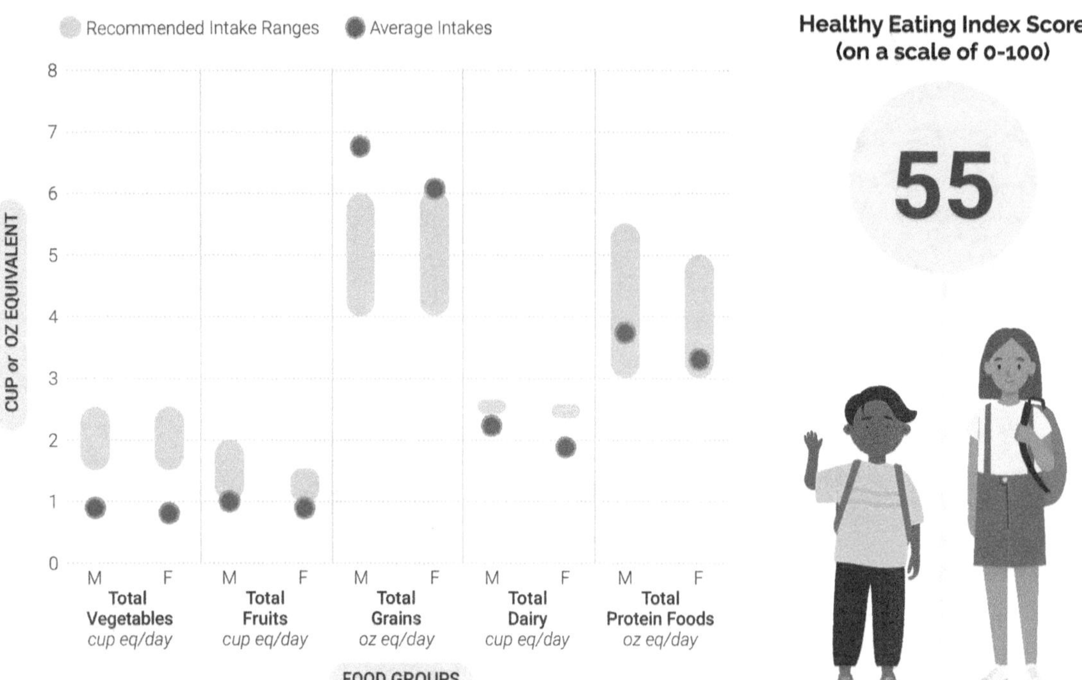

Percent Exceeding Limits of Added Sugars, Saturated Fat, and Sodium

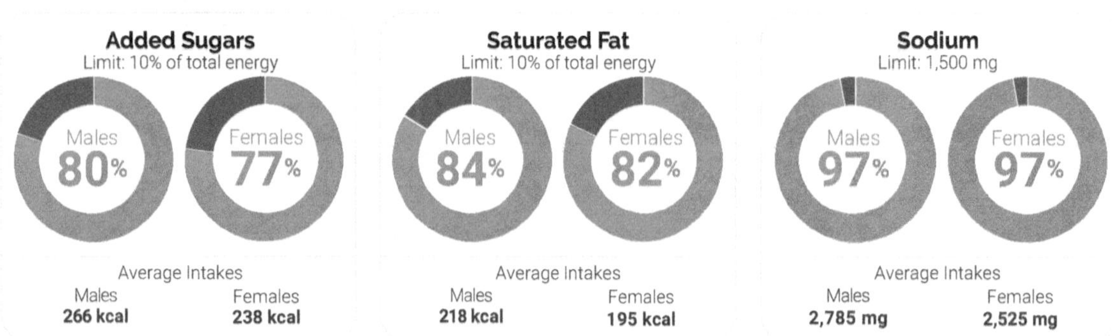

	Added Sugars	Saturated Fat	Sodium
Average Intakes: Males	266 kcal	218 kcal	2,785 mg
Average Intakes: Females	238 kcal	195 kcal	2,525 mg

Data Sources: *Average Intakes and HEI-2015 Scores:* Analysis of What We Eat in America, NHANES 2015-2016, day 1 dietary intake data, weighted. Recommended Intake Ranges: Healthy U.S.-Style Dietary Patterns (see ***Appendix 3***). *Percent Exceeding Limits:* What We Eat in America, NHANES 2013-2016, 2 days dietary intake data, weighted.

AGES 2-18

Figure 3-5
Average Intakes of Subgroups Compared to Recommended Intake Ranges: Ages 5 Through 8

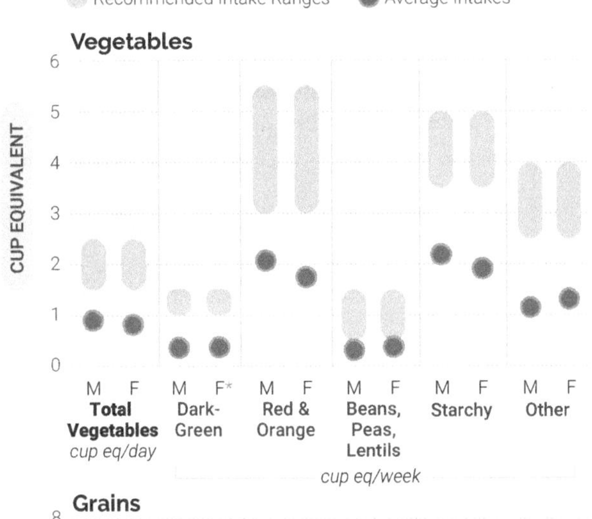

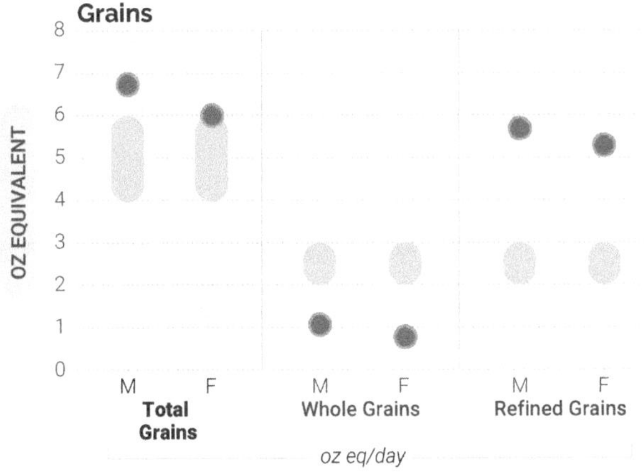

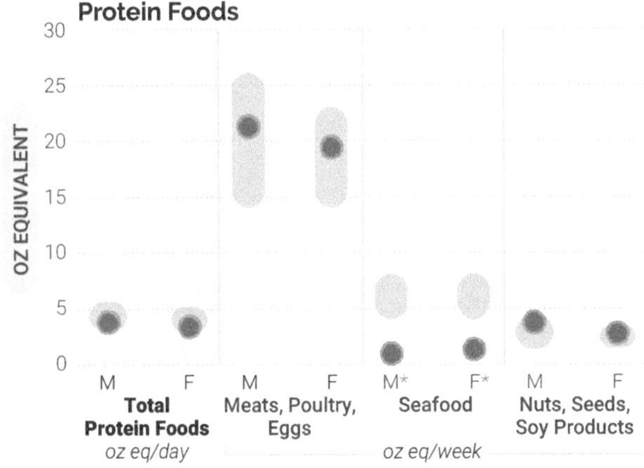

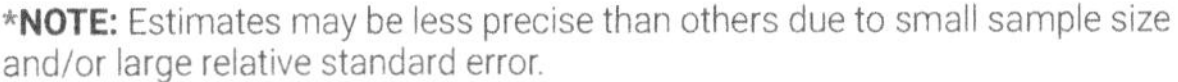

***NOTE:** Estimates may be less precise than others due to small sample size and/or large relative standard error.

Data Sources: *Average Intake:* Analysis of What We Eat in America, NHANES 2015-2016, day 1 dietary intake data, weighted. *Recommended Intake Ranges:* Healthy U.S.-Style Dietary Patterns (see ***Appendix 3***).

AGES 2-18

Children and Adolescents Ages 9 Through 13

In the late childhood and early adolescence stage, females require about 1,400 to 2,200 calories per day and males require about 1,600 to 2,600 calories per day.

Table 3-2

Healthy U.S.-Style Dietary Pattern for Children and Adolescents Ages 9 Through 13, With Daily or Weekly Amounts From Food Groups, Subgroups, and Components

CALORIE LEVEL OF PATTERN[a]	1,400	1,600	1,800	2,000	2,200	2,400	2,600
FOOD GROUP OR SUBGROUP[b]	Daily Amount of Food From Each Group (Vegetable and protein foods subgroup amounts are per week.)						
Vegetables (cup eq/day)	**1 ½**	**2**	**2 ½**	**2 ½**	**3**	**3**	**3 ½**
	Vegetable Subgroups in Weekly Amounts						
Dark-Green Vegetables (cup eq/wk)	1	1 ½	1 ½	1 ½	2	2	2 ½
Red & Orange Vegetables (cup eq/wk)	3	4	5 ½	5 ½	6	6	7
Beans, Peas, Lentils (cup eq/wk)	½	1	1 ½	1 ½	2	2	2 ½
Starchy Vegetables (cup eq/wk)	3 ½	4	5	5	6	6	7
Other Vegetables (cup eq/wk)	2 ½	3 ½	4	4	5	5	5 ½
Fruits (cup eq/day)	**1 ½**	**1 ½**	**1 ½**	**2**	**2**	**2**	**2**
Grains (ounce eq/day)	**5**	**5**	**6**	**6**	**7**	**8**	**9**
Whole Grains (ounce eq/day)	2 ½	3	3	3	3 ½	4	4 ½
Refined Grains (ounce eq/day)	2 ½	2	3	3	3 ½	4	4 ½
Dairy (cup eq/day)	**3**	**3**	**3**	**3**	**3**	**3**	**3**
Protein Foods (ounce eq/day)	**4**	**5**	**5**	**5 ½**	**6**	**6 ½**	**6 ½**
	Protein Foods Subgroups in Weekly Amounts						
Meats, Poultry, Eggs (ounce eq/wk)	19	23	23	26	28	31	31
Seafood (ounce eq/wk)[c]	6	8	8	8	9	10	10
Nuts, Seeds, Soy Products (ounce eq/wk)	3	4	4	5	5	5	5
Oils (grams/day)	**17**	**22**	**24**	**27**	**29**	**31**	**34**
Limit on Calories for Other Uses (kcal/day)[d]	**50**	**100**	**140**	**240**	**250**	**320**	**350**
Limit on Calories for Other Uses (%/day)	4%	6%	8%	12%	11%	13%	13%

[a] Calorie level ranges: Females: 1,400-2,200; Males: 1,600-2,600. Energy levels are calculated based on reference height (median) and reference weight (healthy) corresponding with a healthy body mass index (BMI). Calorie needs vary based on many factors. The DRI Calculator for Healthcare Professionals, available at **nal.usda.gov/fnic/dri-calculator**, can be used to estimate calorie needs based on age, sex, height, weight, and activity level.

[b] Definitions for each food group and subgroup and quantity (i.e., cup or ounce equivalents) are provided in ***Chapter 1*** and are compiled in ***Appendix 3***.

[c] The U.S. Food and Drug Administration (FDA) and the U.S. Environmental Protection Agency (EPA) provide joint advice regarding seafood consumption to limit methylmercury exposure for children. Depending on body weight, some children should choose seafood lowest in methylmercury or eat less seafood than the amounts in the Healthy US-Style Dietary Pattern. More information is available on the FDA and EPA websites at **FDA.gov/fishadvice** and **EPA.gov/fishadvice**.

[d] All foods are assumed to be in nutrient-dense forms; lean or low-fat; and prepared with minimal added sugars, saturated fat, refined starches, or sodium. If all food choices to meet food group recommendations are in nutrient-dense forms, a small number of calories remain within the overall limit of the pattern (i.e., limit on calories for other uses). The number of calories depends on the total calorie level of the pattern and the amounts of food from each food group required to meet nutritional goals. Calories up to the specified limit can be used for added sugars and/or saturated fat, or to eat more than the recommended amount of food in a food group.

NOTE: The total dietary pattern should not exceed *Dietary Guidelines* limits for added sugars and saturated fat; be within the Acceptable Macronutrient Distribution Ranges for protein, carbohydrate, and total fats; and stay within calorie limits. Values are rounded. See ***Appendix 3*** for all calorie levels of the pattern.

AGES 2-18

Current Intakes

Figure 3-6

Current Intakes: Ages 9 Through 13

Average Daily Food Group Intakes Compared to Recommended Intake Ranges

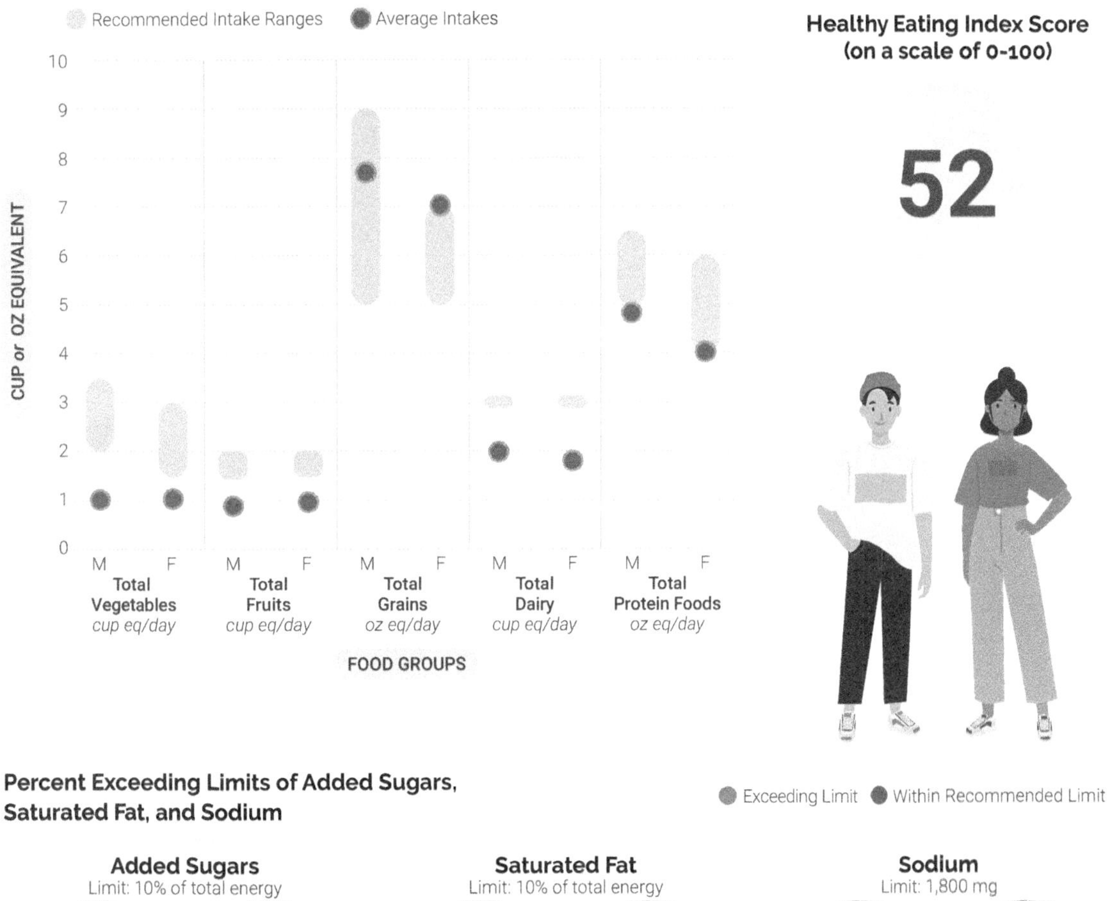

Percent Exceeding Limits of Added Sugars, Saturated Fat, and Sodium

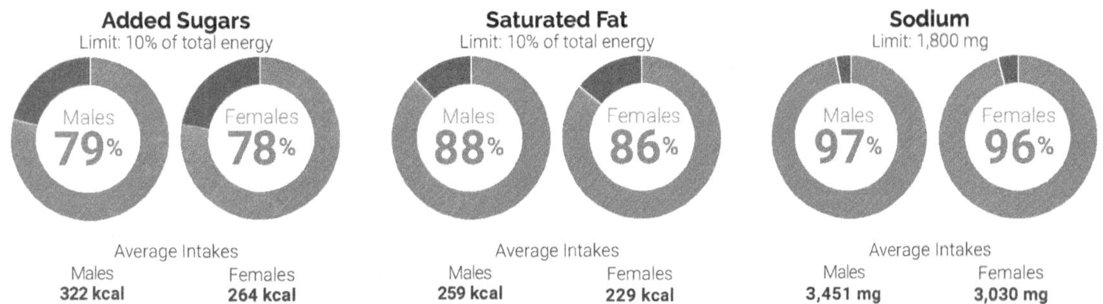

	Average Intakes Males	Average Intakes Females
Added Sugars	322 kcal	264 kcal
Saturated Fat	259 kcal	229 kcal
Sodium	3,451 mg	3,030 mg

Data Sources: *Average Intake and HEI-2015 Scores:* Analysis of What We Eat in America, NHANES 2015-2016, day 1 dietary intake data, weighted. *Recommended Intake Ranges:* Healthy U.S.-Style Dietary Patterns (see ***Appendix 3***). *Percent Exceeding Limits:* What We Eat in America, NHANES 2013-2016, 2 days dietary intake data, weighted.

AGES 2-18

Figure 3-7

Average Intakes of Subgroups Compared to Recommended Intake Ranges: Ages 9 Through 13

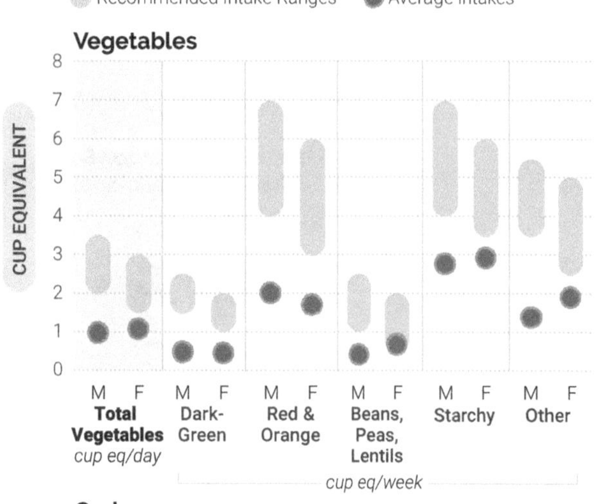

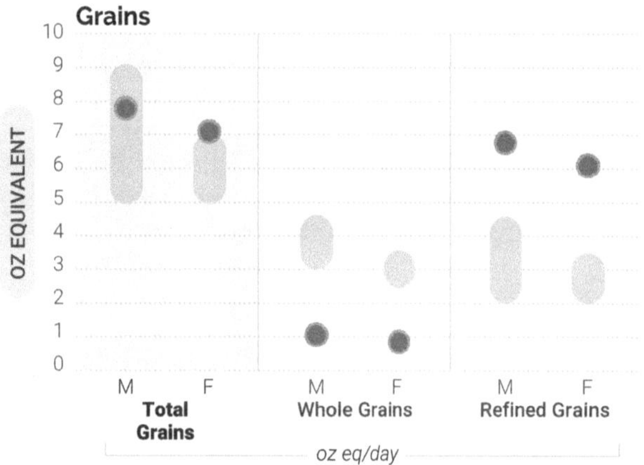

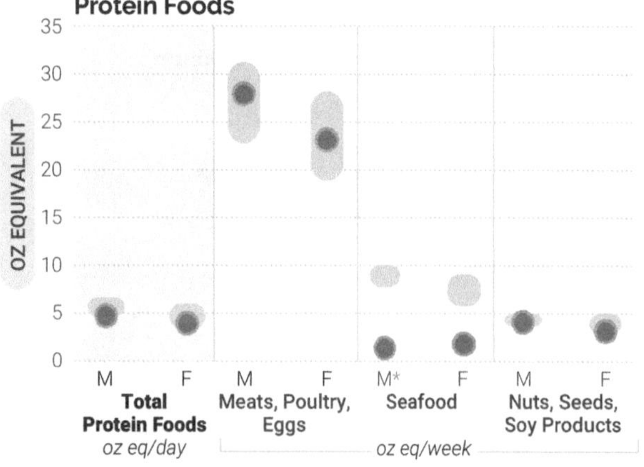

***NOTE:** Estimates may be less precise than others due to small sample size and/or large relative standard error.

Data Sources: *Average Intakes:* Analysis of What We Eat in America, NHANES 2015-2016, day 1 dietary intake data, weighted. *Recommended Intake Ranges:* Healthy U.S.-Style Dietary Patterns (see ***Appendix 3***).

Adolescents Ages 14 Through 18

Adolescent females require about 1,800 to 2,400 calories per day and males require about 2,000 to 3,200 calories per day.

Table 3-3

Healthy U.S.-Style Dietary Pattern for Adolescents Ages 14 Through 18, With Daily or Weekly Amounts From Food Groups, Subgroups, and Components

CALORIE LEVEL OF PATTERN[a]	1,800	2,000	2,200	2,400	2,600	2,800	3,000	3,200
FOOD GROUP OR SUBGROUP[b]	**Daily Amount of Food From Each Group** (Vegetable and protein foods subgroup amounts are per week.)							
Vegetables (cup eq/day)	**2 ½**	**2 ½**	**3**	**3**	**3 ½**	**3 ½**	**4**	**4**
	Vegetable Subgroups in Weekly Amounts							
Dark-Green Vegetables (cup eq/wk)	1 ½	1 ½	2	2	2 ½	2 ½	2 ½	2 ½
Red and Orange Vegetables (cup eq/wk)	5 ½	5 ½	6	6	7	7	7 ½	7 ½
Beans, Peas, Lentils (cup eq/wk)	1 ½	1 ½	2	2	2 ½	2 ½	3	3
Starchy Vegetables (cup eq/wk)	5	5	6	6	7	7	8	8
Other Vegetables (cup eq/wk)	4	4	5	5	5 ½	5 ½	7	7
Fruits (cup eq/day)	**1 ½**	**2**	**2**	**2**	**2**	**2 ½**	**2 ½**	**2 ½**
Grains (ounce eq/day)	**6**	**6**	**7**	**8**	**9**	**10**	**10**	**10**
Whole Grains (ounce eq/day)	3	3	3 ½	4	4 ½	5	5	5
Refined Grains (ounce eq/day)	3	3	3 ½	4	4 ½	5	5	5
Dairy (cup eq/day)	**3**	**3**	**3**	**3**	**3**	**3**	**3**	**3**
Protein Foods (ounce eq/day)	**5**	**5 ½**	**6**	**6 ½**	**6 ½**	**7**	**7**	**7**
	Protein Foods Subgroups in Weekly Amounts							
Meats, Poultry, Eggs (ounce eq/wk)	23	26	28	31	31	33	33	33
Seafood (ounce eq/wk)	8	8	9	10	10	10	10	10
Nuts, Seeds, Soy Products (ounce eq/wk)	4	5	5	5	5	6	6	6
Oils (grams/day)	**24**	**27**	**29**	**31**	**34**	**36**	**44**	**51**
Limit on Calories for Other Uses (kcal/day)[c]	**140**	**240**	**250**	**320**	**350**	**370**	**440**	**580**
Limit on Calories for Other Uses (%/day)	8%	12%	11%	13%	13%	13%	15%	18%

[a] Calorie level ranges: Females: 1,800-2,400 calories; Males: 2,000-3,200 calories. Energy levels are calculated based on reference height (median) and reference weight (healthy) corresponding with a healthy body mass index (BMI). Calorie needs vary based on many factors. The DRI Calculator for Healthcare Professionals, available at **nal.usda.gov/fnic/dri-calculator**, can be used to estimate calorie needs based on age, sex, height, weight, activity level.

[b] Definitions for each food group and subgroup and quantity (i.e., cup or ounce equivalents) are provided in ***Chapter 1*** and are compiled in ***Appendix 3***.

[c] All foods are assumed to be in nutrient-dense forms; lean or low-fat; and prepared with minimal added sugars, saturated fat, refined starches, or sodium. If all food choices to meet food group recommendations are in nutrient-dense forms, a small number of calories remain within the overall limit of the pattern (i.e., limit on calories for other uses). The number of calories depends on the total calorie level of the pattern and the amounts of food from each food group required to meet nutritional goals. Calories up to the specified limit can be used for added sugars and/or saturated fat, or to eat more than the recommended amount of food in a food group.

NOTE: The total dietary pattern should not exceed *Dietary Guidelines* limits for added sugars and saturated fat; be within the Acceptable Macronutrient Distribution Ranges for protein, carbohydrate, and total fats; and stay within calorie limits. Values are rounded. See ***Appendix 3*** for all calorie levels of the pattern.

AGES 2-18

Current Intakes

Figure 3-8

Current Intakes: Ages 14 Through 18

Average Daily Food Group Intakes Compared to Recommended Intake Ranges

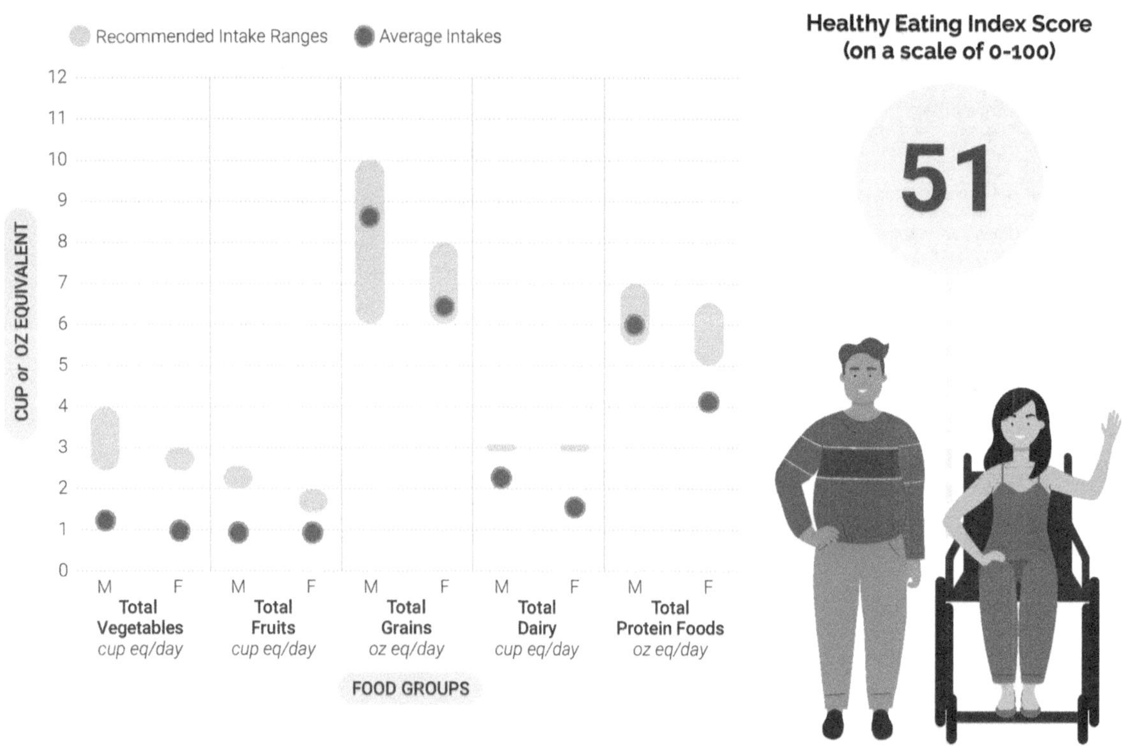

Percent Exceeding Limits of Added Sugars, Saturated Fat, and Sodium

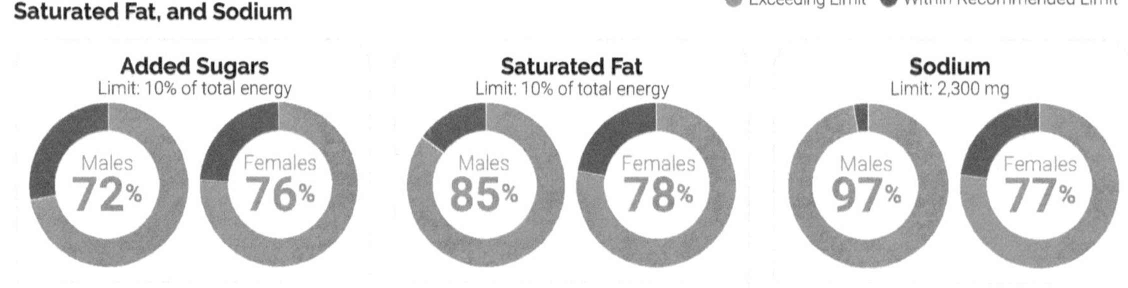

	Added Sugars	Saturated Fat	Sodium
Average Intakes – Males	347 kcal	276 kcal	3,888 mg
Average Intakes – Females	277 kcal	204 kcal	2,875 mg

Data Sources: *Average Intake and HEI-2015 Scores:* Analysis of What We Eat in America, NHANES 2015-2016, day 1 dietary intake data, weighted. *Recommended Intake Ranges:* Healthy U.S.-Style Dietary Patterns (see ***Appendix 3***). *Percent Exceeding Limits:* What We Eat in America, NHANES 2013-2016, 2 days dietary intake data, weighted.

AGES 2-18

Figure 3-9

Average Intakes of Subgroups Compared to Recommended Intake Ranges: Ages 14 Through 18

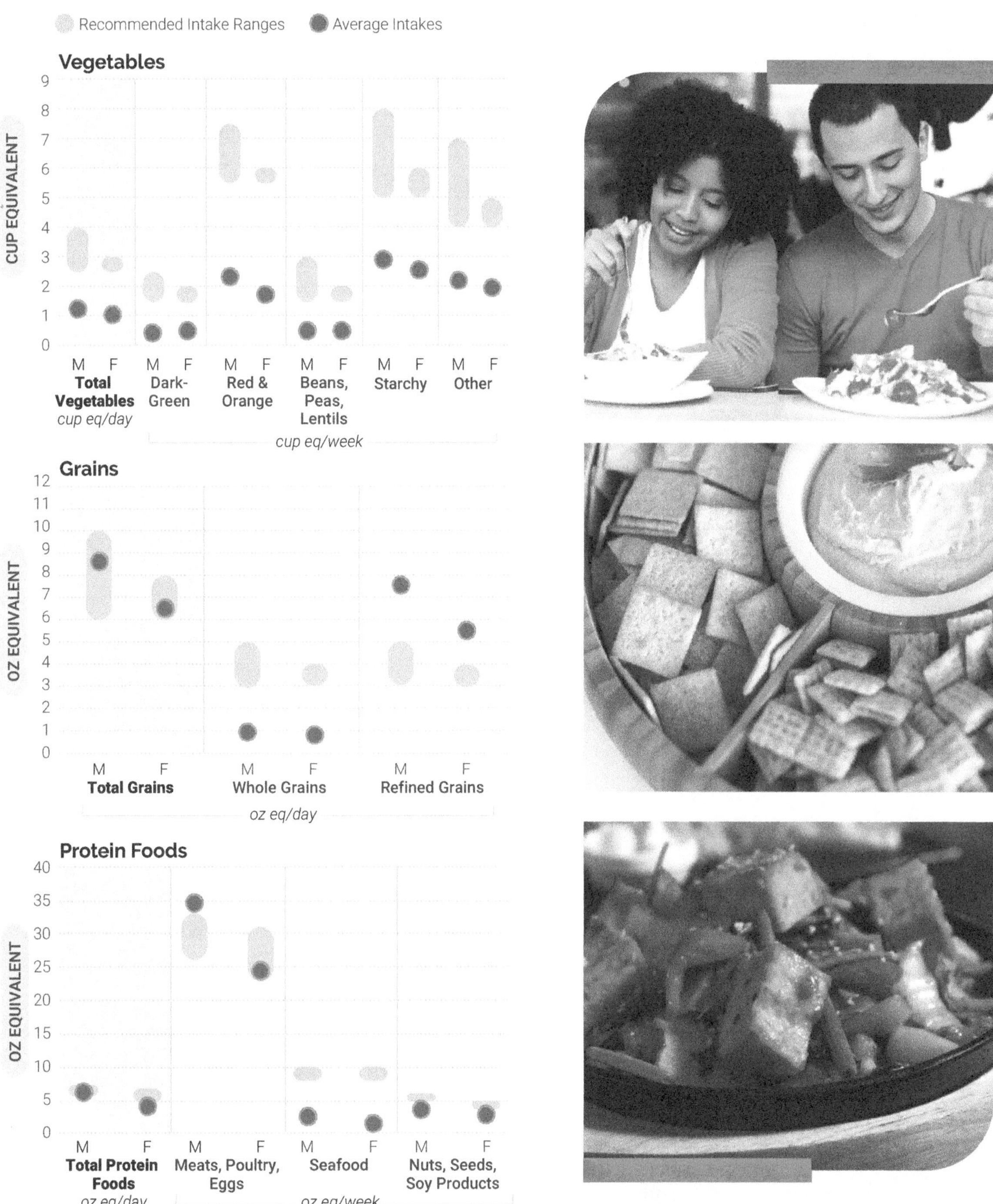

Data Sources: *Average Intakes:* Analysis of What We Eat in America, NHANES 2015-2016, day 1 dietary intake data, weighted. *Recommended Intake Ranges:* Healthy U.S.-Style Dietary Patterns (see ***Appendix 3***).

AGES 2-18

Special Considerations

The nutrition considerations for the general U.S. population described in ***Chapter 1*** apply to children and adolescents. For example, due to low intakes of food groups as described above, the nutrients of public health concern—calcium, vitamin D, potassium, and dietary fiber—apply to these life stages as well. Although the nutritional needs of youth are remarkably similar to their parents, guardians, and caregivers, these age groups do have some special nutrition considerations. Specifically, increasing intakes of sugar-sweetened beverages and decreasing intakes of dairy are dietary components with notable and concerning shifts in consumption throughout youth. Dietary intake patterns for adolescents, particularly females, also are an area of special consideration.

Accounting for the areas of dietary improvement that are important for all children and adolescents, as well as these special considerations, can improve diet quality during a time when food preferences and intake patterns are formed. When consistently followed, these healthy dietary patterns can provide the foundation for healthy dietary patterns in adulthood, promote health among youth, and help prevent the onset of chronic disease later in life.

Sugar-Sweetened Beverages

Sugar-sweetened beverages (e.g., soda, fruit drinks, sports and energy drinks) are not necessary in the child or adolescent diet nor are they a component of the USDA Dietary Patterns. Intake of added sugars increases throughout childhood and adolescence, and sugar-sweetened beverages are a top contributor. As a percent of total daily energy intake, average intake of added sugars is 11 percent among young children and peaks at 15 percent during adolescence. Coinciding with this increase is the contribution of sugar-sweetened beverages to total intake of added sugars. In childhood, sugar-sweetened beverages make up about 15 to 25 percent of total added sugars intake. By adolescence, their contribution is 32 percent and even higher when considering coffee and tea beverages with added sugars (an additional 7 percent). Most sugar-sweetened beverages (e.g., soda, sports drinks) do not contribute to meeting food group goals and often contain a high number of calories.

Decreasing consumption of sugar-sweetened beverages to reduce added sugars intake will help youth achieve a healthy dietary pattern. Beverages that contain no added sugars should be the primary choice for children and adolescents. These include water and unsweetened fat-free or low-fat milk—including low-lactose or lactose-free options or fortified soy beverage—and 100% juice within recommended amounts. Consuming beverages with no added sugars is particularly important for young children ages 2 through 8, when only a small number of calories remains for other uses after meeting food group and nutrient needs with nutrient-dense choices (**Table 3-1**). The number of calories available for other uses increases slightly as energy needs increase throughout adolescence to support growth and development (**Tables 3-2** and **3-3**). However, most adolescents do not consume foods and beverages in their nutrient-dense forms, meaning they have few or no calories remaining for added sugars.

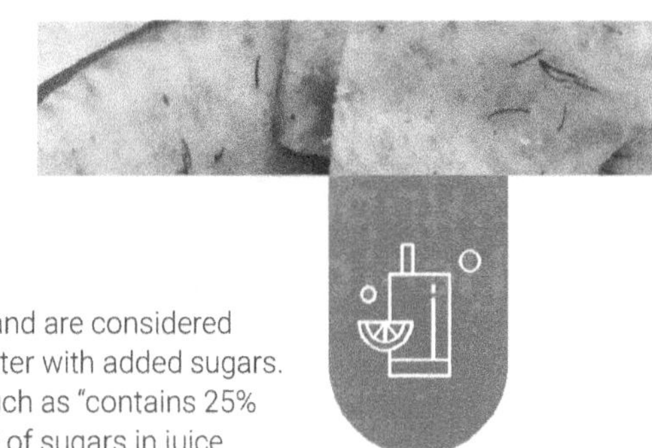

Juice

Many juice products, such as fruit drinks, contain minimal juice content and are considered sugar-sweetened beverages because they are primarily composed of water with added sugars. The percent of juice in a beverage may be found on the package label, such as "contains 25% juice" or "100% fruit juice." The Nutrition Facts label identifies the amount of sugars in juice products that are not naturally occurring (i.e., added sugars). Although 100% fruit juice without added sugars can be part of a healthy dietary pattern, it is lower in dietary fiber than whole fruit. Dietary fiber is a dietary component of public health concern. With the recognition that fruit should mostly be consumed in whole forms, the amount of fruit juice in the USDA Food Patterns ranges from 4 fluid ounces at the lower calorie levels and no more than 10 fluid ounces at the highest calorie levels.

Dairy and Fortified Soy Alternatives

Throughout childhood and adolescence, the types of dairy foods consumed and their contribution to a healthy dietary pattern change. Milk consumption, particularly milk as a beverage, is lower and cheese intake, typically as part of mixed dishes such as sandwiches, pizza, or pasta, is higher among adolescents when compared to younger children. These differences in consumption occur alongside the widening gap between current and recommended intakes of dairy foods that occurs throughout youth. Nutrient-dense options within the dairy group are unsweetened fat-free and low-fat (1%) milk, yogurt, cheese, fortified soy beverages and yogurt, and low-lactose and lactose-free dairy products. Dairy and fortified soy alternatives provide protein and a variety of nutrients that are underconsumed during these life stages. These include three nutrients of public health concern discussed in ***Chapter 1***: potassium, calcium, and vitamin D. The nutrient composition of dairy foods highlights the importance of adequate consumption. This is especially relevant for calcium and vitamin D, given that adolescents have an increased need for consumption to support the accrual of bone mass.

Adolescent Nutrition

The difference between recommended food group amounts and current intakes is greater for adolescents ages 14 through 18 than for any other age group across the lifespan. As a result, adolescents are at greater risk of dietary inadequacy than are other age groups. For adolescent males and females, low intakes of nutrient-dense foods and beverages within the grains, dairy and alternatives, fruits, and vegetables food groups lead to low intakes of phosphorus, magnesium, and choline. Adolescent females also consume less meat, poultry, and eggs than do adolescent males, and in combination with low consumption of seafood and other protein subgroups, including beans, peas, and lentils, this results in the underconsumption of total protein. In addition, adolescent females have low dietary intakes of iron, folate, vitamin B_6, and vitamin B_{12}. The potential for nutrient deficiencies existing alongside underconsumption of nutrients of public health concern for all Americans creates a concerning constellation of nutritional risks at a time of rapid growth and development along with the onset of puberty, menarche, and hormonal changes.

AGES 2-18

Supporting Healthy Eating

The physical, mental, and emotional changes that occur as children transition from pre-school to school-age and into adolescence come with diverse and changing opportunities to support a healthy dietary pattern. Support and active engagement from the various people and places involved in the lives of children and adolescents is necessary to help establish and maintain healthy dietary patterns that support healthy weight and the prevention of chronic disease.

In early childhood, parents, guardians, and caregivers have a primary role in supporting healthy eating because they control the foods and beverages purchased, prepared, and served. Exposing young children to a variety of nutrient-dense foods within each food group helps build a healthy dietary pattern at an age when taste preferences are acquired. Introducing children to a variety of nutrient-dense foods can be challenging. As children grow, their search for a sense of autonomy and desire for independence often manifest through selective or "picky" eating, food neophobia, or food "jags" (eating only one or a few foods for periods of time). Offering the same type of food to children multiple times, in a variety of forms, or prepared in different ways can increase acceptance and intake of healthy foods within food groups. For example, children may show a dislike for vegetables in the cooked form but accept the raw version. Or, children may only accept fruit when it is cut into small, bite-sized pieces. Even with these strategies, parents, guardians, and caregivers of young children should know it may take up to 8 to 10 exposures before a child will accept a new food.

Children's dietary patterns often resemble those of their household, highlighting the importance of their environment in the establishment of a healthy dietary pattern. Shared meals through shopping, cooking, and consumption provides parents, guardians, and caregivers with an opportunity to model healthy eating behaviors and dietary practices. By making nutrient-dense foods and beverages part of the normal household routine, children can observe and learn healthy behaviors that can extend throughout later life stages.

Ideally, children continue to be exposed to a healthy dietary pattern as they experience changes to their daily routines, such as spending time in child care or school settings. As at home, eating occasions in these settings can be used as opportunities to support a healthy dietary pattern. For example, snacks can be used as a way to promote intake of nutrient-dense fruits and vegetables, like carrot sticks and hummus or apple slices, instead of foods like chips or cookies. Using snacks as an opportunity to encourage nutrient-dense food group choices is especially relevant during early childhood when the total volume of food consumed at regular meals is lower and snacking is common.

When exposed to nutrient-dense foods and beverages at an early age and supported in making healthy choices across environments, a healthy dietary pattern can be established and maintained as children transition to the adolescence life stage. With this transition comes increasing autonomy, increased influence of peers, and decreased influence of parents, guardians, and caregivers on food choice. As a result, foods and beverages are more commonly consumed outside of the home, often with a preference for convenience foods that often are not nutrient-dense. Parents, guardians, and caregivers can continue to support healthy eating during this life stage by providing convenient access to nutrient-dense foods; involving children and adolescents in meal decisions, shopping, and cooking; and guiding adolescents' selection of food purchased and consumed outside the home. In schools and community settings, healthy eating can be encouraged by creating an environment that makes healthy choices the norm.

Accessing a Healthy Dietary Pattern

Many resources exist to support healthy growth and development during childhood and adolescence. The following Government programs play an essential role in providing access to healthy meals and educational resources to support healthy dietary patterns for all children and adolescents.

- The **Supplemental Nutrition Assistance Program (SNAP)** provides temporary benefits to families with qualifying incomes for the purchase of foods and beverages. About one-half of all SNAP participants are children.[1]

- Households with young children may be eligible for the **Special Supplemental Nutrition Program for Women, Infants, and Children (WIC)**. WIC can help families with limited resources meet their child's nutritional needs by providing nutritious foods to supplement diets. WIC serves children up to the age of 5 years who are at nutritional risk.

- In childcare and afterschool settings, the **Child and Adult Care Food Program (CACFP)** can support the development of healthy dietary patterns. CACFP is a nutrition program that provides reimbursements for meals and snacks that align with the *Dietary Guidelines* to eligible children enrolled at childcare centers, daycare homes, and in afterschool programs.

- School-age children can benefit from the **National School Lunch Program and School Breakfast Program**. The school meal programs can provide nearly two-thirds of daily calories, and therefore play an influential role in the development of a healthy dietary pattern.

- Outside of the school year, the **Summer Food Service Program (SFSP)** fills the gap by ensuring that children continue to receive nutritious meals when school is not in session. The SFSP operates at sites in a community where children can receive nutritious meals in a safe and supervised environment.

Professionals working with youth and their families can use these, and additional Government and non-Government resources that exist at the community, to support healthy eating during these life stages and to establish the foundation for a healthy dietary pattern that will promote health and support disease prevention in later years.

Looking Toward Chapter 4: Adults

This chapter focused on nutrition issues relevant to children and adolescents. These issues are particularly important because this life stage encompasses significant transitions, from young children who are still dependent on parents, guardians, and caregivers for all their food choices, to adolescents who are highly independent in their food choices. Diet quality tends to decrease as children mature into adolescence, with resulting concerns about underconsumption of nutrients of public health concern. Establishing and maintaining healthy food and beverages choices now can set a firm foundation for healthy dietary patterns that reduce the risk of diet-related chronic disease, an issue of increasing relevance to adults, who are considered in the next chapter.

[1]**Source:** Characteristics of Supplemental Nutrition Assistance Program Households: Fiscal Year 2018. Available at: **www.fns.usda.gov/snap/characteristics-supplemental-nutrition-assistance-program-households-fiscal-year-2018**.

ADULTS AGES 19-59

CHAPTER 4
Adults

ADULTS AGES 19-59

Introduction

The adult life stage (ages 19 through 59) is characterized by independence, opportunity, and increased responsibility—from starting or completing education and training, to managing work and/or family, to planning for the transition to older adulthood. Balancing work or school responsibilities with personal, family, or other commitments can create real or perceived barriers to healthy eating. Constraints on available time and financial resources may make it challenging for adults to adopt and maintain a healthy dietary pattern. Support for healthy food and beverage choices across the multiple places where adults live, work, play, and gather is needed to improve dietary patterns among adults.

Many individuals enter the adult life stage with an unhealthy dietary pattern already established from the childhood and adolescent years. A concerted effort to change this trajectory and support adults in adopting a healthy dietary pattern is needed for better health and to promote the well-being of family and friends across life stages. Learned food and beverage preferences, and norms and values placed on diet, physical activity, and health, can positively or negatively influence health because they can determine an individual's willingness to change and maintain behaviors. These norms and values, including preferences toward certain types of food, attitudes about healthy eating, and beliefs about the importance of physical activity, can extend beyond the individual to larger social networks, influencing the behaviors of friends and older or younger family members. Among adults caring for children, role modeling healthy dietary choices is important because the food components of public health concern observed in earlier life stages are similar for adults.

Following a healthy dietary pattern, engaging in regular physical activity, and managing body weight are critical during this life stage. More than one-half of adults are living with one or more chronic disease—diseases that are often related to poor-quality diets and physical inactivity. Improving dietary patterns in adulthood can play a beneficial role in promoting health and preventing the onset or rate of progression of chronic disease. For adults with overweight or obesity, making healthful changes to dietary patterns and increasing physical activity will improve health and prevent additional weight gain and/or promote weight loss (see "**The Importance of Physical Activity**" and "**Overweight and Obesity**").

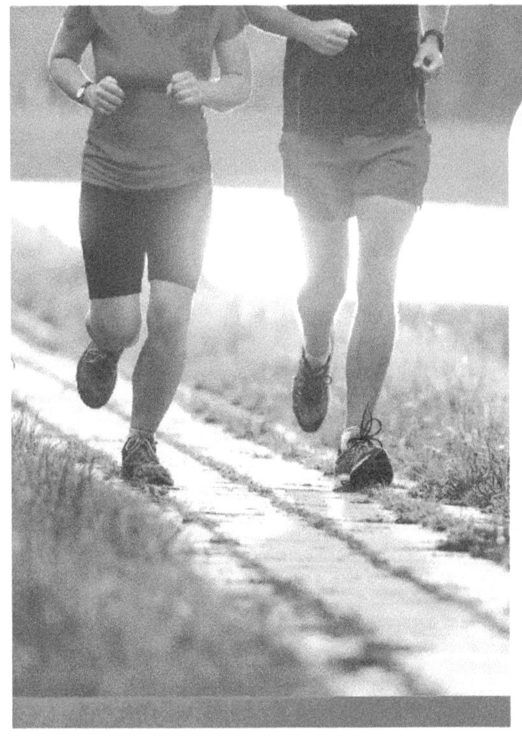

The Importance of Physical Activity

Adults who are physically active are healthier, feel better, and are less likely to develop many chronic diseases than are adults who are inactive. For adults, regular physical activity can provide both immediate benefits (e.g., boost mood, reduce stress, improve sleep) and long-term benefits (e.g., improved bone health and reduced risk of many diseases, such as cardiovascular disease, type 2 diabetes, depression, dementia, and many types of cancer).

Adults should move more and sit less throughout the day. Some physical activity is better than none. To attain the most health benefits from physical activity, adults need at least 150 to 300 minutes of moderate-intensity aerobic activity, like brisk walking or fast dancing, each week. Adults also need muscle-strengthening activity, like lifting weights or doing push-ups, at least 2 days each week.

The U.S. Department of Health and Human Service's *Physical Activity Guidelines for Americans* and related Move Your Way® resources have more information about the benefits of physical activity and tips on how to get started. Available at **health.gov/paguidelines**.

Overweight and Obesity

In the United States, 74 percent of adults have overweight or obesity, creating an increased risk for the development of other chronic health conditions, including cardiovascular disease, type 2 diabetes, and certain types of cancer.

Losing weight and maintaining weight loss is not a simple task. It requires adults to reduce the number of calories they get from foods and beverages and increase the amount expended through physical activity. Weight loss and maintenance are not likely achieved using short-term solutions. They require a commitment to long-term lifestyle change and often need support from healthcare providers, family members, and social networks. Intensive behavioral interventions that use one or more strategies—like group sessions and changes in both diet and physical activity—can be effective for individuals trying to lose a significant amount of weight. In addressing obesity, professionals should be mindful of health problems stemming from obesity-related stigma and discrimination.

The Centers for Disease Control and Prevention's website provides resources to support preventing weight gain (**cdc.gov/healthyweight/prevention/index.html**) and losing weight (**cdc.gov/healthyweight/losing_weight/index.html**).

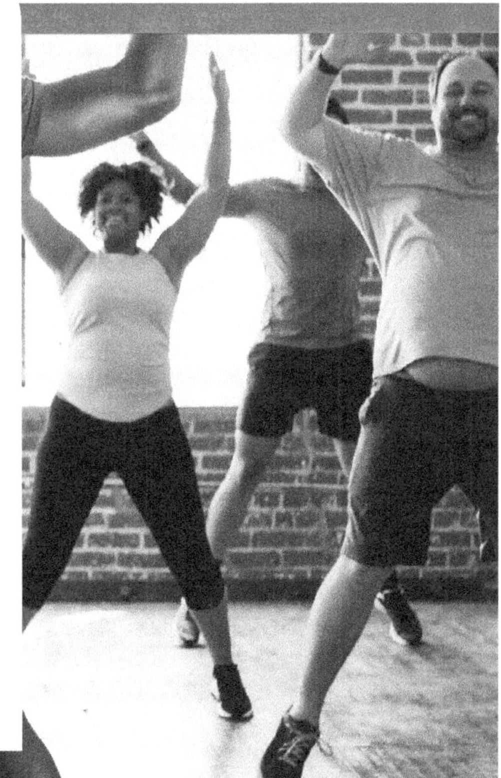

ADULTS AGES 19-59

Healthy Dietary Patterns

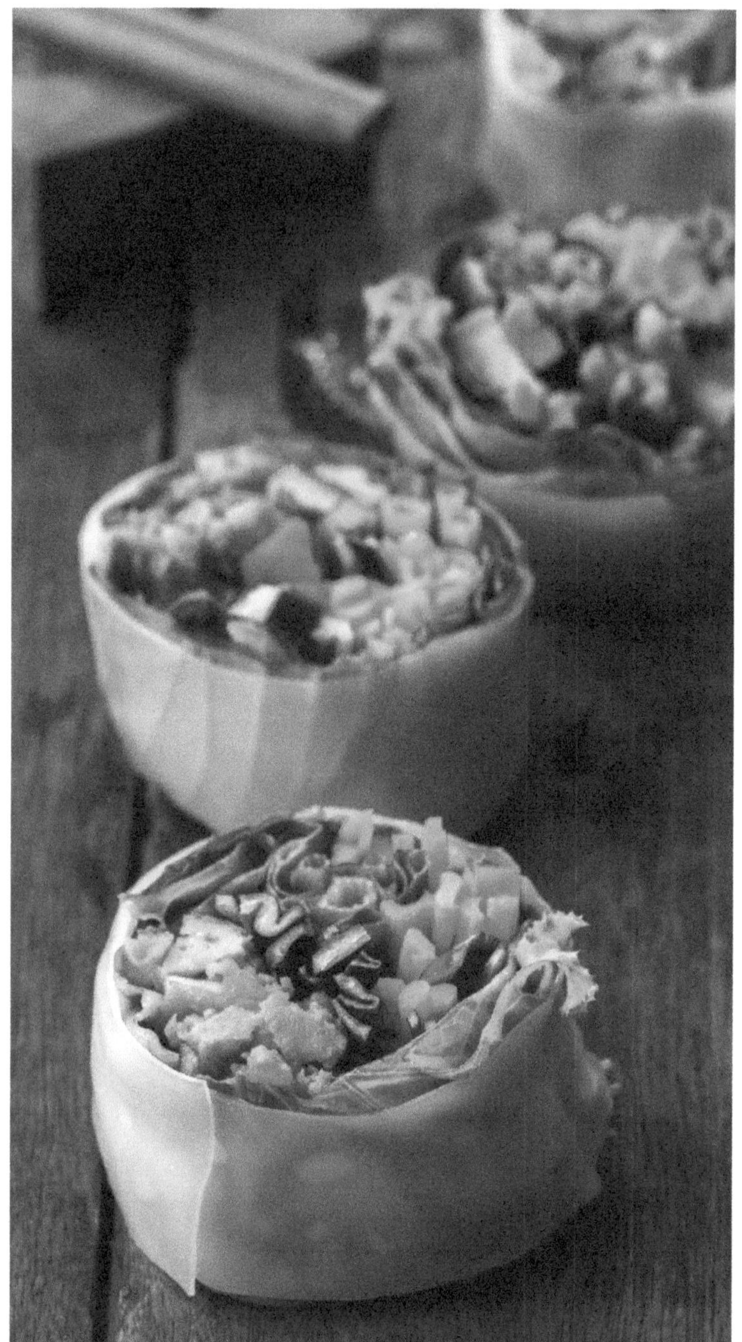

Adults are encouraged to follow the recommendations on the types of foods and beverages that make up a healthy dietary pattern described in ***Chapter 1. Nutrition and Health Across the Lifespan: The Guidelines and Key Recommendations***. The USDA Dietary Patterns provide a framework of nutrient-dense foods and beverages that can be adapted to accommodate budget, culture, and personal preferences to help adults follow a healthy dietary pattern and meet the Guidelines and their Key Recommendations.

Table 4-1 displays the Healthy U.S.-Style Dietary Pattern at eight calorie levels that are appropriate for most adults ages 19 through 59 years to illustrate the specific amounts and limits for food groups and other dietary components that make up healthy dietary patterns. In general, calorie needs are lower for females compared to males. Calorie needs decline throughout adulthood due to changes in metabolism that accompany aging. Level of physical activity, body composition, and the presence of chronic disease are additional factors that affect calorie needs.

Females ages 19 through 30 require about 1,800 to 2,400 calories a day. Males in this age group have higher calorie needs of about 2,400 to 3,000 a day. Calorie needs for adults ages 31 through 59 are generally lower; most females require about 1,600 to 2,200 calories a day and males require about 2,200 to 3,000 calories a day. Additional information on these estimates is provided in **Table 4-1 (footnote a)** and in ***Appendix 2. Estimated Calorie Needs***. The USDA Dietary Patterns are discussed in greater detail in ***Chapter 1*** and ***Appendix 3. USDA Dietary Patterns***.

Nutrient-Dense Foods and Beverages

Nutrient-dense foods and beverages provide vitamins, minerals, and other health-promoting components and have little added sugars, saturated fat, and sodium. Vegetables, fruits, whole grains, seafood, eggs, beans, peas, and lentils, unsalted nuts and seeds, fat-free and low-fat dairy products, and lean meats and poultry—when prepared with no or little added sugars, saturated fat, and sodium—are nutrient-dense foods.

ADULTS AGES 19-59

Table 4-1

Healthy U.S.-Style Dietary Pattern for Adults Ages 19 Through 59, With Daily or Weekly Amounts From Food Groups, Subgroups, and Components

CALORIE LEVEL OF PATTERN[a]	1,600	1,800	2,000	2,200	2,400	2,600	2,800	3,000
FOOD GROUP OR SUBGROUP[b]	Daily Amount of Food From Each Group (Vegetable and protein foods subgroup amounts are per week.)							
Vegetables (cup eq/day)	**2**	**2 ½**	**2 ½**	**3**	**3**	**3 ½**	**3 ½**	**4**
	Vegetable Subgroups in Weekly Amounts							
Dark-Green Vegetables (cup eq/wk)	1 ½	1 ½	1 ½	2	2	2 ½	2 ½	2 ½
Red & Orange Vegetables (cup eq/wk)	4	5 ½	5 ½	6	6	7	7	7 ½
Beans, Peas, Lentils (cup eq/wk)	1	1 ½	1 ½	2	2	2 ½	2 ½	3
Starchy Vegetables (cup eq/wk)	4	5	5	6	6	7	7	8
Other Vegetables (cup eq/wk)	3 ½	4	4	5	5	5 ½	5 ½	7
Fruits (cup eq/day)	**1 ½**	**1 ½**	**2**	**2**	**2**	**2**	**2 ½**	**2 ½**
Grains (ounce eq/day)	**5**	**6**	**6**	**7**	**8**	**9**	**10**	**10**
Whole Grains (ounce eq/day)	3	3	3	3 ½	4	4 ½	5	5
Refined Grains (ounce eq/day)	2	3	3	3 ½	4	4 ½	5	5
Dairy (cup eq/day)	**3**	**3**	**3**	**3**	**3**	**3**	**3**	**3**
Protein Foods (ounce eq/day)	**5**	**5**	**5 ½**	**6**	**6 ½**	**6 ½**	**7**	**7**
	Protein Foods Subgroups in Weekly Amounts							
Meats, Poultry, Eggs (ounce eq/wk)	23	23	26	28	31	31	33	33
Seafood (ounce eq/wk)	8	8	8	9	10	10	10	10
Nuts, Seeds, Soy Products (ounce eq/wk)	4	4	5	5	5	5	6	6
Oils (grams/day)	**22**	**24**	**27**	**29**	**31**	**34**	**36**	**44**
Limit on Calories for Other Uses (kcal/day)[c]	**100**	**140**	**240**	**250**	**320**	**350**	**370**	**440**
Limit on Calories for Other Uses (%/day)	6%	8%	12%	11%	13%	13%	13%	15%

[a] Calorie level ranges: Ages 19 through 30, Females: 1,800-2,400 calories; Males: 2,400-3,000 calories. Ages 31 through 59, Females: 1,600-2,200 calories; Males 2,200-3,000 calories. Energy levels are calculated based on median height and body weight for healthy body mass index (BMI) reference individuals. For adults, the reference man is 5 feet 10 inches tall and weighs 154 pounds. The reference woman is 5 feet 4 inches tall and weighs 126 pounds. Calorie needs vary based on many factors. The DRI Calculator for Healthcare Professionals, available at **nal.usda.gov/fnic/dri-calculator**, can be used to estimate calorie needs based on age, sex, height, weight, and activity level.

[b] Definitions for each food group and subgroup and quantity (i.e., cup or ounce equivalents) are provided in ***Chapter 1*** and are compiled in ***Appendix 3***.

[c] All foods are assumed to be in nutrient-dense forms; lean or low-fat; and prepared with minimal added sugars, refined starches, saturated fat, or sodium. If all food choices to meet food group recommendations are in nutrient-dense forms, a small number of calories remain within the overall limit of the pattern (i.e., limit on calories for other uses). The number of calories depends on the total calorie level of the pattern and the amounts of food from each food group required to meet nutritional goals. Calories up to the specified limit can be used for added sugars, saturated fat, or alcohol, or to eat more than the recommended amount of food in a food group.

NOTE: The total dietary pattern should not exceed *Dietary Guidelines* limits for added sugars, saturated fat, and alcohol; be within the Acceptable Macronutrient Distribution Ranges for protein, carbohydrate, and total fats; and stay within calorie limits. Values are rounded. See ***Appendix 3*** for all calorie levels of the pattern.

ADULTS AGES 19-59

Current Intakes

Figure 4-1

Current Intakes: Ages 19 Through 30

Average Daily Food Group Intakes Compared to Recommended Intake Ranges

Recommended Intake Ranges · Average Intakes

CUP or OZ EQUIVALENT (0–12)

M F Total Vegetables *cup eq/day*
M F Total Fruits *cup eq/day*
M F Total Grains *oz eq/day*
M F Total Dairy *cup eq/day*
M F Total Protein Foods *oz eq/day*

FOOD GROUPS

Healthy Eating Index Score (on a scale of 0-100)

56

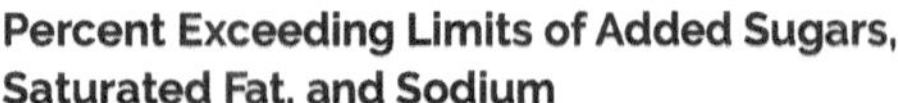

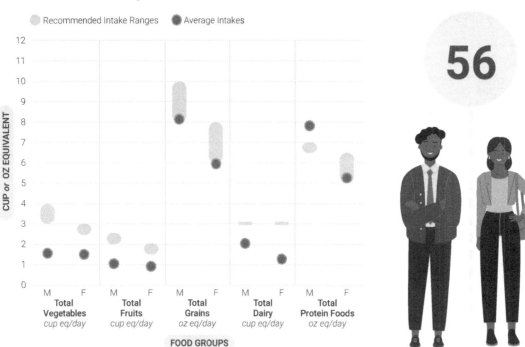

Percent Exceeding Limits of Added Sugars, Saturated Fat, and Sodium

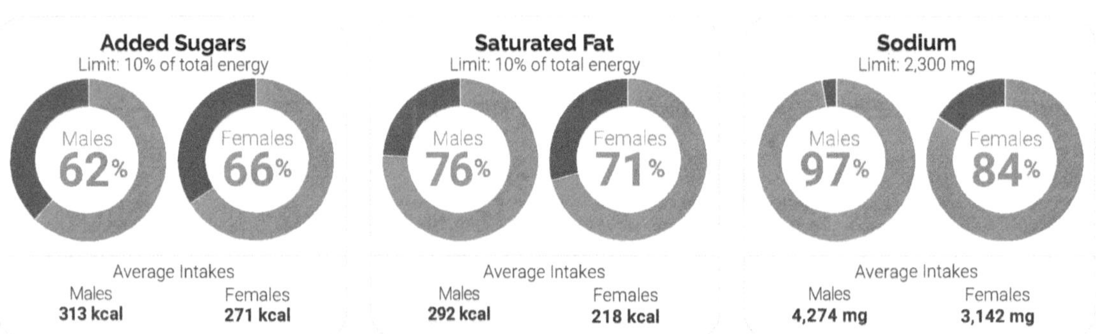

Data Sources: *Average Intakes and HEI-2015 Scores*: Analysis of What We Eat in America, NHANES 2015-2016, day 1 dietary intake data, weighted. *Recommended Intake Ranges*: Healthy U.S.-Style Dietary Patterns (see ***Appendix 3***). *Percent Exceeding Limits*: What We Eat in America, NHANES 2013-2016, 2 days dietary intake data, weighted.

Figure 4-2
Average Intakes of Subgroups Compared to Recommended Intake Ranges: Ages 19 Through 30

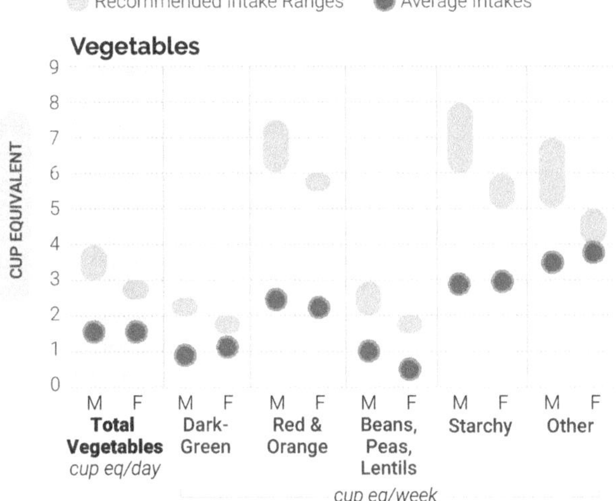

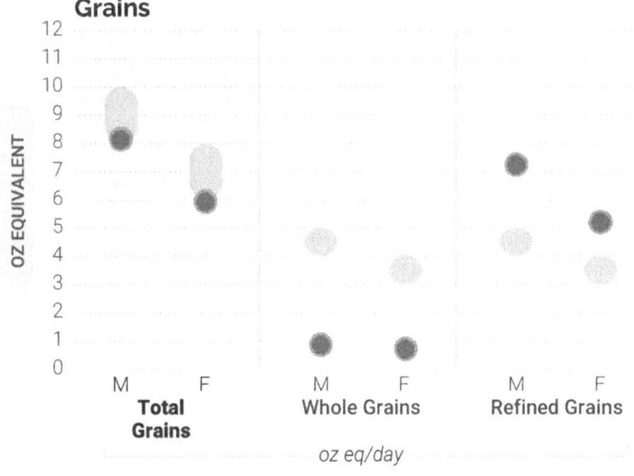

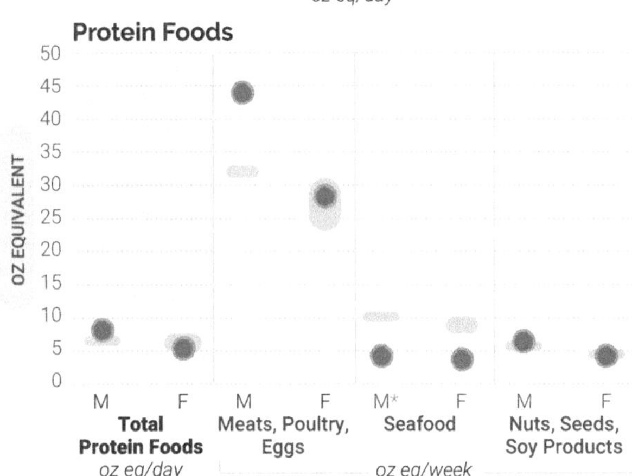

Figures 4-1 to **4-4** highlight the dietary intake of adults, including the Healthy Eating Index-2015 (HEI) score, which is an overall measure of how intakes align with the *Dietary Guidelines*, as well as information on the components of a healthy diet—specifically, the food groups. **Figures 4-1** and **4-3** display the average intakes of the food groups compared to the range of recommended intakes at the calorie levels most relevant to males and females in both adult age groups. Additionally, the percent of adults exceeding the limits for added sugars, saturated fat, and sodium is shown, along with average intakes of these components. Average intakes compared to recommended intake ranges of the subgroups for grains are represented in daily amounts; subgroups for vegetables and protein foods are represented in weekly amounts (see **Figures 4-2** and **4-4**).

The HEI scores in **Figures 4-1** and **4-3** show that adults across this life stage have diets that do not align with the recommendations for food group and nutrient intake as described in ***Chapter 1***. Although intake patterns are generally not consistent with the *Dietary Guidelines*, adults ages 31 through 59 have a slightly higher HEI score (59 out of 100) compared to adults ages 19 through 30 (56 out of 100).

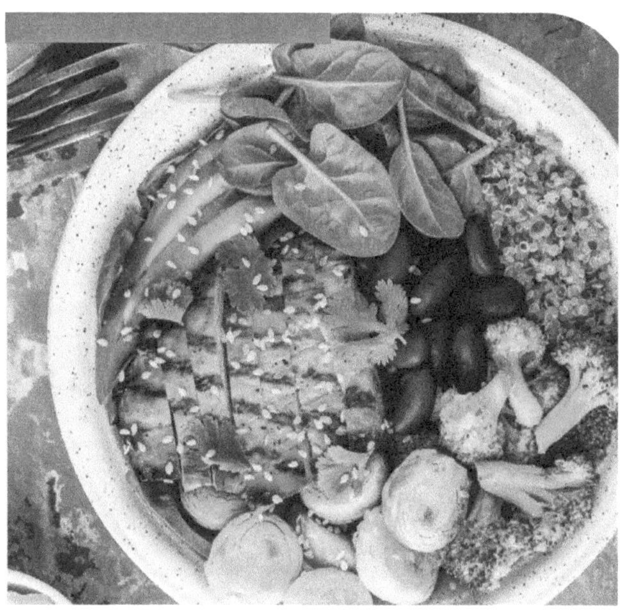

***NOTE:** Estimates may be less precise than others due to small sample size and/or large relative standard error.

Data Sources: *Average Intakes*: Analysis of What We Eat in America, NHANES 2015-2016, day 1 dietary intake data, weighted. *Recommended Intake Ranges*: Healthy U.S.-Style Dietary Patterns (see ***Appendix 3***).

ADULTS AGES 19-59

Figure 4-3

Current Intakes: Ages 31 Through 59

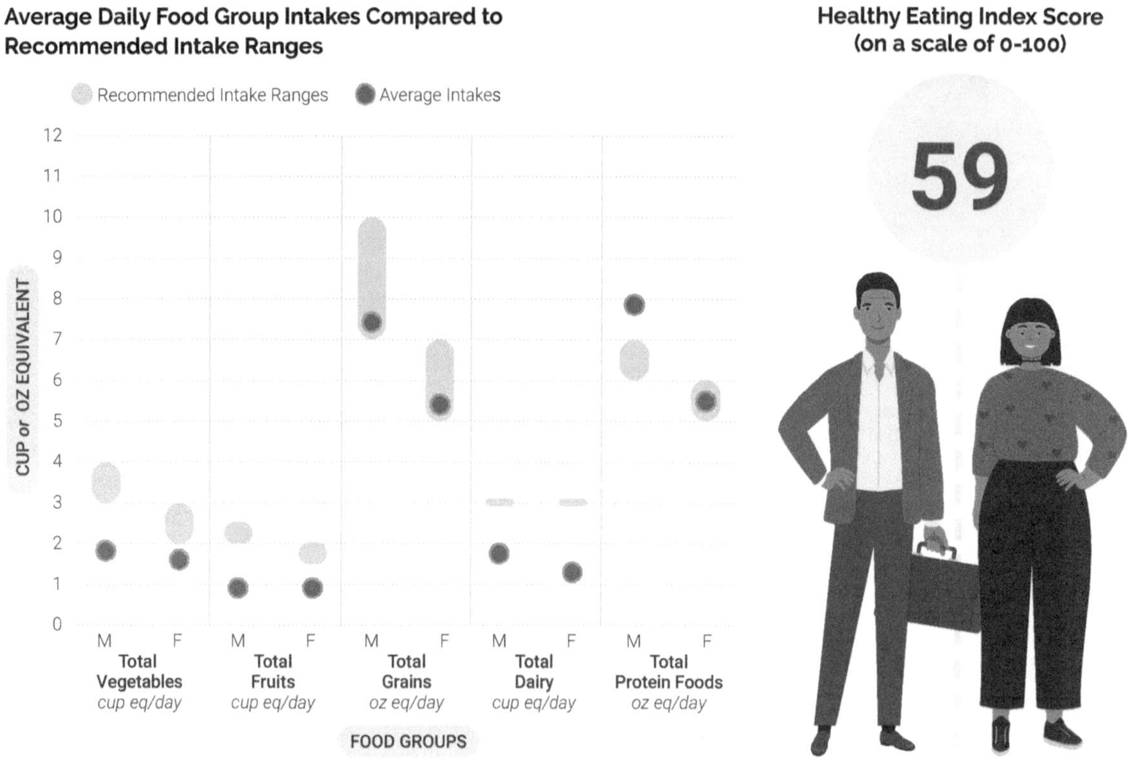

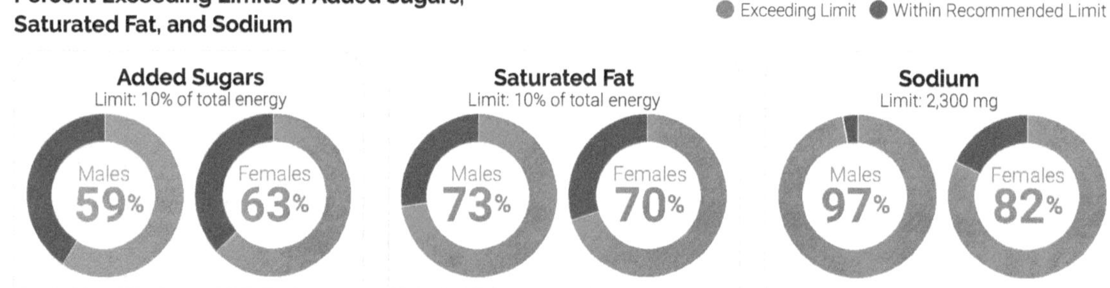

Data Sources: *Average Intakes and HEI-2015 Scores*: Analysis of What We Eat in America, NHANES 2015-2016, day 1 dietary intake data, weighted. *Recommended Intake Ranges*: Healthy U.S.-Style Dietary Patterns (see ***Appendix 3***). *Percent Exceeding Limits*: What We Eat in America, NHANES 2013-2016, 2 days dietary intake data, weighted.

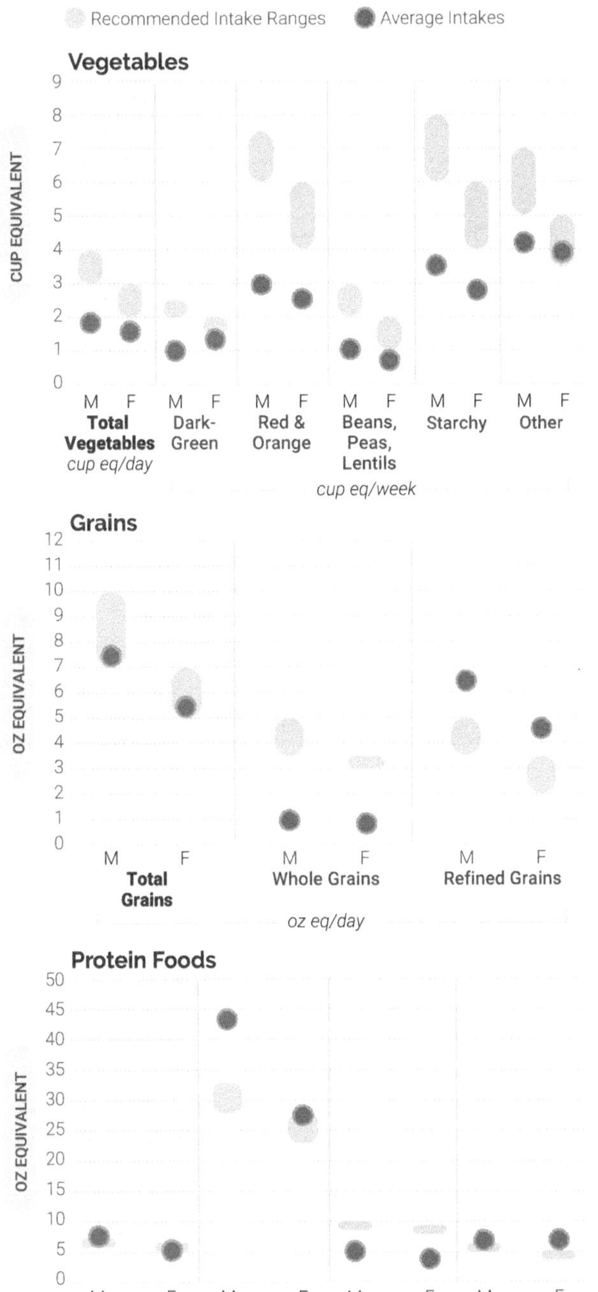

Figure 4-4
Average Intakes of Subgroups Compared to Recommended Intake Ranges: Ages 31 Through 59

Data Sources: *Average Intakes*: Analysis of What We Eat in America, NHANES 2015-2016, day 1 dietary intake data, weighted. *Recommended Intake Ranges*: Healthy U.S.-Style Dietary Patterns (see ***Appendix 3***).

Average intakes of fruits, vegetables, and dairy fall below the range of recommended intakes for all adults. Although average total grains intakes meets recommendations, **Figures 4-2** and **4-4** show that intake of whole grains is well below recommendations, and intakes of refined grains exceeds the upper end of the recommended intake range for adults in both age groups. Intakes of protein foods generally meets or exceeds recommended intake levels. Current patterns generally include meats, poultry, eggs, and nuts, seeds, and soy, while average intake of seafood falls well below recommendations. Beans, peas, and lentils—a subgroup of both the vegetable and protein foods groups—also are underconsumed by most adults.

Figures 4-1 and **4-3** show that adults are exceeding recommendations for added sugars, saturated fat, and sodium. About 60 percent of men and 65 percent of women exceed the limit for intakes of added sugars. This is an average daily intake of about 330 calories from added sugars for men and around 250 calories for women. More than 70 percent of adults are exceeding the recommendations for saturated fat. The average daily intakes of saturated fat is about 290 calories for men and 210 calories for women. The calorie levels relevant to most adults (1,600-3,000 calories) have about 100 to 400 calories remaining after food group recommendations are met through nutrient-dense choices. Combined, these average amounts of calories from added sugars and saturated fat exceed the amount most adults have available—and do not account for calories from alcoholic beverages. For sodium, nearly all men and about 80 percent of women consume too much on a given day. Men generally consume more than 4,000 mg of sodium per day and women more than 3,000 mg.

ADULTS AGES 19-59

Special Considerations

The dietary considerations for the general U.S. population, including adults, are described in ***Chapter 1***. The following sections of this chapter focus on several special considerations to support a healthy dietary pattern for adults that reflect adults' current intake patterns and the prevalence of overweight and obesity and diet-related chronic disease that become more apparent in this life stage. These considerations include a focus on dietary changes to increase intakes of dietary fiber, calcium, and vitamin D and to decrease intakes of added sugars, saturated fat, and sodium. Special considerations related to alcoholic beverages also are discussed.

Dietary Fiber

Dietary patterns that do not meet recommended intakes of fruits, vegetables, and whole grains contribute to low intakes of dietary fiber. More than 90 percent of women and 97 percent of men do not meet recommended intakes for dietary fiber. This aligns with intake patterns where fruits, vegetables, and whole grains are underconsumed by more than 85 percent of adults. ***Appendix 1. Nutritional Goals for Age-Sex Groups*** provides dietary fiber goals for men and women based on the Dietary Reference Intakes. These recommendations are based on levels observed to reduce risk of coronary heart disease. Increasing intakes of fruits, vegetables, and replacing refined grains with whole grains to improve dietary fiber intakes is especially important during this life stage, as the impact of poor diet quality becomes apparent with the onset and/or progression of diet-related chronic diseases. ***Chapter 1*** provides strategies on how to increase intakes of these important food groups. A list of common food sources of dietary fiber is available at **DietaryGuidelines.gov.**

Calcium and Vitamin D

Calcium and vitamin D are important at any age, and most adults do not consume adequate amounts. Close to 30 percent of men and 60 percent of women older than age 19 years do not consume enough calcium, and more than 90 percent do not consume enough vitamin D. Dietary patterns that do not meet recommended intake amounts for food groups and subgroups, which include sources of calcium and vitamin D—such as dairy foods and fortified soy alternatives and seafood—contribute to low intake of these nutrients. Particular attention should be given to consuming adequate amounts of foods with these nutrients during adult years to promote optimal bone health and prevent the onset of osteoporosis. Adequate intake of calcium and vitamin D is particularly important for adults during the time period when peak bone mass is still actively accruing (ages 19 through about 30) and, for women, in the post-menopausal period when rapid bone remodeling occurs.

A healthy dietary pattern with nutrient-dense, calcium-rich foods, such as low-fat milk and yogurt and fortified soy alternatives and canned sardines and salmon, can help adults better meet intake recommendations. Vitamin D aids in the absorption of calcium. Consuming the recommended amount of seafood and choosing foods that are fortified with vitamin D, including milk, fortified soy beverages, and fortified soy yogurt, and some whole-grain cereals, can help adults meet their needs. In addition to dietary sources, the body can make vitamin D from the

sun. However, some individuals may have difficulty producing sufficient vitamin D from sunlight exposure or consuming enough vitamin D from foods and beverages, so a supplement may be recommended by a health professional. ***Appendix 1*** provides calcium and vitamin D goals for men and women based on the Dietary Reference Intakes. A list of common food sources of calcium and vitamin D is available at **DietaryGuidelines.gov**.

Saturated Fat

Chapter 1 explains the importance of limiting intakes of saturated fat to support healthy dietary patterns. Staying within saturated fat limits and replacing saturated fat with unsaturated fat is of particular importance during the adult life stage. The prevalence of coronary heart disease increases with age, and high LDL cholesterol peaks between the ages of 50 to 59 in men and 60 to 69 in women.

About 70 to 75 percent of adults exceed the 10-percent limit on saturated fat as a result of selecting foods and beverages across food groups that are not in nutrient-dense forms. The top sources of saturated fat for adults are sandwiches (e.g., deli sandwiches, burgers, tacos, burritos, grilled cheese, hot dogs) and other grain-based mixed dishes (e.g. spaghetti and meatballs, casseroles, quesadillas) that typically contain ingredients from several food groups that are not in nutrient-dense forms, including grains, protein foods, and dairy. Making changes to the type of ingredients as well as amount and/or frequency of their consumption will help adults lower saturated fat intake without a need to eliminate these foods from the household diet. Strategies include using lean meats and low-fat cheese to prepare these foods or substituting beans in place of meats as the protein source. Saturated fat also can be reduced by substituting certain ingredients with sources of unsaturated fat (e.g., using avocado, nuts, or seeds in a dish instead of cheese). Cooking with oils higher in polyunsaturated and monounsaturated fat (e.g., canola, corn, olive, peanut, safflower, soybean, and sunflower) instead of butter also can reduce intakes of saturated fat.

Sodium

The number of adults exceeding the Chronic Disease Risk Reduction level for sodium (see ***Chapter 1*** or ***Appendix 1***) during this life stage is concerning given that 45 percent of adults ages 18 and older are living with hypertension. During adulthood, prevalence of hypertension increases from about 22 percent of adults ages 18 through 39 to about 55 percent of adults ages 40 through 59.[1] Changing this trend is important because hypertension is a preventable risk factor for cardiovascular disease and stroke. Unlike other factors that cannot be changed, such as genetics and family history, reduced dietary intake of sodium is a modifiable risk factor that can help improve blood pressure control and reduce risk of hypertension.

Overconsumption of sodium occurs for several reasons, as discussed in ***Chapter 1***. Because sodium is found in foods and beverages across all food groups, with most coming from foods that have salt added during commercial processing rather than salt added to foods during or after preparation, reducing sodium consumption will require a joint effort by individuals, the food and beverage industry, and food service and retail establishments.

[1] Ostchega Y, Fryar CD, Nwankwo T, Nguyen DT. Hypertension prevalence among adults aged 18 and over: United States, 2017–2018. NCHS Data Brief, no 364. Hyattsville, MD: National Center for Health Statistics. 2020

ADULTS AGES 19-59

Added Sugars

Most adults exceed recommended limits for added sugars as a result of eating foods and drinking beverages higher in added sugars and selecting foods and beverages across food groups that are not in nutrient-dense forms. Added sugars are of particular concern for adults because exceeding limits contributes to excess calorie intake.

BEVERAGES AS A SOURCE OF ADDED SUGARS

Sugar-sweetened beverages (e.g., soda, sports drinks, energy drinks, fruit drinks) and sweetened coffees and teas (including ready-to-drink varieties) contribute over 40 percent of daily intake of added sugars. More than in earlier life stages, adults consume coffees and teas with additions, such as sugar and flavored syrup. Frequent consumption of these and other beverages containing added sugars can contribute to excess calorie intake. Some sugar-sweetened beverages, such as coffee and tea with milk, contribute to food group intake (e.g., dairy) and can be made without added sugars. Others, such as fruit drinks, can be replaced with nutrient-dense options such as 100% juice to help meet fruit group recommendations.

Most adults' diets include choices across multiple food groups that are not in nutrient-dense forms and therefore cannot accommodate excess calories from sweetened beverages. Intake of sugar-sweetened beverages should be limited to small amounts and most often replaced with beverage options that contain no added sugars, such as water.

OTHER SOURCES OF ADDED SUGARS

A variety of foods and beverages contribute to the remaining added sugars consumed by adults. In addition to the contribution of sugar-sweetened beverages and sweetened coffees and teas, about 30 percent come from desserts and sweet snacks, candies, and sweetened breakfast cereals. The remaining 30 percent of added sugars is consumed in relatively small amounts across many food categories, as discussed in ***Chapter 1***. Many of these food categories have seen market expansion in recent years. For example, over the past decade, beverages, snacks, and bakery foods have continuously topped the list for the most new product introductions.[2] As these and other food categories continue to change and expand, it is vital for individuals to learn how to identify the amount of added sugars in a beverage or food product by reading the Nutrition Facts label (see ***Chapter 1***). Understanding which food choices contribute to intakes of added sugars without contributing to nutrient needs can help individuals remove or replace these foods with better choices that meet food group and nutrient recommendations within calorie needs.

[2] Additional information is available at **ers.usda.gov/topics/food-markets-prices/processing-marketing/new-products.aspx**.

Alcoholic Beverages

Alcoholic beverages are not a component of the USDA Dietary Patterns and their calories are considered discretionary. Regular consumption of alcoholic beverages can make it challenging for adults to meet food group and nutrient needs while not consuming excess calories. The ingredients in certain mixed drinks, including soda, mixers, and heavy cream, also can contribute to intake of added sugars and saturated fat.

The majority of U.S. adults consume alcoholic beverages. About 66 percent of adults ages 21 through 59 report alcoholic beverage consumption in the past month, and of those, approximately half report binge drinking, sometimes multiple times per month. Among adults who choose to drink, average intakes of calories from alcoholic beverages exceed the remaining calorie limit that is available after food group recommendations are met.

There are some adults who should not drink alcoholic beverages at all, such as if they are pregnant or might be pregnant; younger than age 21; or recovering from an alcohol use disorder or if they are unable to control the amount they drink. For those who choose to drink, intakes should be limited to 1 drink or less in a day for women and 2 drinks or less in a day for men, on days when alcohol is consumed. More information in available in ***Chapter 1*** under Alcoholic Beverages.

Supporting Healthy Eating

Individuals need support in making healthy choices at home, work, and in the community to build healthy dietary patterns.

Food retail outlets (e.g., grocery stores, convenience stores, restaurants) provide adults with the option to purchase ingredients to prepare foods themselves or to purchase foods prepared by others. National food expenditures suggest the purchase of prepared foods is a regular habit for most adults, with expenditures outpacing those of foods purchased for household meal preparation.[3] Estimates also suggest that the younger generation of American adults are spending an even larger proportion of their total food dollars on prepared foods than are older generations.[4]

When adults prepare meals themselves, they have more control over the types of food ingredients selected and can focus on choosing nutrient-dense options that contribute to food group goals with little or no added sugars and saturated fat and less sodium. The same is not always true when purchasing prepared foods, despite changes and innovation in the marketplace, such as menu and product labeling or reformulation.

For some adults, preparing and consuming healthy meals at home will mean adopting a new habit and/or learning new skills, such as meal planning. For others, it may entail small changes to current routines. Planning meals and snacks in advance with food groups and nutrient-dense foods and beverages in mind can support healthy eating at home and improve dietary patterns of individuals and families. Preparing meals with family and friends also presents an opportunity for greater connection and enjoyment around food. For adults who are parents, guardians, or caregivers of children or adolescents, preparing meals also provides an opportunity to teach valuable cooking skills and model behaviors that support the adoption of healthy dietary patterns across younger life stages.

[3] Details are available at **ers.usda.gov/webdocs/publications/96957/ap-083.pdf?v=5848.3**.

[4] Details are available at **ers.usda.gov/amber-waves/2017/december/millennials-devote-larger-shares-of-their-grocery-spending-to-prepared-foods-pasta-and-sugar-and-sweets-than-other-generations**.

It is not realistic or desirable to avoid the purchase and consumption of foods prepared by others. Limits on available time and the desire for convenience make restaurant and ready-to-eat meals a part of many household routines. Many of these settings also provide for social enjoyment of food with friends and family. However, foods prepared outside of the home can contribute to the overconsumption of calories as a result of large portion sizes and methods of preparation. Being mindful of the portion sizes and ingredients of prepared foods can help adults achieve a healthy dietary pattern while still enjoying foods prepared by others. Health promotion activities that center on increasing consumer knowledge and access to healthy options in the places where Americans purchase prepared foods are needed to provide support for adults in these efforts.

Health professionals play an important role in supporting adults' healthy eating behaviors. Helping adults become more aware of the foods and beverages that make up their typical dietary patterns and identifying areas for improvement can empower individuals to make changes to the types of foods they purchase or prepare. Teaching skills like cooking and meal planning and helping adults understand how to read labels or make healthy menu substitutions also will support the adoption of a healthy dietary pattern during this life stage.

In settings where adults spend their time, changing organizational practices, approaches, and/or policies to support improved dietary patterns also is needed. Strategies include offering healthy meals and snacks in workplace cafeterias and vending machines, or implementing educational programs tailored to working adults. Or, communities can support farmers markets, community gardens, and related educational programming efforts.

Learn More

The *Federal Foodservice Guidelines* is a resource that food service providers can use to help make healthy choices more available in food service establishments. The Guidelines are available at **cdc.gov/nutrition/healthy-food-environments/food-serv-guide.html**.

Accessing a Healthy Dietary Pattern

A healthy dietary pattern can only be achieved when adequate resources and supports exist in the places where adults live, work, and gather. Food access is crucial for adults to achieve a healthy dietary pattern and is influenced by diverse factors, as discussed in ***Chapter 1***. Food insecurity, which occurs when access to nutritionally adequate and safe food is limited or uncertain, is most prevalent in households with children and in single-parent households. Income is one of the primary characteristics associated with food insecurity. Government programs, such as the **Supplemental Nutrition Assistance Program (SNAP)** or the **Food Distribution Program on Indian Reservations (FDPIR)**, serve as a resource for low-income adults by supplementing food budgets to support healthy lifestyles. Adults with children or those caring for older family members also may benefit from resources discussed in ***Chapters 2***, ***3***, and ***6***.

Additional Government and non-Government resources, such as food banks or community meal sites and programming offered through **SNAP Education (SNAP-Ed)** and the **Expanded Food and Nutrition Education Program (EFNEP)**, play a role in providing food and educational resources to support adults in making healthy food choices within a limited budget. Innovative approaches to support health, such as incentive programs at farmers markets or healthy corner-store initiatives, continue to expand. Continued attention and creativity in approaches to expand food access are needed to support a healthy dietary pattern for adults and the larger social networks that they influence.

Looking Toward Chapter 5: Women Who Are Pregnant or Lactating and Chapter 6: Older Adults

This chapter has discussed the importance of a healthy dietary pattern and related special considerations during the adult life stage. The chapter recognizes that dietary patterns are generally well established by the time individuals reach adulthood and encourages adults to take advantage of the many opportunities available to make changes that support a healthy dietary pattern. Making these changes can have important benefits for achieving a healthy weight status, reducing chronic disease risk, and promoting overall health. These considerations are especially important for the life stages discussed in the next two chapters. ***Chapter 5*** takes a closer look at a special time in the life of many adults—pregnancy and lactation. This chapter echoes the same guidance for adults on following a healthy dietary pattern and discusses several special considerations that arise during this life stage. ***Chapter 6*** then makes the transition from the Adults chapter to a focused look at healthy eating for older adults.

WOMEN WHO ARE PREGNANT OR LACTATING

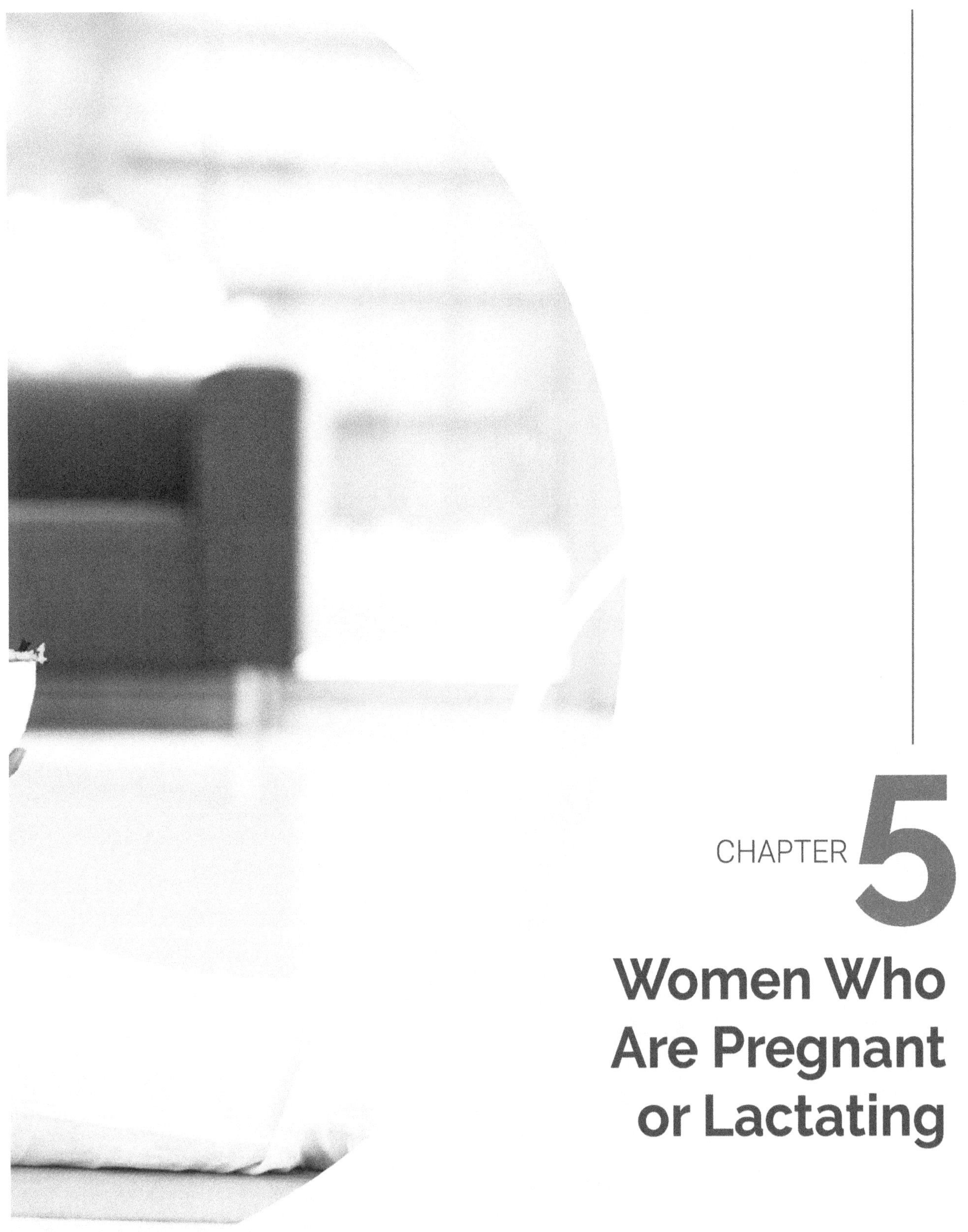

CHAPTER 5

Women Who Are Pregnant or Lactating

WOMEN WHO ARE PREGNANT OR LACTATING

Introduction

Pregnancy and lactation are special stages of life for women, and nutrition plays a vital role before, during, and after these life stages to support the health of the mother and her child. Following a healthy dietary pattern is especially important for those who are pregnant or lactating for several reasons. Increased calorie and nutrient intakes are necessary to support the growth and development of the baby and to maintain the mother's health. Consuming a healthy dietary pattern before and during pregnancy also may improve pregnancy outcomes. In addition, following a healthy dietary pattern before and during pregnancy and lactation has the potential to affect health outcomes for both the mother and child in subsequent life stages.

This chapter addresses some important nutritional considerations for women before pregnancy and contains nutrition guidance for women during pregnancy and lactation. A healthy dietary pattern, along with changing calorie and nutrient needs during pregnancy and lactation, are described throughout the chapter. Special consideration is given to the importance of achieving and maintaining a healthy weight before pregnancy, gaining weight within gestational weight gain guidelines, and returning to a healthy weight during the postpartum period. A healthy weight status during these life stages has short- and long-term health benefits for the mother and her child. The chapter also discusses other considerations important to pregnancy and lactation, including those related to intake of seafood, alcohol, and caffeinated beverages. Finally, during pregnancy, nausea, vomiting, food aversions, and food cravings can make it difficult for some women to achieve optimal dietary intake. The chapter discusses how these can be considered when helping women who are pregnant or lactating make healthy food and beverage choices.

Healthy Dietary Patterns

Women who are pregnant or lactating are encouraged to follow the recommendations on the types of foods and beverages that make up a healthy dietary pattern described in ***Chapter 1. Nutrition and Health Across the Lifespan: The Dietary Guidelines and Key Recommendations.*** The core elements of a healthy diet for women during these life stages are similar to the recommendations for women who are not pregnant. **Table 5-1** shows the Healthy U.S.-Style Dietary Pattern to illustrate the specific amounts and limits for food groups and other dietary components that make up healthy dietary patterns at the six calorie levels most relevant to women who are pregnant or lactating. Following a healthy dietary pattern during these life stages can help women meet the Guidelines and its Key Recommendations. The USDA Dietary Patterns are discussed in greater detail in ***Chapter 1*** and ***Appendix 3. USDA Dietary Patterns.***

Table 5-2 summarizes estimated daily calorie needs during pregnancy and lactation compared to prepregnancy needs for women with a healthy prepregnancy weight. Additional information on estimates of prepregnancy calorie needs is provided in **Table 5-1 (footnote a)** and in ***Appendix 2. Estimated Calorie Needs***. As shown in **Table 5-2**, calorie needs generally increase as pregnancy progresses and remain elevated during lactation. However, it is important to note that women with a prepregnancy weight that is considered overweight or obese have lower weight gain recommendations than do women with a healthy prepregnancy weight (see "**Weight Management**"). Women should follow their healthcare provider's guidance regarding appropriate caloric intake during pregnancy and lactation, as many factors, including prepregnancy weight status, gestational weight gain, and multiple pregnancies, may affect calorie needs. In general, it is important for women who are pregnant to be under the care of a healthcare provider who can monitor their health status and the progress of their pregnancy.

The increased calorie and nutrient needs for these life stages should be met by consuming nutrient-dense food choices as part of a healthy dietary pattern. One way to achieve this is to follow the Healthy U.S.-Style Dietary Pattern throughout pregnancy and lactation, but adjust intake of food groups to reflect higher calorie patterns recommended during the second and third trimesters of pregnancy and throughout lactation. In short, women should meet their increased calorie and nutrient needs with nutrient-dense foods instead of with foods high in added sugars, saturated fat, and sodium.

The customizable components of the USDA Dietary Patterns provide flexibility that allows women—or professionals adapting these patterns—to choose from a variety of foods and beverages within each food group to suit individual preference, lifestyle, traditions, culture, and budget. This flexibility in being able to select among a variety of nutrient-dense options is particularly important for women who experience pregnancy-induced nausea, vomiting, or food aversions.

When making food and beverage choices, women should know that unless it's medically indicated to avoid for her own health, women do *not* need to restrict their choices during pregnancy or lactation to prevent food allergy from developing in their child. However, women who are pregnant should pay attention to some important food safety considerations (see "**Food Safety During Pregnancy**").

Nutrient-Dense Foods and Beverages

Nutrient-dense foods and beverages provide vitamins, minerals, and other health-promoting components and have little added sugars, saturated fat, and sodium. Vegetables, fruits, whole grains, seafood, eggs, beans, peas, and lentils, unsalted nuts and seeds, fat-free and low-fat dairy products, and lean meats and poultry—when prepared with no or little added sugars, saturated fat, and sodium—are nutrient-dense foods.

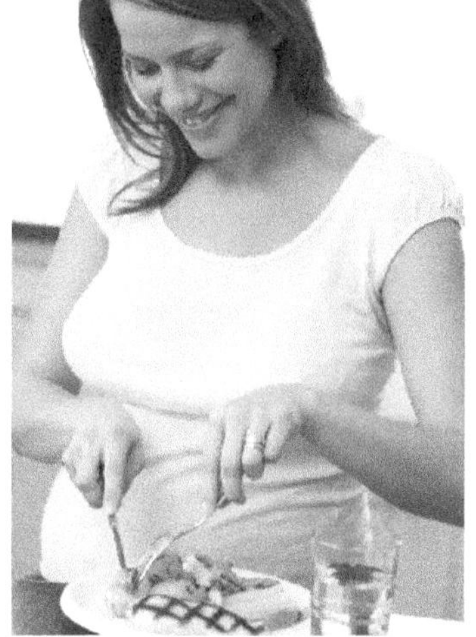

WOMEN WHO ARE PREGNANT OR LACTATING

Table 5-1

Healthy U.S.-Style Dietary Pattern for Women Who Are Pregnant or Lactating, With Daily or Weekly Amounts From Food Groups, Subgroups, and Components

CALORIE LEVEL OF PATTERN[a]	1,800	2,000	2,200	2,400	2,600	2,800
FOOD GROUP OR SUBGROUP[b]	Daily Amount of Food From Each Group (Vegetable and protein foods subgroup amounts are per week.)					
Vegetables (cup eq/day)	**2 ½**	**2 ½**	**3**	**3**	**3 ½**	**3 ½**
	Vegetable Subgroups in Weekly Amounts					
Dark-Green Vegetables (cup eq/wk)	1 ½	1 ½	2	2	2 ½	2 ½
Red & Orange Vegetables (cup eq/wk)	5 ½	5 ½	6	6	7	7
Beans, Peas, Lentils (cup eq/wk)	1 ½	1 ½	2	2	2 ½	2 ½
Starchy Vegetables (cup eq/wk)	5	5	6	6	7	7
Other Vegetables (cup eq/wk)	4	4	5	5	5 ½	5 ½
Fruits (cup eq/day)	**1 ½**	**2**	**2**	**2**	**2**	**2 ½**
Grains (ounce eq/day)	**6**	**6**	**7**	**8**	**9**	**10**
Whole Grains (ounce eq/day)	3	3	3 ½	4	4 ½	5
Refined Grains (ounce eq/day)	3	3	3 ½	4	4 ½	5
Dairy (cup eq/day)	**3**	**3**	**3**	**3**	**3**	**3**
Protein Foods (ounce eq/day)	**5**	**5 ½**	**6**	**6 ½**	**6 ½**	**7**
	Protein Foods Subgroups in Weekly Amounts					
Meats, Poultry, Eggs (ounce eq/wk)	23	26	28	31	31	33
Seafood (ounce eq/wk)[c]	8	8	9	10	10	10
Nuts, Seeds, Soy Products (ounce eq/wk)	4	5	5	5	5	6
Oils (grams/day)	**24**	**27**	**29**	**31**	**34**	**36**
Limit on Calories for Other Uses (kcal/day)[d]	**140**	**240**	**250**	**320**	**350**	**370**
Limit on Calories for Other Uses (%/day)	8%	12%	11%	13%	13%	13%

[a] Calorie level ranges: Prepregnancy energy levels are calculated based on median height and body weight for healthy body mass index (BMI) for a reference woman, who is 5 feet 4 inches tall and weighs 126 pounds. The calorie levels shown in this table include estimates for women during the first trimester of pregnancy, when calorie needs generally do not increase compared to prepregnancy needs, plus the additional calories needed for the later trimesters of pregnancy and during lactation. Calorie needs vary based on many factors. Women with overweight or obesity have lower recommended gestational weight gain during pregnancy, which may affect calorie needs. The DRI Calculator for Healthcare Professionals, available at **nal.usda.gov/fnic/dri-calculator**, can be used to estimate calorie needs based on age, sex, height, weight, activity level, and pregnancy or lactation status.

[b] Definitions for each food group and subgroup and quantity (i.e., cup or ounce equivalents) are provided in ***Chapter 1*** and are compiled in ***Appendix 3***.

[c] The U.S. Food and Drug Administration (FDA) and the U.S. Environmental Protection Agency (EPA) provide joint advice regarding seafood consumption to limit methylmercury exposure for women who might become or are pregnant or lactating. Depending on body weight, some women should choose seafood lowest in methylmercury or eat less seafood than the amounts in the Healthy U.S.-Style Dietary Pattern. More information is available on the FDA and EPA websites at **FDA.gov/fishadvice** and **EPA.gov/fishadvice**.

[d] All foods are assumed to be in nutrient-dense forms; lean or low-fat; and prepared with minimal added sugars, refined starches, saturated fat, or sodium. If all food choices to meet food group recommendations are in nutrient-dense forms, a small number of calories remain within the overall limit of the pattern (i.e., limit on calories for other uses). The number of calories depends on the total calorie level of the pattern and the amounts of food from each food group required to meet nutritional goals. Calories up to the specified limit can be used for added sugars and/or saturated fat, or to eat more than the recommended amount of food in a food group.

NOTE: The total dietary pattern should not exceed *Dietary Guidelines* limits for added sugars and saturated fat; be within the Acceptable Macronutrient Distribution Ranges for protein, carbohydrate, and total fats; and stay within calorie limits. Values are rounded. See ***Appendix 3*** for all calorie levels of the pattern.

Table 5-2

Estimated Change in Calorie Needs During Pregnancy and Lactation for Women With a Healthy[a] Prepregnancy Weight

Stage of Pregnancy or Lactation	Estimated Change in Daily Calorie Needs Compared to Prepregnancy Needs
Pregnancy: 1st trimester	+ 0 calories
Pregnancy: 2nd trimester	+ 340 calories
Pregnancy: 3rd trimester	+ 452 calories
Lactation: 1st 6 months	+ 330 calories[b]
Lactation: 2nd 6 months	+ 400 calories[c]

[a] These estimates apply to women with a healthy prepregnancy weight. Women with a prepregnancy weight that is considered overweight or obese should consult their healthcare provider for guidance regarding appropriate caloric intake during pregnancy and lactation.

[b] The EER for the first 6 months of lactation is calculated by adding 500 calories/day to prepregnancy needs to account for the energy needed for milk production during this time period, then subtracting 170 calories/day to account for weight loss in the first 6 months postpartum.

[c] The EER for the second 6 months of lactation is calculated by adding 400 calories/day to prepregnancy needs to account for the energy needed for milk production during this time period. Weight stability is assumed after 6 months postpartum.

NOTE: Estimates are based on Estimated Energy Requirements (EER) set by the Institute of Medicine. Source: Institute of Medicine. *Dietary Reference Intakes for Energy, Carbohydrate, Fiber, Fat, Fatty Acids, Cholesterol, Protein, and Amino Acids*. Washington, DC: The National Academies Press; 2005.

Weight Management

Weight management is complex, so women should seek advice from a healthcare provider on the best way to achieve their goals. Women should be encouraged to achieve and maintain a healthy weight before becoming pregnant, as well as follow the gestational weight gain guidelines developed by the National Academies of Sciences, Engineering, and Medicine during pregnancy. These guidelines are outlined in **Table 5-3** and serve as a tool to help balance the benefits and risks associated with pregnancy weight change.

Table 5-3

Weight Gain Recommendations for Pregnancy[a]

Pre-pregnancy Weight Category	Body Mass Index	Range of Total Weight Gain (lb)	Rates of Weekly Weight Gain[b] in the 2nd and 3rd Trimesters (mean [range], lbs)
Underweight	Less than 18.5	28-40	1 [1-1.3]
Healthy Weight	18.5-24.9	25-35	1 [0.8-1]
Overweight	25-29.9	15-25	0.6 [0.5-0.7]
Obese	30 and greater	11-20	0.5 [0.4-0.6]

[a] **Reference:** Institute of Medicine and National Research Council. 2009. *Weight Gain During Pregnancy: Reexamining the Guidelines*. Washington, DC: The National Academies Press. **doi.org/10.17226/12584**.

[b] Calculations assume a 1.1 to 4.4 lb weight gain in the first trimester.

It is important to note that about half of women retain 10 pounds or more and nearly 1 in 4 women retain 20 pounds or more at 12 months postpartum. Postpartum weight retention results in about 1 in 7 women moving from a healthy weight classification before pregnancy to an overweight classification postpartum. Current estimates show that about half of women of childbearing age have a weight classification of overweight or obese. Women with overweight or obesity frequently exceed gestational weight gain recommendations during pregnancy, which increases the likelihood of excess postpartum weight retention.

Weight gain is a natural part of pregnancy, which is why it is important to have a plan. Meeting weight management goals may improve pregnancy outcomes, such as increasing the likelihood of delivering a healthy weight infant and improving the long-term health of both mother and child. Women are encouraged to partner with their healthcare provider and other medical professionals to achieve their goals and optimize health outcomes.

WOMEN WHO ARE PREGNANT OR LACTATING

Current Intakes

Figures 5-1 and **5-2** highlight the dietary intakes of women who are pregnant or lactating, including the Healthy Eating Index-2015 score, which is an overall measure of how intakes align with the *Dietary Guidelines*, as well as information on the components of a healthy diet—specifically, the food groups. **Figure 5-1** displays the average intakes of the food groups compared to the range of recommended intakes at the calorie levels most relevant to these life stages.

Figure 5-1

Current Intakes: Women Who Are Pregnant or Lactating

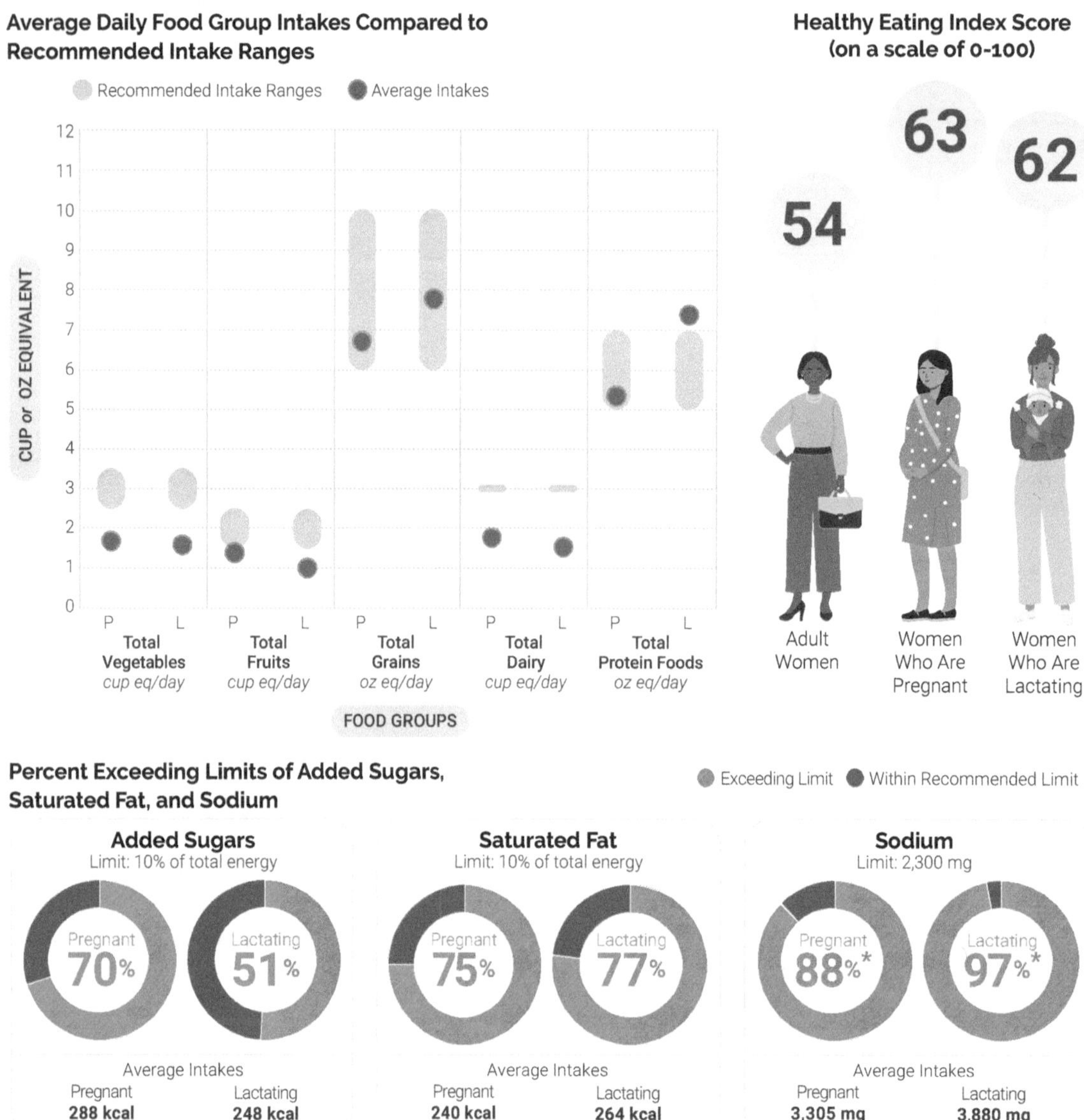

***NOTE:** Estimates may be less precise than others due to small sample size and/or large relative standard error.

Data Sources: *Average Intakes and HEI-2015 Scores*: Analysis of What We Eat in America, NHANES 2013-2016, women ages 20-44, day 1 dietary intake data, weighted. *Recommended Intake Ranges*: Healthy U.S.-Style Dietary Patterns (see ***Appendix 3)***. Percent Exceeding Limits: What We Eat in America, NHANES 2013-2016, 2 days dietary intake data, weighted.

WOMEN WHO ARE PREGNANT OR LACTATING

Figure 5-2
Average Intakes of Subgroups Compared to Recommended Intake Ranges: Women Who Are Pregnant or Lactating

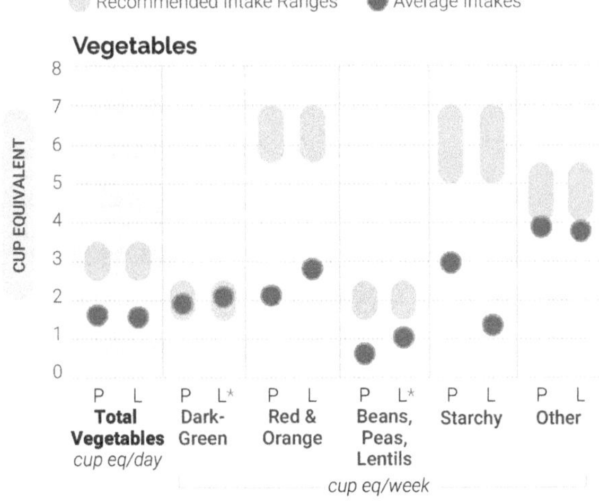

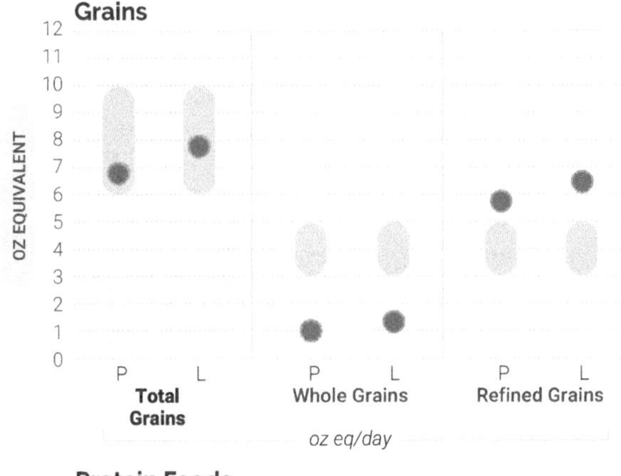

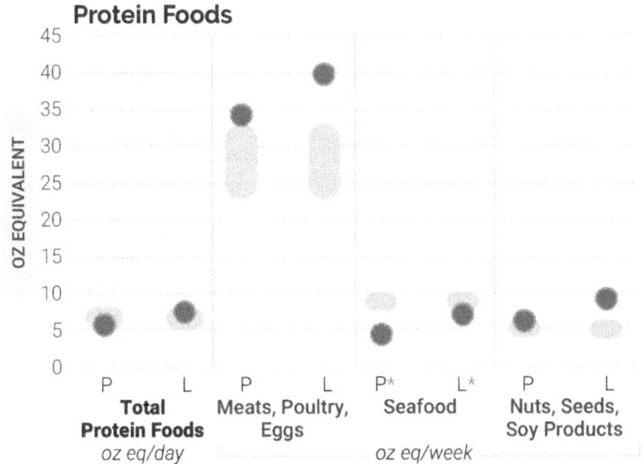

Additionally, the percent of women exceeding the limits for added sugars, saturated fat, and sodium are shown, along with average intakes of these components. Finally, average intakes compared to recommended intake ranges of the subgroups for grains in daily amounts and for vegetables and protein foods in weekly amounts are also provided in **Figure 5-2**.

The Healthy Eating Index score is 63 for women who are pregnant and 62 for women who are lactating. Although diet quality is higher among women during these life stages compared to peers who are not pregnant or lactating (54), intakes are still not optimal. Women who are pregnant or lactating can benefit from making dietary changes to better align with healthy dietary patterns.

As described in ***Chapter 1***, consistent with the general U.S. population, women who are pregnant or lactating are not meeting recommendations for food group and nutrient intake. **Figures 5-1** and **5-2** show average intakes are generally below or in the lower range of recommendations for food groups and subgroups, while exceeding limits for added sugars, saturated fat, and sodium.

***NOTE:** Estimates may be less precise than others due to small sample size and/or large relative standard error.

Data Sources: *Average Intakes*: Analysis of What We Eat in America, NHANES 2013-2016, women ages 20-44, day 1 dietary intake data, weighted. *Recommended Intake Ranges*: Healthy U.S.-Style Dietary Patterns (see ***Appendix 3***).

WOMEN WHO ARE PREGNANT OR LACTATING

Special Considerations

The nutrition considerations for the general U.S. population described in ***Chapter 1*** apply to women who are pregnant or lactating. For example, the nutrients of public health concern—calcium, vitamin D, potassium, and dietary fiber—apply to these life stages as well. In addition, iron is a nutrient of public health concern for women who are pregnant. These life stages also have some special nutrient and dietary considerations regarding folate, iodine, choline, seafood, alcoholic beverages, and caffeinated beverages that are discussed in the following sections of this chapter.

Meeting Nutrient Needs

As discussed in ***Chapter 1***, nutritional needs should be met primarily through foods and beverages. However, this may be difficult for some women, especially those who are pregnant. Most healthcare providers recommend women who are pregnant or planning to become pregnant take a daily prenatal vitamin and mineral supplement in addition to consuming a healthy dietary pattern. This may be especially important to meet folate/folic acid, iron, iodine, and vitamin D needs during pregnancy (see ***Appendix 1. Nutritional Goals for Age-Sex Groups***).

Nutrient needs for women who are lactating differ from those who are pregnant. Continued use of prenatal supplements by women who are lactating may exceed their needs for folic acid and iron. Women who are lactating should not exceed the Tolerable Upper Intake Level (UL) of 1,000 micrograms of folic acid and 45 milligrams of iron. Women should seek guidance from a healthcare provider on appropriate use of prenatal or other dietary supplements during lactation.

Folate/Folic Acid

The RDA for folate is higher during pregnancy and lactation than all other life stages (see ***Appendix 1)***. Adequate folic acid intake is particularly important prior to conception and during the first trimester to help prevent neural tube defects.

The United States Preventative Services Task Force (USPSTF) recommends that all women who are planning or capable of pregnancy take a daily supplement containing 400 to 800 mcg of folic acid. The critical period for supplementation starts at least 1 month before conception and continues through the first 2 to 3 months of pregnancy. Dietary supplements may contain either folic acid or 5-methyltetrahydrofolate (5-MTHF), but only folic acid has been shown to prevent neural tube defects. Most prenatal supplements sold in the United States contain folic acid.

The recommendation for folic acid supplementation is in addition to the amounts of food folate contained in a healthy eating pattern. Folate is found inherently in dark-green vegetables and beans, peas, and lentils. All enriched grains (i.e., bread, pasta, rice, and cereal) and some corn masa flours are fortified with folic acid.

Iron

Iron needs increase during pregnancy compared to prepregnancy. For women who are lactating, before menstruation returns, iron needs fall and then return to prepregnancy levels once menstruation resumes (see ***Appendix 1***).

Iron is a key nutrient during pregnancy that supports fetal development. Iron deficiency affects about 1 in 10 women who are pregnant and 1 in 4 women during their third trimester. Heme iron, which is found in animal source foods (e.g., lean meats, poultry, and some seafood) is more readily absorbed by the body than the non-heme iron found in plant source foods (e.g., beans, peas, lentils, and dark-green vegetables). Additional iron sources include foods enriched or fortified with iron, such as many whole-wheat breads and ready-to-eat cereals. Absorption of iron from non-heme sources is enhanced by consuming them along with vitamin C-rich foods. Food source lists for both heme and non-heme iron are available at **DietaryGuidelines.gov**. Women who are pregnant or who are planning to become pregnant are advised to take a supplement containing iron when recommended by an obstetrician or other healthcare provider.

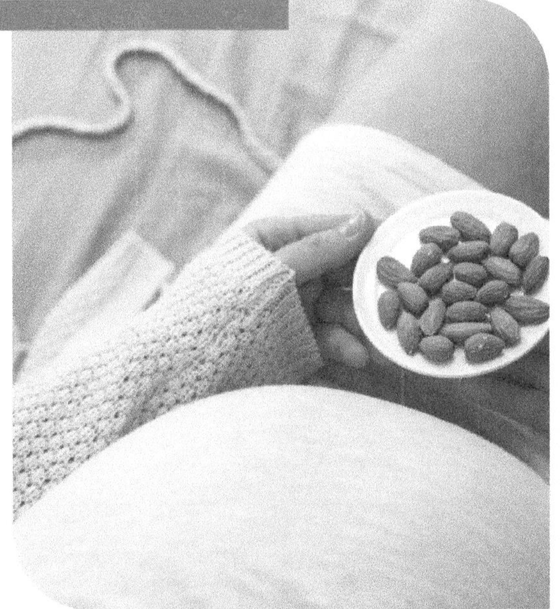

More than half of women continue to use prenatal supplements during lactation. Most prenatal supplements are designed to meet the higher iron needs of pregnancy. Depending on various factors—such as when menstruation returns—prenatal supplements may exceed the iron needs of women who are lactating. Women should seek guidance from a healthcare provider regarding the appropriate level of iron supplementation during lactation based on their unique needs.

Iodine

Iodine needs increase substantially during pregnancy and lactation (see ***Appendix 1***). Adequate iodine intake during pregnancy is important for neurocognitive development of the fetus. Although women of reproductive age generally have adequate iodine intake, some women, particularly those who do not regularly consume dairy products, eggs, seafood, or use iodized table salt, may not consume enough iodine to meet increased needs during pregnancy and lactation.

Women who are pregnant or lactating should not be encouraged to start using table salt if they do not do so already. However, they should ensure that any table salt used in cooking or added to food at the table is iodized. Additionally, women who are pregnant or lactating may need a supplement containing iodine in order to achieve adequate intake. Many prenatal supplements do not contain iodine. Thus, it is important to read the label.

Vegetarian or Vegan Dietary Patterns During Pregnancy and Lactation

Women following a vegetarian or vegan dietary pattern during these life stages may need to take special care to ensure nutrient adequacy. Iron may be of particular concern because plant source foods only contain non-heme iron, which is less bioavailable than heme iron. Food source lists for both heme and non-heme iron are available at **DietaryGuidelines.gov**. Vitamin B_{12} also is of concern because it is present only in animal source foods. Women following a vegetarian or vegan dietary pattern should consult with a healthcare provider to determine whether supplementation of iron, vitamin B_{12}, and/or other nutrients such as choline, zinc, iodine , or EPA/DHA is necessary and if so, the appropriate levels to meet their unique needs.

WOMEN WHO ARE PREGNANT OR LACTATING

Choline

Choline needs also increase during pregnancy and lactation (see ***Appendix 1***). Adequate intake of choline during these life stages helps to both replenish maternal stores and support the growth and development of the child's brain and spinal cord.

Most women do not meet recommended intakes of choline during pregnancy and lactation. Women are encouraged to consume a variety of choline-containing foods during these life stages. Choline can be found throughout many food groups and subgroups. Meeting recommended intakes for the dairy and protein food groups—with eggs, meats, and some seafood being notable sources—as well as the beans, peas, and lentils subgroup can help meet choline needs. Meeting nutrient needs through foods and beverages is preferred, but women who are concerned about meeting recommendations should speak with their healthcare provider to determine whether choline supplementation is appropriate. Many prenatal supplements do not contain choline or only contain small amounts inadequate to meet recommendations.

Seafood

Seafood intake during pregnancy is recommended, as it is associated with favorable measures of cognitive development in young children. Women who are pregnant or lactating should consume at least 8 and up to 12 ounces of a variety of seafood per week, from choices lower in methylmercury. The U.S. Food and Drug Administration (FDA) and the U.S. Environmental Protection Agency (EPA) provide joint advice regarding seafood consumption to limit methylmercury exposure for women who might become or who are pregnant or lactating. Methylmercury can be harmful to the brain and nervous system if a person is exposed to too much of it over time; this is particularly important during pregnancy because eating too much of it can have negative effects on the developing fetus. Based on FDA and EPA's advice, depending on body weight, some women should choose seafood lowest in methylmercury or eat less seafood than the amounts in the Healthy U.S.-Style Dietary Pattern. Additionally, certain species of seafood (e.g., shark, swordfish, king mackerel) should be avoided during pregnancy. More information is available on the FDA or EPA websites at **FDA.gov/fishadvice** and **EPA.gov/fishadvice**.

Alcoholic Beverages

Women who are or who may be pregnant should not drink alcohol. However, consumption of alcohol during pregnancy continues to be of concern in the United States. Among women who are pregnant, about 1 in 10 reported consuming alcohol during the past month, with an average intake of 2 or more drink equivalents on days alcohol is consumed.

It is not safe for women to drink any type or amount of alcohol during pregnancy. Women who drink alcohol and become pregnant should stop drinking immediately and women who are trying to become pregnant should

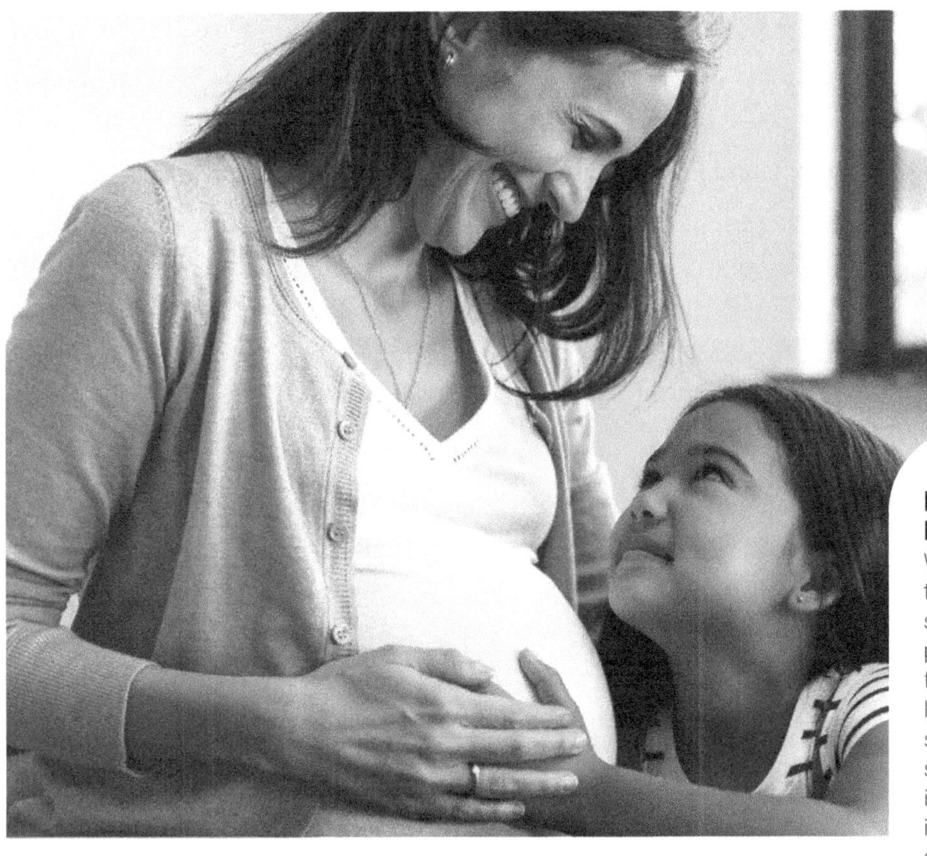

not drink at all. Alcohol can harm the baby at any time during pregnancy, even during the first or second month when a woman may not know she is pregnant.

Not drinking alcohol also is the safest option for women who are lactating. Generally, moderate consumption of alcoholic beverages by a woman who is lactating (up to 1 standard drink in a day) is not known to be harmful to the infant, especially if the woman waits at least 2 hours after a single drink before nursing or expressing breast milk. Additional information on breastfeeding and alcohol can be found at: **cdc.gov/breastfeeding/breastfeeding-special-circumstances/vaccinations-medications-drugs/alcohol.html**. Women considering consuming alcohol during lactation should talk to their healthcare provider.

Caffeine

Many women consume caffeine during pregnancy or lactation. As discussed in ***Chapter 1***, most intake of caffeine in the United States comes from coffee, tea, and soda. Caffeinated beverages vary widely in their caffeine content. Caffeine passes from the mother to infant in small amounts through breast milk, but usually does not adversely affect the infant when the mother consumes low to moderate amounts (about 300 milligrams or less per day, which is about 2 to 3 cups of coffee). More information is available at: **cdc.gov/breastfeeding/breastfeeding-special-circumstances/diet-and-micronutrients/maternal-diet.html**. Women who could be or who are pregnant should consult their healthcare providers for advice concerning caffeine consumption.

Food Safety During Pregnancy

Women who are pregnant and their unborn children are more susceptible than are the general population to the effects of foodborne illnesses, such as listeriosis. They need to take special care to keep foods safe and to not eat foods that increase the risk of foodborne illness. During pregnancy, women should only eat foods containing seafood, meats, poultry, or eggs that have been cooked to recommended safe minimum internal temperatures. They also should take special precautions not to consume unpasteurized (raw) juice or milk, raw sprouts, or some soft cheeses made from unpasteurized milk. Deli and luncheon meats and hot dogs should be reheated to steaming hot or 165°F to kill *Listeria*, the bacteria that causes listeriosis.

Additional food safety resources for pregnant women are available at **fda.gov/media/83740/download and foodsafety.gov/people-at-risk/pregnant-women**, and specific answers to food safety questions are available at **fsis.usda.gov/wps/portal/fsis/topics/food-safety-education/get-answers**.

WOMEN WHO ARE PREGNANT OR LACTATING

Physical Activity During Pregnancy and Postpartum

PREGNANCY

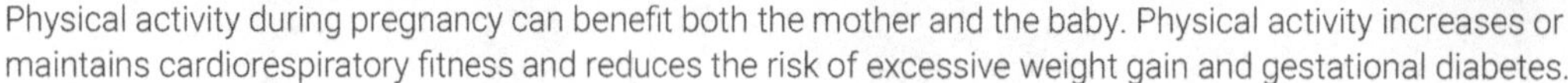

Physical activity during pregnancy can benefit both the mother and the baby. Physical activity increases or maintains cardiorespiratory fitness and reduces the risk of excessive weight gain and gestational diabetes.

For many benefits, healthy women without contraindications should do a least 150 minutes of moderate-intensity aerobic activity a week, as they are able. Women who habitually did vigorous-intensity activity or a lot of aerobic or muscle-strengthening physical activity before pregnancy can continue to do so during pregnancy. Women can consult their healthcare provider about whether or how to adjust their physical activity during pregnancy.

POSTPARTUM

Physical activity following the birth of a child continues to benefit a woman's overall health. Physical activity during the postpartum period increases cardiorespiratory fitness, improves mood, and reduces the symptoms of postpartum depression. Additionally, physical activity can help achieve and maintain a healthy weight and, when combined with caloric restriction, helps promote weight loss.

Women should start slow and build back up to more activity over time. Women should aim for at least 150 minutes of moderate-intensity aerobic activity a week.

The U.S. Department of Health and Human Service's *Physical Activity Guidelines for Americans* and the Move Your Way® communications campaign have information about the benefits of physical activity and tips to get started. Available at **health.gov/paguidelines**.

Supporting Healthy Eating

Many women have increased interest in and motivation to make healthy lifestyle changes during pregnancy and lactation. Furthermore, the dietary choices made during these life stages can affect women's health and the health of their children. Supporting women in adopting healthy dietary patterns during this important time of life and sustaining them thereafter also enables them to serve as role models when their children begin transitioning to complementary foods.

Women who are pregnant or lactating face many real or perceived barriers when trying to meet the recommendations of the *Dietary Guidelines*. Constraints on time and financial resources, limited access to high-quality childcare and family leave policies, as well as inadequate breastfeeding support at home or at work are barriers women may face. These barriers should be considered by all those who support women in their efforts to follow a healthy dietary pattern.

Ensuring women have access to healthy, safe food is vital due to the critical role nutrition plays in health promotion during these life stages. This is particularly critical for families dealing with food insecurity, which is most prevalent in households with children and in single-parent households. Participation in Federal programs, such as the **Special Supplemental Nutrition Program for Women, Infants, and Children (WIC),** which serves low-income pregnant, breastfeeding, and non-breastfeeding postpartum women, and infants and children up to age 5, can help alleviate these challenges and improve dietary intake for many women and children facing economic hardship. The **Supplemental Nutrition Assistance Program (SNAP)** and the **Food Distribution Program on Indian Reservations (FDPIR)** can also serve as resources for low-income women and their families by both supplementing food budgets to support health and by providing nutrition education through the **SNAP-Ed program**. Additionally, USDA's **Healthy Eating on A Budget**[1] can help women and families plan and prepare healthy, inexpensive meals. Other Government and non-Government resources, such as food banks or community meal programs, also provide food and educational resources that can support women in making healthy food choices for themselves and their families.

Support during lactation can help women meet their breastfeeding goals, despite significant demands on their time and energy during this life stage. Worksite programs and policies that allow women adequate time to pump breast milk when away from their child, as well as access to good quality childcare, can allow women who return to work to achieve breastfeeding goals. Access to breastfeeding peer counselors, such as those used in WIC, or free breastfeeding support groups through local hospitals also can support women during this life stage. Additionally, health professionals can promote the **USDA's WIC Breastfeeding Support**[2] and the U.S. Department of Health and Human Services Office of Women's Health (OWH) **Your Guide to Breastfeeding**[3] and their **National Breastfeeding Helpline**[4] (800-994-9662), which are freely accessible to all women.

Health professionals, policymakers, worksite administrators, community leaders, families, and friends should consider these barriers and opportunities when seeking to support women and families. Developing programs and resources that reduce barriers and create opportunities can help women meet their dietary needs and improve their overall health and the health of their children.

For more information on meeting the *Dietary Guidelines* for children during their first 2 years of life, see ***Chapter 2. Infants and Toddlers***

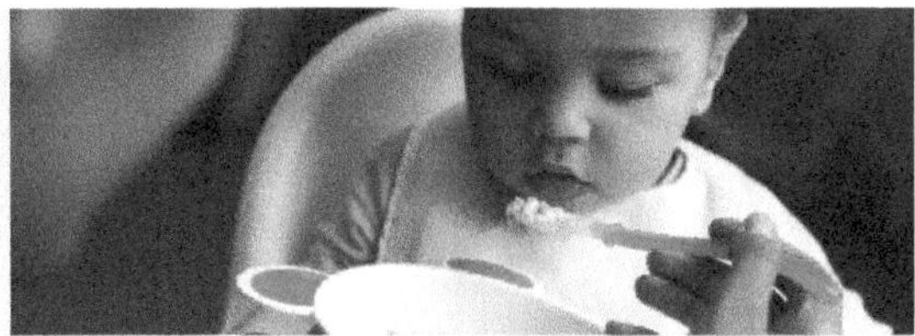

[1] Available at: **MyPlate.gov/budget**

[2] Available at: **wicbreastfeeding.fns.usda.gov/**

[3] Available at: **womenshealth.gov/files/your-guide-to-breastfeeding.pdf**

[4] Available at: **womenshealth.gov/about-us/what-we-do/programs-and-activities/helpline**

ADULTS AGES 60 AND OLDER

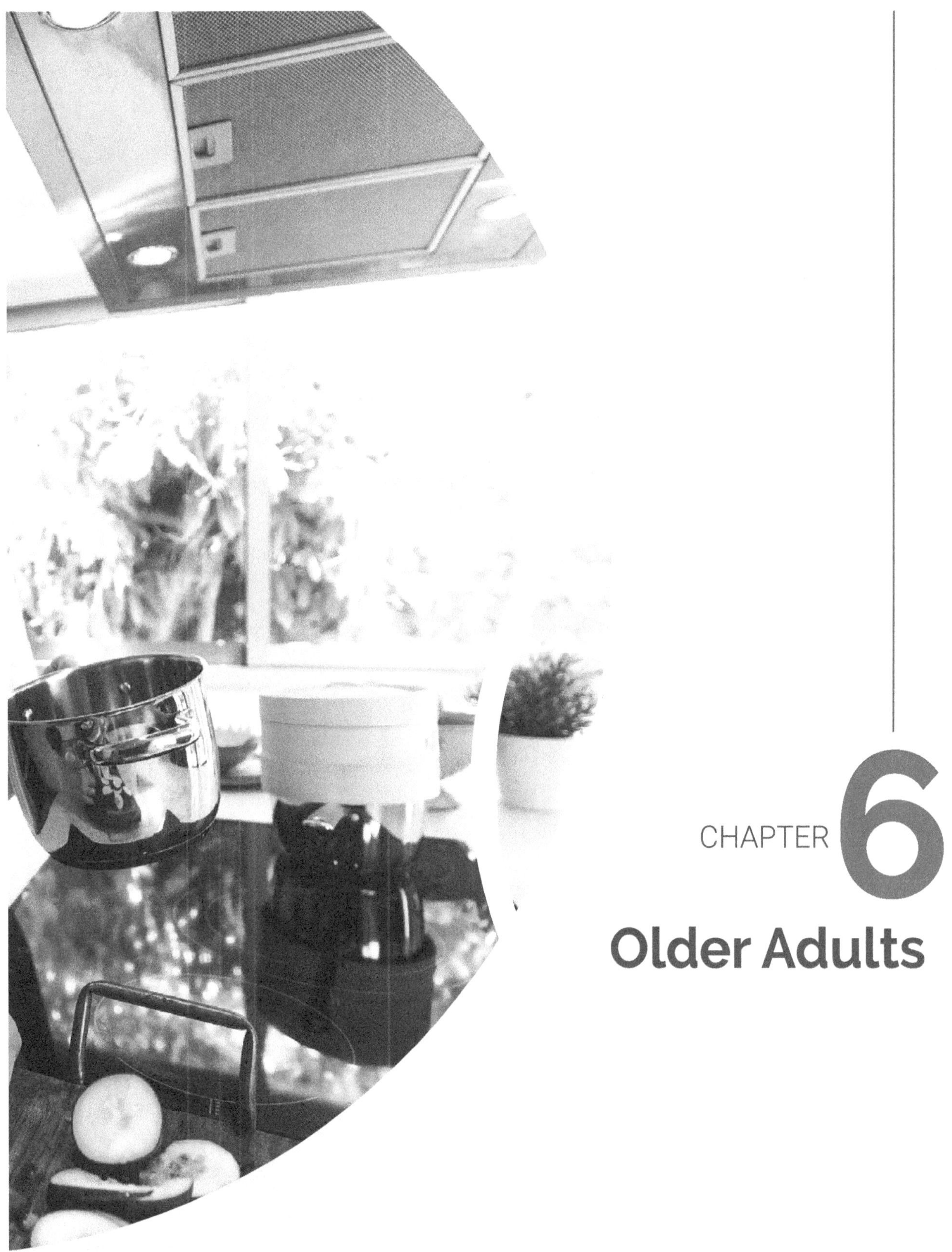

CHAPTER 6
Older Adults

ADULTS AGES 60 AND OLDER

Introduction

Older adults include individuals ages 60 and older—a life stage that includes a broad range of ages and is influenced by a number of health and social changes that affect this population's nutritional status. Compared to younger adults, older adults are at greater risk of chronic diseases, such as cardiovascular disease and cancer, as well as health conditions related to changes in bone and muscle mass, such as osteoporosis and sarcopenia, respectively. An increasing number of older adults start this life stage with excess body weight. Preventing additional weight gain and achieving a healthy weight by following a healthy dietary pattern and adopting an active lifestyle can support healthy aging.

Selecting healthy food and beverage choices is important for people throughout this life stage, regardless of their race or ethnicity or their current health status. It is never too late to make improvements. Older adults should follow a healthy dietary pattern because of the changing dietary needs and the heightened risk of malnutrition that occurs with age. Older adults generally have lower calorie needs but similar or even increased nutrient needs compared to younger adults. The overall nutrient density of dietary patterns is particularly important to this age group. Lower calorie needs result from less physical activity, changes in metabolism, and/or age-related loss in bone and muscle mass. Other factors may affect nutrient needs and absorption of nutrients in older adults, including chronic disease and conditions, use of multiple medications, and changes in body composition. The healthy dietary patterns described below take the unique needs of older adults into account and are further supported by special considerations and strategies for professionals to support healthy aging.

Nutrient-Dense Foods and Beverages

Nutrient-dense foods and beverages provide vitamins, minerals, and other health-promoting components and have little added sugars, saturated fat, and sodium. Vegetables, fruits, whole grains, seafood, eggs, beans, peas, and lentils, unsalted nuts and seeds, fat-free and low-fat dairy products, and lean meats and poultry—when prepared with no or little added sugars, saturated fat, and sodium—are nutrient-dense foods.

Healthy Dietary Patterns

Older adults are encouraged to follow the recommendations on the types of foods and beverages that make up a healthy dietary pattern described in ***Chapter 1. Nutrition and Health Across the Lifespan: The Guidelines and Key Recommendations.*** **Table 6-1** displays the Healthy U.S.-Style Dietary Pattern to illustrate the specific food group amounts and limits for other dietary components that make up healthy dietary patterns at the six calorie levels most relevant to older adults.

Calorie needs are generally lower for females compared to males, and for those who are older, smaller, and less physically active. Females ages 60 and older require about 1,600 to 2,200 calories per day and males ages 60 and older require about 2,000 to 2,600 calories per day. Additional information on these estimates is provided in **Table 6-1 (footnote a)** and in ***Appendix 1. Estimated Calorie Needs***.

The USDA Food Patterns are discussed in greater detail in ***Chapter 1. Nutrition and Health Across the Lifespan: The Guidelines and Key Recommendations*** and ***Appendix 3. USDA Dietary Patterns***. The USDA Dietary Patterns provide a framework to help older adults follow a healthy dietary pattern and meet the Guidelines and their Key Recommendations. The Patterns provide a variety of food and beverage choices that allow individuals to customize their choices within each food group based on lifestyle, traditions, culture, and/or other individual needs.

ADULTS AGES 60 AND OLDER

Table 6-1

Healthy U.S.-Style Dietary Pattern for Adults Ages 60 and Older, With Daily or Weekly Amounts From Food Groups, Subgroups, and Components

CALORIE LEVEL OF PATTERN[a]	1,600	1,800	2,000	2,200	2,400	2,600
FOOD GROUP OR SUBGROUP[b]	Daily Amount of Food From Each Group (Vegetable and protein foods subgroup amounts are per week.)					
Vegetables (cup eq/day)	**2**	**2 ½**	**2 ½**	**3**	**3**	**3 ½**
	Vegetable Subgroups in Weekly Amounts					
Dark-Green Vegetables (cup eq/wk)	1 ½	1 ½	1 ½	2	2	2 ½
Red & Orange Vegetables (cup eq/wk)	4	5 ½	5 ½	6	6	7
Beans, Peas, Lentils (cup eq/wk)	1	1 ½	1 ½	2	2	2 ½
Starchy Vegetables (cup eq/wk)	4	5	5	6	6	7
Other Vegetables (cup eq/wk)	3 ½	4	4	5	5	5 ½
Fruits (cup eq/day)	**1 ½**	**1 ½**	**2**	**2**	**2**	**2**
Grains (ounce eq/day)	**5**	**6**	**6**	**7**	**8**	**9**
Whole Grains (ounce eq/day)	3	3	3	3 ½	4	4 ½
Refined Grains (ounce eq/day)	2	3	3	3 ½	4	4 ½
Dairy (cup eq/day)	**3**	**3**	**3**	**3**	**3**	**3**
Protein Foods (ounce eq/day)	**5**	**5**	**5 ½**	**6**	**6 ½**	**6 ½**
	Protein Foods Subgroups in Weekly Amounts					
Meats, Poultry, Eggs (ounce eq/wk)	23	23	26	28	31	31
Seafood (ounce eq/wk)	8	8	9	9	10	10
Nuts, Seeds, Soy Products (ounce eq/wk)	4	4	5	5	5	5
Oils (grams/day)	**22**	**24**	**27**	**29**	**31**	**34**
Limit on Calories for Other Uses (kcal/day)[c]	**100**	**140**	**240**	**250**	**320**	**350**
Limit on Calories for Other Uses (%/day)	7%	8%	12%	12%	13%	5

[a] Calorie level ranges: Females: 1,600-2,200 calories; Males: 2,000-2,600 calories. Energy levels are calculated based on median height and body weight for healthy body mass index (BMI) reference individuals. For adults, the reference man is 5 feet 10 inches tall and weighs 154 pounds. The reference woman is 5 feet 4 inches tall and weighs 126 pounds. Calorie needs vary based on many factors. The DRI Calculator for Healthcare Professionals, available at **nal.usda.gov/fnic/dri-calculator**, can be used to estimate calorie needs based on age, sex, height, weight, and physical activity level.

[b] Definitions for each food group and subgroup and quantity (e.g., cup or ounce equivalents) are provided in ***Chapter 1*** and are compiled in ***Appendix 3.***

[c] All foods are assumed to be in nutrient-dense forms; lean or low-fat and prepared with minimal added sugars; refined starches, saturated fat, or sodium. If all food choices to meet food group recommendations are in nutrient-dense forms, a small number of calories remain within the overall limit of the pattern (i.e., limit on calories for other uses). The number of calories depends on the total calorie level of the pattern and the amounts of food from each food group required to meet nutritional goals. Calories up to the specified limit can be used for added sugars, saturated fat, and/or alcohol, or to eat more than the recommended amount of food in a food group.

NOTE:** The total dietary pattern should not exceed *Dietary Guidelines* limits for added sugars, saturated fat, and alcohol; be within the Acceptable Macronutrient Distribution Ranges for protein, carbohydrate, and total fats; and stay within calorie limits. Values are rounded. See ***Appendix 3 for all calorie levels of the pattern.

Current Intakes

Figures 6-1 and **6-2** highlight the dietary intakes of older adults, including the Healthy Eating Index-2015 score, which is an overall measure of how intakes align with the *Dietary Guidelines*, as well as information on the components of a healthy diet—specifically, the food groups. **Figure 6-1** displays the average intakes of the food groups compared to the range of recommended intakes at the calorie levels most relevant to males and females in this age group. Additionally, the percent of older adults exceeding the recommended limits for added sugars, saturated fat, and sodium are shown, along with average intakes of these components.

Figure 6-1

Current Intakes: Ages 60 and Older

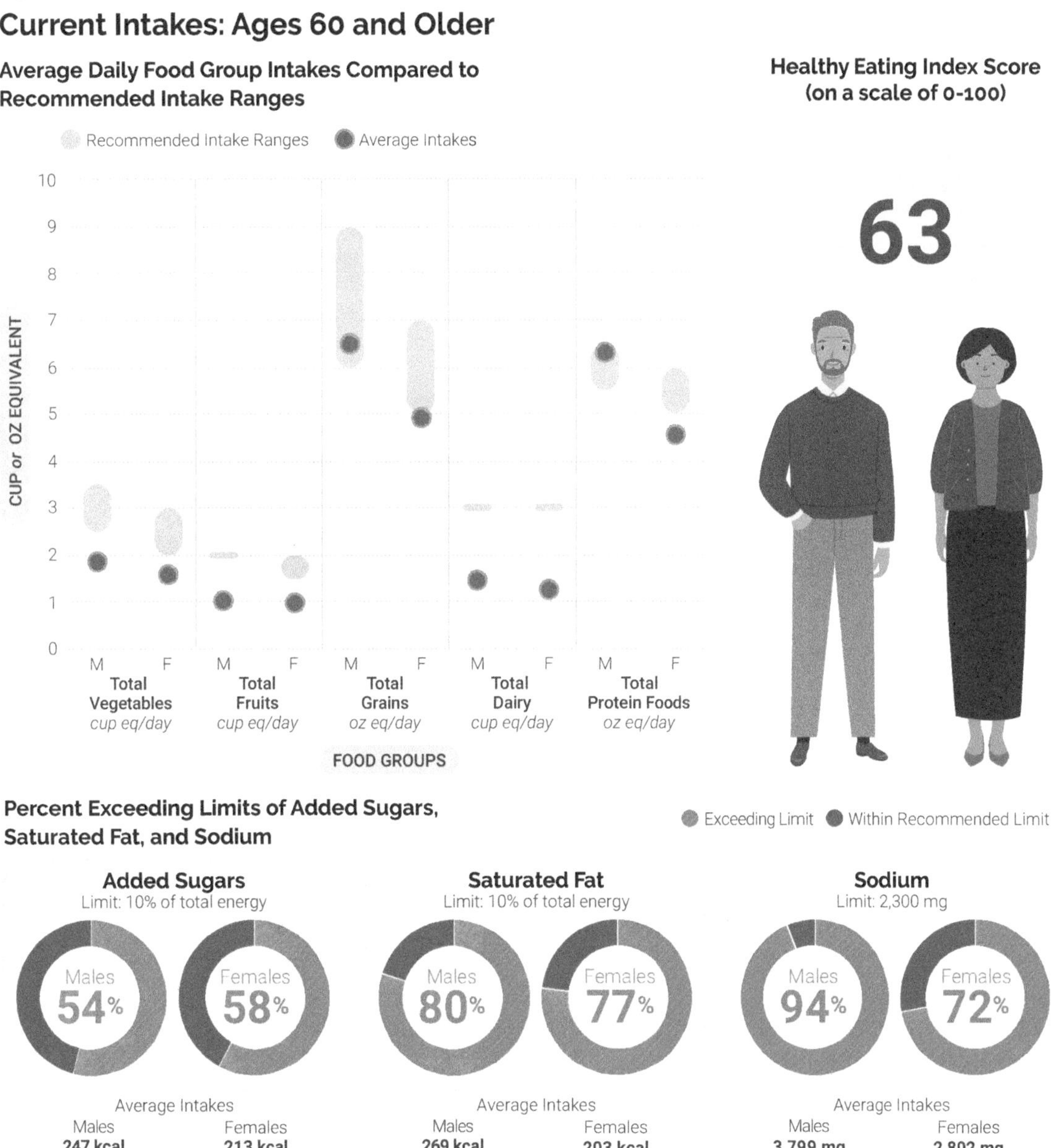

Data Sources: *Average Intakes and HEI-2015 Scores*: Analysis of What We Eat in America, NHANES 2015-2016, day 1 dietary intake data, weighted. *Recommended Intake Ranges*: Healthy U.S.-Style Dietary Patterns (see ***Appendix 3***). *Percent Exceeding Limits*: What We Eat in America, NHANES 2013-2016, 2 days dietary intake data, weighted.

ADULTS AGES 60 AND OLDER

Figure 6-2
Average Intakes of Subgroups Compared to Recommended Intake Ranges: Ages 60 and Older

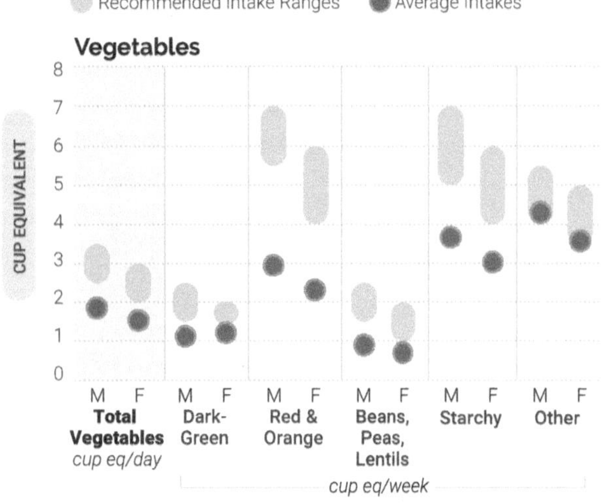

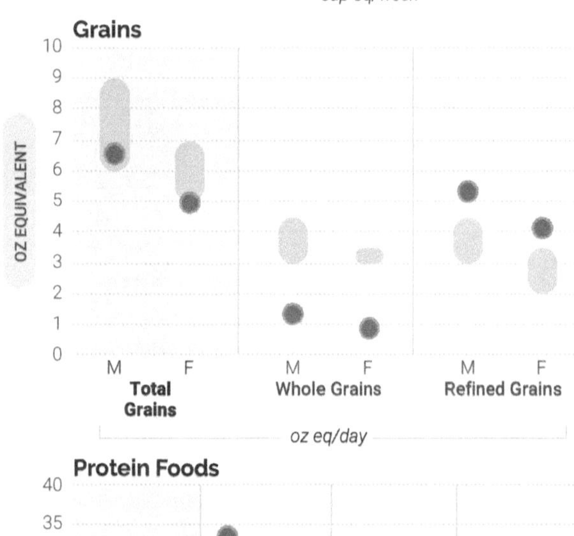

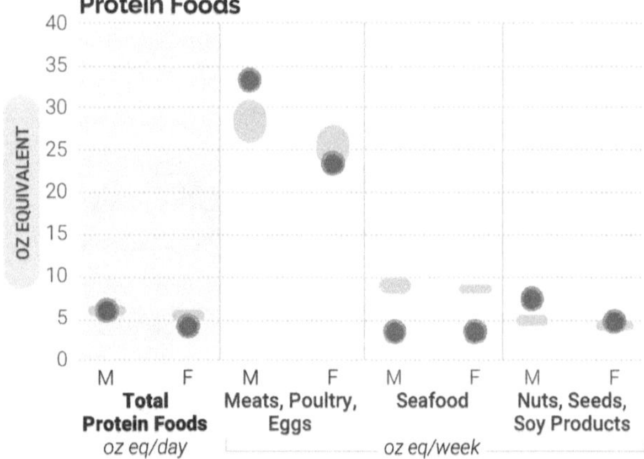

Data Sources: *Average Intakes*: Analysis of What We Eat in America, NHANES 2015-2016, day 1 dietary intake data, weighted. *Recommended Intake Ranges*: Healthy U.S.-Style Dietary Patterns (see ***Appendix 3***).

Average intakes compared to recommended intake ranges of the subgroups for grains are represented in daily amounts; subgroups for vegetables and protein foods are represented in weekly amounts in **Figure 6-2**.

Diet quality is highest among older adults compared to other ages. Consistent with the general U.S. population, however, this age group is not meeting the recommendations for food group and nutrient intakes and has a Healthy Eating Index score of 63 out of 100. Older adults can improve dietary intake by increasing consumption of fruit, vegetables, whole grains, and dairy, while ensuring protein intake meets recommendations. Reducing intakes of added sugars, saturated fat, and sodium also will help older adults achieve recommendations and manage and avoid chronic conditions (**Figure 6-1**). Older adults should choose nutrient-dense options within each food group and consume appropriate portion sizes because calorie needs decline with age.

Special Considerations

The nutrition considerations for the general U.S. population described in ***Chapter 1***. apply to older adults. For example, the nutrients of public concern—calcium, vitamin D, potassium, and dietary fiber—apply to this age group as well. However, this age group also has some special nutrition considerations that are discussed in the following sections of this chapter. For example, several additional nutrients are more likely to be underconsumed during this life stage. These include dietary protein and vitamin B_{12}. Beverage intake, particularly as it relates to hydration status, also is an area of special consideration.

Protein

Consuming enough protein is important to prevent the loss of lean muscle mass that occurs naturally with age. Monitoring protein intake is especially important as older adults transition through this life stage. Intake patterns show average intakes of protein foods is lower for individuals ages 71 and older compared to adults ages 60 through 70. About 50 percent of women and 30 percent of men 71 and older fall short of protein foods recommendations.

The majority of protein in the Healthy U.S.-Style Dietary Pattern is accounted for in the protein foods subgroups: seafood; meats, poultry and eggs; nuts, seeds, and soy products; and the vegetable subgroup of beans, peas, and lentils, which also is considered a protein foods subgroup. The dairy and fortified soy alternatives food group is another source of dietary protein. Most older adults are meeting or exceeding weekly recommendations for meats, poultry, and eggs, making this subgroup a common source of protein foods for older adults (**Table 6-1**). However, seafood, dairy and fortified soy alternatives, and beans, peas, and lentils are underconsumed, yet provide important nutrients that support healthy dietary patterns. For example, the dairy food group provides calcium, vitamin D, and vitamin B_{12} and the beans, peas, and lentils subgroup provides dietary fiber. Many choices within the seafood subgroup also provide vitamins D and B_{12} and calcium (if eaten with bones), and beneficial fatty acids. Food sources of calcium, vitamin D, and dietary fiber are available at **DietaryGuidelines.gov**.

Many older adults can improve their dietary pattern and better meet nutrient needs by choosing from a wider variety of protein sources. In some cases, this may mean using seafood more often in place of meats, poultry, or eggs or using beans, peas, and lentils in mixed dishes, such as soups, rice, or pasta dishes. For others, it may mean maintaining current intakes of protein and finding enjoyable ways to add protein foods from underconsumed food groups and subgroups in order to ensure that overall protein needs are met.

Vitamin B_{12}

Vitamin B_{12} is of concern for some older adults because the ability to absorb this nutrient can decrease with age and use of certain medications can decrease absorption. Older adults are encouraged to meet the recommendations for protein foods, a common source of vitamin B_{12}, and include foods fortified with vitamin B_{12}, such as breakfast cereals. Some individuals also may require vitamin B_{12} dietary supplements. Individuals are encouraged to speak with their healthcare provider to determine what, if any, supplementation is appropriate.

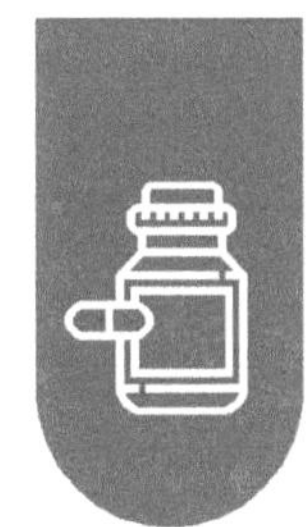

Dietary Supplements

Many adults in the United States take one or more dietary supplements either as a pill or drink. Popular supplements include some nutrients that are underconsumed among older adults, including calcium and vitamins D and B_{12}. All sources of a nutrient or food component—whether from food or a dietary supplement—should be considered when assessing an individual's dietary pattern, including any added sugars that may come from supplement drinks. Older adults should track and discuss all dietary supplement use with their healthcare provider. Beverage supplements should not replace regular food intake unless instructed by a health professional. The National Institutes of Health, Office of Dietary Supplements provides the **My Dietary Supplement and Medicine Record**[1], to help individuals track supplement and medicine use.

[1] Available at: **ods.od.nih.gov/pubs/DietarySupplementandMedicineRecord.pdf**

ADULTS AGES 60 AND OLDER

Beverages

Many older adults do not drink enough fluids to stay hydrated. One reason for this is that the sensation of thirst tends to decline with age. Concerns about bladder control or issues with mobility also may hinder intake of fluids among older adults. Mean intakes of beverages show adults ages 60 and older consume significantly fewer fluid ounces across all beverage types compared to adults ages 59 and under—about 2 fewer cups per day, most of which is due to drinking less water.

It is important that older adults drink plenty of water to prevent dehydration and aid in the digestion of food and absorption of nutrients. In addition to water, choosing unsweetened beverages such as 100% fruit or vegetable juice and low-fat or fat-free milk or fortified soy beverage can support fluid intake to prevent dehydration while helping to achieve food group recommendations. The water that is contained in foods, such as fruits, vegetables, and soups, contributes to hydration status and is a contributor to total fluid intake.

ALCOHOLIC BEVERAGES

The *Dietary Guidelines* do not recommend initiating alcohol consumption for any reason. To help older adults move toward a healthy dietary pattern and minimize risks associated with drinking, older adults can choose not to drink or drink in moderation—limiting intakes to 2 drinks or less in a day for men and 1 drink or less in a day for women, when alcohol is consumed. Older adults who choose to drink may experience the effects of alcohol more quickly than they did when they were younger. This puts older adults at higher risk of falls, car crashes, and other injuries that may result from drinking. In addition, older adults tend to have a greater number of comorbid health conditions than younger adults, and alcohol use or misuse may adversely affect the condition or interfere with management of the disease. Certain older adults should avoid drinking alcohol completely, including those who:

- Plan to drive or operate machinery, or participate in activities that require skill, coordination, and alertness.
- Take certain over-the-counter or prescription medications.
- Have certain medical conditions.
- Are recovering from alcohol use disorder or are unable to control the amount they drink.
- More information on alcoholic beverages and their relationship to health is provided in ***Chapter 1***.

Supporting Healthy Eating

Similar to other life stages, older adults can be supported by professionals, family, and friends to achieve a healthy dietary pattern that accounts for factors such as cost, preferences, traditions, and access. Additional factors to consider when supporting healthy eating for older adults include:

- **Enjoyment of food:** Sharing meals with friends and family can help increase food enjoyment and promote adequacy of dietary intake for older adults.
- **Ability to chew or swallow foods:** Experimenting with the preparation of foods from all food groups can help identify textures that are acceptable, appealing, and enjoyable for adults who have difficulties chewing or swallowing. Good dental health is critical to overall health, as well as the ability to chew foods properly.
- **Food safety:** Practicing safe food handling procedures is of particular importance for older adults due to a decline in immune system function that accompanies age and that increases the risk of foodborne illness. For more information: **Foodsafety.gov** for older adults: **foodsafety.gov/people-at-risk/older-adults** or FDA: **fda.gov/media/83744/download**.

Older adults have access to a variety of Government resources to support a healthy dietary pattern as part of overall healthy aging. Professionals working with older Americans can use these resources to better support access to healthy, safe, and affordable food choices.

- **Congregate Nutrition Services:** The Older Americans Act authorizes meals and related services in congregate settings for any person age 60 and older and their spouse of any age. Program sites offer older individuals healthy meals and opportunities to socialize. Congregate meals are typically provided in senior centers, schools, churches, or other community settings.
- **Supplemental Nutrition Assistance Program (SNAP):** Older adults with limited income may qualify for SNAP, a Federal program that provides temporary benefits to help individuals purchase foods and beverages to support a healthy dietary pattern when resources are constrained.

Physical Activity and Older Adults

The benefits of regular physical activity occur throughout life and are essential for healthy aging. It is never too late to start being physically active. For older adults, regular physical activity supports a number of additional health benefits including improved cognition, balance, and bone strength. These benefits make it easier to perform activities of daily living, preserves function and mobility, and lowers the risk of falls and injuries from falls.

Adults should move more and sit less throughout the day. Some physical activity is better than none. To attain the most health benefits from physical activity, older adults need at least 150 to 300 minutes of moderate-intensity aerobic activity per week. The talk test is a good way to assess moderate intensity for older adults. A person doing moderate-intensity aerobic activity can talk, but not sing. Older adults also need muscle-strengthening activity at least 2 days each week. Older adults should incorporate multicomponent physical activity that includes balance training as well as aerobic and muscle-strengthening activities.

The U.S. Department of Health and Human Service's *Physical Activity Guidelines for Americans* and the related Move Your Way® resources have information about the benefits of physical activity and tips to get started. Available at **health.gov/paguidelines**.

- **Commodity Supplemental Food Program (CSFP):** The CSFP supplements the diets of low-income older adults by providing nutritious USDA packaged food to support a healthy dietary pattern. The CSFP is federally funded, and private and nonprofit institutions facilitate the distribution of monthly CSFP packages to eligible older adults.
- **Home-Delivered Nutrition Services:** The Older Americans Act authorizes meals and related services in a person's home for individuals ages 60 and older and their spouse of any age. Older adults who experience difficulty leaving the home due to frailty, health concerns, or certain medical conditions may benefit from home-delivered meals offered under the Older Americans Act.
- **Child and Adult Care Food Program (CACFP):** The CACFP is a Federal program that provides reimbursements for nutritious meals and snacks to older adults enrolled in daycare facilities. Older adults receiving care at nonresidential care centers may receive meals and snacks that meet nutrition standards of the CACFP.

Additional resources to support older adults exist at the community level. For example, the **Senior Farmers Market Nutrition Program (SFMNP)** provides many low-income seniors with access to fruits and vegetables grown in their local communities. **SNAP Education (SNAP-Ed)** programming may also be offered and teach older adults cooking and shopping skills. Individuals working within these settings must ensure the availability of nutrient-dense foods and assist older adults in choosing a healthy dietary pattern that fits in their cultural and food preferences.

Healthy Eating Through the Lifespan

This chapter has focused on the unique nutritional considerations of the older adult life stage. It also has reinforced the idea that the core elements of a healthy dietary pattern are remarkably consistent across the lifespan and across health outcomes. More than that, a healthy dietary pattern is flexible—people can customize the *Dietary Guidelines* recommendations to suit their personal preferences, cultural traditions, and budget considerations.

Beginning at the earliest life stage—infancy and toddlerhood—a healthy dietary pattern can help people achieve and maintain good health and reduce the risk of chronic diseases. However, it is never too late to make improvements. People at any stage of life can benefit by changing to nutrient-dense forms of foods and beverages across all food groups, in recommended amounts, and within calorie limits. **The bottom line: For lifelong good health, make every bite count with the *Dietary Guidelines for Americans*!**

Appendix 1:

Nutritional Goals[a] for Age-Sex Groups

Table A1-1

Daily Nutritional Goals, Ages 6 Through 11 Months and 12 Through 23 Months

Nutrient	6 Through 11 Months		12 Through 23 Months	
	Goal	Source of Goal[b]	Goal	Source of Goal[b]
Macronutrients				
Protein (g)	11	RDA	13	RDA
Carbohydrate (g)	95	AI	130	RDA
Fiber, total dietary (g)	n/a[d]	n/a[d]	19	AI
Total lipid (% kcal)	n/a[d]	n/a[d]	30-40	AMDR
18:2 Linoleic acid (g)	4.6	AI	7	AI
18:3 Linolenic acid (g)	0.5	AI	0.7	AI
Minerals				
Calcium (mg)	260	AI	700	RDA
Iron (mg)	11	RDA	7	RDA
Magnesium (mg)	75	AI	80	RDA
Phosphorus (mg)	275	AI	460	RDA
Potassium (mg)	860	AI	2,000	AI
Sodium (mg)	370	AI	1,200	CDRR
Zinc (mg)	3	RDA	3	RDA
Vitamins				
Vitamin A (mcg RAE[c])	500	AI	300	RDA
Vitamin E (mg AT[c])	5	AI	6	RDA
Vitamin D (IU[c])	400	AI	600	RDA
Vitamin C (mg)	50	AI	15	RDA
Thiamin (mg)	0.3	AI	0.5	RDA
Riboflavin (mg)	0.4	AI	0.5	RDA
Niacin (mg)	4	AI	6	RDA

Table A1-1 (continued)

Daily Nutritional Goals, Ages 6 Through 11 Months and 12 Through 23 Months

Nutrient	6 Through 11 Months		12 Through 23 Months	
	Goal	Source of Goal[b]	Goal	Source of Goal[b]
Vitamin B-6 (mg)	0.3	AI	0.5	RDA
Vitamin B-12 (mcg)	0.5	AI	0.9	RDA
Choline (mg)	150	AI	200	AI
Vitamin K (mcg)	2.5	AI	30	AI
Folate (mcg DFE[c])	80	AI	150	RDA

[a] Goals reflect Dietary Reference Intakes developed for 7 to 12 months or 6 to 12 months applied to ages 6 to 12 months and DRIs for 1 to 3 years applied to 12 to 24 months.

[b] AI = Adequate Intake, CDRR = Chronic Disease Risk Reduction Level, RDA = Recommended Dietary Allowance.

[c] AT = alpha-tocopherol, DFE = Dietary Folate Equivalent, IU = International Units, RAE = Retinol Activity Equivalents.

[d] n/a = not applicable to this age group.

Sources: Institute of Medicine. *Dietary Reference Intakes: The Essential Guide to Nutrient Requirements.* Washington, DC: The National Academies Press; 2006. Institute of Medicine. *Dietary Reference Intakes for Calcium and Vitamin D.* Washington, DC: The National Academies Press; 2011. National Academies of Sciences, Engineering, and Medicine. *Dietary Reference Intakes for Sodium and Potassium.* Washington, DC: The National Academies Press; 2019.

Table A1-2

Daily Nutritional Goals, Ages 2 and Older

MACRONUTRIENTS, MINERALS & VITAMINS		Age-Sex Groups												
		M/F 2-3	F 4-8	F 9-13	F 14-18	F 19-30	F 31-50	F 51+	M 4-8	M 9-13	M 14-18	M 19-30	M 31-50	M 51+
Calorie Level Assessed	**Source of Goal**[a]	1,000	1,200	1,600	1,800	2,000	1,800	1,600	1,400	1,800	2,200	2,400	2,200	2,000
Macronutrients														
Protein (% kcal)	AMDR	5-20	10-30	10-30	10-30	10-35	10-35	10-35	10-30	10-30	10-30	10-35	10-35	10-35
Protein (g)	RDA	13	19	34	46	46	46	46	19	34	52	56	56	56
Carbohydrate (% kcal)	AMDR	45-65	45-65	45-65	45-65	45-65	45-65	45-65	45-65	45-65	45-65	45-65	45-65	45-65
Carbohydrate (g)	RDA	130	130	130	130	130	130	130	130	130	130	130	130	130
Fiber (g)	14g/ 1,000 kcal	14	17	22	25	28	25	22	20	25	31	34	31	28
Added Sugars (% kcal)	DGA	<10	<10	<10	<10	<10	<10	<10	<10	<10	<10	<10	<10	<10
Total lipid (% kcal)	AMDR	30-40	25-35	25-35	25-35	20-35	20-35	20-35	25-35	25-35	25-35	20-35	20-35	20-35
Saturated Fatty Acids (% kcal)	DGA	<10	<10	<10	<10	<10	<10	<10	<10	<10	<10	<10	<10	<10
18:2 Linoleic acid (g)	AI	7	10	10	11	12	12	11	10	12	16	17	17	14
18:3 Linoleic acid (g)	AI	0.7	0.9	1.0	1.1	1.1	1.1	1.1	0.9	1.2	1.6	1.6	1.6	1.6
Minerals														
Calcium (mg)	RDA	700	1,000	1,300	1,300	1,000	1,000	1,200	1,000	1,300	1,300	1,000	1,000	1,000[b]
Iron (mg)	RDA	7	10	8	15	18	18	8	10	8	11	8	8	8
Magnesium (mg)	RDA	80	130	240	360	310	320	320	130	240	410	400	420	420
Phosphorus (mg)	RDA	460	500	1,250	1,250	700	700	700	500	1,250	1,250	700	700	700
Potassium (mg)	AI	2,000	2,300	2,300	2,300	2,600	2,600	2,600	2,300	2,500	3,000	3,400	3,400	3,400
Sodium (mg)	CDRR	1,200	1,500	1,800	2,300	2,300	2,300	2,300	1,500	1,800	2,300	2,300	2,300	2,300
Zinc (mg)	RDA	3	5	8	9	8	8	8	5	8	11	11	11	11

Table A1-2 (continued)

Daily Nutritional Goals, Ages 2 and Older

MACRONUTRIENTS, MINERALS & VITAMINS		Age-Sex Groups												
		M/F 2-3	F 4-8	F 9-13	F 14-18	F 19-30	F 31-50	F 51+	M 4-8	M 9-13	M 14-18	M 19-30	M 31-50	M 51+
Calorie Level Assessed	**Source of Goal**[a]	1,000	1,200	1,600	1,800	2,000	1,800	1,600	1,400	1,800	2,200	2,400	2,200	2,000
Vitamins														
Vitamin A (mcg RAE[d]**)**	RDA	300	400	600	700	700	700	700	400	600	900	900	900	900
Vitamin E (mg AT[d]**)**	RDA	6	7	11	15	15	15	15	7	11	15	15	15	15
Vitamin D (IU[d]**)**	RDA	600	600	600	600	600	600	600[c]	600	600	600	600	600	600[c]
Vitamin C (mg)	RDA	15	25	45	65	75	75	75	25	45	75	90	90	90
Thiamin (mg)	RDA	0.5	0.6	0.9	1.0	1.1	1.1	1.1	0.6	0.9	1.2	1.2	1.2	1.2
Riboflavin (mg)	RDA	0.5	0.6	0.9	1.0	1.1	1.1	1.1	0.6	0.9	1.3	1.3	1.3	1.3
Niacin (mg)	RDA	6	8	12	14	14	14	14	8	12	16	16	16	16
Vitamin B-6 (mg)	RDA	0.5	0.6	1.0	1.2	1.3	1.3	1.5	0.6	1.0	1.3	1.3	1.3	1.7
Vitamin B-12 (mcg)	RDA	0.9	1.2	1.8	2.4	2.4	2.4	2.4	1.2	1.8	2.4	2.4	2.4	2.4
Choline (mg)	AI	200	250	375	400	425	425	425	250	375	550	550	550	550
Vitamin K (mcg)	AI	30	55	60	75	90	90	90	55	60	75	120	120	120
Folate (mcg DFE[d]**)**	RDA	150	200	300	400	400	400	400	200	300	400	400	400	400

[a] AI = Adequate Intake, CDRR = Chronic Disease Risk Reduction Level, DGA = *Dietary Guidelines for Americans, 2020-2025*, RDA = Recommended Dietary Allowance.

[b] Calcium RDA for males ages 71+ years is 1,200 mg.

[c] Vitamin D RDA for males and females ages 71+ years is 800 IU.

[d] AT = alpha-tocopherol, DFE = Dietary Folate Equivalent, IU = International Units, RAE = Retinol Activity Equivalents.

Sources: Institute of Medicine. *Dietary Reference Intakes: The Essential Guide to Nutrient Requirements.* Washington, DC: The National Academies Press; 2006. Institute of Medicine. *Dietary Reference Intakes for Calcium and Vitamin D.* Washington, DC: The National Academies Press; 2011. National Academies of Sciences, Engineering, and Medicine. *Dietary Reference Intakes for Sodium and Potassium.* Washington, DC: The National Academies Press; 2019.

Table A1-3

Daily Nutritional Goals for Women Who Are Pregnant, by Age Group and Trimester

MACRONUTRIENTS, MINERALS & VITAMINS		Age Group (Years)								
		14-18			19-30			31-50		
		Trimester								
		1st	2nd	3rd	1st	2nd	3rd	1st	2nd	3rd
Calorie Level Assessed	**Source of Goal[a]**	1,800	2,200	2,400	2,000	2,400	2,600	1,800	2,200	2,400
Macronutrients										
Protein (% kcal)	AMDR	10-30	10-30	10-30	10-35	10-35	10-35	10-35	10-35	10-35
Protein (g)	RDA	71	71	71	71	71	71	71	71	71
Carbohydrate (%kcal)	AMDR	45-65	45-65	45-65	45-65	45-65	45-65	45-65	45-65	45-65
Carbohydrate (g)	RDA	175	175	175	175	175	175	175	175	175
Fiber (g)	14g/ 1,000 kcal	25	31	34	28	34	36	25	31	34
Added Sugars (% kcal)	DGA	<10	<10	<10	<10	<10	<10	<10	<10	<10
Total lipid (% kcal)	AMDR	25-35	25-35	25-35	20-35	20-35	20-35	20-35	20-35	20-35
Saturated Fatty Acids (% kcal)	DGA	<10	<10	<10	<10	<10	<10	<10	<10	<10
18:2 Linoleic acid (g)	AI	13	13	13	13	13	13	13	13	13
18:3 Linolenic acid (g)	AI	1.4	1.4	1.4	1.4	1.4	1.4	1.4	1.4	1.4
Minerals										
Calcium (mg)	RDA	1,300	1,300	1,300	1,000	1,000	1,000	1,000	1,000	1,000
Iron (mg)	RDA	27	27	27	27	27	27	27	27	27
Magnesium (mg)	RDA	400	400	400	350	350	350	360	360	360
Phosphorus (mg)	RDA	1,250	1,250	1,250	700	700	700	700	700	700
Potassium (mg)	AI	2,600	2,600	2,600	2,900	2,900	2,900	2,900	2,900	2,900
Sodium (mg)	CDRR	2,300	2,300	2,300	2,300	2,300	2,300	2,300	2,300	2,300
Zinc (mg)	RDA	12	12	12	11	11	11	11	11	11
Iodine (mcg)	RDA	220	220	220	220	220	220	220	220	220
Vitamins										
Vitamin A (mcg RAE[b])	RDA	750	750	750	770	770	770	770	770	770
Vitamin E (mg AT[b])	RDA	15	15	15	15	15	15	15	15	15
Vitamin D (IU[b])	RDA	600	600	600	600	600	600	600	600	600

Table A1-3 (continued)

Daily Nutritional Goals for Women Who Are Pregnant, by Age Group and Trimester

MACRONUTRIENTS, MINERALS & VITAMINS		Age Group (Years)								
		14-18			19-30			31-50		
		Trimester								
		1st	2nd	3rd	1st	2nd	3rd	1st	2nd	3rd
Calorie Level Assessed	**Source of Goal[a]**	1,800	2,200	2,400	2,000	2,400	2,600	1,800	2,200	2,400
Vitamins										
Vitamin C (mg)	RDA	80	80	80	85	85	85	85	85	85
Thiamin (mg)	RDA	1.4	1.4	1.4	1.4	1.4	1.4	1.4	1.4	1.4
Riboflavin (mg)	RDA	1.4	1.4	1.4	1.4	1.4	1.4	1.4	1.4	1.4
Niacin (mg)	RDA	18	18	18	18	18	18	18	18	18
Vitamin B-6 (mg)	RDA	1.9	1.9	1.9	1.9	1.9	1.9	1.9	1.9	1.9
Vitamin B-12 (mcg)	RDA	2.6	2.6	2.6	2.6	2.6	2.6	2.6	2.6	2.6
Choline (mg)	AI	450	450	450	450	450	450	450	450	450
Vitamin K (mcg)	AI	75	75	75	90	90	90	90	90	90
Folate (mcg DFE[b])	RDA	600	600	600	600	600	600	600	600	600

[a] AI = Adequate Intake, CDRR = Chronic Disease Risk Reduction Level, DGA = *Dietary Guidelines for Americans, 2020-2025* , RDA = Recommended Dietary Allowance.

[b] AT = alpha-tocopherol, DFE = Dietary Folate Equivalent, IU= International Units, RAE = Retinol Activity Equivalents.

Sources: Institute of Medicine. *Dietary Reference Intakes: The Essential Guide to Nutrient Requirements.* Washington, DC: The National Academies Press; 2006. Institute of Medicine. *Dietary Reference Intakes for Calcium and Vitamin D.* Washington, DC: The National Academies Press; 2011. National Academies of Sciences, Engineering, and Medicine. *Dietary Reference Intakes for Sodium and Potassium.* Washington, DC: The National Academies Press; 2019.

Table A1-4

Daily Nutritional Goals for Women Who Are Lactating, by Age Group and Months Postpartum

MACRONUTRIENTS, MINERALS & VITAMINS		Age Group (Years)					
		14-18		19-30		31-50	
		Months Postpartum					
		0-6	7-12	0-6	7-12	0-6	7-12
Calorie Level Assessed	Source of Goal[a]	2,200	2,200	2,400	2,400	2,200	2,200
Macronutrients							
Protein (% kcal)	AMDR	10-30	10-30	10-35	10-35	10-35	10-35
Protein (g)	RDA	71	71	71	71	71	71
Carbohydrate (% kcal)	AMDR	45-65	45-65	45-65	45-65	45-65	45-65
Carbohydrate (g)	RDA	210	210	210	210	210	210
Fiber (g)	14g/1,000kcal	31	31	34	34	31	31
Added sugars (% kcals)	DGA	<10	<10	<10	<10	<10	<10
Total lipid (% kcal)	AMDR	25-35	25-35	20-35	20-35	20-35	20-35
Saturated Fatty Acids (% kcal)	DGA	<10	<10	<10	<10	<10	<10
18:2 Linoleic acid (g)	AI	13	13	13	13	13	13
18:3 Linolenic acid (g)	AI	1.3	1.3	1.3	1.3	1.3	1.3
Minerals							
Calcium (mg)	RDA	1,300	1,300	1,000	1,000	1,000	1,000
Iron (mg)	RDA	10	10	9	9	9	9
Magnesium (mg)	RDA	360	360	310	310	320	320
Phosphorus (mg)	RDA	1,250	1,250	700	700	700	700
Potassium (mg)	AI	2,500	2,500	2,800	2,800	2,800	2,800
Sodium (mg)	CDRR	2,300	2,300	2,300	2,300	2,300	2,300
Zinc (mg)	RDA	13	13	12	12	12	12
Iodine (mcg)	RDA	290	290	290	290	290	290

Table A1-4 (continued)

Daily Nutritional Goals for Women Who Are Lactating, by Age Group and Months Postpartum

MACRONUTRIENTS, MINERALS & VITAMINS		Age Group (Years)					
		14-18		19-30		31-50	
		Months Postpartum					
		0-6	7-12	0-6	7-12	0-6	7-12
Calorie Level Assessed	**Source of Goal[a]**	2,200	2,200	2,400	2,400	2,200	2,200
Vitamins							
Vitamin A (mcg RAE[b])	RDA	1,200	1,200	1,300	1,300	1,300	1,300
Vitamin E (mg AT[b])	RDA	19	19	19	19	19	19
Vitamin D (IU[b])	RDA	600	600	600	600	600	600
Vitamin C (mg)	RDA	115	115	120	120	120	120
Thiamin (mg)	RDA	1.4	1.4	1.4	1.4	1.4	1.4
Riboflavin (mg)	RDA	1.6	1.6	1.6	1.6	1.6	1.6
Niacin (mg)	RDA	17	17	17	17	17	17
Vitamin B-6 (mg)	RDA	2	2	2	2	2	2
Vitamin B-12 (mcg)	RDA	2.8	2.8	2.8	2.8	2.8	2.8
Choline (mg)	AI	550	550	550	550	550	550
Vitamin K (mcg)	AI	75	75	90	90	90	90
Folate (mcg DFE[b])	RDA	500	500	500	500	500	500

[a] AI = Adequate Intake, CDRR = Chronic Disease Risk Reduction Level, DGA = *Dietary Guidelines for Americans, 2020-2025*, RDA = Recommended Dietary Allowance.

[b] AT = alpha-tocopherol, DFE = Dietary Folate Equivalent, IU= International Units, RAE = Retinal Activity Equivalents.

Sources: Institute of Medicine. *Dietary Reference Intakes: The Essential Guide to Nutrient Requirements.* Washington, DC: The National Academies Press; 2006. Institute of Medicine. *Dietary Reference Intakes for Calcium and Vitamin D.* Washington, DC: The National Academies Press; 2011. National Academies of Sciences, Engineering, and Medicine. *Dietary Reference Intakes for Sodium and Potassium.* Washington, DC: The National Academies Press; 2019.

Appendix 2:
Estimated Calorie Needs

The total number of calories a person needs each day varies depending on the person's age, sex, height, weight, and level of physical activity. In addition, a need to lose, maintain, or gain weight, and other factors affect how many calories should be consumed. Estimated amounts of calories needed to maintain energy balance for various age and sex groups at three different levels of physical activity are provided in **Table A2-1** for toddlers ages 12 through 23 months and **Table A2-2** for ages 2 and older. These estimates are based on the Estimated Energy Requirements (EER) equations, using reference heights (average) and reference weights (healthy) for each age-sex group. For toddlers, children, and adolescents, reference height and weight vary by age. For adults, the reference man is 5 feet 10 inches tall and weighs 154 pounds. The reference woman is 5 feet 4 inches tall and weighs 126 pounds.

Estimates range from 700 to 1,000 calories for toddlers ages 12 through 23 months. Estimated needs for young children ages 2 through 8 range from 1,000 to 2,000 calories. A wider range of 1,400 to 3,200 calories is estimated for older children and adolescents, with males generally having higher calorie needs than females.

Adult estimated calorie needs range from 1,600 to 2,400 calories per day for females and 2,000 to 3,000 calories per day for males. As shown, males generally require more calories than females. Due to reductions in basal metabolic rate that occur with aging, calorie needs generally decrease for adults as they age.

Estimated calorie needs during the first trimester of pregnancy generally do not increase compared to prepregnancy needs. Additional calories needed for the later trimesters of pregnancy and during lactation are outlined in **Table A2-3** and include approximately 300 to 400 additional calories. It is recommended that women follow their healthcare provider's guidance regarding appropriate caloric intake during pregnancy as many factors, including prepregnancy weight status, gestational weight gain, and multiple pregnancies, may affect calorie needs. Women with overweight or obesity have lower recommended gestational weight gain during pregnancy, which may affect calorie needs.

These calorie needs are only estimates, and approximations of individual calorie needs can be determined with online tools. The DRI Calculator for Healthcare Professionals, available at **nal.usda.gov/fnic/dri-calculator**, can be used to estimate calorie needs based on age, sex, height, weight, activity level, and pregnancy or lactation status.

Table A2-1
Estimated Calorie Needs per Day, by Age and Sex, Ages 12 Through 23 Months

AGE IN MONTHS	Males	Females
12	800	800
15	900	800
18	1,000	900
21 through 23	1,000	1,000

Source: Institute of Medicine. *Dietary Reference Intakes for Energy, Carbohydrate, Fiber, Fat, Fatty Acids, Cholesterol, Protein, and Amino Acids.* Washington (DC): The National Academies Press; 2002.

Table A2-2

Estimated Calorie Needs per Day, by Age, Sex, and Physical Activity Level, Ages 2 and Older

AGE	Males			Females		
	Sedentary[a]	Moderately Active[b]	Active[c]	Sedentary[a]	Moderately Active[b]	Active[c]
2	1,000	1,000	1,000	1,000	1,000	1,000
3	1,000	1,400	1,400	1,000	1,200	1,400
4	1,200	1,400	1,600	1,200	1,400	1,400
5	1,200	1,400	1,600	1,200	1,400	1,600
6	1,400	1,600	1,800	1,200	1,400	1,600
7	1,400	1,600	1,800	1,200	1,600	1,800
8	1,400	1,600	2,000	1,400	1,600	1,800
9	1,600	1,800	2,000	1,400	1,600	1,800
10	1,600	1,800	2,200	1,400	1,800	2,000
11	1,800	2,000	2,200	1,600	1,800	2,000
12	1,800	2,200	2,400	1,600	2,000	2,200
13	2,000	2,200	2,600	1,600	2,000	2,200
14	2,000	2,400	2,800	1,800	2,000	2,400
15	2,200	2,600	3,000	1,800	2,000	2,400
16	2,400	2,800	3,200	1,800	2,000	2,400
17	2,400	2,800	3,200	1,800	2,000	2,400
18	2,400	2,800	3,200	1,800	2,000	2,400
19-20	2,600	2,800	3,000	2,000	2,200	2,400
21-25	2,400	2,800	3,000	2,000	2,200	2,400
26-30	2,400	2,600	3,000	1,800	2,000	2,400
31-35	2,400	2,600	3,000	1,800	2,000	2,200
36-40	2,400	2,600	2,800	1,800	2,000	2,200
41-45	2,200	2,600	2,800	1,800	2,000	2,200
46-50	2,200	2,400	2,800	1,800	2,000	2,200
51-55	2,200	2,400	2,800	1,600	1,800	2,200
56-60	2,200	2,400	2,600	1,600	1,800	2,200

Table A2-2 (continued)

Estimated Calorie Needs per Day, by Age, Sex, and Physical Activity Level, Ages 2 and Older

AGE	Males			Females		
	Sedentary[a]	Moderately Active[b]	Active[c]	Sedentary[a]	Moderately Active[b]	Active[c]
61-65	2,000	2,400	2,600	1,600	1,800	2,000
66-70	2,000	2,200	2,600	1,600	1,800	2,000
71-75	2,000	2,200	2,600	1,600	1,800	2,000
76 and up	2,000	2,200	2,400	1,600	1,800	2,000

[a] Sedentary means a lifestyle that includes only the physical activity of independent living.

[b] Moderately Active means a lifestyle that includes physical activity equivalent to walking about 1.5 to 3 miles per day at 3 to 4 miles per hour, in addition to the activities of independent living.

[c] Active means a lifestyle that includes physical activity equivalent to walking more than 3 miles per day at 3 to 4 miles per hour, in addition to the activities of independent living.

Source: Institute of Medicine. *Dietary Reference Intakes for Energy, Carbohydrate, Fiber, Fat, Fatty Acids, Cholesterol, Protein, and Amino Acids.* Washington (DC): The National Academies Press; 2002.

Table A2-3

Estimated Change in Calorie Needs During Pregnancy and Lactation for Women With a Healthy[a] Prepregnancy Weight

STAGE OF PREGNANCY OR LACTATION	Estimated Change in Daily Calorie Needs Compared to Prepregnancy Needs
Pregnancy: 1st trimester	+ 0 calories
Pregnancy: 2nd trimester	+ 340 calories
Pregnancy: 3rd trimester	+ 452 calories
Lactation: 1st 6 months	+ 330 calories[b]
Lactation: 2nd 6 months	+ 400 calories[c]

[a] These estimates apply to women with a healthy prepregnancy weight. Women with a prepregnancy weight that is considered overweight or obese should consult their healthcare provider for guidance regarding appropriate caloric intake during pregnancy and lactation.

[b] The EER for the first 6 months of lactation is calculated by adding 500 calories/day to prepregnancy needs to account for the energy needed for milk production during this time period, then subtracting 170 calories/day to account for weight loss in the first 6 months postpartum.

[c] The EER for the second 6 months of lactation is calculated by adding 400 calories/day to prepregnancy needs to account for the energy needed for milk production during this time period. Weight stability is assumed after 6 months postpartum.

Note: Estimates are based on Estimated Energy Requirements (EER) set by the Institute of Medicine. Source: Institute of Medicine. *Dietary Reference Intakes for Energy, Carbohydrate, Fiber, Fat, Fatty Acids, Cholesterol, Protein, and Amino Acids.* Washington, DC: The National Academies Press; 2005.

Appendix 3:
USDA Dietary Patterns

The Healthy U.S.-Style Dietary Pattern (**Tables A3-1** and **A3-2**) is based on the types and proportions of foods Americans typically consume but in nutrient-dense forms and appropriate amounts. The Healthy Vegetarian Dietary Pattern (**Tables A3-3** and **A3-4**) and the Healthy Mediterranean-Style Dietary Pattern (**Table A3-5**) are variations that also exemplify a healthy dietary pattern. For the first time, the Healthy U.S.-Style and Healthy Vegetarian Dietary Patterns are provided for toddlers ages 12 through 23 months who are no longer receiving human milk or infant formula. These patterns are designed to meet nutrient needs while not exceeding calorie requirements and while staying within limits for overconsumed dietary components, such as added sugars, saturated fat, and sodium.

The methodology used to develop and update these Patterns builds on the rich history USDA has in developing food guides. This methodology includes using current food consumption data to determine the mix and proportions of foods to include in each group. Food composition data is used to select a nutrient-dense representative for each food and calculate nutrient profiles for each food group. As would be expected, most foods in their nutrient-dense forms do contain some sodium and saturated fat. In a few cases, such as in the case of whole-wheat bread, the most appropriate representative in current Federal databases contains a small amount of added sugars. Detailed information about the representative foods, nutrient profiles, and patterns is available in the online appendix of the *Scientific Report of the 2020 Dietary Guidelines Advisory Committee.*[1]

Amounts of each food group and subgroup within the patterns are based on nutrient and *Dietary Guidelines* standards (see ***Appendix 1. Nutritional Goals for Age-Sex Groups***). Standards for nutrient adequacy aim to meet the Recommended Dietary Allowances (RDA), which are designed to cover the needs of 97 percent of the population, and Adequate Intakes (AI), which are used when an average nutrient requirement cannot be determined. The Patterns meet these standards for almost all nutrients. For a few nutrients (vitamin D and vitamin E for all ages, and choline for ages 2 and older), amounts in the Patterns are marginal or below the RDA or AI standard for many or all age/sex groups. In most cases, an intake of these nutrients below the RDA or AI is not considered to be of public health concern. For more information on dietary components of public health concern, see ***Chapter 1***.

The Patterns have 12 calorie levels to meet the needs of individuals across the lifespan ages 2 and older. For toddlers ages 12 through 23 months, who are no longer receiving either human milk or infant formula, the Patterns are provided at 4 calorie levels. ***Chapters 2***, ***3***, ***4***, ***5***, and ***6*** describe healthy dietary patterns and relevant calorie levels for each life stage. To follow these Patterns, identify the appropriate calorie level, choose a variety of foods in each group and subgroup over time in recommended amounts, and limit choices that are not in nutrient-dense forms so that the overall calorie limit is not exceeded.

[1] Available at: **dietaryguidelines.gov/2020-advisory-committee-report/food-pattern-modeling**

Table A3-1

Healthy U.S.-Style Dietary Pattern for Toddlers Ages 12 Through 23 Months Who Are No Longer Receiving Human Milk or Infant Formula, With Daily or Weekly Amounts From Food Groups, Subgroups, and Components

CALORIE LEVEL OF PATTERN[a]	700	800	900	1,000
FOOD GROUP OR SUBGROUP[b,c]	**Daily Amount of Food From Each Group[d]** (Vegetable and protein foods subgroup amounts are per week.)			
Vegetables (cup eq/day)	**⅔**	**¾**	**1**	**1**
	Vegetable Subgroups in Weekly Amounts			
Dark-Green Vegetables (cup eq/wk)	1	⅓	½	½
Red and Orange Vegetables (cup eq/wk)	1	1 ¾	2 ½	2 ½
Beans, Peas, Lentils (cup eq/wk)	¾	⅓	½	½
Starchy Vegetables (cup eq/wk)	1	1 ½	2	2
Other Vegetables (cup eq/wk)	¾	1 ¼	1 ½	1 ½
Fruits (cup eq/day)	**½**	**¾**	**1**	**1**
Grains (ounce eq/day)	**1 ¾**	**2 ¼**	**2 ½**	**3**
Whole Grains (ounce eq/day)	1 ½	2	2	2
Refined Grains (ounce eq/day)	¼	¼	½	1
Dairy (cup eq/day)	**1 ⅔**	**1 ¾**	**2**	**2**
Protein Foods (ounce eq/day)	**2**	**2**	**2**	**2**
	Protein Foods Subgroups in Weekly Amounts			
Meats, Poultry (ounce eq/wk)	8 ¾	7	7	7 ¾
Eggs (ounce eq/wk)	2	2 ¾	2 ¼	2 ¼
Seafood (ounce eq/wk)[e]	2-3	2-3	2-3	2-3
Nuts, Seeds, Soy Products (ounce eq/wk)	1	1	1 ¼	1 ¼
Oils (grams/day)	**9**	**9**	**8**	**13**

[a] Calorie level ranges: Energy levels are calculated based on median length and body weight reference individuals. Calorie needs vary based on many factors. The DRI Calculator for Healthcare Professionals available at **nal.usda.gov/fnic/dri-calculator/** can be used to estimate calorie needs based on age, sex, and weight.

[b] Definitions for each food group and subgroup and quantity (i.e., cup or ounce equivalents) are provided in ***Chapter 1*** and are compiled in **Table A3-2 (footnote c).**

[c] All foods are assumed to be in nutrient-dense forms and prepared with minimal added sugars, refined starches (which are a source of calories but few or no other nutrients), or sodium. Food are also lean or in low-fat forms with the exception of dairy, which includes whole-fat fluid milk, reduced-fat plain yogurts, and reduced-fat cheese. There are no calories available for additional added sugars, saturated fat, or to eat more than the recommended amount of food in a food group.

[d] In some cases, food subgroup amounts are greatest at the lower calorie levels to help achieve nutrient adequacy when relatively small number of calories are required.

[e] **If consuming up to 2 ounces of seafood per week**, children should only be fed cooked varieties from the "Best Choices" list in the U.S. Food and Drug Administration (FDA) and the U.S. Environmental Protection Agency (EPA) joint "Advice About Eating Fish," available at **FDA.gov/fishadvice** and **EPA.gov/fishadvice**. **If consuming up to 3 ounces of seafood per week**, children should only be fed cooked varieties from the "Best Choices" list that contain even lower methylmercury: flatfish (e.g., flounder), salmon, tilapia, shrimp, catfish, crab, trout, haddock, oysters,

Table A3-1 Footnotes (continued)

sardines, squid, pollock, anchovies, crawfish, mullet, scallops, whiting, clams, shad, and Atlantic mackerel. If consuming up to 3 ounces of seafood per week, many commonly consumed varieties of seafood should be avoided because they cannot be consumed at 3 ounces per week by children without the potential of exceeding safe methylmercury limits; examples that should not be consumed include: canned light tuna or white (albacore) tuna, cod, perch, black sea bass. For a complete list please see: **FDA.gov/fishadvice** and **EPA.gov/fishadvice**.

Table A3-2

Healthy U.S.-Style Dietary Pattern for Ages 2 and Older, With Daily or Weekly Amounts From Food Groups, Subgroups, and Components

CALORIE LEVEL OF PATTERN[a]	1,000	1,200	1,400	1,600	1,800	2,000	2,200	2,400	2,600	2,800	3,000	3,200
FOOD GROUP OR SUBGROUP[b]	**Daily Amount[c] of Food From Each Group** (Vegetable and protein foods subgroup amounts are per week.)											
Vegetables (cup eq/day)	**1**	**1 ½**	**1 ½**	**2**	**2 ½**	**2 ½**	**3**	**3**	**3 ½**	**3 ½**	**4**	**4**
	Vegetable Subgroups in Weekly Amounts											
Dark-Green Vegetables (cup eq/wk)	½	1	1	1 ½	1 ½	1 ½	2	2	2 ½	2 ½	2 ½	2 ½
Red and Orange Vegetables (cup eq/wk)	2 ½	3	3	4	5 ½	5 ½	6	6	7	7	7½	7½
Beans, Peas, Lentils (cup eq/wk)	½	½	½	1	1½	1½	2	2	2 ½	2 ½	3	3
Starchy Vegetables (cup eq/wk)	2	3 ½	3 ½	4	5	5	6	6	7	7	8	8
Other Vegetables (cup eq/wk)	1 ½	2 ½	2 ½	3 ½	4	4	5	5	5 ½	5 ½	7	7
Fruits (cup eq/day)	**1**	**1**	**1 ½**	**1 ½**	**1 ½**	**2**	**2**	**2**	**2**	**2 ½**	**2 ½**	**2 ½**
Grains (ounce eq/day)	**3**	**4**	**5**	**5**	**6**	**6**	**7**	**8**	**9**	**10**	**10**	**10**
Whole Grains (ounce eq/day)[d]	1 ½	2	2 ½	3	3	3	3 ½	4	4 ½	5	5	5
Refined Grains (ounce eq/day)	1 ½	2	2 ½	2	3	3	3 ½	4	4 ½	5	5	5
Dairy (cup eq/day)	**2**	**2 ½**	**2 ½**	**3**	**3**	**3**	**3**	**3**	**3**	**3**	**3**	**3**
Protein Foods (ounce eq/day)	**2**	**3**	**4**	**5**	**5**	**5 ½**	**6**	**6 ½**	**6 ½**	**7**	**7**	**7**
	Protein Foods Subgroups in Weekly Amounts											
Meats, Poultry, Eggs (ounce eq/wk)	10	14	19	23	23	26	28	31	31	33	33	33
Seafood (ounce eq/wk)[e]	2-3[f]	4	6	8	8	8	9	10	10	10	10	10
Nuts, Seeds, Soy Products (ounce eq/wk)	2	2	3	4	4	5	5	5	5	6	6	6
Oils (grams/day)	**15**	**17**	**17**	**22**	**24**	**27**	**29**	**31**	**34**	**36**	**44**	**51**
Limit on Calories for Other Uses (kcal/day)[g]	**130**	**80**	**90**	**100**	**140**	**240**	**250**	**320**	**350**	**370**	**440**	**580**
Limit on Calories for Other Uses (%/day)	13%	7%	6%	6%	8%	12%	11%	13%	13%	13%	15%	18%

[a] Patterns at 1,000, 1,200, and 1,400 kcal levels are designed to meet the nutritional needs of children ages 2 through 8 years. Patterns from 1,600 to 3,200 kcal are designed to meet the nutritional needs of children 9 years and older and adults. If a child 4 through 8 years of age needs more energy and, therefore, is following a pattern at 1,600 calories or more, his/her recommended amount from the dairy group should be 2½ cup eq per day. Amount of dairy for children ages 9 through 18 is 3 cup eq per day regardless of calorie level. The 1,000 and 1,200 kcal level patterns are not intended for children 9 and older or adults. The 1,400 kcal level is not intended for children ages 10 and older or adults.

Table A3-2 Footnotes (continued)

[b] Foods in each group and subgroup are:

Vegetables

Dark-Green Vegetables: All fresh, frozen, and canned dark-green leafy vegetables and broccoli, cooked or raw: for example, amaranth leaves, basil, beet greens, bitter melon leaves, bok choy, broccoli, chamnamul, chrysanthemum leaves, chard, cilantro, collards, cress, dandelion greens, kale, lambsquarters, mustard greens, poke greens, romaine lettuce, spinach, nettles, taro leaves, turnip greens, and watercress.

Red and Orange Vegetables: All fresh, frozen, and canned red and orange vegetables or juice, cooked or raw: for example, calabaza, carrots, red chili peppers, red or orange bell peppers, pimento/pimiento, sweet potatoes, tomatoes, 100% tomato juice, and winter squash such as acorn, butternut, kabocha, and pumpkin.

Beans, Peas, Lentils: All cooked from dry or canned beans, peas, chickpeas, and lentils: for example, black beans, black-eyed peas, bayo beans, brown beans, chickpeas (garbanzo beans), cowpeas, edamame, fava beans, kidney beans, lentils, lima beans, mung beans, navy beans, pigeon peas, pink beans, pinto beans, split peas, soybeans, and white beans. Does not include green beans or green peas.

Starchy Vegetables: All fresh, frozen, and canned starchy vegetables: for example, breadfruit, burdock root, cassava, corn, jicama, lotus root, lima beans, immature or raw (not dried) peas (e.g., cowpeas, black-eyed peas, green peas, pigeon peas), plantains, white potatoes, salsify, tapioca, taro root (dasheen or yautia), water chestnuts, yam, and yucca.

Other Vegetables: All other fresh, frozen, and canned vegetables, cooked or raw: for example, artichoke, asparagus, avocado, bamboo shoots, bean sprouts, beets, bitter melon (bitter gourd, balsam pear), broccoflower, Brussels sprouts, cabbage (green, red, napa, savoy), cactus pads (nopales), cauliflower, celeriac, celery, chayote (mirliton), chives, cucumber, eggplant, fennel bulb, garlic, ginger root, green beans, iceberg lettuce, kohlrabi, leeks, luffa (Chinese okra), mushrooms, okra, onions, peppers (chili and bell types that are not red or orange in color), radicchio, sprouted beans (e.g. sprouted mung beans), radish, rutabaga, seaweed, snow peas, summer squash, tomatillos, turnips, and winter melons.

Fruits

All fresh, frozen, canned, and dried fruits and 100% fruit juices: for example, apples, apricots, Asian pears, bananas, berries (e.g., blackberries, blueberries, cranberries, currants, dewberries, huckleberries, kiwifruit, loganberries, mulberries, raspberries, and strawberries); citrus fruit (e.g., calamondin, grapefruit, kumquats, lemons, limes, mandarin oranges, pomelos, tangerines, and tangelos); cherries, dates, figs, grapes, guava, jackfruit, lychee, mangoes, melons (e.g., cantaloupe, casaba, honeydew, and watermelon); nectarines, papaya, passion fruit, peaches, pears, persimmons, pineapple, plums, pomegranates, prunes, raisins, rhubarb, sapote, soursop, starfruit, and tamarind.

Grains

Whole Grains: All whole-grain products and whole grains used as ingredients: for example, amaranth, barley (not pearled), brown rice, buckwheat, bulgur, millet, oats, popcorn, quinoa, dark rye, triticale, whole-grain cornmeal, whole-wheat bread, whole-wheat chapati, whole-grain cereals and crackers, and wild rice.

Refined Grains: All refined-grain products and refined grains used as ingredients: for example, white breads, refined-grain cereals and crackers, corn grits, cream of rice, cream of wheat, barley (pearled), masa, pasta, and white rice. Refined-grain choices should be enriched.

Dairy

All fluid, dry, or evaporated milk, including lactose-free and lactose-reduced products and fortified soy beverages (soy milk), buttermilk, yogurt, kefir, frozen yogurt, dairy desserts, and cheeses (e.g., brie, camembert, cheddar, cottage cheese, colby, edam, feta, fontina, goat, gouda, gruyere, limburger, Mexican cheeses [queso anejo, queso asadero, queso chihuahua], monterey, mozzarella, muenster, parmesan, provolone, ricotta, and Swiss). Most choices should be fat-free or low-fat. Cream, sour cream, and cream cheese are not included due to their low calcium content.

Protein Foods

Meats, Poultry, Eggs: Meats include beef, goat, lamb, pork, and game meat (e.g., bear, bison, deer, elk, moose, opossum, rabbit, raccoon, squirrel). Poultry includes chicken, Cornish hens, dove, duck, game birds (e.g., ostrich, pheasant, and quail), goose, and turkey. Organ meats include brain, chitterlings, giblets, gizzard, heart, kidney, liver, stomach, sweetbreads, tongue, and tripe. Eggs include chicken eggs and other birds' eggs. Meats and poultry should be lean or low-fat.

Seafood: Seafood examples that are lower in methylmercury include: anchovy, black sea bass, catfish, clams, cod, crab, crawfish, flounder, haddock, hake, herring, lobster, mackerel, mullet, oyster, perch, pollock, salmon, sardine, scallop, shrimp, sole, squid, tilapia, freshwater trout, light tuna, and whiting.

Nuts, Seeds, Soy Products: Nuts and seeds include all nuts (tree nuts and peanuts), nut butters, seeds (e.g., chia, flax, pumpkin, sesame, and sunflower), and seed butters (e.g., sesame or tahini and sunflower). Soy includes tofu, tempeh, and products made from soy flour, soy protein isolate, and soy concentrate. Nuts should be unsalted.

Beans, Peas, Lentils: Can be considered part of the protein foods group as well as the vegetable group, but should be counted in one group only.

[c] Food group amounts shown in cup equivalents (cup eq) or ounce equivalents (ounce eq). Oils are shown in grams. Quantity equivalents for each food group are:

Vegetables, Fruits (1 cup eq): 1 cup raw or cooked vegetable or fruit; 1 cup vegetable or fruit juice; 2 cups leafy salad greens; ½ cup dried fruit or vegetable.

Grains (1 ounce eq): ½ cup cooked rice, pasta, or cereal; 1 ounce dry pasta or rice; 1 medium (1 ounce) slice bread, tortilla, or flatbread; 1 ounce of ready-to-eat cereal (about 1 cup of flaked cereal).

Dairy (1 cup eq): 1 cup milk, yogurt, or fortified soymilk; 1½ ounces natural cheese such as cheddar cheese or 2 ounces of processed cheese.

Protein Foods (1 ounce eq): 1 ounce lean meats, poultry, or seafood; 1 egg; ¼ cup cooked beans or tofu; 1 tbsp nut or seed butter; ½ ounce nuts or seeds.

[d] Amounts of whole grains in the Patterns for children are less than the minimum of 3 ounce-eq in all Patterns recommended for adults.

[e] The U.S. Food and Drug Administration (FDA) and the U.S. Environmental Protection Agency (EPA) provide joint advice regarding seafood consumption to limit methylmercury exposure for women who might become or are pregnant or breastfeeding, and children. Depending on body weight, some women and many children should choose seafood lowest in methylmercury or eat less seafood than the amounts in the Healthy US-Style Eating Pattern. For more information, see the FDA and EPA websites **FDA.gov/fishadvice**; **EPA.gov/fishadvice**.

[f] **If consuming up to 2 ounces of seafood per week**, children should only be fed cooked varieties from the "Best Choices" list in the FDA/EPA joint "Advice About Eating Fish," available at **FDA.gov/fishadvice** and **EPA.gov/fishadvice**. **If consuming up to 3 ounces of seafood per week**, children should only be fed cooked varieties from the "Best Choices" list that contain even lower methylmercury: flatfish (e.g., flounder), salmon, tilapia, shrimp, catfish, crab, trout, haddock, oysters, sardines, squid, pollock, anchovies, crawfish, mullet, scallops, whiting, clams, shad, and Atlantic mackerel. If consuming up to 3 ounces of seafood per week, many commonly consumed varieties of seafood should be avoided because they cannot be consumed at 3 ounces per week by children without the potential of exceeding safe methylmercury limits; examples that should not be consumed include: canned light tuna or white (albacore) tuna, cod, perch, black sea bass. For a complete list please see: **FDA.gov/fishadvice** and **EPA.gov/fishadvice**.

[g] Foods are assumed to be in nutrient-dense forms, lean or low-fat and prepared with minimal added saturated fat, added sugars, refined starches, or salt. If all food choices to meet food group recommendations are in nutrient-dense forms, a small number of calories remain within the overall limit of the pattern (i.e., limit on calories for other uses). The amount of calories depends on the total calorie level of the pattern and the amounts of food from each food group required to meet nutritional goals. Calories up to the specified limit can be used for added sugars, added refined starches, saturated fat, alcohol, or to eat more than the recommended amount of food in a food group.

NOTE: The total dietary pattern should not exceed *Dietary Guidelines* limits for added sugars, saturated fat, and alcohol; be within the Acceptable Macronutrient Distribution Ranges for protein, carbohydrate, and total fats; and stay within calorie limits. Values are rounded.

Table A3-3

Healthy Vegetarian Dietary Pattern for Toddlers Ages 12 Through 23 Months Who Are No Longer Receiving Human Milk or Infant Formula, With Daily or Weekly Amounts From Food Groups, Subgroups, and Components

CALORIE LEVEL OF PATTERN[a]	700	800	900	1,000
FOOD GROUP OR SUBGROUP[b,c]	**Daily Amount of Food From Each Group[d]** (Vegetable and protein foods subgroup amounts are per week.)			
Vegetables (cup eq/day)	**1**	**1**	**1**	**1**
	Vegetable Subgroups in Weekly Amounts			
Dark-Green Vegetables (cup eq/wk)	½	½	½	½
Red and Orange Vegetables (cup eq/wk)	2 ½	2 ½	2 ½	2 ½
Beans, Peas, Lentils (cup eq/wk)	¾	¾	¾	¾
Starchy Vegetables (cup eq/wk)	2	2	2	2
Other Vegetables (cup eq/wk)	1 ½	1 ½	1 ½	1 ½
Fruits (cup eq/day)	**½**	**¾**	**1**	**1**
Grains (ounce eq/day)	**1 ¾**	**2 ¼**	**2 ¾**	**3**
Whole Grains (ounce eq/day)	1 ¼	1 ¾	2	2
Refined Grains (ounce eq/day)	½	½	¾	1
Dairy (cup eq/day)	**1 ½**	**1 ¾**	**1 ¾**	**2**
Protein Foods (ounce eq/day)	**1**	**1**	**1**	**1**
	Protein Foods Subgroups in Weekly Amounts			
Eggs (ounce eq/wk)	3 ½	3 ½	3 ½	3 ½
Nuts, Seeds, Soy Products (ounce eq/wk)	4	4	4	4
Oils (grams/day)	**9**	**8 ½**	**10**	**15**

[a] Calorie level ranges: Energy levels are calculated based on median length and body weight reference individuals. Calorie needs vary based on many factors. The DRI Calculator for Healthcare Professionals available at **nal.usda.gov/fnic/dri-calculator/** can be used to estimate calorie needs based on age, sex, and weight.

[b] Definitions for each food group and subgroup and quantity (i.e., cup or ounce) equivalents are provided in ***Chapter 1*** and are compiled in **Table A3-2 (footnote c)**.

[c] All foods are assumed to be in nutrient-dense forms and prepared with minimal added sugars, refined starches (which are a source of calories but few or no other nutrients), or sodium. Food are also lean or in low-fat forms with the exception of dairy which includes whole-fat fluid milk, reduced-fat plain yogurts, and reduced-fat cheese. There are no calories available for additional added sugars, saturated fat, or to eat more than the recommended amount of food in a food group.

[d] In some cases, food subgroup amounts are greatest at the lower calorie levels to help achieve nutrient adequacy when relatively small number of calories are required.

Table A3-4

Healthy Vegetarian Dietary Pattern for Ages 2 and Older, With Daily or Weekly Amounts From Food Groups, Subgroups, and Components

CALORIE LEVEL OF PATTERN	1,000	1,200	1,400	1,600	1,800	2,000	2,200	2,400	2,600	2,800	3,000	3,200
FOOD GROUP OR SUBGROUP[b]	**Daily Amount[c] of Food From Each Group** (Vegetable and protein foods subgroup amounts[b] are per week.)											
Vegetables (cup eq/day)	**1**	**1 ½**	**1 ½**	**2**	**2 ½**	**2 ½**	**3**	**3**	**3 ½**	**3 ½**	**4**	**4**
	Vegetable Subgroups in Weekly Amounts											
Dark-Green Vegetables (cup eq/wk)	½	1	1	1 ½	1 ½	1 ½	2	2	2 ½	2 ½	2 ½	2 ½
Red and Orange Vegetables (cup eq/wk)	2 ½	3	3	4	5 ½	5½	6	6	7	7	7½	7½
Beans, Peas, Lentils (cup eq/wk)[d]	½	½	½	1	1 ½	1 ½	2	2	2 ½	2 ½	3	3
Starchy Vegetables (cup eq/wk)	2	3 ½	3 ½	4	5	5	6	6	7	7	8	8
Other Vegetables (cup eq/wk)	1 ½	2 ½	2 ½	3 ½	4	4	5	5	5 ½	5 ½	7	7
Fruits (cup eq/day)	**1**	**1**	**1 ½**	**1 ½**	**1 ½**	**2**	**2**	**2**	**2**	**2 ½**	**2 ½**	**2 ½**
Grains (ounce eq/day)	**3**	**4**	**5**	**5 ½**	**6 ½**	**6 ½**	**7 ½**	**8 ½**	**9 ½**	**10 ½**	**10 ½**	**10 ½**
Whole Grains (ounce eq/day)	1 ½	2	2 ½	3	3 ½	3 ½	4	4 ½	5	5 ½	5 ½	5 ½
Refined Grains (ounce eq/day)	1 ½	2	2 ½	2 ½	3	3	3 ½	4	4 ½	5	5	5
Dairy (cup eq/day)	**2**	**2 ½**	**2 ½**	**3**	**3**	**3**	**3**	**3**	**3**	**3**	**3**	**3**
Protein Foods (ounce eq/day)	**1**	**1 ½**	**2**	**2 ½**	**3**	**3 ½**	**3 ½**	**4**	**4 ½**	**5**	**5 ½**	**6**
	Protein Foods Subgroups in Weekly Amounts											
Eggs (ounce eq/wk)	2	3	3	3	3	3	3	3	3	4	4	4
Beans, Peas, Lentils (cup eq/wk)[d]	1	2	4	4	6	6	6	8	9	10	11	12
Soy Products (ounce eq/wk)	2	3	4	6	6	8	8	9	10	11	12	13
Nuts, Seeds (ounce eq/wk)	2	2	3	5	6	7	7	8	9	10	12	13
Oils (grams/day)	**15**	**17**	**17**	**22**	**24**	**27**	**29**	**31**	**34**	**36**	**44**	**51**
Limit on Calories for Other Uses (kcal/day)[e]	**170**	**140**	**160**	**150**	**150**	**250**	**290**	**350**	**350**	**350**	**390**	**500**
Limit on Calories for Other Uses (%/day)	17%	12%	11%	9%	8%	13%	13%	15%	13%	13%	13%	16%

[a, b, c] See **Table A3-2 footnotes**.

[d] About half of beans, peas, lentils are shown as vegetables, in cup eq, and half as protein foods, in ounce eq. Beans, peas, lentils in the patterns, in cup eq, is the amount in the vegetable group plus the amount in protein foods group (in ounce eq) divided by four.

[e] See **Table A3-2 footnotes**.

NOTE: The total dietary pattern should not exceed *Dietary Guidelines* limits for added sugars, saturated fat, and alcohol; be within the Acceptable Macronutrient Distribution Ranges for protein, carbohydrate, and total fats; and stay within calorie limits. Values are rounded.

Table A3-5

Healthy Mediterranean-Style Dietary Pattern for Ages 2 and Older, With Daily or Weekly Amounts From Food Groups, Subgroups, and Components

CALORIE LEVEL OF PATTERN[a]	1,000	1,200	1,400	1,600	1,800	2,000	2,200	2,400	2,600	2,800	3,000	3,200
FOOD GROUP OR SUBGROUP[b]	**Daily Amount[c] of Food From Each Group** (Vegetable and protein foods subgroup amounts are per week.)											
Vegetables (cup eq/day)	**1**	**1 ½**	**1 ½**	**2**	**2 ½**	**2 ½**	**3**	**3**	**3 ½**	**3 ½**	**4**	**4**
	Vegetable Subgroups in Weekly Amounts											
Dark-Green Vegetables (cup eq/wk)	½	1	1	1 ½	1 ½	1 ½	2	2	2 ½	2 ½	2 ½	2 ½
Red and Orange Vegetables (cup eq/wk)	2 ½	3	3	4	5 ½	5 ½	6	6	7	7	7 ½	7 ½
Beans, Peas, Lentils (cup eq/wk)	½	½	½	1	1 ½	1 ½	2	2	2 ½	2 ½	3	3
Starchy Vegetables (cup eq/wk)	2	3 ½	3 ½	4	5	5	6	6	7	7	8	8
Other Vegetables (cup eq/wk)	1 ½	2 ½	2 ½	3 ½	4	4	5	5	5 ½	5 ½	7	7
Fruits (cup eq/day)	**1**	**1**	**1 ½**	**2**	**2**	**2 ½**	**2 ½**	**2 ½**	**2 ½**	**3**	**3**	**3**
Grains (ounce eq/day)	**3**	**4**	**5**	**5**	**6**	**6**	**7**	**8**	**9**	**10**	**10**	**10**
Whole Grains (ounce eq/day)[d]	1 ½	2	2 ½	3	3	3	3 ½	4	4 ½	5	5	5
Refined Grains (ounce eq/day)	1 ½	2	2 ½	2	3	3	3 ½	4	4 ½	5	5	5
Dairy (cup eq/day)[d]	**2**	**2 ½**	**2 ½**	**2**	**2**	**2**	**2**	**2 ½**	**2 ½**	**2 ½**	**2 ½**	**2 ½**
Protein Foods (ounce eq/day)	**2**	**3**	**4**	**5 ½**	**6**	**6 ½**	**7**	**7 ½**	**7 ½**	**8**	**8**	**8**
	Protein Foods Subgroups in Weekly Amounts											
Meats, Poultry, Eggs (ounce eq/wk)	10	14	19	23	23	26	28	31	31	33	33	33
Seafood (ounce eq/wk)[e]	3	4	6	11	15	15	16	16	17	17	17	17
Nuts, Seeds, Soy Products (ounce eq/wk)	2	2	3	4	4	5	5	5	5	6	6	6
Oils (grams/day)	**15**	**17**	**17**	**22**	**24**	**27**	**29**	**31**	**34**	**36**	**44**	**51**
Limit on Calories for Other Uses (kcal/day)[f]	**130**	**80**	**90**	**120**	**140**	**240**	**250**	**280**	**300**	**330**	**400**	**540**
Limit on Calories for Other Uses (%/day)	13%	7%	6%	8%	8%	12%	11%	12%	12%	12%	13%	17%

[a,b,c] See **Table A3-2 footnotes**.

[d] Amounts of dairy recommended for children and adolescents are as follows, regardless of the calorie level of the pattern: for age 2 years, 2 cup-eq per day; for ages 3 through 8 years, 2 ½ cup-eq per day; for ages 9 through 18 years, 3 cup-eq per day.

[e] The U.S. Food and Drug Administration (FDA) and the U.S. Environmental Protection Agency (EPA) provide joint advice regarding seafood consumption to limit methylmercury exposure for women who might become or are pregnant or lactating, and children. Depending on body weight, some women and children should choose seafood lowest in methylmercury or eat less seafood than the amounts in the Healthy U.S.-Style Dietary Pattern. For more information, see the FDA and EPA websites at **FDA.gov/fishadvice** and **EPA.gov/fishadvice**.

[f] Foods are assumed to be in nutrient-dense forms; lean or low-fat; and prepared with minimal added sugars, refined starches (which are a source of calories but few or no other nutrients), saturated fat, or sodium. If all food choices to meet food group recommendations are in nutrient-dense forms, a small number of calories remain within the overall limit of the pattern (i.e., limit on calories for other uses). The amount of calories depends on the total calorie level of the pattern and the amounts of food from each food group required to meet nutritional goals. Calories up to the specified limit can be used for added sugars, saturated fat, and/or alcohol (for nonpregnant adults of legal drinking age only) or to eat more than the recommended amount of food in a food group.

NOTE: The total dietary pattern should not *Dietary Guidelines* limits for added sugars, saturated fat, and alcohol; be within the Acceptable Macronutrient Distribution Ranges for protein, carbohydrate, and total fats; and stay within calorie limits. Values are rounded.

USDA Publication #: USDA-FNS-2020-2025-DGA
HHS Publication #: HHS-ODPHP-2020-2025-01-DGA-A

DASH EATING PLAN

Healthy Eating, Proven Results

The DASH eating plan is flexible and easy to follow with many resources to help you create healthy habits for a lifetime wherever you are on your health journey.

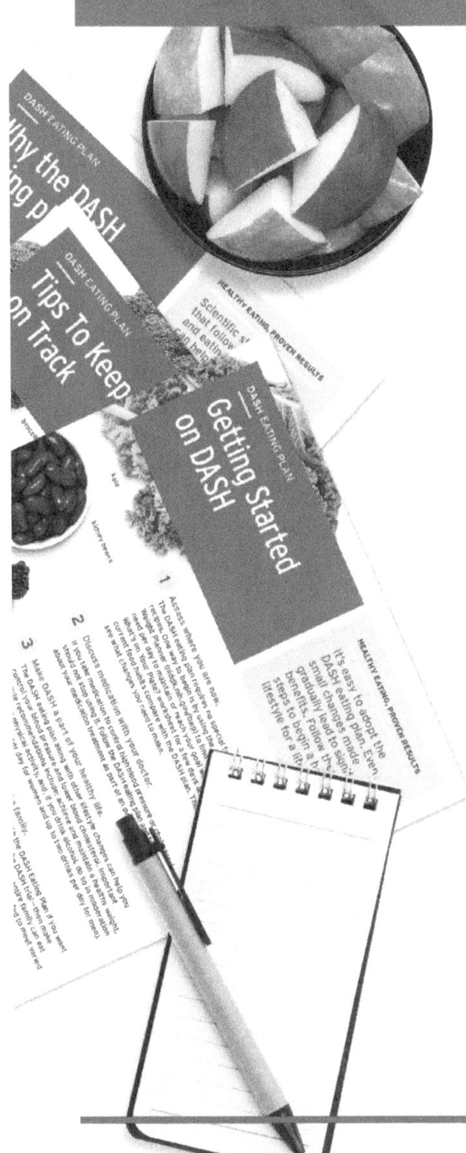

What you choose to eat can affect your chances of developing high blood pressure, also known as hypertension. Following the DASH—Dietary Approaches to Stop Hypertension—eating plan and eating less sodium have been scientifically proven to lower blood pressure and have other health benefits.

Developed through research by the National Heart, Lung, and Blood Institute (NHLBI), the DASH eating plan emphasizes vegetables, fruits, whole grains, fish, poultry, beans, nuts, low-fat dairy, and healthy oils. It focuses on reducing sodium and limiting foods that are high in saturated fat, including fatty meats, full-fat dairy products, and tropical oils. It also limits sweets and sugar-sweetened beverages. The eating plan is aimed, in part, at helping Americans with high blood pressure, a leading risk factor for heart disease, stroke, and other health problems.

The DASH eating plan requires no special foods and has easy recipes. It's flexible and can be adapted for your entire family to meet varied nutritional needs and food preferences.

Daily and weekly nutritional goals are a key part of the DASH eating plan and help you learn about nutrition and keep track of what you eat. Complementing the eating plan with physical activity can help you control high blood pressure and create heart healthy habits for a lifetime.

The DASH Journey

Starting a new way of eating can seem overwhelming, but it doesn't have to be. DASH provides easy-to-understand guidelines, delicious recipes, and lessons to develop the skills to prepare healthy meals at home or make smart choices when dining out. Where are you on your health journey? Consider these three profiles to help you decide which resources to check out first on your way to a heart healthy way of life. Looking for a specific DASH resource? See the complete collection of Tools for a Healthy Life organized by topic following the DASH journey levels.

LEVEL 1

New to DASH

LEARN HOW TO GET STARTED

You have just been diagnosed with high blood pressure and don't know where to begin. You are ready to make a change but it all seems so overwhelming. Everywhere you turn there are quick-fix diets and complicated, expensive eating plans with special foods and many restrictions. Perhaps you discovered DASH through a web search because you are pre-hypertensive and want to learn more about prevention, or maybe your doctor told you to learn more about DASH. Understanding what is happening in your body is the first step, with gradual and easy steps to follow.

What is High Blood Pressure?
Learn the basics about high blood pressure—what it is, who is at risk, how to understand the numbers—so that you can take steps to get it under control.

Getting Started on DASH
Learn how to take the first steps to adopt the DASH eating plan—assess where you are, discuss medication, make it part of your everyday life.

Making the Move to DASH
The DASH eating plan is explained in a single page of simple tips to make the plan work for you—gradually, healthfully, and successfully.

Tips to Reduce Salt and Sodium
Complete with tips for dining out and an easy-to-read chart about sodium content in several foods, learn how to further lower sodium and gain even bigger heart healthy benefits.

Tips to Keep on Track
Follow these steps to help you get back on track even if you slip from the DASH eating plan for a few days.

Nutrition Facts Label Guide
Use this graphical insert to learn about the parts of the Nutrition Facts label and other packaging labels so you can make informed choices based on what's in the food you're buying.

LEVEL 2

Next Level DASH

KEEP IMPROVING ON YOUR HEALTH JOURNEY

You are familiar with the basics of DASH, and you're ready to learn more about how to take it to the next level. You want to exercise more, and are eager to manage your high blood pressure. You have seen benefits from a gradual approach to changing your eating habits and want to learn more about meal planning and adding new foods to your diet. You have started by gradually eating more fruits and vegetables and are seeking information about easy recipes to add variety and keep you motivated.

A Week With the DASH Eating Plan
This comprehensive guide provides a complete set of menus to help you plan healthy, delicious meals for a week.

What's on Your Plate?
These worksheets help you track what you eat and drink and describe serving sizes in each of the major food groups. They can help you can assess your current eating habits or monitor your efforts with DASH based on your caloric needs ranging from 1,200 to 2,600 calories per day.

Tips to Lowering Calories on DASH
Read about easy food substitutions to help you lose weight and maintain it once you do.

Getting More Potassium
Learn about this heart healthy mineral's benefits and find a list of potassium-rich foods to help lower high blood pressure.

Get Active With DASH
Being more active bolsters the benefits of the DASH eating plan. Learn how to gradually move more to make physical activity part of your daily routine and your heart healthy life.

Delicious Heart Healthy Eating Website
In this vast online collection of DASH-friendly recipes, you'll find a variety of cuisines and resources for families, educational videos, and meal planning and cooking tips.

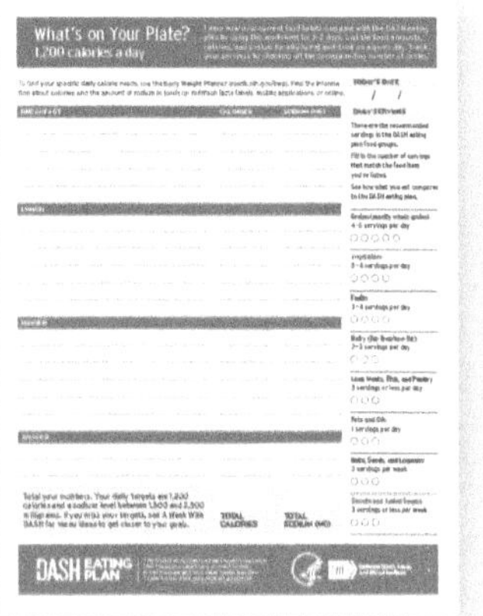

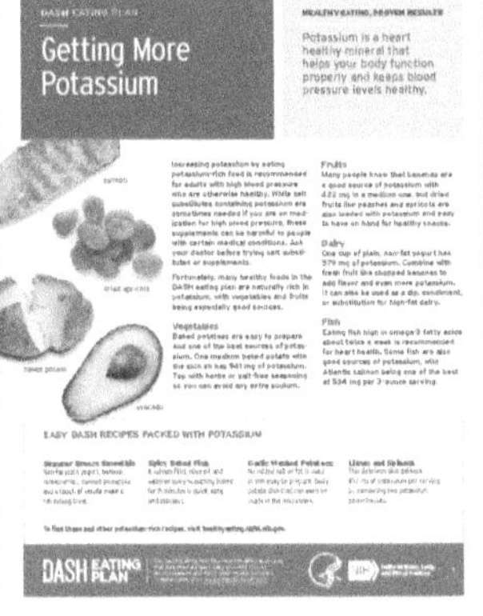

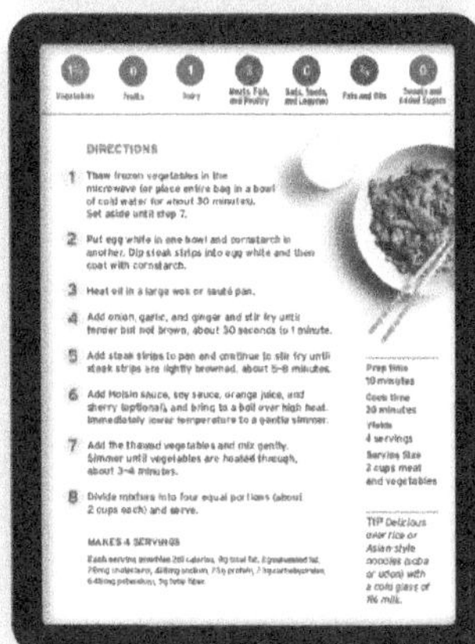

LEVEL 3

DASH Expert

EXPLORE THE SCIENCE BEHIND DASH

You are an expert about DASH from either adopting it in your own life or as a health professional. Perhaps you're a physician, community health advocate, dietitian, or nutrition coach who discusses DASH with clients. Perhaps you simply want to know all of the details about DASH and why it's a proven plan. Health professionals are encouraged to use the entire collection of DASH materials based on client needs. "Why the DASH Eating Plan Works" resource provides a summary of the decades of science behind DASH, while the website delves into multiple studies and links to other medical, scientific, and governmental resources.

Why the DASH Eating Plan Works
The DASH eating plan is based on decades of scientific research and data from multiple studies. Learn about the science behind DASH and why it's so effective.

DASH Website
NHLBI has information about the DASH eating plan, clinical trials, related health topics, and downloads for all of the DASH materials.

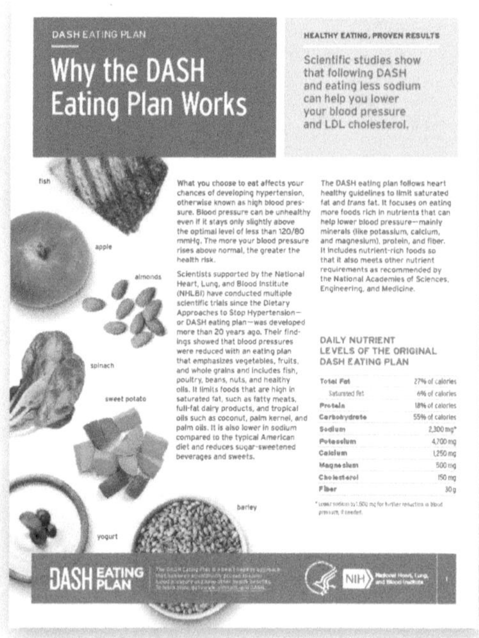

DASH EATING PLAN

Why the DASH Eating Plan Works

HEALTHY EATING, PROVEN RESULTS

Scientific studies show that following DASH and eating less sodium can help you lower your blood pressure and LDL cholesterol.

fish
apple
almonds
spinach
sweet potato
yogurt
barley

What you choose to eat affects your chances of developing hypertension, otherwise known as high blood pressure. Blood pressure can be unhealthy even if it stays only slightly above the optimal level of less than 120/80 mmHg. The more your blood pressure rises above normal, the greater the health risk.

Scientists supported by the National Heart, Lung, and Blood Institute (NHLBI) have conducted multiple scientific trials since the Dietary Approaches to Stop Hypertension—or DASH eating plan—was developed more than 20 years ago. Their findings showed that blood pressures were reduced with an eating plan that emphasizes vegetables, fruits, and whole grains and includes fish, poultry, beans, nuts, and healthy oils. It limits foods that are high in saturated fat, such as fatty meats, full-fat dairy products, and tropical oils such as coconut, palm kernel, and palm oils. It is also lower in sodium compared to the typical American diet and reduces sugar-sweetened beverages and sweets.

The DASH eating plan follows heart healthy guidelines to limit saturated fat and *trans* fat. It focuses on eating more foods rich in nutrients that can help lower blood pressure—mainly minerals (like potassium, calcium, and magnesium), protein, and fiber. It includes nutrient-rich foods so that it also meets other nutrient requirements as recommended by the National Academies of Sciences, Engineering, and Medicine.

DAILY NUTRIENT LEVELS OF THE ORIGINAL DASH EATING PLAN

Total Fat	27% of calories
Saturated fat	6% of calories
Protein	18% of calories
Carbohydrate	55% of calories
Sodium	2,300 mg*
Potassium	4,700 mg
Calcium	1,250 mg
Magnesium	500 mg
Cholesterol	150 mg
Fiber	30 g

* Lower sodium to 1,500 mg for further reduction in blood pressure, if needed.

DASH EATING PLAN

NIH National Heart, Lung, and Blood Institute

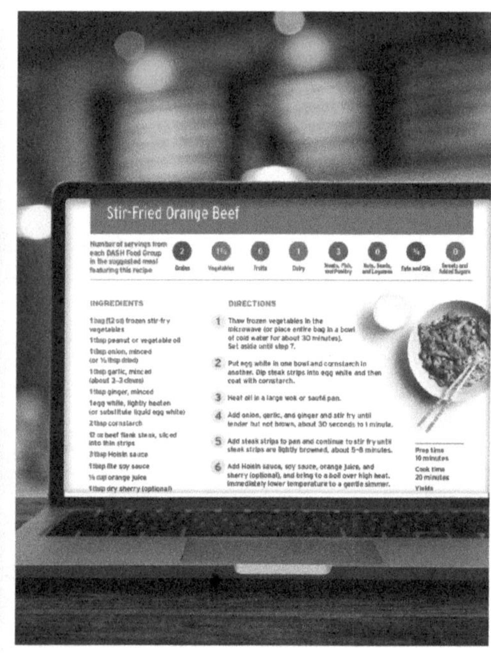

DASH EATING PLAN

Tools for a Healthy Life

HEALTHY EATING, PROVEN RESULTS

The NHLBI has developed many user-friendly materials to help you follow the DASH eating plan, understand how it works, try new foods, and make smart choices on your journey to a healthy lifestyle.

THE SCIENCE BEHIND DASH

Get information about high blood pressure along with scientific research on how DASH works.

What is High Blood Pressure?

Learn the basics about high blood pressure—what it is, who is at risk, how to understand the numbers—so that you can take steps to get it under control.

Why the DASH Eating Plan Works

The DASH eating plan is based on decades of scientific research and data from multiple studies. Learn about the science behind DASH and why it's so effective.

DASH EATING PLAN

What is High Blood Pressure?

HEALTHY EATING, PROVEN RESULTS

The DASH eating plan can help you control high blood pressure and achieve and maintain a healthy weight.

Every time your heart beats, it pumps blood through vessels, called arteries, to the rest of your body. Your blood pressure is how hard your blood pushes against the walls of the arteries. If your blood flows at higher than normal pressure, you may have high blood pressure, also known as hypertension.

If you have high blood pressure, you aren't alone. High blood pressure affects nearly half of U.S. adults. Many people don't even know they have it, which is why it's so important to have your blood pressure checked at least once a year.

Understanding high blood pressure
Blood pressure rises and falls during the day. But when it stays elevated over time, it's called high blood pressure. It's dangerous because the heart is working too hard, and the force of the blood flow can harm arteries and organs. High blood pressure is a major risk factor for heart disease, which is the leading cause of death in the United States.

High blood pressure often has no warning signs or symptoms. That's why it's called a "silent killer." If uncontrolled, it harms your heart and contributes to kidney disease, stroke, blindness, and dementia.

Managing high blood pressure
Sometimes health care providers prescribe medication to manage high blood pressure, which should be taken as directed. If your blood pressure isn't too high, you may be able to control it entirely by following the DASH eating plan, losing even just a little weight, getting regular physical activity, mindfully managing stress, cutting down on alcohol, and not smoking.

Learn more about high blood pressure at www.nhlbi.nih.gov/hypertension.

RISK FACTORS FOR HIGH BLOOD PRESSURE

Age: Blood pressure tends to get higher as we get older. Our blood vessels naturally thicken and stiffen over time. But many younger people, including children and teens, develop high blood pressure, too.

Sex: Before age 60, more men than women have high blood pressure. After age 60, more women than men have it.

Genes: High blood pressure often runs in families.

Race or ethnicity: While anyone can have high blood pressure, African Americans tend to get it at a younger age. Among Hispanic adults, people of Cuban, Puerto Rican, and Dominican backgrounds are at higher risk.

Lifestyle habits: Eating unhealthy foods, especially those with too much salt, drinking too much alcohol or caffeine, being obese, smoking, and not getting enough exercise can raise blood pressure.

DASH EATING PLAN

NIH National Heart, Lung, and Blood Institute

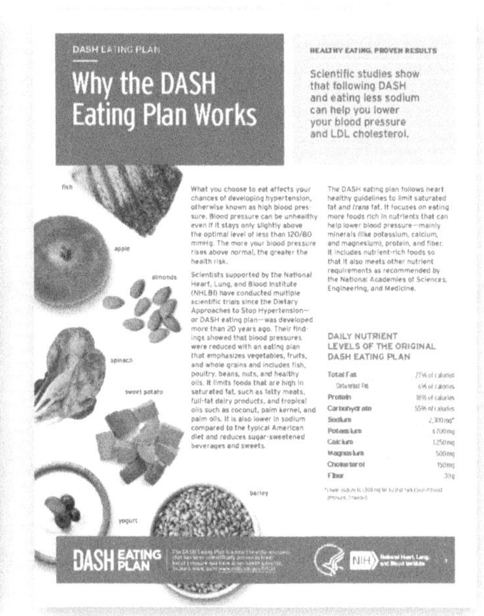

DASH EATING PLAN

Why the DASH Eating Plan Works

HEALTHY EATING, PROVEN RESULTS

Scientific studies show that following DASH and eating less sodium can help you lower your blood pressure and LDL cholesterol.

What you choose to eat affects your chances of developing hypertension, otherwise known as high blood pressure. Blood pressure can be unhealthy even if it stays only slightly above the optimal level of less than 120/80 mmHg. The more your blood pressure rises above normal, the greater the health risk.

Scientists supported by the National Heart, Lung, and Blood Institute (NHLBI) have conducted multiple scientific trials since the Dietary Approaches to Stop Hypertension—or DASH eating plan—was developed more than 20 years ago. Their findings showed that blood pressures were reduced with an eating plan that emphasizes vegetables, fruits, and whole grains and includes fish, poultry, beans, nuts, and healthy oils. It limits foods that are high in saturated fat, such as fatty meats, full-fat dairy products, and tropical oils such as coconut, palm kernel, and palm oils. It is also lower in sodium compared to the typical American diet and reduces sugar-sweetened beverages and sweets.

The DASH eating plan follows heart healthy guidelines to limit saturated fat and *trans* fat. It focuses on eating more foods rich in nutrients that can help lower blood pressure—mainly minerals (like potassium, calcium, and magnesium), protein, and fiber. It includes nutrient-rich foods so that it also meets other nutrient requirements as recommended by the National Academies of Sciences, Engineering, and Medicine.

DAILY NUTRIENT LEVELS OF THE ORIGINAL DASH EATING PLAN

Total Fat	27% of calories
Saturated Fat	6% of calories
Protein	18% of calories
Carbohydrate	55% of calories
Sodium	2,300 mg*
Potassium	4,700 mg
Calcium	1,250 mg
Magnesium	500 mg
Cholesterol	150 mg
Fiber	30 g

DASH EATING PLAN

NIH National Heart, Lung, and Blood Institute

DASH WEB RESOURCES

Comprehensive websites keep you current about how to live a healthy life with DASH.

DASH Website

NHLBI has information about the DASH eating plan, clinical trials, related health topics, and downloads for all of the DASH materials.

Delicious Heart Healthy Eating Website

In this vast online collection of DASH-friendly recipes, you'll find a variety of cuisines and resources for families, educational videos, and meal planning and cooking tips.

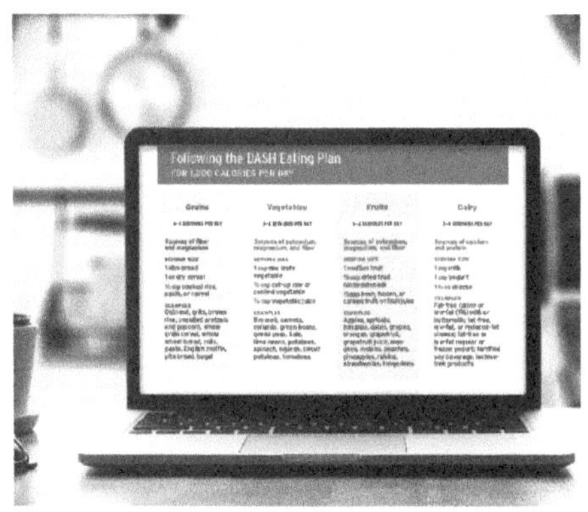

Tools for a Healthy Life

THE HEALTHY BASICS OF DASH

Start your journey to healthy living on DASH with these tools to inform, inspire and motivate.

Getting Started on DASH

Learn how to take the first steps to adopt the DASH eating plan—assess where you are, discuss medication, make it part of your everyday life.

Making the Move to DASH

The DASH eating plan is explained in a single page of simple tips to make the plan work for you—gradually, healthfully, and successfully.

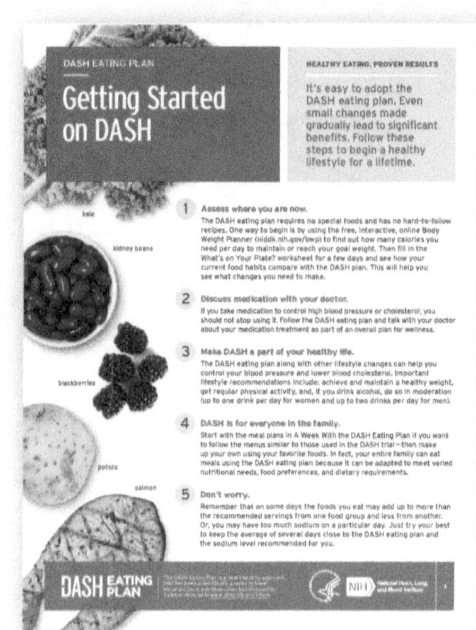

DASH EATING PLAN
Getting Started on DASH
HEALTHY EATING, PROVEN RESULTS
It's easy to adopt the DASH eating plan. Even small changes made gradually lead to significant benefits. Follow these steps to begin a healthy lifestyle for a lifetime.
DASH EATING PLAN

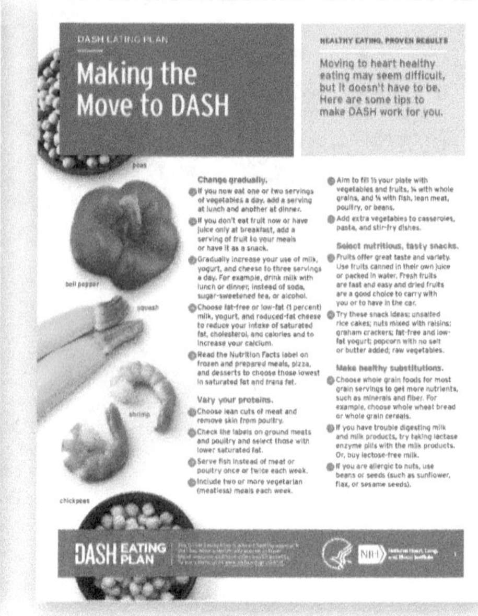

DASH EATING PLAN
Making the Move to DASH
HEALTHY EATING, PROVEN RESULTS
Moving to heart healthy eating may seem difficult, but it doesn't have to be. Here are some tips to make DASH work for you.
DASH EATING PLAN

Tips to Keep on Track

Follow these steps to help you get back on track even if you slip from the DASH eating plan for a few days.

Get Active With DASH

Being more active bolsters the benefits of the DASH eating plan. Learn how to gradually move more to make physical activity part of your daily routine and your heart healthy life.

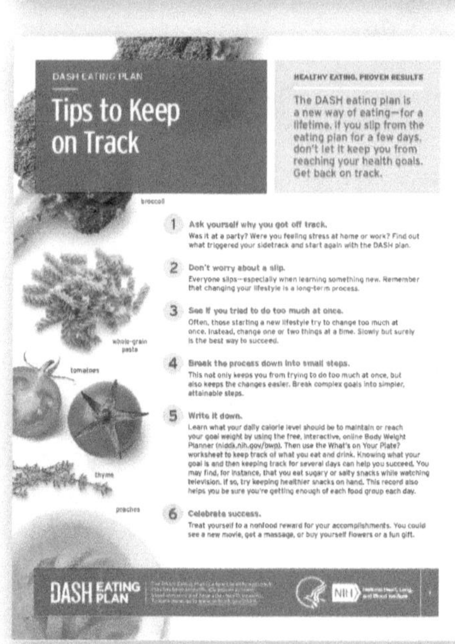

DASH EATING PLAN
Tips to Keep on Track
HEALTHY EATING, PROVEN RESULTS
The DASH eating plan is a new way of eating—for a lifetime. If you slip from the eating plan for a few days, don't let it keep you from reaching your health goals. Get back on track.
DASH EATING PLAN

DASH EATING PLAN
Get Active With DASH
HEALTHY EATING, PROVEN RESULTS
Combining the DASH eating plan and physical activity can lower high blood pressure and make your heart healthier.
DASH EATING PLAN

Tools for a Healthy Life

DASH NUTRITION PLANNING

Learn how to shop for healthy foods and easy tips for dining out and everyday choices on DASH.

Nutrition Facts Label Guide

Use this graphical insert to learn about the parts of the Nutrition Facts label and other packaging labels so you can make informed choices based on what's in the food you're buying.

Getting More Potassium

Learn about this heart healthy mineral's benefits and find a list of potassium-rich foods to help lower high blood pressure.

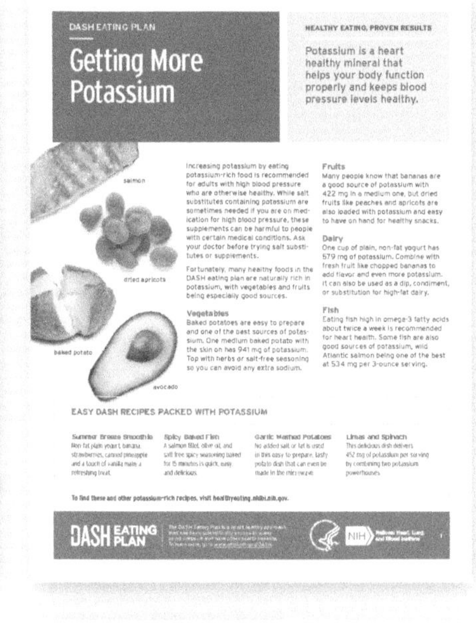

Tips To Reduce Salt and Sodium

Complete with tips for dining out and an easy-to-read chart about sodium content in several foods, learn how to further lower sodium and gain even bigger heart healthy benefits.

Tips to Lowering Calories on DASH

Read about easy food substitutions to help you lose weight and maintain it once you do.

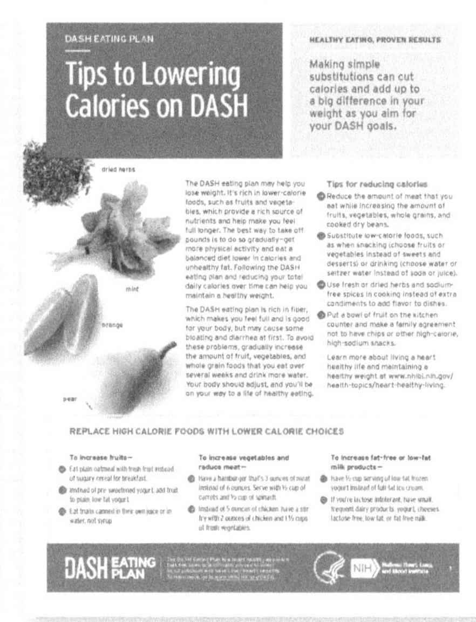

Tools for a Healthy Life

DASH MENUS AND WORKSHEETS

Take the mystery out of weekly meal planning and monitor your individual progress on DASH.

A Week With the DASH Eating Plan
This comprehensive guide provides a complete set of menus to help you plan healthy, delicious meals for a week.

What's on Your Plate?
These worksheets help you track what you eat and drink and describe serving sizes in each of the major food groups. They can help you can assess your current eating habits or monitor your efforts with DASH based on your caloric needs ranging from 1,200 to 2,600 calories per day.

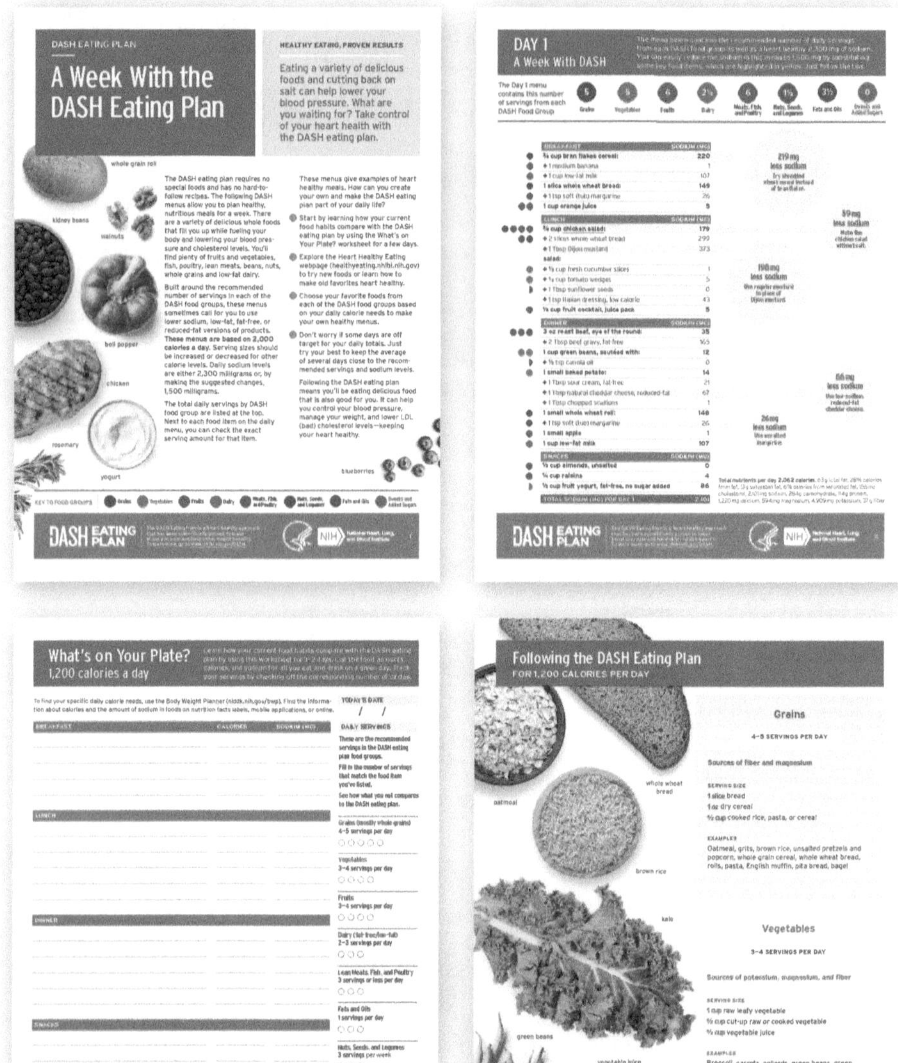

MORE INFORMATION

NHLBI Center for Health Information
P.O. Box 30105, Bethesda, MD 20824-0105
nhlbiinfo@nhlbi.nih.gov
1-877-NHLBI4U (1-877-645-2448)
For access to free Telecommunications Relay Services (TRS), dial 7-1-1 on your telephone.

To learn more about high blood pressure, the DASH eating plan, and NHLBI research in this area, visit NHLBI's high blood pressure webpage: **www.nhlbi.nih.gov/hypertension.**

DASH EATING PLAN

Why the DASH Eating Plan Works

HEALTHY EATING, PROVEN RESULTS

Scientific studies show that following DASH and eating less sodium can help you lower your blood pressure and LDL cholesterol.

What you choose to eat affects your chances of developing hypertension, otherwise known as high blood pressure. Blood pressure can be unhealthy even if it stays only slightly above the optimal level of less than 120/80 mmHg. The more your blood pressure rises above normal, the greater the health risk.

Scientists supported by the National Heart, Lung, and Blood Institute (NHLBI) have conducted multiple scientific trials since the Dietary Approaches to Stop Hypertension—or DASH eating plan—was developed more than 20 years ago. Their findings showed that blood pressures were reduced with an eating plan that emphasizes vegetables, fruits, and whole grains and includes fish, poultry, beans, nuts, and healthy oils. It limits foods that are high in saturated fat, such as fatty meats, full-fat dairy products, and tropical oils such as coconut, palm kernel, and palm oils. It is also lower in sodium compared to the typical American diet and reduces sugar-sweetened beverages and sweets.

The DASH eating plan follows heart healthy guidelines to limit saturated fat and trans fat. It focuses on eating more foods rich in nutrients that can help lower blood pressure—mainly minerals (like potassium, calcium, and magnesium), protein, and fiber. It includes nutrient-rich foods so that it also meets other nutrient requirements as recommended by the National Academies of Sciences, Engineering, and Medicine.

DAILY NUTRIENT LEVELS OF THE ORIGINAL DASH EATING PLAN

Total Fat	27% of calories
Saturated Fat	6% of calories
Protein	18% of calories
Carbohydrate	55% of calories
Sodium	2,300 mg*
Potassium	4,700 mg
Calcium	1,250 mg
Magnesium	500 mg
Cholesterol	150 mg
Fiber	30 g

*Lower sodium to 1,500 mg for further reduction in blood pressure, if needed.

DASH EATING PLAN

The DASH Eating Plan is a heart healthy approach that has been scientifically proven to lower blood pressure and have other health benefits. To learn more, go to www.nhlbi.nih.gov/DASH.

National Heart, Lung, and Blood Institute

The Science Behind the DASH Eating Plan

The importance of eating more vegetables, fruits, whole grains along with low-fat dairy, poultry, fish, beans, and nuts has been proven in multiple research trials. The combination of the DASH eating plan and reduced sodium creates the biggest benefit, lowering blood pressure significantly.

STUDY 1 Original DASH eating plan

The first DASH trial involved 459 adults with systolic blood pressures of less than 160 mmHg and diastolic pressures of 80-95 mmHg. About 27 percent of the participants had high blood pressure. About 50 percent were women and 60 percent were African Americans. It compared three eating plans: one that included foods similar to what many Americans regularly eat; one that included foods similar to what many Americans regularly eat plus more fruits and vegetables; and the DASH eating plan. All three plans included about 3,000 milligrams of sodium daily. None of the plans were vegetarian or used specialty foods.

Results were dramatic. Participants who followed either the plan that included more fruits and vegetables or the DASH eating plan had reduced blood pressure. But the DASH eating plan had the greatest effect, especially for those with high blood pressure. Furthermore, the blood pressure reductions came fast—within 2 weeks of starting the plan.

STUDY 2 Varied sodium levels

The second DASH trial looked at the effect on blood pressure of a reduced dietary sodium intake as participants followed either the DASH eating plan or an eating plan typical of what many Americans consume. This trial involved 412 participants. Participants were randomly assigned to one of the two eating plans and then followed for a month at each of the three sodium levels. The three sodium levels were: a higher intake of about 3,300 milligrams per day (the level consumed by many Americans), an intermediate intake of about 2,300 milligrams per day, and a lower intake of about 1,500 milligrams per day.

Results showed that reducing dietary sodium lowered blood pressure for both eating plans. At each sodium level, blood pressure was lower on DASH than on the typical American eating plan. The greatest blood pressure reductions were for DASH at the sodium intake of 1,500 milligrams per day. Those with high blood pressure saw the greatest reductions.

STUDY 3 Higher protein or healthy fats

As the science around DASH evolves over time, the overall benefits to heart health continue to be evaluated. The OmniHeart (Optimal Macronutrient Intake Trial for Heart Health) trial studied the effect of replacing some daily carbohydrates—or carbs—with either protein (about half from plant sources) or unsaturated fat. This trial included 164 adults who had systolic blood pressure readings of 120 to 159 mmHg. The trial compared three dietary patterns, each containing 2,300 mg of sodium per day—the original DASH plan, substituting 10 percent of daily carbs with protein, and substituting 10 percent of total daily carbs with unsaturated fat.

OmniHeart found that participants who followed either variation of DASH, partially substituting carbs with protein (about half from plant sources) or unsaturated fat, had greater reductions in blood pressure and improvements in blood lipid levels than those who followed the original DASH eating plan.

Success with DASH

DASH along with other lifestyle changes can help you prevent and control high blood pressure. In fact, if your blood pressure is not too high, you may be able to control it entirely by changing your eating habits, losing weight if you are overweight, getting regular physical activity, and cutting down on alcohol. DASH also has other benefits, such as lowering LDL ("bad") cholesterol, and replacing some carbs with protein or unsaturated fat can have an even greater effect. Along with lowering blood pressure, lower cholesterol can reduce your risk for heart disease.

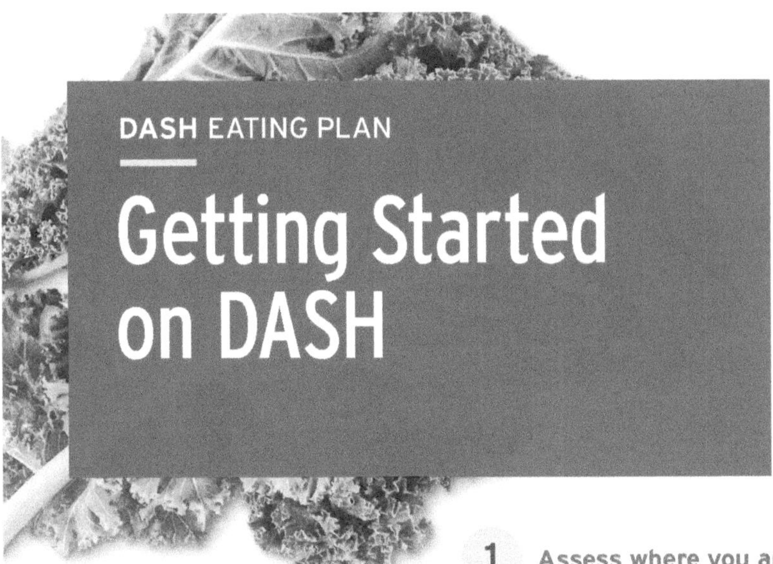

DASH EATING PLAN

Getting Started on DASH

HEALTHY EATING, PROVEN RESULTS

It's easy to adopt the DASH eating plan. Even small changes made gradually lead to significant benefits. Follow these steps to begin a healthy lifestyle for a lifetime.

kale

kidney beans

blackberries

potato

salmon

1 Assess where you are now.

The DASH eating plan requires no special foods and has no hard-to-follow recipes. One way to begin is by using the free, interactive, online Body Weight Planner (niddk.nih.gov/bwp) to find out how many calories you need per day to maintain or reach your goal weight. Then fill in the What's on Your Plate? worksheet for a few days and see how your current food habits compare with the DASH plan. This will help you see what changes you need to make.

2 Discuss medication with your doctor.

If you take medication to control high blood pressure or cholesterol, you should not stop using it. Follow the DASH eating plan and talk with your doctor about your medication treatment as part of an overall plan for wellness.

3 Make DASH a part of your healthy life.

The DASH eating plan along with other lifestyle changes can help you control your blood pressure and lower blood cholesterol. Important lifestyle recommendations include: achieve and maintain a healthy weight, get regular physical activity, and, if you drink alcohol, do so in moderation (up to one drink per day for women and up to two drinks per day for men).

4 DASH is for everyone in the family.

Start with the meal plans in A Week With the DASH Eating Plan if you want to follow the menus similar to those used in the DASH trial—then make up your own using your favorite foods. In fact, your entire family can eat meals using the DASH eating plan because it can be adapted to meet varied nutritional needs, food preferences, and dietary requirements.

5 Don't worry.

Remember that on some days the foods you eat may add up to more than the recommended servings from one food group and less from another. Or, you may have too much sodium on a particular day. Just try your best to keep the average of several days close to the DASH eating plan and the sodium level recommended for you.

DASH EATING PLAN

The DASH Eating Plan is a heart healthy approach that has been scientifically proven to lower blood pressure and have other health benefits. To learn more, go to www.nhlbi.nih.gov/DASH.

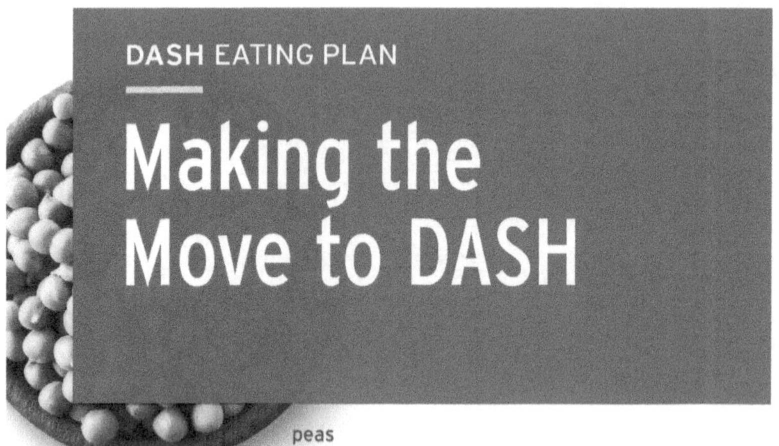

DASH EATING PLAN

Making the Move to DASH

peas

HEALTHY EATING, PROVEN RESULTS

Moving to heart healthy eating may seem difficult, but it doesn't have to be. Here are some tips to make DASH work for you.

bell pepper

squash

shrimp

chickpeas

Change gradually.

- If you now eat one or two servings of vegetables a day, add a serving at lunch and another at dinner.
- If you don't eat fruit now or have juice only at breakfast, add a serving of fruit to your meals or have it as a snack.
- Gradually increase your use of milk, yogurt, and cheese to three servings a day. For example, drink milk with lunch or dinner, instead of soda, sugar-sweetened tea, or alcohol.
- Choose fat-free or low-fat (1 percent) milk, yogurt, and reduced-fat cheese to reduce your intake of saturated fat, cholesterol, and calories and to increase your calcium.
- Read the Nutrition Facts label on frozen and prepared meals, pizza, and desserts to choose those lowest in saturated fat and *trans* fat.

Vary your proteins.

- Choose lean cuts of meat and remove skin from poultry.
- Check the labels on ground meats and poultry and select those with lower saturated fat.
- Serve fish instead of meat or poultry once or twice each week.
- Include two or more vegetarian (meatless) meals each week.
- Aim to fill ½ your plate with vegetables and fruits, ¼ with whole grains, and ¼ with fish, lean meat, poultry, or beans.
- Add extra vegetables to casseroles, pasta, and stir-fry dishes.

Select nutritious, tasty snacks.

- Fruits offer great taste and variety. Use fruits canned in their own juice or packed in water. Fresh fruits are fast and easy and dried fruits are a good choice to carry with you or to have in the car.
- Try these snack ideas: unsalted rice cakes; nuts mixed with raisins; graham crackers; fat-free and low-fat yogurt; popcorn with no salt or butter added; raw vegetables.

Make healthy substitutions.

- Choose whole grain foods for most grain servings to get more nutrients, such as minerals and fiber. For example, choose whole wheat bread or whole grain cereals.
- If you have trouble digesting milk and milk products, try taking lactase enzyme pills with the milk products. Or, buy lactose-free milk.
- If you are allergic to nuts, use beans or seeds (such as sunflower, flax, or sesame seeds).

DASH EATING PLAN

The DASH Eating Plan is a heart healthy approach that has been scientifically proven to lower blood pressure and have other health benefits. To learn more, go to www.nhlbi.nih.gov/DASH.

National Heart, Lung, and Blood Institute

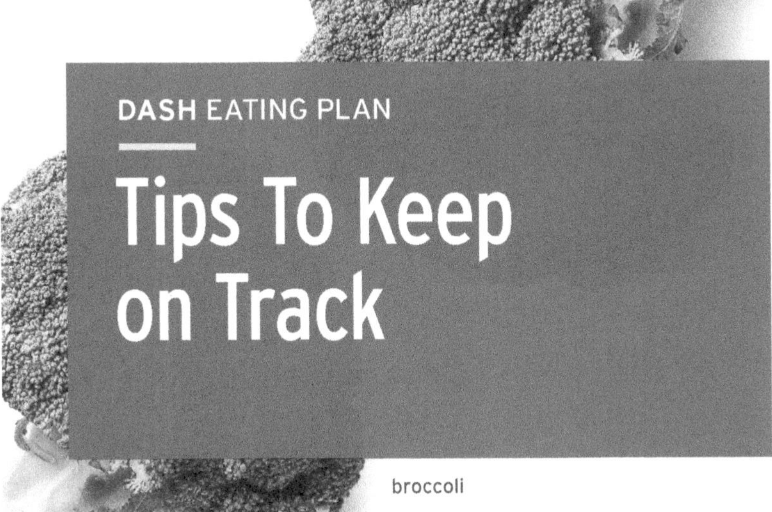

DASH EATING PLAN

Tips To Keep on Track

HEALTHY EATING, PROVEN RESULTS

The DASH eating plan is a new way of eating—for a lifetime. If you slip from the eating plan for a few days, don't let it keep you from reaching your health goals. Get back on track.

broccoli

whole-grain pasta

tomatoes

thyme

peaches

1 **Ask yourself why you got off track.**

Was it at a party? Were you feeling stress at home or work? Find out what triggered your sidetrack and start again with the DASH plan.

2 **Don't worry about a slip.**

Everyone slips—especially when learning something new. Remember that changing your lifestyle is a long-term process.

3 **See if you tried to do too much at once.**

Often, those starting a new lifestyle try to change too much at once. Instead, change one or two things at a time. Slowly but surely is the best way to succeed.

4 **Break the process down into small steps.**

This not only keeps you from trying to do too much at once, but also keeps the changes easier. Break complex goals into simpler, attainable steps.

5 **Write it down.**

Learn what your daily calorie level should be to maintain or reach your goal weight by using the free, interactive, online Body Weight Planner (niddk.nih.gov/bwp). Then use the What's on Your Plate? worksheet to keep track of what you eat and drink. Knowing what your goal is and then keeping track for several days can help you succeed. You may find, for instance, that you eat sugary or salty snacks while watching television. If so, try keeping healthier snacks on hand. This record also helps you be sure you're getting enough of each food group each day.

6 **Celebrate success.**

Treat yourself to a nonfood reward for your accomplishments. You could see a new movie, get a massage, or buy yourself flowers or a fun gift.

DASH EATING PLAN

The DASH Eating Plan is a heart healthy approach that has been scientifically proven to lower blood pressure and have other health benefits. To learn more, go to www.nhlbi.nih.gov/DASH.

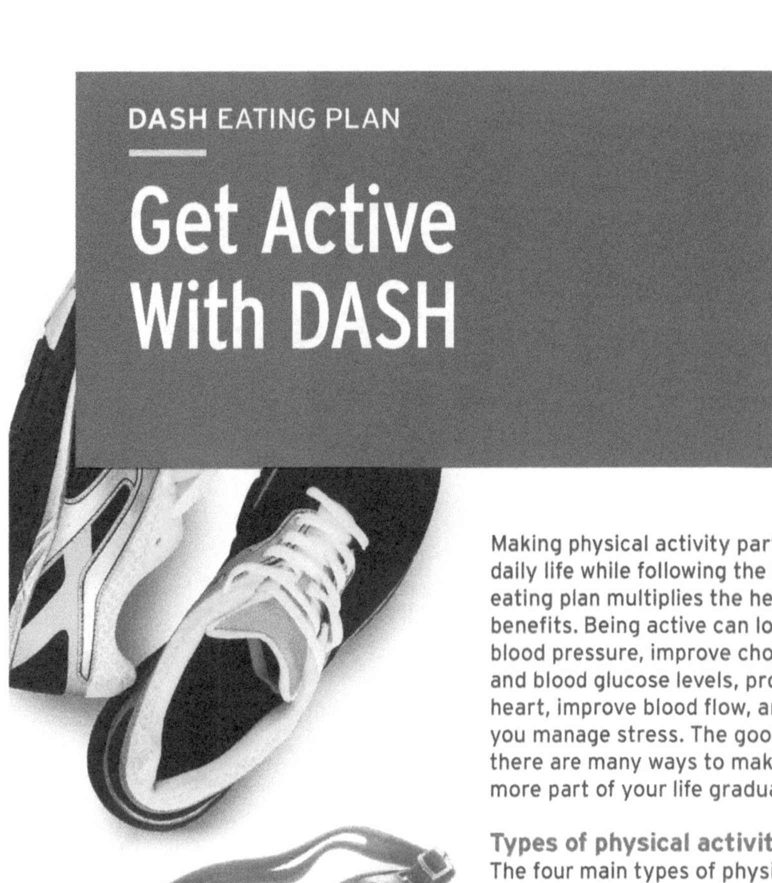

DASH EATING PLAN

Get Active With DASH

HEALTHY EATING, PROVEN RESULTS

Combining the DASH eating plan and physical activity can lower high blood pressure and make your heart healthier.

Making physical activity part of your daily life while following the DASH eating plan multiplies the health benefits. Being active can lower high blood pressure, improve cholesterol and blood glucose levels, protect your heart, improve blood flow, and help you manage stress. The good news is there are many ways to make moving more part of your life gradually.

Types of physical activity

The four main types of physical activity are aerobic, muscle-strengthening, bone-strengthening, and stretching.

- **Aerobic.** Also called endurance activity, aerobic activity benefits your heart and lungs the most. Brisk walking, running, bicycling, jumping rope, and swimming are all examples.
- **Muscle-strengthening.** Resistance training and weight lifting improve your power and endurance. You can also use elastic bands or body weight for resistance, like doing push-ups.
- **Bone-strengthening.** Weight-bearing activities such as running, walking, jumping rope, and lifting weights, make your bones strong.
- **Stretching.** Stretching improves your flexibility and your ability to fully move your joints making all other activity possible. Touching your toes, side stretches, and yoga are some examples.

How much activity is needed?

Adults should get at least 2½ hours of physical activity a week to help lower and control blood pressure. That's just 30 minutes a day, 5 days a week. If you don't have high blood pressure, being physically active can help keep it that way.

Increase activity to multiply the benefits

If you have high blood pressure, the benefits of physical activity are actually greater than in those with normal blood pressure. Both aerobic and muscle-strengthening activities are beneficial. Moderate-intensity activity for about 90 minutes a week or 45 minutes of vigorous-intensity activity helps to substantially lower your risk of heart disease. If you have high blood pressure, work with your doctor as you increase your physical activity, as adjustments to medication may be needed.

Everyone can benefit by being active

If you don't have high blood pressure but still aren't active, you can benefit from increasing your physical activity to recommended levels. Physical activity can help lower blood pressure and reduce your risk of becoming overweight or obese or developing diabetes.

DASH EATING PLAN

The DASH Eating Plan is a heart healthy approach that has been scientifically proven to lower blood pressure and have other health benefits. To learn more, go to www.nhlbi.nih.gov/DASH.

Tips to Make Moving More Part of Your Life Every Day

Getting started
If you're inactive, start slow. For example, start with a short walk each day. Gradually build up and set new goals to stay motivated. The important thing is to find something you enjoy, and do it safely. And remember—trying too hard at first can lead to injury and cause you to give up. If you have a chronic health problem, be sure to talk with your doctor before beginning a new physical activity program.

1 **Set a schedule.**
Physical activity can help improve your mood and your overall well-being. Planning time for exercise helps make it part of a routine.

2 **Build activities into your day.**
Go for a walk during a break from work or do strength training while watching TV. Think about transforming your everyday activities so you move more.

3 **Move for a short time a few times a day.**
Don't have a full half hour? Move for few minutes at a time. Walk briskly for 5 minutes, turn around and walk back. Dance (standing or seated) to three songs. Do some squats. Break up sitting time. Even light-intensity activity is beneficial for your health.

4 **Get a friend or family member to join you.**
Go on walks or take a yoga or other fitness class together. Motivate each other to keep it up. Share your goals and celebrate your accomplishments together.

5 **Do what you love.**
Love the outdoors? Try gardening, hiking, biking, or golf. Play with the children in your life. Walk on a track at a nearby school or dance to music that lifts your spirits.

Learn more about the benefits of physical activity and living a heart-healthy life at **www.nhlbi.nih.gov/health-topics/heart-healthy-living.**

DASH EATING PLAN | The DASH Eating Plan is a heart healthy approach that has been scientifically proven to lower blood pressure and have other health benefits. To learn more, go to www.nhlbi.nih.gov/DASH.

National Heart, Lung, and Blood Institute

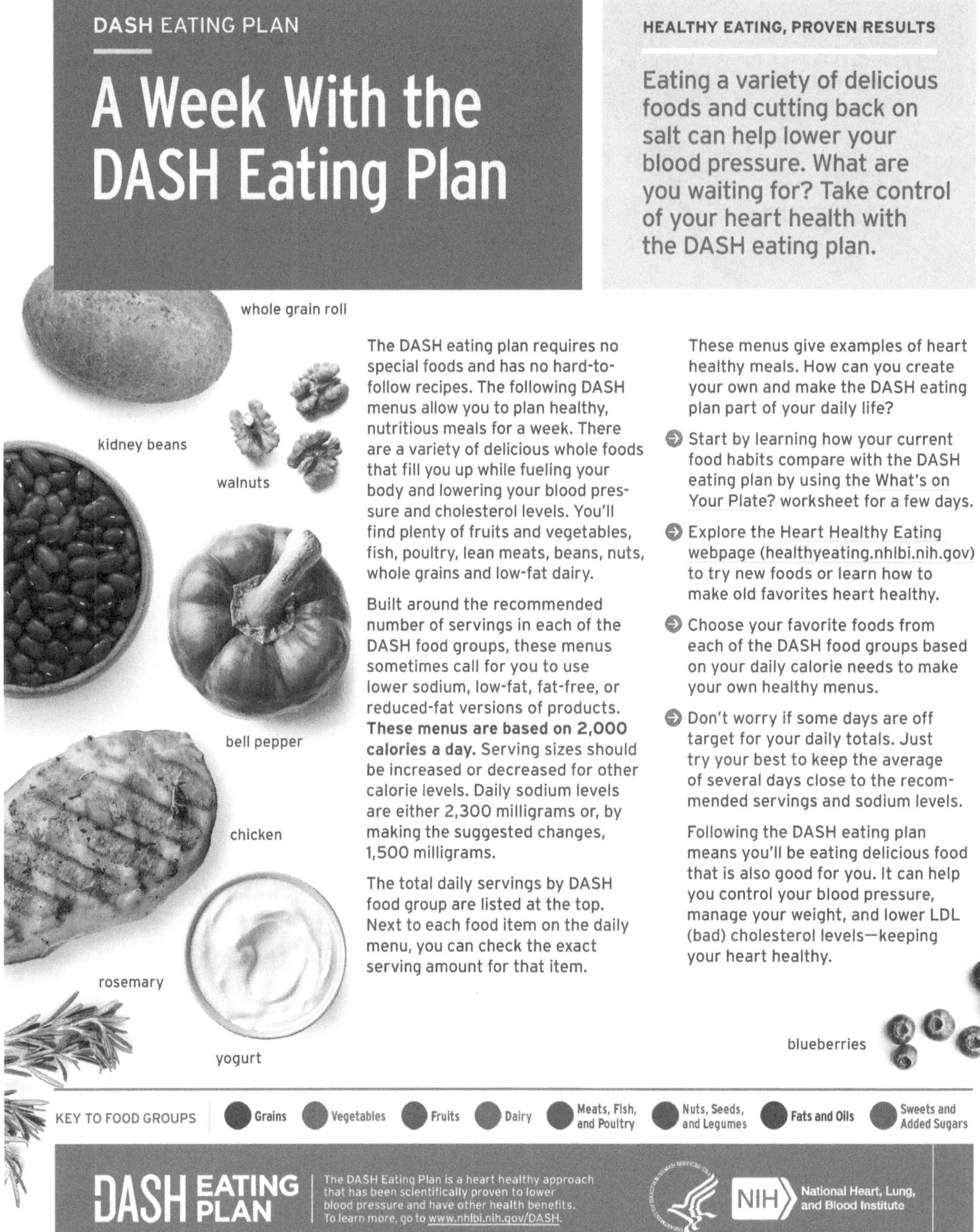

DASH EATING PLAN

A Week With the DASH Eating Plan

HEALTHY EATING, PROVEN RESULTS

Eating a variety of delicious foods and cutting back on salt can help lower your blood pressure. What are you waiting for? Take control of your heart health with the DASH eating plan.

The DASH eating plan requires no special foods and has no hard-to-follow recipes. The following DASH menus allow you to plan healthy, nutritious meals for a week. There are a variety of delicious whole foods that fill you up while fueling your body and lowering your blood pressure and cholesterol levels. You'll find plenty of fruits and vegetables, fish, poultry, lean meats, beans, nuts, whole grains and low-fat dairy.

Built around the recommended number of servings in each of the DASH food groups, these menus sometimes call for you to use lower sodium, low-fat, fat-free, or reduced-fat versions of products. **These menus are based on 2,000 calories a day.** Serving sizes should be increased or decreased for other calorie levels. Daily sodium levels are either 2,300 milligrams or, by making the suggested changes, 1,500 milligrams.

The total daily servings by DASH food group are listed at the top. Next to each food item on the daily menu, you can check the exact serving amount for that item.

These menus give examples of heart healthy meals. How can you create your own and make the DASH eating plan part of your daily life?

- Start by learning how your current food habits compare with the DASH eating plan by using the What's on Your Plate? worksheet for a few days.
- Explore the Heart Healthy Eating webpage (healthyeating.nhlbi.nih.gov) to try new foods or learn how to make old favorites heart healthy.
- Choose your favorite foods from each of the DASH food groups based on your daily calorie needs to make your own healthy menus.
- Don't worry if some days are off target for your daily totals. Just try your best to keep the average of several days close to the recommended servings and sodium levels.

Following the DASH eating plan means you'll be eating delicious food that is also good for you. It can help you control your blood pressure, manage your weight, and lower LDL (bad) cholesterol levels—keeping your heart healthy.

KEY TO FOOD GROUPS: Grains · Vegetables · Fruits · Dairy · Meats, Fish, and Poultry · Nuts, Seeds, and Legumes · Fats and Oils · Sweets and Added Sugars

DASH EATING PLAN | The DASH Eating Plan is a heart healthy approach that has been scientifically proven to lower blood pressure and have other health benefits. To learn more, go to www.nhlbi.nih.gov/DASH.

NIH National Heart, Lung, and Blood Institute

DAY 1
A Week With DASH

The menu below contains the recommended number of daily servings from each DASH food group as well as a heart healthy 2,300 mg of sodium. You can easily reduce the sodium in this menu to 1,500 mg by substituting some key food items, which are highlighted in yellow. Just follow the tips.

The Day 1 menu contains this number of servings from each DASH Food Group

Grains

Vegetables

Fruits

Dairy

Meats, Fish, and Poultry

Nuts, Seeds, and Legumes

Fats and Oils

Sweets and Added Sugars

BREAKFAST	SODIUM (MG)
¾ cup bran flakes cereal:	**220**
+ 1 medium banana	1
+ 1 cup low-fat milk	107
1 slice whole wheat bread:	**149**
+ 1 tsp soft (tub) margarine	26
1 cup orange juice	**5**
LUNCH	**SODIUM (MG)**
¾ cup chicken salad:	**179**
+ 2 slices whole wheat bread	299
+ 1 Tbsp Dijon mustard	373
salad:	
+ ½ cup fresh cucumber slices	1
+ ½ cup tomato wedges	5
+ 1 Tbsp sunflower seeds	0
+ 1 tsp Italian dressing, low calorie	43
½ cup fruit cocktail, juice pack	**5**
DINNER	**SODIUM (MG)**
3 oz roast beef, eye of the round:	**35**
+ 2 Tbsp beef gravy, fat-free	165
1 cup green beans, sautéed with:	**12**
+ ½ tsp canola oil	0
1 small baked potato:	**14**
+ 1 Tbsp sour cream, fat-free	21
+ 1 Tbsp natural cheddar cheese, reduced-fat	67
+ 1 Tbsp chopped scallions	1
1 small whole wheat roll:	**148**
+ 1 tsp soft (tub) margarine	26
1 small apple	**1**
1 cup low-fat milk	**107**
SNACKS	**SODIUM (MG)**
⅓ cup almonds, unsalted	**0**
¼ cup raisins	**4**
½ cup fruit yogurt, fat-free, no sugar added	**86**
TOTAL SODIUM (MG) FOR DAY 1	**2,101**

219 mg less sodium
Try shredded wheat cereal instead of bran flakes.

59 mg less sodium
Make the chicken salad without salt.

198 mg less sodium
Use regular mustard in place of Dijon mustard.

66 mg less sodium
Use low-sodium, reduced-fat cheddar cheese.

26 mg less sodium
Use unsalted margarine.

Total nutrients per day 2,062 calories, 63 g total fat, 28% calories from fat, 13 g saturated fat, 6% calories from saturated fat, 155 mg cholesterol, 2,101 mg sodium, 284 g carbohydrate, 114 g protein, 1,220 mg calcium, 594 mg magnesium, 4,909 mg potassium, 37 g fiber

DAY 2
A Week With DASH

The menu below contains the recommended number of daily servings from each DASH food group as well as a heart healthy 2,300 mg of sodium. You can easily reduce the sodium in this menu to 1,500 mg by substituting some key food items, which are highlighted in yellow. Just follow the tips.

The Day 2 menu contains this number of servings from each DASH Food Group

Grains	Vegetables	Fruits	Dairy	Meats, Fish, and Poultry	Nuts, Seeds, and Legumes	Fats and Oils	Sweets and Added Sugars
6	5¼	7	3	3	1½	1½	0

BREAKFAST	SODIUM (MG)
½ cup instant oatmeal	**54**
1 mini whole wheat bagel:	**84**
+ 1 Tbsp peanut butter	81
1 medium banana	**1**
1 cup low-fat milk	**107**

49 mg less sodium Use regular oatmeal with 1 tsp cinnamon.

LUNCH	SODIUM (MG)
chicken breast sandwich:	
+ 3 oz cooked chicken breast, skinless	65
+ 2 slices whole wheat bread	299
+ 1 slice (¾ oz) natural cheddar cheese, reduced-fat	202
+ 1 large leaf romaine lettuce	1
+ 2 slices tomato	2
+ 1 Tbsp mayonnaise, low-fat	101
1 cup cantaloupe chunks	**26**
1 cup apple juice	**21**

199 mg less sodium Use reduced-fat, low-sodium, natural Swiss cheese instead of reduced-fat, natural cheddar cheese.

DINNER	SODIUM (MG)
1 cup spaghetti:	**1**
+ ¾ cup vegetarian spaghetti sauce	479
+ 3 Tbsp Parmesan cheese	287
spinach salad:	
+ 1 cup fresh spinach leaves	24
+ ¼ cup fresh carrots, grated	19
+ ¼ cup fresh mushrooms, sliced	1
+ 1 Tbsp vinaigrette dressing	1
½ cup corn, cooked from frozen	**1**
½ cup canned pears, juice pack	**5**

226 mg less sodium Use low-sodium tomato paste in the vegetarian spaghetti sauce recipe.

SNACKS	SODIUM (MG)
⅓ cup almonds, unsalted	**0**
¼ cup dried apricots	**3**
1 cup fruit yogurt, fat-free, no sugar added	**173**
TOTAL SODIUM (MG) FOR DAY 2	2,035

Total nutrients per day 2,027 calories, 64 g total fat, 28% calories from fat, 13 g saturated fat, 6% calories from saturated fat, 114 mg cholesterol, 2,035 mg sodium, 288 g carbohydrate, 99 g protein, 1,370 mg calcium, 535 mg magnesium, 4,715 mg potassium, 34 g fiber

DAY 3
A Week With DASH

The menu below contains the recommended number of daily servings from each DASH food group as well as a heart healthy 2,300 mg of sodium. You can easily reduce the sodium in this menu to 1,500 mg by substituting some key food items, which are highlighted in yellow. Just follow the tips.

The Day 3 menu contains this number of servings from each DASH Food Group

Grains

Vegetables

Fruits

Dairy

Meats, Fish, and Poultry

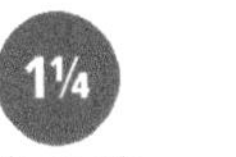

Nuts, Seeds, and Legumes

Fats and Oils

0
Sweets and Added Sugars

BREAKFAST	SODIUM (MG)
¾ cup bran flakes cereal:	**220**
+ 1 medium banana	1
+ 1 cup low-fat milk	107
1 slice whole wheat bread:	**149**
+ 1 tsp soft (tub) margarine	26
1 cup orange juice	**6**
LUNCH	**SODIUM (MG)**
beef barbeque sandwich:	
+ 2 oz roast beef, eye of round	26
+ 1 Tbsp barbeque sauce	156
+ 2 slices (1½ oz) natural cheddar cheese, reduced-fat	405
+ 1 hamburger bun	183
+ 1 large leaf romaine lettuce	1
+ 2 slices tomato	2
1 cup new potato salad	**17**
1 medium orange	**0**
DINNER	**SODIUM (MG)**
3 oz cod:	**70**
+ 1 tsp lemon juice	1
½ cup brown rice	**5**
1 cup spinach, cooked from frozen, sautéed with:	**184**
+ 1 tsp canola oil	0
+ 1 Tbsp almonds, slivered	0
1 small cornbread muffin, made with oil:	**119**
+ 1 tsp soft (tub) margarine	26
SNACKS	**SODIUM (MG)**
1 cup fruit yogurt, fat-free, no sugar added	**173**
1 Tbsp sunflower seeds, unsalted	**0**
2 large graham cracker rectangles:	**156**
+ 1 Tbsp peanut butter	81
TOTAL SODIUM (MG) FOR DAY 3	**2,114**

219 mg less sodium
Try puffed wheat cereal instead of bran flakes.

26 mg less sodium
Use unsalted margarine.

396 mg less sodium
Use low-sodium natural cheddar cheese instead of reduced-fat natural cheddar cheese.

26 mg less sodium
Use unsalted margarine.

Total nutrients per day 1,997 calories, 56 g total fat, 25% calories from fat, 12 g saturated fat, 6% calories from saturated fat, 140 mg cholesterol, 2,114 mg sodium, 289 g carbohydrate, 103 g protein, 1,537 mg calcium, 630 mg magnesium, 4,676 mg potassium, 34 g fiber

DAY 4
A Week With DASH

The menu below contains the recommended number of daily servings from each DASH food group as well as a heart healthy 2,300 mg of sodium. You can easily reduce the sodium in this menu to 1,500 mg by substituting some key food items, which are highlighted in yellow. Just follow the tips.

The Day 4 menu contains this number of servings from each DASH Food Group

Grains

Vegetables

Fruits

Dairy

Meats, Fish, and Poultry

Nuts, Seeds, and Legumes

Fats and Oils

Sweets and Added Sugars

BREAKFAST	SODIUM (MG)
1 slice whole wheat bread:	**149**
+ 1 tsp soft (tub) margarine	26
1 cup fruit yogurt, fat-free, no sugar added	**173**
1 medium peach	**0**
½ cup grape juice	**4**
LUNCH	**SODIUM (MG)**
ham and cheese sandwich:	
+ 2 oz ham, low-fat, low-sodium	549
+ 2 slices whole wheat bread	299
+ 1 large leaf romaine lettuce	1
+ 2 slices tomato	2
+ 1 slice (¾ oz) natural cheddar cheese, reduced-fat	202
+ 1 Tbsp mayonnaise, low-fat	101
1 cup carrot sticks	**84**
DINNER	**SODIUM (MG)**
chicken and Spanish rice	**341**
1 cup green peas, sautéed with:	**115**
+ 1 tsp canola oil	0
1 cup cantaloupe chunks	**26**
1 cup low-fat milk	**107**
SNACKS	**SODIUM (MG)**
⅓ cup almonds, unsalted	**0**
1 cup apple juice	**21**
¼ cup apricots	**3**
1 cup low-fat milk	**107**
TOTAL SODIUM (MG) FOR DAY 4	**2,312**

26 mg less sodium
Use unsalted margarine.

526 mg less sodium
Try roast beef tenderloin instead of low-fat, low-sodium ham.

198 mg less sodium
Use reduced-fat, low-sodium natural cheddar cheese.

126 mg less sodium
Use low-sodium tomato sauce in Spanish rice recipe.

Total nutrients per day 2,024 calories, 59 g total fat, 26% calories from fat, 12 g saturated fat, 5% calories from saturated fat, 148 mg cholesterol, 2,312 mg sodium, 279 g carbohydrate, 110 g protein, 1,417 mg calcium, 538 mg magnesium, 4,575 mg potassium, 35 g fiber

DAY 5
A Week With DASH

The menu below contains the recommended number of daily servings from each DASH food group as well as a heart healthy 2,300 mg of sodium. You can easily reduce the sodium in this menu to 1,500 mg by substituting some key food items, which are highlighted in yellow. Just follow the tips.

The Day 5 menu contains this number of servings from each DASH Food Group

Grains	Vegetables	Fruits	Dairy	Meats, Fish, and Poultry	Nuts, Seeds, and Legumes	Fats and Oils	Sweets and Added Sugars
5	6¼	5	2¼	6	1¾	2	0

BREAKFAST	SODIUM (MG)
1 cup whole grain oat rings cereal:	**273**
+ 1 medium banana	1
+ 1 cup low-fat milk	107
1 medium raisin bagel:	**272**
+ 1 Tbsp peanut butter	81
1 cup orange juice	**5**

LUNCH	SODIUM (MG)
tuna salad plate:	
+ ½ cup tuna salad	171
+ 1 large leaf romaine lettuce	1
+ 1 slice whole wheat bread	149
cucumber salad:	
+ 1 cup fresh cucumber slices	2
+ ½ cup tomato wedges	5
+ 1 Tbsp vinaigrette dressing	133
½ cup cottage cheese, low-fat:	**459**
+ ½ cup canned pineapple, juice pack	1
+ 1 Tbsp almonds, unsalted	0

DINNER	SODIUM (MG)
3 oz turkey meatloaf	**205**
1 small baked potato:	**14**
+ 1 Tbsp sour cream, fat-free	21
+ 1 Tbsp natural cheddar cheese, reduced-fat, grated	67
+ 1 scallion stalk, chopped	1
1 cup collard greens, sautéed with:	**85**
+ 1 tsp canola oil	0
1 small whole wheat roll	**148**
1 medium peach	**0**

SNACKS	SODIUM (MG)
1 cup fruit yogurt, fat-free, no sugar added	**173**
2 Tbsp sunflower seeds, unsalted	**0**
TOTAL SODIUM (MG) FOR DAY 5	**2,373**

269 mg less sodium — Try frosted shredded wheat instead of whole grain oat rings cereal.

67 mg less sodium — Use unsalted peanut butter.

96 mg less sodium — Use 6 low-sodium whole wheat crackers.

67 mg less sodium — Use fat-free yogurt dressing.

131 mg less sodium — Use low-sodium ketchup in turkey meatloaf.

66 mg less sodium — Use low-sodium, reduced-fat cheese.

147 mg less sodium — Use 6 small melba toast crackers instead of a whole wheat roll.

Total nutrients per day 1,976 calories, 57 g total fat, 26% calories from fat, 11 g saturated fat, 5% calories from saturated fat, 158 mg cholesterol, 2,373 mg sodium, 275 g carbohydrate, 111 g protein, 1,470 mg calcium, 495 mg magnesium, 4,769 mg potassium, 30 g fiber

DAY 6
A Week With DASH

The menu below contains the recommended number of daily servings from each DASH food group as well as a heart healthy 2,300 mg of sodium. You can easily reduce the sodium in this menu to 1,500 mg by substituting some key food items, which are highlighted in yellow. Just follow the tips.

The Day 6 menu contains this number of servings from each DASH Food Group

Grains

Vegetables

Fruits

Dairy

Meats, Fish, and Poultry

Nuts, Seeds, and Legumes

Fats and Oils

Sweets and Added Sugars

BREAKFAST	SODIUM (MG)
1 low-fat granola bar	**81**
1 medium banana	**1**
½ cup fruit yogurt, fat-free, no sugar added	**86**
1 cup orange juice	**5**
1 cup low-fat milk	**107**
LUNCH	**SODIUM (MG)**
turkey breast sandwich:	
+ 3 oz cooked turkey breast	48
+ 2 slices whole wheat bread	299
+ 1 large leaf romaine lettuce	1
+ 2 slices tomato	2
+ 2 tsp mayonnaise, low-fat	67
+ 1 Tbsp Dijon mustard	373
1 cup steamed broccoli, cooked from frozen	**11**
1 medium orange	**0**
DINNER	**SODIUM (MG)**
3 oz spicy baked fish	**50**
1 cup scallion rice	**18**
spinach sauté:	
+ ½ cup spinach, cooked from frozen, sautéed with:	92
+ 2 tsp canola oil	0
+ 1 Tbsp almonds, slivered, unsalted	0
1 cup carrots, cooked from frozen	**84**
1 small whole wheat roll:	**148**
+ 1 tsp soft (tub) margarine	26
1 small cookie	**60**
SNACKS	**SODIUM (MG)**
2 Tbsp peanuts, unsalted	**1**
1 cup low-fat milk	**107**
¼ cup dried apricots	**3**
TOTAL SODIUM (MG) FOR DAY 6	**1,671**

198 mg less sodium
Use 1 Tbsp regular mustard instead of Dijon mustard.

Total nutrients per day 1,939 calories, 58g total fat, 27% calories from fat, 12g saturated fat, 6% calories from saturated fat, 171mg cholesterol, 1,671mg sodium, 268g carbohydrate, 105g protein, 1,210mg calcium, 548mg magnesium, 4,710mg potassium, 36g fiber

DAY 7
A Week With DASH

The menu below contains the recommended number of daily servings from each DASH food group as well as a heart healthy 2,300 mg of sodium. You can easily reduce the sodium in this menu to 1,500 mg by substituting some key food items, which are highlighted in yellow. Just follow the tips.

The Day 7 menu contains this number of servings from each DASH Food Group

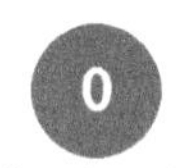

8¼	4¾	5	4	3	1½	2½	0
Grains	Vegetables	Fruits	Dairy	Meats, Fish, and Poultry	Nuts, Seeds, and Legumes	Fats and Oils	Sweets and Added Sugars

BREAKFAST	SODIUM (MG)
1 cup whole grain oat rings:	**273**
+ 1 medium banana	1
+ 1 cup low-fat milk	107
1 cup fruit yogurt, fat-free, no sugar added	173
LUNCH	**SODIUM (MG)**
tuna salad sandwich:	
+ ½ cup tuna, drained, rinsed	39
+ 1 Tbsp mayonnaise, low-fat	101
+ 1 large leaf romaine lettuce	1
+ 2 slices tomato	2
+ 2 slices whole wheat bread	299
1 medium apple	**1**
1 cup low-fat milk	**107**
DINNER	**SODIUM (MG)**
⅙ recipe zucchini lasagna	**368**
salad:	
+ 1 cup fresh spinach leaves	24
+ 1 cup tomato wedges	9
+ 2 Tbsp croutons, seasoned	62
+ 1 Tbsp vinaigrette dressing, reduced calorie	133
+ 1 Tbsp sunflower seeds	0
1 small whole wheat roll:	**148**
+ 1 tsp soft (tub) margarine	45
1 cup grape juice	**8**
SNACKS	**SODIUM (MG)**
⅓ cup almonds, unsalted	**0**
¼ cup dry apricots	**3**
6 whole wheat crackers	**166**
TOTAL SODIUM (MG) FOR DAY 7	**2,069**

268 mg less sodium
Try regular oatmeal Instead of whole grain oat rings.

203 mg less sodium
Use low-fat, no salt added cottage cheese in zucchini lasagna recipe.

26 mg less sodium
Use unsalted margarine.

132 mg less sodium
Use low-sodium vinaigrette in salad recipe.

Total nutrients per day 1,993 calories, 64 g total fat, 29% calories from fat, 13 g saturated fat, 6% calories from saturated fat, 71 mg cholesterol, 2,069 mg sodium, 283 g carbohydrate, 93 g protein, 1,616 mg calcium, 537 mg magnesium, 4,693 mg potassium, 32 g fiber

Mediterranean Diet

Choosing a diet similar to one eaten by people living around the Mediterranean Sea may lower the risk of cardiovascular disease and have additional health benefits. The diet is mostly plant-based with high amounts of fresh vegetables, fruits, nuts, dried beans, olive oil, and fish. Follow these tips to eat the Mediterranean way!

Food/Food Group	**Recommended Intake***	Tips
Vegetables	4 or more servings each day (one portion each day should be raw vegetables)	A serving is 1 cup raw or ½ cup cooked vegetables. Eat a variety of colors and textures.
Fruits	3 or more servings each day	Make fruit your dessert
Grains	4 or more servings each day	Choose mostly whole grains. 1 serving = 1 slice bread or ½ cup cooked oatmeal
Fats/Oils	Olive Oil: 4 Tablespoons or more each day	Choose extra virgin olive oil (EVOO) and use in salad dressings and cooking; choose avocado or natural peanut butter instead of butter or margarine
Dried Beans/Nuts/Seeds	Nuts/Seeds: 3 or more servings each week Beans/Legumes: 3 or more servings each week	1 ounce or 1 serving = 23 almonds or 14 walnut halves; 1 serving of beans = ½ cup
Fish and Seafood	2-3 times each week	Choose salmon, sardines, and tuna which are rich in Omega-3 fatty acids
Herbs and Spices	Use daily	Season foods with herbs, garlic, onions and spices instead of salt
Yogurt/Cheese/Egg Poultry	Choose daily to weekly	Choose low-fat yogurt and cheeses; choose skinless chicken or turkey in place of red meat
Alcohol/Wine	Men: 1-2 glasses each day Women: 1 glass each day	Always ask your medical team if alcohol is ok for you to consume.

***Serving sizes should be individualized to meet energy and nutrient needs.**

- ❖ Red meats, processed meats, and sweets should be limited

08/2015

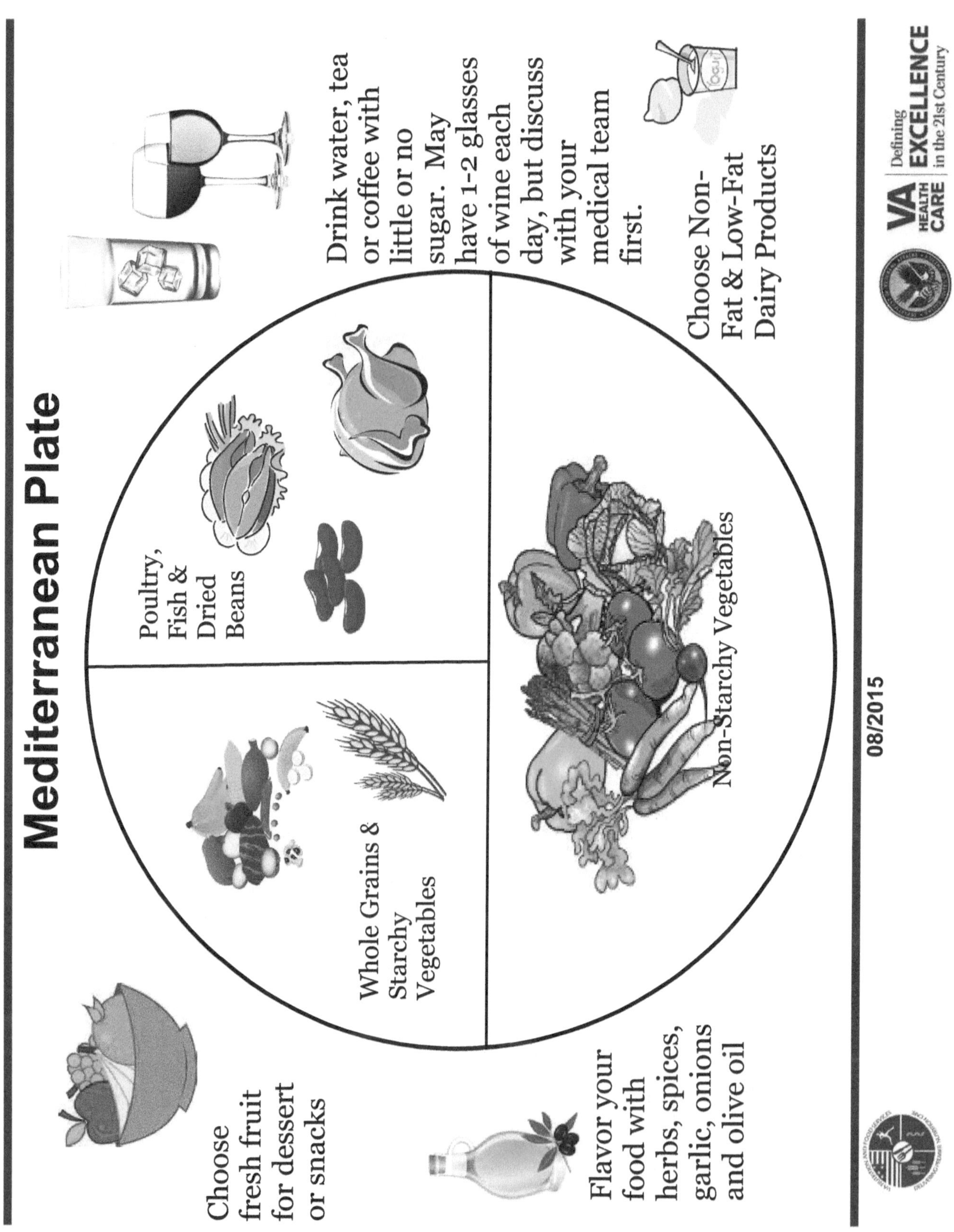
Mediterranean Plate
Choose fresh fruit for dessert or snacks
Flavor your food with herbs, spices, garlic, onions and olive oil
Whole Grains & Starchy Vegetables
Poultry, Fish & Dried Beans
Non-Starchy Vegetables
Drink water, tea or coffee with little or no sugar. May have 1-2 glasses of wine each day, but discuss with your medical team first.
Choose Non-Fat & Low-Fat Dairy Products
08/2015
VA HEALTH CARE
Defining EXCELLENCE in the 21st Century

Sample Menu

Breakfast

1 cup Greek yogurt with ¾ cup berries or fresh fruit and ¼ cup walnuts
1 slice whole wheat toast with ¼ cup mashed avocado or 2 teaspoons natural nut butter
Coffee or tea

Lunch

1 cup lentil or minestrone soup
1 whole wheat pita
2 Tablespoon hummus
1/2 cup tomatoes, 1/2 cup cucumber with 2 Tablespoons olive oil, balsamic vinegar, and basil
Water with lemon wedge
1 apple, peach, or orange

Snack

1 ounce low-fat mozzarella cheese and 15 grapes

Dinner

3-4 ounces broiled fish brushed with olive oil, seasoned with lemon and dill
1 cup brown rice, cooked
1 cup steamed carrots
1-2 cups baby spinach and arugula salad with 2 Tablespoons olive oil vinaigrette dressing
Decaf green tea or 5 ounce wine (if cleared by medical team)

Snack

1 ounce dark chocolate

Nutrition Information: 2200 calories (8% saturated fat, 11% polyunsaturated fat, 19% Monounsaturated fat), 43 grams fiber. 4 Tablespoons olive oil each day provides 480 of 2200 calories.

08/2015

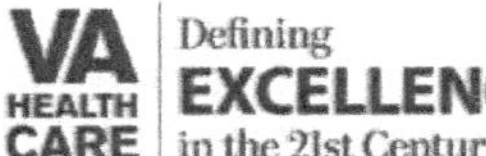

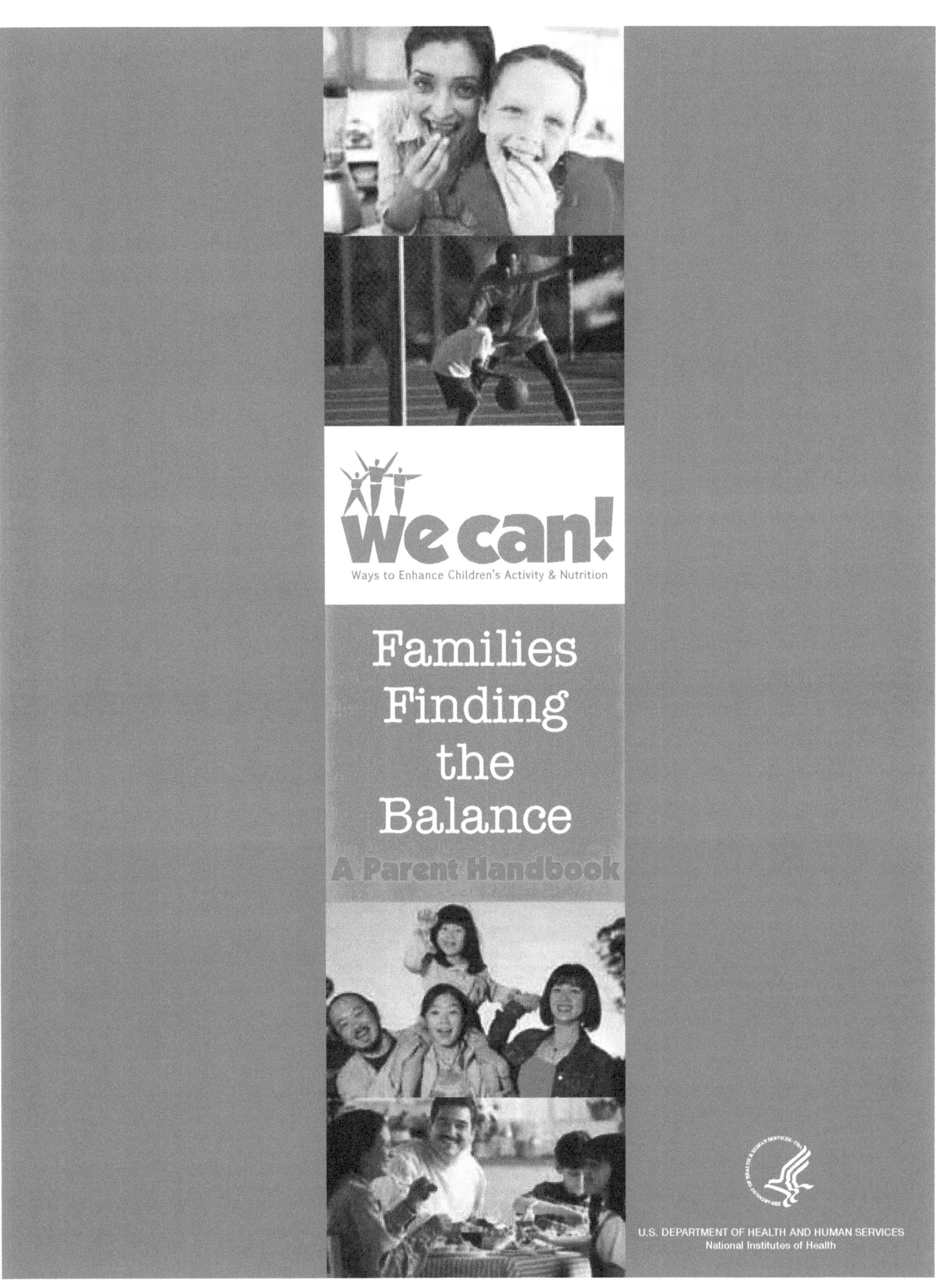
We can!
Ways to Enhance Children's Activity & Nutrition
Families Finding the Balance
A Parent Handbook
U.S. DEPARTMENT OF HEALTH AND HUMAN SERVICES
National Institutes of Health

We Can! (Ways to Enhance Children's Activity & Nutrition) is a new public education outreach program designed to help children 8–13 years old stay at a healthy weight through improving food choices, increasing physical activity, and reducing screen time. The program is a collaboration of four Institutes of the National Institutes of Health (NIH): the National Heart, Lung, and Blood Institute (NHLBI), National Institute of Diabetes and Digestive and Kidney Diseases (NIDDK), National Institute of Child Health and Human Development (NICHD), and National Cancer Institute (NCI).

We Can! is unique because it focuses on parents and families in home and community settings. Research shows that parents and families have a big impact on shaping the behavior of children. They can do much to help children maintain a healthy weight and prevent overweight. ***We Can!*** is harnessing that power through:

- Programs in local communities throughout the country
- Partnerships with other national organizations that care about children and their health
- A comprehensive Web site for parents (**http://wecan.nhlbi.nih.gov**)

Read on to understand why overweight is a problem for children as well as adults in the United States. Learn about energy balance—the key to managing weight—and get lots of ideas and tips to help you and your children eat right and be physically active. And find out about places to go for further information and more strategies.

We Can! Families Finding the Balance: A Parent Handbook

Table of Contents

1- Why Should We Care About Our Weight?

These days, it seems as though everybody is talking about overweight and obesity and what to do about it. Why is it such a big deal?

Because, as a Nation, we've been getting steadily heavier. As the two maps on page 2 show, the number of adults who are obese has increased dramatically, even in the past decade or so. And it's not just a slightly larger waistline that might come with middle age. It's weight gain that damages our health. According to national data analyzed in 2002, it's estimated that 65 percent of Americans are now overweight or obese, and more than 61 million adults are obese.

Adults aren't the only ones who've been getting heavier. Children have been getting heavier as well. The percentage of children and teens who are overweight has more than doubled since the 1970s. About 16 percent of children and teens are overweight.

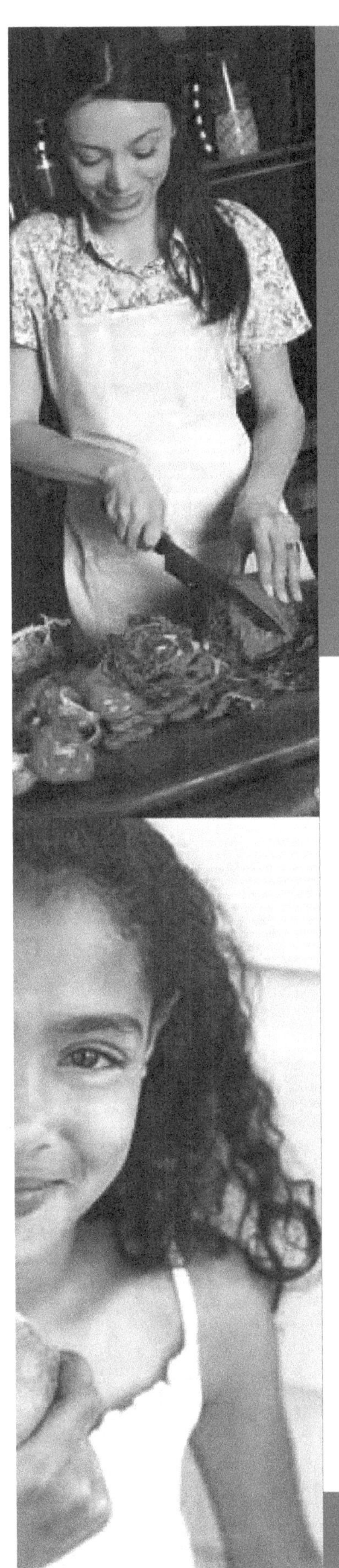

How America Has Changed

1990. In 10 States, fewer than 10 percent of adults were obese. In 33 States, 10 to 14 percent of adults were obese. In no State were more than 15 percent of adults obese.

Flash forward to 2003. In every State, at least 15 percent of adults were obese. In 15 States, 15 to 19 percent of adults were obese. In 31 States, 20 to 24 percent of adults were obese. In four States, more than 25 percent of adults were obese.

Obesity Trends Among U.S. Adults

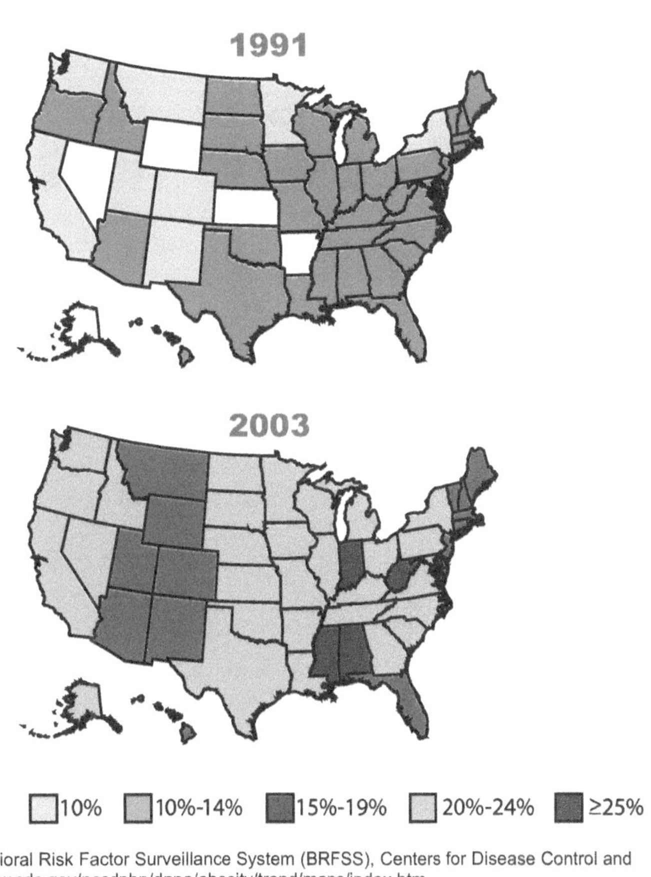

Source: Behavioral Risk Factor Surveillance System (BRFSS), Centers for Disease Control and Prevention, www.cdc.gov/nccdphp/dnpa/obesity/trend/maps/index.htm

The Downside of Overweight

People have lots of reasons to care if they weigh too much, both in the short run and over the long haul. In the short run, when a child is overweight, it can be hard to keep up with friends, play outside at recess, or wear the latest styles. Other kids at school can sometimes tease. Excess weight can be hard for adults, too. Clothes feel too tight, it's not always easy to be active, and one can tire easily.

Those extra pounds also have long-term consequences for both adults and children. Overweight is linked to increased risk of heart disease, type 2 diabetes, high blood pressure, high cholesterol, certain cancers, and other chronic conditions. Health experts are especially concerned about the long-term consequences of excess weight in children. For example, type 2 diabetes was once rare in children. Now, it is estimated to account for 8 to 45 percent of newly diagnosed cases of childhood diabetes. Most cases of type 2 diabetes in children occur in those who are overweight. And overweight children are likely to become overweight or obese adults.

2-What Can My Family and I Do to Encourage a Healthy Weight?

It's one thing to think about the national epidemic of obesity, but as a parent, what can you do about it? The two main ways to encourage and maintain a healthy weight and prevent overweight are to make smart food choices and to be physically active. That's what this ***We Can!*** handbook is all about—giving you lots of ideas that can help you and your family take action for a healthy weight.

Why parents? Because as parents, you make a big difference in what children think and do. Your children look up to you as role models. If you eat right and are physically active, you have a good chance of helping your children make those choices, too.

Why families? As a family, ***We Can!*** be more successful in adopting healthy choices and making changes. It's hard to make changes on your own. Creating family habits around smart eating and physical activity can make it easier for everyone to maintain a healthy weight.

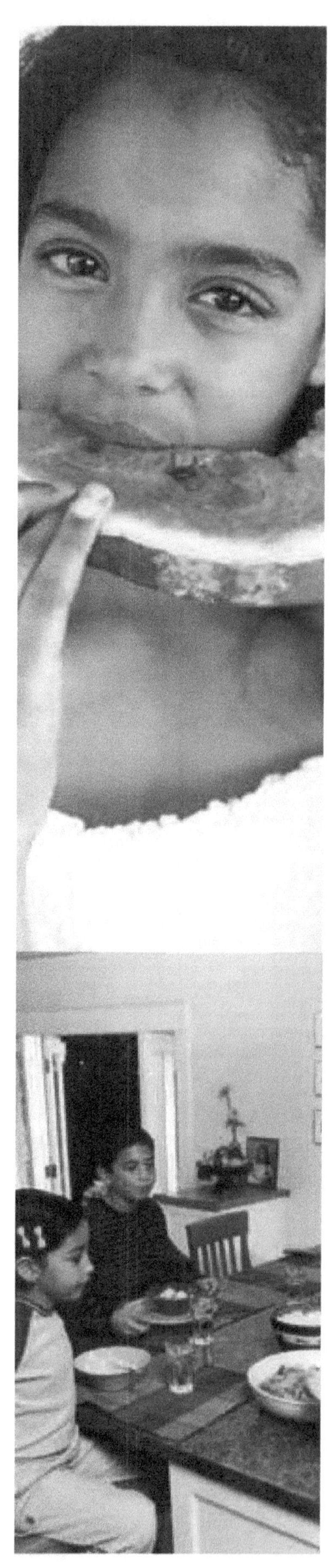

For example,

- Planning regular family time that involves physical activity means that everyone is supported and encouraged to be active.
- Putting a bowl of fruit on the kitchen counter and making a family agreement not to have chips or other high-calorie snacks in the house can change everyone's snacking habits.

Strategies for Real Life

If you're interested in jump-starting your family on a healthy lifestyle by making some nutrition and physical activity changes, here are a few strategies to get you started:

- **Recognize that you have more control than you might think.** You **can** turn off the TV and the video game. You **can** choose to get off the bus one stop earlier than usual and walk the rest of the way, especially when you are with your kids. You **can** give your family more vegetables for dinner.

- **Think about the immediate benefits.** If reducing future heart disease risk seems a bit abstract, focus on the good things that can happen right now. You won't feel so full if you have a smaller portion or skip dessert. Going hiking with your teenager might lead to a wonderful talk

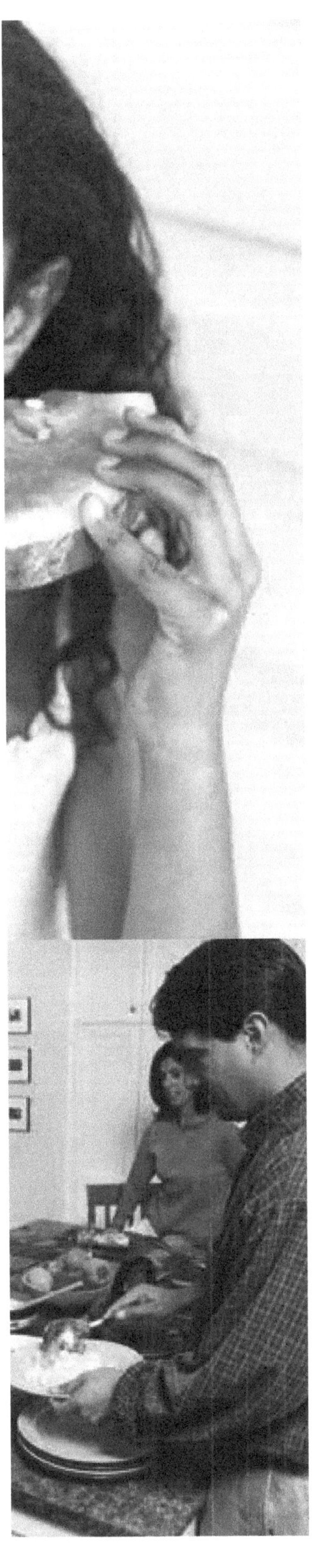

that neither of you anticipated. A fruit salad tastes great and looks beautiful. Dancing with your spouse is lots of fun and can give you a great workout.

- **Make small, easy changes over time.** Suggesting that family members take a run together every day will probably get you lots of eye-rolling and "no-thank-you's." It's easier and more appealing to start out with some new approaches to nutrition and physical activity that the whole family is really willing to try. For example, take a walk after dinner a couple of nights a week instead of turning on the TV. And, instead of chocolate cake with frosting, enjoy sliced strawberries over angel food cake.

- **Try a variety of strategies.** No one will notice if you use part-skim mozzarella cheese instead of whole-milk mozzarella in your lasagna, but you'll be reducing the calories and fat for everyone who eats it. Combine "invisible" strategies like this with strategies that actively involve other family members: See if everyone will commit to eating healthy dinners together at least four times a week. Get your children involved in the process of shopping for and preparing these healthy dinners. Make a plan with your child to walk to school together or to walk after dinner 2 days a week.

What is a "Healthy Weight?"

People have different ideas about what a "healthy" weight is. Some think that a model–thin physique is a healthy weight; others think that they can have some extra padding around the middle and still be at a healthy weight. That's why health experts have developed standards that define normal weight, overweight, and obesity.

For adults, a normal, or healthy, weight is defined as an appropriate weight in relation to height. This ratio of weight to height is known as the body mass index (BMI). People who are overweight might have too much body weight for their height. People who are obese almost always have a large amount of extra body fat in relation to their height. There are some exceptions. Big athletes with lots of muscle might have a BMI greater than 30 but would not be considered obese from the perspective of health risk.

For adults, BMI falls into the following categories:

Weight Status	BMI
Normal, or healthy, weight	18.5–24.9
Overweight	25–29.9
Obese	30.0 and above

For example, a woman who is 5'5" and weighs 132 pounds has a BMI of 22— healthy weight. If she weighs 162 pounds, she'd have a BMI of 27 (overweight). If she weighs 186 pounds, she'd have a BMI of 31 (obese). To find out more about BMI and how to calculate your own number, try NHLBI's calculator at **www.nhlbisupport.com/bmi/bmicalc.htm.**

For **children and teens**, overweight is defined differently than it is for adults. Because children are still growing, and boys and girls develop at different rates, BMIs for children 2–20 years old are determined by comparing their weight and height against growth charts that take their age and gender into account. A child's "BMI-for-age" shows how his or her BMI compares with other girls or boys of the same age. A child or teen who is between the 85th and 95th percentile on the growth chart is considered at risk of overweight. A child or teen who is at the 95th percentile or above is considered overweight. Ask your family doctor, pediatrician, or health care provider about your child's BMI-for-age. For more information about BMI-for-age and growth charts for children, visit **www.cdc.gov/nccdphp/dnpa/bmi/bmi-for-age.htm.**

3-Energy Balance: The Heart of the Matter

A person's weight is the result of many things working together—height, genes, metabolism (the way your body converts food and oxygen into energy), behavior, and environment. Changes in our environment that make it harder to engage in healthy behaviors have a lot to do with the overall increase in weight over the past few decades:

- We're an in-the-car and sit-behind-a-desk society. For many of us—parents and children alike—daily life doesn't involve a lot of physical activity. If we want to be active, we have to make an effort.

- Food is everywhere, along with messages telling us to eat and drink. We can even get something to eat at places where food was never available before—like the gas station. Going out to eat or buying carryout is easy.

- Food portions in restaurants and at home are bigger than they used to be.

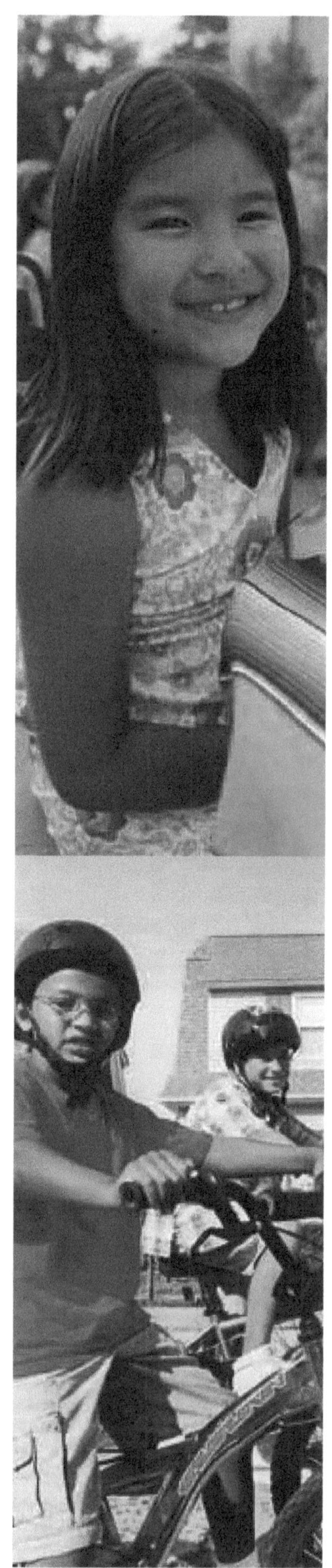

Becoming overweight doesn't happen overnight. It develops over time when the energy we take in by eating is not in balance with the energy we burn from physical activity.

What Is Energy Balance?

Energy is just another word for calories. Whenever you eat or drink, **ENERGY** (in the form of calories) is coming **IN**. At the same time, your body is constantly working, so **ENERGY** (in the form of calories) is going **OUT**. Your body burns a certain number of calories just to carry out basic functions like breathing and digesting. Children also need extra calories to help them grow and develop. A big person burns more calories every day than a small person. You also burn a certain number of calories through your daily activities. For example, children burn calories being students. Adults burn calories being office workers, kindergarten teachers, construction workers, stay-at-home parents, and everything in between. People with active lifestyles burn more calories than those with not-so-active lifestyles. Finally, people burn calories through extra physical activity, from lifting weights to running to playing on the playground. Vigorous physical activity (such as running) burns more calories than moderate or low-intensity physical activity (such as walking). See the Estimated Calorie Requirements on page 11.

To imagine energy balance, think of a scale…

Energy balance means that your ENERGY IN (all the calories from the foods and drinks you consume every day) equals your ENERGY OUT (all the calories you burn to keep your body going and carry out your activities).

The same amount of energy IN and energy OUT over ***time = weight stays the same***

More IN than OUT over time = weight gain

More OUT than IN over time = weight loss

Your energy IN and OUT don't have to balance exactly every day. It's the balance over time that determines whether you can maintain a healthy weight in the long run. And, because children need energy to grow properly, energy balance in children happens when the amount of energy IN and energy OUT supports natural growth without promoting excess weight gain.

Estimated Calorie Requirements

(In Kilocalories) for Each Gender and Age Group at Three Levels of Physical Activity[a]

	Activity Level [b,c,d]			
Gender	**Age (years)**	**Sedentary[b]**	**Moderately Active[c]**	**Active[d]**
Child	2–3	1,000	1,000–1,400[e]	1,000–1,400[e]
Female	4–8	1,200	1,400–1,600	1,400–1,800
	9–13	1,600	1,600–2,000	1,800–2,200
	14–18	1,800	2,000	2,400
	19–30	2,000	2,000–2,200	2,400
	31–50	1,800	2,000	2,200
	51+	1,600	1,800	2,000–2,200
Male	4–8	1,400	1,400–1,600	1,600–2,000
	9–13	1,800	1,800–2,200	2,000–2,600
	14–18	2,200	2,400–2,800	2,800–3,200
	19–30	2,400	2,600–2,800	3,000
	31–50	2,200	2,400–2,600	2,800–3,000
	51+	2,000	2,200–2,400	2,400–2,800

Source: HHS/USDA Dietary Guidelines for Americans, 2005

[a] These levels are based on Estimated Energy Requirements (EER) from the Institute of Medicine Dietary Reference Intakes macronutrients report, 2002, calculated by gender, age, and activity level for reference-sized individuals. "Reference size," as determined by IOM, is based on median height and weight for ages up to age 18 years of age and median height and weight for that height to give a BMI of 21.5 for adult females and 22.5 for adult males.

[b] Sedentary means a lifestyle that includes only the light physical activity associated with typical day-to-day life.

[c] Moderately active means a lifestyle that includes physical activity equivalent to walking about 1.5 to 3 miles per day at 3 to 4 miles per hour, in addition to the light physical activity associated with typical day-to-day life

[d] Active means a lifestyle that includes physical activity equivalent to walking more than 3 miles per day at 3 to 4 miles per hour, in addition to the light physical activity associated with typical day-to-day life.

[e] The calorie ranges shown are to accommodate needs of different ages within the group. For children and adolescents, more calories are needed at older ages. For adults, fewer calories are needed at older ages.

TIP:

Here are a few small and easy things that you and your family can do to get energy IN and energy OUT in balance. Give them a try! You also can visit the ***We Can!*** Web site at **http://wecan.nhlbi.nih.gov** for lots more ideas just like them.

ENERGY IN

- Choose food portions no larger than your fist.
- Choose a checkout line without a candy display.
- Eat a low-fat, high-fiber breakfast—it may make you less hungry later in the day.
- Cut high-calorie foods like cheese and chocolate into small pieces and eat fewer pieces.

ENERGY OUT

- Take the long way to the water cooler.
- Buy a set of hand weights and play a round of Simon Says with your children—you do it with the weights, they do it without.
- Choose "labor-spending" devices instead of "labor-saving" devices: wash the car by hand instead of going through an automatic car wash.
- Go on a family bike ride or hike.

A Real-Life Example of Energy Balance

Consuming 150 calories a day more than you burn in activity can lead to a gain of 5 pounds in 6 months, or 10 pounds in a year. To prevent that from happening, you can either reduce your energy IN or increase your energy OUT. Doing both is another great idea:

Two easy ways to reduce energy IN by 150 calories:

- Drink water instead of a 12-ounce regular soda.
- Downsize a medium french fries to a small, or substitute a salad.

Two easy ways to increase energy OUT by 150 calories*:

- Shoot hoops for 30 minutes.
- Walk 2 miles in 30 minutes.

*Calories burned by a 150-pound person. People who weigh less will burn fewer calories doing these activities; people who weigh more will burn more.

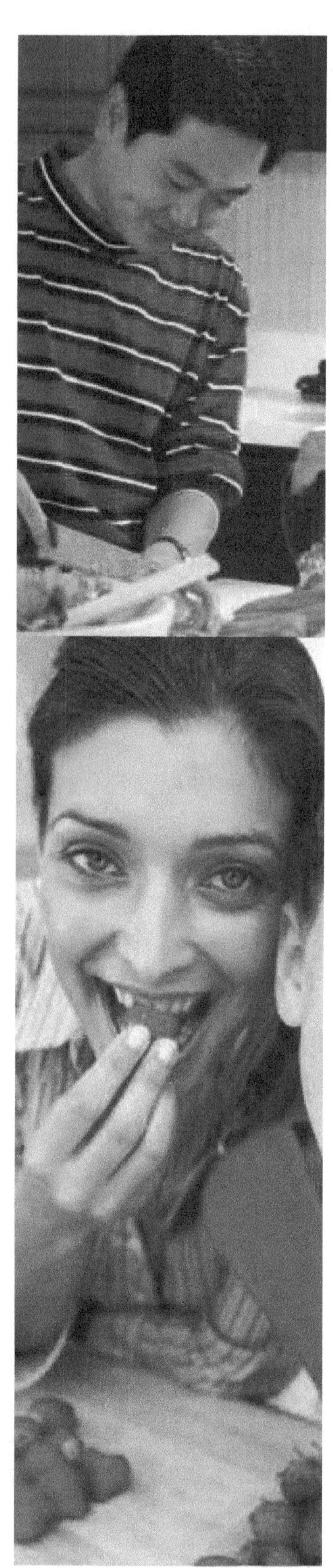

4-Energy IN: Focusing on Food Choices and Portion Size

And the most important tip of all....

- Acknowledge and reward your efforts: spend the afternoon with a friend. Buy fresh flowers for your home. Do something special just for you.

Calories do count, no matter what kind of food or drink they come from. The trick to controlling energy IN is to:

- Choose foods that are low or moderate in calories.
- Enjoy small portions at home and at restaurants.

Focus on Food Choices

An eating plan that can help you and your family maintain a healthy weight is one that gives everyone the nutrients they need while keeping calories under control. One way to put this plan into action is to think about food choices in terms of GO, SLOW, and WHOA foods:*

*Adapted from CATCH: Coordinated Approach to Child Health, 4th Grade Curriculum, University of California and Flaghouse, Inc., 2002

GO foods are the lowest in fat and added sugar. They also are "nutrient dense," which means that they are rich in nutrients (vitamins, minerals, and other components important to health) and relatively low in calories. Enjoy GO foods almost anytime.

Fruits and vegetables are great GO foods.

- **GO for color**—choose dark green, deep yellow, orange, red, blue, and purple.
- **GO for sensory appeal**—juicy, crunchy, tart, crisp, sweet, yummy.
- **GO for variety**—berries, other fruits, leafy greens, dry beans and peas, starchy vegetables (like potatoes), and other vegetables.

SLOW foods are higher in fat, added sugar, and calories than GO foods. Have SLOW foods sometimes, at most several times a week.

WHOA foods are the highest in fat and added sugar. They are "calorie dense" (high in calories), and many are low in nutrients as well. Have WHOA foods only once in a while or on special occasions. And, when you do have them, have small portions.

Translating GO, SLOW, and WHOA into daily food choices means:

- Emphasizing fruits, vegetables, whole grains, and fat-free or low-fat milk and milk products.
- Including lean meat, poultry, fish, beans, eggs, and nuts.
- Cutting back on foods and drinks that are high in fat and added sugar.

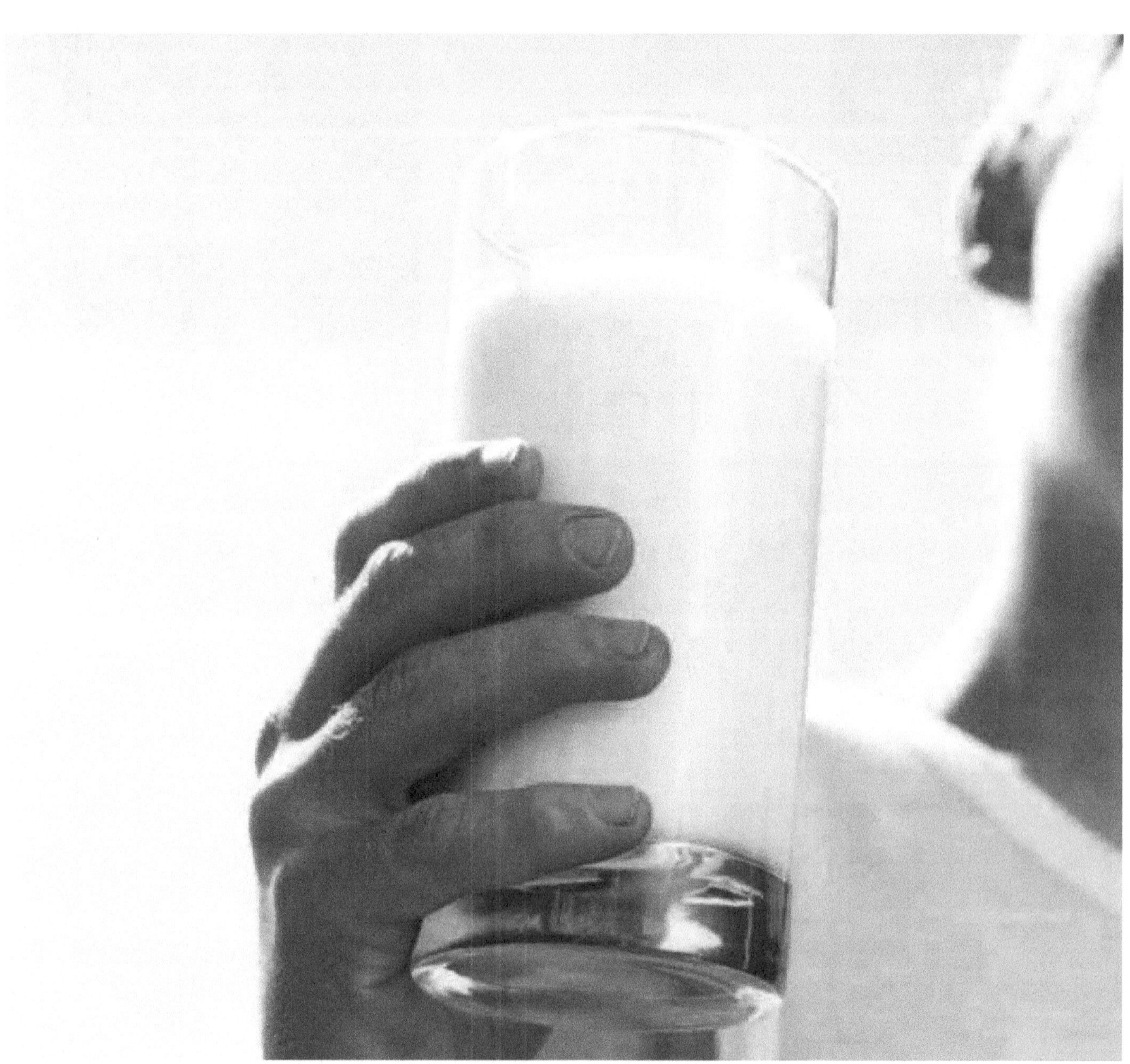

GO, SLOW, and WHOA Foods

Use this chart as a guide to help you and your family make smart food choices. Post it on your refrigerator at home or take it with you to the store when you shop. Refer to the Estimated Calorie Requirements on page 11 to determine how much of these foods to eat to maintain energy balance.

- **GO Foods**—Eat almost anytime.
- **SLOW Foods**—Eat sometimes, at most several times a week.
- **WHOA Foods**—Eat only once in a while or on special occasions.

Food Group	GO (Almost Anytime Foods)	SLOW (Sometimes Foods)	WHOA (Once in a While Foods)
	Nutrient-Dense ⟵	⟶	Calorie-Dense
Vegetables	Almost all fresh, frozen, and canned vegetables without added fat and sauces	All vegetables with added fat and sauces; oven-baked french fries; avocado	Fried potatoes, like french fries or hash browns; other deep-fried vegetables
Fruits	All fresh, frozen, canned (in juice)	100 percent fruit juice; fruits canned in light syrup; dried fruits	Fruits canned in heavy syrup
Breads and Cereals	Whole-grain breads, pita bread, tortillas, and pasta; brown rice; hot and cold unsweetened whole-grain breakfast cereals	White refined flour bread, rice, and pasta; French toast; taco shells; cornbread; biscuits; granola; waffles and pancakes	Croissants; muffins; doughnuts; sweet rolls; crackers made with trans fats; sweetened breakfast cereals
Milk and Milk Products	Fat-free or 1 percent reduced-fat milk; fat-free or low-fat yogurt; part-skim, reduced fat, and fat-free cheese; low-fat or fat-free cottage cheese	2 percent low-fat milk; processed cheese spread	Whole milk; full-fat American, cheddar, Colby, Swiss, cream cheese; whole-milk yogurt
Meats, Poultry, Fish, Eggs, Beans, and Nuts	Trimmed beef and pork; extra lean ground beef; chicken and turkey without skin; tuna canned in water; baked, broiled, steamed, grilled fish and shellfish; beans, split peas, lentils, tofu; egg whites and egg substitutes	Lean ground beef, broiled hamburgers; ham, Canadian bacon; chicken and turkey with skin; low-fat hot dogs; tuna canned in oil; peanut butter; nuts; whole eggs cooked without added fat	Untrimmed beef and pork; regular ground beef; fried hamburgers; ribs; bacon; fried chicken, chicken nuggets; hot dogs, lunch meats, pepperoni, sausage; fried fish and shellfish; whole eggs cooked with fat
Sweets and Snacks*	Ice milk bars; frozen fruit juice bars; low-fat frozen yogurt and ice cream; fig bars, ginger snaps; baked chips; low-fat microwave popcorn; pretzels		Cookies and cakes; pies; cheese cake; ice cream; chocolate; candy; chips; buttered microwave popcorn
Fats	Vinegar; ketchup; mustard; fat-free creamy salad dressing; fat-free mayonnaise; fat-free sour cream;vegetable oil, olive oil, and oil-based salad dressing**	Low-fat creamy salad dressing; low-fat mayonnaise; low-fat sour cream	Butter, margarine; lard; salt pork; gravy; regular creamy salad dressing; mayonnaise; tartar sauce; sour cream; cheese sauce; cream sauce; cream cheese dips
Beverages	Water, fat-free milk, or 1 percent reduced-fat milk; diet soda; diet iced teas and lemonade	2 percent low-fat milk; 100 percent fruit juice; sports drinks	Whole milk; regular soda; sweetened iced teas and lemonade; fruit drinks with less than 100 percent fruit juice

*Though some of the foods in this row are lower in fat and calories, all sweets and snacks need to be limited so as not to exceed one's daily calorie requirements.
**Vegetable and olive oils contain no saturated *or trans* fats and can be consumed daily, but in limited portions, to meet daily calorie needs (about 6 teaspoons a day for the 2,000-calorie level). *(HHS/USDA Dietary Guidelines for Americans)*

Source: Adapted from CATCH: Coordinated Approach to Child Health, 4th Grade Curriculum, University of California and Flaghouse, Inc., 2002.

"A Spoonful (or More) of Sugar"

Fat has twice as many calories as protein or carbohydrate, so it's easy to see why cutting back on fat can help control weight. But why should we cut back on added sugar?

Sugar is present naturally in some foods (like the fructose in fruit or the lactose in milk). It's also added to foods at the table or during processing and preparation (like the high-fructose corn syrup in sweetened beverages and breakfast cereal). Health experts have several reasons for saying that we should cut back on added sugar:

- Studies show that people who consume many foods and drinks with added sugar tend to consume more calories than people who consume fewer of these foods. They also show a link between weight gain and drinking sweetened beverages. Cutting back on added sugars, especially from sweetened beverages such as regular soda and fruit punch, can help you and your family maintain a healthy weight.
- Added sugar provides calories but no additional nutrients. An eating plan that helps you and your family maintain a healthy weight is one that focuses on getting plenty of nutrients within your calorie needs.
- Many children and teens, especially girls, don't get enough calcium, a mineral that's important for strong bones and teeth and other body functions. Giving your children fat-free or low-fat milk instead of sweetened beverages can give their bodies a boost.

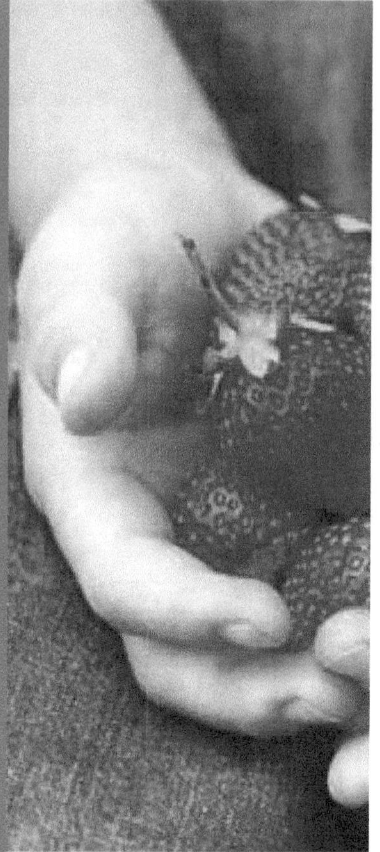

Focus on Portion Size

Anyone who has eaten out lately is likely to notice how big the portions are. It's hard to find "small" anymore—"supersize" is more like it. Sometimes your plate arrives, and there's enough food for two or even three people. These ever-larger portions have changed what we think of as a "normal" portion, and that affects how much we eat at home as well. Cutting back on portion size is a surefire way to help keep energy IN and energy OUT in balance:

- Order a medium pizza instead of a large. Everyone gets the same number of slices as before; they're just smaller.
- Order an appetizer instead of an entrée at a restaurant.
- Use tall, narrow glasses instead of short, wide glasses. You will drink less.
- Put a smaller portion on a smaller plate; it won't look so skimpy.
- Share a portion with a family member or friend.
- Instead of giving your child an entire bottle of fruit juice or soda, pour a small amount (½ cup) into a cup.

What's the Difference Between a Portion and a Recommended Serving Size?

Portion

A "portion" is the amount of a food that you choose to eat for a meal or snack. It can be big or small—you decide.

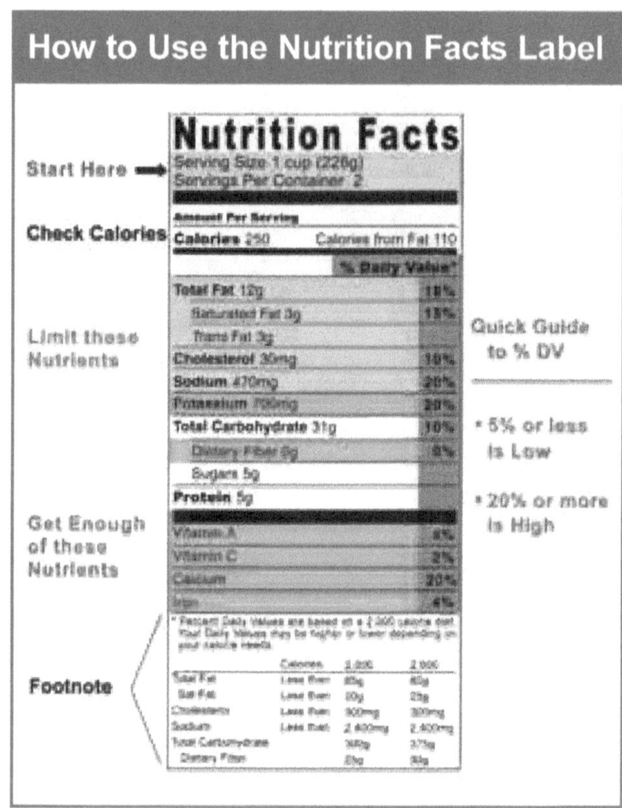

Serving

A "serving" is a measured amount of food or drink, such as one slice of bread or 1 cup of milk. Some foods that most people consume as a single serving actually contain multiple serving sizes (e.g. a 20-ounce soda, or a 3-ounce bag of chips). Nutrition recommendations use serving sizes to help people know how much of different types of foods they should eat to get the nutrients they need. The Nutrition Facts Label on packaged foods also lists a serving size. The serving sizes on packaged foods are not always the same as those included in nutrition recommendations. However, serving sizes are standardized to make it easier to compare similar foods. To get an idea of how big recommended serving sizes really are, check out NHLBI's Serving Size Card at **http://hin.nhlbi.nih.gov/portion/servingcard7.pdf.** And, for help on using the Nutrition Facts Label, visit the Food and Drug Administration (FDA) Web site at **www.cfsan.fda.gov/~dms/foodlab.html#see1**.

My, How They've Grown!

Here are just a few examples of how much average portion sizes have grown over the past 20 years. For more eye-opening examples, visit NHLBI's Portion Distortion website at **http://hin.nhlbi.nih.gov/portion/index.htm**

	20 Years Ago	
	Portion	Calories
Bagel	3" diameter	140
Cheeseburger	1	333
Spaghetti and meatballs	1 cup spaghetti; 3 small meatballs	500
Soda	6.5 ounces	85
Blueberry muffin	1.5 ounces	210

	Today	
	Portion	Calories
Bagel	6" diameter	350
Cheeseburger	1	590
Spaghetti and meatballs	2 cup spaghetti; 3 large meatballs	1,020
Soda	20 ounces	250
Blueberry muffin	5 ounces	500

TIP:

For more information and tips about food choices and portion sizes that can help you and your family maintain a healthy weight, check out the following Web sites:

- NHLBI's Keep an Eye on Portion Size: **http://hin.nhlbi.nih.gov/portion/keep.htm**
- U.S. Department of Health and Human Services and U.S. Department of Agriculture (HHS/USDA) Dietary Guidelines for Americans: **www.health-ierus.gov/ dietaryguidelines**

5-Energy OUT: Physical Activity and Screen Time

Americans aren't very physically active. They sit a lot and spend hours in front of TVs, video games, and computers. Studies show that people often eat when they are in front of a screen, and that habit can be a double whammy for a person's weight—very little energy OUT to burn off all that energy IN.

To maintain a healthy weight, being physically active is just as important as eating right. ***We Can!*** benefit a lot from physical activity. It can:

- Keep your body healthy.
- Burn off calories, which can help you stay at a healthy weight.
- Make your bones and muscles strong.
- Make you feel energetic.
- Build strength and endurance.
- Help relieve stress.
- Help you sleep better.
- Help your mental health.

- Help you feel good about yourself.
- Give you something to do when you are bored.
- Be a fun way to spend time with family and friends.

How Much Physical Activity Should We Get?

The HHS/USDA Dietary Guidelines for Americans recommend that children and teens be physically active for at least 60 minutes on most, if not all, days.

The Guidelines also recommend that adults engage in at least 30 minutes of moderate-intensity physical activity, above usual activity, on most days of the week in order to reduce the risk of chronic disease in adulthood. And 60 minutes of moderate- to vigorous-intensity physical activity on most days of the week will help adults avoid gradual weight gain.

Combined with eating right, this level of physical activity can help you and your children stay at a healthy weight and prevent gradual weight gain over time.

Sometimes, Life Gets in the Way... But It Doesn't Have To.

Trying to get in 60 minutes of moderate- to vigorous-intensity physical activity on most days may seem like a lot. But you can do it, and doing it with the family can make it easier.

Get Away From the Screen

- Turn off Saturday morning cartoons and take your child roller-blading or to the zoo.
- Make a family agreement to limit TV/DVD/video watching or gaming to 2 hours (or less) a day.
- Play with a ball instead of a video game.
- Take the TV out of your child's bedroom.

Make Screen Time Active Time

- If you do watch TV, stretch, do yoga, or even lift weights at the same time.
- Have a contest with your children. Who can do the most push-ups or jumping jacks during a commercial break?
- Pop in your favorite aerobics exercise tape or DVD to get your heart pumping!

Make Family Time Active Time

- Bike to the library together.
- Go to your children's sports events and cheer for them. Have them come to yours and cheer for you.
- Celebrate a birthday or anniversary with something active—a hike, a volleyball game, a Frisbee™ match.
- Make a plan with your spouse or child to train together to walk or run a 5K race.

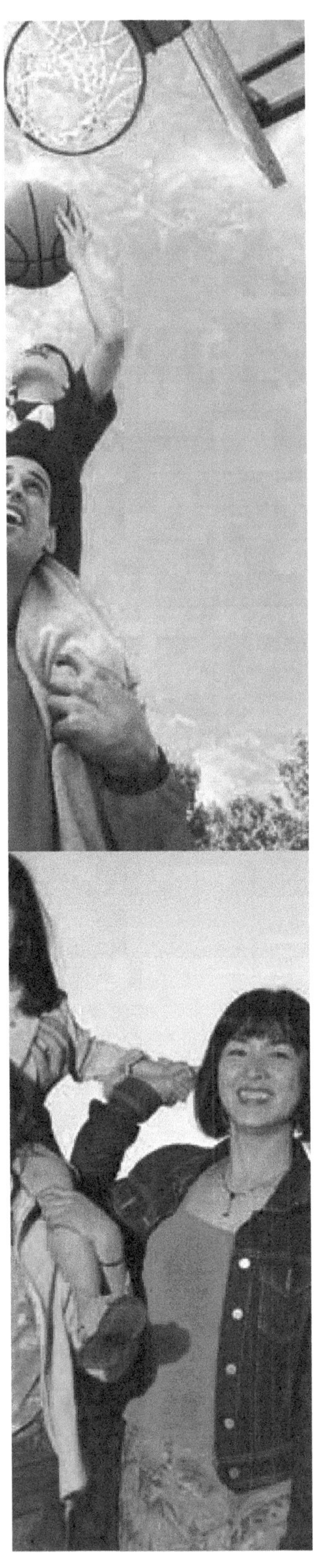

Be Physically Active in Small Chunks

- Instead of e-mailing or phoning colleagues, walk to their offices and back again.
- Challenge your child to jump rope for 5 minutes. When he or she is done, enjoy a big hug and then you try it!
- Play outside with the dog for 20 minutes after work.

Did You Know!

- Every day, on average, 8 to 18-year-olds spend
  - Nearly 4 hours watching TV, videos, DVDs, and prerecorded shows
  - Just over an hour on the computer
  - About 50 minutes playing video games
- 2/3 of young people have a TV in their bedroom; have a video game player and nearly 1/3 have a computer in their bedroom
- Youth who have TVs in their rooms spend almost 1½ hours or more a day watching TV than youth without a set in their room.

Source: Henry J. Kaiser Foundation. Generation M: Media in the Lives of 8-18 Year Olds, March 2005. **www.kff.org/entmedia/entmedia030905pkg.cfm**

Kick It Up a Notch

- When you're out walking, pick up your pace. Go faster than you usually do.
- Take the stairs instead of the elevator or escalator. Jog up the stairs rather than walk.
- Play singles tennis rather than doubles.
- If you swim laps, do the last two as fast as you can. Finish in a glorious burst of speed!

A Handy Guide to Calories Burned in Common Activities

This chart shows how many calories you would burn in 30 minutes for these common activities:

Activity	Calories Burned Per 30 minutes*
Walking (Leisurely), 2 miles per hour	85
Walking (Brisk), 4 miles per hour	170
Gardening	135
Raking Leaves	145
Dancing	190
Bicycling (Leisurely) 10 miles per hour	205
Swimming Laps, medium level	240
Jogging, 5 miles per hour	275

*For a healthy 150-pound person. A lighter person burns fewer calories; a heavier person burns more.

Each of these activities burns approximately 150 calories*:

Examples of moderate amounts of physical activity		
Common Chores	**Sporting Activities**	**Less Vigorous, More Time** ↑
Washing and waxing a car for 45–60 minutes	Playing volleyball for 45–60 minutes	
	Playing touch football for 45 minutes	
Washing windows or floors for 45–60 minutes	Walking 1½ miles in 35 minutes (20 minutes/mile)	
Gardening for 30–45 minutes	Basketball (shooting baskets) 30 minutes	
	Bicycling 5 miles in 30 minutes	
Wheeling self in wheelchair 30–40 minutes	Dancing fast (social) for 30 minutes	
	Walking 2 miles in 30 minutes (15 minutes/mile)	
Pushing a stroller 1½ miles in 30 minutes	Water aerobics for 30 minutes	
Raking leaves for 30 minutes	Swimming laps for 20 minutes	
	Basketball (playing game) for 15–20 minutes	
Shoveling snow for 15 minutes	Bicycling 4 miles in 15 minutes	
	Jumping rope for 15 minutes	
Stairwalking for 15 minutes	Running 1½ miles in 15 minutes (10 minutes/mile)	↓ **More Vigorous, Less Time**

* Source: Adapted from Surgeon General's Call to Action to Prevent and Decrease Overweight and Obesity, 2001; **www.surgeongeneral.gov/topics/obesity/**

6-Resources

Congratulations! If you've come to this point in the ***We Can!*** *Families Finding the Balance: A Parent Handbook*, you've got everything you need to start—or continue—helping your family maintain a healthy weight. If you're ready to try additional ideas or want other ***We Can!*** ways to help your family eat well and get more physically active, call 1-866-35-WECAN or visit the ***We Can!*** Web site at **http://wecan.nhlbi.nih.gov.** The Web site is full of information about maintaining a healthy weight, nutrition, and physical activity. You also can visit the Web site for recipes, healthy tips, and additional resources.

Check out these other great resources:

NHLBI, **www.nhlbi.nih.gov**

- Aim For a Healthy Weight, **www.nhlbi.nih.gov/health/public/heart/obesity/lose_wt/index.htm**
- Portion Distortion Quiz, **http://hin.nhlbi.nih.gov/portion**
- Body Mass Index (BMI) Calculator, **www.nhlbisupport.com/bmi**
- Heart Healthy Latino Recipes, **www.nhlbi.nih.gov/health/public/heart/other/sp_recip.htm**
- Heart Healthy Home Cooking African American Style, **www.nhlbi.nih.gov/health/public/heart/other/chdblack/cooking.htm**

NIDDK, **www.niddk.nih.gov**

- Weight-control Information Network, **http://win.niddk.nih.gov**

NICHD, **www.nichd.nih.gov**

- Milk Matters, **www.nichd.nih.gov/milk**

NCI, **www.nci.nih.gov**

- Cancer Control PLANET, **http://cancercontrolplanet.cancer.gov/physical_activity.html**
- Eat 5-to-9 a Day, **http://5aday.gov/homepage/index_content.html**
- Body and Soul, **http://5aday.nci.nih.gov/about/print_key_soul.html**

FACTS

Food Allergies: *What You Need to Know*

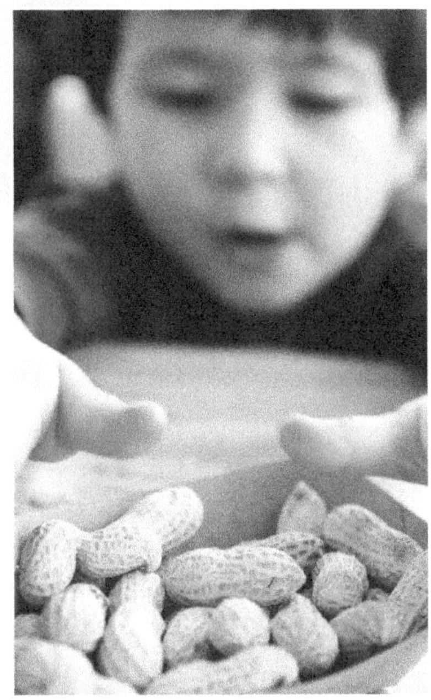

Millions of Americans have food allergies and may experience adverse reactions to products that have food allergens. Most reactions cause mild symptoms, but some are severe and may even be life-threatening.

Although new treatments are being developed, there is no cure for food allergies. Medical diagnosis to find out which foods cause an individual to have an allergic reaction and strictly avoiding those foods are important ways to prevent serious adverse health effects.

What Are the *Major Food Allergens?*

While many different foods can cause allergic reactions, the Food Allergen Labeling and Consumer Protection Act of 2004 (FALCPA) identifies the eight most common allergenic foods. These major food allergens make up 90 percent of food allergic reactions in the United States:

1. **Milk**
2. **Eggs**
3. **Fish** (e.g., bass, flounder, cod)
4. **Crustacean shellfish** (e.g., crab, lobster, shrimp)
5. **Tree nuts** (e.g., almonds, walnuts, pecans)
6. **Peanuts**
7. **Wheat**
8. **Soybeans**

Allergen Labeling

The FDA enforces FALCPA in the labeling of foods the agency regulates, which include all foods except poultry, most meats, certain egg products, and most alcoholic beverages (all of which are regulated by other Federal agencies). FALCPA requires that food labels clearly identify the food source names of any ingredients that are one of the eight major food allergens or contain protein derived from a major food allergen.

Proper labeling of foods helps allergic consumers identify foods or ingredients that they should avoid.

How Major Food Allergens Are Listed

FALCPA requires that food labels identify the food source names of all major food allergens used to make the food. This requirement is met if the common or usual name of an ingredient (e.g., buttermilk) that is a major food allergen already identifies that allergen's food source name (i.e., milk). Otherwise, the allergen's food source name must be declared at least once on the food label in **one of two ways:**

1. In parentheses following the name of the ingredient in the ingredient list.
   Examples: "lecithin (soy)," "flour (wheat)," and "whey (milk)"

– OR –

2. Immediately after or next to to the list of ingredients in a "Contains" statement.
   Example: "Contains soy, wheat, and milk..."

FOOD FACTS

Know the Symptoms of Food Allergies

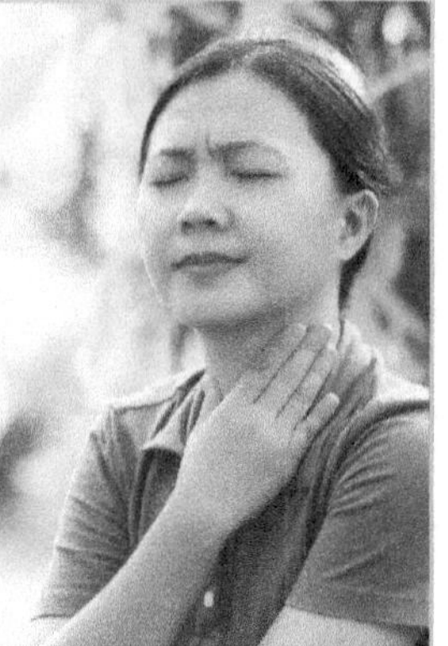

If you are allergic to a food you have eaten, you may experience a variety of symptoms. These symptoms are not always present or the same for every person or reaction and can vary depending on a number of actors, including the amount of food allergen eaten.

If you are allergic to a food that you have eaten, symptoms may appear from within a few minutes to a few hours.

Symptoms of food allergies (allergic reactions), can include:

- Hives
- Flushed skin or rash
- Tingling or itchy sensation in the mouth
- Face, tongue, or lip swelling
- Vomiting and/or diarrhea
- Abdominal cramps
- Coughing or wheezing
- Dizziness and/or lightheadedness
- Swelling of the throat and vocal cords
- Difficulty breathing
- Loss of consciousness

Food Allergies Can Be Life-Threatening

While most symptoms from food allergies are mild and limited to skin or digestive discomfort, some may progress to a severe, life-threatening allergic reaction called **anaphylaxis**.

This can lead to:

- constricted airways in the lungs
- severe lowering of blood pressure and shock ("**anaphylactic shock**")
- suffocation by swelling of the throat and larynx

If you have a known food allergy and start having symptoms of an allergic reaction:

- Stop eating the food immediately
- Evaluate the need for emergency treatment (such as epinephrine)
- Seek medical attention

Symptoms of anaphylaxis may start out as relatively mild but, if not treated promptly, symptoms can become life-threatening in a short amount of time.

Recognizing early symptoms of anaphylaxis and prompt injection of the drug epinephrine and other medical care or intervention can help prevent life-threatening consequences.

It is important to understand that a mild allergic reaction does not always mean the allergy is mild. Any allergic reaction has potential to lead to anaphylaxis. Allergic individuals are taught to always monitor symptoms and seek medical care if needed when symptoms occur.

What to Do If Symptoms Occur

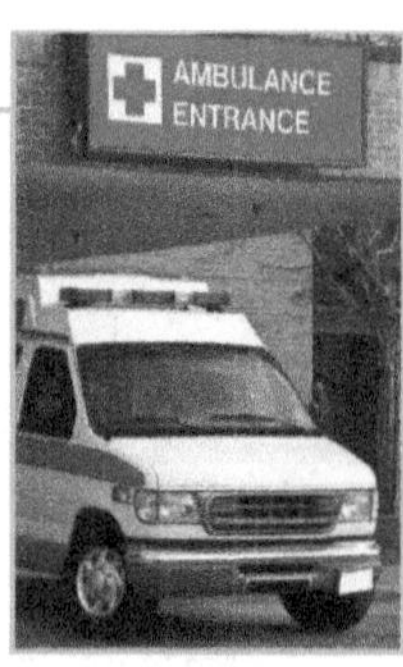

The appearance of symptoms after eating certain foods may be a sign of a food allergy. The food(s) that caused these symptoms should be avoided, and the affected person should contact a health care provider for appropriate testing and evaluation.

If you or a loved one has food allergies, use these 4 tips to help reduce your risk of getting sick:

1. Always read food labels.
2. Avoid foods that you are allergic to.

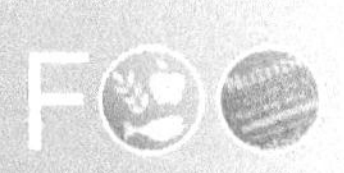

FACTS

3. Learn to recognize the early symptoms of an allergic reaction, in case of accidental ingestion.
4. Know what to do in case an allergic reaction occurs. Plan to have ready access to the appropriate treatment measures and medical care.

Reporting Adverse Reactions and Labeling Concerns

If you or a family member has had an allergic reaction after eating an FDA-regulated food or food product with unclear labeling or a possible allergen, discuss this with your health care provider. Keep any food packages because they may contain important information. You may want to contact the manufacturer. Also, report the suspected reaction or labeling concerns to the FDA in one of these ways:

- Consumers and manufacturers can submit reports detailing product reactions or other complaints to an FDA Consumer Complaint Coordinator for the state where the food was purchased. A list of FDA Consumer Complaint Coordinators is available at https://www.fda.gov/safety/report-problem-fda/consumer-complaint-coordinators#section-nav,
- Call FDA at 1-888-SAFEFOOD, or
- Submit a report using FDA's MedWatch Online reporting form for consumers, which can be found here: https://www.accessdata.fda.gov/scripts/medwatch/index.cfm.

Reports submitted to FDA should include as much information as possible:

- Who is reporting the incident and who was affected? Please provide names, addresses, and phone numbers.
- The name and address of the place where the product was purchased.
- A clear description of the reaction, including:
  - o Date the reaction occurred.
  - o All symptoms experienced.
  - o How long after you ate or drank the product that the reaction occurred.
  - o Medications used to treat symptoms.
  - o Whether the reaction required further medical care, and if so, what kind. Please provide contact information for the doctor or hospital.
- A complete description of the product, including:
  - o Date of purchase.
  - o Any codes or identifying marks on the label or container, such as lot number, expiration date, and UPC code.
  - o Photos of the product, label, ingredient statement, and lot code.

Consumer reports of adverse events help FDA identify problem products and better protect all consumers.

For more information on food allergies, visit
https://www.fda.gov/food/food-labeling-nutrition/food-allergies

On Your Way to Preventing Type 2 Diabetes

Welcome!

If you're interested in preventing type 2 diabetes, this guide can help you get started. Congratulations on taking the first step! By reading this, **you're already on your way.**

Prediabetes puts you on the road to possibly getting type 2 diabetes.

Find out now, in less than 1 minute, if you may have prediabetes by taking the **Prediabetes Risk Test:** https://www.cdc.gov/prediabetes/takethetest/

How did it go?

If your result shows you're at high risk for type 2 diabetes, talk to your doctor about getting a simple blood sugar test to confirm it. Then, if you're diagnosed with prediabetes, consider joining a lifestyle change program offered by the National Diabetes Prevention Program (National DPP). This program is proven to cut the risk for type 2 diabetes in half. You can find out more at **CDC's Lifestyle Change Program website**: https://www.cdc.gov/diabetes/prevention/lifestyle-program/participating.html

Not quite ready to join a lifestyle change program? Use this guide to help you take the first steps toward preventing type 2 diabetes.

Why is prevention so important? Because type 2 diabetes is a serious, chronic health condition that can lead to other serious health issues such as heart disease, stroke, blindness, and kidney failure. If you can prevent or even delay getting type 2 diabetes, you can lower your risk for all those other conditions. **That's a pretty great deal.**

This guide will help you take small, practical steps that add up to a healthy lifestyle you can stick with and enjoy, including:

- ✓ **Starting point:** Assess where you stand with eating and your activity level right now.
  - ✓ Set a weight loss goal.
- ✓ **First stop:** Make a nutrition plan for healthier eating.
  - ✓ Develop winning lifestyle habits.
  - ✓ Master the skills of food measurement.
  - ✓ Choose the best foods.
  - ✓ Make work, home, grocery stores, and restaurants work for you.
- ✓ **Keep moving:** Set a fitness goal for healthier movement.
- ✓ **Track your progress:** Watch yourself succeed with a few easy steps.
- ✓ **Prepare for the long run:** Understand the support you have to keep you going.

By making some healthy changes, including eating healthier and getting active, you can prevent or delay type 2 diabetes and improve your physical and mental health overall.

And you don't have to wait to feel the benefits—when you start making healthy changes, you get rewards right away. After taking just one walk, your blood sugar goes down. Make physical activity a habit and see how your sleep improves. Enjoy the taste of fresh, healthy food. Figure out what to do with all of your extra energy. Maybe even get closer to friends and family if you invite them along for the ride!

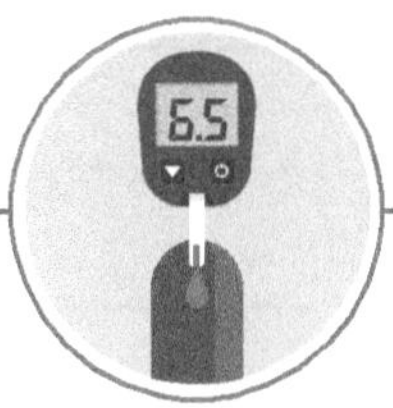

A little background.

More than 30 million Americans have diabetes, and 84 million have prediabetes. Generally, people who get type 2 diabetes started out with prediabetes. But the good news is prediabetes can be reversed! And this guide will help to teach you the basics.

What is prediabetes?

If you have prediabetes, your blood sugar is higher than normal but not high enough yet to be diagnosed as type 2 diabetes. Prediabetes is really a wake-up call to turn things around, get healthier, and not get type 2 diabetes down the road.

Considering joining a lifestyle change program?

A CDC-recognized National DPP lifestyle change program is the gold standard for preventing type 2 diabetes. A trained lifestyle coach helps guide you to make healthy changes that can cut your type 2 diabetes risk in half. You also have a support group of other people who have similar goals and challenges. This guide can't substitute for this lifestyle change program. But if you can't join one right now, or if you want a jumpstart before your program begins, we can help you get going.

Starting Point: Assess Where You Are and Where You Need to Go

Let's assess where you stand right now when it comes to nutrition and physical activity. Write down your answers to these questions to make it easier for you to figure out which of your habits are helpful and which habits you might want to work on.

Think About How You Eat in a Typical Week	Think About How You Move in a Typical Week
Do other people, such as friends, family, or coworkers, influence what you eat?	How much of your commute is spent walking or biking?
Do you prepare your meals ahead of time, or decide in the moment what to eat?	How much time do you make for physical activity around the house, such as walking the dog, cleaning the house, or gardening?
How comfortable are you with reading a nutrition label?	How often do you dedicate 30 minutes per day for physical activity, such as walking, biking, or swimming?
How often do you eat out and where?	What are your favorite ways to be active?
What makes it easier for you to eat healthier?	What makes it easier or more enjoyable for you to move more?
What makes it harder?	What makes it harder?

Set a Weight Loss Goal

With your starting point in mind, set a weight loss goal. If you are overweight and have prediabetes, shedding just 5% of your weight can help reverse prediabetes.

Here's an example to help calculate a weight loss goal of 5%.

Action	Example
Weigh yourself first thing in the morning for the most accurate results and record the number.	**240 pounds**
Determine 5% of your current weight.	Take off last digit of your weight: 24 Divide in half: 12 **To lose 5%, a 240-pound person would need to lose 12 pounds.**
Subtract that number from your current weight to determine your goal weight.	**240 - 12 = 228** A 240-pound person's goal weight would be 228 pounds.

Now it's your turn. Calculate your personal weight loss goal here:

My current weight is ________ pounds.

5% of my weight is ________ pounds.

My goal is to lose ________ pounds, for a goal weight of __________ pounds.

Now that you've assessed your habits and preferences around eating and being active and have set a healthy weight loss goal, you're better prepared to hit the road on your way to wellness. The following pages will help you improve your current habits, gain new ones, and set yourself up for success.

First Stop: Make a Nutrition Plan for Healthier Eating

Winning Habits: Make over your meals with a plan, the right ingredients, and life hacks.

Make a plan. You've probably noticed that someone who follows a popular diet plan might quickly lose weight, but has a hard time keeping it off long term. This is common and discouraging, so let's design a plan that you can follow for life. It doesn't need to be popular or have a name.

Your plan only needs two key ingredients to work:

1. **It should be based on healthy eating.**
2. **It should be something you can keep doing.**

People often need to try different things to create a plan that works for them. Some may cut back on sugar and eat more protein to stay fuller longer. Others may focus on crowding out unhealthy food with extra fruits and vegetables. Still others take the guesswork and temptation out of life by sticking to just a few breakfast and lunch choices that they know are nutritious. The details will depend on what you like and what fits in best with your life.

Eat well. Good food in the right amounts does so much more for you than just helping you lose the pounds; it helps you feel better and even think better. **All good things!**

Some basics to get started:

Choose these foods and drinks **more often:**

Non-starchy vegetables such as peppers, mushrooms, asparagus, broccoli, and spinach

Fruits

Lean protein such as fish, chicken, turkey, tofu, eggs, and yogurt

Whole grains such as quinoa, brown rice, and steel cut oatmeal

Water and unsweetened beverages

Choose these foods and drinks **less often:**

     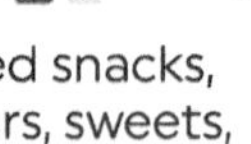

Processed foods such as packaged snacks, packaged meat, chips, granola bars, sweets, and fast foods

Trans fat, found in things such as margarine, snack food, packaged baked goods, and many fried foods

Sugary drinks such as fruit juice, sports drinks, and soda

Alcohol

Meaningful Changes That Take Minimal Effort:

Make time to cook. You'll gain impressive skills that you'll keep for a lifetime, save money, and take the guesswork out of the ingredients.

Look online for recipes that meet your skill level, time, and budget. Many have user reviews to help you decide on a recipe.

Plan a week's worth of meals before you go grocery shopping. You'll thank yourself later.

Swap boring veggie recipes for exciting ones. Watch online cooking videos to learn the secrets of making vegetables tastier with different spices or methods of cooking.

Make the same food for you and your family. Healthy eating is good for everyone!

Try Meatless Monday. Beans and lentils are cheap, tasty, and pack a protein punch.

Make family favorites with a twist. Substitute veggies for grains or starchy carbohydrates (zucchini noodles, anyone?) or blend veggies and add to sauces.

Try not to drink your calories. They won't fill you up! Reduce fruit juice and sports drinks, and limit alcohol.

Dress smart. Dress salads with oil (a healthy one like olive oil) and vinegar, choose low-fat or fat-free yogurt over sour cream, and mustard instead of mayonnaise.

Make spices your secret weapon. They add flavor without adding calories.

Freeze! Freeze single servings of a big batch of healthy food for work lunches or when you're too tired to cook.

Think ahead. Think about the times you're most likely to eat junk food, like after a stressful day at work. Make a plan in advance to swap out the unhealthy snack you might eat—such as a candy bar—with a healthy one, like an apple.

Master the Skills of Food Measurement: Portion Sizes and Food Labels

Size it up: get a handle on portion size. Most of us don't know just how much we're eating. One way to help manage portion size is by using the plate method.

Using a basic 9-inch dinner plate:

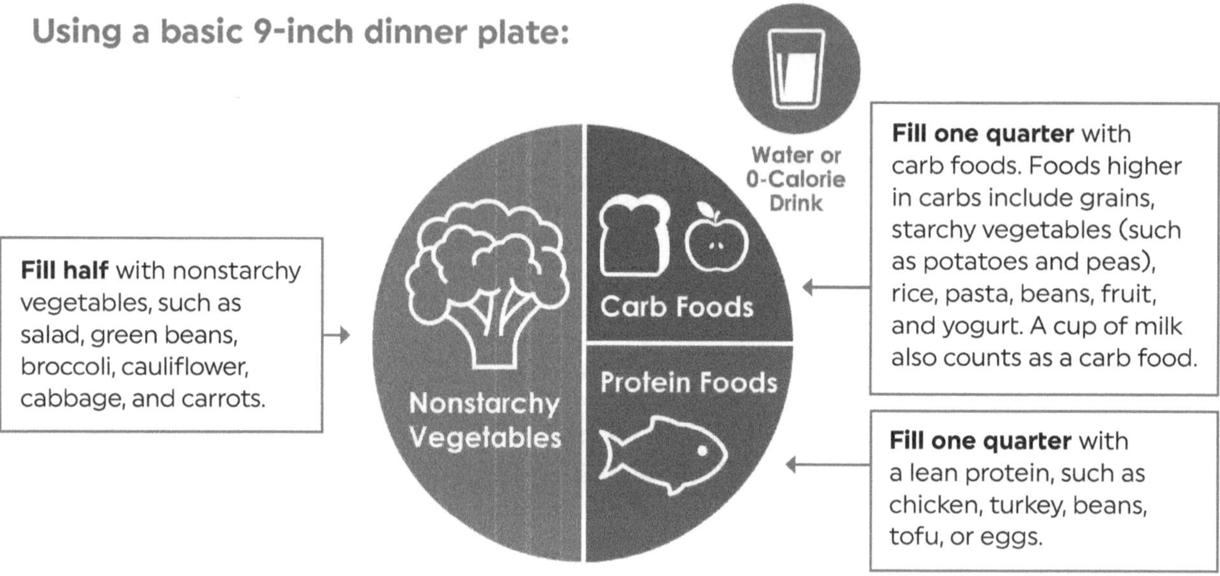

Fill half with nonstarchy vegetables, such as salad, green beans, broccoli, cauliflower, cabbage, and carrots.
Nonstarchy Vegetables
Carb Foods
Protein Foods
Water or 0-Calorie Drink
Fill one quarter with carb foods. Foods higher in carbs include grains, starchy vegetables (such as potatoes and peas), rice, pasta, beans, fruit, and yogurt. A cup of milk also counts as a carb food.
Fill one quarter with a lean protein, such as chicken, turkey, beans, tofu, or eggs.

Then choose water or a low-calorie drink such as unsweetened iced tea to go with your meal.

If you're not using a plate, this "handy" guide will help you estimate portion size:

1. **3 ounces of meat, fish, or poultry**
   Palm of hand (no fingers)
2. **1 ounce of meat or cheese**
   Thumb (tip to base)
3. **1 cup or 1 medium fruit**
   Fist
4. **1–2 ounces of nuts or pretzels**
   Cupped hand
5. **1 tablespoon**
   Thumb tip (tip to 1st joint)
6. **1 teaspoon**
   Fingertip (tip to 1st joint)

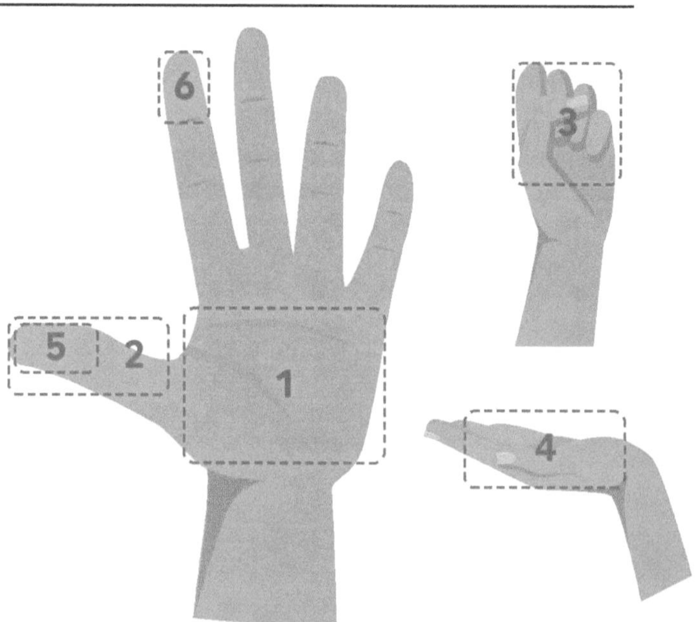

Choose the Best Foods: Decoding Food Labels, Eating a Healthy Variety, and Quality Calories

Put foods that don't have labels first on your grocery list. Visit the produce section to stock up on fresh veggies and fruit. (Just watch out for packaged food tucked away between the apples and asparagus, such as salad toppings and snack foods.) Then, shop the outside aisles of the store for dairy, eggs, and lean meat. Some packaged food will be on your list. **Use the Nutrition Facts label to see how many calories and grams of carbs, sugars, and fat are in the food you choose.**

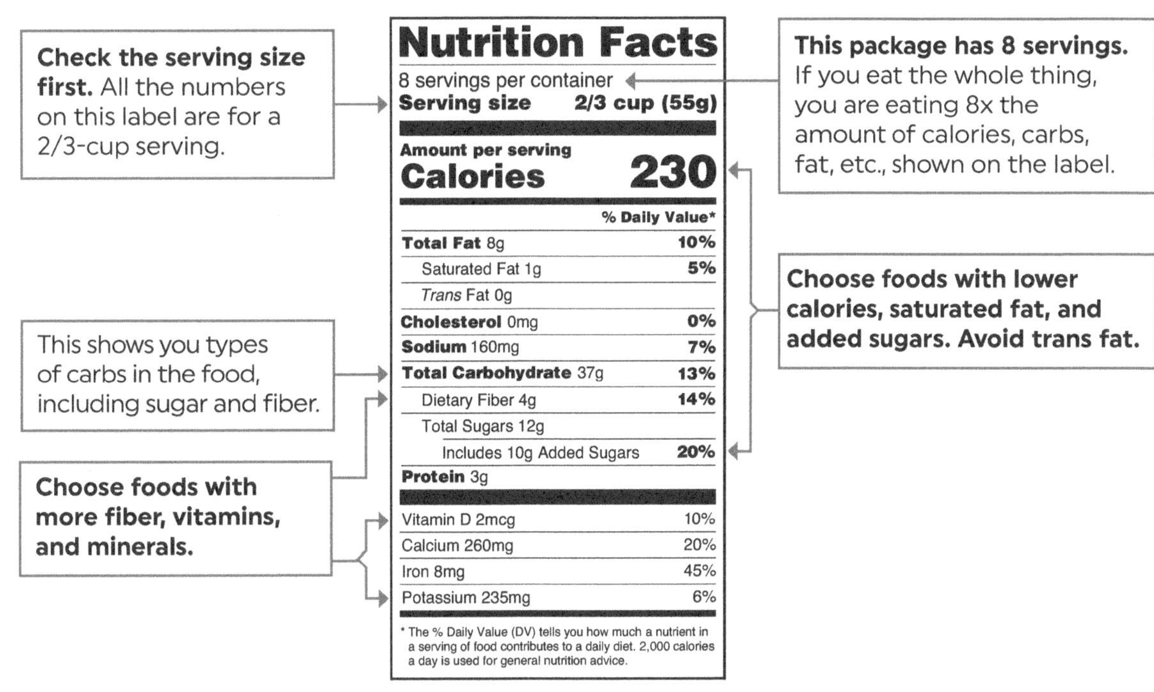

Check the serving size first. All the numbers on this label are for a 2/3-cup serving.
This shows you types of carbs in the food, including sugar and fiber.
Choose foods with more fiber, vitamins, and minerals.
Nutrition Facts
8 servings per container
Serving size 2/3 cup (55g)
Amount per serving
Calories 230
% Daily Value*
Total Fat 8g 10%
Saturated Fat 1g 5%
Trans Fat 0g
Cholesterol 0mg 0%
Sodium 160mg 7%
Total Carbohydrate 37g 13%
Dietary Fiber 4g 14%
Total Sugars 12g
Includes 10g Added Sugars 20%
Protein 3g
Vitamin D 2mcg 10%
Calcium 260mg 20%
Iron 8mg 45%
Potassium 235mg 6%
* The % Daily Value (DV) tells you how much a nutrient in a serving of food contributes to a daily diet. 2,000 calories a day is used for general nutrition advice.
This package has 8 servings. If you eat the whole thing, you are eating 8x the amount of calories, carbs, fat, etc., shown on the label.
Choose foods with lower calories, saturated fat, and added sugars. Avoid trans fat.

Eat a variety of healthy foods. Eat all kinds of different foods from the major food groups: veggies, fruits, grains, dairy or dairy alternatives such as low-fat or fat-free milk, yogurt, and other products made from soy, almonds, and cashews, and lean protein. Eating a variety of foods helps to make sure you get the vitamins and minerals you need. You don't need to eat all food groups at each meal.

Count what counts.

Don't get too hung up on calories, but definitely count them in. Cutting calories from your meals and adding physical activity to your routine can help you lose weight. But don't cut back too far. If you get too hungry, you won't stay on your plan. And remember, if you're more active, you're burning more calories.

The National Institutes of Health offers an interactive **Body Weight Planner** (https://www.niddk.nih.gov/bwp) that can help you determine the number of calories you should eat each day to get you to your goal weight and to maintain it.

Make Work, Home, Grocery Stores, and Restaurants Work for You

Take the work out of eating at work.

From office pastries to afternoon snacks to increase energy, the workplace can be a challenge for staying on course to eat healthy. **A little food preparation goes a long way.**

- ✔ Bring your lunch to work. This can often be healthier than buying it.
- ✔ Keep fruit and vegetables in a plastic container in the fridge at work for snacks.
- ✔ Bring groceries in on Mondays and keep them in a refrigerator to make your lunch at work if you don't want to bring lunch each day.
- ✔ Package high-power snacks, such as nuts, in small containers so you don't get famished or eat too much.

Make home your healthy place.

Sticking to a healthy plan is a lot easier when you can rely on having nutritious food available at home.

- ✔ Avoid "hiding" treats. You'll know where to find them.
- ✔ Prepare a few healthy snacks and keep them on hand as soon as you get home from the grocery store. Chop strips of peppers or celery or fruit so that healthy snacks are readily available when you get a food craving.
- ✔ Create a cooking ritual at home. Whether it's calling a friend, listening to music, or catching up on a TV show while you cook, pairing cooking with another rewarding activity makes it all the more enticing and beneficial.

Create a grocery store game plan.

The grocery store is your key to success. Plan before you go, and let an entire healthy week unfold.

- ✔ Make a shopping list based on your weekly meal plan, and stick to it.
- ✔ Focus on shopping the outer aisles where the fresh food is located. The inner aisles contain a lot of processed food and snacks that aren't as heathy. This also helps prevent temptation if you bring your kids shopping with you.
- ✔ You know this one: shop on a full stomach so you're not tempted to buy unhealthy processed food or junk food.

Restaurants: Order with ease.

- ✔ Look at the menu and nutrition info online before you go.
- ✔ Decide what you're going to order before you go to a restaurant so you're not tempted by the look and smell of less healthy choices.
- ✔ Avoid buffets.
- ✔ Ask your server how food is prepared before deciding what to order.
- ✔ Ask for veggies instead of fries or other high-calorie side dishes.
- ✔ Choose baked, steamed, grilled, or broiled instead of fried.
- ✔ Share your main dish with a friend or eat half of it and wrap up the rest to take home to eat later.
- ✔ Order sauces, salad dressing, or spreads on the side, and use sparingly.
- ✔ Avoid items that seem healthy but aren't, such as salads loaded with dressing, cheese, croutons, and bacon.

Keep Moving: Set a Fitness Goal for Healthier Movement

Get active. Our bodies are made to move, and we feel better when we do. That said, getting started can be a challenge. One thing is for sure—you won't stick with something that you don't like doing, and you shouldn't have to.

There are lots of ways to get moving; for example, walking is a great physical activity, and just about anyone can do it. Just be sure to check with your doctor about which activities are best for you and if there are any you should avoid.

So, set a goal that works for you! And gradually work up to being active at a moderate intensity at least 150 minutes per week. One way to do this is to aim for 30 minutes, 5 days a week. Moderate-intensity activities are those that make you breathe harder and make your heart beat faster, such as a brisk walk.

Goals:	Number of days a week being active:	How many active minutes each time:	Total number of active minutes each week:	Goal date:
My physical activity goal for now:				
My intermediate physical activity goal:				
My ultimate physical activity goal:				

Make a Plan! Put it on the calendar and choose the same time or location for your daily activity. The more regular you are physically active, the quicker being active becomes a habit.

Some Pointers:

Make it easy. Put your walking shoes and the dog's leash by the door; lay out your workout clothes the night before.

Sit less. Get up every hour and move. Set a timer on your phone with movement reminders. Walk around the room or stretch when you're watching TV or talking on the phone. Go talk to a coworker instead of sending an e-mail.

Try an activity tracker. Many of these apps are free, and it feels great to watch your steps add up.

Make goals specific. Instead of "I'm going to get in shape," think "I'm going to walk after dinner on weekdays."

Find a physical activity that you like, or you won't keep doing it. Physical activity should feel more like summer camp than boot camp (unless you like boot camp). Dance, hike, or play—do what's fun for you.

Start small. Little successes, like choosing physical activity over TV, pave the way for taking on bigger goals. Also, take it slow at first—you're still beating everyone on the couch!

Work out with a friend. When someone else is counting on you to show up, you'll likely hit the trail or the treadmill more often. There's nothing wrong with a little friendly competition.

Reward yourself. Think of a way to reward yourself for your great work. Maybe put a dollar in a jar every time you meet your daily physical activity goal. At the end of the month, treat yourself to a new outfit or a trip to the movies (just skip the buttery popcorn and candy).

Write any other strategies you plan to use for keeping active here:

____

____

____

____

____

____

Track Your Progress: Watch Yourself Succeed With a Few Easy Steps

The best way to stick with your goals and keep building on them is to measure them! Research shows that people who keep track of their food, activity, and weight reach their goals more often than people who don't.

There are lots of free tracking apps for your phone or tablet. Good old-fashioned pen and paper work too. Some people swear by taking photos of everything they eat and drink to keep them accountable.

Here's an example log:

Activity

Date: Monday, January 28	
Walking	10 minutes
Stationary bike	20 minutes
Climbing stairs	10 minutes
Total	**40 minutes**

Weight

Starting weight	240
Week 1*	239
Week 2	236
Week 3	234
Goal weight	**228**

Food

Date: Monday, January 28

Time	Amount	Food Item	Calories
8:00 am	1 cup	Oatmeal	160
	½ cup	Strawberries	25
	7 oz.	Greek yogurt	150
	1 cup	Tea with sugar-free sweetener	0
11:00 am	10	Almonds	70
12:30 pm	1 piece	Pita bread	190
	2 pieces	Falafel (baked)	80
	¼ cup	Hummus	160
	2 leaves	Romaine lettuce	5
	5	Cherry tomatoes	15
	Single-serve bag	Baked chips	120
	1 cup	Water with lemon	0
4:00 pm	2 cups	Popcorn	60
6:30 pm	1 cup	Shrimp scampi	230
	1 cup	Cooked broccoli with 1 tablespoon of parmesan cheese	100
	½ cup	Brown rice	110
	1 cup	Nonfat milk	90
Total			**1,565 calories**

*Weighing yourself more or less often is fine too if you prefer

Prepare for the Long Run: Get Support and Look Ahead

Get support. Share your healthy goals and why they're important with your friends and family. Having their support and encouragement can help you stay on track.

Consider these few examples of support:

- ✔ Ask if a friend would like to walk with you after dinner.
- ✔ Invite your kids to cook a healthy meal with you, or make a date night out of cooking with a partner.
- ✔ Talk to friends about struggles you're having and ask if they have advice.
- ✔ Share your successes with people you can trust to encourage you.

Who knows, you could even be helping someone you care about prevent type 2 diabetes along with you.

Go online.

There are lots of free online resources that can boost your motivation and confidence too. A quick Internet search will show you no-cost communities with people who share your goals and challenges, and who could learn from your experience (and you from theirs). If you share your health goals with others, you'll be more likely to stick to them.

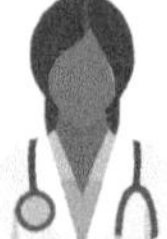

Remember, your doctor, physician assistant, or nurse practitioner can help you meet your goals.

If you retake the risk test and find that you're at a higher risk, or just feel like you're struggling and not seeing the results you want, consider asking for your health care provider's advice and direction. They could also refer you to specialists, such as a registered dietitian or mental health counselor, who can help you deal with a specific challenge. If you have prediabetes, ask your doctor if joining the National DPP might be a helpful step for you.

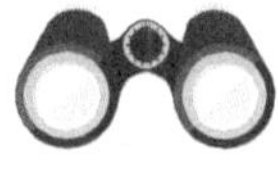

Look ahead.

We hope this guide has helped you get started down the road to not only preventing type 2 diabetes, but also having more energy, better checkups, and better mental health.

Making lifestyle changes can take time, but if you add in small steps towards your goals every week, you can start to make living healthy a habit.

CS324366-A

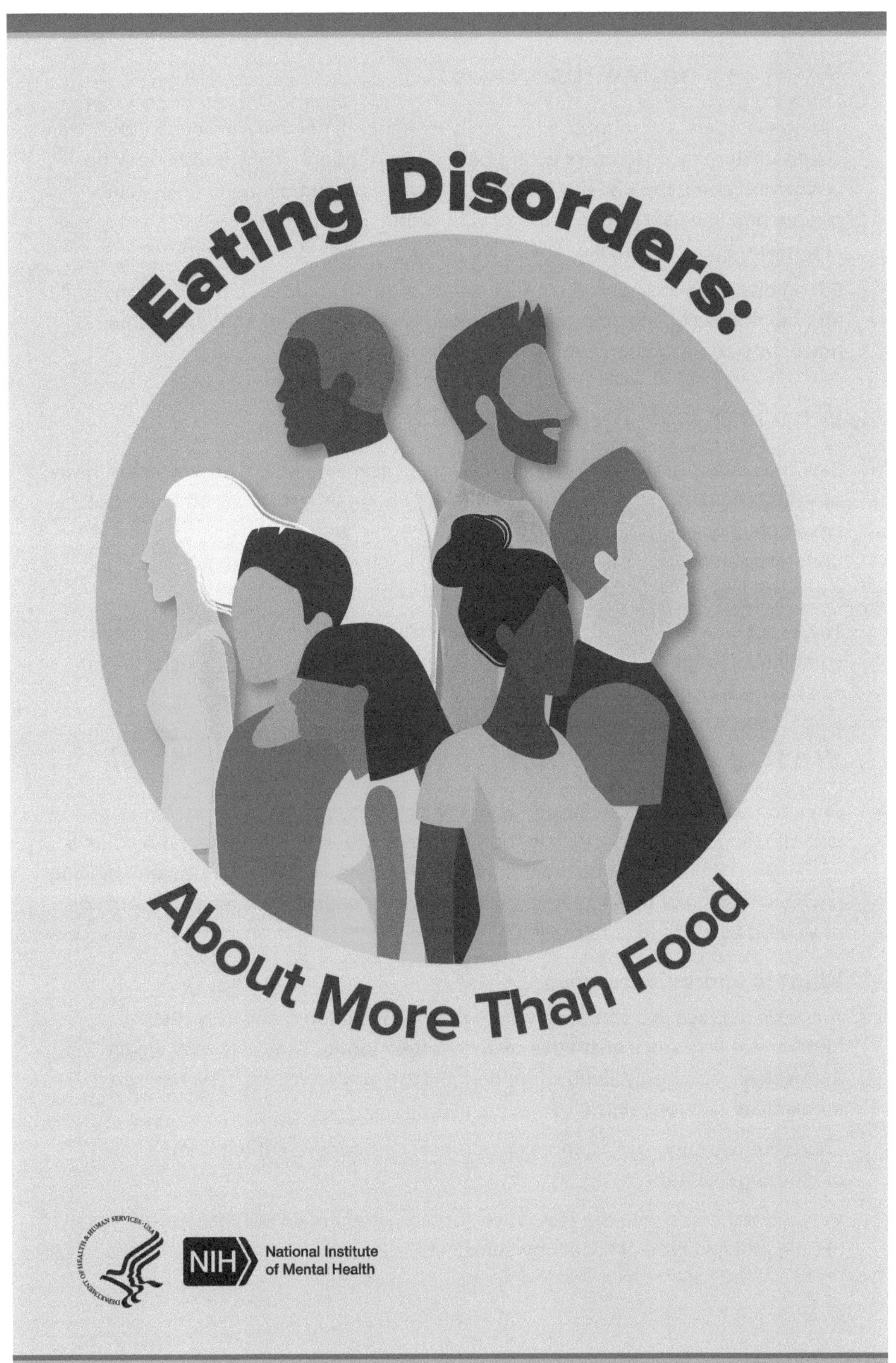
Eating Disorders:
About More Than Food
DEPARTMENT OF HEALTH & HUMAN SERVICES • USA
NIH
National Institute
of Mental Health

What are eating disorders?

Eating disorders are serious, biologically influenced medical illnesses marked by severe disturbances to one's eating behaviors. Although many people may be concerned about their health, weight, or appearance from time to time, some people become fixated or obsessed with weight loss, body weight or shape, and controlling their food intake. These may be signs of an eating disorder.

Eating disorders are not a choice. These disorders can affect a person's physical and mental health. In some cases, they can be life-threatening. With treatment, however, people can recover completely from eating disorders.

Who is at risk for eating disorders?

Eating disorders can affect people of all ages, racial and ethnic backgrounds, body weights, and genders. Even people who appear healthy, such as athletes, can have eating disorders and be extremely ill. People with eating disorders can be underweight, normal weight, or overweight. In other words, you can't tell if someone has an eating disorder by looking at them.

The exact cause of eating disorders is not fully understood. Research suggests a combination of genetic, biological, behavioral, psychological, and social factors can raise a person's risk.

What are the common types of eating disorders?

Common eating disorders include anorexia nervosa, bulimia nervosa, binge-eating disorder, and avoidant restrictive food intake disorder. Each of these disorders is associated with different but sometimes overlapping symptoms. People exhibiting any combination of these symptoms may have an eating disorder and should be evaluated by a health care provider.

What is anorexia nervosa?

Anorexia nervosa is a condition where people avoid food, severely restrict food, or eat very small quantities of only certain foods. They also may weigh themselves repeatedly. Even when dangerously underweight, they may see themselves as overweight.

There are two subtypes of anorexia nervosa: a *restrictive* subtype and a *binge-purge* subtype.

Restrictive: People with the restrictive subtype of anorexia nervosa severely limit the amount and type of food they consume.

Binge-Purge: People with the binge-purge subtype of anorexia nervosa also greatly restrict the amount and type of food they consume. In addition, they may have binge-eating and purging episodes—eating large amounts of food in a short time followed by vomiting or using laxatives or diuretics to get rid of what was consumed.

Symptoms of anorexia nervosa include:

- Extremely restricted eating and/or intensive and excessive exercise
- Extreme thinness (emaciation)
- A relentless pursuit of thinness and unwillingness to maintain a normal or healthy weight
- Intense fear of gaining weight
- Distorted body or self-image that is heavily influenced by perceptions of body weight and shape
- Denial of the seriousness of low body weight

Over time, anorexia nervosa can lead to numerous serious health consequences, including:

- Thinning of the bones (osteopenia or osteoporosis)
- Mild anemia
- Muscle wasting and weakness
- Brittle hair and nails
- Dry and yellowish skin
- Growth of fine hair all over the body (lanugo)
- Severe constipation
- Low blood pressure
- Slowed breathing and pulse
- Damage to the structure and function of the heart
- Drop in internal body temperature, causing a person to feel cold all the time
- Lethargy, sluggishness, or feeling tired all the time
- Infertility
- Brain damage
- Multiple organ failure

Anorexia nervosa can be fatal. It has an extremely high death (mortality) rate compared with other mental disorders. People with anorexia are at risk of dying from medical complications associated with starvation. Suicide is the second leading cause of death for people diagnosed with anorexia nervosa.

If you or someone you know is in immediate distress or is thinking about hurting themselves, call the **National Suicide Prevention Lifeline** toll-free at 1-800-273-TALK (8255). You also can text the **Crisis Text Line** (HELLO to 741741) or use the Lifeline Chat at the **National Suicide Prevention Lifeline** website at **https://suicidepreventionlifeline.org**. If you suspect a medical emergency, seek medical attention or call 911 immediately.

What is bulimia nervosa?

Bulimia nervosa is a condition where people have recurrent episodes of eating unusually large amounts of food and feeling a lack of control over their eating. This binge eating is followed by behaviors that compensate for the overeating to prevent weight gain, such as forced vomiting, excessive use of laxatives or diuretics, fasting, excessive exercise, or a combination of these behaviors. Unlike those with anorexia nervosa, people with bulimia nervosa may maintain a normal weight or be overweight.

Symptoms and health consequences of bulimia nervosa include:

- Chronically inflamed and sore throat
- Swollen salivary glands in the neck and jaw area
- Worn tooth enamel and increasingly sensitive and decaying teeth from exposure to stomach acid when vomiting
- Acid reflux disorder and other gastrointestinal problems
- Intestinal distress and irritation from laxative abuse
- Severe dehydration from purging
- Electrolyte imbalance (too low or too high levels of sodium, calcium, potassium, and other minerals), which can lead to stroke or heart attack

What is binge-eating disorder?

Binge-eating disorder is a condition where people lose control of their eating and have reoccurring episodes of eating unusually large amounts of food. Unlike bulimia nervosa, periods of binge eating are not followed by purging, excessive exercise, or fasting. As a result, people with binge-eating disorder are often overweight or obese.

Symptoms of binge-eating disorder include:

- Eating unusually large amounts of food in a short amount of time, for example, within two hours
- Eating rapidly during binge episodes
- Eating even when full or not hungry
- Eating until uncomfortably full
- Eating alone or in secret to avoid embarrassment
- Feeling distressed, ashamed, or guilty about eating
- Frequent dieting, possibly without weight loss

What is avoidant restrictive food intake disorder?

Avoidant restrictive food intake disorder (ARFID), previously known as selective eating disorder, is a condition where people limit the amount or type of food eaten. Unlike anorexia nervosa, people with ARFID do not have a distorted body image or extreme fear of gaining weight. ARFID is most common in middle childhood and usually has an earlier onset than other eating disorders. Many children go through phases of picky eating, but a child with ARFID does not eat enough calories to grow and develop properly, and an adult with ARFID does not eat enough calories to maintain basic body function.

Symptoms of ARFID include:

- Dramatic restriction of types or amount of food eaten
- Lack of appetite or interest in food
- Dramatic weight loss
- Upset stomach, abdominal pain, or other gastrointestinal issues with no other known cause
- Limited range of preferred foods that becomes even more limited ("picky eating" that gets progressively worse)

How are eating disorders treated?

Eating disorders can be treated successfully. Early detection and treatment are important for a full recovery. People with eating disorders are at higher risk for suicide and medical complications.

A person's family can play a crucial role in treatment. Family members can encourage the person with eating or body image issues to seek help. They also can provide support during treatment and can be a great ally to both the individual and the health care provider. Research suggests that incorporating the family into treatment for eating disorders can improve treatment outcomes, particularly for adolescents.

Treatment plans for eating disorders include psychotherapy, medical care and monitoring, nutritional counseling, medications, or a combination of these approaches. Typical treatment goals include:

- Restoring adequate nutrition
- Bringing weight to a healthy level
- Reducing excessive exercise
- Stopping binge-purge and binge-eating behaviors

People with eating disorders also may have other mental disorders (such as depression or anxiety) or problems with substance use. It's critical to treat any co-occurring conditions as part of the treatment plan.

Specific forms of psychotherapy ("talk therapy") and cognitive-behavioral approaches can treat certain eating disorders effectively. For general information about psychotherapies, visit **www.nimh.nih.gov/psychotherapies**.

Research also suggests that medications may help treat some eating disorders and co-occurring anxiety or depression related to eating disorders. Information about medications changes frequently, so talk to your health care provider. Visit the U.S. Food and Drug Administration (FDA) website at **www.fda.gov/drugsatfda** for the latest warnings, patient medication guides, and FDA-approved medications.

Where can I find help?

If you're unsure where to get help, your health care provider is a good place to start. Your health care provider can refer you to a qualified mental health professional, such as a psychiatrist or psychologist, who has experience treating eating disorders.

You can learn more about getting help and finding a health care provider on the National Institute of Mental Health (NIMH) webpage, Help for Mental Illnesses, at **www.nimh.nih.gov/findhelp**. If you need help identifying a provider in your area, call the Substance Abuse and Mental Health Services Administration (SAMHSA) Treatment Referral Helpline at 1-800-662-HELP (4357). You also can search SAMHSA's online Behavioral Health Treatment Services Locator (**https://findtreatment.samhsa.gov**), which lists facilities and programs that provide mental health services.

For tips on talking with your health care provider about your mental health, read NIMH's fact sheet, Taking Control of Your Mental Health: Tips for Talking With Your Health Care Provider, at **www.nimh.nih.gov/talkingtips**.

For additional resources, visit the Agency for Healthcare Research and Quality website at **www.ahrq.gov/questions**.

Are there clinical trials studying eating disorders?

NIMH supports a wide range of research, including clinical trials that look at new ways to prevent, detect, or treat diseases and conditions, including eating disorders. Although individuals may benefit from being part of a clinical trial, participants should be aware that the primary purpose of a clinical trial is to gain new scientific knowledge so that others may be better helped in the future.

Researchers at NIMH and around the country conduct clinical trials with patients and healthy volunteers. Talk to your health care provider about clinical trials, their benefits and risks, and whether one is right for you. For more information about clinical research and how to find clinical trials being conducted around the country, visit **www.nimh.nih.gov/clinicaltrials**.

Phosphorus

Tips for People with Chronic Kidney Disease (CKD)

What Is Phosphorus?

Phosphorus is a mineral that helps keep your bones healthy. It also helps keep blood vessels and muscles working. Phosphorus is found naturally in foods rich in protein, such as meat, poultry, fish, nuts, beans, and dairy products. Phosphorus is also added to many processed foods.

Why Is Phosphorus Important for People with CKD?

When you have CKD, phosphorus can build up in your blood, making your bones thin, weak, and more likely to break. It can cause itchy skin, and bone and joint pain. Most people with CKD need to eat foods with less phosphorus than they are used to eating.

Your health care provider may talk to you about taking a phosphate binder with meals to lower the amount of phosphorus in your blood.

Foods *Lower* in Phosphorus

- Fresh fruits and vegetables
- Rice milk (not enriched)
- Breads, pasta, rice

- Corn and rice cereals
- Light-colored sodas/pop
- Home-brewed iced tea

Foods *Higher* in Phosphorus

- Meat, poultry, fish
- Dairy foods
- Beans, lentils, nuts

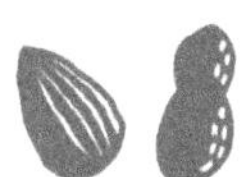

- Bran cereals and oatmeal
- Colas
- Some bottled iced tea

Phosphorus

How Do I Lower Phosphorus in My Diet?

- Know what foods are lower in phosphorus (see page 1).
- Eat smaller portions of foods high in protein at meals and for snacks.
  - **Meat, poultry, and fish:** A cooked portion should be about 2 to 3 ounces or about the size of a deck of cards.

  - **Dairy foods:** Keep your portions to ½ cup of milk or yogurt, or one slice of cheese.

  - **Beans and lentils:** Portions should be about ½ cup of cooked beans or lentils.
  - **Nuts:** Keep your portions to about ¼ cup of nuts.
- Eat fresh fruits and vegetables—if you have not been told to watch your potassium
- Many packaged foods have added phosphorus. Look for phosphorus, or for word with PHOS, on ingredient labels, like the one below. Choose a different food when the ingredient list has PHOS on the label.

> **Ingredients:** Potatoes, Vegetable Oil (Partially Hydrogenated Soybean Oil), Salt, Dextrose, Disodium Dihydrogen Pyro**phos**phate...

Examples of Foods that May Have Added Phosphorus	
• Fresh* and frozen uncooked meats and poultry	• Frozen baked goods
• Chicken nuggets	• Cereals, cereal bars
• Baking mixes	• Instant puddings and sauces

*Ask the butcher to show you which fresh meats do not have added phosphorus.

For more information, visit *www.niddk.nih.gov* or call 1-800-860-8747.

This content is provided as a service of the National Institute of Diabetes and Digestive and Kidney Diseases (NIDDK), part of the National Institutes of Health. The NIDDK translates and disseminates research findings to increase knowledge and understanding about health and disease among patients, health professionals, and the public. Content produced by the NIDDK is carefully reviewed by NIDDK scientists and other experts.

NIH Publication No. 10-7407 • April 2010

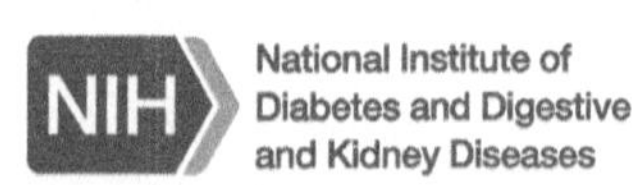

Potassium

Tips for People with Chronic Kidney Disease (CKD)

What Is Potassium?

Potassium is a mineral that helps your nerves and muscles work the right way.

Why Is Potassium Important for People with CKD?

In some people with CKD, the kidneys may not remove extra potassium from the blood. Some medicines also can raise your potassium level. Your food choices can help you lower your potassium level.

How Do I Know My Potassium Is High?

People often do not feel any different when their potassium is high. Your health care provider will check the level of potassium in your blood and the medicines you take. The level of potassium in your blood should be between **3.5 to 5.0**.*

How Do I Lower Potassium in My Diet?

- Eat smaller portions of foods high in protein at meals and for snacks: meat, poultry, fish, beans, dairy, and nuts.
- Use spices and herbs in cooking and at the table. Salt substitutes often contain potassium and should not be used.
- **Potassium chloride** can be used in place of salt in some packaged foods, like canned soups and tomato products. Limit foods with potassium chloride on the ingredient list.
- Drain canned fruits and vegetables before eating.
- If you have diabetes, choose apple, grape, or cranberry juice when your blood sugar goes down.

Eat These Foods	Instead of These Foods
• White rice	• Brown and wild rice
• White bread and pasta	• Whole wheat bread and pasta
• Cooked rice and wheat cereals	• Bran cereals
• Rice milk (not enriched)	• Cow's milk

*Normal ranges may vary.

Potassium

How Do I Lower Potassium in My Diet? (continued)

- Choose fruits and vegetables that are lower in potassium. Have very small portions of foods that are higher in potassium, like one slice of tomato on a sandwich, a few slices of banana on cereal, or half of an orange.

Fruits and Vegetables *Lower* in Potassium (200 mg or less*)

FRUITS

- Apples/apple juice/applesauce
- Apricots (canned)/apricot nectar
- Berries
- Cranberry juice
- Fruit cocktail
- Grapes/grape juice
- Grapefruit/grapefruit juice
- Honeydew melon
- Lemons and limes
- Mangoes
- Papayas
- Pears
- Peaches
- Plums
- Pineapple
- Rhubarb
- Tangerines
- Watermelon

VEGETABLES

- Alfalfa sprouts
- Bell peppers
- Bamboo shoots (canned)
- Broccoli (fresh)
- Cabbage
- Carrots
- Cauliflower
- Celery and onions (raw)
- Corn
- Cucumber
- Eggplant
- Green beans
- Kale
- Lettuce
- Mushrooms (fresh)
- Okra
- Summer squash (cooked)

*Potassium level is based on one serving. One serving of fruit is one small piece; ½ cup fresh, canned, canned, or cooked fruit; ¼ cup dried fruit; or ½ cup juice. **One serving of vegetables** is ½ cup fresh or cooked vegetables, 1 cup raw leafy vegetables, or ½ cup juice.

Potassium

Fruits and Vegetables *Higher* in Potassium (More than 200 mg*)
FRUITS • Apricots (fresh) • Bananas • Cantaloupe • Dates • Nectarines • Kiwi • Prunes/prune juice • Oranges/orange juice • Raisins
VEGETABLES • Acorn and butternut squash • Avocado • Baked beans • Beet and other greens • Broccoli (cooked) • Brussels sprouts (cooked) • Chard • Chile peppers • Mushrooms (cooked) • Potatoes • Pumpkin • Spinach (cooked) • Split peas, lentils, beans • Sweet potatoes, yams • Vegetable juice • Tomatoes/tomato juice/tomato sauce

*Potassium level is based on one serving. **One serving of fruit** is one small piece; ½ cup fresh, canned, or cooked fruit; ¼ cup dried fruit; or ½ cup juice. **One serving of vegetables** is ½ cup fresh or cooked vegetables, 1 cup raw leafy vegetables, or ½ cup juice.

Protein

Tips for People with Chronic Kidney Disease (CKD)

What Is Protein?

Protein is in many foods that you eat. Protein can be found in foods from animals and from plants. Most diets include both types of protein. Protein provides the building blocks that help maintain and repair muscles, organs, and other parts of the body.

Animal-protein Foods

- Meat, such as pork, beef, chicken, turkey, duck
- Eggs
- Dairy products, such as milk, yogurt, cheese
- Fish

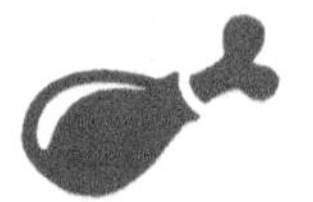

Plant-protein Foods

High Protein	Low Protein
• Beans, peas, lentils • Soy foods, such as soy milk, tofu • Nuts and nut spreads, such as almond butter, peanut butter, soy nut butter • Sunflower seeds 	• Bread, tortillas • Oatmeal, grits, cereals • Pasta, noodles, rice • Rice milk (not enriched) 

Why Is Protein Important for People with CKD?

When your body uses protein, it produces waste. This waste is removed by the kidneys. Too much protein can make the kidneys work harder, so people with CKD may need to eat less protein.

Animal protein includes all of the building blocks that your body needs. Plant proteins need to be combined to get all of the building blocks that your body needs.

Protein

How Do I Eat the Right Amount of Protein?

Your dietitian will tell you what amount and types of protein are right for you. Here is some general information about protein types and serving sizes:

- Eat smaller portions of meat and dairy. This will also help you lower the amount of phosphorus in your diet, because phosphorus is found in meat and dairy foods.
  - **Meat, poultry, and fish:** A cooked portion should be about 2 to 3 ounces or about the size of a deck of cards.

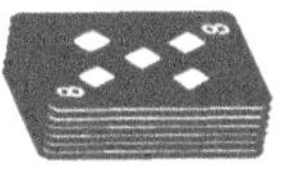

  - **Dairy foods:** A portion is ½ cup of milk or yogurt, or one slice of cheese.
- Plant proteins should make up the rest of the protein that you eat. A serving is:
  - ½ cup of cooked beans
  - ¼ cup of nuts
  - a slice of bread
  - ½ cup of cooked rice or noodles

What if I Am a Vegetarian?

There are many good sources of protein for people who do not eat meat or dairy foods. Talk to your dietitian about how to combine plant proteins to be sure you are getting all of the building blocks your body needs.

Notes: ______________________________

____

____

____

For more information, visit *www.niddk.nih.gov* or call 1-800-860-8747.

This content is provided as a service of the National Institute of Diabetes and Digestive and Kidney Diseases (NIDDK), part of the National Institutes of Health. The NIDDK translates and disseminates research findings to increase knowledge and understanding about health and disease among patients, health professionals, and the public. Content produced by the NIDDK is carefully reviewed by NIDDK scientists and other experts.

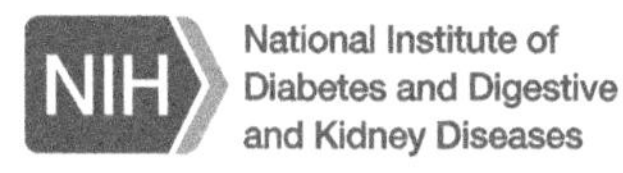

NIH Publication No. 10-7407 • April 2010

Sodium

Foods *Higher* in Sodium

- Bacon, corned beef, ham, hot dogs, luncheon meat, sausage
- Bouillon, canned, and instant soups
- Boxed mixes, like hamburger meals and pancake mix
- Canned beans, chicken, fish and meat
- Canned tomato products, including juice
- Canned and pickled vegetables, vegetable juice
- Cottage cheese
- Frozen meals
- Frozen vegetables with sauce
- Olives, pickles, relish
- Pretzels, chips, crackers, salted nuts
- Salt and salt seasonings, like garlic salt
- Seasoning mix and sauce packets
- Soy sauce
- Salad dressings, bottled sauces, marinades
- Some ready-to-eat cereals, baked goods, breads
- Ready-to-eat boxed meals and side dishes

How Do I Lower the Sodium in My Diet?

- Buy fresh foods more often.
- Cook foods from scratch, instead of eating prepared foods, "fast" foods, frozen dinners, and canned foods that are higher in sodium.
- Use spices, herbs, and sodium-free seasonings in place of salt. Check with your health care provider about using salt substitutes.
- Rinse canned vegetables, beans, meats, and fish with water to remove extra sodium.

Sodium

Always read the Nutrition Facts label to compare foods. Choose foods with the lowest Percent Daily Value (%DV) for sodium. The %DV lets you see if a food is high or low in sodium. **5% or less is low and 20% or more is high.**

- Check the label on fresh meats and poultry. Sodium additives can be used to make meat last longer.

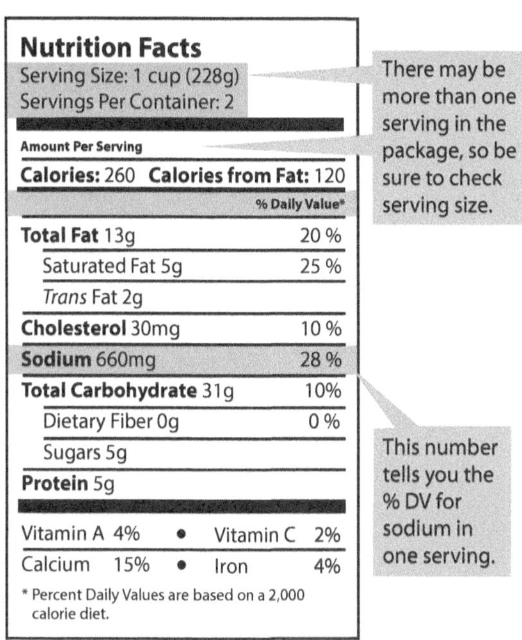

Nutrition Facts

Serving Size: 1 cup (228g)
Servings Per Container: 2

Amount Per Serving

Calories: 260 **Calories from Fat:** 120

	% Daily Value*
Total Fat 13g	20 %
Saturated Fat 5g	25 %
Trans Fat 2g	
Cholesterol 30mg	10 %
Sodium 660mg	28 %
Total Carbohydrate 31g	10%
Dietary Fiber 0g	0 %
Sugars 5g	
Protein 5g	

Vitamin A 4% • Vitamin C 2%
Calcium 15% • Iron 4%

* Percent Daily Values are based on a 2,000 calorie diet.

- Look for foods labeled: sodium free, salt free, very low sodium, low sodium, reduced or less sodium, light in sodium, no salt added, unsalted, and lightly salted.

Check the Ingredient Label for Added Sodium

- Salt (sodium chloride)
- Monosodium glutamate or MSG
- Baking soda (sodium bicarbonate)
- Baking powder
- Sodium nitrate
- Sodium sulfite
- Sodium phosphate
- Sodium alginate
- Sodium benzoate
- Sodium hydroxide
- Sodium propionate

How to
avoid
portion size
pitfalls
to help manage
your weight.
When eating at many restaurants, it's hard to miss that portion sizes have gotten larger in the last few years. The trend has also spilled over into the grocery store and vending machines, where a bagel has become a **BAGEL** and an "individual" bag of chips can easily feed more than one. Research shows that people unintentionally consume more calories when faced with larger portions. This can mean significant excess calorie intake, especially when eating high-calorie foods.
Here are some tips to help you avoid some common portion-size pitfalls:
Popcorn
GUEST CHECK
RIDICULOUSLY LARGE
DEPARTMENT OF HEALTH AND HUMAN SERVICES
CENTERS FOR DISEASE CONTROL AND PREVENTION
CDC

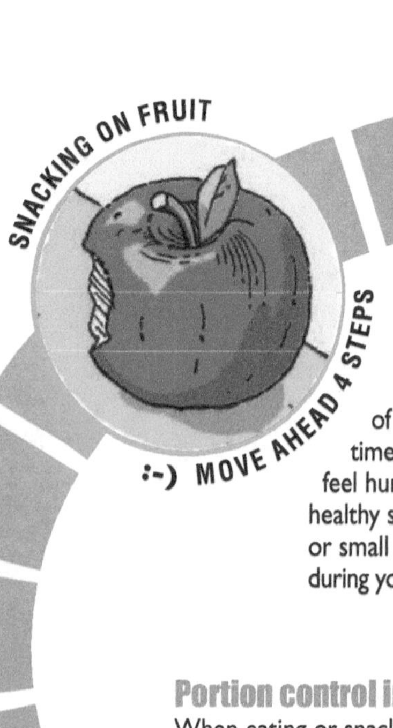

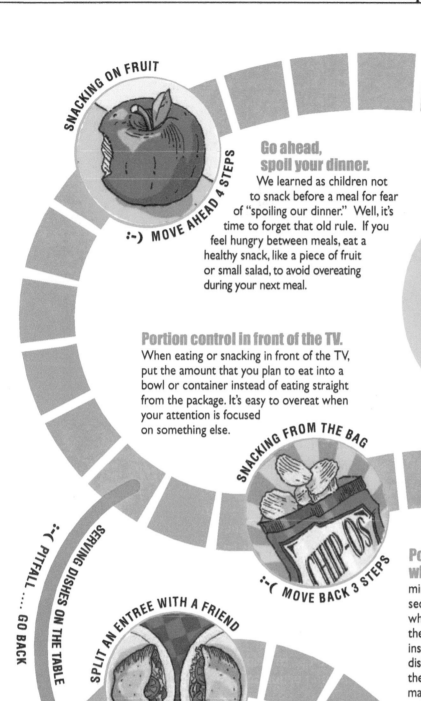

Go ahead, spoil your dinner. We learned as children not to snack before a meal for fear of "spoiling our dinner." Well, it's time to forget that old rule. If you feel hungry between meals, eat a healthy snack, like a piece of fruit or small salad, to avoid overeating during your next meal.

Directions

Do you get caught in portion size pitfalls? Roll the dice and move along the path. (Use dice and players from another board game.) Follow the instructions for each shortcut or pitfall you land on. The turn then moves to the next player. **Get on the path to proper portion control!**

Portion control in front of the TV. When eating or snacking in front of the TV, put the amount that you plan to eat into a bowl or container instead of eating straight from the package. It's easy to overeat when your attention is focused on something else.

SNACKING FROM THE BAG

CHIP-OS

:-(MOVE BACK 3 STEPS

Portion control when eating in. To minimize the temptation of second and third helpings when eating at home, serve the food on individual plates, instead of putting the serving dishes on the table. Keeping the excess food out of reach may discourage overeating.

SPLIT AN ENTREE WITH A FRIEND

:-) MOVE AHEAD 3 STEPS

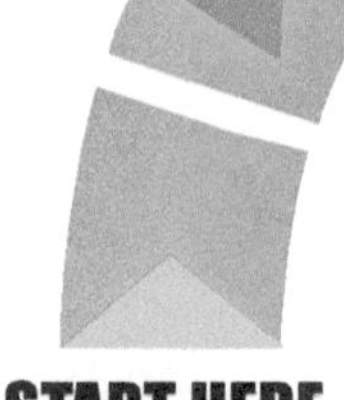

Portion control when eating out. Many restaurants serve more food than one person needs at one meal. Take control of the amount of food that ends up on your plate by splitting an entrée with a friend. Or, ask the wait person for a "to-go" box and wrap up half your meal as soon as it's brought to the table.

START HERE

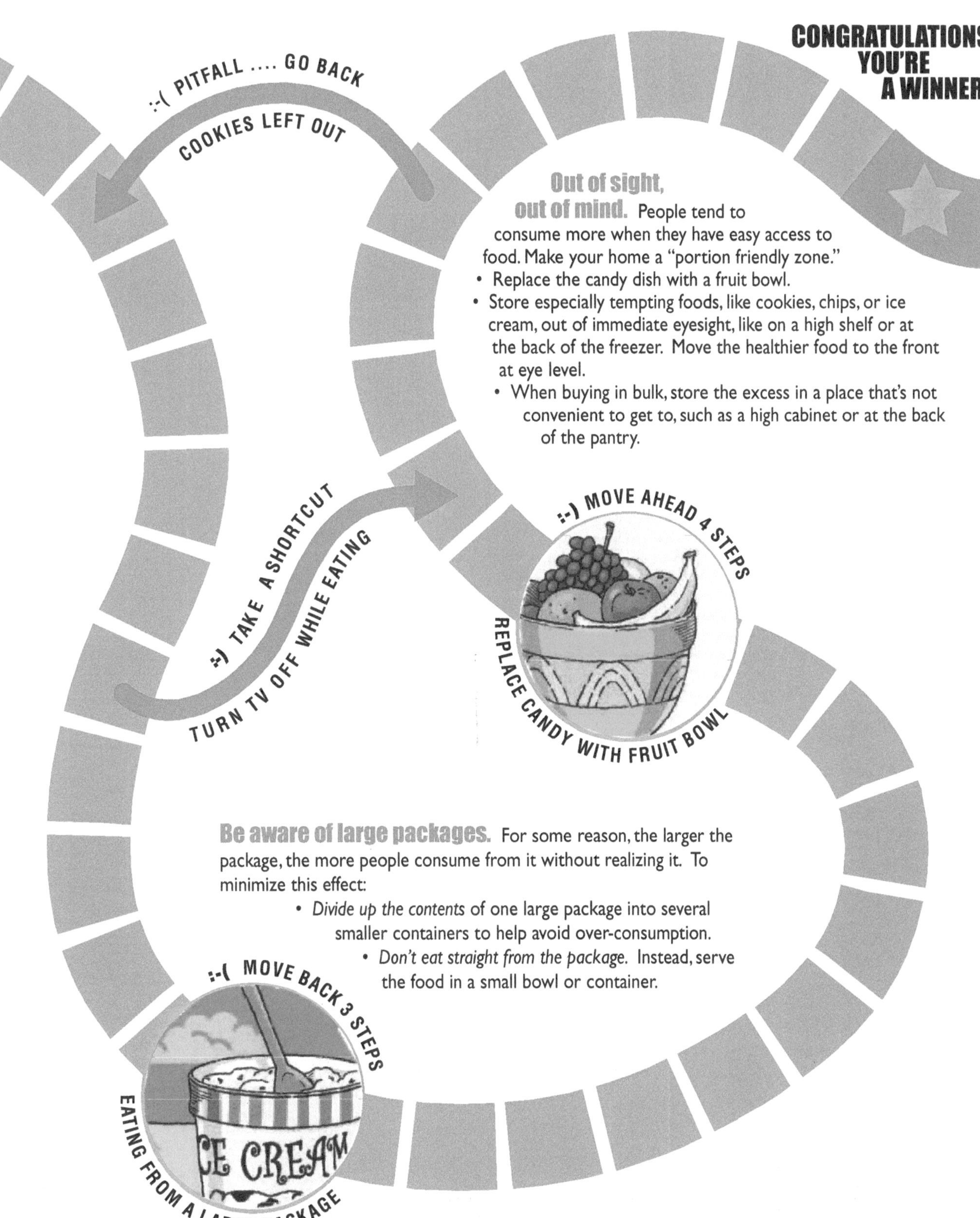

Out of sight, out of mind. People tend to consume more when they have easy access to food. Make your home a "portion friendly zone."

- Replace the candy dish with a fruit bowl.
- Store especially tempting foods, like cookies, chips, or ice cream, out of immediate eyesight, like on a high shelf or at the back of the freezer. Move the healthier food to the front at eye level.
- When buying in bulk, store the excess in a place that's not convenient to get to, such as a high cabinet or at the back of the pantry.

Be aware of large packages. For some reason, the larger the package, the more people consume from it without realizing it. To minimize this effect:

- *Divide up the contents* of one large package into several smaller containers to help avoid over-consumption.
- *Don't eat straight from the package.* Instead, serve the food in a small bowl or container.

Check out these websites for more portion size tips

- The Portion Distortion Quiz from the National Heart Lung and Blood Institute (NHLBI) (http://hin.nhlbi.nih.gov/portion/) shows how portion sizes of some common foods have changed over the years.
- Food labels can help you understand that portion sizes are often larger than you think. Click the links below to learn how to use the Nutrition Facts Label on food packages:
  - > How to Understand and Use the Nutrition Facts Label, Food and Drug Administration, Center for Food Safety and Applied Nutrition. http://www.cfsan.fda.gov/~dms/foodlab.html
  - > Test Your Food Label Knowledge (quiz), Food and Drug Administration, Center for Food Safety and Applied Nutrition. http://www.cfsan.fda.gov/~dms/flquiz1.html
- Take the NHLBI Visual Reality quiz (http://nhlbisupport.com/chd1/visualreality/visualreality.htm) to test your skills at estimating serving sizes.
- Use this handy Serving Size Wallet card from NHLBI (http://hin.nhlbi.nih.gov/portion/servingcard7.pdf) to help estimate the right amount to eat. Or check out www.MyPyramid.gov for detailed information on how much to eat from each food group without eating more calories than you need.

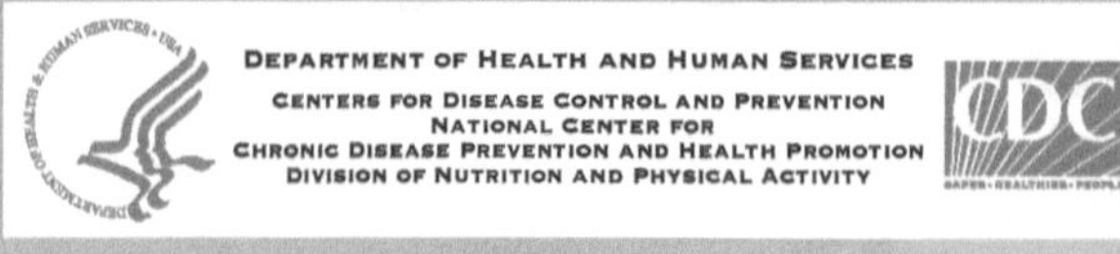

Department of Health and Human Services
Centers for Disease Control and Prevention
National Center for
Chronic Disease Prevention and Health Promotion
Division of Nutrition and Physical Activity
CDC

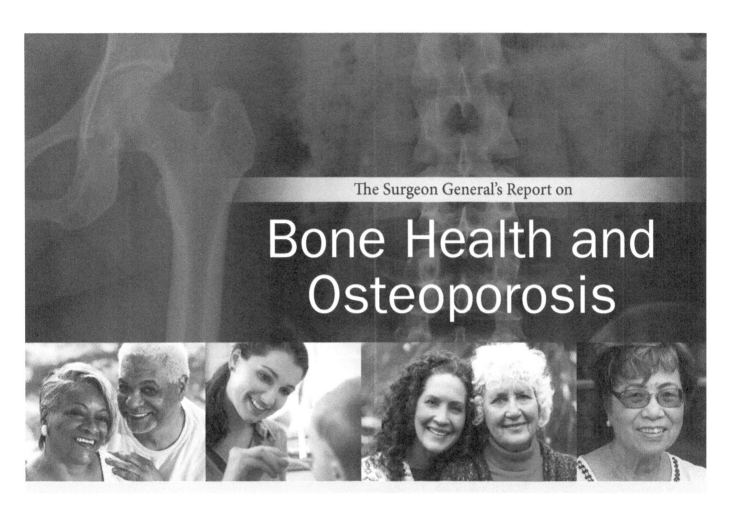

The Surgeon General's Report on

Bone Health and Osteoporosis

what it means to you

Strong bones begin in childhood. With good habits and medical attention when needed, we can have strong bones throughout our lives. People who have weak bones are at higher risk for fractures.

You can improve your bone health by getting enough calcium, vitamin D, and physical activity. If you have osteoporosis or another bone disease, your doctor can detect and treat it. This can help prevent painful fractures.

"...with good habits and medical attention when needed, we can have strong bones throughout our lives."

"Bones may begin to weaken early in life. Prevent this with a healthy diet and the right kinds of physical activity."

Why Healthy Bones Are Important to You

Strong bones support us and allow us to move. They protect our heart, lungs, and brain from injury. Our bones are also a storehouse for vital minerals we need to live. Weak bones break easily, causing terrible pain. You might lose your ability to stand or walk. And as bones weaken, you might lose height.

Silently and without warning, bones may begin to weaken early in life if you do not have a healthy diet and the right kinds of physical activity. Many people already have weak bones and don't know it. Others are making choices that will weaken their bones later.

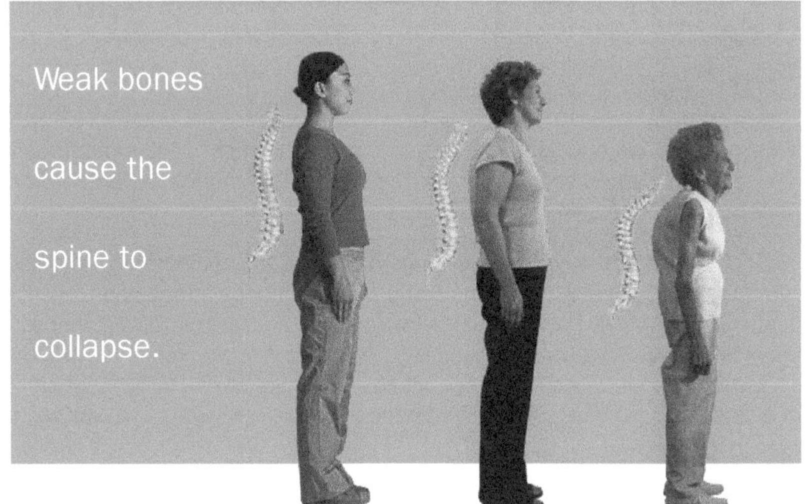
Weak bones
cause the
spine to
collapse.

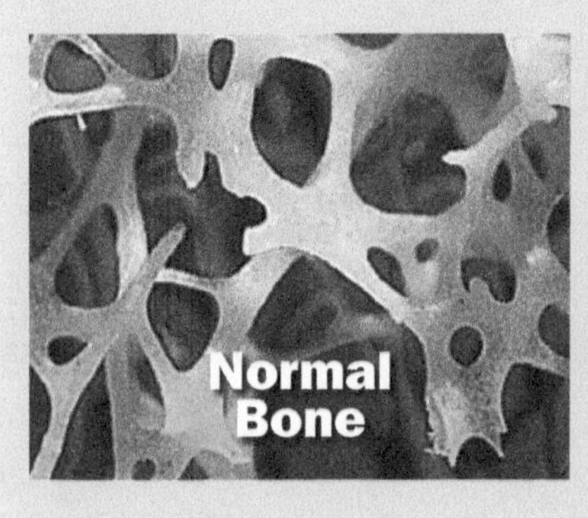

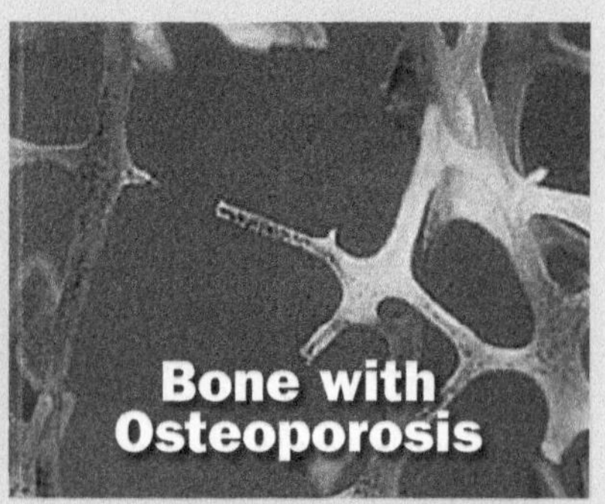

Osteoporosis causes weak bones.

"...you are never too old or too young to improve your bone health."

There are several kinds of bone disease. The most common is osteoporosis. In this disease, bones lose minerals like calcium. They become fragile and break easily. With osteoporosis, your body's frame becomes like the frame of a house damaged by termites. Termites weaken your house like osteoporosis weakens your bones. If you have severe fractures from osteoporosis, you risk never walking again. Weak bones can break easily. This can be fatal.

Fragile bones are not painful at first. Unfortunately, most people don't realize they have weakened bones until one breaks. By that time, it is hard to make your bones strong again.

The good news is that you are never too old or too young to improve your bone health. There are many things you can do to keep bones strong and prevent fractures. At all ages, a diet with enough calcium and vitamin D, together with weight-bearing and resistance exercises, can help prevent problems later. You can work with your doctor to check out warning signs or risk factors. When you are older, you can have your bones tested and take medicine to strengthen them.

"Staying active helps strengthen bones."

Don't Risk Your Bones

Many things weaken bones. Some are outside your control. If you have a family member who has bone problems, you could also be at risk. Some medical conditions can also make you prone to bone disease.

There are some things you can control:

- **Get enough calcium and vitamin D** in your diet at every age.
- **Be physically active.**
- **Reduce hazards in your home** that could increase your risk of falling and breaking bones.
- **Talk with your doctor about medicines** you are taking that could weaken bones, like medicine for thyroid problems or arthritis. Also talk about ways to take medicines that are safe for bones. Discuss ways to protect bones while treating other problems.
- **Maintain a healthy weight.** Being underweight raises the risk of fracture and bone loss.
- **Don't smoke.** Smoking can reduce bone mass and increase your risks for a broken bone.
- **Limit alcohol use.** Heavy alcohol use reduces bone mass and increases your risk for broken bones.

FAST FACT

Many types of physical activity can contribute to bone health, but most people are not active enough.

Bones Are Not What You Think They Are

When you think of bones, you might imagine a hard, brittle skeleton. In reality, your bones are living organs. They are alive with cells and flowing body fluids. Bones are constantly renewed and grow stronger with a good diet and physical activity.

The amount of calcium that makes up your bones is the measure of how strong they are. But your muscles and nerves must also have calcium and phosphorus to work. If these are in short supply from foods you eat, your body simply takes them from your bones.

Each day calcium is deposited and withdrawn from your bones. If you don't get enough calcium, you could be withdrawing more than you're depositing. Our bodies build up calcium in our bones efficiently until we are about 30 years old. Then our bodies stop adding new bone. But healthy habits can help us keep the bone we have.

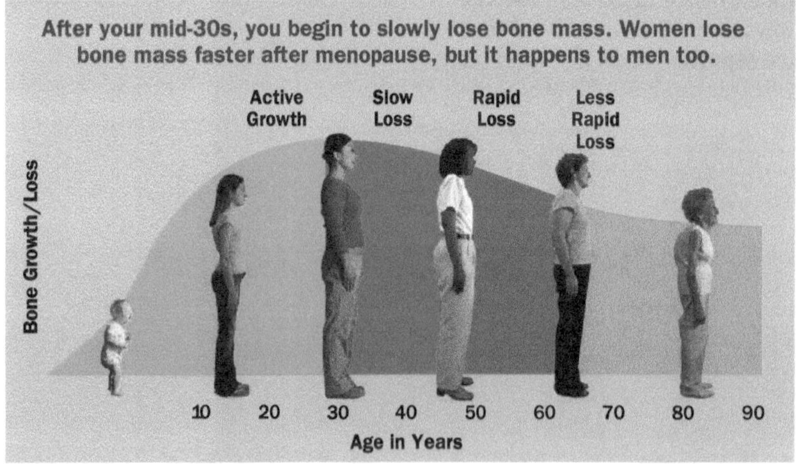

"Do you spend your free evenings on the sofa or taking a walk?"

"The most common breaks in weak bones are in the wrist, spine, and hip."

When Bones Break

There is some natural bone loss as women and men age. As we grow older, bones can break or weaken if we don't take steps to keep them strong. The most common breaks in weak bones are in the wrist, spine, and hip.

Broken bones in your spine can be painful and very slow to heal. People with weak bones in their spine gradually lose height and their posture becomes hunched over. Over time a bent spine can make it hard to walk or even sit up.

Broken hips are a very serious problem as we age. They greatly increase the risk of death, especially during the year after they break.

People who break a hip might not recover for months or even years. Because they often cannot care for themselves, they are more likely to have to live in a nursing home.

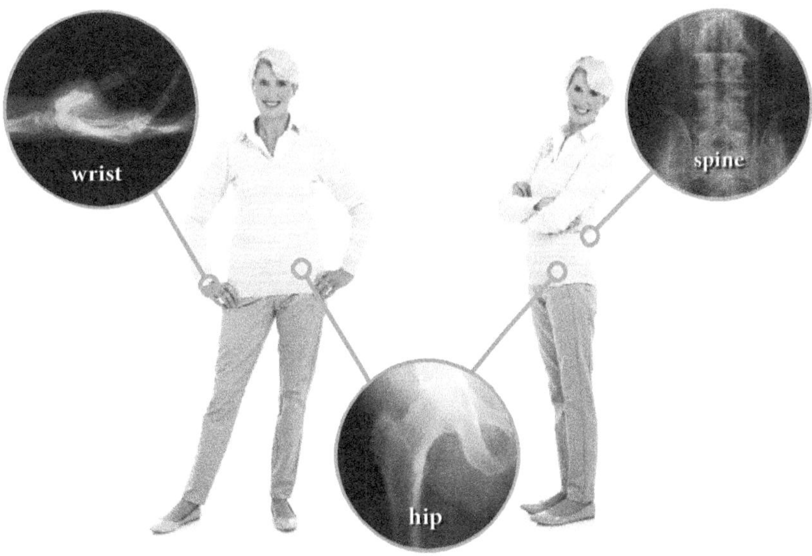

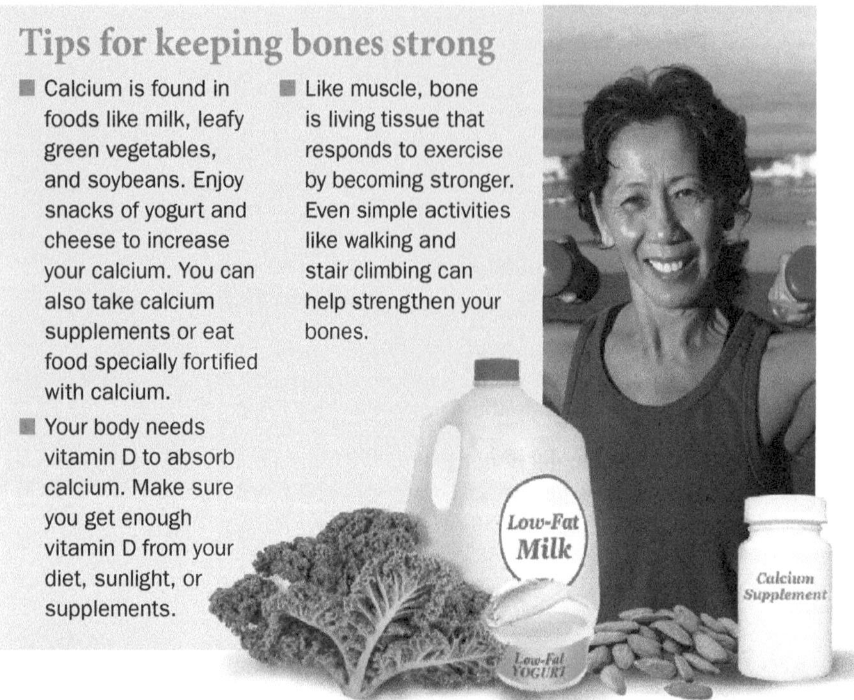

Tips for keeping bones strong
Calcium is found in foods like milk, leafy green vegetables, and soybeans. Enjoy snacks of yogurt and cheese to increase your calcium. You can also take calcium supplements or eat food specially fortified with calcium.
Your body needs vitamin D to absorb calcium. Make sure you get enough vitamin D from your diet, sunlight, or supplements.
Like muscle, bone is living tissue that responds to exercise by becoming stronger. Even simple activities like walking and stair climbing can help strengthen your bones.
Low-Fat Milk
Low-Fat Yogurt
Calcium Supplement

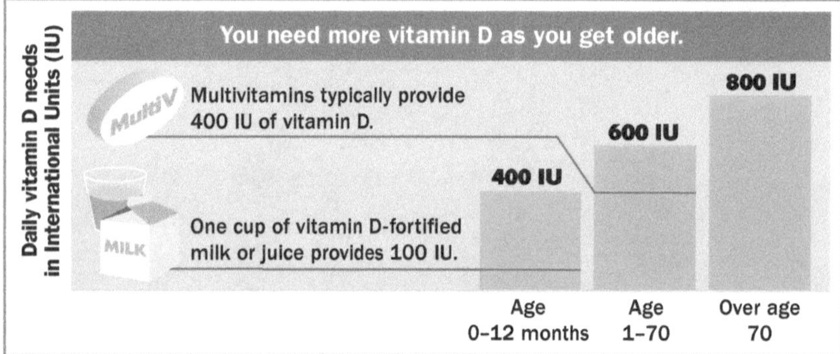

You need more vitamin D as you get older.

Multivitamins typically provide 400 IU of vitamin D.
One cup of vitamin D-fortified milk or juice provides 100 IU.

Age 0–12 months

Over age 70

> "If you have any kind of a fracture after age 50, talk to your doctor about getting your bone density checked."

You Could Be at Risk

Too many of us assume we are not at risk for bone loss or fractures. We believe that if we haven't had any signs of bone damage, then our bones are strong. Because there are no obvious warning signs, even doctors often miss signs of the problem. Most of us have our blood pressure and cholesterol checked for heart health. Testing bone density is an important way to check for bone health.

The risk of osteoporosis is highest among women. It is also higher for whites and Asians than other groups. However, it's important to remember that it is a real risk for older men and women of all backgrounds.

Here are some clues that you are at risk:

- Your older relatives have had fractures.
- You have had illnesses or have been on medications that might weaken bones.
- You are underweight.

That's why it is important to know the risks for poor bone health at all ages. There are many "red flags" that are signs that you are at risk for weak bones. (See page 19 for a checklist.) In addition, your calcium and vitamin D intake, level of physical activity, and medications should all be evaluated.

Why being active makes your bones strong

When you jump, run, or lift a weight, it puts stress on your bones. This sends a signal to your body that your bones need to be made stronger. New cells are added to strengthen your bones. If you are right-handed, the bones in your right arm are slightly larger and stronger from the extra use.

Bone Up on Your Diet

Calcium

To keep your bones strong, eat foods rich in calcium. Some people have trouble digesting the lactose found in milk and other dairy foods, including cheese and yogurt. Most supermarkets sell lactose-reduced dairy foods. Many nondairy foods are also calcium-rich.

Vitamin D

Vitamin D helps your body absorb calcium. As you grow older, your need for vitamin D goes up. Vitamin D is made by your skin when you are in the sun. For many, especially seniors, getting enough vitamin D from sunlight is not practical. Almost all milk and some other foods are fortified with vitamin D. If you are not getting enough calcium and vitamin D in your diet, supplements can be bone savers.

Your body needs calcium and vitamin D.

If this is your age, then you need this much calcium and vitamin D each day.

	Calcium (mg)	Vitamin D (IU)
Infants 0 to 6 months	200	400
Infants 6 to 12 months	260	400
1 to 3 years	700	600
4 to 8 years	1,000	600
9 to 13 years	1,300	600
14 to 18 years	1,300	600
19 to 30 years	1,000	600
31 to 50 years	1,000	600
51- to 70-year-old males	1,000	600
51- to 70-year-old females	1,200	600
>70 years	1,200	800
14 to 18 years, pregnant/lactating	1,300	600
19 to 50 years, pregnant/lactating	1,000	600

mg = milligrams; IU = International Units (40 IU = 1 mcg)

Source: Food and Nutrition Board, Institute of Medicine, National Academy of Sciences, 2010.

Nutrition Facts

8 servings per container

Serving size **2/3 cup (55g)**

Amount per serving

Calories **230**

	% Daily Value*
Total Fat 8g	**10%**
Saturated Fat 1g	**5%**
Trans Fat 0g	
Cholesterol 0mg	**0%**
Sodium 160mg	**7%**
Total Carbohydrate 37g	**13%**
Dietary Fiber 4g	**14%**
Total Sugars 12g	
Includes 10g Added Sugars	**20%**
Protein 3g	
Vitamin D 2mcg	10%
Calcium 260mg	20%
Iron 8mg	45%
Potassium 235mg	6%

* The % Daily Value (DV) tells you how much a nutrient in a serving of food contributes to a daily diet. 2,000 calories a day is used for general nutrition advice.

Food labels tell you how much calcium and vitamin D you get per serving.

Source: U.S. Food and Drug Administration

Calcium-Rich Foods

Help your bones. Choose foods that are high in calcium. Here are some examples.

Fortified oatmeal, 1 packet, 350 mg

Orange juice, fortified with calcium, 6 oz., 200–260 mg (varies)

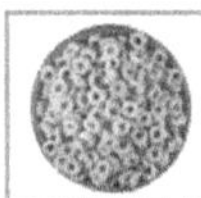
Ready-to-eat cereal, fortified with calcium, 1 cup, 100–1,000 mg (varies)

Sardines, canned in oil, with edible bones, 3 oz., 324 mg

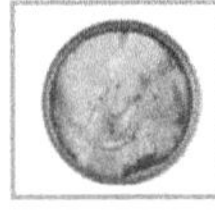
Salmon, canned, with edible bones, 3 oz., 181 mg

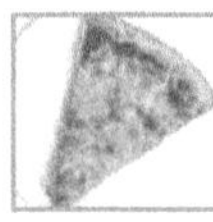
Cheese pizza, 1 slice, 100 mg

Cheddar cheese, 1½ oz. shredded, 306 mg

Pudding, instant (chocolate, banana, etc.) made with 2% milk, ½ cup, 153 mg

Fortified waffles (2), 100 mg

Milk, nonfat, 1 cup, 302 mg

Baked beans, 1 cup, 142 mg

Turnip greens, boiled, ½ cup, 99 mg

Milkshake, 1 cup, 300 mg

Cottage cheese, 1% milk fat, 1 cup, 138 mg

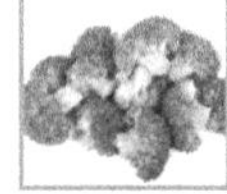
Broccoli, raw, 1 cup, 90 mg

Yogurt, plain, low-fat, 1 cup, 300 mg

Spaghetti or lasagna, 1 cup, 125 mg

Ice cream, vanilla, ½ cup, 85 mg

Soybeans, cooked, 1 cup, 261 mg

Frozen yogurt, vanilla, soft-serve, ½ cup, 103 mg

Soy or rice milk, fortified with calcium, 1 cup, 80–500 mg (varies)

Tofu, firm, with calcium, ½ cup, 204 mg

Protect Your Bones at Every Age

People of all ages need to know what they can do to have strong bones. You are never too old or too young to improve your bone health.

Babies

Bone growth starts before babies are born. Premature and low-birth-weight infants often need extra calcium, phosphorus, and protein to help them catch up on the nutrients they need for strong bones. Breastfed babies get the calcium and nutrients they need for good bone health from their mothers. That's why mothers who breastfeed need extra vitamin D. Most baby formula contains calcium and vitamin D.

Children

Good bone health starts early in life with good habits. While children and young adults rarely get bone diseases, kids can develop habits that endanger their health and bones. Parents can help by encouraging kids to eat healthful food and get at least an hour of physical activity every day. Jumping rope, running, and sports are fun activities that are great for building strong bones. Children need the amount of calcium equal to 3 servings of low-fat milk each day. If your child doesn't drink enough milk, try low-fat cheese, yogurt, or other foods that are high in calcium. If your child is allergic to milk or lactose intolerant, talk to your pediatrician about milk substitutes.

What if your toddler doesn't like to drink milk?

- Include some low-fat cheese chunks or yogurt for snacks.
- Make a cheesy sauce for vegetables or for a dip.
- Offer strawberry or chocolate milk as an afternoon treat.

"Your teen years are very important for strengthening bones through healthy eating and physical activity."

Teens

Teens are especially at risk for not developing strong bones because their bones are growing so rapidly. Boys and girls from ages 9 to 18 need 1,300 milligrams of calcium each day, more than any other age group. Parents can help teens by making sure they eat 4 servings of calcium-rich and vitamin D-fortified foods a day. At least 1 hour a day of physical activities—like running, skateboarding, sports, and dance—is also critical. But take note: extreme physical exercise, when combined with undereating, can weaken teens' bones. In young women, this situation can lead to a damaging lack of menstrual periods. Teens who miss adding bone to their skeletons during these critical years may never make it up.

Adults

Adulthood is a time when we need to look carefully at our bone health. As adults, we need 1,000 to 1,200 milligrams of calcium every day, depending on our age, and at least 2 hours and 30 minutes per week of moderate-intensity physical activity. Activity that puts some stress on your bones is very important.

Many women over age 50 are at risk for bone disease, but few know it. At menopause, which usually happens in women over age 50, a woman's hormone production drops sharply. Because hormones help protect bones, menopause can lead to bone loss. Hormone therapy was widely used to

FAST FACT

Children and teens should get at least an hour of physical activity every day. Adults should get at least 2 hours and 30 minutes each week.

prevent this loss, but now it is known to increase other risks. Your doctor can help advise you on protecting bone health around menopause.

Seniors

Seniors can take steps to help prevent bone problems. Physical activity and diet are vital to bone health in older adults. Calcium, together with vitamin D, helps reduce bone loss. Activities that put stress on bones keep them strong. Find time for activities like walking, dancing, and gardening. Strengthening your body helps prevent falls. Protecting yourself against falls is key to avoiding a broken hip or wrist. All women over age 65 should have a bone density test.

Seniors should also know that recent studies conclude that anyone over age 50 should increase his or her vitamin D intake to 600 International Units (IU) per day. After age 70, 800 IU per day are needed.

Adults: Keep your bones strong with physical activity.

- Physical activity at least 2 hours and 30 minutes each week
- Muscle strengthening activities on 2 days a week
- Older adults should do exercises that maintain or improve balance if they are at risk of falling

"You are buying lunch. Do you choose milk or a soft drink?"

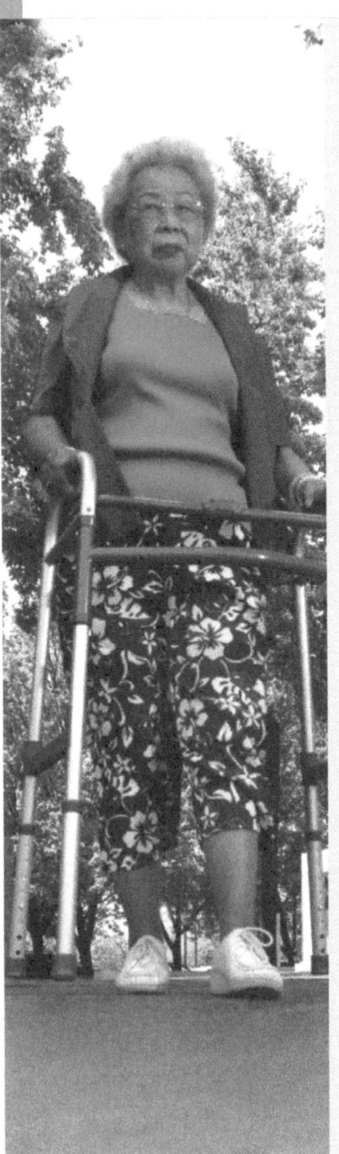

Falls break bones

You can prevent most falls.

Falls are not just the result of getting older. But as you age, falls become more dangerous. Most falls can be prevented. By changing some of the things listed here, you can lower the chances of falling for you or someone you love.

1. Begin a regular exercise program.

Exercise is one of the most important ways to reduce your chances of falling. It makes you stronger and helps you feel better. Exercises that improve balance and coordination, like dancing and Tai Chi, are the most helpful. Consider joining an organized program at your local community center or gym.

2. Make your home safer.

- Remove things you can trip over from stairs and places where you walk.
- Remove all small rugs.
- Don't use step stools. Keep items you need within easy reach.
- Have grab bars put in next to your toilet and in the bathtub or shower.
- Use nonslip mats in the bathtub and shower.
- Use brighter light bulbs in your home.
- Add handrails and light in all staircases.
- Wear shoes that give good support and have nonslip soles.

3. Ask a health care professional to review your medicines.

Ask your doctor, nurse, pharmacist, or other health care professional to review all the medicines you are taking. Make sure to mention over-the-counter medicine, such as cold medicine. As you get older, the way some medicines work in your body can change. Some medicines, or combinations of medicines, can make you drowsy or light-headed, which can lead to a fall.

4. Have your vision checked.

Poor vision increases your risk of falling. You could be wearing the wrong glasses or have a condition such as glaucoma or cataracts that limits your vision.

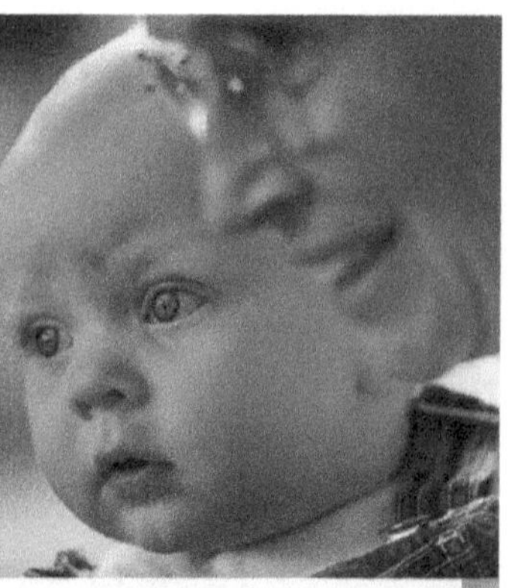

Live Well, Live Strong, Live Long

The average American eats too little calcium. And nearly half of us do not get enough physical activity to strengthen our bones.

The same healthy lifestyle that strengthens your bones strengthens your whole body. You might not hear as much about bone health as other health concerns. But healthy habits are good for all your organs, including your bones.

- **Be physically active every day**—at least 60 minutes for children and teens, and 2 hours and 30 minutes each week for adults. Do strength-building, weight-bearing, and resistance exercises to build strong bones.
- **Eat a healthy diet.** Educate yourself on proper nutrition. Be aware that certain foods are naturally rich in calcium and vitamin D. Get the recommended amounts of calcium and vitamin D daily.
- **Reduce your risks of falling.** Check your home for loose rugs, poor lighting, etc. Take classes that increase balance and strength—like Tai Chi or yoga. Make stretching a part of your workout.

Even people who know better don't always do what's good for their bones. Make yourself an exception. Be aware of your risks and work to reduce them. Get help from your family and friends and your doctor, nurse, pharmacist, or other health care professional. Building healthy bones begins at birth and lasts your whole life.

"It's never too late or too early to improve your bone health."

"All women over age 65 should have a bone density test."

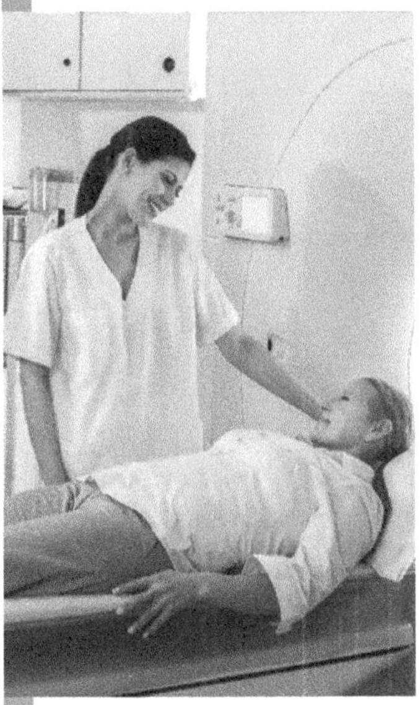

Your Doctor Can Help Protect Your Bones

Talk to your doctor about bone health. Together you can evaluate your risks. Some things to discuss include your current health, your diet and physical activity levels, and your family background.

Your doctor can look at your age, weight, height, and medical history. From that he or she can determine if you need a bone density test. Broken bones are a "red flag" for your doctor. If you break a bone after the age of 50, talk to your doctor about measuring your bone density. Even if you broke a bone in an accident, you might have weak bones. It is worth checking.

Your doctor might recommend a medical test called a bone mineral density test. These tests are quick (5 to 10 minutes), safe, and painless. They will give you and your doctor an idea of how strong your bones are. All women over age 65 should have a bone density test. Women who are younger than age 65 and at high risk for fractures should also have a bone density test.

Your doctor might also want to do a blood test to check for a vitamin D deficiency or abnormal calcium levels.

If your doctor finds that your bones are becoming weaker, there are things you can do to make them stronger. You can be more physically active, change your diet, and take calcium and vitamin D supplements. If your bones are already weak, there are medicines that stop bone loss. They can even build new bone and make it less likely that you will suffer a broken bone.

Your doctor might suggest medications to help you build stronger bones. To reduce the chance that you might fall, have your vision checked. When you speak to your doctor, be prepared with a list of questions and concerns. The list on the next page should help get you started.

See Your Doctor

Although osteoporosis is the most common disease that harms bones, certain other conditions can also be harmful. Your doctor can help you learn if you are at risk and can help you treat these conditions.

- Rickets and osteomalacia—Too little vitamin D causes these diseases in children and adults. They can lead to bone deformities and fractures.
- Kidney disease—Renal osteodystrophy can cause fractures.
- Paget's disease of bone—Bones become deformed and weak, which can be caused by genetic and environmental factors.
- Genetic abnormalities—Disorders like osteogenesis imperfecta cause bones to grow abnormally and break easily.
- Endocrine disorders—Overactive glands can cause bone disease.

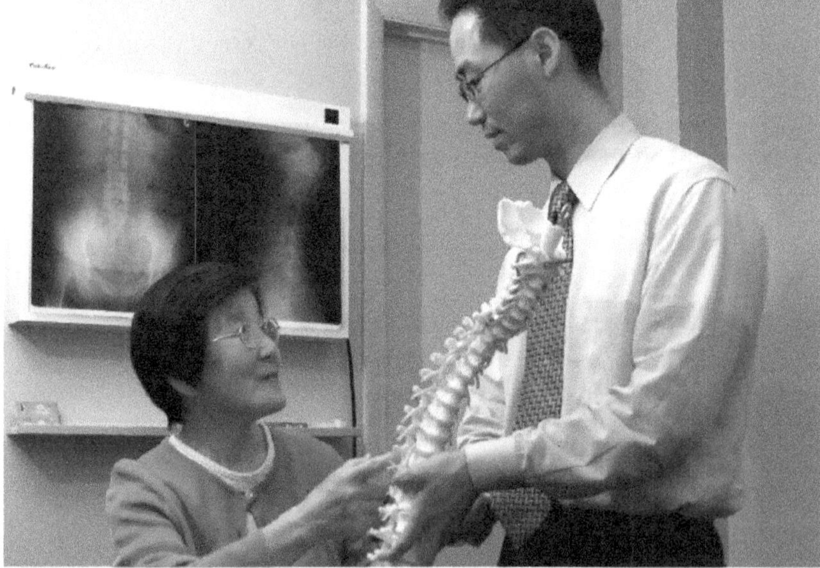

"A 50-year-old woman breaks her wrist when she trips on a rug. Should she ask for a bone density test even if her doctor doesn't bring it up? YES!"

What to discuss with your doctor

Talk with your doctor, nurse, or other health care professional about your bone health. Use this checklist to start your discussion.

- ☐ Ask to check your risk for bone disease.
- ☐ Discuss your need for a bone density test.
- ☐ Talk about any fall, even ones in which you were not hurt. Tell him or her about any broken bones you've had.
- ☐ If you have fallen, ask about the need for a full evaluation. Tests include vision, balance, walking, muscle strength, heart function, and blood pressure.
- ☐ Go over all the medications you are taking (including over-the-counter ones). Do this at least once a year. This helps avoid dangerous drug interactions and taking higher doses of drugs than you need, which can lead to falls.
- ☐ Ask if your doctor checks vision. Annual vision checks can help eliminate bone-breaking falls.
- ☐ Know your calcium and vitamin D intake. Report your totals to your doctor.
- ☐ If you would like to try a new physical activity, ask about the best choices for you.

FAST FACT

Bone disease is often a "silent" disorder until it causes a fracture.

Are you at risk for weak bones?

Check any of these that apply to you.

- ☐ I'm older than 65.
- ☐ I've broken a bone after age 50.
- ☐ My close relative has osteoporosis or has broken a bone.
- ☐ My health is "fair" or "poor."
- ☐ I smoke.
- ☐ I am underweight for my height.
- ☐ I started menopause before age 45.
- ☐ I've never gotten enough calcium.
- ☐ I have more than two drinks of alcohol several times a week.
- ☐ I have poor vision, even with glasses.
- ☐ I sometimes fall.
- ☐ I'm not active.
- ☐ I have one of these medical conditions:
  - ☐ Hyperthyroidism
  - ☐ Chronic lung disease
  - ☐ Cancer
  - ☐ Inflammatory bowel disease
  - ☐ Chronic hepatic or renal disease
  - ☐ Hyperparathyroidism
  - ☐ Vitamin D deficiency
  - ☐ Cushing's disease
  - ☐ Multiple sclerosis
  - ☐ Rheumatoid arthritis
- ☐ I take one of these medicines:
  - ☐ Oral glucocorticoids (steroids)
  - ☐ Cancer treatments (radiation, chemotherapy)
  - ☐ Thyroid medicine
  - ☐ Antiepileptic medications
  - ☐ Gonadal hormone suppression
  - ☐ Immunosuppressive agents

If you have any of these "red flags," you could be at high risk for weak bones. Talk to your doctor, nurse, pharmacist, or other health care professional.

Obesity Trends Among U.S. Adults Between 1985 and 2010

Definitions:

- Obesity: Body Mass Index (BMI) of 30 or higher.

- Body Mass Index (BMI): A measure of an adult's weight in relation to his or her height, specifically the adult's weight in kilograms divided by the square of his or her height in meters.

Obesity Trends Among U.S. Adults Between 1985 and 2010

Source of the data:

- The data shown in these maps were collected through CDC's Behavioral Risk Factor Surveillance System (BRFSS). Each year, state health departments use standard procedures to collect data through a series of telephone interviews with U.S. adults. Height and weight data are self-reported.

- Prevalence estimates generated for the maps may vary slightly from those generated for the states by BRFSS (http://aps.nccd.cdc.gov/brfss) as slightly different analytic methods are used.

- In 1990, among states participating in the Behavioral Risk Factor Surveillance System, 10 states had a prevalence of obesity less than 10% and no state had prevalence equal to or greater than 15%.
- By 2000, no state had a prevalence of obesity less than 10%, 23 states had a prevalence between 20–24%, and no state had prevalence equal to or greater than 25%.
- In 2010, no state had a prevalence of obesity less than 20%. Thirty-six states had a prevalence equal to or greater than 25%; 12 of these states (Alabama, Arkansas, Kentucky, Louisiana, Michigan, Mississippi, Missouri, Oklahoma, South Carolina, Tennessee, Texas, and West Virginia) had a prevalence equal to or greater than 30%.

Citations

- Mokdad AH, et al. The spread of the obesity epidemic in the United States, 1991–1998. *JAMA* 1999;282:16:1519–22.
- Mokdad AH, et al. The continuing epidemics of obesity and diabetes in the United States. *JAMA* 2001;286:10:1519–22.
- Mokdad AH, et al. Prevalence of obesity, diabetes, and obesity-related health risk factors, 2001. *JAMA* 2003;289:1:76–9.
- CDC. State-specific prevalence of obesity among adults — United States, 2005. *MMWR* 2006;55(36):985–8.
- CDC. State-specific prevalence of obesity among adults — United States, 2007. *MMWR* 2008;57(28):765–8.
- CDC. Vital signs: State-specific prevalence of obesity among adults — United States, 2009. *MMWR* 2010;59:1–5.

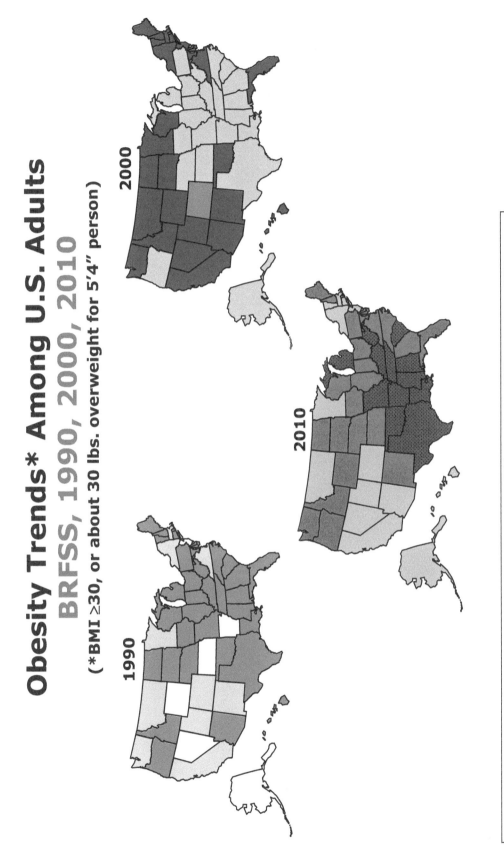

Obesity Trends* Among U.S. Adults

BRFSS, 1990, 2000, 2010

(*BMI ≥30, or about 30 lbs. overweight for 5'4" person)

1990

2000

2010

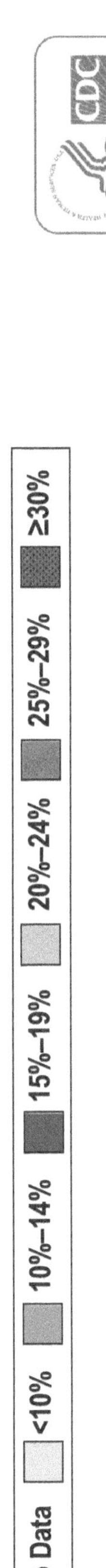

CDC

Source: Behavioral Risk Factor Surveillance System, CDC.

Prevalence of Self-Reported Obesity Among U.S. Adults by State and Territory

Definitions

- Obesity: Body Mass Index (BMI) of 30 kg/m^2 or higher.

- Body Mass Index (BMI): A measure of an adult's weight in relation to his or her height, calculated by using the adult's weight in kilograms divided by the square of his or her height in meters.

Prevalence of Self-Reported Obesity Among U.S. Adults by State and Territory

Source of the Data

- The data were collected through the Behavioral Risk Factor Surveillance System (BRFSS), an ongoing, state-based, telephone interview survey conducted by state health departments with assistance from CDC.
- Height and weight data used in the BMI calculations were self-reported.

Prevalence of Self-Reported Obesity Among U.S. Adults by State and Territory

BRFSS Methodological Changes Started in 2011

- New sampling frame that included both landline and cell phone households.
- New weighting methodology used to provide a closer match between the sample and the population.

Prevalence of Self-Reported Obesity Among U.S. Adults by State and Territory

Exclusion Criteria Used Beginning with 2011 BRFSS Data

Records with the following were excluded:

- ❑ **Height: <3 feet or ≥8 feet**
- ❑ **Weight: <50 pounds or ≥650 pounds**
- ❑ **BMI: <12 kg/m^2 or ≥ 100 kg/m^2**
- ❑ **Pregnant women**

Prevalence¶ of Self-Reported Obesity Among U.S. Adults by State and Territory, BRFSS, 2011

¶ Prevalence estimates reflect BRFSS methodological changes started in 2011. These estimates should not be compared to prevalence estimates before 2011.

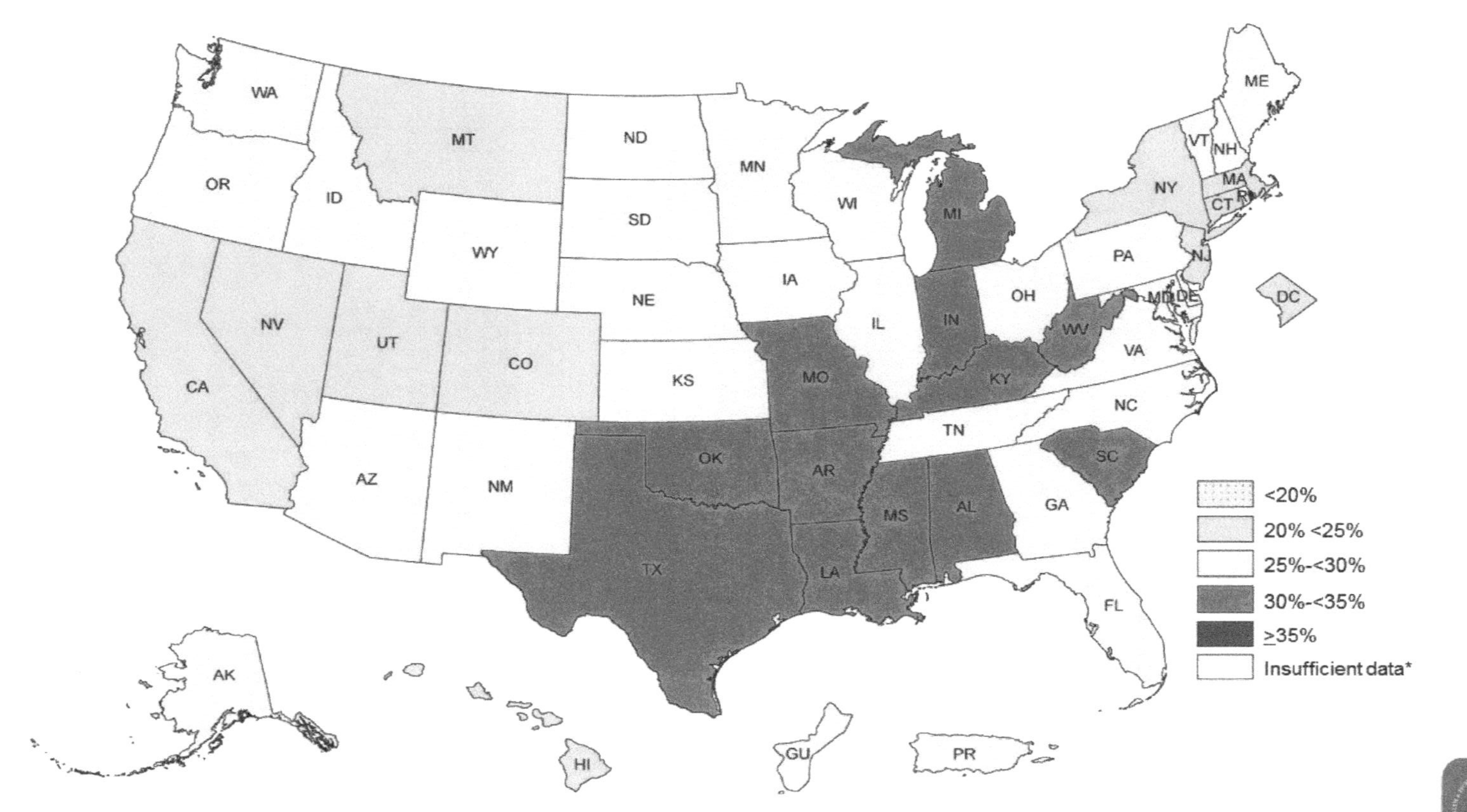

***Sample size <50, the relative standard error (dividing the standard error by the prevalence) ≥30%, or no data in a specific year.**

Prevalence¶ of Self-Reported Obesity Among U.S. Adults by State and Territory, BRFSS, 2012

¶ Prevalence estimates reflect BRFSS methodological changes started in 2011. These estimates should not be compared to prevalence estimates before 2011.

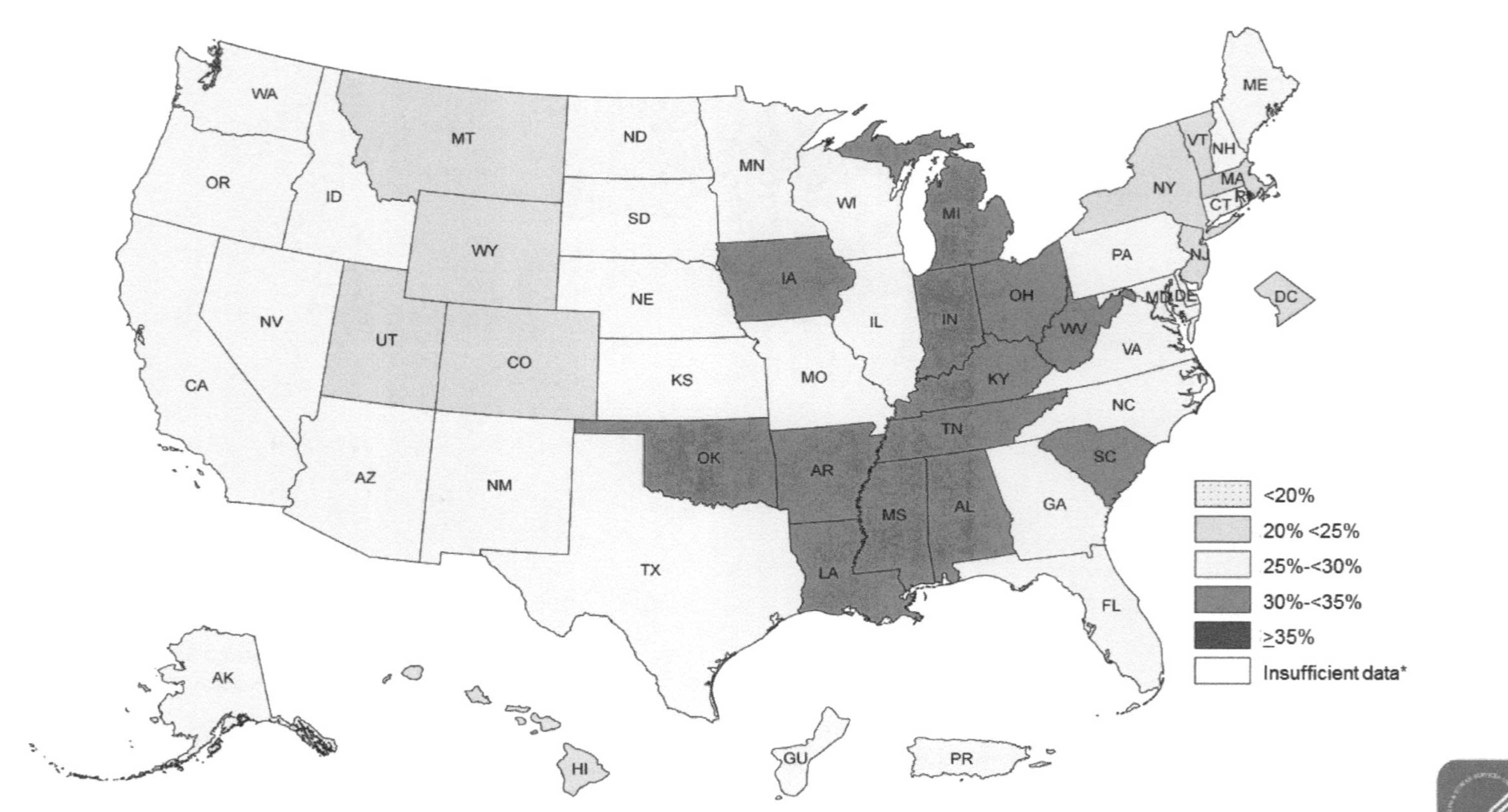

***Sample size <50, the relative standard error (dividing the standard error by the prevalence) ≥30%, or no data in a specific year.**

Prevalence¶ of Self-Reported Obesity Among U.S. Adults by State and Territory, BRFSS, 2013

¶ Prevalence estimates reflect BRFSS methodological changes started in 2011. These estimates should not be compared to prevalence estimates before 2011.

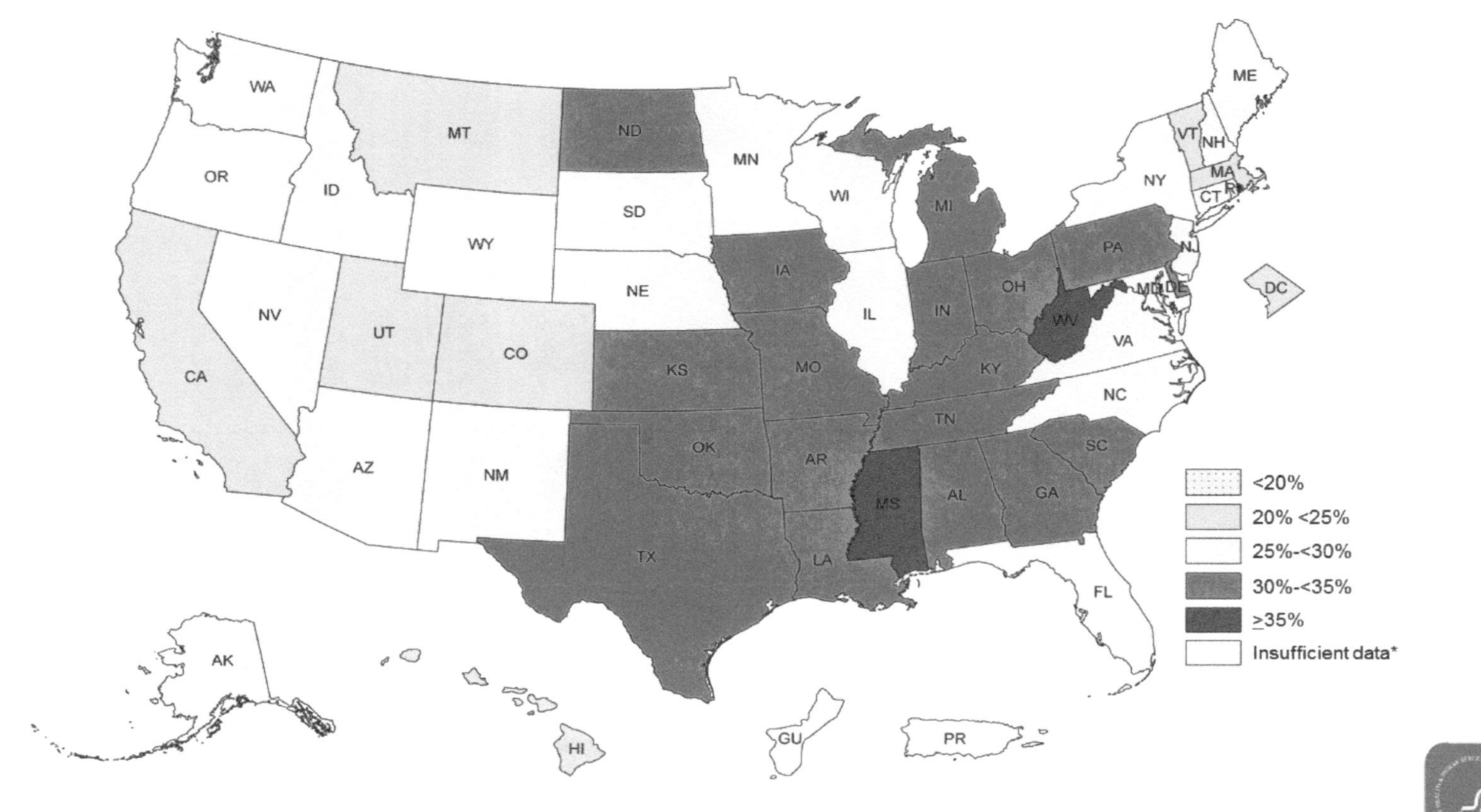

*Sample size <50, the relative standard error (dividing the standard error by the prevalence) ≥30%, or no data in a specific year.

Prevalence¶ of Self-Reported Obesity Among U.S. Adults by State and Territory, BRFSS, 2014

¶ Prevalence estimates reflect BRFSS methodological changes started in 2011. These estimates should not be compared to prevalence estimates before 2011.

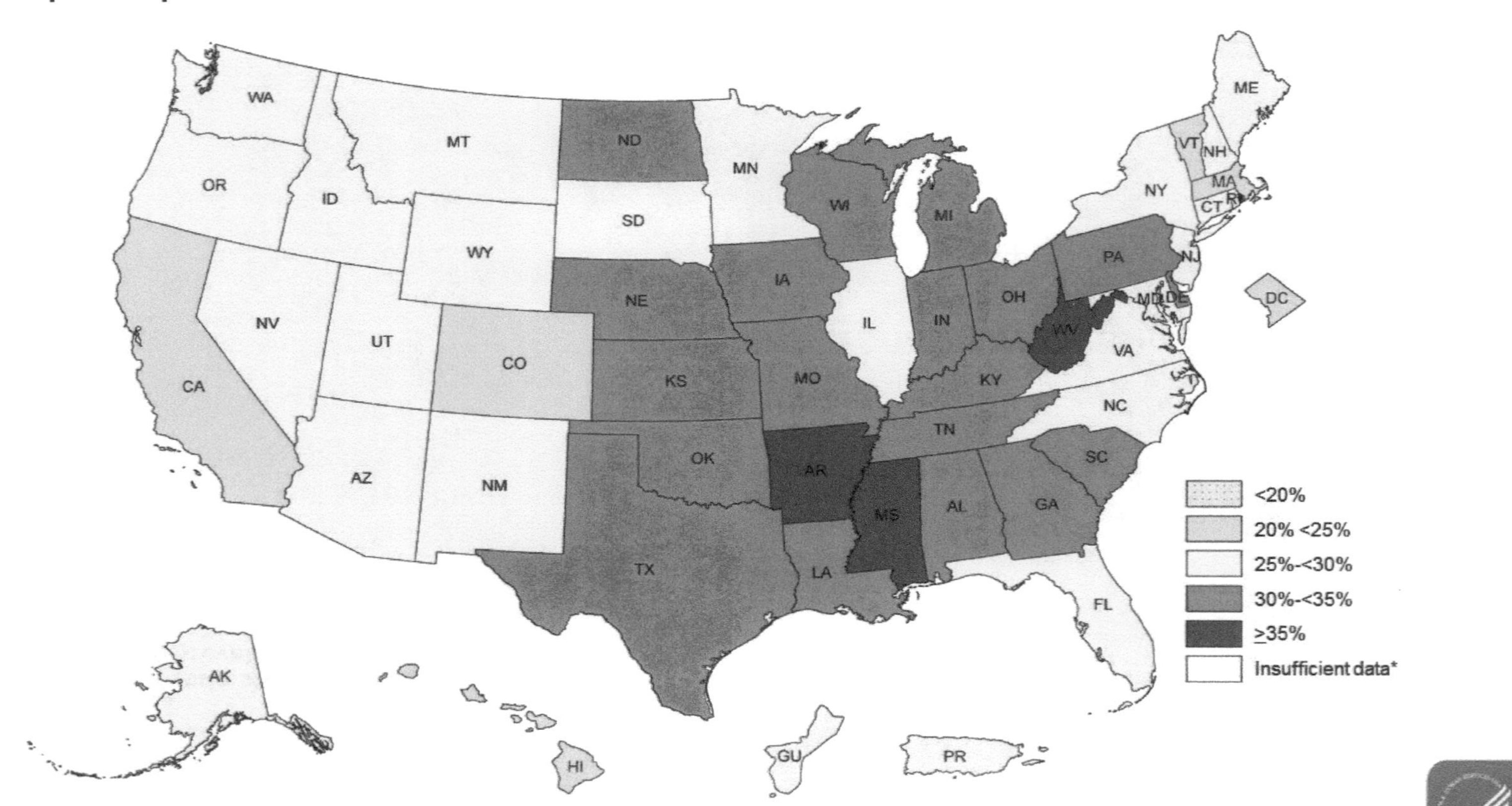

*Sample size <50, the relative standard error (dividing the standard error by the prevalence) ≥30%, or no data in a specific year.

Prevalence¶ of Self-Reported Obesity Among U.S. Adults by State and Territory, BRFSS, 2015

¶ Prevalence estimates reflect BRFSS methodological changes started in 2011. These estimates should not be compared to prevalence estimates before 2011.

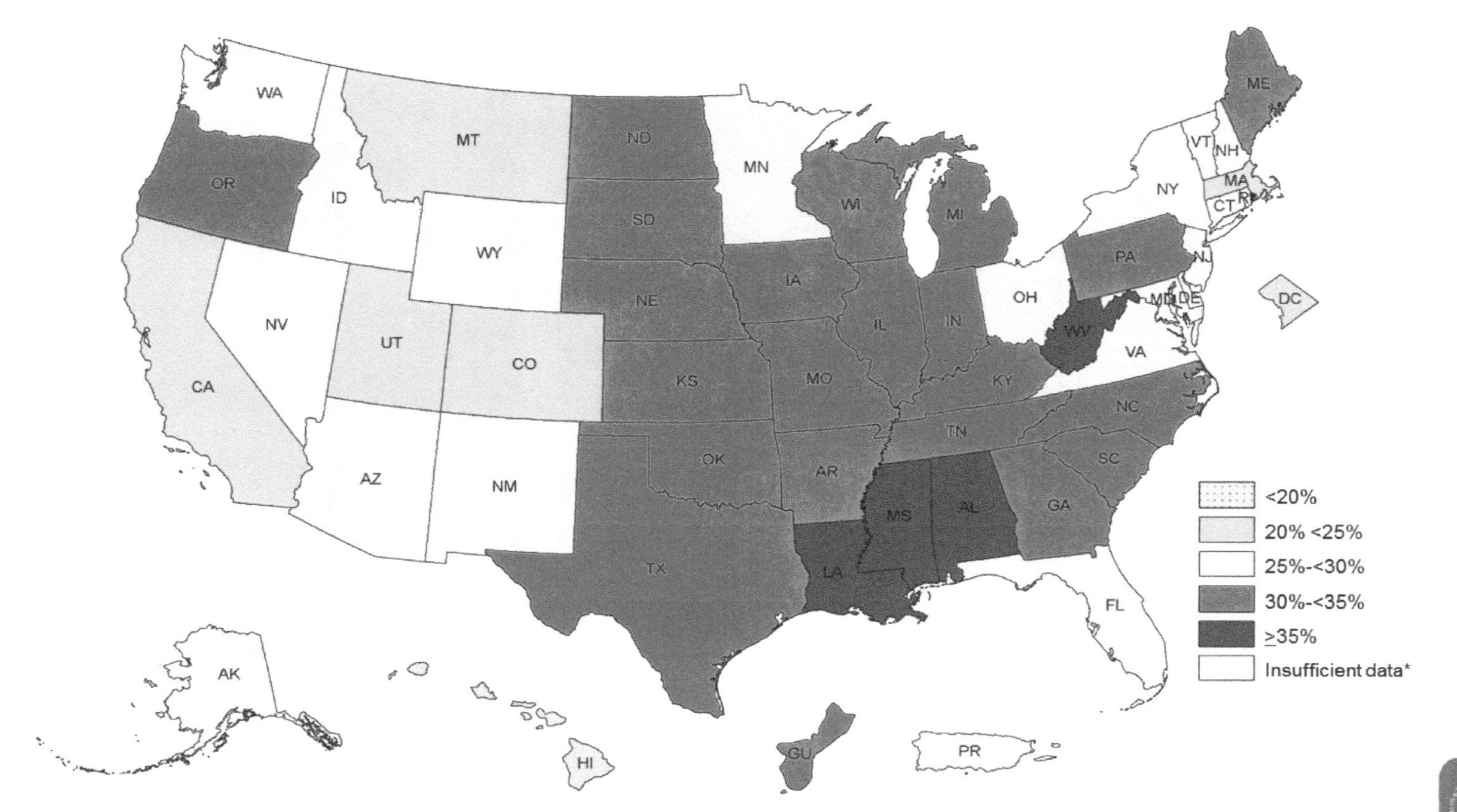

*Sample size <50, the relative standard error (dividing the standard error by the prevalence) ≥30%, or no data in a specific year.

Prevalence¶ of Self-Reported Obesity Among U.S. Adults by State and Territory, BRFSS, 2016

¶ Prevalence estimates reflect BRFSS methodological changes started in 2011. These estimates should not be compared to prevalence estimates before 2011.

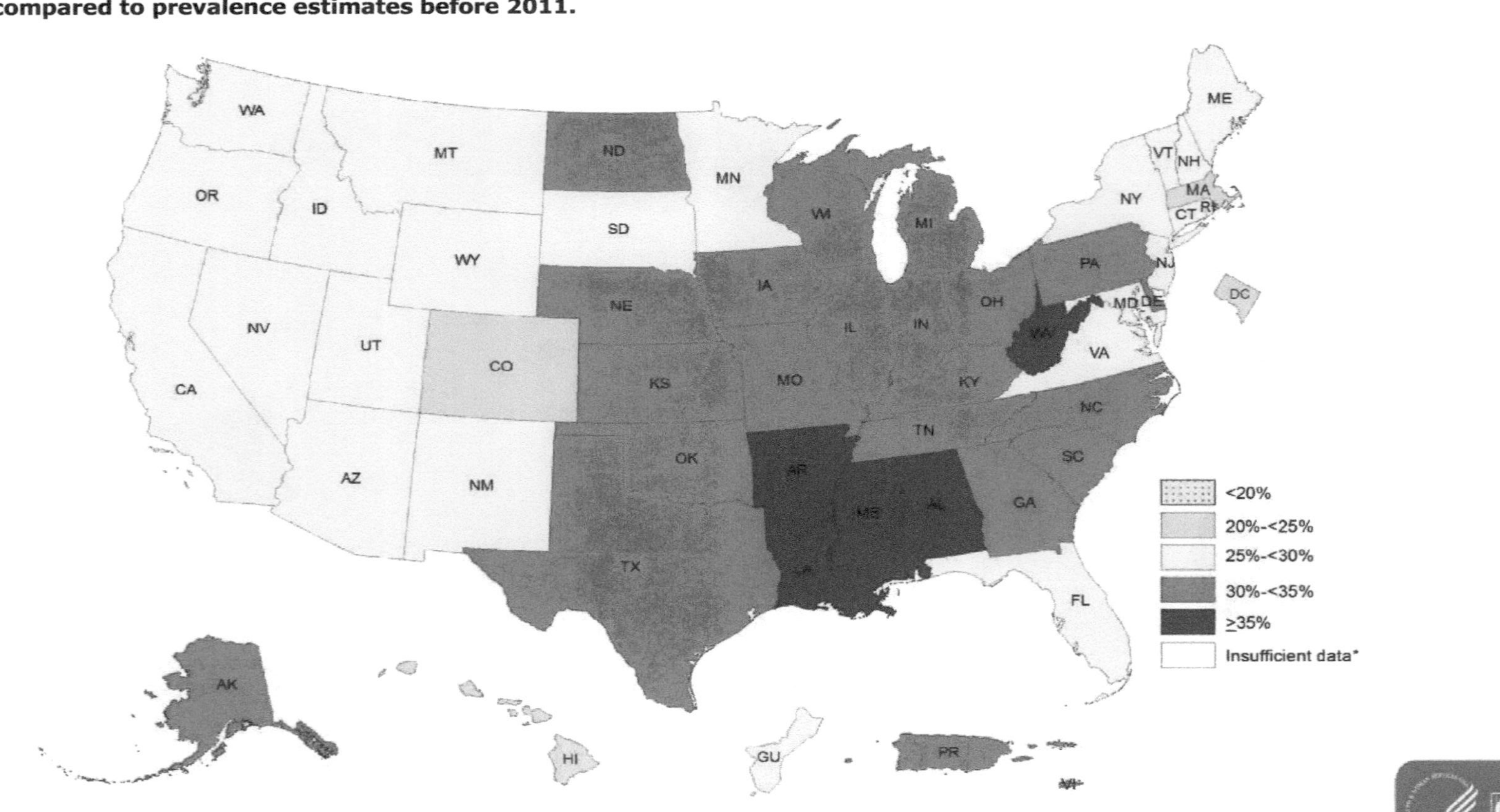

*Sample size <50, the relative standard error (dividing the standard error by the prevalence) ≥30%, or no data in a specific year.

Prevalence¶ of Self-Reported Obesity Among U.S. Adults by State and Territory, BRFSS, 2017

¶ Prevalence estimates reflect BRFSS methodological changes started in 2011. These estimates should not be compared to prevalence estimates before 2011.

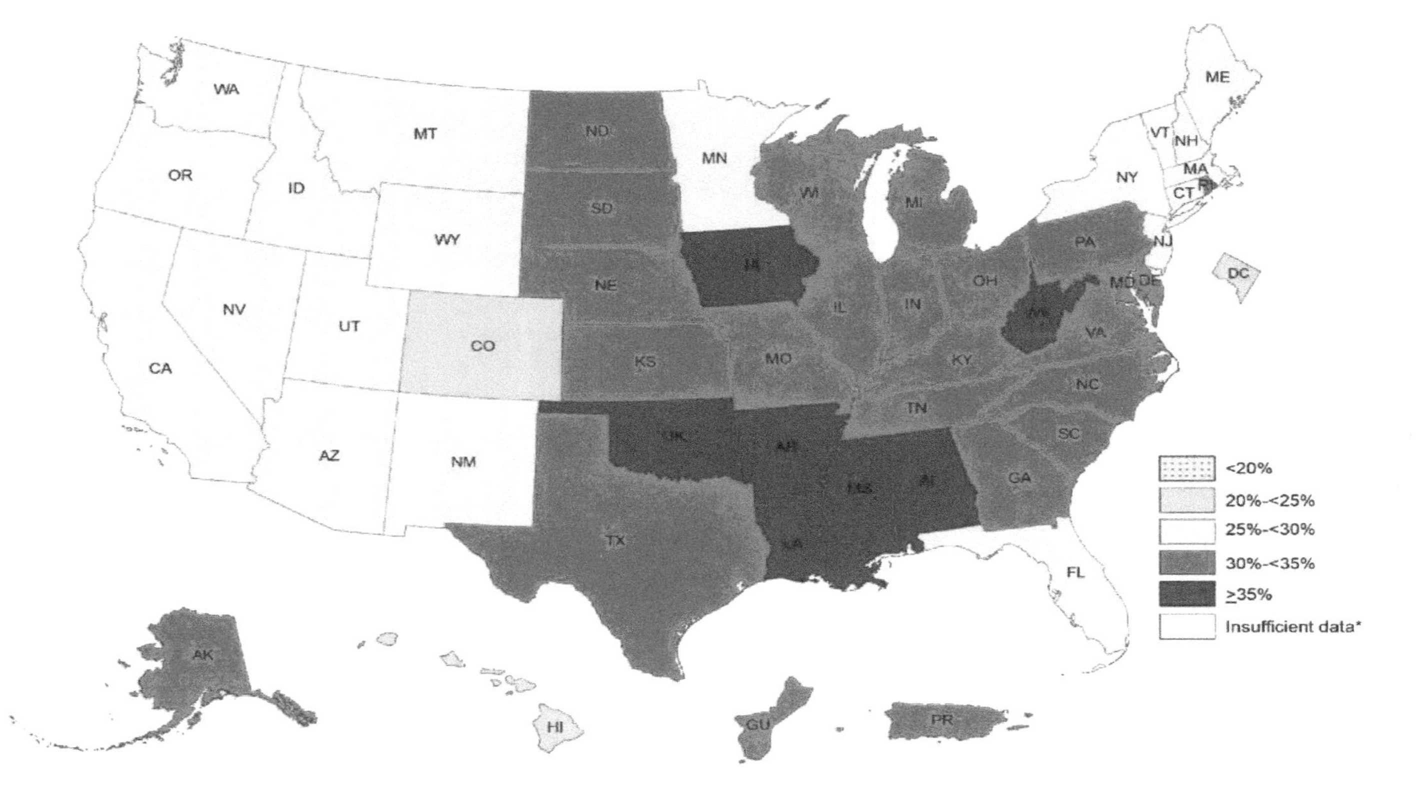

*Sample size <50, the relative standard error (dividing the standard error by the prevalence) ≥30%, or no data in a specific year.

Prevalence[¶] of Self-Reported Obesity Among U.S. Adults by State and Territory, BRFSS, 2018

¶ Prevalence estimates reflect BRFSS methodological changes started in 2011. These estimates should not be compared to prevalence estimates before 2011.

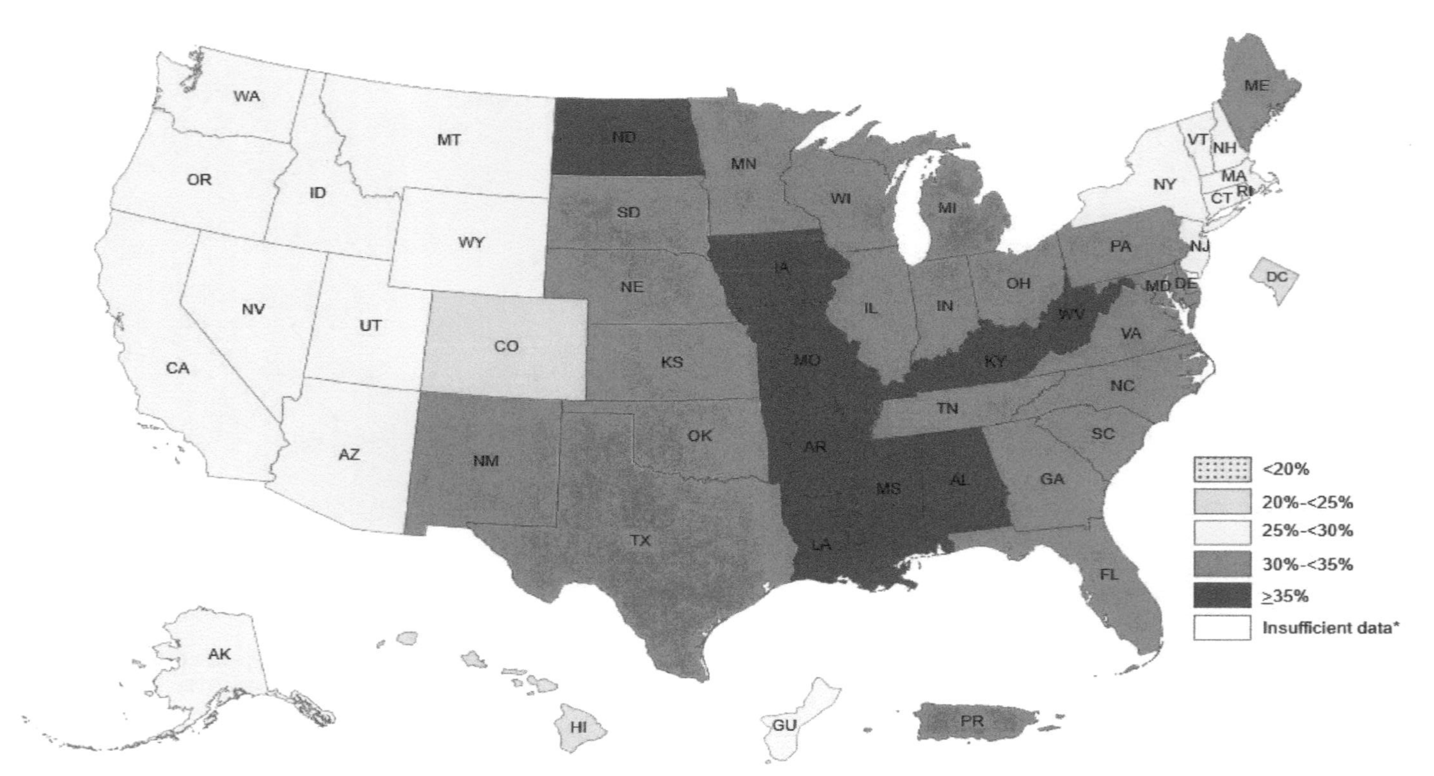

*Sample size <50, the relative standard error (dividing the standard error by the prevalence) ≥30%, or no data in a specific year.

Prevalence¶ of Self-Reported Obesity Among U.S. Adults by State and Territory, BRFSS, 2019

¶ Prevalence estimates reflect BRFSS methodological changes started in 2011. These estimates should not be compared to prevalence estimates before 2011.

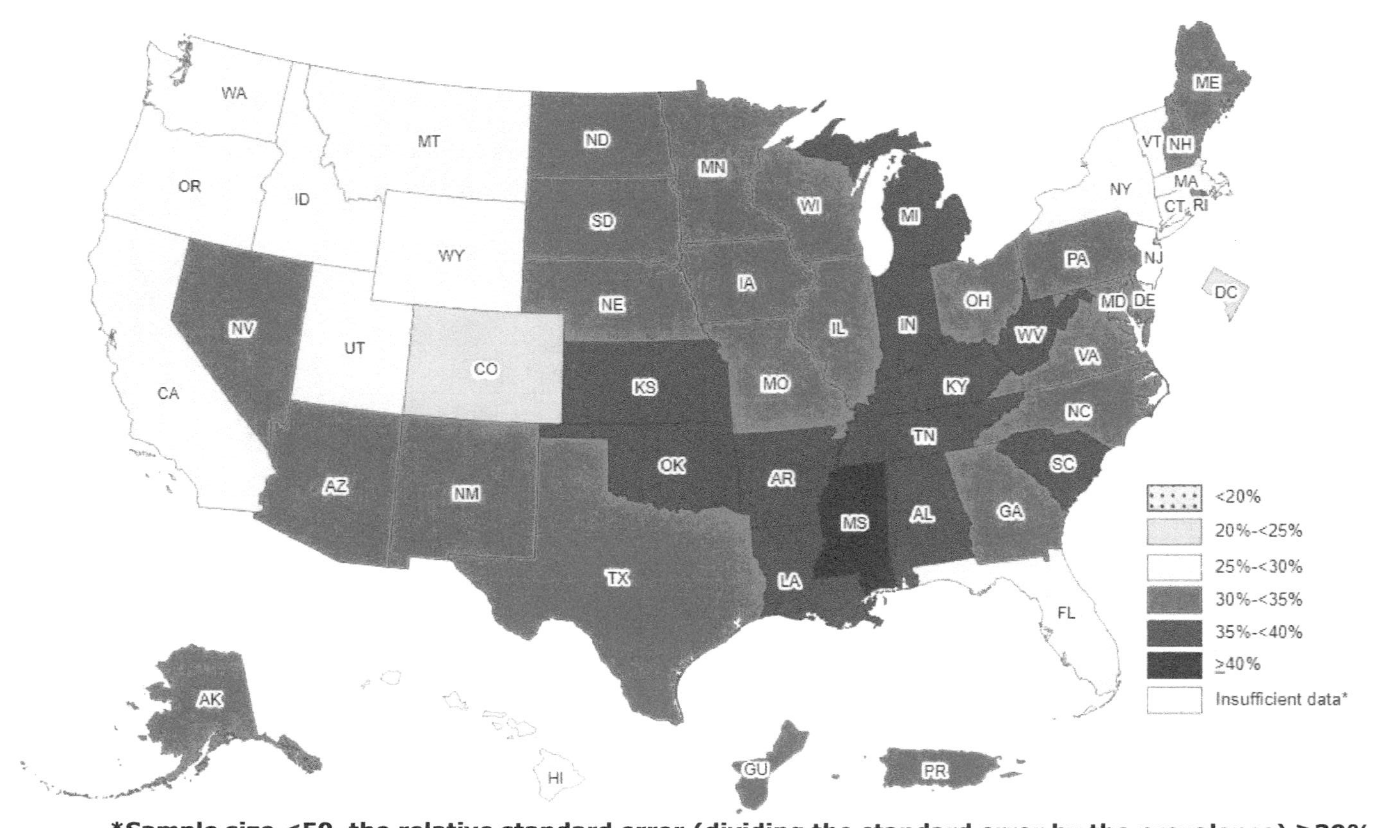

*Sample size <50, the relative standard error (dividing the standard error by the prevalence) ≥30%, or no data in a specific year.

Prevalence¶ of Self-Reported Obesity Among U.S. Adults by State and Territory, BRFSS, 2020

¶ Prevalence estimates reflect BRFSS methodological changes started in 2011. These estimates should not be compared to prevalence estimates before 2011.

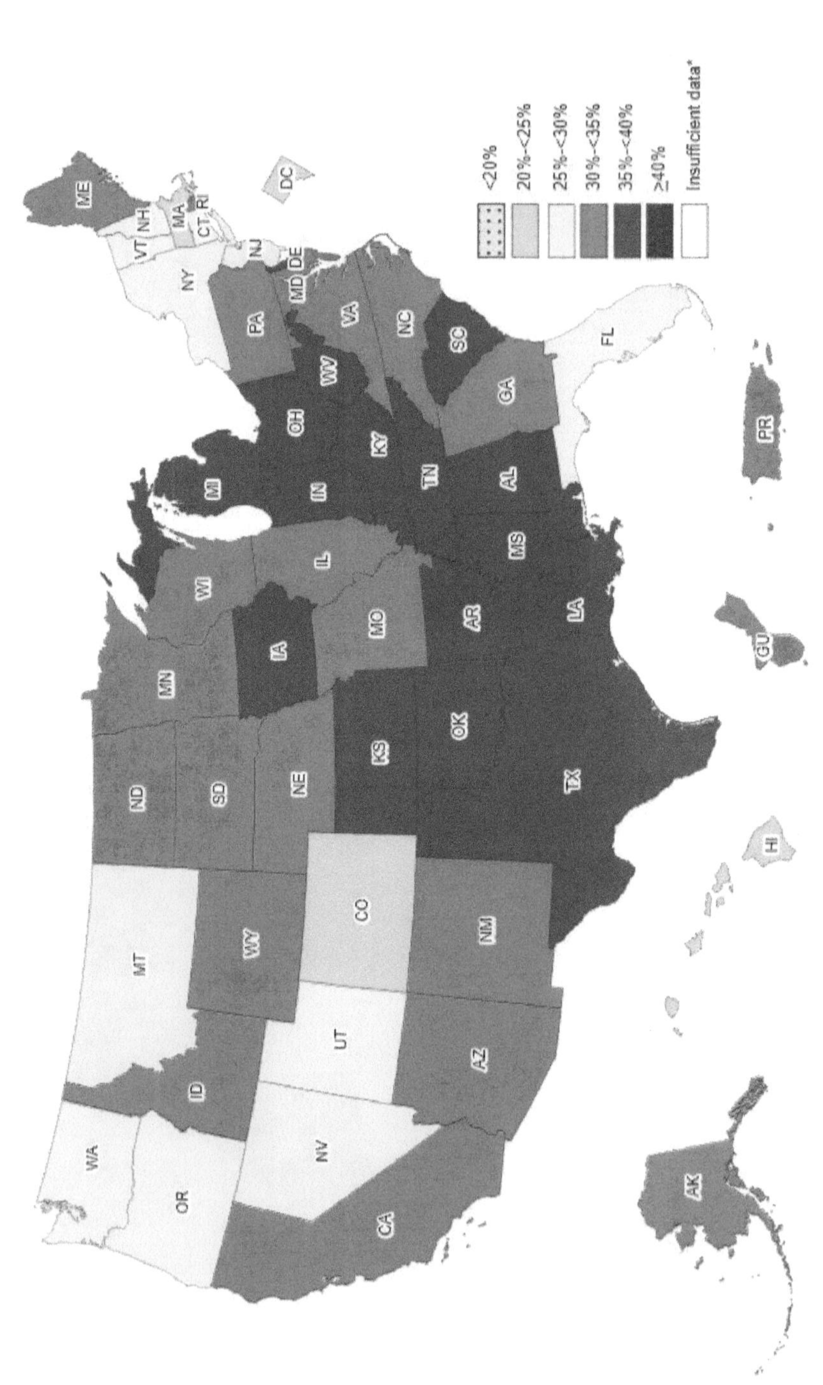

***Sample size <50, the relative standard error (dividing the standard error by the prevalence) ≥30%, or no data in a specific year.**

Prevalence¶ of Self-Reported Obesity Among U.S. Adults by State and Territory, BRFSS, 2011

State	Prevalence	95% Confidence Interval
Alabama	32.0	(30.5, 33.5)
Alaska	27.4	(25.3, 29.7)
Arizona	25.1	(23.0, 27.3)
Arkansas	30.9	(28.8, 33.1)
California	23.8	(22.9, 24.7)
Colorado	20.7	(19.7, 21.8)
Connecticut	24.5	(23.0, 26.0)
Delaware	28.8	(26.9, 30.7)
District of Columbia	23.7	(21.9, 25.7)
Florida	26.6	(25.4, 27.9)
Georgia	28.0	(26.6, 29.4)
Guam	27.4	(24.8, 30.2)
Hawaii	21.8	(20.4, 23.4)
Idaho	27.0	(25.3, 28.9)
Illinois	27.1	(25.4, 28.9)
Indiana	30.8	(29.5, 32.3)
Iowa	29.0	(27.6, 30.3)
Kansas	29.6	(28.7, 30.4)
Kentucky	30.4	(28.9, 31.9)
Louisiana	33.4	(32.0, 34.9)
Maine	27.8	(26.8, 28.9)
Maryland	28.3	(26.9, 29.7)
Massachusetts	22.7	(21.8, 23.7)
Michigan	31.3	(30.0, 32.6)
Minnesota	25.7	(24.6, 26.8)
Mississippi	34.9	(33.5, 36.3)

State	Prevalence	95% Confidence Interval
Missouri	30.3	(28.6, 32.0)
Montana	24.6	(23.3, 26.0)
Nebraska	28.4	(27.6, 29.2)
Nevada	24.5	(22.5, 26.6)
New Hampshire	26.2	(24.7, 27.7)
New Jersey	23.7	(22.7, 24.8)
New Mexico	26.3	(25.1, 27.6)
New York	24.5	(23.2, 25.9)
North Carolina	29.1	(27.7, 30.6)
North Dakota	27.8	(26.3, 29.4)
Ohio	29.6	(28.3, 31.0)
Oklahoma	31.1	(29.7, 32.5)
Oregon	26.7	(25.2, 28.3)
Pennsylvania	28.6	(27.3, 29.8)
Puerto Rico	26.3	(25.0, 27.7)
Rhode Island	25.4	(23.9, 27.0)
South Carolina	30.8	(29.6, 32.1)
South Dakota	28.1	(26.3, 30.1)
Tennessee	29.2	(26.8, 31.7)
Texas	30.4	(29.1, 31.8)
Utah	24.4	(23.4, 25.5)
Vermont	25.4	(24.1, 26.8)
Virginia	29.2	(27.5, 30.9)
Washington	26.5	(25.3, 27.7)
West Virginia	32.4	(30.9, 34.0)
Wisconsin	27.7	(25.8, 29.7)
Wyoming	25.0	(23.5, 26.6)

¶ Prevalence estimates reflect BRFSS methodological changes started in 2011. These estimates should not be compared to prevalence estimates before 2011. *Source:* Behavioral Risk Factor Surveillance System, CDC.

Prevalence¶ of Self-Reported Obesity Among U.S. Adults by State and Territory, BRFSS, 2012

State	Prevalence	95% Confidence Interval
Alabama	33.0	(31.5, 34.4)
Alaska	25.7	(23.9, 27.5)
Arizona	26.0	(24.3, 27.8)
Arkansas	34.5	(32.7, 36.4)
California	25.0	(23.9, 26.0)
Colorado	20.5	(19.5, 21.4)
Connecticut	25.6	(24.3, 26.9)
Delaware	26.9	(25.2, 28.6)
District of Columbia	21.9	(19.8, 24.0)
Florida	25.2	(23.6, 26.7)
Georgia	29.1	(27.4, 30.8)
Guam	29.1	(26.3, 31.9)
Hawaii	23.6	(22.0, 25.1)
Idaho	26.8	(24.8, 28.8)
Illinois	28.1	(26.4, 29.9)
Indiana	31.4	(30.1, 32.7)
Iowa	30.4	(29.1, 31.8)
Kansas	29.9	(28.7, 31.0)
Kentucky	31.3	(29.9, 32.6)
Louisiana	34.7	(33.1, 36.4)
Maine	28.4	(27.2, 29.5)
Maryland	27.6	(26.3, 28.9)
Massachusetts	22.9	(22.0, 23.8)
Michigan	31.1	(29.8, 32.3)
Minnesota	25.7	(24.7, 26.8)
Mississippi	34.6	(33.0, 36.2)

State	Prevalence	95% Confidence Interval
Missouri	29.6	(28.0, 31.2)
Montana	24.3	(23.1, 25.5)
Nebraska	28.6	(27.7, 29.6)
Nevada	26.2	(24.3, 28.1)
New Hampshire	27.3	(25.8, 28.8)
New Jersey	24.6	(23.6, 25.6)
New Mexico	27.1	(25.9, 28.3)
New York	23.6	(22.0, 25.1)
North Carolina	29.6	(28.5, 30.7)
North Dakota	29.7	(27.9, 31.4)
Ohio	30.1	(29.0, 31.2)
Oklahoma	32.2	(30.8, 33.6)
Oregon	27.3	(25.7, 29.0)
Pennsylvania	29.1	(28.1, 30.1)
Puerto Rico	28.4	(27.0, 29.7)
Rhode Island	25.7	(24.1, 27.4)
South Carolina	31.6	(30.4, 32.8)
South Dakota	28.1	(26.5, 29.8)
Tennessee	31.1	(29.6, 32.7)
Texas	29.2	(27.8, 30.5)
Utah	24.3	(23.3, 25.3)
Vermont	23.7	(22.3, 25.1)
Virginia	27.4	(26.0, 28.7)
Washington	26.8	(25.8, 27.8)
West Virginia	33.8	(32.2, 35.4)
Wisconsin	29.7	(27.8, 31.6)
Wyoming	24.6	(22.8, 26.4)

¶ Prevalence estimates reflect BRFSS methodological changes started in 2011. These estimates should not be compared to prevalence estimates before 2011. *Source:* Behavioral Risk Factor Surveillance System, CDC.

Prevalence¶ of Self-Reported Obesity Among U.S. Adults by State and Territory, BRFSS, 2013

State	Prevalence	95% Confidence Interval
Alabama	32.4	(30.8, 34.1)
Alaska	28.4	(26.5, 30.4)
Arizona	26.8	(24.3, 29.4)
Arkansas	34.6	(32.7, 36.6)
California	24.1	(23.0, 25.3)
Colorado	21.3	(20.4, 22.2)
Connecticut	25.0	(23.5, 26.4)
Delaware	31.1	(29.3, 32.8)
District of Columbia	22.9	(21.0, 24.8)
Florida	26.4	(25.3, 27.4)
Georgia	30.3	(28.9, 31.8)
Guam	27.0	(24.4, 29.8)
Hawaii	21.8	(20.4, 23.2)
Idaho	29.6	(27.8, 31.4)
Illinois	29.4	(27.7, 31.2)
Indiana	31.8	(30.6, 33.1)
Iowa	31.3	(29.9, 32.7)
Kansas	30.0	(29.2, 30.7)
Kentucky	33.2	(31.8, 34.6)
Louisiana	33.1	(31.1, 35.2)
Maine	28.9	(27.5, 30.2)
Maryland	28.3	(27.0, 29.5)
Massachusetts	23.6	(22.5, 24.8)
Michigan	31.5	(30.4, 32.6)
Minnesota	25.5	(24.1, 26.8)
Mississippi	35.1	(33.5, 36.8)

State	Prevalence	95% Confidence Interval
Missouri	30.4	(28.8, 32.1)
Montana	24.6	(23.4, 25.8)
Nebraska	29.6	(28.4, 30.7)
Nevada	26.2	(24.0, 28.6)
New Hampshire	26.7	(25.3, 28.3)
New Jersey	26.3	(25.1, 27.5)
New Mexico	26.4	(25.1, 27.7)
New York	25.4	(24.2, 26.6)
North Carolina	29.4	(28.1, 30.7)
North Dakota	31.0	(29.5, 32.5)
Ohio	30.4	(29.2, 31.6)
Oklahoma	32.5	(31.2, 33.9)
Oregon	26.5	(24.9, 28.1)
Pennsylvania	30.0	(28.9, 31.2)
Puerto Rico	27.9	(26.4, 29.5)
Rhode Island	27.3	(25.8, 28.8)
South Carolina	31.7	(30.5, 33.1)
South Dakota	29.9	(28.0, 31.8)
Tennessee	33.7	(31.9, 35.5)
Texas	30.9	(29.5, 32.3)
Utah	24.1	(23.2, 25.1)
Vermont	24.7	(23.4, 26.1)
Virginia	27.2	(25.9, 28.5)
Washington	27.2	(26.0, 28.3)
West Virginia	35.1	(33.6, 36.6)
Wisconsin	29.8	(28.0, 31.6)
Wyoming	27.8	(26.2, 29.5)

¶ Prevalence estimates reflect BRFSS methodological changes started in 2011. These estimates should not be compared to prevalence estimates before 2011.
Source: Behavioral Risk Factor Surveillance System, CDC.

Prevalence¶ of Self-Reported Obesity Among U.S. Adults by State and Territory, BRFSS, 2014

State	Prevalence	95% Confidence Interval
Alabama	33.5	(32.1, 35.0)
Alaska	29.7	(27.8, 31.7)
Arizona	28.9	(27.7, 30.2)
Arkansas	35.9	(33.8, 38.0)
California	24.7	(23.5, 25.9)
Colorado	21.3	(20.4, 22.2)
Connecticut	26.3	(24.9, 27.7)
Delaware	30.7	(28.6, 32.8)
District of Columbia	21.7	(19.5, 24.0)
Florida	26.2	(25.0, 27.5)
Georgia	30.5	(28.9, 32.1)
Guam	28.0	(25.6, 30.5)
Hawaii	22.1	(20.7, 23.5)
Idaho	28.9	(27.1, 30.8)
Illinois	29.3	(27.6, 31.1)
Indiana	32.7	(31.6, 34.0)
Iowa	30.9	(29.6, 32.3)
Kansas	31.3	(30.3, 32.2)
Kentucky	31.6	(30.2, 33.1)
Louisiana	34.9	(33.4, 36.4)
Maine	28.2	(26.9, 29.5)
Maryland	29.6	(28.1, 31.1)
Massachusetts	23.3	(22.3, 24.4)
Michigan	30.7	(29.4, 32.0)
Minnesota	27.6	(26.8, 28.5)
Mississippi	35.5	(33.4, 37.6)

State	Prevalence	95% Confidence Interval
Missouri	30.2	(28.6, 31.9)
Montana	26.4	(24.9, 27.9)
Nebraska	30.2	(29.2, 31.3)
Nevada	27.7	(25.4, 30.1)
New Hampshire	27.4	(25.8, 29.1)
New Jersey	26.9	(25.7, 28.1)
New Mexico	28.4	(27.0, 30.0)
New York	27.0	(25.6, 28.5)
North Carolina	29.7	(28.4, 31.0)
North Dakota	32.2	(30.5, 34.0)
Ohio	32.6	(31.2, 34.1)
Oklahoma	33.0	(31.7, 34.3)
Oregon	27.9	(26.3, 29.6)
Pennsylvania	30.2	(28.9, 31.4)
Puerto Rico	28.3	(26.8, 29.8)
Rhode Island	27.0	(25.4, 28.6)
South Carolina	32.1	(30.9, 33.3)
South Dakota	29.8	(27.9, 31.8)
Tennessee	31.2	(29.3, 33.2)
Texas	31.9	(30.6, 33.3)
Utah	25.7	(24.9, 26.6)
Vermont	24.8	(23.5, 26.1)
Virginia	28.5	(27.2, 29.7)
Washington	27.3	(26.0, 28.5)
West Virginia	35.7	(34.2, 37.2)
Wisconsin	31.2	(29.6, 32.8)
Wyoming	29.5	(27.5, 31.5)

¶ Prevalence estimates reflect BRFSS methodological changes started in 2011. These estimates should not be compared to prevalence estimates before 2011.
Source: Behavioral Risk Factor Surveillance System, CDC.

Prevalence¶ of Self-Reported Obesity Among U.S. Adults by State and Territory, BRFSS, 2015

State	Prevalence	95% Confidence Interval
Alabama	35.6	(34.1, 37.2)
Alaska	29.8	(27.5, 32.3)
Arizona	28.4	(26.9, 30.0)
Arkansas	34.5	(32.2, 36.9)
California	24.2	(23.2, 25.2)
Colorado	20.2	(19.1, 21.3)
Connecticut	25.3	(24.1, 26.4)
Delaware	29.7	(27.6, 31.8)
District of Columbia	22.1	(19.7, 24.8)
Florida	26.8	(25.5, 28.1)
Georgia	30.7	(28.8, 32.6)
Guam	31.6	(28.2, 35.1)
Hawaii	22.7	(21.3, 24.1)
Idaho	28.6	(26.9, 30.4)
Illinois	30.8	(29.2, 32.4)
Indiana	31.3	(29.5, 33.1)
Iowa	32.1	(30.5, 33.8)
Kansas	34.2	(33.4, 35.0)
Kentucky	34.6	(32.9, 36.3)
Louisiana	36.2	(34.3, 38.1)
Maine	30.0	(28.6, 31.4)
Maryland	28.9	(27.2, 30.7)
Massachusetts	24.3	(23.0, 25.6)
Michigan	31.2	(29.9, 32.4)
Minnesota	26.1	(25.3, 27.0)
Mississippi	35.6	(33.8, 37.5)

State	Prevalence	95% Confidence Interval
Missouri	32.4	(30.8, 34.0)
Montana	23.6	(22.1, 25.2)
Nebraska	31.4	(30.3, 32.5)
Nevada	26.7	(24.1, 29.5)
New Hampshire	26.3	(24.8, 27.9)
New Jersey	25.6	(24.3, 26.9)
New Mexico	28.8	(27.1, 30.6)
New York	25.0	(24.0, 26.1)
North Carolina	30.1	(28.7, 31.5)
North Dakota	31.0	(29.3, 32.8)
Ohio	29.8	(28.4, 31.2)
Oklahoma	33.9	(32.2, 35.6)
Oregon	30.1	(28.4, 31.8)
Pennsylvania	30.0	(28.4, 31.6)
Puerto Rico	29.5	(28.0, 31.1)
Rhode Island	26.0	(24.3, 27.7)
South Carolina	31.7	(30.5, 33.0)
South Dakota	30.4	(28.5, 32.3)
Tennessee	33.8	(31.9, 35.7)
Texas	32.4	(30.9, 33.9)
Utah	24.5	(23.5, 25.5)
Vermont	25.1	(23.8, 26.6)
Virginia	29.2	(27.9, 30.6)
Washington	26.4	(25.5, 27.4)
West Virginia	35.6	(34.1, 37.1)
Wisconsin	30.7	(29.0, 32.4)
Wyoming	29.0	(27.0, 31.1)

¶ Prevalence estimates reflect BRFSS methodological changes started in 2011. These estimates should not be compared to prevalence estimates before 2011.

Source: Behavioral Risk Factor Surveillance System, CDC.

Prevalence¶ of Self-Reported Obesity Among U.S. Adults by State and Territory, BRFSS, 2016

State	Prevalence	95% Confidence Interval
Alabama	35.7	(34.2, 37.3)
Alaska	31.4	(28.5, 34.4)
Arizona	29.0	(27.5, 30.6)
Arkansas	35.7	(33.3, 38.1)
California	25.0	(23.9, 26.1)
Colorado	22.3	(21.4, 23.2)
Connecticut	26.0	(24.8, 27.2)
Delaware	30.7	(28.7, 32.8)
District of Columbia	22.6	(20.9, 24.3)
Florida	27.4	(26.4, 28.5)
Georgia	31.4	(29.7, 33.2)
Guam	28.3	(25.1, 31.7)
Hawaii	23.8	(22.5, 25.2)
Idaho	27.4	(25.6, 29.3)
Illinois	31.6	(29.9, 33.3)
Indiana	32.5	(31.2, 33.8)
Iowa	32.0	(30.5, 33.4)
Kansas	31.2	(30.1, 32.3)
Kentucky	34.2	(32.7, 35.6)
Louisiana	35.5	(33.4, 37.7)
Maine	29.9	(28.5, 31.3)
Maryland	29.9	(28.9, 31.0)
Massachusetts	23.6	(22.3, 24.9)
Michigan	32.5	(31.4, 33.6)
Minnesota	27.8	(26.9, 28.6)
Mississippi	37.3	(35.4, 39.1)
Missouri	31.7	(30.0, 33.4)

State	Prevalence	95% Confidence Interval
Montana	25.5	(23.9, 27.2)
Nebraska	32.0	(30.8, 33.2)
Nevada	25.8	(23.9, 27.8)
New Hampshire	26.6	(25.0, 28.2)
New Jersey	27.4	(25.7, 29.1)
New Mexico	28.3	(26.6, 30.1)
New York	25.5	(24.6, 26.5)
North Carolina	31.8	(30.4, 33.3)
North Dakota	31.9	(30.3, 33.6)
Ohio	31.5	(30.2, 32.8)
Oklahoma	32.8	(31.2, 34.3)
Oregon	28.7	(27.3, 30.3)
Pennsylvania	30.3	(28.8, 31.8)
Puerto Rico	30.7	(29.0, 32.5)
Rhode Island	26.6	(24.9, 28.4)
South Carolina	32.3	(31.0, 33.6)
South Dakota	29.6	(27.6, 31.7)
Tennessee	34.8	(33.0, 36.7)
Texas	33.7	(31.9, 35.4)
Utah	25.4	(24.2, 26.5)
Vermont	27.1	(25.5, 28.7)
Virgin Islands	32.5	(28.6, 36.6)
Virginia	29.0	(27.7, 30.3)
Washington	28.6	(27.6, 29.6)
West Virginia	37.7	(36.3, 39.0)
Wisconsin	30.7	(29.0, 32.5)
Wyoming	27.7	(25.7, 29.8)

¶ Prevalence estimates reflect BRFSS methodological changes started in 2011. These estimates should not be compared to prevalence estimates before 2011.
Source: Behavioral Risk Factor Surveillance System, CDC.

Prevalence¶ of Self-Reported Obesity Among U.S. Adults by State and Territory, BRFSS, 2017

State	Prevalence	95% Confidence Interval
Alabama	36.3	(34.7, 38.0)
Alaska	34.2	(31.4, 37.1)
Arizona	29.5	(28.5, 30.5)
Arkansas	35.0	(32.6, 37.5)
California	25.1	(23.8, 26.4)
Colorado	22.6	(21.6, 23.7)
Connecticut	26.9	(25.6, 28.1)
Delaware	31.8	(29.7, 34.0)
District of Columbia	22.9	(21.1, 24.7)
Florida	28.4	(27.0, 29.9)
Georgia	31.6	(30.0, 33.3)
Guam	34.3	(31.2, 37.6)
Hawaii	23.8	(22.4, 25.2)
Idaho	29.3	(27.5, 31.2)
Illinois	31.1	(29.5, 32.7)
Indiana	33.6	(32.5, 34.7)
Iowa	36.4	(35.1, 37.7)
Kansas	32.4	(31.5, 33.2)
Kentucky	34.3	(32.6, 36.0)
Louisiana	36.2	(34.4, 38.1)
Maine	29.1	(27.7, 30.6)
Maryland	31.3	(30.0, 32.6)
Massachusetts	25.9	(24.1, 27.7)
Michigan	32.3	(31.1, 33.4)
Minnesota	28.4	(27.5, 29.4)
Mississippi	37.3	(35.3, 39.3)
Missouri	32.5	(30.9, 34.0)

State	Prevalence	95% Confidence Interval
Montana	25.3	(23.8, 26.9)
Nebraska	32.8	(31.6, 34.0)
Nevada	26.7	(24.5, 29.0)
New Hampshire	28.1	(26.3, 29.9)
New Jersey	27.3	(25.8, 28.7)
New Mexico	28.4	(26.8, 30.0)
New York	25.7	(24.6, 26.9)
North Carolina	32.1	(30.4, 34.0)
North Dakota	33.2	(31.6, 34.7)
Ohio	33.8	(32.5, 35.1)
Oklahoma	36.5	(34.9, 38.1)
Oregon	29.4	(27.9, 30.9)
Pennsylvania	31.6	(30.0, 33.2)
Puerto Rico	32.9	(31.0, 34.9)
Rhode Island	30.0	(28.1, 31.9)
South Carolina	34.1	(32.8, 35.4)
South Dakota	31.9	(29.8, 34.1)
Tennessee	32.8	(31.1, 34.6)
Texas	33.0	(31.2, 34.9)
Utah	25.3	(24.2, 26.4)
Vermont	27.6	(26.0, 29.2)
Virginia	30.1	(28.7, 31.4)
Washington	27.7	(26.6, 28.7)
West Virginia	38.1	(36.4, 39.7)
Wisconsin	32.0	(30.3, 33.8)
Wyoming	28.8	(27.1, 30.6)

¶ Prevalence estimates reflect BRFSS methodological changes started in 2011. These estimates should not be compared to prevalence estimates before 2011.
Source: Behavioral Risk Factor Surveillance System, CDC.

Prevalence¶ of Self-Reported Obesity Among U.S. Adults by State and Territory, BRFSS, 2018

State	Prevalence	95% Confidence Interval
Alabama	36.2	(34.6, 37.9)
Alaska	29.5	(27.0, 32.2)
Arizona	29.5	(27.8, 31.3)
Arkansas	37.1	(35.1, 39.1)
California	25.8	(24.8, 26.9)
Colorado	23.0	(21.9, 24.0)
Connecticut	27.4	(26.2, 28.7)
Delaware	33.5	(31.7, 35.4)
District of Columbia	24.7	(22.9, 26.5)
Florida	30.7	(29.1, 32.3)
Georgia	32.5	(31.2, 33.8)
Guam	29.8	(26.6, 33.3)
Hawaii	24.9	(23.6, 26.3)
Idaho	28.4	(26.3, 30.5)
Illinois	31.8	(30.2, 33.4)
Indiana	34.1	(32.6, 35.6)
Iowa	35.3	(34.2, 36.5)
Kansas	34.4	(33.2, 35.6)
Kentucky	36.6	(34.9, 38.4)
Louisiana	36.8	(34.9, 38.7)
Maine	30.4	(28.9, 31.9)
Maryland	30.9	(29.8, 32.1)
Massachusetts	25.7	(24.3, 27.2)
Michigan	33.0	(31.8, 34.2)
Minnesota	30.1	(29.2, 30.9)
Mississippi	39.5	(37.8, 41.2)
Missouri	35.0	(33.3, 36.8)

State	Prevalence	95% Confidence Interval
Montana	26.9	(25.2, 28.5)
Nebraska	34.1	(32.9, 35.3)
Nevada	29.5	(27.1, 32.0)
New Hampshire	29.6	(27.9, 31.4)
New Jersey	25.7	(23.3, 28.2)
New Mexico	32.3	(30.7, 34.0)
New York	27.6	(26.7, 28.6)
North Carolina	33.0	(31.2, 34.8)
North Dakota	35.1	(33.3, 37.0)
Ohio	34.0	(32.7, 35.3)
Oklahoma	34.8	(33.1, 36.6)
Oregon	29.9	(28.4, 31.4)
Pennsylvania	30.9	(29.4, 32.5)
Puerto Rico	32.9	(31.2, 34.7)
Rhode Island	27.7	(26.0, 29.5)
South Carolina	34.3	(33.0, 35.6)
South Dakota	30.1	(28.1, 32.1)
Tennessee	34.4	(32.5, 36.3)
Texas	34.8	(32.8, 36.8)
Utah	27.8	(26.7, 28.9)
Vermont	27.5	(25.9, 29.2)
Virginia	30.4	(29.1, 31.6)
Washington	28.7	(27.6, 29.8)
West Virginia	39.5	(37.8, 41.3)
Wisconsin	32.0	(30.2, 33.8)
Wyoming	29.0	(27.3, 30.8)

¶ Prevalence estimates reflect BRFSS methodological changes started in 2011. These estimates should not be compared to prevalence estimates before 2011.
Source: Behavioral Risk Factor Surveillance System, CDC.

Prevalence¶ of Self-Reported Obesity Among U.S. Adults by State and Territory, BRFSS, 2019

State	Prevalence	95% Confidence Interval
Alabama	36.1	(34.6, 37.7)
Alaska	30.5	(27.8, 33.4)
Arizona	31.4	(29.7, 33.2)
Arkansas	37.4	(35.5, 39.4)
California	26.2	(25.1, 27.2)
Colorado	23.8	(22.7, 24.9)
Connecticut	29.1	(27.8, 30.5)
Delaware	34.4	(32.1, 36.6)
District of Columbia	23.8	(21.7, 25.9)
Florida	27.0	(25.6, 28.5)
Georgia	33.1	(31.3, 35.0)
Guam	33.6	(30.5, 37.0)
Hawaii	25.0	(23.7, 26.3)
Idaho	29.5	(27.6, 31.4)
Illinois	31.6	(30.1, 33.1)
Indiana	35.3	(34.0, 36.7)
Iowa	33.9	(32.8, 35.1)
Kansas	35.2	(34.1, 36.4)
Kentucky	36.5	(34.7, 38.2)
Louisiana	35.9	(34.1, 37.7)
Maine	31.7	(30.3, 33.1)
Maryland	32.3	(31.1, 33.4)
Massachusetts	25.2	(23.9, 26.5)
Michigan	36.0	(34.7, 37.3)
Minnesota	30.1	(29.2, 31.1)
Mississippi	40.8	(39.0, 42.7)
Missouri	34.8	(33.2, 36.4)

State	Prevalence	95% Confidence Interval
Montana	28.3	(27.0, 29.7)
Nebraska	34.1	(33.0, 35.2)
Nevada	30.6	(28.2, 33.1)
New Hampshire	31.8	(30.0, 33.6)
New Jersey	Insufficient data*	Insufficient data*
New Mexico	31.7	(30.0, 33.5)
New York	27.1	(26.0, 28.2)
North Carolina	34.0	(32.2, 35.8)
North Dakota	34.8	(33.0, 36.7)
Ohio	34.8	(33.5, 36.1)
Oklahoma	36.8	(35.2, 38.4)
Oregon	29.0	(27.5, 30.4)
Pennsylvania	33.2	(31.7, 34.7)
Puerto Rico	32.5	(31.0, 34.0)
Rhode Island	30.0	(28.2, 31.9)
South Carolina	35.4	(33.8, 36.9)
South Dakota	33.0	(30.6, 35.5)
Tennessee	36.5	(34.8, 38.3)
Texas	34.0	(32.2, 35.7)
Utah	29.2	(28.2, 30.3)
Vermont	26.6	(25.0, 28.3)
Virginia	31.9	(30.6, 33.2)
Washington	28.3	(27.3, 29.4)
West Virginia	39.7	(38.0, 41.5)
Wisconsin	34.2	(32.4, 36.1)
Wyoming	29.7	(27.7, 31.7)

¶ Prevalence estimates reflect BRFSS methodological changes started in 2011. These estimates should not be compared to prevalence estimates before 2011.
Source: Behavioral Risk Factor Surveillance System, CDC.
*Sample size <50, the relative standard error (dividing the standard error by the prevalence) ≥30%, or no data in a specific year.

Prevalence¶ of Self-Reported Obesity Among U.S. Adults by State and Territory, BRFSS, 2020

State	Prevalence	95% Confidence Interval	State	Prevalence	95% Confidence Interval
Alabama	39.0	(37.3, 40.8)	Montana	28.5	(27.1, 30.0)
Alaska	31.9	(29.4, 34.4)	Nebraska	34.0	(32.8, 35.2)
Arizona	30.9	(29.5, 32.3)	Nevada	28.7	(26.2, 31.3)
Arkansas	36.4	(34.5, 38.4)	New Hampshire	29.9	(28.2, 31.6)
California	30.3	(28.3, 32.2)	New Jersey	27.7	(26.5, 28.9)
Colorado	24.2	(23.1, 25.2)	New Mexico	30.9	(29.0, 32.8)
Connecticut	29.2	(27.7, 30.8)	New York	26.3	(25.3, 27.4)
Delaware	36.5	(34.3, 38.8)	North Carolina	33.6	(32.0, 35.2)
District of Columbia	24.3	(22.3, 26.4)	North Dakota	33.1	(31.1, 35.1)
Florida	28.4	(26.7, 30.2)	Ohio	35.5	(34.3, 36.7)
Georgia	34.3	(32.5, 36.0)	Oklahoma	36.4	(34.7, 38.2)
Guam	34.4	(30.8, 38.2)	Oregon	28.1	(26.6, 29.6)
Hawaii	24.5	(23.2, 25.9)	Pennsylvania	31.5	(29.8, 33.2)
Idaho	31.1	(29.4, 32.9)	Puerto Rico	31.4	(29.5, 33.3)
Illinois	32.4	(30.2, 34.6)	Rhode Island	30.1	(28.2, 32.1)
Indiana	36.8	(35.4, 38.1)	South Carolina	36.2	(34.2, 38.3)
Iowa	36.5	(35.3, 37.7)	South Dakota	33.2	(30.7, 35.8)
Kansas	35.3	(34.0, 36.5)	Tennessee	35.6	(33.6, 37.6)
Kentucky	36.6	(34.6, 38.6)	Texas	35.8	(33.9, 37.7)
Louisiana	38.1	(36.2, 40.1)	Utah	28.6	(27.4, 29.7)
Maine	31.0	(29.6, 32.5)	Vermont	26.3	(24.6, 27.9)
Maryland	31.0	(29.8, 32.2)	Virginia	32.2	(30.8, 33.6)
Massachusetts	24.4	(23.0, 25.9)	Washington	28.0	(27.0, 29.1)
Michigan	35.2	(33.7, 36.7)	West Virginia	39.1	(37.5, 40.7)
Minnesota	30.7	(29.8, 31.7)	Wisconsin	32.3	(30.4, 34.2)
Mississippi	39.7	(38.1, 41.3)	Wyoming	30.7	(28.7, 32.7)
Missouri	34.0	(32.7, 35.4)			

¶ Prevalence estimates reflect BRFSS methodological changes started in 2011. These estimates should not be compared to prevalence estimates before 2011.
Source: Behavioral Risk Factor Surveillance System, CDC.

Prevalence¶ of Self-Reported Obesity Among U.S. Adults by State and Territory, BRFSS, 2020

Summary

- No state or territory had a prevalence of obesity less than 20%.
- 3 states (Colorado, Hawaii, Massachusetts) and the District of Columbia had a prevalence of obesity between 20% and <25%.
- 11 states had a prevalence of obesity between 25% and <30%.
- 20 states, Guam, and Puerto Rico had a prevalence of obesity between 30% and <35%.
- 16 states (Alabama, Arkansas, Delaware, Indiana, Iowa, Kansas, Kentucky, Louisiana, Michigan, Mississippi, Ohio, Oklahoma, South Carolina, Tennessee, Texas, and West Virginia) had a prevalence of obesity of 35% or greater.

¶ Prevalence estimates reflect BRFSS methodological changes started in 2011. These estimates should not be compared to prevalence estimates before 2011.

http://www.cdc.gov/obesity/data/prevalence-maps.html

SECTION TWO: CONDITIONS DIRECTLY RELATED TO NUTRITION

ALLERGIES & NUTRITION

There are three primary diseases and disorders that may be defined as allergic diseases according to the National Institutes of Health: asthma, eczema (atopic dermatitis) and food allergy. Asthma is a chronic disease with episodes of airway narrowing resulting in wheezing, coughing and shortness of breath. Eczema is a non-contagious skin disorder characterized by dry, itchy skin and blisters. Food allergy is a condition that affects almost 5 percent of children and adults in the United States. With a food allergy, the immune system reacts abnormally to the food or food component and may produce a life-threatening response. While all three conditions may require medication and other interventions, nutrition may play a vital role in improving the body's response to asthma, eczema and, of course, food allergies. Consultation with a clinical, registered dietician is highly recommended if one of the three conditions is diagnosed.

Asthma is a chronic, long-term disease that interferes with the ability to move air into and out of the lungs. The airways may become inflamed and narrowed causing wheezing, coughing, shortness of breath and chest tightness. An asthma attack is when these symptoms worsen. Genetics and environment may play a factor, but the underlying cause of asthma is unknown. Triggers vary by individual and may include dust, pollen, certain medications, infections and tobacco smoke. The diagnosis of asthma is made through physical examination and medical history, lung function tests and allergy skin or blood tests. Treatments include avoiding triggers, short-term relief and control medicines and proper nutrition. While there is no diet that will eliminate asthma symptoms, eating to maintain a healthy weight, consuming plenty of fruits and vegetables, avoiding allergy-triggering foods, increasing vitamin D intake and avoiding sulfites such as those in wine, pickles, shrimp and dried fruits are recommended. Restricting salt and eating foods rich in omega-3 fatty acids such as cold-water fish may also reduce asthma symptoms. Consultation with a registered dietician is recommended once a diagnosis is established.

Eczema or atopic dermatitis is a non-contagious inflammatory skin condition causing dry, itchy skin that may weep fluid if the rash is scratched. Bacterial, fungal and viral infections may occur in individuals with eczema. Eczema affects almost 1/3 of the U.S. population, mostly children and young adults. Both genetic and environmental factors may contribute to eczema development. Food allergies are associated with 30 percent of children with atopic dermatitis and many also have asthma and other respiratory allergies. Treatment involves medications, appropriate skin care, avoiding triggers such as pollen, emotional stress, skin contact with known allergens, and avoiding foods known to be allergic to the individual.

Food is defined as any substance intended for human consumption and includes beverages, chewing gum, food additives, dietary supplements and processed, semi-processed and raw foods. Some allergens cause a reaction only when eaten raw, while some cause a reaction whether raw or cooked. Foods that are similar to a known food allergen may also cause an allergic reaction. A reaction may occur after years of consuming a certain food with no problems. Individuals may outgrow certain food allergies or may receive therapy to eliminate a reaction. Peanut allergies and allergic reactions to shell fish are present in between 1.1 and 2 percent of the population.

There is no cure for food allergy, but experimental immunotherapies may decrease symptoms. Avoiding the food that causes the allergic reaction is the most effective treatment. Medication may also be used to manage symptoms, including antihistamines. Consultation with a clinical dietician is highly recommended, who will provide information on food allergens and emergency management of reactions. The National Institute for Allergies and Infectious Diseases does not recognize food restriction during pregnancy or lactation as a strategy for preventing food allergies in children.

See page 225 for more information on food allergies.

Agencies & Associations

2 **Academy of Nutrition & Dietetics**
120 South Riverside Plaza 312-899-0040
Chicago, IL 60606-6995 800-877-1600
media@eatright.org
www.eatright.org
Offers information and support to allergy sufferers. Serves the public through the promotion of optimal nutrition, health, and well-being. Formerly the American Dietetic Association.
Patricia M. Babjak, Chief Executive Officer

3 **Agency for Toxic Substances and Disease Registry**
1200 Pennsylvania Avenue NW 800-232-4636
Washington, DC 20460 www.atsdr.cdc.gov
The Agency for Toxic Substances and Disease Registry (ATSDR), based in Atlanta, Georgia, is a federal public health agency of the U.S. Department of Health and Human Services. ATSDR serves the public by using the best science, taking responsive public health actions, and providing trusted health information to prevent harmful exposures and diseases related to toxic substances.
Patrick Breysse, Director

4 **Allergy & Asthma Network**
8229 Boone Boulevard 800-878-4403
Vienna, VA 22182 www.allergyasthmanetwork.org
Non-profit membership organization dedicated to eliminating suffering and death due to asthma, allergies and related conditions through education, advocacy, community outreach, and research.
Tonya Winders, President & CEO
Marcela Gieminiani, Director, Development

5 **American Academy of Allergy, Asthma & Immunology**
555 East Wells Street 414-272-6071
Milwaukee, WI 53202-3823 info@aaaai.org
www.aaaai.org
Strives to serve the public through information on asthma and allergies, as well as referrals to allergists.
Giselle S. Mosnaim, President
Jonathan A. Bernstein, Secretary-Treasurer

6 **American Academy of Environmental Medicine**
PO Box 195 316-684-5500
Ashland, MO 65010 www.aaemonline.org
The AAEM Promotes the education of healthcare professionals in the interaction between humans and the environment. Offers names of Clinical Ecologists and Allergy Specialists in the United States.
Lauren Grohs, Executive Director

7 **American College of Allergy, Asthma & Immunology**
www.acaai.org
Focuses on research and public awareness of allergies, asthma, and immunology. Distributes informational brochures and pamphlets, offers referrals and counseling services, as well as patient care.
Rick Slawny, Executive Diector
Kevin Bragaw, Chief Financial Officer

8 **American Lung Association**
55 W Wacker Drive 800-586-4872
Chicago, IL 60601 info@lung.org
www.lung.org
A voluntary organization interested in the prevention and control of lung disease. Promotes and distributes public awareness information on a variety of lung disorders, including allergies, and complications can that arise from them.
Harold Wimmer, President & CEO

9 **Asthma Canada**
124 Merton Street 416-787-4050
Toronto, Ontario, M4S-2Z2 866-787-4050
info@asthma.ca
www.asthma.ca
National, volunteer-led organization devoted to enhancing the quality of life for individuals with athsma and respiratory allergies.
Vanessa Foran, President & CEO
Kristin Valois, Manager, Communications & Programs

10 **Birth Defect Research for Children, Inc.**
976 Lake Baldwin Lane 407-895-0802
Orlando, FL 32814 staff@birthdefects.org
www.birthdefects.org/allergies
A non-profit organization providing parents and soon-to-be parents with information resources about birth defects, and support services for their children. Offers fact sheets on allergies.

11 **Canadian Society of Allergy and Clinical Immunology**
PO Box 51045 613-986-5869
Orleans, Ontario, K1E-3W4 info@csaci.ca
www.csaci.ca
Promotes the advancement of the knowledge and practice of allergy, clinical immunology, and asthma for optimal patient care.
Tim Vander Leek, President
Louise Tremblay, Executive Director

12 **Centers for Disease Control & Prevention: Division of Adolescent & School Health**
1600 Clifton Road 800-232-4636
Atlanta, GA 30329 TTY: 888-232-6348
www.cdc.gov/HealthyYouth
CDC promotes the health and well-being of children and adolescents to enable them to become healthy and productive adults.

13 **Centers for Medicare & Medicaid Services**
7500 Security Boulevard www.cms.gov
Baltimore, MD 21244
U.S. federal agency which administers Medicare, Medicaid, and the State Children's Health Insurance Program.
Chiquita Brooks-LaSure, Administrator
Jonathan Blum, COO

14 **Food Allergy Research & Education**
7901 Jones Branch Drive 703-691-3179
McLean, VA 22102 800-929-4040
www.foodallergy.org
FARE aims to increase public awareness about food allergies and anaphylaxis, advance research, and provide education, emotional support and coping strategies to patients. It also serves as the communication link between the food industry, the government and the airline industry.
Lisa Gable, Chief Executive Officer
Ruchi Gupta, MD, MPH, Chief Medical Officer for Public Health

15 **Food Safety and Inspection Service**
U.S. Department of Agriculture
1400 Independence Avenue SW fsis.webmaster@usda.gov
Washington, DC 20250 www.fsis.usda.gov
The Food Safety and Inspection Service (FSIS) is the public health agency in the U.S. Department of Agriculture responsible for ensuring that the nation's commercial supply of meat, poultry, and egg products is safe, wholesome, and correctly labeled and packaged.
Paul Kiecher, Administrator
Terri Nintemann, Deputy Administrator

16 **National Eczema Association**
505 San Marin Drive 415-499-3474
Novato, CA 94945 800-818-7546
www.nationaleczema.org
Engages in research, support, and education to better the lives of individuals with eczema, including information on allergies.
Julie Block, President & CEO
Scott Sanford, COO

17 **National Institute for Occupational Safety and Health**
Patriots Plaza 1
395 E Street SW 800-232-4636
Washington, DC 20201 www.cdc.gov/niosh
The National Institute for Occupational Safety and Health (NIOSH) is the U.S. federal agency that conducts research and makes recommendations to prevent worker injury and illness.
John Howard, MD, Director

18 **National Institute of Allergy and Infectious Diseases**
NIAID Office of Communications & Govt Relations

5601 Fishers Lane 301-496-5717
Bethesda, MD 20892-9806 866-284-4107
TDD: 800-877-8339
ocpostoffice@niaid.nih.gov
www.niaid.nih.gov

Conducts and supports research on allergies; focused on understanding what happens to the body during the allergic process. Educates patients and health care workers in controlling allergic disease; offers various research centers that conduct and evaluate educational programs focused on methods to control allergic diseases.
Anthony S. Fauci, MD, Director

19 **National Institute of Environmental Health Sciences**
PO Box 12233 919-541-3345
Research Triangle Park, NC 27709 www.niehs.nih.gov
The mission of the NIEHS is to discover how the environment affects people in order to promote healthier lives.
Rick Woychik, PhD, Director
Gwen W. Collman, PhD, Acting Deputy Director

20 **National Institute of Food and Agriculture**
1400 Independence Avenue SW nifa.usda.gov
Washington, DC 20250-2201
National Institute of Food and Agriculture (NIFA) provides leadership and funding for programs that advance agriculture-related sciences.
Carrie Castille, Director
William Hoffman, Chief of Staff

21 **National Institute of General Medical Sciences**
45 Center Drive 301-496-7301
Bethesda, MD 20892-6200 info@nigms.nih.gov
www.nigms.nih.gov
The National Institute of General Medical Sciences (NIGMS) supports basic research that increases understanding of biological processes and lays the foundation for advances in disease diagnosis, treatment and prevention.
Jon R. Lorsch, PhD, Director
Dorit Zuk, PhD, Acting Deputy Director

22 **Nurse Practitioners in Women's Health**
PO Box 15837 202-543-9693
Washington, DC 20003 info@npwh.org
www.npwh.org
Ensures the delivery and accessibility of primary and specialty healthcare to women of all ages by women's health and women's health focused nurse practitioners.
Heather L. Maurer, CEO
Donna Ruth, Director, Education

23 **U.S. Food and Drug Administration**
10903 New Hampshire Avenue 888-463-6332
Silver Spring, MD 20993-0002 www.fda.gov
FDA is responsible for protecting the public health by assuring the safety, efficacy and security of human and veterinary drugs, biological products, medical devices, the nation's food supply, cosmetics, and products that emit radiation.
Janet Woodcock, MD, Acting Commissioner

24 **World Allergy Organization**
555 East Wells Street 414-276-1791
Milwaukee, WI 53202 info@worldallergy.org
www.worldallergy.org
International organization building global alliance of allergy societies to advance excellence in care, research, education and training.
Justin Dodge, Executive Director

Alabama

25 **American Lung Association: Alabama**
1678 Montgomery Highway 205-258-5367
Birmingham, AL 35216 alaal@lungse.org
www.lung.org

Alaska

26 **American Lung Association: Alaska**
500 W International Airport Road 907-276-5864
Anchorage, AK 99518 www.lung.org

Arizona

27 **American Lung Association: Arizona**
102 W McDowell Road 602-258-7505
Phoenix, AZ 85003 azinfo@lungs.org
www.lung.org

Arkansas

28 **American Lung Association: Arkansas**
2020 W 3rd Street www.lung.org
Little Rock, AR 72225

California

29 **American Lung Association: California**
2020 Camino Del Rio North 619-297-3901
San Diego, CA 92108 ellen.sherwood@lung.org
www.lung.org

Colorado

30 **American Lung Association: Colorado**
5600 Greenwood Plaza Boulevard 303-388-4327
Greenwood Village, CO 80111 coinfo@lungs.org
www.lung.org

Connecticut

31 **American Lung Association: Connecticut**
45 Ash Street 860-289-5401
East Hartford, CT 06108 www.lung.org

Delaware

32 **American Lung Association: Delaware**
630 Churchmans Road 302-565-2071
Newark, DE 19702 www.lung.org

District of Columbia

33 **American Lung Association: District of Columbia**
1331 Pennsylvania Avenue NW 202-785-3355
Washington, DC 20004 www.lung.org

Florida

34 **American Lung Association: Florida**
2701 N Australian Avenue 561-659-7644
West Palm Beach, FL 33407 alafse@lungse.org
www.lung.org

Georgia

35 **American Lung Association: Georgia**
2452 Spring Road 770-544-0521
Smyrna, GA 30080 www.lung.org

Hawaii

36 **American Lung Association: Hawaii**
201 Merchant Street 808-537-5966
Honolulu, HI 96813 www.lung.org

Idaho

37 **American Lung Association: Idaho**
1412 W Idaho Street 208-345-5864
Boise, ID 83702 www.lung.org

Illinois

38 **American Lung Association: Illinois**
3000 Kelly Lane — 217-787-5864
Springfield, IL 62711 — www.lung.org

Indiana

39 **American Lung Association: Indiana**
115 West Washington Street — 317-819-1181
Indianapolis, IN 46204 — www.lung.org

Iowa

40 **American Lung Association: Iowa**
2530 73rd Street — 515-309-9507
Des Moines, IA 50322 — www.lung.org

Kansas

41 **American Lung Association: Kansas**
8400 W 110th Street — 913-353-9165
Overland Park, KS 66210 — www.lung.org

Kentucky

42 **American Lung Association: Kentucky**
10168 Linn Station Road — 502-363-2652
Louisville, KY 40223 — www.lung.org

Louisiana

43 **American Lung Association: Louisiana**
2325 Severn Avenue — 504-828-5864
Metairie, LA 70001 — www.lung.org

Maine

44 **American Lung Association: Maine**
122 State Street — 207-622-6394
Augusta, ME 04330 — www.lung.org

Maryland

45 **American Lung Association: Maryland**
211 E Lombard Street — 302-565-2074
Baltimore, MD 21202 — www.lung.org

Massachusetts

46 **American Lung Association: Massachusetts**
1661 Worcester Road — 781-890-4262
Farmingham, MA 01701 — www.lung.org

Michigan

47 **American Lung Association: Michigan**
1475 E 12 Mile Road — 248-784-2000
Madison Heights, MI 48071 — www.lung.org

Minnesota

48 **American Lung Association: Minnesota**
490 Concordia Avenue — 651-227-8014
St. Paul, MN 55103 — info@lungmn.org
www.lung.org

Mississippi

49 **American Lung Association: Mississippi**
438 Katherine Drive — 601-206-5810
Flowood, MS 39232 — www.lung.org

Missouri

50 **American Lung Association: Missouri**
7745 Carondelet Avenue — 314-627-5505
Clayton, MO 63105 — www.lung.org

Montana

51 **American Lung Association: Montana**
c/o American Lung Association — 206-441-5100
Seattle, WA 98109 — infomtp@lung.org
www.lung.org

Nebraska

52 **American Lung Association: Nebraska**
11225 Davenport Street — 402-502-4950
Omaha, NE 68154 — www.lung.org

Nevada

53 **American Lung Association: Nevada**
3552 W Cheyenne Avenue — 702-431-3590
North Las Vegas, NV 89032 — www.lung.org

New Hampshire

54 **American Lung Association: New Hampshire**
36 Maplewood Avenue — 603-369-3977
Portsmouth, NH 03801 — www.lung.org

New Jersey

55 **American Lung Association: New Jersey**
PO Box 10188 — 908-685-8040
Newark, NJ 07101 — jgrinwald@lunginfo.org
www.lung.org

New Mexico

56 **American Lung Association: New Mexico**
5911 Jefferson Street NE — 505-265-0732
Albuquerque, NM 87109 — www.lung.org

New York

57 **American Lung Association: New York**
21 W 38th Street — 212-938-6889
New York, NY 10018 — www.lung.org

North Carolina

58 **American Lung Association: North Carolina**
514 Daniels Street — 919-792-1641
Raleigh, NC 27605 — alanc-r@lungsc.org
www.lung.org

North Dakota

59 **American Lung Association: North Dakota**
212 N Second Street — 701-354-9719
Bismarck, ND 58501 — www.lung.org

Ohio

60 **American Lung Association: Ohio**
7720 Rivers Edge Drive — 614-279-1700
Columbus, OH 43235 — www.lung.org

Oklahoma

61 **American Lung Association: Oklahoma**
710 W Wilshire Boulevard — 405-748-4674
Oklahoma City, OK 73116 — www.lung.org

Oregon

62 **American Lung Association: Oregon**
16037 SW Upper Boones Ferry Road — 800-732-9339
Tigard, OR 97224 — www.lung.org

Pennsylvania

63 **American Lung Association: Pennsylvania**
Marywood University
Scranton, PA 18509
570-346-1784
adelonti@lunginfo.org
www.lung.org

Rhode Island

64 **American Lung Association: Rhode Island**
260 West Exchange Street
Providence, RI 02903
401-421-6487
www.lung.org

South Carolina

65 **American Lung Association: South Carolina**
2030 North Church Place
Spartanburg, SC 29303
864-764-1777
upstate@lungse.org
www.lung.org

South Dakota

66 **American Lung Association: South Dakota**
108 E 38th Street
Sioux Falls, SD 57105
605-336-7222
www.lung.org

Tennessee

67 **American Lung Association: Tennessee**
One Vantage Way
Nashville, TN 37228
615-329-1151
www.lung.org

Texas

68 **American Lung Association: Texas**
8207 Callaghan Road
San Antonio, TX 78230
210-308-8978
txinfo@lungs.org
www.lung.org

Utah

69 **American Lung Association: Utah**
3920 South 1100 E
Salt Lake City, UT 84124
801-484-4456
www.lung.org

Vermont

70 **American Lung Association: Vermont**
372 Hurricane Lane
Williston, VT 05495
802-876-6500
www.lung.org

Virginia

71 **American Lung Association: Virginia**
1331 Pennsylvania Avenue NW
Washington, DC 20004
202-785-3355
www.lung.org

Washington

72 **American Lung Association: Washington**
5601 6th Avenue
Seattle, WA 98108
206-441-5100
www.lung.org

West Virginia

73 **American Lung Association: West Virginia**
2102 Kanawha Boulevard E
Charleston, WV 25311
304-342-6600
www.lung.org

Wisconsin

74 **American Lung Association: Wisconsin**
13100 W Lisbon Road
Brookfield, WI 53005
262-703-4200
www.lung.org

Wyoming

75 **American Lung Association: Wyoming**
c/o American Lung Association
Seattle, WA 98109
206-441-5100
infomtp@lung.org
www.lung.org

Foundations & Research Centers

76 **American Academy of Allergy, Asthma & Immunology Foundation**
555 East Wells Street
Milwaukee, WI 53202-3823
414-272-6071
lwiensch@aaaai.org
www.aaaaifoundation.org
Funds research in an effort to prevent and cure asthma and allergic/immunologic diseases.
Lee Wiensch, Executive Director
Anne Koenings, Development Manager

77 **American College of Allergy, Asthma & Immunology Foundation**
85 West Algonquin Road
Arlington Heights, IL 60005
847-427-1200
mail@acaai.org
college.acaai.org/acaai-foundation
Funds faculty research grants and travel scholarships.
Richard Weber, President
Stanley Fineman, Vice President

78 **Asthma and Allergy Foundation of America**
8201 Corporate Drive
Landover, MD 20785
202-466-7643
800-727-8462
info@aafa.org
www.aafa.org
The AAFA is a non-profit patient organization dedicated to improving the quality of life for people with asthma and allergies and their caregivers, through education, advocacy, funding, and research.
Richard Murray, Chair
Kenneth Mendez, Chief Executive Officer

79 **Columbia University Irving Center for Clinical Research**
Columbia University
622 West 168th Street
New York, NY 10032
212-305-2071
irving_institute@cumc.columbia.edu
www.columbia.edu/
Multidisciplinary studies of human disease and clinical pharmacology. Areas include arrhythmia control, heart failure, atherosclerosis, nutrition, metabolism, clinical pharmacology, dermatology, endocrinology, hypertension, immunology, mineral metabolism and skeletal disease, neuromuscular disease, physiology, pulmonary disease, pulmonary physiology, reproductive research studies, neurology (including dementia, stroke, and seizure disorders).
Muredach P. Pollinger, Director

80 **Creighton University Allergic Disease Center**
601 N 30th Street
Omaha, NE 68131-0001
402-280-4403
casalej@creighton.edu
medicine.creighton.edu
Robert G Townley, Investigator
Thomas B Casale, Chief

81 **Duke University School of Medicine**
Duke University
PO Box 3854
Durham, NC 27708
919-684-8111
Fax: 919-681-8829
medicine.duke.edu/divisions/cardiology
Multidisciplinary, clinical research into the cause, progression, prevention, control, and cure of human disease. Sample projects have studied immunodeficiency diseases, Alzheimer's disease, food allergy, X-linked hypophosphatemic rickets, and cardiovascular disease.
Manesh Patel, MD, Chief
Nick Nguyen, MHA, Division Administrator

82 **Immune Deficiency Foundation**
110 West Road
Towson, MD 21204-4841
800-296-4433
info@primaryimmune.org
www.primaryimmune.org

A national charitable organization aimed at fighting the primary immune deficiency diseases. The founders included parents of children with primary immune deficiency, immunologists who treat immune deficient patients, and other individuals with an immune deficiency.
John G. Boyle, President & CEO
Kara Moran, Vice President, Communications

83 **Kids with Food Allergies**
4259 W Swamp Road 215-230-5394
Doylestown, PA 18902 awaldron@aafa.org
www.kidswithfoodallergies.org
A division of the Asthma and Allergy Foundation of America, KFA provides support to families with children suffering from food allergies.
Angel Waldron, Senior Communications Manager

84 **Mayo Clinic and Foundation: Division of Allergic Diseases**
Department of Immunology
200 First Street SW 507-284-2511
Rochester, MN 55905 www.mayoclinic.org
Provides a focus for research into the causes prevention and management of allergic diseases.
John H Noseworthy MD, President
William C Rupp MD, Vice President, CEO

85 **National Human Genome Research Institute**
Building 31, Room 4B09 301-402-0911
Bethesda, MD 20892-2152 www.genome.gov
The National Human Genome Research Institute began as the National Center for Human Genome Research (NCHGR), which was established in 1989 to carry out the role of the National Institutes of Health (NIH) in the International Human Genome Project (HGP).
Eric D. Green, M.D., Ph.D., Director
Lawrence Brody, Ph.D., Director, Division of Genomics & Society

86 **National Jewish Center for Immunology and Respiratory Medicine**
Goodman Building Room 611 303-398-1287
Denver, CO 80206 800-423-8891
www.nationaljewish.org
Basic and clinical research into the causes and treatments of asthmatic disorders.
Tom Gart, Chairman
Michael Salem, President & CEO

87 **Nationwide Children's Hospital**
700 Childrens Drive 614-722-2000
Columbus, OH 43205 800-792-8401
www.nationwidechildrens.org
Global referral hospital for pediatric care, specializing in rare diseases and overall population health.

88 **Research Institute of Palo Alto Medical Foundation**
795 El Camino Real 650-326-8120
Palo Alto, CA 94301-2302 www.pamf.org/research
Clinical and general medical sciences research including allergy and immunology disorders.
Jane Risser, Director
Andrea Norcia, Assistant Director

89 **Scripps Research Institute**
10550 N Torrey Pines Road 858-784-1000
La Jolla, CA 92037 www.scripps.edu
William Burfitt, President
Alex Bruner, Executive Vice President and Chief Opera

90 **Texas Children's Allergy and Immunology Clinic**
Clinical Care Center
6701 Fannin Street 832-824-1000
Houston, TX 77030 800-364-5437
pediai@texaschildrenshospital.org
www.texaschildrenshospital.org
Mark A Wallace, President & CEO
Mark W Kline MD, Physician In Chief

91 **University of Cincinnati Department of Pathology & Laboratory Medicine**
234 Goodman Street 513-584-7284
Cincinnati, OH 45219-0533 Fax: 513-584-3892
pathology@uc.edu
pathology.uc.edu
Research to understand the causes of disease and develop treatments for infectious diseases, diabete, obesity and lipid disorders, cancer and cardiovascular diseases.
Dani Zander, MD, Chair of Pathology
Michelle Cooper, Executive Director, Business & Admin

92 **University of Florida: General Clinical Research Center**
University of Florida
1600 SW Archer Road 352-273-5500
Gainesville, FL 32610-0322 888-635-0763
thomprd@ufl.edu
www.med.ufl.edu
Studies on allergies and immunology.
Robert Thompson, Program Director

93 **University of Kansas Allergy and Immunology Clinic**
University of Kansas Medical Center
3901 Rainbow Boulevard 913-588-5000
Kansas City, KS 66160 TTY: 913-588-7963
TDD: 913-588-7963
dstechsc@kumc.edu
www.kumc.edu
This service provides complete evaluation of patients with allergic diseases such as rhinitis and asthma immunological deficiencies food and drug intolerances and autoimmune dysfunctions.
Barbara F Atkinson MD, Executive Vice Chancellor
Shelley Gebar, RN, MHA, Chief of Staff

94 **University of Michigan Montgomery: John M. Sheldon Allergy Society**
Alllergy & Clinical Immunology
24 Frank Lloyd Wright Drive 734-232-2154
Ann Arbor, MI 48106-0380 echoreed@med.umich.edu
www.med.umich.edu/sheldonsociety
Travis A Miller, President

95 **University of Pittsburgh Medical Center**
200 Lothrop Street 412-647-8762
Pittsburgh, PA 15213 800-533-8762
upmc.com
The University of Pittsburgh Medical Center is a health care provider and insurer focused on developing new models of patient-centered care. Its mission is to engage in clinical research, education and innovation to ensure excellence in patient care.
G Nicholas Beckwith III, Chairperson
Jeffrey A Romoff, President and CEO

96 **University of Rochester: Clinical Research Center**
601 Elmwood Avenue 585-275-2907
Rochester, NY 14642-0001 Fax: 585-256-3805
germaine_reinhardt@urmc.rochester.edu
www.urmc.rochester.edu/crc/
Studies of normal tissue functions pertaining to heart diseases.
Nancy M. Bennett, MD, Co-Director
Martin S. Zand, MD, Co-Director

97 **University of Texas Southwestern Medical Center**
5323 Harry Hines Boulevard 214-645-8300
Dallas, TX 75390-9151 www.utsouthwestern.edu
Daniel K Podolsky, MD, President
J. Gregory Fitz, Executive Vice President

98 **University of Texas Southwestern Medical Center at Dallas**
University of Texas Southwestern Medical Center
5323 Harry Hines Boulevard 214-648-3111
Dallas, TX 75390 news@utsouthwestern.edu
www.utsouthwestern.edu
Immunodermatology department researching allergies and immune disorders.
Daniel K Podolsky MD, President

99 **Warren Grant Magnuson Clinical Center**
National Institute of Health

9000 Rockville Pike 301-496-2563
Bethesda, MD 20892 800-411-1222
TTY: 866-411-1010
prpl@mail.cc.nih.gov
www.cc.nih.gov
Established in 1953 as the research hospital of the National Institutes of Health. Designed so that patient care facilities are close to research laboratories so new findings of basic and clinical scientists can be quickly applied to the treatment of patients. Upon referral by physicians, patients are admitted to NIH clinical studies.
Michael J Klag MD, Chair
David K Henderson MD, Clinical Director

100 **Washington University School of Medicine**
660 S Euclid Avenue 314-362-5000
St. Louis, MO 63110-1016 www.medicine.wustl.edu
Washington University School of Medicine is a leader in improving human health throughout the world. As noted leaders in patient care, research and education, our outstanding faculty members have contributed many discoveries and innovations to the field of science since the founding of the School of Medicine in 1891. The School of Medicine is one of seven schools of Washington University in St. Louis.
David H. Perlmutter, M.D, Dean

Support Groups & Hotlines

101 **ASTHMA Hotline**
American Academy of Allergy, Asthma and Immunology
2275 East Bayshore Road 650-328-3123
Palo Alto, CA 53202 800-822-2762
www.aaai.org
Referral line offering information on allergy and asthma treatments, referrals to an allergy/immunology specialist, lay organization or support groups across the country.

102 **National Health Information Center**
Office of Disease Prevention & Health Promotion
1101 Wootton Pkwy Fax: 240-453-8281
Rockville, MD 20852 odphpinfo@hhs.gov
www.health.gov/nhic
Supports public health education by maintaining a calendar of National Health Observances; helps connect consumers and health professionals to organizations that can best answer questions and provide up-to-date contact information from reliable sources; updates on a yearly basis toll-free numbers for health information, Federal health clearinghouses and info centers.
Don Wright, MD, MPH, Director

Journals

103 **Allergy & Asthma Today**
Allergy & Asthma Network
8229 Boone Boulevard 800-878-4403
Vienna, VA 22182 www.allergyasthmanetwork.org
Medically reviewed magazine for people living with asthma, allergies and other respiratory conditions. Free with Allergy & Asthma Network membership.
40 pages

104 **Food & Nutrition**
120 South Riverside Plaza 312-899-0040
Chicago, IL 60606-6995 800-877-1600
foodandnutrition@eatright.org
www.eatright.org
Formerly the ADA Times, Food & Nutrition is the member and professional magazine of the Academy of Nutrition & Dietetics.

105 **Food Allergy News**
Food Allergy and Anaphylaxis Network
7901 Jones Branch Dr. 703-691-3179
McLean, VA 22102-2208 800-929-4040
faan@foodallergy.org
www.foodallergy.org
Contains allergy free recipes, practical tips such as birthday party, trick-or-treating and travel tips, a dietitian's column, medical information and product information.
12 pages
James R. Baker, Jr., MD, CEO
Donna McKelvey, Senior VP and Chief Development Officer

106 **Journal of the Academy of Nutrition and Dietetics**
120 South Riverside Plaza 312-899-4831
Chicago, IL 60606-6995 journal@eatright.org
www.eatright.org
Official research publication of the Academy of Nutrition and Dietetics.

107 **MA Report**
Allergy and Asthma Network/Mothers of Asthmatics
8229 Boone Boulevard 703-641-9595
Vienna, VA 22182 800-878-4403
editor@aanma.org
www.allergyasthmanetwork.org
Provides up-to-date medical news, emotional support and practical strategies for overcoming asthma and allergies.
8 pages

108 **Understanding Anaphylaxis**
Allergy & Asthma Network
8229 Boone Boulevard 800-878-4403
Vienna, VA 22182 www.allergyasthmanetwork.org
Magazine focusing on how to recognize and prevent anaphylaxis.
40 pages

Digital Resources

109 **Advice From Your Allergist**
American College of Allergy & Immunology
85 W Algonguin Road 847-359-2800
Alrlington Heights, IL 60005 www.allergy.mcg.edu
Offers information on the effects, triggers and causes of allergies including house dust, pets, hay fever, hives and exercise.

110 **Alexander, the Elephant Who Couldn't Eat Peanuts**
Food Allergy and Anaphylaxis Network
7901 Jones Branch Dr. 800-929-4040
McLean, VA 22102-3309 www.foodallergy.org
Helps children cope with their own allergies and teach other children about tolerance. Both videos combine colorful animation with interviews of real-life children with food allergies who talk about their experiences.
James R. Baker, Jr., MD, CEO
Donna McKelvey, Senior VP and Chief Development Officer

111 **Allergic Rhinitis**
American Academy of Allergy, Asthma and Immunology
555 East Wells Street 414-272-6071
Milwaukee, WI 53202-3889 800-822-2762
www.aaaai.org
Allergic rhinitis, often called hay fever, affects the quality of life of millions of Americans. This video covers the causes and symptoms of seasonal and chronic allergic rhinitis, as well as environmental controls and treatments.

112 **Allergic Rhinitis: Nothing to Sneeze At!**
Asthma and Allergy Foundation of America
8201 Corporate Drive 202-466-7643
Landover, MD 20785-2330 800-727-8462
info@aafa.org
www.aafa.org
The basics of allergic rhinitis, with a touch of humor. Common allergens, environmental control, skin testing and immunotherapy medications.

113 **Allergic Skin Reactions**
American Academy of Allergy, Asthma and Immunology
555 East Wells Street 414-272-6071
Milwaukee, WI 53202-3889 800-822-2762
www.aaaai.org
In some people, allergy symptoms include itching redness, rashes, or hives. This video describes the symptoms, triggers, and treat-

ment for common skin reactions such as dermatitis, hives and angioedema.

114 **An Overview of Allergy**
American College of Allergy & Immunology
800 E NW Highway 847-359-2800
Palatine, IL 60067-6580
Strengthen relationships with patients by providing them with the essential information they need.

115 **Immunotherapy**
American Academy of Allergy, Asthma and Immunology
555 East Wells Street 414-272-6071
Milwaukee, WI 53202-3889 800-822-2762
www.aaaai.org
Immunotherapy, of allergy shots, is a long-term allergy and asthma treatment program that helps control allergic symptoms and reduces the need for medications. Learn more about immunotherapy through this video, which includes information on allergy testing and how your allergist determines if immunotherapy is right for you.

116 **Sinusitis and Sinus Surgery**
Milner-Fenwick
119 Lakefront Drive 410-252-1700
Hunt Valley, MD 21030-3100 800-432-8433
mail@milner-fenwick.com
www.milner-fenwick.com
Discusses sinusitis symptoms, causes, evaluation and treatments. Animation depicts how sinuses function and how irritants, allergies, colds or structural abnormalities cause sinus blockages. Also explains the role of medical therapy and irrigation in managing acute sinusitis.
Dolores McKee, Advertising Director

117 **Stinging Insect Allergy**
American Academy of Allergy, Asthma and Immunology
555 East Wells Street 414-272-6071
Milwaukee, WI 53202-3889 800-822-2762
www.aaaai.org
Although many people are afraid of stinging insects such as bees, the stings of these insects actually cause some people to have serious allergic reactions. This video tells how to recognize and avoid stinging insects, what to do if you are stung and how to identify symptoms of an allergic reaction and get medical help.

118 **Understanding Allergic Reactions**
American Academy of Allergy, Asthma and Immunology
555 East Wells Street 414-272-6071
Milwaukee, WI 53202-3889 800-822-2762
www.aaaai.org
During an allergic reaction, your body responds to a substance generally considered harmless to most people. This video portrays what happens in you body's immune system during an allergic reaction, how to avoid allergic substances, and methods your allergist uses to treat your allergies.

Web Sites

119 **Academy of Nutrition & Dietetics**
www.eatright.org
Offers information and support to allergy sufferers. Serves the public through the promotion of optimal nutrition, health, and well-being. Formerly the American Dietetic Association.

120 **Allergy & Asthma Network**
www.allergyasthmanetwork.org
Non-profit membership organization dedicated to eliminating suffering and death due to asthma, allergies and related conditions through education, advocacy, community outreach, and research.

121 **American Academy of Allergy, Asthma & Immunology**
www.aaaai.org
Strives to serve the public through information on asthma and allergies, as well as referrals to allergists.

122 **American College of Allergy, Asthma & Immunology**
www.acaai.org
Focuses on research and public awareness of allergies, asthma, and immunology. Distributes informational brochures and pamphlets, offers referrals and counseling services, as well as patient care.

123 **Asthma and Allergy Foundation of America**
www.aafa.org
The AAFA is a non-profit patient organization dedicated to improving the quality of life for people with asthma and allergies and their caregivers, through education, advocacy, funding, and research.

124 **Birth Defect Research for Children, Inc.**
www.birthdefects.org
Provides parents and expectant parents with information about birth defects and support services for their children

125 **Dietary Guidelines for Americans**
www.dietaryguidelines.gov
Publishes the Dietary Guidelines for Americans, a guide providing nutritional advice to promote health and prevent disease. Updated versions of the Dietary Guidelines are released by the US Departments of Agriculture (USDA) and Health & Human Services (HHS) every five years.

126 **Everyday Health**
www.everydayhealth.com
Provides evidence-based health information from physicians and healthcare providers.

127 **FamilyDoctor.org**
www.familydoctor.org
Medical advice and information provided by the American Academy of Family Physicians. Resources include a medical dictionary, a symptom checker tool, a BMI calculator, and medication information.

128 **Food Allergy Research & Education**
www.foodallergy.org
FARE aims to increase public awareness about food allergies and anaphylaxis, advance research, and provide education, emotional support and coping strategies to patients. It also serves as the communication link between the food industry, the government and the airline industry.

129 **Healing Well**
www.healingwell.com
A social network and support community for patients, caregivers, and families coping with the daily struggles of diseases, disorders and chronic illness.

130 **Health Finder**
www.healthfinder.gov
Government website where individuals can find information and tools to hel you and those you care about stay healthy.

131 **Healthline**
www.healthline.com
Provides medical and health articles and information.

132 **Healthlink USA**
www.healthlinkusa.com
Health information concerning treatment, cures, prevention, diagnosis, risk factors, research, support groups, email lists, personal stories and much more. Updated regularly.

133 **Immune Deficiency Foundation**
www.primaryimmune.org
The national patient organization dedicated to improving the diagnosis, treatment and quality of life of persons with primary immunodeficiency diseases through advocacy, education and research.

134 **MedicineNet**
www.medicinenet.com
An online resource for consumers providing easy-to-read, authoritative medical and health information.

135 **MedlinePlus**
www.medlineplus.gov
A service of the National Library of Medicine, MedlinePlus is an online resource providing health and wellness information in both English and Spanish.

136 **Medscape**

www.medscape.com

Medscape offers specialists, primary care physicians, and other health professionals the Web's most robust and integrated medical information and educational tools.

137 **MyPlate**

www.myplate.gov

Created and managed by the US Department of Agriculture's Center for Nutrition Policy & Promotion, MyPlate is a dietary guide providing resources and recipes to promote healthy eating for all Americans.

138 **Nutrition.gov**

www.nutrition.gov

Sponsored by the United States Department of Agriculture (USDA), Nutrition.gov offers information on topics in food and nutrition, including healthy eating, physical activity, and food safety.

139 **Science Daily**

www.sciencedaily.com

Provides information on the latest news and research in science, health, the environment, and technology.

140 **The Nutrition Source**

hsph.harvard.edu/nutritionsource

From the Harvard T.H. Chan School of Public Health, The Nutrition Source provides news, information, and guidance for nutrition and healthy eating.

141 **UnlockFood**

www.unlockfood.ca

A website from Dietitians of Canada. Provides videos, recipes, and information on food and nutrition, as well as helps Canadians connect with a dietitian.

142 **Verywell**

www.verywellhealth.com

Offers health, medicine, and wellness information from health professionals.

143 **WebMD**

www.webmd.com

Provides credible information, supportive communities, and in-depth reference material about health subjects. A source for original and timely health information as well as material from well known content providers.

144 **World Health Organization**

www.who.int

An agency of the United Nations, World Health Organization (WHO) serves to promote global health. The WHO website provides fact sheets, publications, media, and other resources on various health topics.

DIABETES (TYPE 2)

The most common form of diabetes is type 2 diabetes, in which the body is unable to use insulin properly. Insulin regulates blood sugar levels after eating. In a healthy body, carbohydrates such as bread and pasta are broken down into sugar, also referred to as glucose, the body's major source of energy. In type 2 diabetes, the pancreas may not produce enough insulin to handle the glucose load after eating and the body's cells may not take in enough sugar to function. Being overweight and not getting enough activity may contribute to type 2 diabetes that generally develops in older adults. There is no cure for type 2 diabetes but losing weight, eating healthy foods and getting exercise may help manage the disease. If these activities don't manage the blood sugar levels, diabetes medications or insulin injections may be needed. A simple blood test to measure blood sugar and A1C can diagnose pre-diabetes or type 2 diabetes.

One in three American adults are considered pre-diabetic, meaning that, without intervention, they are likely to develop type 2 diabetes. The symptoms of type 2 diabetes are slow to develop and may occur over years. Symptoms of increased thirst, excessive hunger, frequent urination, unexplained weight loss and fatigue are usually the first noticeable symptoms — hopefully enough for an individual to see a doctor for a diagnostic work-up. If ignored, additional symptoms such as blurred vision, sores that are slow to heal, frequent infections, tingling and numbness in the hands and feet and discolored skin may develop.

Insulin is produced by beta cells in the pancreas. When the pancreas does not produce enough insulin to regulate how the body uses sugar, type 2 diabetes may occur. A second cause of type 2 diabetes is related to cells, such as those in the muscles, fat and liver not interacting appropriately with insulin. When this occurs, cells don't take in enough glucose for the energy needed to function. After eating, the glucose in the bloodstream is absorbed into cells with the help of insulin. Liver cells store glucose as glycogen and then converts glycogen to glucose and releases it as the body needs it. In type 2 diabetes, the process of food providing sugar for energy does not work well. As a result, the body demands more insulin to function, and the pancreas, working overtime to try to keep up production of insulin, will eventually shut down. The mechanism of why this happens is not known, but obesity and lack of exercise are major contributing factors.

Nutrition plays a key role in both preventing type 2 diabetes and managing the early stages of the disease. Being overweight or obese is the most significant risk factor for developing type 2 diabetes. Poor nutrition coupled with low levels of high-density lipoprotein (HDL), the good cholesterol, inactivity, family history of the disease, age over 45, and being of non-white race all increase the risk of developing type 2 diabetes. As the pancreas tries to provide sufficient insulin, especially if calorie intake is higher than needed resulting in weight gain, the blood sugar level may be higher than normal but not enough to be diagnosed with type 2 disease. This condition is pre-diabetes and is a warning sign that if ignored, type 2 diabetes may develop. There are also pregnancy related risks, and risks related to polycystic ovary disease.

Weight management, whether maintaining a healthy weight or losing weight to get to a healthy weight, is needed to both prevent and manage type 2 diabetes. When fat is stored around the abdomen rather than other body locations such as hips or thighs, the risk is greater. The goal is a body weight that makes you feel better and keeps blood sugar levels within normal limits. You can calculate your weight category — and therefore your risk factor — using your body mass index (BMI) or your waist circumference. A readily available BMI chart on the Centers for Disease Control website uses height and weight to measure BMI — 18.5 to 24.9 is normal, 25-29.9 is overweight, and 30 or greater is obese. Using waist circumference, a man's waist above 40 inches, and a woman's waist above 35 inches raises the risk of development of the disease. Losing just 5-10 percent of body weight can improve health and make you feel better.

Two important things to remember when following a weight-loss diet: it needs to be based on healthy foods, and it needs to be an eating plan you can follow for life. It may involve cutting out sugary foods and drinks and eating more protein. Increasing vegetables and fruits may decrease your appetite for processed or junk food. Your eating plan must meet your lifestyle and caloric needs based on your level of activity. For example, a busy working person may eat more meals away from home so learning how to select healthy restaurant choices is important. A mother cooking for her family will need to find foods that are both healthy and that her family will eat.

Talking to your doctor, a registered dietician or diabetes educator will help if you are concerned about your risk for type 2 diabetes or have been diagnosed with prediabetes. You can start by taking these simple steps: control what foods you have available at work or home; read labels for calories, sugar content and nutrients; avoid buffets, fried foods and fast food; eat healthy snacks between meals to avoid overeating at meals; schedule time to exercise; get enough sleep; keep a food journal.

If you are diagnosed with type 2 diabetes, a doctor will determine if you can attempt to manage your disease with weight management and increased exercise or if you need medications or insulin. A professional will also help you with an eating plan that will provide sufficient nutrition to balance the requirements of the disease or treatment. Talk with your physician about your risk of type 2 diabetes and what actions are appropriate to decrease your risk of developing the disease, including a healthy diet and appropriate exercise.

See page 229 for more information on type 2 diabetes.

Agencies & Associations

146 **American Association of Clinical Endocrinology**
904-353-7878
800-393-2223
www.aace.com
A professional community of physicians specializing in endocrinology, diabetes, and metabolism. Referrals and patient information available.
Paul Markowski, Chief Executive Officer
Tom Conway, Chief Financial Officer

147 **American Diabetes Association**
2451 Crystal Drive 800-342-2383
Arlington, VA 22202 askada@diabetes.org
www.diabetes.org
Voluntary organization concerned with diabetes and its complications. The mission of the organization is to prevent and cure diabetes and to improve the lives of persons with diabetes. Offers a network of offices nationwide.
Tracey D. Brown, MBA, BChE, Chief Executive Officer
Charles Henderson, Chief Development Officer

148 **Association of Diabetes Care & Education Specialists**
125 South Wacker Drive 800-338-3633
Chicago, IL 60606 www.diabeteseducator.org
An independent, multidisciplinary organization of health professionals involved in teaching persons with diabetes. The mission is to enhance the competence of health professionals who teach persons with diabetes, advance the specialty practice of diabetes education, and to improve the quality of diabetes education and care for all those affected by diabetes.
Charles Macfarlane, Chief Executive Officer
Brad Neal, Chief Administrative Officer

149 **Centers for Medicare & Medicaid Services**
7500 Security Boulevard www.cms.gov
Baltimore, MD 21244
U.S. federal agency which administers Medicare, Medicaid, and the State Children's Health Insurance Program.
Chiquita Brooks-LaSure, Administrator
Jonathan Blum, COO

150 **Certification Board for Diabetes Care & Education**
330 E Algonquin Road 847-228-9795
Arlington Heights, IL 60005 info@ncbde.org
www.ncbde.org
The CBDCE is dedicated to promoting excellence in the field of diabetes education through the development, maintenance, and protection of the certified Diabetes Educator credential and the certification process.
Ben Klein, Chair
Sheryl Traficano, Chief Executive Officer

151 **Diabetes Action Network**
National Federation of the Blind
200 East Wells Street 573-268-6989
Baltimore, MD 21230 www.nfb.org
DAN is a division of the National Federation of the Blind. It is a support and information organization of persons losing vision due to diabetes. Provides personal contact and resource information with other blind diabetics about non-visual techniques of independently managing diabetes and monitoring glucose levels.
Debbie Wunder, President

152 **Diabetes Care and Education**
Academy of Nutrition & Dietetics
120 South Riverside Plaza www.dce.org
Chicago, IL 60606
Responds to the needs of diabetes organizations and industry with regard to diabetes nutrition issues, promotes clinical and educational research to imrpove diabetes management, develop guideleines for the nutritional management of diabetes and maintain a network of practicing dieticians available for consultation services to health professionals and people with diabetes.
Janice Macleod, Chair
Laura Russell, Secretary

153 **Endocrine Society**
2055 L Street NW 202-971-3636
Washington, DC 20036 888-363-6274
info@endocrine.org
www.endocrine.org
Mission is to promote excellence in research, education, and the clinical practice endocrinology.
Kate Fryer, Chief Executive Officer
Paul Hedrick, Chief Financial Officer

154 **International Society of Endocrinology**
625 N North Court www.isendo.org
Palatine, IL 60067
Serves to advance education, science, and patient care in endocrinology worldwide.
Margaret Wierman, Chair
Helen van Oers, Executive Director

155 **National Eye Institute**
31 Center Drive 301-496-5248
Bethesda, MD 20892 2020@nei.nih.gov
nei.nih.gov
Mission is to promote public and professional awareness of the importance of diagnosis and treatment of diabetic eye disease. NEHEP is a partnership with various public and private organizations that plan and implemtn eye health education programs targeted to a variety of high-risk audiences.
Michael F. Chiang, Director
Santa Tumminia, Deputy Director

156 **National Institute of Diabetes & Digestive & Kidney Diseases**
9000 Rockville Pike 800-860-8747
Bethesda, MD 20892 TTY: 866-569-1162
healthinfo@niddk.nih.gov
www.niddk.nih.gov
Research areas include diabetes, digestive diseases, endocrine and metabolic diseases, hematologic diseases, kidney disease, liver disease, urologic diseases, as well as matters relating to nutrition and obesity.
Griffin P. Rodgers, MD, MACP, Director
Gregory Germino, MD, Deputy Director

157 **National Institute of General Medical Sciences**
45 Center Drive 301-496-7301
Bethesda, MD 20892-6200 info@nigms.nih.gov
www.nigms.nih.gov
The National Institute of General Medical Sciences (NIGMS) supports basic research that increases understanding of biological processes and lays the foundation for advances in disease diagnosis, treatment and prevention.
Jon R. Lorsch, PhD, Director
Dorit Zuk, PhD, Acting Deputy Director

158 **Nurse Practitioners in Women's Health**
PO Box 15837 202-543-9693
Washington, DC 20003 info@npwh.org
www.npwh.org
Ensures the delivery and accessibility of primary and specialty healthcare to women of all ages by women's health and women's health focused nurse practitioners.
Heather L. Maurer, CEO
Donna Ruth, Director, Education

159 **Nutrition Science Initiative**
6020 Cornerstone Court W 858-914-5400
San Diego, CA 92121 www.nusi.org
Nutrition Science Initiative (NuSI) works to combat obesity, diabetes, and related metabolic diseases by supporting and improving the quality of nutrition research.
Gary Taubes, Chair

160 **Pediatric Endocrine Society**
6728 Old McLean Village Drive 703-718-6023
McLean, VA 22101 Fax: 703-556-8729
info@pedsendo.org
www.pedsendo.org
Works to advance the endocrine health of children and adolescents.
Maureen Thompson, Executive Director
Jessica Widing, Associate Executive Director

Alabama

161 **American Diabetes Association: Alabama**
3918 Montclair Rd
Birmingham, AL 35213
205-870-5172
800-342-2383
Fax: 205-879-2903
www.diabetes.org

Stephanie Willis, Market Director

Alaska

162 **American Diabetes Association: Alaska**
801 W Fireweed Lane
Anchorage, AK 99503
907-272-1424
800-342-2383
Fax: 907-272-1428
www.diabetes.org

Michelle Cassano, Executive Director
Cyrese Gorrin, Manager, Development

Arizona

163 **American Diabetes Association: Arizona**
5333 N 7th St
Phoenix, AZ 85014
602-861-4731
800-342-2383
Fax: 602-995-1344
www.diabetes.org

Anne Dennis, Area Director
Thomas Donohue, Regional Director, Proj. Mngmnt.

Arkansas

164 **American Diabetes Association: Arkansas**
320 Executive Court
Little Rock, AR 72205
501-221-7444
800-342-2383
Fax: 501-221-3138
www.diabetes.org

Rick Selig, Director
Becki Swindell, Manager

California

165 **American Diabetes Association: No. California**
1970 Broadway
Oakland, CA 94612
510-654-4499
800-342-2383
Fax: 510-893-2376
www.diabetes.org

Michael Chae, Executive Director
Tom Hall, Director, Tour de Cure

166 **American Diabetes Association: So. California**
611 Wilshire Boulevard
Los Angeles, CA 90017
323-966-2890
800-342-2383
Fax: 213-489-4375
www.diabetes.org

Cassie Shafer, Regional Director, So. Calif.
Jennifer Campbell, Area Director

167 **Diabetes Society of Santa Clara Valley**
4040 Moorpark Avenue
San Jose, CA 95117
408-241-1922
888-DIA-BETE
www.diabetes.org

Douglas Metz DPM/MPH, Executive Director
Thomas Smith, Program/Camp Director

Colorado

168 **American Diabetes Association: Colorado**
2460 W 26th Avenue
Denver, CO 80211
720-855-1102
800-342-2383
Fax: 720-855-1302
www.diabetes.org

Sue Glass, Vice President, Western Division
Jennifer Klass, Area Director, CO/MT/WY

Connecticut

169 **American Diabetes Association: Connecticut & Western Massachusetts**
2080 Silas Deane Highway
Rocky Hill, CT 06067
203-639-0385
800-342-2383
Fax: 860-257-4320
www.diabetes.org

Patti Clair, Associate Director
Hope Jays, Manager, Special Events

District of Columbia

170 **American Diabetes Association: District of Columbia**
1400 16th Street NW
Washington, DC 20036
202-331-8303
800-342-2383
Fax: 202-331-1402
www.diabetes.org

Mary Merritt, Executive Director
Kim Cameron, Associate Director, Tour de Cure

Florida

171 **American Diabetes Association: Central Florida**
2290 Lucien Way
Maitland, FL 32751
407-660-1926
800-342-2383
Fax: 407-660-1080
www.diabetes.org

Carly Zampiceni, Regional Director, Florida
Nicole Donelson, Area Director, Ctrl & SW Florida

Georgia

172 **American Diabetes Association: Georgia**
Harris Tower
233 Peachtree Street
Atlanta, GA 30303
404-320-7100
800-342-2383
Fax: 404-581-1904
www.diabetes.org

Rena Cozart, Regional Director, South
Tiffany Kirkland, Area Director, Georgia

Hawaii

173 **American Diabetes Association: Hawaii**
Pioneer Plaza
Honolulu, HI 96813
808-947-5979
800-342-2383
Fax: 808-546-7502
www.diabetes.org

Leslie Lam, Executive Director
Danielle Tuata, Events Director

Iowa

174 **American Diabetes Association: Iowa**
317 7th Avenue SE
Cedar Rapids, IA 52401
319-247-5124
800-342-2383
Fax: 319-247-5125
www.diabetes.org

Kansas

175 **American Diabetes Association: Kansas**
608 W Douglas Avenue
Wichita, KS 67203
316-684-6091
800-342-2383
www.diabetes.org

Kentucky

176 **American Diabetes Association: Kentucky**
161 St. Matthews Avenue
Louisville, KY 40207
502-452-6072
800-342-2383
Fax: 502-893-2698
www.diabetes.org

Louisiana

177 **American Diabetes Association: Louisiana & Mississippi**
2424 Edenborn Avenue 888-342-2383
Metairie, LA 70001 Fax: 504-834-2797
www.diabetes.org

John Guzzardo, Executive Director

Maryland

178 **American Diabetes Association: Maryland**
2002 Clipper Park Road 410-265-0075
Baltimore, MD 21211 800-342-2383
Fax: 410-235-4048
www.diabetes.org

Kathy Rogers, Executive Director

Massachusetts

179 **American Diabetes Association: Maine, Massachusetts, New Hampshire, Rhode Isl.**
10 Speen Street 617-482-4580
Framingham, MA 01701 800-342-2383
Fax: 508-626-4260
www.diabetes.org

Chris Boynton, Executive Director, New England

Michigan

180 **American Diabetes Association: Michigan**
300 Galleria Officentre 248-433-3830
Southfield, MI 48034 800-342-2383
Fax: 248-352-0261
www.diabetes.org

Debbie O'Leary, Sr. Executive Director

Minnesota

181 **American Diabetes Association: Minnesota & North Dakota**
8000 W 78th Street 763-593-5333
Edina, MN 55439 800-342-2383
Fax: 952-582-9000
www.diabetes.org

David Becker, Executive Director

Missouri

182 **American Diabetes Association: Missouri**
2833-B East Battlefield Road 417-890-8400
Springfield, MO 65804 800-342-2383
Fax: 417-890-8484
www.diabetes.org

Renee Steele-Paulsell, Regional Director

Montana

183 **American Diabetes Association: Montana**
112 S First Avenue 406-256-0616
Laurel, MT 59044 800-342-2383
Fax: 877-684-7059
www.diabetes.org

Nebraska

184 **American Diabetes Association: Nebraska & South Dakota**
14216 Dayton Circle 402-571-1101
Omaha, NE 68137 800-342-2383
Fax: 402-572-8141
www.diabetes.org

Doug Bickford, Executive Director
Ellen Myer, Manager, Tour de Cure (Nebraska)

New Jersey

185 **American Diabetes Association: New Jersey**
CenterPointe II 732-469-7979
Bridgewater, NJ 08807 800-342-2383
Fax: 908-722-4887
www.diabetes.org

Denise Andersen, Regional Director

New York

186 **American Diabetes Association: New York**
333 7th Avenue 212-725-4925
New York, NY 10001 800-342-2383
Fax: 212-725-8916
www.diabetes.org

Elaine Curran, VP, Development
Gina Ihne, Director, Corp. Development

North Carolina

187 **American Diabetes Association: North Carolina**
1300 Baxter Street 704-373-9111
Charlotte, NC 28204 800-342-2383
Fax: 704-373-9113
www.diabetes.org

Dianne Roth, Executive Director

Ohio

188 **American Diabetes Association: Central Ohio**
1900 Crown Park Court 614-436-1917
Columbus, OH 43235 800-342-2383
Fax: 614-221-0348
www.diabetes.org

Lori Butterfield, Executive Director, Greater Ohio
William Hesse, Campaign Manager, Tour de Cure

189 **American Diabetes Association: Northeast Ohio**
4500 Rockside Road 216-328-9989
Independence, OH 44131 800-342-2383
Fax: 216-328-0007
www.diabetes.org

Lori Butterfield, Executive Director, Greater Ohio

Oklahoma

190 **American Diabetes Association: Oklahoma**
4334 NW Expressway 405-840-3881
Oklahoma City, OK 73116 800-342-2383
Fax: 405-810-8427
www.diabetes.org

Oregon

191 **American Diabetes Association: Oregon**
4380 SW Macadam Avenue 503-736-2770
Portland, OR 97239 800-342-2383
Fax: 503-227-2090
www.diabetes.org

Andrea Bruno, Regional Director, Northwest
Alison Bruun, Market Director

Pennsylvania

192 **American Diabetes Association: Eastern Pennsylvania & Delaware**
150 Monument Road 610-828-5003
Philadelphia, PA 19004 800-342-2383
Fax: 610-667-1761
bala_office@diabetes.org
www.diabetes.org

Denise Andersen, Regional Director

193 **American Diabetes Association: Western Pennsylvania**
100 W Station Square Drive 412-824-1181
Pittsburgh, PA 15219 800-342-2383
Fax: 412-471-1315
pittsburgh@diabetes.org
www.diabetes.org
Julie Keller Heverly, Executive Director

Tennessee

194 **American Diabetes Association: Tennessee**
220 Great Circle Road 615-298-3066
Nashville, TN 37228 800-342-2383
Fax: 615-271-2151
www.diabetes.org

Texas

195 **American Diabetes Association: Central Texas**
Building 2 512-472-9838
Austin, TX 78759 800-342-2383
Fax: 512-472-9672
ctxinfo@diabetes.org
www.diabetes.org
Michelle Peacock, Executive Director, Ctrl. Texas

196 **American Diabetes Association: North Texas**
4100 Alpha Road 972-392-1181
Dallas, TX 75244 800-342-2383
Fax: 972-392-1366
www.diabetes.org
Quin Neal, Sr. Exec. Director, North Texas

197 **American Diabetes Association: West Texas & New Mexico**
8008 Slide Road 806-794-0691
Lubbock, TX 79424 800-342-2383
Fax: 806-794-1394
www.diabetes.org

Utah

198 **American Diabetes Association: Utah & Nevada**
4424 South 700 East 801-363-3024
Salt Lake City, UT 84107 800-342-2383
Fax: 801-261-3005
www.diabetes.org
Jeff Bird, Market Director, UT/NV

Virginia

199 **American Diabetes Association: Virginia**
Greenbrier Tower II 757-424-6662
Chesapeake, VA 23320 800-342-2383
Fax: 757-420-0490
www.diabetes.org
Deanie Eldridge, Executive Director
Amie Holman, Associate Director, Tour de Cure

Washington

200 **American Diabetes Association: Washington**
2815 Eastlake Avenue E 206-282-4616
Seattle, WA 98102 800-342-2383
Fax: 206-282-4732
www.diabetes.org
Paul Tobin, Market Director

West Virginia

201 **American Diabetes Association: West Virginia**
PO Box 21903 859-268-9129
Lexington, KY 40522 800-342-2383
Fax: 502-714-7313
www.diabetes.org

Wisconsin

202 **American Diabetes Association: Wisconsin**
375 Bishop's Way 414-778-5500
Brookfield, WI 53005 800-342-2383
Fax: 262-797-9270
www.diabetes.org

Wyoming

203 **American Diabetes Association: Wyoming**
2460 W 26th Avenue 720-855-1102
Denver, CO 80211 800-342-2383
Fax: 720-855-1302
www.diabetes.org
Sue Glass, Vice President, Western Division
Jennifer Klass, Area Director, CO/MT/WY

Libraries & Resource Centers

204 **Diabetes Control Program**
California Department of Health Services
PO Box 997413 916-552-9888
Sacramento, CA 95899-7413 http://www.caldiabetes.org/
Our mission is to prevent diabetes and its complications in California's diverse communities.
Susan Lopez-Payan, Interim Chief

205 **Division of Diabetes Translation**
National Center for Chronic Disease Prevention
1600 Clifton Rd 800-232-4636
Atlantia, GA 30333-3717 TTY: 888-232-6348
cdcinfo@cdc.gov
www.cdc.gov/diabetes
The Division of Diabetes Translation's (DDT) goal is to reduce the burden of diabetes in the United States. The division works to achieve this goal by combining support for public health-oriented diabetes prevention and control programs (DPCPs) and translating diabetes research findings into widespread clinical and public health practice.

206 **Health Science Library**
Marshall University
1600 Medical Center Drive 304-691-1700
Huntington, WV 25701 www.musom.marshall.edu/library
The Health Sciences Library's primary mission is serving the informational needs of the students, faculty, and staff at Marshall University and the Cabell-Huntington Hospital. The Library also plays an important role in providing information services to hospitals and healthcare professionals in the Huntington and the Tri-State area.
Edward Dzierzak, Director

207 **National Diabetes Information Clearinghouse**
One Information Way 800-860-8747
Bethesda, MD 20892-3560 TTY: 866-8569-116
ndic@info.niddk.nih.gov
diabetes.niddk.nih.gov
To serve as a diabetes informational, educational, and referral resource for health professionals and the public. NDIC is a service of the NIDDK.

Foundations & Research Centers

208 **Barbara Davis Center for Childhood Diabetes**
13001 E 17th Place 303-724-2323
Aurora, CO 80045-6511 www.uchsc.edu/misc/diabetes
Research and educational organization.
Marian Rewers, Clinical Director
George S Eisenbarth, Executive Director

209 **Baylor College of Medicine: Children's General Clinical Research Center**
One Baylor Plaza 713-798-4780
Houston, TX 77030 pedi-webmaster@bcm.edu
www.bcm.edu/pediatrics

Offers research into juvenile aspects of immunology and infectious diseases including diabetes research activities.
Lisa Bomgaars, Medical Director
Mark A Ward, Director

210 **Benaroya Research Institute Virginia Mason Medical Center**
Virginia Mason Medical Center
1201 9th Avenue 206-583-6525
Seattle, WA 98101-2795 info@benaroyaresearch.org
www.benaroyaresearch.org
Immunology and diabetes research.
Robert B Lemon, Chair
Gerald Nepom, Director

211 **Columbia University Irving Center for Clinical Research**
Columbia University
622 West 168th Street 212-305-2071
New York, NY 10032 irving_institute@cumc.columbia.edu
www.columbia.edu/
Multidisciplinary studies of human disease and clinical pharmacology. Areas include arrhythmia control, heart failure, atherosclerosis, nutrition, metabolism, clinical pharmacology, dermatology, endocrinology, hypertension, immunology, mineral metabolism and skeletal disease, neuromuscular disease, physiology, pulmonary disease, pulmonary physiology, reproductive research studies, neurology (including dementia, stroke, and seizure disorders).
Muredach P. Pollinger, Director

212 **Diabetes Education and Research Center The Franklin House**
The Franklin House
PO Box 897 215-829-3426
Philadelphia, PA 19105 www.diabeteseducationandresearchcenter.o
Is a non-profit organization serving the needs of people living in Philadelphia PA and surrounding communities. The goal of the Foundation is to improve the health of people with diabetes.

213 **Diabetes Research and Training Center: University of Alabama at Birmingham**
Department of Medicine
1530 3rd Avenue S 205-934-4011
Birmingham, AL 35294-1150 www.main.uab.edu
The DRTC works to develop and evaluate new models of diabetes care and to facilitate translational diabetes research.
Dr Carol Garrison, President
William Ferniany, CEO

214 **Diabetes Youth Foundation of Indiana**
7311 Tousley Drive 317-750-9310
Indianapolis, IN 46256-9212 dyfjulie@yahoo.com
www.dyfofindiana.org
This nonprofit group whose mission is to improve the lives of children with diabetes and their families.
Julie Shutt, Executive Director
Rick Crosslin, Camp Director

215 **Division on Endocrinology Northwestern University Feinberg School**
Northwestern University Feinberg School of Medicin
251 East Huron Street 312-926-6895
Chicago, IL 60611 help@medicine.northwestern.edu
www.medicine.northwestern.edu
Nonprofit organization focusing research activities on endocrinology metabolism nutrition and specializing in diabetes.
Joe Bass, MD, PhD, Chief of the Division of Endocrinology
Grazia Aleppo, MD, Director, Endocrinology Clinical Practic

216 **Endocrinology Research Laboratory Cabrini Medical Center**
Cabrini Medical Center
227 E 19th Street 212-222-7464
New York, NY 10003-7457 www.cabrininy.org
Focuses on the effects of insulin and insulin-like growth factors on human body functions.
Dr Leonid Poretsky, Director

217 **Indiana University: Area Health Education Center**
714 N Senate Avenue 317-278-8893
Indianapolis, IN 46202 ahec@iupui.edu
www.ahec.iupui.edu
A collaborative statewide system for community-based primary health care professions education that fosters the continuing improvement of health care services for all citizens in Indiana.
Richard D Kiovsky, MD, Director
Jonathan C Barclay, Associate Director

218 **Indiana University: Center for Diabetes Research**
340 West 10th Street 317-274-8157
Indianapolis, IN 46202-3082 rconsidi@iupui.edu
www.medicine.iu.edu
Our goal is to promote the training of scientists whose research will develop new understandings of the basis of the disease and its complications and to cultivate basic science research that can speed the discovery of more effective therapies.
Robert Considine, Associate Professor of Medicine
D Craig Brater MD, Dean

219 **Indiana University: Pharmacology Research Laboratory**
Division of Clinical Pharmacology
1001 W 10th Street 317-630-8795
Indianapolis, IN 46202 www.medicine.iupui.edu/clinpharm
We will train highly skilled compassionate and altruistic professionals both generalists and specialists to be future leaders in medical practice academia and industry.
David A Flockhart, Division Director
John T Callaghan, Associate Professor of Medicine

220 **International Diabetes Center at Nicollet**
3800 Park Nicollet Boulevard 952-993-3393
Saint Louis Park, MN 55416-2533 888-825-6315
idcdiabetes@parknicollet.com
www.parknicollet.com/diabetes
Research center which improves the quality of life of individuals with diabetes and those at risk of developing diabetes by undertaking clinical care education research and outreach activities that stimulate and support health.
Richard Berg MD, Executive Director

221 **Joslin Center at University of Maryland Medicine**
22 S Greene Street 800-492-5538
Baltimore, MD 21201 TDD: 800735225800
www.umm.edu/joslindiabetes
The Joslin Center at University of Maryland Medicine meets the highest standards of care for people with diabetes. Its programs reflect a philosophy which have been the hallmark of Joslin's care — a comprehensive team approach to diabetes treatment with programs designed to help children and adults with diabetes take charge of their own health and well-being.
Thomas W Donner, MD, Director

222 **Joslin Diabetes Center**
One Joslin Place 617-732-2400
Boston, MA 02215-5306 800-567-5461
diabetes@joslin.harvard.edu
www.joslin.org
An internationally recognized leader in diabetes and endocrine disease treatment research and patient and professional education affiliated with Harvard Medical School. In addition to its headquarters in Boston's Longwood Medical area Joslin has affiliated treatment centers across the nation. Established in 1898.
John L Brooks, Chairman of the Board
Martin J Abrahamson, Senior VP, Medical Director

223 **Metabolic Research Institute**
1515 N Flagler Drive 561-802-3060
West Palm Beach, FL 33401 www.metabolic-institute.com
The Metabolic Research Institute specializes in clinical studies involving endocrinology disorders complications of endocrinology disorders metabolic problems and selected renal disease.
William A Kaye, Co-Director
Barry Horowitz, Co-Director

224 **Naomi Berrie Diabetes Center at Columbia University Medical Center**
Russ Berrie Medical Science Pavillion
1150 St. Nicholas Avenue 212-851-5494
New York, NY 10032 diabetes@columbia.edu
nbdiabetes.org
The special focus of the Naomi Berrie Diabetes Center is on families — a concept that differentiates it from almost every other dia-

betes treatment facility in America. People with diabetes are strongly encouraged to involve their entire families in the treatment process.
Robin Goland, MD, Co-Director
Rudolph Liebel, Co-Director

225 **Sansum Diabetes Research Institute**
2219 Bath Street 805-682-7638
Santa Barbara, CA 93105-4321 info@sansum.org
www.sansum.org
A research institute devoted to the prevention treatment and cure of diabetes.
Lois Jovanovich, CEO & Chief Scientific Officer
Wendy Bevier, Associate Investigator

226 **Schulze Diabetes Institute**
University of Minnesota
420 Delaware Street SE 612-626-3016
Minneapolis, MN 55455 diitinfo@umn.edu
www.med.umn.edu
Formerly the Diabetes Institute for Immunology and Transplantation
David Sutherland MD, PhD, Director
Bernard Hering, Director

227 **Tallahassee Memorial Diabetes Center**
Tallahassee Memorial Health Care
1300 Miccosukee Road 850-431-5404
Tallahassee, FL 32308 800-662-4278
www.tmh.org/diabetes
TMH provides comprehensive, patient-centered services to both children and adults. The Diabetes Center uses a team approach that involves the patient, physicians, nurse educators, registered dietitians with access to a diabetes counselor and registered pharmacists and social worker.
Richard M Bergenstal, MD, Medical Director

228 **University of Chicago: Comprehensive Diabetes Center**
5841 S Maryland Avenue 773-702-2371
Chicago, IL 60637 800-989-6740
diabetes@uchospitals.edu
www.kovlerdiabetescenter.org
The University of Chicago Kovler Diabetes Center offers a unique fully comprehensive approach to diagnosing and treating diabetes. Focuses on children adolescents and adults with diabetes as well as individuals at the highest risk for serious complications.
Louis H Philipson, Medical Director
Christopher Rhodes, Kovler Diabetes Center Pediatric Program

229 **University of Cincinnati Department of Pathology & Laboratory Medicine**
234 Goodman Street 513-584-7284
Cincinnati, OH 45219-0533 Fax: 513-584-3892
pathology@uc.edu
pathology.uc.edu
Research to understand the causes of disease and develop treatments for infectious diseases, diabete, obesity and lipid disorders, cancer and cardiovascular diseases.
Dani Zander, MD, Chair of Pathology
Michelle Cooper, Executive Director, Business & Admin

230 **University of Colorado: General Clinical Research Center, Pediatric**
13001 E 17th Place 720-777-2957
Aurora, CO 80045 www.uchsc.edu/pedsgcrc
Focuses on developmental studies and diabetes research.
Ronald J Sokol, Program Director
Philip S Zeitler, Associate Program Director

231 **University of Iowa: Diabetes Research Center**
Department of Internal Medicine
200 Hawkins Drive 319-353-7842
Iowa City, IA 52242 www.int-med.uiowa.edu
The Diabetes Research Center combines the talents of experienced clinical investigators molecular biologists and vascular physiologists in an integrated multidisciplinary approach toward the study and treatment of abnormalities of vascular reactivity which characterize diabetes mellitus.
Ken Kates, Chief Executive Officer
John Swenning, Associate Director

232 **University of Kansas Cray Diabtetes Center**
3901 Rainbow Boulevard 913-588-5000
Kansas City, KS 66160-7376 TTY: 913-588-7963
geaks@kumc.edu
www.kumc.edu
The KU Medical Center is a complex institution whose basic functions include research education patient care and community service involving multiple constituencies at state and national levels.
Barbara Atkinson, Executive Vice Chancellor

233 **University of Massachusetts: Diabetes and Endocrinology Research Center**
55 Lake Avenue N 508-856-8989
Worcester, MA 01655 evelyn.vignola@umassmed.edu
www.umassmed.edu
UMMS has exploded onto the national scene as a major center for research, and in the past four decades, UMMS researchers have made pivotal advances in HIV, cancer, diabetes, infectious disease and in understanding the molecular basis of disease.
Micheal F Collins MD, Senior VP
Michael P Czech, Professor and Chair

234 **University of Miami: Diabetes Research Institute**
200 S Park Road 954-964-4040
Hollywood, FL 33021 800-321-3437
info@drif.org
www.diabetesresearch.org
The Diabetes Research Institute (DRI) is an innovator in many fields of diabetes research but one of its primary strengths lies in islet cell transplantation, a cellular therapy that restores insulin production to normalize blood sugar control.
Thomas D Stern, Chairman
Camillo Ricordi, DRI Scientific Director

235 **University of New Mexico General Clinical Research Center**
University of New Mexico Hospital
The University of New Mexico 505-277-0111
Albuquerque, NM 87131-2240 mburge@salud.unm.edu
hsc.unm.edu/som/gcrc
Diabetes research.
Steve McKernan, CEO
Richard Larson, Vice President for Research

236 **University of Pennsylvania Diabetes and Endocrinology Research Center**
700 Clinical Research Building (CRB 215-898-4365
Philadelphia, PA 19104 www.med.upenn.edu/idom/derc
The Penn Diabetes and Endocrinology Research Center (DERC) participates in the nationwide inter-disciplinary program established over two decades ago by the NIDDK to foster research and training in the areas of diabetes and related endocrine and metabolic disorders.
Mitchell A Lazar, Director
Morris J Birnbaum, Co Director

237 **University of Pittsburgh Medical Center**
200 Lothrop Street 412-647-8762
Pittsburgh, PA 15213 800-533-8762
upmc.com
The University of Pittsburgh Medical Center is a health care provider and insurer focused on developing new models of patient-centered care. Its mission is to engage in clinical research, education and innovation to ensure excellence in patient care.
G Nicholas Beckwith III, Chairperson
Jeffrey A Romoff, President and CEO

238 **University of Tennessee: General Clinical Research Center**
1265 Union Avenue 901-516-2212
Memphis, TN 38104 www.utmem.edu/crc
Congress directed the National Institutes of Health to establish clinical research centers throughout the United States to launch an all-out attack on human diseases.
Bruce S Alpert MD, Program Director
Teresa Carr, Research Nurses

239 **University of Texas General Clinical Research Center**
7400 Merton Minter Boulevard 409-772-1950
San Antonio, TX 78229 public.affairs@utmb.edu
www.utmb.edu/gcrc

Focuses on diabetes and infectious disease research.
Michael Lich MD, Program Director
Garland D Anderson, Principal Investigator

240 **University of Vermont Medical Center**
111 Colchester Avenue 802-847-0000
Burlington, VT 05401 800-358-1144
www.uvmhealth.org/medcenter
Melinda L Estes, MD, President/CEO
Richarad Magnuson, CFO

241 **University of Washington Diabetes: Endocrinology Research Center**
DVA Puget Sound Health Care System
1660 S Columbian Way 206-616-4860
Seattle, WA 98108 derc@u.washington.edu
www.depts.washington.edu/diabetes
The primary purpose of the DERC is to facilitate and enhance the diabetes-related research of approximately 100 Affiliate Investigators at the University of Washington
Jerry P Palmer MD, Director
David E Cummings, Deputy Director

242 **Vanderbilt University Diabetes Center**
1211 Medical Center Drive 615-322-5000
Nashville, TN 37232 dc.brown@vanderbilt.edu
www.mc.vanderbilt.edu/diabetes/vdc
The Vanderbilt Diabetes Center provides complete care for children and adults with diabetes under one roof
Joe C Davis, Chair in Biomedical Sciences
Alvin C Powers, Director Vanderbilt Diabetes Center

243 **Veterans Affairs Medical Center: Research Service**
500 Foothill Drive 801-582-1565
Salt Lake City, UT 84148 www.va.gov
Diabetes and cancer research.
James Floyd, Director
Byron Bair, Director

244 **Warren Grant Magnuson Clinical Center**
National Institute of Health
9000 Rockville Pike 301-496-4000
Bethesda, MD 20892 800-411-1222
TTY: 866-411-1010
prpl@mail.cc.nih.gov
clinicalcenter.nih.gov
Established in 1953 as the research hospital of the National Institutes of Health. Designed so that patient care facilities are close to research laboratories so new findings of basic and clinical scientists can be quickly applied to the treatment of patients. Upon referral by physicians, patients are admitted to NIH clinical studies.
John Gallin, Director
David Henderson, Deputy Director for Clinical Care

245 **Washington University: Diabetes Research and Training Center**
School of Medicine
660 S Euclid Avenue 314-362-0558
Saint Louis, MO 63110 drtc.im.wustl.edu
DRTC investigators were involved in conducting 60 investigator-initiated diabetes-related clinical research protocols on the WU GCRC
Jean Schaffer MD, Professor of Medicine
Kristin E Mondy, Medicine/Infectious Diseases

Support Groups & Hotlines

246 **American Diabetes Association**
2451 Crystal Drive 888-342-2383
Arlington, VA 22202 askada@diabetes.org
www.diabetes.org
Voluntary organization concerned with diabetes and its complications. The mission of the organization is to prevent and cure diabetes and to improve the lives of persons with diabetes. Offers a network of offices nationwide.
Tracey D. Brown, MBA, BChE, Chief Executive Officer
Eloise Scavella, MA, Chief Operating & Strategy Officer

247 **National Health Information Center**
Office of Disease Prevention & Health Promotion
1101 Wootton Pkwy odphpinfo@hhs.gov
Rockville, MD 20852 www.health.gov/nhic
Supports public health education by maintaining a calendar of National Health Observances; helps connect consumers and health professionals to organizations that can best answer questions and provide up-to-date contact information from reliable sources; updates on a yearly basis toll-free numbers for health information, Federal health clearinghouses and info centers.
Don Wright, MD, MPH, Director

Journals

248 **Countdown**
Juvenile Diabetes Foundation International
432 Park Avenue S 212-889-7575
New York, NY 10016-8013
Offers the latest news and information in diabetes research and treatment to everyone from an international arena of diabetes investigators to parents of small children with diabetes, from physicians to school teachers, from pharmacists to corporate executives.
Sandy Dylak, Editor

249 **Diabetes**
American Diabetes Association
2451 Crystal Drive 800-342-2383
Arlington, VA 22202 www.diabetes.org
A peer-reviewed journal focusing on laboratory research.
Brenda Montgomery, President, Health Care & Education

250 **Diabetes Advisor**
American Diabetes Association
2451 Crystal Drive 703-549-1500
Arlington, VA 22202 800-342-2383
askada@diabetes.org
www.diabetes.org
Offers informative articles and research in the area of diabetes for professionals and patients. Offers facts and research on diagnosis, symptoms, technology and the newest devices for persons with diabetes, as well as referral and hotline numbers.
Brenda Montgomery, President, Health Care & Education

251 **Diabetes Care**
American Diabetes Association
2451 Crystal Drive 800-342-2383
Arlington, VA 22202 www.diabetes.org
A peer-reviewed journal emphasizing reviews, commentaries and original research on topics of interest to clinicians.
Brenda Montgomery, President, Health Care & Education

252 **Diabetes Dateline**
National Diabetes Information Clearinghouse
1 Information Way 301-496-3583
Bethesda, MD 20205 800-860-8747
www.niddk.nih.gov

253 **Diabetes Educator**
American Association of Diabetes Educators
444 N Michigan Avenue 312-644-2233
Chicago, IL 60611-3959 www.aadenet.org
Offers information to health professionals working with persons with diabetes.
James J Balija, Executive Director

254 **Diabetes Forecast**
American Diabetes Association
2451 Crystal Drive 800-342-2383
Arlington, VA 22202 www.diabetes.org
The monthly lifestyle magazine for people with diabetes, featuring complete, in-depth coverage of all aspects of living with diabetes.
Brenda Montgomery, President, Health Care & Education

255 **Diabetes Spectrum: From Research to Practice**
American Diabetes Association
2451 Crystal Drive 800-342-2383
Arlington, VA 22202 www.diabetes.org
A journal translating research into practice and focusing on diabetes education and counseling.
Brenda Montgomery, President, Health Care & Education

256 **Joslin Magazine**
Joslin Diabetes Center
1 Joslin Place 617-732-2400
Boston, MA 02215-5306 diabetes@joslin.harvard.edu
www.joslin.org

257 **Kid's Corner**
American Diabetes Association
2451 Crystal Drive 800-342-2383
Arlington, VA 22202 www.diabetes.org
A mini-magazine for kids that offers word searches, puzzles and jokes - plus an encouraging story in each issue about kids with diabetes.
8 pages
Brenda Montgomery, President, Health Care & Education

258 **Voice of the Diabetic**
Ed Bryant, author
National Federation of the Blind
200 East Wells Street 410-659-9314
Baltimore, MD 21230-4998 www.nfb.org
The leading publication in the diabetes field. Each issue addresses the problems and concerns of diabetes, with a special emphasis for those who have lost vision due to diabetes. Available in print and on cassette.
28 pages
Eileen Ley, Director of Publishing
Elizabeth Lunt, Editor

Digital Resources

259 **ADA Clinical Education Series on CD-Rom**
American Diabetes Association
2451 Crystal Drive 800-342-2383
Arlington, VA 22202 www.diabetes.org
Features complete texts of Medical Management of Type 1 Diabetes, Medical Management of Type 2 Diabetes, Therapy for Diabetes Mellitus and Related Disorders, 2nd Ed., and Medical Management of Pregnancy Complicated by Diabetes, 2nd Ed.
Brenda Montgomery, President, Health Care & Education

260 **Black Experience**
American Diabetes Association
2451 Crystal Drive 703-549-1500
Arlington, VA 22202 800-342-2383
www.diabetes.org
Designed to increase awareness of diabetes in the black community.
Brenda Montgomery, President, Health Care & Education

261 **Diabetes & Exercise Video**
American Diabetes Association
2451 Crystal Drive 800-342-2383
Arlington, VA 22202 www.diabetes.org
A video offering information on how to maintain good health and exercise in controlling diabetes.
Brenda Montgomery, President, Health Care & Education

262 **Label Reading and Shopping**
American Diabetes Association
2451 Crystal Drive 703-549-1500
Arlington, VA 22202 800-342-2383
www.diabetes.org
Provides practical information on how to shop and what to look for on labels.
Brenda Montgomery, President, Health Care & Education

263 **Living Well with Diabetes**
American Diabetes Association
2451 Crystal Drive 800-342-2383
Arlington, VA 22202 www.diabetes.org
Presents two patient role models who are successfully following a treatment plan for noninsulin dependent diabetes.
Brenda Montgomery, President, Health Care & Education

264 **On Top of My Game: Living with Diabetes**
American Diabetes Association
2451 Crystal Drive 800-342-2383
Arlington, VA 22202 www.diabetes.org
Six patients and their families share their day-to-day frustrations and successes in managing diabetes.
Brenda Montgomery, President, Health Care & Education

265 **Physicians Guide to Type I Diabetes**
American Diabetes Association
2451 Crystal Drive 800-342-2383
Arlington, VA 22202 www.diabetes.org
Principles of good care in the diagnosis and management of Type I.
Brenda Montgomery, President, Health Care & Education

266 **Survival Skills for Diabetic Children**
Ajn Company
20 West 44th Street 212-686-7220
New York, NY 10036-2961 800-226-6256
www.chamber.nyc
How to provide insulin-dependent children with education, supervision, and support.

267 **Understanding Diabetes: A User's Guide to Novolin**
American Diabetes Association
2451 Crystal Drive 800-342-2383
Arlington, VA 22202 www.diabetes.org
Basic information about diabetes and the role insulin plays in blood glucose control.
Brenda Montgomery, President, Health Care & Education

Web Sites

268 **American Diabetes Association**
www.diabetes.org
Voluntary organization concerned with diabetes and its complications. The mission of the organization is to prevent and cure diabetes and to improve the lives of persons with diabetes. Offers a network of offices nationwide.
Tracey D. Brown, MBA, BChE, Chief Executive Officer
Eloise Scavella, MA, Chief Operating & Strategy Officer

269 **Association of Diabetes Care & Education Specialists**
www.diabeteseducator.org
An independent, multidisciplinary organization of health professionals involved in teaching persons with diabetes. The mission is to enhance the competence of health professionals who teach persons with diabetes and advance the specialty practice of diabetes.

270 **Diabetes Action Network for the Blind**
1501 Langford Road 410-215-8587
Gwynn Oak, MD 21207 bernienfb75@gmail.com
www.nfb.org
Bernadette M Jacobs, President

271 **Diabetes Dictionary**
diabetes.niddk.nih.gov
A publication of National Diabetes Information Clearinghouse. The Clearinghouse provides information about diabetes to people with diabetes and to their families, health care professionals, and the public. The NDIC answers inquiries, develops and distributes publications, and works closely with professional and patient organizations and Government agencies to coordinate resources about diabetes.

272 **Diabetes Exercise**
www.diabetes-exercise.org
Exists to enhance the quality of life for people with diabetes through exercise and physical fitness.

273 **Dietary Guidelines for Americans**
www.dietaryguidelines.gov
Publishes the Dietary Guidelines for Americans, a guide providing nutritional advice to promote health and prevent disease. Updated versions of the Dietary Guidelines are released by the US Departments of Agriculture (USDA) and Health & Human Services (HHS) every five years.

274 **EndocrineWeb**
www.endocrineweb.com
A website of Remedy Health Media, EndocrineWeb provides information about endocrine disorders, including thyroid disorders, diabetes, obesity, Addison's disease, and more.

275 **Everyday Health**
www.everydayhealth.com
Aims to provide evidence-based health information from physicians and healthcare providers.

276 **FamilyDoctor.org**
www.familydoctor.org
Medical advice and information provided by the American Academy of Family Physicians. Resources include a medical dictionary, a symptom checker tool, a BMI calculator, and medication information.

277 **Healing Well**
www.healingwell.com
An online health resource guide to medical news, chat, information and articles, newsgroups and message boards, books, disease-related web sites, medical directories, and more for patients, friends, and family coping with disabling diseases, disorders, or chronic illnesses.

278 **Health Finder**
www.healthfinder.gov
Searchable, carefully developed web site offering information on over 1000 topics. Developed by the US Department of Health and Human Services, the site can be used in both English and Spanish.

279 **Healthline**
www.healthline.com
Provides medical and health articles and information.

280 **Healthlink USA**
www.healthlinkusa.com
Health information concerning treatment, cures, prevention, diagnosis, risk factors, research, support groups, email lists, personal stories and much more. Updated regularly.

281 **Hormone Health Network**
www.hormone.org
Online support and resources for patients, with focus on hormone health, disease and treatment. Provided by the Endocrine Society.

282 **MedicineNet**
www.medicinenet.com
An online resource for consumers providing easy-to-read, authoritative medical and health information.

283 **MedlinePlus**
www.medlineplus.gov
A service of the National Library of Medicine, MedlinePlus is an online resource providing health and wellness information in both English and Spanish.

284 **Medscape**
www.medscape.com
Medscape offers specialists, primary care physicians, and other health professionals the Web's most robust and integrated medical information and educational tools.

285 **MyPlate**
www.myplate.gov
Created and managed by the US Department of Agriculture's Center for Nutrition Policy & Promotion, MyPlate is a dietary guide providing resources and recipes to promote healthy eating for all Americans.

286 **National Diabetes Information Clearinghouse**
www.niddk.nih.gov

287 **Nutrition.gov**
www.nutrition.gov
Sponsored by the United States Department of Agriculture (USDA), Nutrition.gov offers information on topics in food and nutrition, including healthy eating, physical activity, and food safety.

288 **Science Daily**
www.sciencedaily.com
Provides information on the latest news and research in science, health, the environment, and technology.

289 **The Nutrition Source**
hsph.harvard.edu/nutritionsource
From the Harvard T.H. Chan School of Public Health, The Nutrition Source provides news, information, and guidance for nutrition and healthy eating.

290 **UnlockFood**
www.unlockfood.ca
A website from Dietitians of Canada. Provides videos, recipes, and information on food and nutrition, as well as helps Canadians connect with a dietitian.

291 **Verywell**
www.verywellhealth.com
Offers health, medicine, and wellness information from health professionals.

292 **WebMD**
www.webmd.com
Provides credible information, supportive communities, and in-depth reference material about health subjects. A source for original and timely health information as well as material from well known content providers.

293 **World Health Organization**
www.who.int
An agency of the United Nations, World Health Organization (WHO) serves to promote global health. The WHO website provides fact sheets, publications, media, and other resources on various health topics.

EATING DISORDERS

Eating disorders, far from a lifestyle choice, are serious illnesses, and classified as mental illness. Eating disorders are usually defined by a severe disturbance in eating patterns and related emotions leading to preoccupation with food and body image. The most common disorders are anorexia nervosa, bulimia and binge-eating disorder. Pica, rumination and avoidant restrictive food intake disorder (ARFID) are other disorders discussed below. While food and nutrition are at the center of all eating disorders, treatment is not effective unless the underlying mental health issue is treated. Maintaining a healthy diet is difficult without interventions designed to treat the associated mental health issues that use food as a control mechanism. An eating disorder can develop for anyone at any age, of any body type, and at any time. Genes and family history, mental and emotional stress, environment and culture may all contribute to eating disorder development.

Anorexia Nervosa (AN) is considered a mental disorder in which individuals see themselves as overweight even when they are dangerously underweight. People with AN weigh themselves excessively, severely restrict the food they eat, often exercise to extreme and may use laxatives or forced vomiting to lose weight. Physical complications develop over time including bone loss, constipation, low blood pressure, heart and brain damage, and multi-organ failure. Psychosocial issues include distorted body image, poor self-esteem and denial of the seriousness of low body weight. AN has the highest mortality rate of any mental disorder, often from complications of starvation or death by suicide.

Individuals with Bulimia Nervosa (BN) have recurrent and frequent episodes of eating large amounts of food and feeling no ability to control themselves. Binging episodes are followed by purging (forced vomiting), excessive use of laxatives or diuretics, and excessive exercise. People with BN may be underweight, overweight or of normal weight. They experience chronic sore throat, worn enamel on the teeth, acid reflux disorder and other gastrointestinal disorders, and dehydration and electrolyte imbalance which can lead to stroke or heart attack.

Unlike BN, individuals with Binge-eating Disorder (B-ED) lose control over eating but do not self-induce vomiting, over exercise or follow with periods of fasting. They are often overweight or obese. B-ED is the most common eating disorder in the United States, and is defined as consuming unusually large amounts of food in a specific time frame, such as the equivalent of several meals, in a two-hour period. Eating fast, eating until uncomfortably full, hiding while eating and frequently dieting without weight loss are all symptoms.

PICA is an eating disorder that involves eating non-food items such as dirt, hair, clay and paint chips. Testing for anemia, gastrointestinal issues and blockage, nutritional and mineral deficiencies and toxic side effects of consumed items is usually indicated. PICA can occur in any age group but often occurs in developing countries.

Rumination disorder is when recently eaten food is regurgitated (or flows backward), caused by involuntary contraction of stomach muscles, triggered by a virus, emotional distress or physical injury. This usually occurs 15-30 minutes after eating and does not involve gagging or retching.

Avoidant restrictive food intake disorder (ARFID) was formerly known as selective eating disorder. Being a picky eater may result in insufficient caloric intake to maintain basic body functioning. Behavioral symptoms include a lack of interest in eating, avoidance of certain foods based on smell or consistency, and poor psychosocial functioning. People with autism spectrum conditions are more likely to develop ARFID. Physical symptoms may include weight loss, nutritional deficiency, gastrointestinal complaints, menstrual irregularities including lack of periods, dizziness, hair loss, and others.

Treatment for all eating disorders may include combinations of psychotherapy, medications and nutritional counseling along with medical monitoring of laboratory tests and behaviors. Because eating disorders are considered mental health disorders, psychotherapies and medication may be the first line of treatment. Individual and family therapy, cognitive behavioral therapy, meditation and other strategies are often recommended. Some disorders may be treated with medications that treat symptoms. For example, antidepressants, antipsychotics and mood stabilizers may be used as part of the behavioral therapy to treat eating disorders when depression and anxiety are present, baclofen may be used to treat rumination disorder, and antacids and other gastrointestinal medications may be indicated. Outpatient, residential or inpatient hospital care may be necessary.

The role of nutrition in eating disorders, while significant, is only effective if the underlying issues causing the eating disorder is first addressed. Counseling with a registered dietician, approaches such as the Maudsley approach, where parents of adolescents with AN actually feed the teen, teaching healthy nutrition choices and the complications of not eating sufficient calories and, in some cases, intravenous or nasogastric feeding in an inpatient treatment facility may be indicated.

See page 243 for more information on eating disorders.

Agencies & Associations

295 **Academy for Eating Disorders**
11130 Sunrise Valley Drive 703-234-4079
Reston, VA 20191 info@aedweb.org
www.aedweb.org
AED is an association of multidisciplinary professionals promoting effective treatment, developing prevention initiatives, advocating for the field, stimulating research and sponsoring an annual conference.
Dawn Gannon, Operations Director

296 **Academy of Nutrition & Dietetics**
120 South Riverside Plaza 312-899-0040
Chicago, IL 60606-6995 800-877-1600
media@eatright.org
www.eatright.org
Serves the public through the promotion of optimal nutrition, health, and well-being. Formerly the American Dietetic Association.
Patricia M. Babjak, Chief Executive Officer

297 **Administration for Children and Families**
330 C Street SW 202-401-9200
Washington, DC 20201 www.acf.hhs.gov
The Administration for Children & Families (ACF) is a division of the U.S. Department of Health & Human Services (HHS). ACF promotes the economic and social well-being of families, children, individuals and communities.
JooYeun Chang, Acting Assistant Secretary
Larry Handerhan, Chief of Staff

298 **Alliance for Eating Disorders Awareness**
4400 North Congress Avenue 866-662-1235
West Palm Beach, FL 33407 info@allianceforeatingdisorders.com
www.allianceforeatingdisorders.com
Nonprofit organization dedicated to supporting those with eating disorders through outreach, education, early intervention and advocacy.
Johanna Kandel, Founder & CEO
Joann Hendelman, Clinical Director

299 **Association of Gastrointestinal Motility Disorders**
140 Pleasant Street 781-275-1300
Lexington, MA 02421 info@agmdhope.org
www.agmdhope.org
A non-profit international organization which serves as an integral educational resource concerning digestive motility diseases and disorders. Also functions as an important information base for members of the medical and scientific communities. Also provides a forum for patients suffering from digestive motility diseases and disorders as well as their families and members of the medical, scientific, and nutritional communities.
Mary Angela DeGrazia-DiTucci, President

300 **Body Brave**
1047 Main Street E 905-312-9628
Hamilton, Ontario, L8M-1N5 info@bodybrave.ca
www.bodybrave.ca
A charitable organization focusing on accessible treatment and support for individuals recovering from an eating disorder.
Sonia Kumar-Seguin, Chief Executive Officer
Karen Trollope-Kumar, MD, PhD, Chief Medical Officer

301 **Bulimia Anorexia Nervosa Association**
1500 Ouellette Avenue 519-969-2112
Windsor, Ontario, N8X-1K7 855-969-5530
www.bana.ca
BANA facilitates, advocates, and coordinates support for any individual directly or indirectly affected by eating disorders, and raises public awareness through improved communication and the provision of education within the community.
Luciana Rosu Sieza, Executive Director
Patrick Kelly, Communications & Office Administrator

302 **Centers for Disease Control & Prevention: Division of Adolescent & School Health**
1600 Clifton Road 800-232-4636
Atlanta, GA 30329 TTY: 888-232-6348
www.cdc.gov/HealthyYouth
CDC promotes the health and well-being of children and adolescents to enable them to become healthy and productive adults.

303 **Eat Breathe Thrive**
www.eatbreathethrive.org
Eat Breathe Thrive aims to provide skills and resources to prevent and help individuals recover from eating disorders. The organization offers online and in-person courses, events, resources, and more.
Chelsea Roff, Founder & Director
Samantha Christodoulou, Director, Operations

304 **Eating Disorder Hope**
www.eatingdisorderhope.com
Eating Disorder Hope offers information and resources to individuals with eating disorders, their families, and treatment providers.
Jacquelyn Ekern, President
Baxter Ekern, Chief Executive Officer

305 **Eating Disorder Recovery Support**
911 Lakeville Street info@edrecoverysupport.org
Petaluma, CA 94952 www.edrecoverysupport.org
Aims to promote the recovery of everyone impacted by eating disorders by offering support, information, and education to individuals, families, and professionals.
Corinne Dobbas, President
Shelly Kamboj, Vice President

306 **Eating Disorders Anonymous**
PO Box 55876 info@eatingdisordersanonymous.org
Phoenix, AZ 85078-5876 www.eatingdisordersanonymous.org
EDA provides support group services for people recovering from eating disorders.

307 **Eating Disorders Association of Canada**
Calgary, Alberta www.edac-atac.com
Comprised of professionals in the eating disorders field, EDAC seeks to best serve individuals who are impacted by eating disorders.
Lea Thaler, President
Gisele Marcoux-Louie, Secretary-Treasurer

308 **Eating Disorders Coalition for Research, Policy and Action**
PO Box 96503-98807 202-543-9570
Washington, DC 20090 www.eatingdisorderscoalition.org
Advocates at the federal level on behalf of people with eating disorders, their families, and professionals working with these populations. Promotes federal support for improved access to care.
David Jaffe, Executive Director

309 **Eating Disorders Treatment Accountability Council**
www.eatingdisorderstreatmentreviews.org
A community-based research initiative aiming to identify effective eating disorder treatment options and improve treatment outcomes.

310 **Families Empowered and Supporting Treatment for Eating Disorders**
136 Everett Road 855-503-3278
Albany, NY 12205 info@feast-ed.org
www.feast-ed.org
F.E.A.S.T. is a nonprofit organization for parents and families of persons with eating disorders. Its mission is to provide information and support, and to promote research and evidence-based treatment.
Judy Krasna, Executive Director

311 **Footsteps For Recovery**
4801 McKnight Road 412-215-7967
Pittsburgh, PA 15237 pened1@aol.com
www.footstepsforrecovery.com
A nonprofit organization providing education, support, and referral information to the general and professional public.

312 **Healthy Weight Network**
402 S 14th Street 701-567-2646
Hettinger, ND 58639 www.healthyweight.net
Promotes information and resources pertaining to the Health at Any Size paradigm.
Frances M. Berg, MS, Founder/Editor

313 **Jessie's Legacy**
1111 Lonsdale Avenue 604-988-5281
North Vancouver, BC, V7M-2H4 jessieslegacy.com
A program of Family Services of the North Shore, Jessie's Legacy seeks to support youth, families, and professionals involved in body image and eating disorders in BC.
Joanna Zelichowska, Manager

314 **KMB for Answers**
Livonia, NY kmbforanswers1@gmail.com
www.kmbforanswers.com
A nonprofit organization offering resources, programs, and support services to school and mental health professionals, treatment centers, and individuals with eating disorders and their families.
Ellen Bennett, Director
Luke Costanza, Co-Director

315 **MindWise Innovations**
270 Bridge Street 781-239-0071
Dedham, MA 02026 info@mindwise.org
www.mindwise.org
Formerly known as Screening For Mental Health, MindWise Innovations provides resources to schools, workplaces, and communities to address mental health issues, eating disorders, substance abuse, and suicide.
Bryan Kohl, Executive Director
Marjie McDaniel, Vice President

316 **Moonshadow's Spirit**
776 Saffron Lane 585-353-2205
Webster, NY 14580 www.moonshadowsspirit.org
Offers need-based financial assistance to individuals receiving eating disorder treatment at residential facilities or intensive partial hospitalization program facilities.
Sharon Mathiason, President & Secretary
David Mathiason, Treasurer

317 **Multi-Service Eating Disorders Association**
1320 Centre Street 617-558-1881
Newton, MA 02459 888-350-4049
www.medainc.org
A nonprofit organization dedicated to the treatment and prevention of eating disorders. MEDA provides help line resource and referral, assessments, client consultations, individual therapy, support groups and an intensive evening treatment program.
Monika Ostroff, Executive Director
Carolyn Judge, Director, Operations

318 **Nalgona Positivity Pride**
www.nalgonapositivitypride.com
Nalgona Positivity Pride is an organization dedicated to raising awareness and providing resources on eating disorders and body positivity, with focus on the specific needs of Black, Indigenous, and communities of color (BICC).
Gloria Lucas, Chief Executive Officer

319 **National Association of Anorexia Nervosa and Associated Disorders**
PO Box 409047 312-262-6897
Chicago, IL 60640 hello@anad.org
www.anad.org
Works to prevent eating disorders and provides numerous programs — all free — to help victims and families including hotlines, support groups, referrals, information packets and newsletters. Educational/prevention programs include presentations and early detection.
Lynn Slawsky, MPA, PMP, Executive Director
Giva Ann Wilkerson, Program Director

320 **National Eating Disorder Information Centre**
200 Elizabeth Street 416-340-4156
Toronto, Ontario, M5G-2C4 866-633-4220
nedic@uhn.ca
www.nedic.ca
NEDIC promotes healthy lifestyles, including both healty eating and appropriate, enjoyable exercise, through outreach and education, direct client support, and other programs.
Suzanne Phillips, Program Manager
Sara Marini, Administrative Coordinator

321 **National Eating Disorders Association**
1500 Broadway 212-575-6200
New York, NY 10036 800-931-2237
info@nationaleatingdisorders.org
www.nationaleatingdisorders.org
NEDA aims to eliminate eating disorders and body dissatisfaction through prevention efforts, education, referral and support services, advocacy training, and research.
Elizabeth Thompson, Interim Chief Executive Officer
Lauren Smolar, Senior Director, Programs

322 **National Initiative for Eating Disorders**
Toronto, Ontario info@nied.ca
www.nied.ca
Provides educational and informational resources for people affected by eating disorders and related mental illnesses in Canada.
Wendy Preskow, Co-Founder & President
Lynne Koss, Co-Founder & Vice President

323 **Nurse Practitioners in Women's Health**
PO Box 15837 202-543-9693
Washington, DC 20003 info@npwh.org
www.npwh.org
Ensures the delivery and accessibility of primary and specialty healthcare to women of all ages by women's health and women's health focused nurse practitioners.
Heather L. Maurer, CEO
Donna Ruth, Director, Education

324 **Office of Women's Health**
200 Independence Avenue SW 202-690-7650
Washington, DC 20201 800-994-9662
womenshealth@hhs.gov
www.womenshealth.gov
Government agency under the Department of Health & Human Services, with free health information for women.
Dorothy Fink, MD, Deputy Asst. Secretary, Women's Health
Richelle West Marshall, Deputy Director

325 **Ophelia's Place**
PO Box 621 833-721-0605
Liverpool, NY 13088 www.opheliasplace.org
Aims to support individuals affected by eating disorders, diet culture, and body oppression by providing free phone support, support groups, and information about treatment services.
Holli Zehring, Chief Executive Officer
Brittany Cannon, Chief Program Officer

326 **Overeaters Anonymous**
6075 Zenith Court NE 505-891-2664
Rio Rancho, NM 87174-4727 www.oa.org
A fellowship of individuals who meet in order to help solve their eating behaviors.

327 **Project HEAL**
PO Box 160185 contact@theprojectheal.org
New York, NY 11216 www.theprojectheal.org
Project HEAL's mission is to break down barriers to eating disorder treatment and help all individuals receive the care they need. Project HEAL offers three treatment access programs: Insurance Navigation, Treatment Placement, and Cash Assistance.
Rebecca Eyre, Chief Executive Officer
Ashlee Knight, Program Director

328 **REDC**
555 8th Avenue 646-553-1340
New York, NY 10018 info@redcconsortium.org
www.redcconsortium.org
Formerly the Residential Eating Disorders Consortium, the REDC is a professional association focused on maintaining and improving standards, policy, research, and best practices in eating disorders care.
Jillian Lampert, President
Sharon Zimbler, Vice President

329 **Renewed Eating Disorders Support**
1101 17th Avenue South 615-831-9838
Nashville, TN 37212 info@renewedsupport.org
www.renewedsupport.org

Provides free referrals and support to anyone impacted by an eating disorder, as well as educational training to healthcare professionals.
Lauran Sauter, Executive Director
Courtney Grimes, Clinical Director

330 **Renfrew Center**
475 Spring Lane 800-736-3739
Philadelphia, PA 19128 www.renfrewcenter.com
The Renfrew Center is a pioneering treatment center for individuals with eating disorders. The residential program has 19 locations throughout the country, and the Center also engages in research activities through its foundation.
Samuel E. Menaged, Founder & President

331 **Rock Recovery**
PO Box 100923 571-255-9906
Arlington, VA 22201 info@rockrecoveryed.org
www.rockrecoveryed.org
Rock Recovery aims to bridge gaps in eating disorder treatment by providing quality clinical care and removing barriers in treatment. Rock Recovery offers support services, educational workshops, therapy programs, and more.
Christie Dondero Bettwy, Executive Director
Kristyn Y. Soto, Director, Community Partnerships

332 **Up Against Eating Disorders**
upagainsted.com
Provides services to loved ones of people with eating disorders, and training to treatment professionals.
Joe Kelly, Founder

333 **WithAll**
2265 Como Avenue 651-379-6123
St Paul, MN 55108 hello@withall.org
www.withall.org
A nonprofit organization seeking to prevent eating disorders and support recovery by providing tools to help adults talk with children about food and the body.
Lisa Radzak, Executive Director
Erin Martin, Director, Engagement & Programming

California

334 **Renfrew Center - Los Angeles**
12121 Wilshire Boulevard 800-736-3739
Los Angeles, CA 90025 www.renfrewcenter.com

Florida

335 **Renfrew Center - Coconut Creek**
7700 Renfrew Lane 800-736-3739
Coconut Creek, FL 33073 www.renfrewcenter.com

336 **Renfrew Center - Orlando**
3452 Lake Lynda Drive 800-736-3739
Orlando, FL 32817 www.renfrewcenter.com

337 **Renfrew Center - West Palm Beach**
1515 North Flagler Drive 800-736-3739
West Palm Beach, FL 33401 www.renfrewcenter.com

Georgia

338 **Renfrew Center - Atlanta**
50 Glenlake Parkway 800-736-3739
Atlanta, GA 30328 www.renfrewcenter.com

Illinois

339 **Renfrew Center - Chicago**
5 Revere Drive 800-736-3739
Northbrook, IL 60062 www.renfrewcenter.com

Maryland

340 **Renfrew Center - Baltimore**
1122 Kenilworth Drive 800-736-3739
Towson, MD 21204 www.renfrewcenter.com

341 **Renfrew Center - Bethesda**
4416 East-West Highway 800-736-3739
Bethesda, MD 20814 www.renfrewcenter.com

Massachusetts

342 **Renfrew Center - Boston**
870R Commonwealth Avenue 800-736-3739
Boston, MA 02215 www.renfrewcenter.com

New Jersey

343 **Renfrew Center - Mount Laurel**
15000 Midlantic Drive 800-736-3739
Mount Laurel, NJ 08054 www.renfrewcenter.com

344 **Renfrew Center - Paramus**
1 Kalisa Way 800-736-3739
Paramus, NJ 07652 www.renfrewcenter.com

New York

345 **Renfrew Center - New York**
38 East 32nd Street 800-736-3739
New York, NY 10016 www.renfrewcenter.com

346 **Renfrew Center - White Plains**
1025 Westchester Avenue 800-736-3739
White Plains, NY 10604 www.renfrewcenter.com

North Carolina

347 **Renfrew Center - Charlotte**
6633 Fairview Road 800-736-3739
Charlotte, NC 28210 www.renfrewcenter.com

Pennsylvania

348 **Renfrew Center - Center City**
1528 Walnut Street 800-736-3739
Philadelphia, PA 19102 www.renfrewcenter.com

349 **Renfrew Center - Pittsburgh**
201 North Craig Street 800-736-3739
Pittsburgh, PA 15213 www.renfrewcenter.com

350 **Renfrew Center - Radnor**
320 King of Prussia Road 800-736-3739
Radnor, PA 19087 www.renfrewcenter.com

Tennessee

351 **Renfrew Center - Nashville**
1624 Westgate Circle 800-736-3739
Brentwood, TN 37027 www.renfrewcenter.com

Libraries & Resource Centers

352 **Eating Disorder Resource Center**
330 W 58th Street 212-989-3987
New York, NY 10019 info@edrcnyc.org
www.edrcnyc.org
A specialized treatment program for women and men who were suffering from bulimia. Now EDRC treats eating disorders of all kinds, offering individual, group, family and couples treatment for those challenged by bulimia, binge eating disorder, anorexia and other kinds of body dysmorphia.
Judith Brisman, Director & Founder
Senna Lauer, Marketing Assistant

353 **Weight-Control Information Network**
National Institutes of Health
31 Center Drive 800-860-8747
Bethesda, MD 20892-2560 TTY: 866-569-1162
healthinfo@niddk.nih.gov
www.win.niddk.nih.gov
WIN provides the general public, health professionals, and the media with up-to-date, science-based information on obesity, weight control, physical activity, and related nutritional issues. WIN pro-

vides tip sheets, fact sheets, and brochures for a range of audiences. Some of WIN's content is available in Spanish.

Foundations & Research Centers

354 **Academy for Eating Disorders**
11130 Sunrise Valley Drive 703-234-4079
Reston, VA 20191 info@aedweb.org
www.aedweb.org
AED is an association of multidisciplinary professionals promoting effective treatment, developing prevention initiatives, advocating for the field, stimulating research and sponsoring an annual conference.
Elissa Myers, Executive Director
Dawn Gannon, Deputy Executive Director

355 **Breaking the Chains Foundation**
16647 Sunburst Street www.breakingthechainsfoundation.org
North Hills, CA 91343
The foundation uses art to advocate for the prevention, intervention, and destigmatization of eating disorders, as well as to provide support for those recovering from eating disorders.
Debra Hopkins, Founder & President

356 **Center for the Study of Anorexia and Bulimia**
1841 Broadway at 60th Street 212-333-3444
New York, NY 10023 www.icpnyc.org
The Institute is composed of a group of 150 professionally trained licensed psychotherapists who offer a full range of psychotherapeutic services including individual and group psychotherapy and psychoanalysis in addition to more specialized treatment services.
Jim M Pollack CSW, Executive Director/Director of Treatment
Ron Taffel, Chair

357 **Division of Digestive & Liver Diseases of Cloumbia University**
630 W 168th Street 212-305-5960
New York, NY 10032-3784 hjw14@columbia.edu
www.cumc.columbia.edu
The Division's faculty members are devoted to research and the clinical care of patients with gastrointestinal, liver and nutritional disorders. The Division is also responsible for the Gastroenterology Training Program at the medical center and for teaching medical students, interns, residents, fellows and attending physicians aspects of gastrointestinal and liver diseases.
Howard J Worman MD, Division Director
Karen Wisdom, Director

358 **Eating Disorder Foundation**
1901 East 20th Avenue 303-322-3373
Denver, CO 80205 info@eatingdisorderfoundation.org
www.eatingdisorderfoundation.org
Seeks to prevent and eliminate eating disorders by engaging in education and advocacy initiatives, and providing support to individuals with eating disorders and their families.
Daniella Gilady, Executive Director
Sabrina Scanga, Program Director

359 **Harris Center for Education and Advocacy in Eating Disorders**
2 Longfellow Place 617-726-8470
Boston, MA 02114 www.harriscentermgh.org
Conducts research provides a newsletter and information.
David B Herzog MD, Director
David B Herzog, Director

360 **International Association of Eating Disorders Professionals Foundation**
PO Box 1295 309-346-3341
Pekin, IL 61555-1295 800-800-8126
iaedpmembers@earthlink.net
www.iaedp.com
IAEDP Offers professional counseling and assistance to the medical community, courts, law enforcement officials and social welfare agencies.
Bonnie Harken, Managing Director
Blanche Williams, Director, International Development

361 **Kirsten Haglund Foundation**
PO Box 2701 www.kirstenhaglundfoundation.org
Farmington Hills, MI 48333
The Kirsten Haglund Foundation aims to provide support for individuals with eating disorders through networking and financial aid.
Kirsten Haglund, Founder
Iora Haglund, President

362 **Renfrew Center Foundation**
475 Spring Lane 800-736-3739
Philadelphia, PA 19128 www.renfrewcenter.com
Non-profit organization aiming to increase awareness of eating disorders as a public health issue. It seeks to accomplish this through educating policy makers and to remove barriers to treatment. It also conducts research into the pathology and recovery patterns of people with eating disorders.
Samuel E. Menaged, Founder & President

Support Groups & Hotlines

363 **AABA Support Group**
Chippenham Medican Center
7101 Jahnke Rd. 804-320-3911
Richmond, VA 23225
Elliot Spanier, Contact

364 **About Kids GI Disorders**
IFFGD
PO Box 170864 414-964-1799
Milwaukee, WI 53217-8076 888-964-2001
iffgd@iffgd.org
www.aboutkidsgi.org
About Kids is the pediatric branch of the International Foundation for Functional Gastrointestinal Disorders (IFFGD), a registered nonprofit education and research organization founded in 1991. Their mission is to inform, assist, and support those affected by gastrointestinal (GI) disorders, addressing issues of digestive health in children through support of education and research. IFFGD promotes awareness among the public, health care providers, researchers, and regulators.
Nancy J Norton, President/Founder

365 **Alliance for Eating Disorders Awareness**
4400 North Congress Avenue 866-662-1235
West Palm Beach, FL 33407 info@allianceforeatingdisorders.com
www.allianceforeatingdisorders.com
Nonprofit organization dedicated to supporting those with eating disorders through outreach, education, early intervention and advocacy.
Johanna Kandel, Founder & CEO
Joann Hendelman, Clinical Director

366 **Association of Gastrointestinal Motility Disorders**
12 Roberts Drive 781-275-1300
Bedford, MA 01730 digestive.motility@gmail.com
www.agmd-gimotility.org
A non-profit international organization which serves as an integral educational resource concerning digestive motility diseases and disorders. Also functions as an important information base for members of the medical and scientific communities. Also provides a forum for patients suffering from digestive motility diseases and disorders as well as their families and members of the medical, scientific, and nutritional communities.
Mary Angela DeGrazia-DiTucci, President/Patient/Founder

367 **Coconut Creek Eating Disorders Support Group**
Renfrew Center
7700 NW 48th Avenue 954-698-9222
Coconut Creek, FL 33073-3508 877-367-3383
www.renfrew.org

368 **First Presbyterian Church in the City of New York Support Groups**
First Presbyterian Church in the City of New York
12 West 12th Street 212-675-6150
New York, NY 10011 fpcnyc@fpcnyc.org
www.fpcnyc.org

The First Presbyterian Church in the City of New York provides numerous programs and supports groups for both adults and children including an educational program for autistic children.
Jon M Walton, Senior Pastor
Sarah Segal Mccaslin, Associate Pastor

369 Holliswood Hospital Psychiatric Care, Serv ices and Self-Help/Support Groups
87-37 Palermo Street 718-776-8181
Holliswood, NY 11423 800-486-3005
HolliswoodInfo@libertymgt.com
www.holliswoodhospital.com/
The Holliswood Hospital, a 110-bed private psychiatric hospital located in a quiet residential Queens community, is a leader in providing quality, acute inpatient mental health care for adult, adolescent, geriatric and dually diagnosed patients. Holliswood Hospital treats patients with a broad range of psychiatric disorders. Additionally, specialized services are available for patients with psychiatric diagnoses compounded by chemical dependency, or a history of physical or sexual abuse.
Susan Clayton, Support Group Coordinator
Angela Hurtado, Support Group Coordinator

370 National Association of Anorexia Nervosa and Associated Disorders Helpline
220 N. Green Street 630-577-1330
Chicago, IL 60607 hello@anad.org
www.anad.org
Works to prevent eating disorders and provides numerous programs — all free — to help victims and families including hotlines, support groups, referrals, information packets, and online content. Educational/prevention programs include presentations and early detection.
Lynn Slawsky, MPA, PMP, Executive Director
Kristen Portland, Operations Manager

371 National Eating Disorder Information Centre Helpline
ES 7-421, 200 Elizabeth Street 416-340-4156
Toronto, Ontario, M5G-2C4 866-633-4220
nedic@uhn.ca
www.nedic.ca
NEDIC promotes healthy lifestyles, including both healty eating and appropriate, enjoyable exercise, through outreach and education, direct client support, and other programs, including a helpline.
Suzanne Phillips, Program Manager
Rekha Wijayaratna, Development Officer

372 National Eating Disorders Association Helpline
1500 Broadway 212-575-6200
New York, NY 10036 800-931-2237
info@NationalEatingDisorders.org
www.nationaleatingdisorders.org
NEDA aims to eliminate eating disorders and body dissatisfaction through prevention efforts, education, referral and support services, advocacy training, and research. Also provides a Helpline.
Elizabeth Thompson, Interim CEO

373 National Health Information Center
Office of Disease Prevention & Health Promotion
1101 Wootton Pkwy odphpinfo@hhs.gov
Rockville, MD 20852 www.health.gov/nhic
Supports public health education by maintaining a calendar of National Health Observances; helps connect consumers and health professionals to organizations that can best answer questions and provide up-to-date contact information from reliable sources; updates on a yearly basis toll-free numbers for health information, Federal health clearinghouses and info centers.
Don Wright, MD, MPH, Director

374 Renewed Eating Disorders Support
1101 17th Avenue South 615-831-9838
Nashville, TN 37212 info@renewedsupport.org
www.renewedsupport.org
Provides free referrals and support to anyone impacted by an eating disorder, as well as educational training to healthcare professionals.
Lauran Sauter, Executive Director
Courtney Grimes, Clinical Director

375 Richmond Support Group
Warwick Medical & Professional Ctr 804-320-7881
Richmond, VA

376 Rock Recovery
PO Box 100923 571-255-9906
Arlington, VA 22201 info@rockrecoveryed.org
www.rockrecoveryed.org
Rock Recovery aims to bridge gaps in eating disorder treatment by providing quality clinical care and removing barriers in treatment. Rock Recovery offers support services, educational workshops, therapy programs, and more.
Christie Dondero Bettwy, Executive Director
Kristyn Y. Soto, Director, Community Partnerships

Journals

377 BANA Be Yourself Magazine
1500 Ouellette Avenue 519-969-2112
Windsor, Ontario, N8X-1K7 855-969-5530
www.bana.ca
A publication of the Bulimia Anorexia Nervosa Association (BANA), this magazine provides resources for clinicians, educators, and mental health professionals.

378 BASH Magazine
Bulimia Anorexia Self-Help/Behavior Adaptation
PO Box 39903 800-762-3334
Saint Louis, MO 63139-8903
A journal of eating and mood disorders.

379 Eating Disorders Review
Gurze Books
PO Box 2238 800-756-7533
Carlsbad, CA 92018-9883 gzcatl@aol.com
www.bulimia.com
Presents current clinical information for the professional treating eating disorders. Features summeries of relevant research from journals and unpublished studies, abstracts, nutritional notes, questions and answers, book reviews and reproducible client handouts.
8 pages
Joel Yager MD, Editor-in-Chief
Liegh Cohn, Publisher

380 Food & Nutrition
120 South Riverside Plaza 312-899-0040
Chicago, IL 60606-6995 800-877-1600
foodandnutrition@eatright.org
www.eatright.org
Formerly the ADA Times, Food & Nutrition is the member and professional magazine of the Academy of Nutrition & Dietetics.

381 Journal of the Academy of Nutrition and Dietetics
120 South Riverside Plaza 312-899-4831
Chicago, IL 60606-6995 journal@eatright.org
www.eatright.org
Official research publication of the Academy of Nutrition and Dietetics.

382 The Eating Disorder Journal
www.edreferral.com
Focuses on clinical research and up-to-date information related to the eating disorders field.

383 Working Together
Anorexia Nervosa and Associated Disorders
PO Box 7 847-831-3438
Highland Park, IL 60035-0007 www.thesaurus.com
Designed for individuals, families, group leaders and professionals concerned with eating disorders. Provides updates on treatments, resources, conferences, programs, articles by therapists, recovered victims, group members and leaders.
Michele Turner, CEO
Jim Conning, SVP of Engineering

Digital Resources

384 **Bulimia: A Guide to Recovery**
Gurze Books
PO Box 2238 800-756-7533
Carlsbad, CA 92018-2238 gzcatl@aol.com
www.bulimia.com
This newly rediscovered tape is an inspirational talk by Lindsey Hall on the relationship between bulimia, self-esteem and love. This was one of Lindsey's last public appearances, where she addressed a 1991 eating disorers conference in Colorado Springs.

385 **WIN Notes**
Weight-control Information Network
1 WIN Way 202-828-1025
Bethesda, MD 20892-3665 877-946-4627
win@mathewsgroup.com
www.niddk.nih.gov/health/nutrit/win.htm
Addresses the health information needs of individuals with weight-control problems. Available on the WIN web site.
Griffin P. Rodgers, Director

Web Sites

386 **Academy of Nutrition & Dietetics**
www.eatright.org
Serves the public through the promotion of optimal nutrition, health, and well-being. Formerly the American Dietetic Association.

387 **Anorexia Nervosa & Related Eating Disorders**
www.anred.com
A nonprofit organization that provides information about anorexia nervosa, bulimia nervosa, binge eating disorder, and other less-well-known food and weight disorders.

388 **BulimiaGuide**
www.bulimiaguide.org
Provides information and resources about bulimia nervosa.

389 **Dietary Guidelines for Americans**
www.dietaryguidelines.gov
Publishes the Dietary Guidelines for Americans, a guide providing nutritional advice to promote health and prevent disease. Updated versions of the Dietary Guidelines are released by the US Departments of Agriculture (USDA) and Health & Human Services (HHS) every five years.

390 **Eating Disorder Referral and Information Center**
www.edreferral.com
Provides information for individuals with eating disorders.

391 **Eating Disorders Treatment Accountability Council**
www.eatingdisorderstreatmentreviews.org
A community-based research initiative aiming to identify effective eating disorder treatment options and improve treatment outcomes.

392 **Everyday Health**
www.everydayhealth.com
Aims to provide evidence-based health information from physicians and healthcare providers.

393 **FamilyDoctor.org**
www.familydoctor.org
Medical advice and information provided by the American Academy of Family Physicians. Resources include a medical dictionary, a symptom checker tool, a BMI calculator, and medication information.

394 **GERD Information Resource Center**
www.gerd.com
A resource center with educational resources on Gastroesophageal Reflux Disease (GERD).

395 **Gastroenterology Therapy Online**
www.gastrotherapy.com
An informational website with resources for many kinds of diseases.

396 **Healing Well**
www.healingwell.com
An online health resource guide to medical news, chat, information and articles, newsgroups and message boards, books, disease-related web sites, medical directories, and more for patients, friends, and family coping with disabling diseases, disorders, or chronic illnesses.

397 **Health Finder**
www.healthfinder.gov
Searchable, carefully developed web site offering information on over 1000 topics. Developed by the US Department of Health and Human Services, the site can be used in both English and Spanish.

398 **Healthline**
www.healthline.com
Provides medical and health articles and information.

399 **Healthlink USA**
www.healthlinkusa.com
Health information concerning treatment, cures, prevention, diagnosis, risk factors, research, support groups, email lists, personal stories and much more. Updated regularly.

400 **International Association of Eating Disorders Professionals Foundation**
www.iaedp.com
Supplies printed information and sponsors meetings and other activities. Publishes a directory of speech instructors and maintains a list of sources for supplies for laryngectomee.

401 **MedicineNet**
www.medicinenet.com
An online resource for consumers providing easy-to-read, authoritative medical and health information.

402 **MedlinePlus**
www.medlineplus.gov
A service of the National Library of Medicine, MedlinePlus is an online resource providing health and wellness information in both English and Spanish.

403 **Medscape**
www.medscape.com
Medscape offers specialists, primary care physicians, and other health professionals the Web's most robust and integrated medical information and educational tools.

404 **Mirror Mirror**
www.mirror-mirror.org
Offers information on eating disorders and eating disorder treatment.

405 **MyPlate**
www.myplate.gov
Created and managed by the US Department of Agriculture's Center for Nutrition Policy & Promotion, MyPlate is a dietary guide providing resources and recipes to promote healthy eating for all Americans.

406 **National Association of Anorexia Nervosa and Associated Disorders**
www.anad.org
Works to prevent eating disorders and provides numerous programs — all free — to help victims and families including hotlines, support groups, referrals, information packets, and online content. Educational/prevention programs include presentations and early detection.

407 **National Eating Disorders Association**
www.nationaleatingdisorders.org
NEDA aims to eliminate eating disorders and body dissatisfaction through prevention efforts, education, referral and support services, advocacy training, and research.

408 **Nutrition.gov**
www.nutrition.gov
Sponsored by the United States Department of Agriculture (USDA), Nutrition.gov offers information on topics in food and nutrition, including healthy eating, physical activity, and food safety.

409 Science Daily

www.sciencedaily.com

Provides information on the latest news and research in science, health, the environment, and technology.

410 UnlockFood

www.unlockfood.ca

A website from Dietitians of Canada. Provides videos, recipes, and information on food and nutrition, as well as helps Canadians connect with a dietitian.

411 Verywell

www.verywellhealth.com

Offers health, medicine, and wellness information from health professionals.

412 WebMD

www.webmd.com

Provides credible information, supportive communities, and in-depth reference material about health subjects. A source for original and timely health information as well as material from well known content providers.

413 Weight-Control Information Network

www.win.niddk.nih.gov

The Weight-control Information Network (WIN) provides the general public, health professionals, and the media with up-to-date, science-based information on obesity, weight control, physical activity, and related nutritional issues. WIN provides tip sheets, fact sheets, and brochures for a range of audiences. Some of WIN's content is available in Spanish.

GASTROINTESTINAL DISORDERS

Gastrointestinal (GI) diseases are diseases of the digestive tract. When digestion occurs, food and beverages are broken down into nutrients or small pieces that the body can absorb to make energy and use as the building blocks for cells. The GI tract includes the esophagus, stomach, large and small intestines, liver, pancreas and gallbladder. Diseases related to the GI tract include Celiac disease, Crohn's disease, irritable bowel syndrome (IBS) and lactose intolerance. These conditions may cause trouble swallowing, bleeding, bloating, diarrhea, constipation, incontinence, belly pain, nausea and vomiting with weight gain or loss. Diseases may be mild or serious. Adequate nutrition can be challenging when gastrointestinal diseases are caused or whose symptoms worsen by certain foods. Healthcare providers, especially registered clinical dieticians, are often needed to determine a diet that can balance the body's nutritional needs with disease management.

Many diseases have a gastrointestinal component. Celiac, Crohn's, IBS and lactose intolerance have a major gastrointestinal component. Others have less, or varying degrees of gastrointestinal involvement, like gallstones, rectal problems, strictures, gastritis and gastric ulcers, liver problems including hepatitis B and C, cirrhosis and alcoholic hepatitis, pancreatitis, polyps, cancer, ulcerative colitis, gastroesophageal reflux disease (GERD) and hiatal hernia. Diagnosis is based on patient history and a physical examination conducted by a healthcare provider, tests including colonoscopy, upper GI endoscopy, and endoscopic examinations including retrograde cholangiopancreatography and ultrasound and blood work. Often a gastroenterologist (physician specializing in GI diseases), is involved in the diagnostic process. Maintaining a healthy diet is a key component in any disease affecting the gastrointestinal tract.

Celiac disease impacts the small intestine, and is triggered by foods that contain gluten, which triggers an abnormal immune response. It is a chronic, autoimmune disorder and causes long-term problems that prevent the body from getting critical nutrients. Symptoms vary, but usually include bloating, chronic diarrhea, constipation, loose, greasy, foul-smelling stools, nausea and vomiting, lactose intolerance due to damage to the small intestine, and pain in the abdomen. Other symptoms may include fatigue, joint or bone pain, depression, headaches, seizures and peripheral neuropathy, reproductive problems and missed menstrual periods. Symptoms are improved and may be alleviated altogether by following a gluten-free diet. Gluten, a protein found in wheat, rye, barley and other foods, serves as a type of glue that binds foods together. Gluten-free foods include fruit, some grains and flours such as corn, rice and quinoa, a number of dairy foods, and anything labeled gluten free. A clinical dietician will work out a healthy eating plan for patients that provides needed nutrients without the gluten.

Crohn's disease is a chronic disease of the digestive tract that causes inflammation and irritation. Common symptoms include diarrhea, cramping and pain in the abdomen as well as weight loss. The causes are unclear. Diagnosis requires tests, a through family history and physical examination. Treatment may involve medications, bowel rest, and surgery. The goal of treatment is decreasing inflammation in the intestines and is individualized to the patient. A variety of treatment medications are available including aminosalicylates, corticosteroids, immunomodulators, and biologic modifiers. Other drugs may be prescribed to manage the symptoms of the disease. Bowel rest involves drinking only certain fluids for a specified period of time, and may require hospitalization and intravenous fluid therapy. Surgery is necessary in up to 60 percent of patients living with Chron's for 20 or more years. Changing diet, including avoiding carbonated beverages, popcorn, nuts and high-fiber foods, and drinking more liquids, eating small, more frequent meals may reduce symptoms. Keeping a food diary is recommended, as is an eating plan/diet that is high in calories, lactose-free, and low in fat, fiber, and salt. Nutritional supplements and vitamins may be recommended.

Irritable bowel syndrome (IBS) does not include visible damage to the gastrointestinal tract, but symptoms include pain in the abdomen and changes in bowel patterns such as diarrhea and constipation or both. There are three types of IBS: with constipation; with diarrhea; and with mixed bowel habits. About 12 percent of the U.S. population have IBS, with women twice as likely as men to develop the condition. The cause of IBS is unknown. Stress, difficult early life events, certain mental disorders such as depression and anxiety, bacterial infections and food intolerances and sensitivities are suspected as contributing factors. Eating and lifestyle changes, medications and mental health therapies are often indicated treatments. A clinical dietician, doctor and patient will design a diet with more fiber and no gluten, often called the FODMAP diet, which reduces or avoids certain carbohydrate containing foods that are hard to digest such as certain fruits and vegetables, dairy products, wheat and rye products, foods with high-fructose levels, and products containing any sweetener that ends in "ol" such as xylitol, sorbitol, maltitol and mannitol. If symptoms improve after a few weeks on the FODMAP diet, certain foods may be reintroduced while monitoring IBS symptoms.

Lactose intolerance (LI) creates digestive symptoms such as bloating, diarrhea and gas, after eating foods that contain lactose, which is a sugar found in milk. Individuals with LI may be able to tolerate differing amounts of lactose before symptoms occur. LI is not a milk allergy (which is an immune system disorder) but rather intolerance to lactose contained in dairy products. It is caused by lactose malabsorption that occurs when the small intestine can not produce sufficient lactase to break down consumed lactose. Diagnosis is based on family history, symptoms and eating habits. LI can be managed by limiting or avoiding foods with lactose such as milk and milk products. A doctor may recommend taking lactese tablets or drops prior to consuming milk products. It is important to work with a dietician to be sure the patient is getting sufficient nutrients, like vitamin D and calcium. There are many lactose-free and lactose-reduced milk and milk products currently available. Lactose may also be found in products other than dairy such as baked goods, bread, processed foods, meal replacement liquids and nondairy liquid and powdered coffee creamers and whipped toppings, making it important to read labels and keep a food diary of what causes symptoms.

Nutrition plays a significant role in all gastrointestinal disorders as the GI tract is how the body consumes, breaks down and absorbs nutrients. Consultation with a physician and clinical dietician is highly recommended if you have symptoms of GI disease.

Agencies & Associations

415 **Academy of Nutrition & Dietetics**
120 South Riverside Plaza 312-899-0040
Chicago, IL 60606-6995 800-877-1600
media@eatright.org
www.eatright.org
Serves the public through the promotion of optimal nutrition, health, and well-being. Formerly the American Dietetic Association.
Patricia M. Babjak, Chief Executive Officer

416 **American Academy of Pain Medicine**
1705 Edgewater Drive 800-917-1619
Orlando, FL 32804 Fax: 407-749-0714
info@painmed.org
www.painmed.org
The AAPM is a medical specialty society representing physicians and healthcare professionals practicing in the field of pain medicine. Its mission is to promote and advance pain care, education, training, advocacy, and research.
W. Michael Hooten, MD, President
Farshad M. Ahadian, MD, Treasurer

417 **American Celiac Society**
266 Midway Drive 504-305-2968
River Ridge, LA 70123 www.americanceliacsociety.org
Promotes education, research, and mutual support for people with dietary disorders.
Annette Bentley, President
James Bentley, Vice President

418 **American Chronic Pain Association**
11936 West 119th Street 913-991-4740
Overland Park, KS 66213-2216 acpa@theacpa.org
www.theacpa.org
The ACPA facilitates peer support and education for individuals with chronic pain in its many forms, in order to increase quality of life. Also raises awareness among the healthcare community, and with policy makers.
Kathy Sapp, Chief Executive Officer
Scott Farmer, Chief Operating Officer

419 **American College of Gastroenterology**
6400 Goldsboro Road 301-263-9000
Bethesda, MD 20817 www.gi.org
ACG serves clinical and scientific information needs of member physicians and surgeons, who specialize in digestive and related disorders. Emphasis is on scholarly practice, teaching and research.
David A. Greenwald, MD, FACG, President
Amy S. Oxentenko, MD, FACG, Secretary

420 **American Gastroenterological Association**
4930 Del Ray Avenue 301-654-2055
Bethesda, MD 20814 Fax: 301-654-5920
member@gastro.org
www.gastro.org
AGA fosters the development and application of the science of gastroenterology by providing leadership and aid including patient care, research, teaching, continuing education, scientific communication and matters of national health policy.
Tom Serena, Chief Executive Officer
Nancy Chill, Vice President, Business Development

421 **American Hemochromatosis Society**
PO Box 950871 407-829-4488
Lake Mary, FL 32795-0871 888-655-4766
mail@americanhs.org
www.americanhs.org
Educates the public, the medical community and the media by distributing the most current information available on hereditary hemochromatosis (HH) including DNA screening for HH and pediatric HH; also facilitates patient empowerment through an online network.
Sandra Thomas, President

422 **American Neurogastroenterology & Motility Society**
45685 Harmony Lane 734-699-1130
Belleville, MI 48111 Fax: 734-699-1136
admin@motilitysociety.org
www.motilitysociety.org
Promotes research and sponsors professional education seminars about gastrointestinal motility topics including disorders of esophageal, gastric, small intestinal, and colonic function; and sponsors biennial meetings (even years), syposia and courses.
John Pandolfino, MD, President
Lori Ennis, Executive Director

423 **American Pancreatic Association**
2508 West 71st Street 913-402-7102
Prairie Village, KS 66208 apa@apapancreas.org
www.american-pancreatic-association.org
Provides forum for presentation of scientific research related to the pancreas.
O. Joe Hines, MD, President
Ashok Saluja, Secretary-Treasurer

424 **American Society for Gastrointestinal Endoscopy**
3300 Woodcreek Drive 630-573-0600
Downers Grove, IL 60515 800-353-2743
Fax: 630-963-8332
info@asge.org
www.asge.org
ASGE provides information, training, and practice guidelines about gastrointestinal endoscopic techniques.
Douglas K. Rex, MD, MASGE, President
Donald J. Palmisano, JD, CAE, Chief Executive Officer

425 **American Society for Parenteral and Enteral Nutrition (ASPEN)**
8401 Colesville Road 301-587-6315
Silver Spring, MD 20910 Fax: 301-587-2365
aspen@nutritioncare.org
www.nutritioncare.org
Offers information and continuing medical education to professionals involved in the care of parenterally and enterally fed patients. Membership includes complimentary subscriptions to two peer reviewed journals.
Wanda Johnson, Chief Executive Officer
Joanne Kieffer, Senior Director, Finance

426 **Association of Gastrointestinal Motility Disorders**
140 Pleasant Street 781-275-1300
Lexington, MA 02421 info@agmdhope.org
www.agmdhope.org
A non-profit international organization which serves as an integral educational resource concerning digestive motility diseases and disorders. Also functions as an important information base for members of the medical and scientific communities. Also provides a forum for patients suffering from digestive motility diseases and disorders as well as their families and members of the medical, scientific, and nutritional communities.
Mary Angela DeGrazia-DiTucci, President

427 **Canadian Celiac Association**
1450 Meyerside Drive 905-507-6208
Mississauga, Ontario, L5T-2N5 800-363-7296
info@celiac.ca
www.celiac.ca
A national organization dedicated to providing services and support to persons with celiac disease and dermatitis herpetiformis through programs of awareness, advocacy, education, and research.
Janet Bolton, President
Melissa Secord, Executive Director

428 **Celiac Society**
www.celiacsociety.com
Volunteer organization seeking to raise awareness about and provide information on celiac disease and other gluten-related disorders.

429 **Centers for Medicare & Medicaid Services**
7500 Security Boulevard www.cms.gov
Baltimore, MD 21244

U.S. federal agency which administers Medicare, Medicaid, and the State Children's Health Insurance Program.
Chiquita Brooks-LaSure, Administrator
Jonathan Blum, COO

430 **Cyclic Vomiting Syndrome Association**
PO Box 270341 414-342-7880
Milwaukee, WI 53227 cvsa@cvsaonline.org
www.cvsaonline.org
CVSA provides opportunities for patients, families and professionals to offer and receive support and share knowledge about cyclic vomiting syndrome; actively promotes and facilitates medical research about nausea and vomiting.
Blynda Killian, President
Kristin Koch, Secretary

431 **Digestive Disease National Coalition**
507 Capitol Court NE 202-544-7497
Washington, DC 20002 www.ddnc.org
Informs the public and the health care community about digestive disorders; seeks Federal funding for research, education, and training; and represents members' interests regarding Federal and State legislation that affects digestive diseases research.
Bryan Green, President
James DeGerome, MD, Director, Development

432 **Gastrointestinal Society - Canadian Society of Intestinal Research**
231 - 3665 Kingsway 604-873-4876
Vancouver, BC, V5R-5W2 866-600-4875
Fax: 855-875-4429
www.badgut.org
Aims to improve the lives of people with gastrointestinal and liver diseases and disorders by funding research, advocating for patient access to healthcare, and providing evidence-based information for patients.
Gail Attara, Chief Executive Officer
Kwynn Vodnak, Associate Director

433 **Gluten Intolerance Group**
31214 124th Avenue SE 253-833-6655
Auburn, WA 98092 customerservice@gluten.org
gluten.org
Provides instructional and general information materials, as well as counseling and access to gluten-free products and ingredients to persons with celiac sprue and their families; operates telephone information and referral service, and conducts educational seminars.
Cynthia Kupper, RD, CD, Chief Executive Officer
Channon Quinn, Chief Operating Officer

434 **Inflammatory Bowel Disease Program**
Digestive Health Center
Chicago, IL 60611 312-695-5620
www.nm.org
A fully integrated clinical GI program that is part of the Northwestern Medicine Digestive Health Center.

435 **National Celiac Association**
20 Pickering Street 617-262-5422
Needham, MA 02492 888-423-5422
info@nationalceliac.org
nationalceliac.org
Dedicated to helping individuals with celiac disease and gluten sensitivities through education, advocacy, and awareness.
Lee Graham, Executive Director
Kimberly Buckton, Managing Director

436 **National Institute of Biomedical Imaging and Bioengineering**
9000 Rockville Pike 301-496-8859
Bethesda, MD 20892 info@nibib.nih.gov
www.nibib.nih.gov
The mission of the National Institute of Biomedical Imaging and Bioengineering (NIBIB) is to improve health by leading the development and accelerating the application of biomedical technologies.
Bruce J. Tromberg, PhD, Director
Jill Heemskerk, PhD, Deputy Director

437 **National Institute of Diabetes & Digestive & Kidney Diseases**
9000 Rockville Pike 800-860-8747
Bethesda, MD 20892 TTY: 866-569-1162
healthinfo@niddk.nih.gov
www.niddk.nih.gov
Research areas include diabetes, digestive diseases, endocrine and metabolic diseases, hematologic diseases, kidney disease, liver disease, urologic diseases, as well as matters relating to nutrition and obesity.
Griffin P. Rodgers, MD, MACP, Director
Gregory Germino, MD, Deputy Director

438 **National Institute of General Medical Sciences**
45 Center Drive 301-496-7301
Bethesda, MD 20892-6200 info@nigms.nih.gov
www.nigms.nih.gov
The National Institute of General Medical Sciences (NIGMS) supports basic research that increases understanding of biological processes and lays the foundation for advances in disease diagnosis, treatment and prevention.
Jon R. Lorsch, PhD, Director
Dorit Zuk, PhD, Acting Deputy Director

439 **North American Society for Pediatric Gastroenterology, Hepatology & Nutrition**
714 N. Bethlehem Pike 215-641-9800
Ambler, PA 19002 naspghan@naspghan.org
www.naspghan.org
Promotes research and provides a forum for professionals in the areas of pediatric GI liver disease, gastroenterology, and nutrition. Associated with fellow organizations in Europe and Australia (ESPGAN, AUSPGAN).
Margaret K. Stallings, Executive Director
Kim Rose, Associate Director

440 **Northwestern Medicine Digestive Health Center**
Digestive Health Center
Chicago, IL 60611 312-695-5620
www.nm.org
Multifaceted program to meet the needs of people who suffer from gastrointestinal problems; offers literature, videotapes and educational meetings and, if medical care is needed, appropriate referrals are made.

441 **Nurse Practitioners in Women's Health**
PO Box 15837 202-543-9693
Washington, DC 20003 info@npwh.org
www.npwh.org
Ensures the delivery and accessibility of primary and specialty healthcare to women of all ages by women's health and women's health focused nurse practitioners.
Heather L. Maurer, CEO
Donna Ruth, Director, Education

442 **Society for Surgery of the Alimentary Tract**
500 Cummings Center 978-927-8330
Beverly, MA 01915 www.ssat.com
SSAT provides a forum for exchange of information among physicians specializing in alimentary tract surgery.
Mark P. Callery, MD, Chair

443 **Society for the Study of Celiac Disease**
3300 Woodcreek Drive 630-522-7886
Downers Grove, IL 60515 info@theceliacsociety.org
www.theceliacsociety.org
Professional organization of physicians, nurses, dietitians, and other healthcare workers in North America, with specialties in treating celiac disease and gluten-related disorders.
Marty Roth, Executive Director
Michael Dellutri, Project Administrator

444 **Society of American Gastrointestinal Endoscopic Surgeons**
11300 W Olympic Boulevard 310-437-0544
Los Angeles, CA 90064 webmaster@sages.org
www.sages.org
SAGES encourages study and practice of gastrointestinal endoscopy laparoscopy and minimal access surgery.
Liane S. Feldman, MD, President
Brent D. Matthews, MD, Secretary

445 **Society of Gastroenterology Nurses and Associates**
330 N Wabash Avenue 312-321-5165
Chicago, IL 60611 info@sgna.org
www.sgna.org
SGNA provides members with continuing education opportunities practice and training guidelines, and information about trends and development in the field of gastroenterology.
Kim Eskew, MBA, CAE, Executive Director
Martha O'Hanlon, Operations Manager

446 **United Ostomy Associations of America, Inc**
PO Box 525 800-826-0826
Kennebunk, ME 04043 www.ostomy.org
A national network for bowel and urinary diversion support groups in the United States. Its goal is to provide a non-profit association that will serve to unify and strengthen its member support groups, which are organized for the benefit of people who have, or will have intestinal or urinary diversions and their caregivers.
Christine Ryan, Executive Director
Jeanine Gleba, Advocacy Manager

447 **Wound Ostomy and Continence Nurses Society**
1120 Route 73 888-224-9626
Mt Laurel, NJ 08054 info@wocn.org
www.wocn.org
Membership comprises nurses that specialize in enterostomal therapy.
Nicolette Zuecca, Chief Staff Executive
Anna Shnayder, Chief Operations Officer

Alabama

448 **CCFA Alabama Chapter**
244 Goodwin Crest Drive 205-941-9900
Birmingham, AL 35259 800-249-1993
www.ccfa.org/chapters/alabama/
Crohn's and Colitis Foundation of America is a non-profit, volunteer-driven organization dedicated to finding the cure for Crohn's disease and ulcerative colitis.
Pat Talty, Executive Director

Arizona

449 **CCFA Southwest Chapter: Arizona**
8098 Via de Negocio 480-246-3676
Scottsdale, AZ 85258 877-259-2104
southwest@ccfa.org
www.ccfa.org/chapters/southwest/
Crohn's and Colitis Foundation of America is a non-profit volunteer-driven organization dedicated to finding the cure for Crohn's disease and ulcerative colitis.
Kathie Gadberry, Executive Director
Bernadette Sewer, Development Coordinator

California

450 **CCFA California: Greater Los Angeles Chapter**
1640 S Sepulveda Boulevard 310-478-4500
Los Angeles, CA 90025 866-831-9157
losangeles@ccfa.org
www.ccfa.org/chapters/losangeles/
Crohn's and Colitis Foundation of America is a non-profit volunteer-driven organization dedicated to finding the cure for Crohn's disease and ulcerative colitis.
Iyad Zabaneh, Development Coordinator
Kerri Yoder, Education Manager

Colorado

451 **CCFA Rocky Mountain Chapter**
1777 S Bellaire Street 303-639-9163
Denver, CO 80222 866-768-2232
rockymountain@ccfa.org
www.ccfa.org/chapters/rockymountain/
Crohn's and Colitis Foundation of America is a non-profit volunteer-driven organization dedicated to finding the cure for Crohn's disease and ulcerative colitis.
Nancy Freimuth, Walk Manager
Mackenzie Lyle, Interim Executive Director

Connecticut

452 **CCFA Central Connecticut Chapter**
P O Box 275 203-208-3130
Branford, CT 06405 mgrande@ccfa.org
www.ccfa.org/chapters/centralct/
Crohn's and Colitis Foundation of America is a non-profit volunteer-driven organization dedicated to finding the cure for Crohn's disease and ulcerative colitis.
Sally Connolly, Board President

453 **CCFA Northern Connecticut Affiliate Chapter**
PO Box 370614 212-679-1570
W Hartford, CT 06137-0614 800-932-2423
info@ccfa.org
www.ccfa.org/chapters/northernct/
Crohn's and Colitis Foundation of America is a non-profit volunteer-driven organization dedicated to finding the cure for Crohn's disease and ulcerative colitis.
Marilyn Hagg Blohm, Executive Director National Headquarters
Jeff Neale, Public Relations National Headquarters

Florida

454 **CCFA Florida Chapter**
2250 N Druid Hills Road 404-982-0616
Boca Raton, FL 30329-2391 877-664-2929
kkeohane@ccfa.org
www.ccfa.org/chapters/florida/
Crohn's and Colitis Foundation of America is a non-profit volunteer-driven organization dedicated to finding the cure for Crohn's disease and ulcerative colitis.
Deborah Barnard, Development Manager
Lacy Woods, Administrator

Georgia

455 **CCFA Georgia Chapter**
2250 N Druid Hills Road 404-982-0616
Atlanta, GA 30329 800-472-6795
georgia@ccfa.org
www.ccfa.org/chapters/georgia/
Crohn's and Colitis Foundation of America is a non-profit volunteer-driven organization dedicated to finding the cure for Crohn's disease and ulcerative colitis.
Marcia Greenburg, Executive Director
Karen Rittenbaum, Development Director

Illinois

456 **CCFA Illinois: Carol Fisher Chapter**
2250 E Devon Avenue 847-827-0404
Des Plaines, IL 60018 800-886-6664
Illinois@ccfa.org
www.ccfa.org/chapters/illinois/
Crohn's and Colitis Foundation of America is a non-profit volunteer-driven organization dedicated to finding the cure for Crohn's disease and ulcerative colitis.
Marianne Floriano, Executive Director
Kristina Sickles, Development Coordinator

Indiana

457 **CCFA Indiana Chapter**
931 E 86th Street 317-259-8071
Indianapolis, IN 46240 800-332-6029
indiana@ccfa.org
www.ccfa.org/chapters/indiana/
Crohn's and Colitis Foundation of America is a non-profit volunteer-driven organization dedicated to finding the cure for Crohn's disease and ulcerative colitis.
Scott Baumruck, Development Director
Dawn Drinkut, Development Assistant

Iowa

458 **CCFA Iowa Chapter**
PO Box 1184 515-664-8961
Johnston, IA 50131-0016 iowa@ccfa.org
www.ccfa.org/chapters/iowa/
Crohn's and Colitis Foundation of America is a non-profit volunteer-driven organization dedicated to finding the cure for Crohn's disease and ulcerative colitis.
Tony Kline, Chapter President
Abbie Hansen, Vice President Communications

Kansas

459 **CCFA Mid-America Chapter: Kansas**
1034 S Brentwood 314-863-4747
St Louis, MO 63117 800-783-8006
sskodak@ccfa.org
www.ccfa.org/chapters/midamerica/
Crohn's and Colitis Foundation of America is a non-profit volunteer-driven organization dedicated to finding the cure for Crohn's disease and ulcerative colitis.
Steve Skodak, Executive Director
Andi Harrington, Development Manager

Louisiana

460 **CCFA Louisiana Chapter**
7611 Maple Street 504-861-3433
New Orleans, LA 70118 866-382-2232
lams@ccfa.org
www.ccfa.org/chapters/louisiana
Crohn's and Colitis Foundation of America is a non-profit volunteer-driven organization dedicated to finding the cure for Crohn's disease and ulcerative colitis.
David Lee Thomas, Development Director
Gail C Smith, Development Assistant

Maryland

461 **CCFA Maryland Chapter**
10400 Little Patuxent Parkway 443-276-0861
Columbia, MD 21044 800-618-5583
maryland@ccfa.org
www.ccfa.org/chapters/md-southdc
Crohn's and Colitis Foundation of America is a non-profit volunteer-driven organization dedicated to finding the cure for Crohn's disease and ulcerative colitis.
Robert J Milanchus, Regional Executive Director
Mary Glagola, President

Massachusetts

462 **CCFA New England Chapter: Massachusetts**
280 Hillside Avenue 781-449-0324
Needham, MA 02494 800-314-3459
ne@ccfa.org
www.ccfa.org/chapters/ne
Crohn's and Colitis Foundation of America is a non-profit volunteer-driven organization dedicated to finding the cure for Crohn's disease and ulcerative colitis.
Jess Adani, Development Manager
Kristin Patmos, Education Manager

Michigan

463 **CCFA Michigan Chapter: Farmington Hills**
31313 N Western Highway 248-737-0900
Farmington Hills, MI 78334 michigan@ccfa.org
www.ccfa.org/chapters/michigan
Crohn's and Colitis Foundation of America is a non-profit volunteer-driven organization dedicated to finding the cure for Crohn's disease and ulcerative colitis.
Bernard L Riker, Executive Director
Gilda Hauser, Development Manager

Minnesota

464 **CCFA Minnesota Chapter**
1885 University Avenue W 651-917-2424
Saint Paul, MN 55104 888-422-3266
Minnesota@ccfa.org
www.ccfa.org/chapters/minnesota
Crohn's and Colitis Foundation of America is a non-profit volunteer-driven organization dedicated to finding the cure for Crohn's disease and ulcerative colitis.
Maggie Brown, Take Steps Manager
Ruby Lanoux, Development Manager

Missouri

465 **CCFA Mid-America Chapter: Missouri**
1034 S Brentwood 314-863-4747
Saint Louis, MO 63117 800-783-8006
info@ccfa.org
www.ccfa.org/chapters/midamerica
Crohn's and Colitis Foundation of America is a non-profit volunteer-driven organization dedicated to finding the cure for Crohn's disease and ulcerative colitis.
Steve Skodak, Executive Director
Andi Harrington, Development Manager

New Jersey

466 **CCFA New Jersey Chapter**
45 Wilson Avenue 732-786-9960
Manalapan, NJ 07726 newjersey@ccfa.org
www.ccfa.org/chapters/newjersey
Crohn's and Colitis Foundation of America is a non-profit volunteer-driven organization dedicated to finding the cure for Crohn's disease and ulcerative colitis.
Rosemarie Golombos, Executive Director
Barbara Fedorchak, Chapter Development Manager

New York

467 **CCFA Greater New York Chapter: National Headquarters**
386 Park Avenue S 800-932-2423
New York, NY 10016-8804 800-932-2423
info@ccfa.org
www.ccfa.org
Crohn's and Colitis Foundation of America is a non-profit volunteer-driven organization dedicated to finding the cure for Crohn's disease and ulcerative colitis.
Marilyn Hagg Blohm, Executive Director
Jeff Neale, Public Relations/Media Director

468 **CCFA Long Island Chapter**
585 Stewart Avenue 516-222-5530
Garden City, NY 11530 longisland@ccfa.org
www.ccfa.org/chapters/longisland
Crohn's and Colitis Foundation of America is a non-profit volunteer-driven organization dedicated to finding the cure for Crohn's disease and ulcerative colitis.
Marilyn Hagg Blohm, Executive Director National Office
Jeff Neale, Public Relations/Media National Office

469 **CCFA Rochester/Southern Tier Chapter**
2117 Buffalo Road 585-617-4771
Rochester, NY 14624 800-932-2423
rochester@ccfa.org
www.ccfa.org/chapters/rochester
Crohn's and Colitis Foundation of America is a non-profit volunteer-driven organization dedicated to finding the cure for Crohn's disease and ulcerative colitis.
Marilyn Hagg Blohm, Executive Director National Headquarters
Jeff Neale, Public Relations

470 **CCFA Upstate/Northeastern New York Chapter**
4 Normanskill Boulevard 518-439-0252
Delmar, NY 12054 upstateny@ccfa.org
www.ccfa.org/chapters/upstateny

Crohn's and Colitis Foundation of America is a non-profit volunteer-driven organization dedicated to finding the cure for Crohn's disease and ulcerative colitis.
Linda Winston, Chapter President
Peter Purcel MD, Medical Advisory Chair

471 **CCFA Western New York Chapter**
2714 Sheridan Drive 716-833-2870
Tonawanda, NY 14150-0224 800-932-2423
jpetri@ccfa.org
www.ccfa.org/chapters/westernny
Crohn's and Colitis Foundation of America is a non-profit volunteer-driven organization dedicated to finding the cure for Crohn's disease and ulcerative colitis.
Marilyn Hagg Blohm, Executive Director National Headquarters
Jeff Neale, Public Relations

North Carolina

472 **CCFA Carolinas Chapter**
2901 N Davidson Street 704-332-1611
Charlotte, NC 28205 877-332-1611
carolinas@ccfa.org
www.ccfa.org/chapters/carolinas
Crohn's and Colitis Foundation of America is a non-profit volunteer-driven organization dedicated to finding the cure for Crohn's disease and ulcerative colitis.
Angela Parks, Development Director
Julie Perkins, Special Events/Development Manager

Ohio

473 **CCFA Central Ohio Chapter**
5008 Pine Creek Drive 614-865-1933
Westerville, OH 43081 800-625-5977
centralohio@ccfa.org
www.ccfa.org/chapters/centralohio
Crohn's and Colitis Foundation of America is a non-profit volunteer-driven organization dedicated to finding the cure for Crohn's disease and ulcerative colitis.
Janelle Gasaway, Take Steps Manager
Kelly Bush, Development Coordinator

474 **CCFA Northeast Ohio Chapter**
23775 Commerce Park Road 216-831-2692
Beachwood, OH 44122 866-345-2232
neohio@ccfa.org
www.ccfa.org/chapters/neohio
Crohn's and Colitis Foundation of America is a non-profit volunteer-driven organization dedicated to finding the cure for Crohn's disease and ulcerative colitis.
Kristin Knipp, Development Coordinator
Patty Kaplan, Development Manager NE Ohio Chapter

475 **CCFA Southwest Ohio Chapter**
8 Triangle Park Drive 513-772-3550
Cincinnati, OH 45246 877-283-7513
SWOhio@ccfa.org
www.ccfa.org/chapters/swohio
Crohn's and Colitis Foundation of America is a non-profit volunteer-driven organization dedicated to finding the cure for Crohn's disease and ulcerative colitis.
Rachel Spradlin, Take Steps Manager
Jenny Southers, Development Manager SE Ohio Chapter

Oklahoma

476 **CCFA Oklahoma Chapter**
4504 E 67th Street 918-523-8540
Tulsa, OK 74136 800-658-1533
jsummers@ccfa.org
www.ccfa.org/chapters/oklahoma
Crohn's and Colitis Foundation of America is a non-profit volunteer-driven organization dedicated to finding the cure for Crohn's disease and ulcerative colitis.
Judy Summers, Regional Executive Director
Christopher Woods, President

Pennsylvania

477 **CCFA Philadelphia/Delaware Valley Chapter**
367 E Street Road 215-396-9100
Trevose, PA 19053 888-340-4744
Philadelphia@ccfa.org
www.ccfa.org/chapters/philadelphia
Crohn's and Colitis Foundation of America is a non-profit volunteer-driven organization dedicated to finding the cure for Crohn's disease and ulcerative colitis.
Barbara Berman, Executive Director
Suzanne Rhodeside, Development Director

478 **CCFA Western Pennsylvania/West Virginia Chapter**
300 Penn Center Boulevard 412-823-8272
Pittsburgh, PA 15235 877-823-8272
wpawv@ccfa.org
www.ccfa.org/chapters/wpawv
Crohn's and Colitis Foundation of America is a non-profit volunteer-driven organization dedicated to finding the cure for Crohn's disease and ulcerative colitis.
10-12 pages
Jamie Rhoades, Development Manager
Susan Kukic, Executive Director

South Carolina

479 **CCFA South Carolina Chapter**
2901 N Davidson Street 704-332-1611
Charlotte, NC 28205 877-632-1611
carolinas@ccfa.org
www.ccfa.org/chapters/carolinas
Crohn's and Colitis Foundation of America is a non-profit volunteer-driven organization dedicated to finding the cure for Crohn's disease and ulcerative colitis.
Angela Parks, Development Manager
Tewanna Sanders, Education & Support Manager

Tennessee

480 **CCFA Tennessee Chapter**
95 White Bridge Road 615-356-0444
Nashville, TN 37205 866-814-2232
tennessee@ccfa.org
www.ccfa.org/chapters/tennessee
Crohn's and Colitis Foundation of America is a non-profit volunteer-driven organization dedicated to finding the cure for Crohn's disease and ulcerative colitis.
Michelle J Chianese, Education & Support Manager
Nicole Boisvert, Walk Manager

Texas

481 **CCFA Houston Gulf Coast/South Texas Chapter**
5120 Woodway 713-572-2232
Houston, TX 77056 800-785-2232
infohouston@ccfa.org
www.ccfa.org/chapters/houston
Crohn's and Colitis Foundation of America is a non-profit volunteer-driven organization dedicated to finding the cure for Crohn's disease and ulcerative colitis.
Brandy Bendele, Walk Manager
Erin Fagan, Development Manager

482 **CCFA North Texas Chapter**
12801 N Central Expressway 972-386-0607
Dallas, TX 75243 ntexas@ccfa.org
www.ccfa.org/chapters/ntexas
Crohn's and Colitis Foundation of America is a non-profit volunteer-driven organization dedicated to finding the cure for Crohn's disease and ulcerative colitis.
Rachel Wallace, Development Manager
Sharon Seagraves, Executive Director

Virginia

483 **CCFA Greater Washington DC/Virginia Chapter**
4085 Chain Bridge Road 703-865-6130
Fairfax, VA 22314 877-807-5271
washingtondc@ccfa.org
www.ccfa.org/chapters/washingtondc
Crohn's and Colitis Foundation of America is a non-profit volunteer-driven organization dedicated to finding the cure for Crohn's disease and ulcerative colitis.
Eileen Pugh, Executive Director
Stephanie Campbell, Development Coordinator

Washington

484 **CCFA Washington State Chapter**
9 Lake Bellevue Drive 425-451-8455
Bellevue, WA 98005 877-703-6900
northwest@ccfa.org
www.ccfa.org/chapters/northwest
Crohn's and Colitis Foundation of America is a non-profit volunteer-driven organization dedicated to finding the cure for Crohn's disease and ulcerative colitis.
Linda Huse, Executive Director
Jennifer Simmons, Development Manager

Wisconsin

485 **CCFA Wisconsin Chapter**
1126 S 70th Street 414-475-5520
W Allis, WI 53214 877-586-5588
wisconsin@ccfa.org
www.ccfa.org/chapters/wisconsin
Crohn's and Colitis Foundation of America is a non-profit volunteer-driven organization dedicated to finding the cure for Crohn's disease and ulcerative colitis.
Jan Lenz, Executive Director
Nadine Davis, Development Coordinator

Libraries & Resource Centers

486 **National Digestive Diseases Information Clearinghouse**
2 Information Way 800-891-5389
Bethesda, MD 20892-3570 TTY: 866-569-1162
nddic@info.niddk.nih.gov
www.digestive.niddk.nih.gov
Established to increase knowledge and understanding about digestive diseases among people with these conditions and their families, health care professionals, and the general public. To carry out this mission, NDDIC works closely with a coordinating panel of representatives from Federal agencies, voluntary organizations on the national level, and professional groups to identify and respond to informational needs about digestive diseases.

Foundations & Research Centers

487 **ACG Institute for Clinical Research and Education**
6400 Goldsboro Road 301-263-9000
Bethesda, MD 20817 gi.org/acg-institute
Innovation center and source of funding for clinically oriented research and education into gastroenterology.
Nicholas J. Shaheen, MD, MPH, FACG, Director

488 **American Pancreatic Association Foundation**
3904 West 126th Street 913-402-7102
Leawood, KS 66209 apa@apapancreas.org
www.american-pancreatic-association.org
Aims to cure pancreatic disease by supporting and promoting research.
Fred Gorelick, Chair
Ashok Saluja, Secretary-Treasurer

489 **Baylor College of Medicine: General Clinical Research Center for Adults**
One Baylor Plaza 713-798-4951
Houston, TX 77030 dbier@bcm.edu
www.bcm.edu/pediatrics
Endocrinology, genetics and gastroenterology research.
Dennis M Bier MD, Program Director
Paul Klotman, President

490 **Celiac Disease Foundation**
20350 Ventura Boulevard 818-716-1513
Woodlands Hills, CA 91364 www.celiac.org
Provides services and support to persons with celiac disease and dermatitis herpetiformis, through programs of awareness, education, advocacy and research; telephone information and referral services; medical advisory board annual educational conference and quarterly newsletters.
Marilyn Grunzweig Geller, Chief Executive Officer
Deborah J. Ceizler, Chief Development Officer

491 **Columbus Children's Research Institute**
700 Children's Drive 614-722-2000
Columbus, OH 43205 John.Barnard@NationwideChildrens.org
www.nationwidechildrens.org
Research institute dedicated to enhancing the health of children by engaging in the high quality cutting-edge research according to the highest scientific and ethical standards.
John A Barnard, Research Institute President
Steve Allen MD, CEO

492 **Crohn's & Colitis Foundation**
733 Third Avenue 800-932-2423
New York, NY 10017 info@crohnscolitisfoundation.org
www.crohnscolitisfoundation.org
CCF's mission is to cure and prevent Crohn's disease and ulcerative colitis through research, and to improve the quality of life of children and adults affected by the disease through education and support. The foundation offers patient and professional support.
Michael Osso, President & CEO
Allison Coffrey, Chief Development Officer

493 **Digestive Disorders Associates Ridgely Oaks Professional Center**
Ridgely Oaks Professional Center
621 Ridgely Avenue 41 -22 -488
Annapolis, MD 21401 800-273-0505
TTY: 800-735-2258
www.dda.net
Specialize in the diagnosis and treatment of diseases of the entire digestive system including esophagus stomach small and large intestine colon liver pancreas and gall bladder.
Michael S Epstein, Founder
Charles E King, Doctor

494 **Division of Digestive & Liver Diseases of Cloumbia University**
630 W 168th Street 212-305-5960
New York, NY 10032-3784 hjw14@columbia.edu
www.cumc.columbia.edu
The Division's faculty members are devoted to research and the clinical care of patients with gastrointestinal, liver and nutritional disorders. The Division is also responsible for the Gastroenterology Training Program at the medical center and for teaching medical students, interns, residents, fellows and attending physicians aspects of gastrointestinal and liver diseases.
Howard J Worman MD, Division Director
Karen Wisdom, Director

495 **Gastro-Intestinal Research Foundation**
70 E Lake Street 312-332-1350
Chicago, IL 60601-5915 info@girf.org
www.giresearchfoundation.org
Founded to help combat gastrointestinal diseases. Raises funds to support research at the Center for study of the Digestive Diseases at the University of Chicago Medical Center and to support advanced training for scientists. Sponsors educational activities for the public.
Kimberly Coady, Executive Director
Eric Berlin, President

496 **Hahnemann University, Krancer Center for Inflammatory Bowel Disease Research**
230 N Broad St 215-762-7000
Philadelphia, PA 19102 www.hahnemannhospital.com
Research into the causes and treatments of ulcerative colitis and Crohn's disease.
Dr. Harris Clearfield, Director

497 **Hemochromatosis Foundation**
www.hemochromatosis.org
Provides information to the public, families, and professionals about hereditary hemochromatosis (HH); conducts and raises funds for research; encourages early screening for HH; holds symposiums and meetings; and offers genetic counseling along with support for patients, families, and professionals.

498 **International Foundation for Functional Gastrointestinal Disorders (IFFGD)**
PO Box 170864 414-964-1799
Milwaukee, WI 53217 888-964-2001
iffgd@iffgd.org
www.iffgd.org
Non-profit education, support, and research organization devoted to increasing awareness and understanding of functional gastrointestinal disorders, including irritable bowel syndrome (IBS), constipation, diarrhea, pain, and incontinence. Mission is to inform, assist and support people affected by these disorders.
Nancy J. Norton, Founder
Ceciel T. Rooker, President

499 **NASPGHAN Foundation**
714 N. Bethlehem Pike 215-641-9800
Ambler, PA 19002 naspghan@naspghan.org
www.naspghan.org
The foundation's sole mission is to improve treatment and management of gastrointestinal, hepatobiliary, pancreatic, and nutritional disorders in children.

500 **Oley Foundation**
43 New Scotland Ave 518-262-5079
Albany, NY 12208-3478 800-776-6539
www.oley.org
Promotes and advocates education and research in home parenteral and enteral nutrition; provides support and networking to patients through information clearinghouse and regional volunteer networks; sponsors meetings and conferences, including annual patient/clinician conference; maintains speakers bureau.
Joan Bishop, Executive Director
Roslyn Dahl, Communications & Development

501 **Society for Surgery of the Alimentary Foundation**
500 Cummings Center 978-927-8330
Beverly, MA 01915 ssat.com/foundation
Provides funding for surgeon-scientists.
Jeffrey B. Matthews, MD, Chair

502 **The C.H.I.L.D. Foundation**
2150 Western Parkway 604-736-0645
Vancouver, BC, V6T-1V6 Fax: 604-228-0066
www.child.ca
The C.H.I.L.D. Foundation supports research to help children with intestinal and liver disorders, including Crohn's disease and ulcerative colitis.
Mary Parsons, President & CEO

503 **University of California: Davis Gastroenterology & Nutrition Center**
Pediatric GI Medical Center
4900 Broadway www.ucdmc.ucdavis.edu
Sacramento, CA 95820-2214
Research into gastrointestinal mobility and electro-physiology nutrition support and references for the public and patient evaluations.
Bonnie Hyatt, Assistant Director
Jenny Carrick, Senior Director of Communications and Ma

504 **University of California: Los Angeles Center for Ulcer Research**
LA Medical Center
Building 115 Room 117 310-312-9284
Los Angeles, CA 90073 cureadmn@mednet.ucla.edu
www.cure.med.ucla.edu
Offers basic and clinical research related to peptic ulcer disease including causes checks and balances and stress-ulcer relationships.
Enrique Rozengurt, Director
Emeran Mayer, Co-Director

505 **University of Michigan Michigan Gastrointestinal Peptide Research Ctr.**
U-M Health System
1500 E Medical Center Drive 734-936-4000
Ann Arbor, MI 48109 www.med.umich.edu/mgpc
Research into gastroenterology including chemistry of gut hormones is studied.
Chung Owyang MD, Director
Juanita Merc MD PhD, Associate Director

506 **University of Pennsylvania: Harrison Department of Surgical Research**
3400 Spruce Street 215-662-4000
Philadelphia, PA 19104 800-789-PENN
www.uphs.upenn.edu/surgery/res/harrisonr
Offers research and studies on surgical transplantations gastrointestinal physiology.
Julie Hagan Koehler MBA, Business Director
Georgina Suarez, Administrative Assistant

507 **University of Pittsburgh Medical Center**
200 Lothrop Street 412-647-8762
Pittsburgh, PA 15213 800-533-8762
upmc.com
The University of Pittsburgh Medical Center is a health care provider and insurer focused on developing new models of patient-centered care. Its mission is to engage in clinical research, education and innovation to ensure excellence in patient care.
G Nicholas Beckwith III, Chairperson
Jeffrey A Romoff, President and CEO

508 **University of Vermont Medical Center**
111 Colchester Avenue 802-847-0000
Burlington, VT 05401 800-358-1144
www.uvmhealth.org/medcenter
Melinda L Estes, MD, President/CEO
Richarad Magnuson, CFO

Support Groups & Hotlines

509 **Association of Gastrointestinal Motility Disorders**
AGMD International Corporate Headquarters
12 Roberts Drive 781-275-1300
Bedford, MA 01730 digestive.motility@gmail.com
www.agmd-gimotility.org
A non-profit international organization which serves as an integral educational resource concerning digestive motility diseases and disorders. Also functions as an important information base for members of the medical and scientific communities. Also provides a forum for patients suffering from digestive motility diseases and disorders as well as their families and members of the medical, scientific, and nutritional communities.
Mary Angela DeGrazia-DiTucci, President/Patient/Founder

510 **Celiac Disease Foundation**
20350 Ventura Boulevard 818-716-1513
Woodlands Hills, CA 91364 www.celiac.org
Provides services and support to persons with celiac disease and dermatitis herpetiformis, through programs of awareness, education, advocacy and research; telephone information and referral services; medical advisory board annual educational conference and quarterly newsletters.
Marilyn Grunzweig Geller, Chief Executive Officer
Deborah J. Ceizler, Chief Development Officer

511 **National Health Information Center**
Office of Disease Prevention & Health Promotion
1101 Wootton Pkwy odphpinfo@hhs.gov
Rockville, MD 20852 www.health.gov/nhic
Supports public health education by maintaining a calendar of National Health Observances; helps connect consumers and health professionals to organizations that can best answer questions and provide up-to-date contact information from reliable sources; updates on a yearly basis toll-free numbers for health information, Federal health clearinghouses and info centers.
Don Wright, MD, MPH, Director

512 **Pull-thru Network**
2312 Savoy Street 205-978-2930
Hoover, AL 35226-1528 www.pullthrough.org
Dedicated to the needs of those born wutith anorectal malformation or colon disease and any of the associated diagnoses.

Journals

513 **American Journal of Gastroenterology**
American College of Gastroenterology
6400 Goldsboro Rd 301-263-9000
Bethesda, MD 20817 gi.org/journals-publications
Serves clinical and scientific information needs of member physicians and surgeons, who specialize in digestive and related disorders. Emphasis is on scholarly practice, teaching, and research.

514 **American Journal of Gastrointestinal Surgery**
Society for Surgery of the Alimentary Tract
500 Cummings Center 978-927-8330
Beverly, MA 01915 ssat@prri.com
www.ssat.com
Provides information for physicians specializing in gastrointestinal surgery.
Robin S. McLeod, Chair
Fabrizio Michelassi, President

515 **Clinical Gastroenterology & Hepatology**
American Gastroenterological Association
4930 Del Ray Avenue 301-654-2055
Bethesda, MD 20814 member@gastro.org
www.gastro.org
Focuses on research, medical and professional developments in the science of gastroenterology.
John I. Allen, President
Michael Camilleri, President-Elect

516 **Clinical Updates**
American Society for Gastrointestinal Endoscopy
3300 Woodcreek Dr. 630-573-0600
Downers Grove, IL 60515 info@asge.org
www.asge.org
Provides information, training, and practice guidelines about gastrointestinal endoscopic techniques.
Colleen M. Schmitt, President
Douglas O. Faigel, President-elect

517 **Colon and Rectal Surgery**
International Academy of Proctology
PO Box 1716 765-342-3686
Martinsville, IN 46151
Information for professionals involved with colon and rectal surgery.
George Donnally MD

518 **Crohn's Disease, Ulcerative Colitis, and School**
Pediatric Crohn's & Colitis Association
PO Box 188 617-489-5854
Newton, MA 02468 questions@pcca.hypermart.net
pcca.hypermart.net
Information on Crohn's Disease and Ulcerative Colitis, including medical, nutritional, psychological and social factors.

519 **Digestive Health Matters**
Intl. Foundation for Gastrointestinal Disorders
PO Box 170864 414-964-1799
Milwaukee, WI 53217 888-964-2001
iffgd@iffgd.org
www.iffgd.org
Quarterly journal focuses on upper and lower gastrointestinal disorders in adults and children. Educational pamphlets and factsheets are available. Patient and professional membership.
Nancy Norton, President

520 **Food & Nutrition**
120 South Riverside Plaza 312-899-0040
Chicago, IL 60606-6995 800-877-1600
foodandnutrition@eatright.org
www.eatright.org
Formerly the ADA Times, Food & Nutrition is the member and professional magazine of the Academy of Nutrition & Dietetics.

521 **Foundation Focus**
Crohn's & Colitis Foundation of America
386 Park Avenue S 212-685-3440
New York, NY 10016-8804 800-932-2423
info@ccfa.org
www.ccfa.org
Magazine for CCFA supporters.

522 **GIG Quarterly Magazine**
Gluten Intolerance Group: GIG
31214 124th Avenue SE 253-833-6655
Auburn, WA 98092-3667 customerservice@gluten.org
www.gluten.net
Member magazine. Offers updated medical and technological information for patients with celiac disease, their families and healthcare professionals.
Cynthia Kupper RDCD, Executive Director

523 **Gastroenterology**
American Gastroenterological Association
4930 Del Ray Avenue 301-654-2055
Bethesda, MD 20814-3002 member@gastro.org
www.gastro.org
Focuses on research, medical and professional developments in the science of gastroenterology.
John I. Allen, President
Michael Camilleri, President-Elect

524 **Gastroenterology Nursing**
Society of Gastroenterology Nurses and Associates
330 N. Wabash Ave. 312-321-5165
Chicago, IL 60611 800-245-7462
sgna@sba.com
www.sgna.org
Provides members with information about trends and development in the field of gastroenterology nursing.
Colleen Keith, President
Lisa Fonkalsrud, President-Elect

525 **Gastrointestinal Endoscopy**
American Society for Gastrointestinal Endoscopy
3300 Woodcreek Dr. 630-573-0600
Downers Grove, IL 60515 866-353-2743
info@asge.org
www.asge.org
Provides information, training, and practice guidelines about gastrointestinal endoscopic techniques.
Adjournia Jones, Manager of Operations
Angela Saylor, Accounting Assistant Manager

526 **Hemochromatosis Awareness**
Hemochromatosis Foundation
PO Box 8569 518-489-0972
Albany, NY 12208 www.hemochromatosis.org
Provides information to the public, families, professionals and government agencies about hereditary hemochromatosis (HH); conducts and raises funds for research; encourages early screening for HH; holds symposiums and meetings; and offers genetic counseling along with support for patients, families, and professionals.
Margit Krikker MD, Medical Director

527 **IBD File**
Crohn's & Colitis Foundation of America
386 Park Avenue S 212-685-3440
New York, NY 10016-8804 800-932-2423
info@ccfa.org
www.ccfa.org
Offers updated information and the latest medical news about Crohn's Disease and Colitis.

528 **Inner Circle**
Reach Out for Youth with Ileitis and Colitis
84 Northgate Circle 516-293-3102
Melville, NY 11747 www.rightdiagnosis.com
Provides information to patients with ileitis and colitis and their families.

529 **Inside Story**
Reach Out for Youth with Ileitis and Colitis
84 Northgate Circle 516-293-3102
Melville, NY 11747 www.rightdiagnosis.com
Provides information to patients with ileitis and colitis and their families.

530 **Ironic Blood**
Iron Overload Diseases Association
433 Westward Drive 561-840-8512
Taylors, SC 29687-5123 info@irondisorders.org
www.irondisorders.org
Information for hemochromatosis patients and families.

531 **Journal of Parenteral and Enteral Nutrition**
ASPEN
8630 Fenton Street 301-587-6315
Silver Spring, MD 20910-3805 aspen@nutr.org
www.nutritioncare.org
Offers information to professionals involved in the care of parenterally and enterally fed patients.
100 pages
Adrian Nickel, Director Communications/Marketing

532 **Journal of Pediatric Gastroenterology and Nutrition**
N American Society for Pediatric Gastroenterology
6900 Grove Road 609-848-1000
Thorofare, NJ 08086 www.jpgn.org/
Provides information for professionals in the areas of pediatric GI liver disease, gastroenterology, and nutrition.

533 **Journal of the Academy of Nutrition and Dietetics**
120 South Riverside Plaza 312-899-4831
Chicago, IL 60606-6995 journal@eatright.org
www.eatright.org
Official research publication of the Academy of Nutrition and Dietetics.

534 **Nutrition in Clinical Practice**
ASPEN
8630 Fenton Street 301-587-6315
Silver Spring, MD 20910-3805 aspen@nutr.org
www.nutritioncare.org
Offers information to professionals involved in the care of parenterally and enterally fed patients.
100 pages
Adrian Nickel, Director Communications/Marketing

535 **Ostomy Quarterly**
United Ostomy Association
P.O. Box 512 800-826-0826
Northfield, MN 55057 info@uoa.org
www.uoa.org
First person stories, ostomy management advice from an ET and MD, organization news and ostomy product information.
72 pages
Susan Burns, President
Jim Murray, 1st Vice President

536 **Pancreas**
American Pancreatic Association
3 Bethesda Metro Center 301-961-1508
Bethesda, MD 20814-6904 866-726-2737
info@pancreasfoundation.org
pancreasfoundation.org
Provides information on scientific research related to the pancreas.
Joseph M. Titlebaum, Chair
Jessica Kruse, Secretary

537 **Phoenix Magazine**
United Ostomy Association of America
PO Box 512 800-826-0826
Northfield, MN 55057 info@uoaa.org
www.uoa.org
America's leading ostomy patient magazine providing colostomy, ileostomy, urostomy and continent diversion information, management techniques, new products and much more.
David Rudzin, President

538 **Pull-thru Network News**
Pull-thru Network
4 Woody Lane 203-221-7530
Westport, CT 06880 Pullthrunw@aol.com
members.aol.com/pullthrunw/Pullthru.html
Provides information to patients and families of children who have had or will have pull-through surgery to correct an imperforate anus or associated malformation, Hirschsprung's disease, or other fecal incontinence problems.

539 **SGNA News**
Society of Gastroenterology Nurses and Associates
330 N. Wabash Ave. 312-321-5165
Chicago, IL 60611 800-245-7462
www.sgna.org
Provides members with information about trends and development in the field of gastroenterology.

540 **Whooo's Report**
American Celiac Society
PO Box 23455 504-737-3293
New Orleans, LA 70183 amerceliacsoc@netscape.net
Provides practical assistance to members and individuals with celiac disease and information about the disease to the public.

Digital Resources

541 **A Day in the Life of a Child**
Albany Medical Center 518-262-5079
Albany, NY 12208-3478 800-776-6539
www.oley.org
In this video you are welcomed into the household of the Miller family. The Millers have three children, one of whom is tube fed. Jessica has been dependent on tube-feedings since birth, and her family is prepared to show you just what that means. They share tips for keeping a sterile environment in a house with three children, and tips for helping Jessica fit in with her peers.
Joan Bishop, Executive Director

542 **CD-A NIH Consensus Conference**
Celiac Sprue Association/USA
PO Box 31700 402-558-0600
Omaha, NE 68131 877-272-4272
www.csaceliacs.org
Celiac Disease - A NIH Consensus Conference - Reaching Out to Improve the Health of Millions.
Mary Schluckebier, Executive Director

543 **Cleveland Clinic Teaching Conference**
Hemochromatosis Foundation
PO Box 8569 518-489-0972
Albany, NY 12208 www.hemochromatosis.org
Provides information to the public, families, and professionals about hereditary hemochromatosis.

544 **Family Teaching Conference**
Hemochromatosis Foundation
PO Box 8569 518-489-0972
Albany, NY 12208 www.hemochromatosis.org
Provides information to the public, families, and professionals about hereditary hemochromatosis.

545 **Inflammatory Bowel Disease**
Gastro-Intestinal Research Foundation
70 E Lake Street 312-332-1350
Chicago, IL 60601 info@girf.org
www.giresearchfoundation.org

546 **Life with Mic-Key**
Albany Medical Center 518-262-5079
Albany, NY 12208-3478 800-776-6539
www.oley.org
Serves as an informative and introductory guide for adapting to life with a Mic-key low profile feeding tube. Low profile means that the Mic-key tube lies very close to the patient's body and does not stick out. It's slim design allows more air to circulate around the stoma site and makes it easy to care for. The Mic-key tube uses a balloon to hold it in place and comes with several important accessories, including two types of extensions sets and an anti-reflux valve.
Joan Bishop, Executive Director

547 **Mealtime Notions - The 'Get Permission' Approach to Mealtimes and Oral Motor**
Marsha Dunn Klein, MED, OTR/L, author
Albany Medical Center 518-262-5079
Albany, NY 12208-3478 800-776-6539
www.oley.org
This video explores the development of trusting feeding relationships, understanding the child's pace, and strategies for increasing permissive behavior. Tools discussed in this video include an introduction to the sensory continuum, a description of the around the bowl technique, and tips for removing the stress from your child's mealtime.
Joan Bishop, Executive Director

548 **WIN Notes**
Weight-control Information Network
1 WIN Way 301-496-3583
Bethesda, MD 20892-3665 877-946-4627
www.niddk.nih.gov/health/nutrit/win.htm
Addresses the health information needs of individuals with weight-control problems. Available on the WIN web site.

Web Sites

549 **Academy of Nutrition & Dietetics**
www.eatright.org
Serves the public through the promotion of optimal nutrition, health, and well-being. Formerly the American Dietetic Association.

550 **American Celiac Society**
www.americanceliacsociety.org
Promotes education, research, and mutual support for people with dietary disorders.

551 **American College of Gastroenterology**
www.gi.org
ACG serves clinical and scientific information needs of member physicians and surgeons, who specialize in digestive and related disorders. Emphasis is on scholarly practice, teaching, and research.

552 **American Gastroenterological Association**
www.gastro.org
AGA fosters the development and application of the science of gastroenterology by providing leadership and aid including patient care, research, teaching, continuing education, scientific communication and matters of national health policy.

553 **American Hemochromatosis Society**
www.americanhs.org
Educates the public, the medical community, and the media by distributing the most current information available on hereditary hemochromatosis (HH), including DNA screening for HH and pediatric HH; also facilitates patient empowerment through an online network.

554 **American Pseudo-Obstruction and Hirschsprung's Disease Society**
Promotes public awareness of gastrointestinal motility disorders, in particular intestinal pseudo-obstruction and Hirschsprung's Disease; provides education and support to individuals and families of children who have been diagnosed with these disorders through parent-to-parent contact, publications, and educational symposia; and encourages and supports medical research in the area of gastrointestinal motility disorders.

555 **American Society for Gastrointestinal Endoscopy**
www.asge.org
ASGE provides information, training, and practice guidelines about gastrointestinal endoscopic techniques.

556 **American Society of Abdominal Surgeons**
www.abdominalsurg.org
ASAS sponsors extensive continuing education program for physicians in the field of abdominal surgery and maintains library.

557 **Background on Functional Gastrointestinal Disorders**
www.med.unc.edu
Statistical background information on gastrointestinal disorders.

558 **Celiac Disease & Gluten-Free Diet Online Resource Center**
www.celiac.com
Internet based support organization that provides important resources and information for people on gluten-free diets due to celiac disease, gluten intolerance or wheat allergy.

559 **Celiac Disease Foundation**
www.celiac.org
Provides services and support to persons with celiac disease and dermatitis herpetiformis, through programs of awareness, education, advocacy and research; telephone information and referral services; medical advisory board annual educational conference and quarterly newsletters.

560 **Children's Motility Disorder Foundation**
www.motility.org
CMDF works to increase awareness of pediatric motility disorders in the general public and among the physicians most likely to encounter children suffering from these conditions, such as pediatricians and family practice doctors. Supports medical research regarding the causes, treatment, and potentially life-threatening disorders.

561 **Crohn's & Colitis Foundation**
www.crohnscolitisfoundation.org
CCF's mission is to cure and prevent Crohn's disease and ulcerative colitis through research, and to improve the quality of life of children and adults affected by the disease through education and support. The foundation offers patient and professional support.

562 **Cyclic Vomiting Syndrome Association**
www.cvsaonline.org
CVSA provides opportunities for patients, families and professionals to offer and receive support and share knowledge about cyclic vomiting syndrome; actively promotes and facilitates medical research about nausea and vomiting.

563 **Dietary Guidelines for Americans**
www.dietaryguidelines.gov
Publishes the Dietary Guidelines for Americans, a guide providing nutritional advice to promote health and prevent disease. Updated versions of the Dietary Guidelines are released by the US Departments of Agriculture (USDA) and Health & Human Services (HHS) every five years.

564 **Everyday Health**
www.everydayhealth.com
Aims to provide evidence-based health information from physicians and healthcare providers.

565 **FamilyDoctor.org**
www.familydoctor.org
Medical advice and information provided by the American Academy of Family Physicians. Resources include a medical dictionary, a symptom checker tool, a BMI calculator, and medication information.

566 **Gastroenterology Therapy Online**
www.gastrotherapy.com
An informational website with resources for many kinds of diseases.

567 **Gastrointestinal Research Foundation**
www.giresearchfoundation.org
Founded to help combat gastrointestinal diseases. Raises funds to support research at the Center for the study of the Digestive Diseases at the University of Chicago Medical Center and to support advanced training for scientists. Sponsors educational activities for the public.

568 **Gastrointestinal Society - Canadian Society of Intestinal Research**
www.badgut.org
Aims to improve the lives of people with gastrointestinal and liver diseases and disorders by funding research, advocating for patient access to healthcare, and providing evidence-based information for patients.

569 **Gluten Intolerance Group**
gluten.org
Provides instructional and general information materials, as well as counseling and access to gluten-free products and ingredients to

persons with celiac sprue and their families; operates telephone information and referral service, and conducts educational seminars.

570 **Healing Well**

www.healingwell.com

An online health resource guide to medical news, chat, information and articles, newsgroups and message boards, books, disease-related web sites, medical directories, and more for patients, friends, and family coping with disabling diseases, disorders, or chronic illnesses.

571 **Health Finder**

www.healthfinder.gov

Searchable, carefully developed web site offering information on over 1000 topics. Developed by the US Department of Health and Human Services, the site can be used in both English and Spanish.

572 **Healthline**

www.healthline.com

Provides medical and health articles and information.

573 **Healthlink USA**

www.healthlinkusa.com

Health information concerning treatment, cures, prevention, diagnosis, risk factors, research, support groups, email lists, personal stories and much more. Updated regularly.

574 **Hemochromatosis Foundation**

www.hemochromatosis.org

Provides information to the public, families, and professionals about hereditary hemochromatosis (HH); conducts and raises funds for research; encourages early screening for HH; holds symposiums and meetings; and offers genetic counseling along with support for patients, families, and professionals.

575 **International Foundation for Functional Gastrointestinal Disorders (IFFGD)**

www.iffgd.org

Non-profit education, support, and research organization devoted to increasing awareness and understanding of functional gastrointestinal disorders, including irritable bowel syndrome (IBS), constipation, diarrhea, pain, and incontinence. Mission is to inform, assist and support people affected by these disorders.

576 **MedicineNet**

www.medicinenet.com

An online resource for consumers providing easy-to-read, authoritative medical and health information.

577 **MedlinePlus**

www.medlineplus.gov

A service of the National Library of Medicine, MedlinePlus is an online resource providing health and wellness information in both English and Spanish.

578 **Medscape**

www.medscape.com

Medscape offers specialists, primary care physicians, and other health professionals the Web's most robust and integrated medical information and educational tools.

579 **MyPlate**

www.myplate.gov

Created and managed by the US Department of Agriculture's Center for Nutrition Policy & Promotion, MyPlate is a dietary guide providing resources and recipes to promote healthy eating for all Americans.

580 **National Celiac Association**

nationalceliac.org

Dedicated to helping individuals with celiac disease and gluten sensitivities through education, advocacy, and awareness.
Lee Graham, Executive Director
Kimberly Buckton, Managing Director

581 **National Digestive Diseases Information Clearinghouse**

www.digestive.niddk.nih.gov

Offers various educational information, resources and reprints focusing on Colitis, Ulcerative Colitis and Crohn's disease.

582 **North American Society for Pediatric Gastroenterology, Hepatology & Nutrition**

www.naspghan.org

NASPGHAN strives to improve the care of infants, children and adolescents with digestive disorders by promoting advances in clinical care, research and education.

583 **Nutrition in Clinical Practice**

www.nutritioncare.org

NCP is indexed by PubMed (MEDLINE), Cumulative Index to Nursing and Allied Health Literature, International Nursing Index, International Pharmaceutical Index, Reference Update, Silver Platter, TOXLINE and UMI.

584 **Nutrition.gov**

www.nutrition.gov

Sponsored by the United States Department of Agriculture (USDA), Nutrition.gov offers information on topics in food and nutrition, including healthy eating, physical activity, and food safety.

585 **Oley Foundation**

www.oley.org

Enriches the lives of those requiring home IV & tube feeding through education, outreach, & networking.

586 **Pediatric Crohn's and Colitis Association**

pcca.hypermart.net

Focuses on all aspects of pediatric and adolescent Crohn's disease and ulcerative colitis, including medical, nutritional, psychological and social factors. Activities include information sharing, educational forums, newsletters and hospital outreach programs, as well as support of research.

587 **Pull-thru Network**

www.pullthrunetwork.org

Pull-thru Network (PTN) was founded in 1988 and has grown to be one of the largest organizations in the world dedicated to the needs of those born with an anorectal malformation or colon disease and any of the associated diagnoses

588 **Science Daily**

www.sciencedaily.com

Provides information on the latest news and research in science, health, the environment, and technology.

589 **Society for Surgery of the Alimentary Tract**

www.ssat.com

SSAT provides a forum for exchange of information among physicians specializing in alimentary tract surgery.

590 **Society of American Gastrointestinal Endoscopic Surgeons**

www.sages.org

SAGES encourages study and practice of gastrointestinal endoscopy, laparoscopy and minimal acces surgery.

591 **The Inside Tract**

theinsidetract.sgna.org

Content brand of the Society of Gastroenterology Nurses and Associates, with an online portal featuring analysis, editorials, behind the scenes, education, and more.

592 **The Nutrition Source**

hsph.harvard.edu/nutritionsource

From the Harvard T.H. Chan School of Public Health, The Nutrition Source provides news, information, and guidance for nutrition and healthy eating.

593 **United Ostomy Associations of America, Inc**

www.ostomy.org

A national network for bowel and urinary diversion support groups in the United States. Its goal is to provide a non-profit association that will serve to unify and strengthen its member support groups, which are organized for the benefit of people who have, or will have intestinal or urinary diversions and their caregivers.

594 **UnlockFood**

www.unlockfood.ca

A website from Dietitians of Canada. Provides videos, recipes, and information on food and nutrition, as well as helps Canadians connect with a dietitian.

595 **Verywell**

www.verywellhealth.com

Offers health, medicine, and wellness information from health professionals.

596 **WebMD**

www.webmd.com

Provides credible information, supportive communities, and in-depth reference material about health subjects. A source for original and timely health information as well as material from well known content providers.

597 **World Health Organization**

www.who.int

An agency of the United Nations, World Health Organization (WHO) serves to promote global health. The WHO website provides fact sheets, publications, media, and other resources on various health topics.

HEART DISEASE & NUTRITION

Cardiovascular disease includes heart disease, heart attacks, stroke, heart failure, arrythmias (abnormal heart rhythm) and heart valve problems. In the fight against cardiovascular disease, a healthy diet and lifestyle are most important. Choosing a healthy eating plan, being physically active and educated about warning signs of heart disease, heart attack and stroke may help prevent heart disease. In consultation with a physician and clinical dietician, an understanding of calories necessary to maintain or manage weight is the first step in approaching heart healthy behaviors. Depending on age, activity level and gender, the number of calories needed will vary by individual. Activity should be appropriate to the individual but a goal of 150 minutes of moderate physical activity or 75 minutes of vigorous activity (or a combination of the two) a week is recommended by the American Heart Association.

Heart disease causes one in four deaths in the United States. This risk can be greatly reduced with lifestyle changes and medications. There are a variety of conditions that make up heart disease but the most common in the United States is coronary artery disease (CAD). Often the first sign of CAD is a heart attack. It is caused by plaque buildup in the coronary artery walls, the arteries that provide blood to the heart and other parts of the body. Plaque comes from cholesterol deposits that narrow the arteries over time (atherosclerosis). Symptoms of CAD include chest pain and discomfort (angina), light-headedness, nausea, pain in the arms or shoulder, and shortness of breath. Being overweight, not getting enough physical activity, unhealthy eating and smoking are risk factors for CAD that can be managed. A family history of CAD with individuals demonstrating symptoms at 50 or younger also increases risk.

Measuring blood cholesterol levels, blood sugar levels and blood pressure may help identify CAD risks. If at high risk, additional testing may be indicated including an electrocardiogram (ECG or EKG) or echocardiogram, an exercise stress test, chest X-ray, cardiac catheterization, coronary angiogram and a coronary artery calcium scan.

Preventing heart disease and managing CAD are similar. Lifestyle changes such as eating a healthy diet, increasing physical activity, reaching a healthy weight and stopping smoking are both preventive and assist in managing existing CAD. Medicines may be used to treat high cholesterol, high blood pressure and an irregular heartbeat. There are some surgeries that may enhance or restore blood flow to the heart.

It is important to know your personal risk of heart disease. If you are between the ages of 40 and 75 with no history of stroke or heart attack, you can calculate your risk using a calculator, "Check.Change.Control.Calculator"™, that is available on the American Heart Association website. In addition to a healthy diet, physical activity, and no tobacco use, it is important to manage any health conditions that put you at risk, including hypertension, high cholesterol and diabetes with high blood sugar. Taking prescribed medications exactly as ordered is critical. Aspirin should be used only if prescribed by the doctor. Work with your healthcare provider on a prevention plan. Living a healthy life can delay or avoid may heart related diseases.

If your physician determines that you are at risk for heart disease, a common first recommendation is a healthy diet and meeting with a registered dietician. The DASH diet is recommended most often for managing the risks of heart disease. It is flexible and balanced, requires no special foods and provides daily and weekly goals. DASH recommends eating fruits, vegetables and whole grains, fat-free or low-fat dairy products, fish, poultry, beans, nuts and vegetable oils, limiting foods high in saturated fats, and sugar-sweetened beverages and foods. Sodium is limited to 1,500-2,300 mg a day and foods should be low in saturated and trans fats, rich in potassium, magnesium, calcium, fiber and protein. A physician and dietician will provide guidance on specific foods, based on your individual needs. Online, you can find eating plans, meal planning tools and tips for success.

Nutrition can play a key role in a variety of health conditions, especially in managing heart disease. A heart healthy diet, adequate activity and healthy lifestyle choices will prevent the development of heart disease. Prevention is the key to living a long and healthy life, free of heart disease and many other diseases. Good nutrition plays a significant role.

See page 167 for more information on the DASH diet.

Agencies & Associations

599 **Active Healthy Kids Global Alliance**
401 Smyth Road info@activehealthykids.org
Ottawa, Ontario, K1H-8L1 www.activehealthykids.org
Advocates the importance of quality, accessible, and enjoyable physical activity participation exercises for children and youth.
Mark Tremblay, President
Peter Katzmarzyk, Vice President

600 **American Autoimmune Related Diseases Association**
19176 Hall Road 586-776-3900
Clinton Township, MI 48038 aarda@aarda.org
www.aarda.org
Awareness, education, referrals for patients with any type of autoimmune disease.
Molly Murray, President & CEO
Laura Simpson, Chief Operating Officer

601 **American College of Cardiology**
2400 N Street NW 202-375-6000
Washington, DC 20037 800-253-4636
Fax: 202-375-6842
membercare@acc.org
www.acc.org
The mission of the American College of Cardiology is to advocate for quality cardiovascular care, through education, research promotion, development and application of standards and guidelines, and to influence health care policy.
Cathleen C. Gates, Chief Executive Officer
Brendan Mullen, Senior Executive Vice President

602 **American Heart Association**
7272 Greenville Avenue 800-242-8721
Dallas, TX 75231 www.heart.org
The American Heart Association is the nation's oldest, largest volunteer organization devoted to fighting cardiovascular diseases and stroke. Funds research and raises public awareness of heart diseases.
Nancy Brown, Chief Executive Officer
Suzie Upton, Chief Operating Officer

603 **Canadian Adult Congenital Heart Network**
222 Queen Street 877-569-3407
Ottawa, Ontario, K1P-5V9 cachnet@ccs.ca
www.cachnet.org
Organization founded to share knowledge and skills among congenital heart disease professionals in order to create a community committed to caring for individuals with congenital heart disease.
Ariane Marelli, MD, President
Candice Silversides, MD, Vice President

604 **Center for Science in the Public Interest**
1220 L Street NW 202-332-9110
Washington, DC 20005 cspi@cspinet.org
www.cspinet.org
The nation's leading consumer group concerned with food and nutrition issues. Focuses on diseases that result from consuming too many calories, too much fat, sodium and sugar such as cancer and heart disease.
Peter Lurie, President
Sara Ghaith, Chief Operating Officer

605 **Centers for Medicare & Medicaid Services**
7500 Security Boulevard www.cms.gov
Baltimore, MD 21244
U.S. federal agency which administers Medicare, Medicaid, and the State Children's Health Insurance Program.
Chiquita Brooks-LaSure, Administrator
Jonathan Blum, COO

606 **Children's Heart Society**
12122 68 Street NW 780-454-7665
Edmonton, Alberta, T5B-1R1 childrensheart@shaw.ca
www.childrensheart.ca
Supports families of children with acquired and congenital heart disease.
Gerry Cruz, President
Dariel Maclean, Vice President

607 **Heart and Stroke Canada**
1525 Carling Avenue 888-473-4636
Ottawa, Ontario, K1Z-8R9 www.heartandstroke.ca
Leading authority on cardiovascular disease, providing resources for individuals and funding scientific research on heart disease and stroke.
Doug Roth, Chief Executive Officer

608 **National Heart, Lung & Blood Institute**
31 Center Drive 877-645-2448
Bethesda, MD 20892 nhlbiinfo@nhlbi.nih.gov
www.nhlbi.nih.gov
Trains, conducts research, and educates in order to promote the prevention and treatment of heart, lung, and blood disorders.
Gary H. Gibbons, MD, Director

609 **National Institute of Biomedical Imaging and Bioengineering**
9000 Rockville Pike 301-496-8859
Bethesda, MD 20892 info@nibib.nih.gov
www.nibib.nih.gov
The mission of the National Institute of Biomedical Imaging and Bioengineering (NIBIB) is to improve health by leading the development and accelerating the application of biomedical technologies.
Bruce J. Tromberg, PhD, Director
Jill Heemskerk, PhD, Deputy Director

610 **National Institute of General Medical Sciences**
45 Center Drive 301-496-7301
Bethesda, MD 20892-6200 info@nigms.nih.gov
www.nigms.nih.gov
The National Institute of General Medical Sciences (NIGMS) supports basic research that increases understanding of biological processes and lays the foundation for advances in disease diagnosis, treatment and prevention.
Jon R. Lorsch, PhD, Director
Dorit Zuk, PhD, Acting Deputy Director

611 **Nurse Practitioners in Women's Health**
PO Box 15837 202-543-9693
Washington, DC 20003 info@npwh.org
www.npwh.org
Ensures the delivery and accessibility of primary and specialty healthcare to women of all ages by women's health and women's health focused nurse practitioners.
Heather L. Maurer, CEO
Donna Ruth, Director, Education

612 **Office of Women's Health**
200 Independence Avenue SW 202-690-7650
Washington, DC 20201 800-994-9662
womenshealth@hhs.gov
www.womenshealth.gov
Government agency under the Department of Health & Human Services, with free health information for women.
Dorothy Fink, MD, Deputy Asst. Secretary, Women's Health
Richelle West Marshall, Deputy Director

613 **Pulmonary Hypertension Association (PHA)**
8401 Colesville Road 301-565-3004
Silver Spring, MD 20910 800-748-7274
pha@phassociation.org
www.phassociation.org
A non-profit organization for pulmonary hypertension patients, families, caregivers and PH-treating medical professionals. PHA works to provide support, education, and find a cure for pulmonary hypertension.
Matt J. Granato, President & CEO
Azalea Candelaria, Vice President, Development

614 **St. Joseph's Medical Center**
7601 Osler Drive 410-337-1000
Towson, MD 21204 www.umms.org/sjmc
Thomas B. Smyth, MD, President & CEO

Alabama

615 **American Heart Association: Birmingham**
217 County Club Park 205-510-1500
Mountain Brook, AL 35213 www.heart.org

616 **American Heart Association: Huntsville**
6275 University Boulevard 800-257-6941
Huntsville, AL 35806 www.heart.org

617 **American Heart Association: Montgomery**
9154 E Chase Parkway 800-257-6941
Montgomery, AL 36117 www.heart.org

Alaska

618 **American Heart Association: Anchorage**
3700 Woodland Drive 907-865-5300
Anchorage, AK 99517 www.heart.org

619 **American Heart Association: Fairbanks**
PO Box 71717 907-456-3659
Fairbanks, AK 99707 www.heart.org

Arizona

620 **American Heart Association: Phoenix**
1910 W University Drive 602-414-5353
Tempe, AZ 85281 www.heart.org

621 **American Heart Association: Southern Arizona**
3443 N Campbell Avenue 520-917-7520
Tucson, AZ 85719 www.heart.org

Arkansas

622 **American Heart Association: Central Arkansas**
909 W 2nd Street 501-707-6600
Little Rock, AR 72201 www.heart.org

623 **American Heart Association: Northwest Arkansas**
108 E Sunbridge 479-439-6800
Fayetteville, AR 72703 www.heart.org

California

624 **American Heart Association: Central Coast**
212 W Figueroa Street 805-963-8862
Santa Barbara, CA 93101 www.heart.org

625 **American Heart Association: Central Valley & Kern County**
7425 N Palm Buffs Avenue 559-650-4010
Fresno, CA 93711 www.heart.org

626 **American Heart Association: Coachella Valley**
PO Box 5417 www.heart.org
Irvine, CA 92616

627 **American Heart Association: Greater Bay Area**
1111 Broadway 510-903-4050
Oakland, CA 94607 www.heart.org

628 **American Heart Association: Inland Empire**
PO Box 5417 www.heart.org
Irvine, CA 92616

629 **American Heart Association: Los Angeles**
816 S Figueroa Street 213-291-7000
Los Angeles, CA 90017 www.heart.org

630 **American Heart Association: North Bay**
1710 Gilbreth Road 707-890-3590
Burlingame, CA 94010 www.heart.org

631 **American Heart Association: Orange County**
4600 Campus Drive 949-856-3555
Irvine, CA 92617 www.heart.org

632 **American Heart Association: Sacramento**
2007 O Street 916-446-6505
Sacramento, CA 95811 www.heart.org

633 **American Heart Association: San Diego**
9404 Genesee Avenue 858-410-3850
San Diego, CA 92037 www.heart.org

634 **American Heart Association: Stockton & Modesto**
2007 O Street 209-477-2683
Sacramento, CA 95811 www.heart.org

Colorado

635 **American Heart Association: Denver**
1777 S Harrison Street 303-801-4630
Denver, CO 80210 www.heart.org

Connecticut

636 **American Heart Association: Norwalk**
501 Merritt 7, PH 203-295-2942
Norwalk, CT 06851 www.heart.org

637 **American Heart Association: Wallingford**
5 Brookside Drive 203-303-3300
Wallingford, CT 06492 www.heart.org

Delaware

638 **American Heart Association: Delaware**
131 Continental Drive 302-454-0613
Newark, DE 19713 877-750-4276
www.heart.org

District of Columbia

639 **American Heart Association: District of Columbia**
4601 N Fairfax Drive 703-248-1700
Arlington, VA 22203 www.heart.org

Florida

640 **American Heart Association: Alachua County**
3324 W University Avenue 800-257-6941
Gainesville, FL 32607 www.heart.org

641 **American Heart Association: Bay County**
653 W 23rd Street 800-257-6941
Panama City, FL 32405 www.heart.org

642 **American Heart Association: Brevard County**
1982 State Road 44 407-843-1330
New Smyrna Beach, FL 32168 www.heart.org

643 **American Heart Association: Charlotte County**
1767 Lakewood Ranch Boulevard 941-232-8308
Bradenton, FL 34211 www.heart.org

644 **American Heart Association: First Coast**
7751 Baymeadows Road E 904-903-5205
Jacksonville, FL 32256 www.heart.org

645 **American Heart Association: Marion County**
1202 SW 17th Street 800-257-6941
Ocala, FL 34471 www.heart.org

646 **American Heart Association: Okaloosa County**
548 Mary Esther Cut-off 800-257-6941
Ft. Walton Beach, FL 32548 www.heart.org

647 **American Heart Association: Orlando**
5224 W State Road 46 407-481-6300
Sanford, FL 32771-9230 www.heart.org

648 **American Heart Association: Palm Beach County**
2300 Centrepark W Drive 561-697-6600
West Palm Beach, FL 33409 www.heart.org

649 **American Heart Association: Polk County**
10460 Roosevelt Boulevard N 314-283-1726
St. Petersburg, FL 33716 www.heart.org

650 **American Heart Association: South Florida**
4000 Hollywood Boulevard 954-364-5000
Hollywood, FL 33021 www.heart.org

651 **American Heart Association: Southwest Florida**
9200 Estero Parks Commons Blvd. 239-495-4900
Estero, FL 33928 www.heart.org

652 **American Heart Association: Suncoast**
1767 Lakewood Ranch Boulevard 800-257-6941
Bradenton, FL 34211 www.heart.org

653 **American Heart Association: Tallahassee**
2851 Remington Green Circle — 850-536-8960
Tallahassee, FL 32308 — www.heart.org

654 **American Heart Association: Tampa Bay**
11207 Blue Heron Boulevard N — 727-563-8000
St. Petersburg, FL 33716 — www.heart.org

655 **American Heart Association: Volusia County**
1982 State Road 44 — 407-481-6300
New Smyrna Beach, FL 32168 — www.heart.org

Georgia

656 **American Heart Association: Athens**
1720 Epps Bridge Parkway — 800-257-6941
Athens, GA 30606 — www.heart.org

657 **American Heart Association: Atlanta**
10 Glenlake Parkway — 678-224-2000
Atlanta, GA 30328 — www.heart.org

658 **American Heart Association: Central Georgia**
5962 Zebulon Road — 800-257-6941
Macon, GA 31210 — www.heart.org

659 **American Heart Association: Greater Columbus**
1639 Bradley Park Drive — 800-257-6941
Columbus, GA 31904 — www.heart.org

660 **American Heart Association: Hall County**
821 Dawsonville Highway — 800-257-6941
Gainesville, GA 30501 — www.heart.org

Hawaii

661 **American Heart Association: Hawaii**
707 Richards Street — 808-377-6630
Honolulu, HI 96813 — www.heart.org

Idaho

662 **American Heart Association: Idaho**
208-501-7800
www.heart.org

Illinois

663 **American Heart Association: Chicago**
300 South Riverside Plaza — 312-346-4675
Chicago, IL 60606 — www.heart.org

664 **American Heart Association: Springfield**
2141 W White Oaks Drive — 217-331-6773
Springfield, IL 62704 — www.heart.org

Indiana

665 **American Heart Association: Indianapolis**
6500 Technology Center Drive — 317-732-4700
Indianapolis, IN 46278 — www.heart.org

Iowa

666 **American Heart Association: Des Moines**
5000 Westown Parkway — 515-414-3200
West Des Moines, IA 50266 — www.heart.org

667 **American Heart Association: Eastern Iowa**
1035 N Center Point Road — 319-536-3900
Hiawatha, IA 52233 — www.heart.org

Kansas

668 **American Heart Association: Kansas City**
13851 W 63rd Street — 913-652-1913
Shawnee, KS 66216 — www.heart.org

669 **American Heart Association: Wichita**
1861 North Rock Road — 316-768-3830
Wichita, KS 67206 — www.heart.org

Kentucky

670 **American Heart Association: Lexington**
354 Waller Avenue — 859-317-6880
Lexington, KY 40504 — www.heart.org

671 **American Heart Association: Louisville**
240 Whittington Parkway — 877-693-6208
Louisville, KY 40222 — www.heart.org

Louisiana

672 **American Heart Association: Baton Rouge**
14241 Coursey Boulevard — 225-248-7700
Baton Rouge, LA 70817 — www.heart.org

673 **American Heart Association: Lafayette**
139-B James Comeaux Road — 225-666-4297
Lafayette, LA 70508 — www.heart.org

674 **American Heart Association: New Orleans**
110 Veterans Boulevard — 504-872-3500
Metairie, LA 70005 — www.heart.org

675 **American Heart Association: Northeast Louisiana**
4830 McWillie Circle — 601-321-1200
Jackson, MS 39206 — www.heart.org

676 **American Heart Association: Northwest Louisiana**
4830 Line Avenue — 770-612-6168
Shreveport, LA 71106 — www.heart.org

Maine

677 **American Heart Association: Maine**
5 Brookside Drive — 207-289-2391
Wallingford, CT 06492 — www.heart.org

Maryland

678 **American Heart Association: Baltimore**
1100 E Fayette Street — 410-685-7074
Baltimore, MD 21202 — www.heart.org

Massachusetts

679 **American Heart Association: Massachusetts**
300 5th Avenue — 781-373-4500
Waltham, MA 02451-8750 — www.heart.org

Michigan

680 **American Heart Association: Detroit**
27777 Franklin Road — 248-936-5800
Southfield, MI 48034 — www.heart.org

681 **American Heart Association: West Michigan**
3940 Peninsular Drive SE — 616-482-1503
Grand Rapids, MI 49546 — www.heart.org

Minnesota

682 **American Heart Association: Minnesota**
2750 Blue Water Road — 952-835-3300
Eagan, MN 55121 — www.heart.org

Mississippi

683 **American Heart Association: Gulf Coast**
2159 E Pass Road — 228-604-5300
Gulfport, MS 39507 — www.heart.org

684 **American Heart Association: Jackson**
4830 McWillie Circle — 601-321-1200
Jackson, MS 39206 — www.heart.org

Missouri

685 **American Heart Association: St. Louis**
460 N Lindbergh Boulevard — 314-692-5635
St. Louis, MO 63141 — www.heart.org

Montana

686 **American Heart Association: Montana**
PO Box 8951
Missoula, MT 59807
406-273-8023
www.heart.org

Nebraska

687 **American Heart Association: Lincoln**
1540 S 70th Street
Lincoln, NE 68506
402-875-7382
www.heart.org

688 **American Heart Association: Omaha**
9900 Nicholas Street
Omaha, NE 68114
402-810-6870
www.heart.org

Nevada

689 **American Heart Association: Las Vegas**
816 S Figueroa Street
Los Angeles, CA 90017
702-789-4370
www.heart.org

New Hampshire

690 **American Heart Association: New Hampshire**
2 Wall Street
Manchester, NH 03101
603-263-8318
www.heart.org

New Jersey

691 **American Heart Association: New Jersey**
250 Pehle Avenue
Saddle Brook, NJ 07663
609-208-0020
newjersey@heart.org
www.heart.org

New Mexico

692 **American Heart Association: New Mexico**
2201 San Pedro NE
Albuquerque, NM 87110
505-485-1330
www.heart.org

New York

693 **American Heart Association: Buffalo**
25 Circle Street
Rochester, NY 14607-1007
716-243-4600
buffaloaha@heart.org
www.heart.org

694 **American Heart Association: Capital Region**
PO Box 3049
Syracuse, NY 13220
518-626-8750
www.heart.org

695 **American Heart Association: Hudson Valley**
301 Manchester Road
Poughkeepsie, NY 12603
845-867-5370
www.heart.org

696 **American Heart Association: Long Island**
125 E Bethpage Road
Plainview, NY 11803
516-962-0800
www.heart.org

697 **American Heart Association: Mohawk Valley**
125 Business Park Drive
Utica, NY 13502
315-580-3950
www.heart.org

698 **American Heart Association: New York City**
10 E 40th Street
New York, NY 10016
212-878-5900
www.heart.org

699 **American Heart Association: Rochester**
25 Circle Street
Rochester, NY 14607-1007
585-371-3227
rochesteraha@heart.org
www.heart.org

700 **American Heart Association: Syracuse**
2 Clinton Square
Syracuse, NY 13202
315-728-7540
www.heart.org

North Carolina

701 **American Heart Association: Charlotte**
401 Hawthorne Lane
Charlotte, NC 28204
704-417-5750
www.heart.org

702 **American Heart Association: Triangle**
5001 S Miami Boulevard
Durham, NC 27703
919-463-8300
www.heart.org

North Dakota

703 **American Heart Association: North Dakota**
PO Box 90545
Sioux Falls, SD 57109
605-360-2542
www.heart.org

Ohio

704 **American Heart Association: Columbus**
5455 N High Street
Columbus, OH 43214
614-848-6676
www.heart.org

705 **American Heart Association: Northeast Ohio & Western Pennsylvania**
1575 Corporate Woods Parkway
Uniontown, OH 44685
330-396-5800
www.heart.org

Oklahoma

706 **American Heart Association: Oklahoma City**
3401 NW 63rd Street
Oklahoma City, OK 73116
405-415-3030
www.heart.org

707 **American Heart Association: Tulsa**
2227 E Skelly Drive
Tulsa, OK 74105
918-877-8359
www.heart.org

Oregon

708 **American Heart Association: Oregon & Southwest Washington**
4380 SW Macadam Avenue
Portland, OR 97239
503-820-5300
www.heart.org

Pennsylvania

709 **American Heart Association: Harrisburg**
4250 Crums Mill Road
Harrisburg, PA 17112
717-730-1700
www.heart.org

710 **American Heart Association: Philadelphia**
1617 JFK Boulevard
Philadelphia, PA 19103
215-575-5200
www.heart.org

711 **American Heart Association: Pittsburgh**
444 Liberty Avenue
Pittsburgh, PA 15222-1207
412-208-3550
www.heart.org

Rhode Island

712 **American Heart Association: Southern New England**
1 State Street
Providence, RI 02908
401-228-2320
www.heart.org

South Carolina

713 **American Heart Association: Lowcountry**
887 Johnnie Dodds Boulevard
Mt. Pleasant, SC 29464
843-480-4900
www.heart.org

714 **American Heart Association: Midlands**
701 Gervais Street
Columbia, SC 29201
803-738-9540
www.heart.org

715 **American Heart Association: Upstate**
864-627-4158
upstateaha@heart.org
www.heart.org

South Dakota

716 **American Heart Association: South Dakota**
PO Box 90545
Sioux Falls, SD 57109
605-360-2542
www.heart.org

Tennessee

717 **American Heart Association: Chattanooga**
519 E 4th Street
Chattanooga, TN 37403
423-763-4400
www.heart.org

718 **American Heart Association: Knoxville**
4708 Papermill Drive
Knoxville, TN 37909
865-293-5100
www.heart.org

719 **American Heart Association: Mid-South & West Tennessee**
5384 Poplar Avenue
Memphis, TN 38119
901-248-7950
www.heart.org

720 **American Heart Association: Nashville**
1818 Patterson Street
Nashville, TN 37203
615-340-4100
www.heart.org

721 **American Heart Association: Tri-Cities**
3101 Browns Mill Road
Johnson City, TN 37604
800-257-6941
www.heart.org

Texas

722 **American Heart Association: Austin**
12345 N Lamar Boulevard
Austin, TX 78753
512-338-2400
www.heart.org

723 **American Heart Association: Corpus Christi**
12345 N Lamar Boulevard
Austin, TX 78753
www.heart.org

724 **American Heart Association: Dallas**
105 Decker Court
Irving, TX 75062
214-441-4200
www.heart.org

725 **American Heart Association: El Paso**
512-338-2400
elpasotx@heart.org
www.heart.org

726 **American Heart Association: Houston**
10060 Buffalo Speedway
Houston, TX 77054
832-918-4000
www.heart.org

727 **American Heart Association: Midland**
10900-B Stonelake Boulevard
Austin, TX 78759
866-698-5414
www.heart.org

728 **American Heart Association: San Antonio**
8415 Wurzbach Road
San Antonio, TX 78229
210-810-3100
www.heart.org

729 **American Heart Association: South Texas**
10900-B Stonelake Boulevard
Austin, TX 78759
512-338-2400
www.heart.org

730 **American Heart Association: Tarrant County**
2630 West Freeway
Fort Worth, TX 76102
817-698-5400
www.heart.org

Utah

731 **American Heart Association: Utah**
465 South 400 East
Salt Lake City, UT 84111
801-702-4420
www.heart.org

Vermont

732 **American Heart Association: Vermont**
5 Brookside Drive
Wallingford, CT 06492
802-497-1855
www.heart.org

Virginia

733 **American Heart Association: Hampton Roads**
4217 Park Place Court
Glen Allen, VA 23060
757-628-2610
www.heart.org

734 **American Heart Association: Richmond**
4217 Park Place Court
Glen Allen, VA 23060
804-747-8334
www.heart.org

735 **American Heart Association: Roanoke**
3140 Chaparral Drive
Roanoke, VA 24018
540-989-2810
www.heart.org

Washington

736 **American Heart Association: Puget Sound**
710 2nd Avenue
Seattle, WA 98104
206-336-7200
puget.sound@heart.org
www.heart.org

737 **American Heart Association: South Sound**
1142 Broadway
Tacoma, WA 98402
253-240-3310
www.heart.org

738 **American Heart Association: Spokane**
710 2nd Avenue
Seattle, WA 98104
206-336-7200
www.heart.org

West Virginia

739 **American Heart Association: West Virginia**
4217 Park Place Court
Glen Allen, VA 23060
757-628-2610
www.heart.org

Wisconsin

740 **American Heart Association: Madison**
2850 Dairy Road
Madison, WI 53718
608-709-4930
www.heart.org

741 **American Heart Association: Milwaukee**
1555 N RiverCenter Drive
Milwaukee, WI 53212
414-271-9999
milwaukee@heart.org
www.heart.org

Wyoming

742 **American Heart Association: Wyoming**
2120 Capitol Avenue
Cheyenne, WY 82001
www.heart.org

Libraries & Resource Centers

743 **American Heart Association Interactive Cardiovascular Library**
7272 Greenville Avenue
Dallas, TX 75231
214-373-6300
800-242-8721
Fax: 214-706-1341
inquire@amhrt.org
watchlearnlive.heart.org

Features illustrations and animations about a variety of heart disease and stroke-related conditions, treatments, and procedures.
Nancy Brown, CEO
Mitchell Elkind, President

744 **American Heart Association eBooks**
7272 Greenville Avenue
Dallas, TX 75231
214-373-6300
800-242-8721
Fax: 214-706-1341
inquire@amhrt.org
ebooks.heart.org

Online store featuring guidelines, handbooks, manuals, and more, in a variety of languages.
Nancy Brown, CEO
Mitchell Elkind, President

Foundations & Research Centers

745 **Albert Einstein College Of Medicine Cardiothoracic & Vascular Surgery**
Montefiore Medical Center
3400 Bainbridge Avenue
Bronx, NY 10467
718-920-7000
Fax: 718-231-7113
www.einstein.yu.edu

Cardiovascular research.
Robert E. Michler, MD, Chair
Daniel Goldsteinn, MD, Vice Chair, MD

746 **Arizona Heart Institute**
2632 N 20th Street 602-266-2200
Phoenix, AZ 85006-1300 800-345-4278
www.azheart.com
Edward Diethrich, Medical Director and Founder

747 **Baylor College of Medicine: Cardiovascular Research Institute**
Texas Medical Center
1 Baylor Plaza 713-798-6941
Houston, TX 77030-3411 Fax: 713-798-3692
cvri@bcm.edu
www.bcm.tmc.edu
Research activities have an emphasis on therapeutic intervention and prevention of heart disease.
Xander Wehrens MD, Director
Biykem Bozkurt MD, Associate Director

748 **Baylor College of Medicine: Debakey Heart Center**
Texas Medical Center
1 Baylor Plaza 713-798-4710
Houston, TX 77030-3411 president@bcm.edu
www.bcm.tmc.edu
Research activities have an emphasis on therapeutic intervention and prevention of heart disease.
James T Hackett, Chair
Paul Klotman MD, President

749 **Bees-Stealy Research Foundation**
2001 4th Avenue 619-235-8744
San Diego, CA 92101-2303
Basic cardiac research.
HD Peabody Jr, Director

750 **Biltmore Cardiology**
4444 h 32nd Street 888-431-9846
Phoenix, AZ 85018 Fax: 602-224-9119
biltmorecardiology.com
Specializes in heart treatment for patients in Arizona. Part of the Abrazo Medical Group.

751 **Bockus Research Institute Graduate Hospital**
Graduate Hospital
415 S 19th Street 215-893-2000
Philadelphia, PA 19146-1464
Offers research in cardiovascular diseases with emphasis on muscle tissue studies.
Dr Robert Cox, Director

752 **Boston University, Whitaker Cardiovascular Institute**
715 Albany Street 617-638-4887
Boston, MA 02118 www.bumc.bu.edu
Offers basic and clinical care research relating to cardiovascular diseases.
Gary J Balady MD, Clinical Investigator

753 **Cardiovascular Center at University of Utah**
50 North Medical Drive 801-585-7676
Salt Lake City, UT 84132 uofuhealth.utah.edu
Heart care, heart surgery, and treatment for all types of heart disease. Specialties are cardiology, cardiothoracic surgery, vascular surgery, and others.
Michael Good, CEO
Will Dere, AVP, Research

754 **Cardiovascular Research Center: University of California at LA**
UCLA Cardiovascular Center
100 UCLA Medical Plaza 310-825-9011
Los Angeles, CA 90095 uclahealth.org/heart
Cardiovascular and heart disease disorders and illness research.
Jamil A. Aboulhosn MD, Director, Congenital Heart Disease
Daniel Levi MD, Director, Ped. Cardiology Fellowship

755 **Cardiovascular Research Foundation**
1700 Broadway, 9th Floor 646-434-4500
New York, NY 10019 info@crf.org
www.crf.org
A nonprofit organization with a mission to improve the survival and quality of life for people with cardiovascular disease through research and education.
Juan F. Granada, MD, President & CEO

756 **Cardiovascular Research and Training Center University of Alabama**
THT Room 311 205-934-3624
Birmingham, AL 35294-6
Robert C Bueourge, Director

757 **Children's Heart Institute of Texas**
PO Box 3966 512-887-4505
Corpus Christi, TX 78463-3966
Offers research and statistical information on pediatric cardiology.
Laura Berlanga, Director

758 **Cleveland Clinic Lerner Research Institute**
9500 Euclid Avenue 216-444-3900
Cleveland, OH 44195 dicorlp@ccf.org
www.lerner.ccf.org
Research institute focusing on diseases of the cardiovascular system.
Paul E DiCorleto PhD, Institute Chairman
Guy M Chisolm, III, PhD, Institute Vice-Chair

759 **Columbia University Irving Center for Clinical Research Adult Unit**
Presbyterian Hospital
116 Street and Broadway 212-854-1754
New York, NY 10027 askcuit@columbia.edu
www.columbia.edu
Research center focusing on pulmonary diseases.
Lee C Bollinger, President
John H Coatsworth, Provost

760 **Congenital Heart Disease Anomalies Support, Education & Resources CHASER**
2112 N Wilkins Road 419-825-5575
Swanton, OH 43558-9445 www.csun.edu
An organization established to meet the emotional and educational needs of parents and professionals who deal with congenital heart disease in children. Offers resource materials and support for parent to parent networking.

761 **Creighton University Cardiac Center**
3006 Webster Street 402-280-4566
Omaha, NE 68131-2137 800-237-7828
thecardiaccenter.creighton.edu
Research into the clinical aspects of cardiology and heart disease.
Tami Ward, Nurse Practitioner
Kimberly Harm, Nurse Practitioner

762 **Creighton University School Of Medicine Division Of Cardiology**
7710 Mercy Road 402-280-4526
Omaha, NE 68124 Fax: 402-280-4850
thecardiaccenter.creighton.edu
Research into the clinical aspects of cardiology and heart disease.
Amy J. Arouni MD, Professor
Michael G. Del Core MD, Professor

763 **Dalton Cardiovascular Research Center**
School of Medicine
134 Research Park Dr. 573-882-7588
Columbia, MO 65211 dalton@missouri.edu
www.missouri.edu
Research includes hypertension, cancer, cystic fibrosis and heart disease.
Micheal A. Hill, Director

764 **Duke University Pediatric Cardiac Catheterization Laboratory**
T901/Children's Health Center 919-681-4080
Durham, NC 27705-0001 john.rhodes@duke.edu
pediatrics.duke.edu
Research into pediatric cardiology.
Joseph St Geme, III, MD, Chair
Kay Marshall, Chief Administrator

765 **Duke University School of Medicine: Cardiology Division**
Duke University
PO Box 3854 919-684-8111
Durham, NC 27708 Fax: 919-681-8829
medicine.duke.edu/divisions/cardiology
Multidisciplinary, clinical research into the cause, progression, prevention, control, and cure of human disease. Sample projects have studied immunodeficiency diseases, Alzheimer's disease,

food allergy, X-linked hypophosphatemic rickets, and cardiovascular disease.
Manesh Patel, MD, Chief
Nick Nguyen, MHA, Division Administrator

766 **Florida Heart Research Institute**
4770 Biscayne Boulevard 305-674-3020
Miami, FL 33137 pak@floridaheart.org
www.miamiheartresearch.org
General cardiovascular research.
Kathleen T DuCasse, Chief Executive Officer

767 **Framingham Heart Study**
73 Mount Wayte Avenue 508-935-3418
Framingham, MA 01702-5828 LLehmann1@partners.org
www.framinghamheartstudy.org
Lisa Soleymani Lehmann, M.D.,, Chair

768 **Francois M Abboud Cardiovascular Research Center**
285 Newton Road 319-335-9305
Iowa City, IA 52242 acrc@uiowa.edu
www.medicine.uiowa.edu
Barry London, MD, Director

769 **General Clinical Research Center at Beth Israel Hospital**
330 Brookline Avenue 617-667-7000
Boston, MA 02215-5400 800-667-5356
TDD: 800-439-0183
www.bidmc.org
Studies into cardiology pulmonary disorders and heart disease.
Stephen B Kay, Chair
Kevin Tabb, MD, President & Chief Executive Officer

770 **General Clinical Research Center: University of California at LA**
Center for Health Sciences
10833 Le Conte Avenue 310-825-7177
Los Angeles, CA 90095 www.gcrc.medsch.ucla.edu
Cardiovascular and heart disease disorders and illness research.
Isidro Salus MD, Program Director
Gerald Levey, Principal Investigator

771 **Hahnemann University Likoff Cardiovascular Institute**
Broad & Vine Streets 215-854-8100
Philadelpia, PA 19102
Diseases of the heart and vessels.
William S Frankl MD, Director

772 **Harvard Throndike Laboratory Harvard Medical Center**
Harvard Medical Center
330 Brookline Avenue 617-735-3020
Boston, MA 02215-5400
Dr James Morgan, Director

773 **Heart Disease Research Foundation**
50 Court Street 718-649-6210
Brooklyn, NY 11201-4801
Robert A Teters, Director

774 **Heart Research Foundation of Sacramento**
1007 39th Street 916-456-3365
Sacramento, CA 95816-5502 www.hrfsac.org
Dr Frink, Founder/Principal Investigator

775 **Henry Ford Hospital: Hypertension and Vascular Research Division**
2799 W Grand Boulevard 313-972-1693
Detroit, MI 48202-2689 Fax: 313-876-1479
ocarret1@hfhs.org
www.hypertensionresearch.org
Basic biomedical research seeks to understand: The role of vasoconstrictors and vasodilators (angiotensin II bradykinin nitric oxide natriuretic peptides) in the regulation of blood pressure development of hypertension and development of target organ damage (myocardial infarction heart failure vascular injury and renal disease); The generation of reactive oxygen species by blood vessels and kidney cells and how this contributes to target organ damage; and The mechanisms by which therape
Pablo A. Ortiz, Ph.D., Division Head

776 **Hope Heart Institute**
1380 112th Ave. NE 425-456-8700
Bellvue, WA 98004 info@hopeheart.org
www.hopeheart.org
Heart and blood vessel research.
Dr Lester R Sauvage MD, Founder
Cherie Skager, Interim Executive Director

777 **John L McClellan Memorial Veterans' Hospital Research Office**
4300 W 7th Street 501-257-1000
Little Rock, AR 72205-5446 www2.va.gov
Karl David Straub MD, Chief Staff

778 **Krannert Institute of Cardiology**
1801 N Senate Boulevard 317-962-0500
Indianapolis, IN 46202-4832 800-843-2786
medicine.iupui.edu/krannert
The cardiovascular program at the Indiana University School of Medicine is recognized throughout the world for its commitment to excellence in patient care research and education. While we're known for our experience and ability to take care of the most complex cardiovascular problems we are equally focused on prevention and early detection.
Peng-Sheng Chen, MD, Division Director
Eric Williams, MD, Associate Dean

779 **Leon H. Charney Division Of Cardiology**
435 East 30th Street 212-263-3967
New York, NY 10016 Fax: 212-263-3972
www.med.nyu.edu
Externally funded basic, translational, and clinical research programs.
Glenn I. Fishman, MD, Director
Anna Yick, MPA, Administrative Manager

780 **Loyola University of Chicago Cardiac Transplant Program**
2160 S 1st Avenue 708-216-9000
Maywood, IL 60153-3304 888-584-7888
www.loyolamedicine.org/
Loyola University Health System is committed to excellence in patient care and the education of health professionals. They believe that our Catholic heritage and Jesuit traditions of ethical behavior academic distinction and scientific research lead to new knowledge and advance our healing mission in the communities we serve.
Larry M Goldberg, President & CEO
Wendy S Leutgens, Senior Vice President and COO

781 **MedStar Heart & Vascular Institute**
MedStar Georgetown University Hospital
3800 Reservoir Road NW 202-342-2400
Washington, DC 20007 888-354-3422
www.medstarheartinstitute.org
Studies of medical sciences with particular emphasis on heart disease.
Dr Richard Goldberg, President

782 **Medstar Georgetown University Hospital Facility**
3800 Reservoir Road NW 202-444-2000
Washington, DC 20007-2195 www.georgetownuniversityhospital.org
Studies of medical sciences with particular emphasis on heart disease.
Dr Richard Goldberg, President

783 **Mount Sinai Medical Center**
4300 Alton Road 305-674-2121
Miami Beach, FL 33140-2997 www.msmc.com
General cardiovascular research.
Steven D Sonenreich, President & Chief Executive Officer

784 **National Human Genome Research Institute**
Building 31, Room 4B09 301-402-0911
Bethesda, MD 20892-2152 www.genome.gov
The National Human Genome Research Institute began as the National Center for Human Genome Research (NCHGR), which was established in 1989 to carry out the role of the National Institutes of Health (NIH) in the International Human Genome Project (HGP).
Eric D. Green, M.D., Ph.D., Director
Lawrence Brody, Ph.D., Director, Division of Genomics & Society

785 **Oklahoma Medical Research Foundation: Cardiovascular Research Program**
825 NE 13th Street 405-271-6673
Oklahoma City, OK 73104-5097 800-522-0211
contact@omrf.org
www.omrf.ouhsc.edu
The Cardiovascular Biology Research Program investigates fundamental mechanisms involved in blood coagulation inflammation and atherogenesis with special emphasis on the regulation of theses processes.
Dr Stephen M Prescott, President
Mike D Morgan, Executive Vice President & COO

786 **Penn CVI Cardiovascular Institute**
3400 Civic Center Blvd. 215-746-4635
Philadelphia, PA 19104 emily.schuster@pennmedicine.upenn.edu
med.upenn.edu/cvi
The Hospital of the University of Pennsylvania (HUP) is world-renowned for its clinical and research excellence, forging the way for newer and better ways to diagnose and treat illnesses and disorders. The world-class faculty and staff of the Hospital of the University of Pennsylvania are dedicated to superior patient care, education and research for a better, healthier future. Their significant and groundbreaking contributions to medicine are recognized both nationally and internationally.
Daniel P. Kelly MD, Director
Mark L. Kahn MD, Director, Center For Vascular Biology

787 **Pennsylvania State University Artificial Heart Research Project**
Milton S Hershey Medical Center
500 University Drive 717-531-8407
Hershey, PA 17033-2391 www.psu.edu
William S Pierce MD, Director

788 **Preventive Medicine Research Institute**
900 Bridgeway 415-332-2525
Sausalito, CA 94965-2158 Tandis@pmri.org
www.pmri.org
Nonprofit organization focusing on prevention and treatment of heart disease through modification of diet exercise and relaxation techniques.
Dean Ornish, MD, Founder & President
Anne Ornish, Vice President, Director of Program Deve

789 **Purdue University William A Hillenbrand Biomedical Engineering Center**
AA Potter Engineering Center
206 S. Martin Jischke Drive 765-494-2995
W Lafayette, IN 47907-2032 877-598-4233
WeldonBME@purdue.edu
engineering.purdue.edu/BME
Cardiology and heart disease research.
Brian J Knoy, Director of Development
Kathryn Copper, Secretary

790 **Rockefeller University Laboratory of Cardiac Physiology**
1230 York Avenue 212-327-8000
New York, NY 10065 pubinfo@rockefeller.edu
www.rockefeller.edu
Causes of cardiac arrhythmias and prevention of heart disease.
David Rockfeller, Honorary Chair
Russell L Carson, Chair

791 **San Francisco Heart & Vascular Institute**
1900 Sullivan Avenue 650-991-6712
Daly City, CA 94015-2200 800-82H-EART
www.sfhi.com
At Seton Medical Center we are committed to providing a full range of high quality services and state-of-the-art cardiovascular treatments for our patients. Our medical nursing and social services staff provide quality care and compassion as a coordinated team focusing on the medical emotional and spiritual needs of patients and their families.
Colman J Ryan, MD, Executive Medical Director
Michael Girolami, MD, Chief of Cardiology

792 **Sharp Rees-Stealy Medical Group**
2929 Health Center Drive 858-499-2600
San Diego, CA 92123 sharp.com/rees-stealy
Basic cardiac research.
Stacey Hrountas, Ceo

793 **Specialized Center of Research in Ischemic Heart Disease**
1802 6th Avenue South 205-934-4011
Birmingham, AL 35294-0001 800-822-8816
www.health.uab.edu
Coronary artery disease.
Will Ferniany, CEO
Becky Armstrong, Program Manager

794 **Texas Heart Institute St Lukes Episcopal Hospital**
St Lukes Episcopal Hospital
6770 Bertner Avenue 832-355-4011
Houston, TX 77030-0345 800-292-2221
www.texasheartinstitute.org
Denton A Cooley MD, President Emeritus
James T Willerson MD, President, Medical Director

795 **University of Alabama at Birmingham: Congenital Heart Disease Center**
1720 2nd Avenue South 205-934-4011
Birmingham, AL 35294 www.uab.edu
Ray L Watts, MD, President
Linda Lucas, PhD, Provost

796 **University of California San Diego General Clinical Research Center**
UCSD Medical Center
200 W Arbor Drive 619-543-3102
San Diego, CA 92103-1910 858-657-7000
www.health.ucsd.edu
General clinical research.
Paul Viviano, Chief Executive Officer and Associate Vi
Margarita Baggett, Interim Chief Operating Officer and Chie

797 **University of California: Cardiovascular Research Laboratory**
Center for Health Sciences
UCLA Medical Center 310-825-6824
Los Angeles, CA 90024
Cellular and subcellular cardiac conditions.
Dr Glenn Langer, Director

798 **University of Cincinnati Department of Pathology & Laboratory Medicine**
234 Goodman Street 513-584-7284
Cincinnati, OH 45219-0529 pathology@uc.edu
pathology.uc.edu
Fred V Lucas, MD, Chair of Pathology
James Hill, Business Manager

799 **University of Iowa: Iowa Cardiovascular Center**
College of Medicine
200 Hawkins Drive 319-335-8588
Iowa City, IA 52242 www.int-med.uiowa.edu
The purpose is to coordinate the cardiovascular programs of the College into a more cohesive unit to permit us to 1) utilize our cardiovascular resources optimally 2) intensify expand and integrate basic and clinical research programs in areas related to cardiovascular research and 3) evaluate the role of new measures for prevention diagnosis and treatment of cardiovascular disease.
Barry London, MD, PhD, Director Cardiovascular Medicine

800 **University of Michigan Pulmonary and Critical Care Division**
University Hospital
1500 E Medical Center Drive 734-647-9342
Ann Arbor, MI 48109 888-287-1084
www2.med.umich.edu/healthcenters/clinic_
Kevin Michael Chan, MD, Division Director

801 **University of Michigan: Cardiovascular Medicine**
1500 E. Medical Center Drive 734-647-9000
Ann Arbor, MI 48109 Fax: 734-936-0133
intmedcardiology@umich.edu
Focuses on the diagnosis, treatment and prevention of cardiovascular and heart diseases.
Kim Allen Eagle, MD, Division Director

802 **University of Missouri Columbia Division of Cardiothoracic Surgery**
School of Medicine

Columbia, MO 65212 573-882-2121
AldenM@missouri.edu
www.missouri.edu
Cardiac surgery research.
Mike Alden, Director
Brian Foster, Provost

803 **University of Pittsburgh Medical Center**
200 Lothrop Street 412-647-8762
Pittsburgh, PA 15213 800-533-8762
upmc.com
The University of Pittsburgh Medical Center is a health care provider and insurer focused on developing new models of patient-centered care. Its mission is to engage in clinical research, education and innovation to ensure excellence in patient care.
G Nicholas Beckwith III, Chairperson
Jeffrey A Romoff, President and CEO

804 **University of Pittsburgh: Human Energy Research Laboratory**
4200 Fifth Avenue 412-624-4141
Pittsburgh, PA 15260-0001 www.pitt.edu
Focuses on exercise and cardiac rehabilitation.
Mark A Nordenberg, Chancellor
Patricia E Beeson, Provost and Senior Vice Chancellor

805 **University of Rochester: Clinical Research Center**
601 Elmwood Avenue 585-275-2907
Rochester, NY 14642-0001germaine_reinhardt@urmc.rochester.edu
www.urmc.rochester.edu/crc/
Studies of normal tissue functions pertaining to heart diseases.
Thomas A Pearson, MD, MPH, PhD, Director, Principal Investigator
Giovanni Schifitto , MD, Program Director

806 **University of Southern California: Coronary Care Research**
1200 N State Street 213-226-7242
Los Angeles, CA 90033-1029
Dr. L Julian Haywood, Director

807 **University of Tennessee Medical Center: Heart Lung Vascular Institute**
1940 Alcoa Hwy 865-305-9000
Knoxville, TN 37920 www.utmedicalcenter.org
Hospital dedicated to heart health.

808 **University of Tennessee: Division of Cardiovascular Diseases**
920 Madison Avenue 901-448-5750
Memphis, TN 38163-0001 www.utmem.edu\cardiology
Cardiovascular system disorders including heart disease prevention and treatment.
Karl T Weber MD, Director

809 **University of Texas Southwestern Medical Center**
5323 Harry Hines Boulevard 214-645-8300
Dallas, TX 75390-9151 www.utsouthwestern.edu
Daniel K Podolsky, MD, President
J. Gregory Fitz, Executive Vice President

810 **University of Texas Southwestern Medical Center at Dallas**
University of Texas
5323 Harry Hines Boulevard 214-648-3111
Dallas, TX 75390-7208 www.utsouthwestern.edu
Cardiology department research.
Daniel K Podolsky, MD, President
J. Gregory Fitz, MD, Executive Vice President

811 **University of Utah: Artificial Heart Research Laboratory**
50 North Medical Drive 801-581-2121
Salt Lake City, UT 84132-1414 healthsciences.utah.edu
Cardiac and blood vessel research.
Allen Stephens, Associate Director

812 **University of Utah: Cardiovascular Genetic Research Clinic**
420 Chipeta Way 801-581-3888
Salt Lake City, UT 84132-0001 www.medicine.utah.edu
Cardiovascular genetics research.
Dr Roger Williams, Founder

813 **University of Vermont Medical Center**
111 Colchester Avenue 802-847-0000
Burlington, VT 05401 800-358-1144
www.uvmhealth.org/medcenter
Melinda L Estes, MD, President/CEO
Richarad Magnuson, CFO

814 **Urban Cardiology Research Center**
2300 Garrison Boulevard 410-945-8600
Baltimore, MD 21216-2308
Causes diagnosis and treatment of cardiovascular diseases.
Arthur White MD, Director

815 **Wake Forest School of Medicine Heart & Vascular Center**
Wake Forest School of Medicine
Medical Center Boulevard 336-716-5819
Winston-Salem, NC 27157 www.wakehealth.edu
This center works towards developing a comprehensive collection of basic science and clinical research in the field of cardiology.
David Zhao, Director

816 **Warren Grant Magnuson Clinical Center**
National Institute of Health
10 Center Drive MSC 1078 301-496-3311
Bethesda, MD 20892 800-411-1222
TTY: 866-411-1010
mmichael@cc.nih.gov
www.dnrc.nih.gov/reports/programs/ncc.as
Established in 1953 as the research hospital of the National Institutes of Health. Designed so that patient care facilities are close to research laboratories so new findings of basic and clinical scientists can be quickly applied to the treatment of patients. Upon referral by physicians, patients are admitted to NIH clinical studies.
Madeline Michael, Chief, Clinical Nutrition Services

817 **Weldon School of Biomedical Engineering**
AA Potter Engineering Center
206 S. Martin Jischke Drive 765-494-2995
W Lafayette, IN 47907-2032 877-598-4233
Fax: 765-494-6628
WeldonBME@purdue.edu
engineering.purdue.edu/BME
Cardiology and heart disease research.
Brian J Knoy, Director of Development
Kathryn Copper, Secretary

818 **Yeshiva University General Clinical Research Center**
500 West 185th Street 212-960-5400
New York, NY 10033 www.yu.edu
Cardiovascular research.
Dr Henry Kressel, Chairman
Richard M Joel, President

Support Groups & Hotlines

819 **Mended Hearts**
8150 N. Central Expressway 214-206-9259
Dallas, TX 75206 888-432-7899
info@mendedhearts.org
www.mendedhearts.org
Mutual support for persons who have heart disease, their families, friends, and other interested persons.
Gordon Littlefield, President of the Board
Donnette Smith, Executive Vice President

820 **Mitral Valve Prolapse Program of Cincinnati Support Group**
10525 Montgomery Road 513-745-9911
Cincinnati, OH 45242 kscordo@wright.edu
www.nursing.wright.edu
Brings together persons frightened by their symptoms in order to learn to better cope with MVP. Fosters use of non-drug therapies. Supervised exercise sessions, diagnostic evaluations and specialized testing. Information and referrals, conferences, literature, group meetings, MVP Hot Line, and assistance in starting groups.

821 **National Health Information Center**
Office of Disease Prevention & Health Promotion
1101 Wootton Pkwy odphpinfo@hhs.gov
Rockville, MD 20852 www.health.gov/nhic

Supports public health education by maintaining a calendar of National Health Observances; helps connect consumers and health professionals to organizations that can best answer questions and provide up-to-date contact information from reliable sources; updates on a yearly basis toll-free numbers for health information, Federal health clearinghouses and info centers.
Don Wright, MD, MPH, Director

822 **National Society for MVP and Dysautonomia**
880 Montclair Road 205-595-8229
Birmingham, AL 35213 866-595-8229
nancysawyermd@bellsouth.net
Assists individuals suffering from mitral valve prolapse syndrome and dysautonomia to find support and understanding. Education on symptoms and treatment. Other areas of focus are Fibromyalgia and Sjogren's Syndrome.
Nancy Sawyer, MD

823 **Pulmonary Hypertension Association**
801 Roeder Road 301-565-3004
Silver Spring, MD 20910 800-748-7274
PHCR@PHAssociation.org
www.phassociation.org
A nonprofit organization funded and for pulmonary hypertension patients. Our mission is to seek a cure, provide hope, support, education and to promote awareness and advocate for the PH community.
Brad Wong, President & CEO
Kelly Williams, VP, Communications & Marketing

824 **Society of Mitral Valve Prolapse Syndrome**
PO Box 431 630-250-9327
Itasca, IL 60143-0431 bonnie0107@aol.com
www.mitralvalveprolapse.com/
Provides support and education to patients, families and friends about mitral valve prolapse syndrome.
Jim Durante, Co-Founder
Bonnie Durante, Co-Founder

Journals

825 **American Heart Association News**
American Heart Association
7272 Greenville Avenue 214-706-1162
Dallas, TX 75231-5129 800-242-8721
www.heart.org
News reports and journal reports on the latest information concerning heart disease.

826 **Arteriosclerosis, Thrombosis, and Vascular Biology**
7272 Greenville Avenue atvb@atvb.org
Dallas, TX 75231 ahajournals.org/atvb
Journal for academic cardiologists, vascular biologists, physiologists, pharmacologists, and hematologists
Alan Daugherty, PhD, DSc, Editor-in-Chief
Melissa Arey, Managing Editor

827 **Circulation**
Circulation
200 Fifth Avenue 410-528-4000
Waltham, MA 02451 circ@circulationjournal.org
ahajournals.org/journal/circ
Publishes original research manuscripts, review articles, and other content related to cardiovascular health and disease, including observational studies, clinical trials, epidemiology, health services and outcome studies, and advances in basic and translational research.
Joseph A. Hill, Editor-In-Chief
David Rivera, Managing Editor

828 **Circulation Research: Journal of the American Heart Association**
3355 Keswick Rd circres@circresearch.org
Baltimore, MD 21211 ahajournals.org/res
Biweekly peer-reviewed medical journal that cover research on all aspects of the cardiovascular.
Jane E. Freedman, MD, Editor-in-Chief
Gemma Bridges-Lyman, Managing Editor

829 **Circulation: Arrhythmia and Electrophysiology**
200 Fifth Avenue 781-902-4400
Waltham, MA 02451 circ@circulationjournal.org
ahajournals.org/circep
Articles related to research in and the practice of clinical cardiac electrophysiology and the diagnosis and management of cardiac arrhythmias, including observational studies, clinical trials, epidemiology, and advances in applied (translational) research.
Paul J. Wang, MD, Editor-in-Chief

830 **Circulation: Cardiovascular Imaging**
200 Fifth Avenue circ@circulationjournal.org
Waltham, MA 02451 ahajournals.org/circimaging
High-quality, patientcentric articles focusing on observational stuies, clinical trials, and advances in applied (translational) research featuring innovative, multimodality approaches diagnosis and risk stratification of cardiovascular disease.
Robert J. Gropler, MD, Editor-in-Chief
Victor G. Davila-Roman, MD, Executive Editor

831 **Circulation: Cardiovascular Interventions**
200 Fifth Avenue circ@circulationjournal.org
Waltham, MA 02451 ahajournals.org/circinterventions
Focuses on inteventional techniques pertaining to coronary artery disease, structural heart disease, and vascular disease, with priority placed on original research and on randomized trials and large registry studies.
Sunil V. Rao, MD, Editor-in-Chief
Subhash Banerjee, MD, Deputy Editor

832 **European Heart Journal**
Oxford University Press
2001 Evans Road 800-852-7323
Cary, NC 27513 Fax: 919-677-1714
academic.oup.com/eurheartj
An international, English language. peer-reviewed journal dealing with cardiovascular medicine. It is an official journal of the European Society of Cardiology and is published weekly.
Filippo Crea, Editor-In-Chief
Amelia Meier-Batschelet, Lead Managing Editor

833 **Heartstyle**
American Heart Association
7272 Greenville Avenue 214-706-1162
Dallas, TX 75231-5129 800-242-8721
www.heart.org
Reports on heart and blood vessel diseases and stroke.

834 **JACC: Cardiovascular Imaging**
American College of Cardiology
2400 North Street NW 202-375-6136
Washington, DC 20037 Fax: 202-375-6819
jaccimg@acc.org
jacc.org/journal/imaging
Monthly journal that publishes research articles on current and future applications of non-invasive and invasive imaging techniques, including echocardiography, computed tomography, cardiovascular magnetic resonance imaging, nuclear, angiography and other novel techniques.
Y.S. Chandrashekhar, Editor-in-Chief

835 **JACC: Cardiovascular Interventions**
American College of Cardiology
2400 North Street NW 202-375-6136
Washington, DC 20037 202-375-6819
jaccint@acc.org
jacc.org/journal/interventions
Journal that covers entire field of interventional cardiovascular medicine, including coronary, structural, peripheral and cerebrovascular interventions.
David J. Moliterno, MD, Editor-in-Chief

836 **JACC: Case Reports**
American College of Cardiology
2400 North Street NW jacc@acc.org
Washington, DC 20037 jacc.org/journal/case-reports
Open access journal serving as a forum for promoting clinical cases and clinical problem solving.
Julia Grapsa, MD, Editor-in-Chief

837 **JAMA Cardiology**
Subscriber Services Center
P.O. Box subscriptions@jamanetwork.org
Chicago, IL 60654 jamanetwork.com
A monthly peer-reviewed medical journal covering cardiology.
Robert O. Bonow, MD, Editor

838 **Journal of the American College of Cardiology**
American College Of Cardiology
2400 North Street NW 202-375-6136
Washington, DC 20037 Fax: 202-375-6819
jacc@acc.org
jacc.org/journal/jacc
The JACC publishes peer-eviewed articles highlighting all aspects of cardiovascular disease, including original clinical studies, experimental investigations with clear clinical relevance, state-of-the-art papers and viewpoints. Publishes 50 issues per year.
Valentine Furster, MD, PhD, Editor-in-Chief

839 **Journal of the American Heart Association**
200 5th Ave jaha@journalaha.org
Waltham, MA 02451 ahajournals.org/jaha
Online-only journal for healthcare professionals interested and involved with cardiovascular and cerebrovascular diseases, vascular and endovascular medicine, pediatric cardiology, and neurology.
Barry London, MD, PhD, Editor-in-Chief
Kathleen Sullivan, Managing Editor

840 **MVPS & Anxiety**
Society of Mitral Valve Prolapse Syndrome
PO Box 431 630-250-9327
Itasca, IL 60143-0431 bonnie0107@aol.com
www.mitralvalveprolapse.com
6 pages

841 **Nature Reviews Cardiology**
4 Crinan Street nrcardio@nature.com
London, UK www.nature.com/nrcardio
Publishes research, news, and perspectives relevant to practising cardiologists and cardiovascular research scientists.
Gregory Lim, Chief Editor

Web Sites

842 **American Heart Association**
www.heart.org
Supports research, education and community service programs with the objective of reducing premature death and disability from cardiovascular diseases and stroke; coordinates the efforts of health professionals, and other engaged in the fight against heart and circulatory disease.

843 **Dietary Guidelines for Americans**
www.dietaryguidelines.gov
Publishes the Dietary Guidelines for Americans, a guide providing nutritional advice to promote health and prevent disease. Updated versions of the Dietary Guidelines are released by the US Departments of Agriculture (USDA) and Health & Human Services (HHS) every five years.

844 **Everyday Health**
www.everydayhealth.com
Aims to provide evidence-based health information from physicians and healthcare providers.

845 **FamilyDoctor.org**
www.familydoctor.org
Medical advice and information provided by the American Academy of Family Physicians. Resources include a medical dictionary, a symptom checker tool, a BMI calculator, and medication information.

846 **Healing Well**
www.healingwell.com
An online health resource guide to medical news, chat, information and articles, newsgroups and message boards, books, disease-related web sites, medical directories, and more for patients, friends, and family coping with disabling diseases, disorders, or chronic illnesses.

847 **Health Finder**
www.healthfinder.gov
Searchable, carefully developed web site offering information on over 1000 topics. Developed by the US Department of Health and Human Services, the site can be used in both English and Spanish.

848 **Healthline**
www.healthline.com
Provides medical and health articles and information.

849 **Healthlink USA**
www.healthlinkusa.com
Health information concerning treatment, cures, prevention, diagnosis, risk factors, research, support groups, email lists, personal stories and much more. Updated regularly.

850 **Hormone Health Network**
www.hormone.org
Online support and resources for patients, with focus on hormone health, disease and treatment. Provided by the Endocrine Society.

851 **MedicineNet**
www.medicinenet.com
An online resource for consumers providing easy-to-read, authoritative medical and health information.

852 **MedlinePlus**
www.medlineplus.gov
A service of the National Library of Medicine, MedlinePlus is an online resource providing health and wellness information in both English and Spanish.

853 **Medscape**
www.medscape.com
Medscape offers specialists, primary care physicians, and other health professionals the Web's most robust and integrated medical information and educational tools.

854 **MyPlate**
www.myplate.gov
Created and managed by the US Department of Agriculture's Center for Nutrition Policy & Promotion, MyPlate is a dietary guide providing resources and recipes to promote healthy eating for all Americans.

855 **National Heart, Lung and Blood Institute**
www.nhlbi.nih.gov
Primary responsibility of this organization is the scientific investigation of heart, blood vessel, lung and blood disorders. Oversees research, demonstration, prevention, education, control and training activities in these fields and emphasizes the prevention and control of heart diseases.

856 **Nutrition.gov**
www.nutrition.gov
Sponsored by the United States Department of Agriculture (USDA), Nutrition.gov offers information on topics in food and nutrition, including healthy eating, physical activity, and food safety.

857 **Science Daily**
www.sciencedaily.com
Provides information on the latest news and research in science, health, the environment, and technology.

858 **The Nutrition Source**
hsph.harvard.edu/nutritionsource
From the Harvard T.H. Chan School of Public Health, The Nutrition Source provides news, information, and guidance for nutrition and healthy eating.

859 **UnlockFood**
www.unlockfood.ca
A website from Dietitians of Canada. Provides videos, recipes, and information on food and nutrition, as well as helps Canadians connect with a dietitian.

860 **Verywell**
www.verywellhealth.com

Offers health, medicine, and wellness information from health professionals.

861 **WebMD**

www.webmd.com

Provides credible information, supportive communities, and in-depth reference material about health subjects. A source for original and timely health information as well as material from well known content providers.

862 **World Health Organization**

www.who.int

An agency of the United Nations, World Health Organization (WHO) serves to promote global health. The WHO website provides fact sheets, publications, media, and other resources on various health topics.

HYPERTENSION

Hypertension, also known as high blood pressure, is a common disease characterized by blood flow through the body's arteries at higher-than-normal pressures. When the ventricles pump blood out of the heart it is referred to as systolic pressure. The pressure between heartbeats, when the heart is filling with blood, is diastolic pressure. A measurement higher than 120 (systolic) over 80 (diastolic) is considered high blood pressure. To control blood pressure, doctors recommend a heart-healthy lifestyle, including a nutritious diet such DASH, detailed below. Increased activity is also a way to control blood pressure. Medication may be necessary to lower BP. Controlling BP may delay, or prevent, health problems such as heart failure, heart attack, kidney disease, stroke and perhaps vascular dementia.

The risk of high blood pressure is often increased by unhealthy lifestyle habits. Other risk factors include family history and genetics, age, race, ethnicity and sex. BP tends to increase with age because blood vessels naturally thicken over time making it harder to pump blood. Excess weight also increases the risk of high blood pressure, especially in children and teens. Hypertension often runs in families as does a high sensitivity to salt in the diet which can increase BP through fluid retention. Income, education, geography, and work settings may all contribute to hypertension risk.

Lifestyle habits can be managed to prevent or control hypertension. Poor nutrition, such as eating unhealthy foods with too much salt and not enough potassium, may increase the risk. African Americans, seniors, and people with diabetes or chronic kidney disease are often more sensitive to salt in their diet. Retaining fluid increases the workload on the heart. Too much alcohol or caffeine, low physical activity, poor sleep, smoking and drug misuse all contribute to high blood pressure. Medicines that may raise blood pressure include antidepressants, birth control pills, non-steroidal anti-inflammatory drugs (aspirin or ibuprofen), and decongestants.

Regular BP checks are recommended. If hypertension is detected (numbers higher than 120/80), a doctor may advise a heart-healthy lifestyle to prevent development of life-threatening hypertension. A dietician can suggest heart-healthy foods low in sodium and rich in potassium such as fruits and vegetables. Regular physical activity, healthy weight, not smoking, good sleep and low stress levels are all strategies to manage blood pressure.

The DASH heart-healthy eating plan is often recommended for blood pressure management. It is flexible and balanced, requires no special foods and provides daily and weekly goals. The plan recommends eating fruits, vegetables and whole grains, fat-free or low-fat dairy products, fish, poultry, beans, nuts and vegetable oils, and limiting foods high in saturated fats and sugar-sweetened beverages and foods. Sodium is limited to 1500-2300 mg and foods should be low in saturated and transfats, and rich in potassium, magnesium, calcium, fiber and protein.

Nutrition can play a key role in a variety of health conditions, especially in blood pressure management. A heart-healthy diet, adequate activity and healthy lifestyle choices will help prevent the development of hypertension.

See page 167 for more information on the DASH diet and other nutrition concerns.

Agencies & Associations

864 **American Stroke Association**
7272 Greenville Avenue 800-242-8721
Dallas, TX 75231 www.stroke.org
A division of the American Heart Association. Aims to reduce the incidence of stroke by supporting research, offering information, and advocating for stronger public health policies.
Nancy Brown, Chief Executive Officer
Suzie Upton, Chief Operating Officer

865 **Centers for Medicare & Medicaid Services**
7500 Security Boulevard www.cms.gov
Baltimore, MD 21244
U.S. federal agency which administers Medicare, Medicaid, and the State Children's Health Insurance Program.
Chiquita Brooks-LaSure, Administrator
Jonathan Blum, COO

866 **National Heart, Lung & Blood Institute**
31 Center Drive 877-645-2448
Bethesda, MD 20892 nhlbiinfo@nhlbi.nih.gov
www.nhlbi.nih.gov
Trains, conducts research, and educates in order to promote the prevention and treatment of heart, lung, and blood disorders.
Gary H. Gibbons, MD, Director

867 **National Institute of Biomedical Imaging and Bioengineering**
9000 Rockville Pike 301-496-8859
Bethesda, MD 20892 info@nibib.nih.gov
www.nibib.nih.gov
The mission of the National Institute of Biomedical Imaging and Bioengineering (NIBIB) is to improve health by leading the development and accelerating the application of biomedical technologies.
Bruce J. Tromberg, PhD, Director
Jill Heemskerk, PhD, Deputy Director

868 **Nurse Practitioners in Women's Health**
PO Box 15837 202-543-9693
Washington, DC 20003 info@npwh.org
www.npwh.org
Ensures the delivery and accessibility of primary and specialty healthcare to women of all ages by women's health and women's health focused nurse practitioners.
Heather L. Maurer, CEO
Donna Ruth, Director, Education

869 **Office of Women's Health**
200 Independence Avenue SW 202-690-7650
Washington, DC 20201 800-994-9662
womenshealth@hhs.gov
www.womenshealth.gov
Government agency under the Department of Health & Human Services, with free health information for women.
Dorothy Fink, MD, Deputy Asst. Secretary, Women's Health
Richelle West Marshall, Deputy Director

870 **Pulmonary Hypertension Association (PHA)**
8401 Colesville Road 301-565-3004
Silver Spring, MD 20910 800-748-7274
pha@phassociation.org
www.phassociation.org
A non-profit organization for pulmonary hypertension patients, families, caregivers and PH-treating medical professionals. PHA works to provide support, education, and find a cure for pulmonary hypertension.
Matt J. Granato, President & CEO
Azalea Candelaria, Vice President, Development

Foundations & Research Centers

871 **Columbia University Irving Center for Clinical Research**
Columbia University
622 West 168th Street 212-305-2071
New York, NY 10032 irving_institute@cumc.columbia.edu
www.columbia.edu/
Multidisciplinary studies of human disease and clinical pharmacology. Areas include arrhythmia control, heart failure, atherosclerosis, nutrition, metabolism, clinical pharmacology, dermatology, endocrinology, hypertension, immunology, mineral metabolism and skeletal disease, neuromuscular disease, physiology, pulmonary disease, pulmonary physiology, reproductive research studies, neurology (including dementia, stroke, and seizure disorders).
Muredach P. Pollinger, Director

872 **Creighton University Midwest Hypertension Research Center**
601 N 30th Street 402-280-4507
Omaha, NE 68131-2137
Dr William PhD, Director

873 **Hahnemann University: Division of Surgical Research**
230 N Broad Street 215-762-7000
Philadelphia, PA 19102 866-884-4HUH
www.hahnemannhospital.com
Studies hypertension and management of stress ulcers.
Teuro Matsum Carretero, Division Head
William H Beierwaltes, Scientist

874 **Henry Ford Hospital: Hypertension and Vascular Research Division**
2799 W Grand Boulevard 313-972-1693
Detroit, MI 48202-2689 ocarret1@hfhs.org
www.hypertensionresearch.org
Basic biomedical research seeks to understand: The role of vasoconstrictors and vasodilators (angiotensin II bradykinin nitric oxide natriuretic peptides) in the regulation of blood pressure development of hypertension and development of target organ damage (myocardial infarction heart failure vascular injury and renal disease); The generation of reactive oxygen species by blood vessels and kidney cells and how this contributes to target organ damage; and The mechanisms by which therape
William H Beierwaltes, Ph.D., Faculty
Oscar A Carretero, Faculty

875 **Indiana University: Hypertension Research Center**
425 University Boulevard 317-274-4591
Indianapolis, IN 46202-0001 800-274-4862
www.indiana.edu/medical
The mission of the Center is to conduct research in the causes diagnosis treatment and prevention of high blood pressure and its complications.
Dr Myron Rom MPH, Director
Eric Schips, Divisional Administrator

876 **Nevada Kidney Disease & Hypertension Centers**
210 S Desplaines Street 312-654-2720
Chicago, IL 60661 charlotte.chapple@ainmd.com
www.ainmd.com/
A medical group practicing nephrology in the Chicago metropolitan area and it suburbs. Includes 21 nephrologists with expertise in many areas in the field of nephrology including hypertension chronic and acute renal failure hemodialysis and peritoneal dialysis glomerulonephritis acid base disturbances fluid and electrolytes management. Provides personal high quality care to patients with kidney diseases.
Eduardo Kantor MD, Founder

877 **New York University General Clinical Research Center**
NYU Medical Center
550 First Avenue 212-263-7300
New York, NY 10016 www.med.nyu.edu
Focuses in the areas of hypertension and studies into endocrinology.
Robert I Grossman, MD, Dean & CEO
Steven B Abramson, MD, Senior Vice President and Vice Dean for

878 **University of Michigan: Division of Hypertension**
1500 E Medical Center 734-615-0863
Ann Arbor, MI 48109 855-855-0863
www.med.umich.edu
Excellence in medical education patient care and research.
Douglas L Stoulil, Study Coordinator

879 **University of Minnesota: Hypertensive Research Group**
611 Beacon Street SE 612-624-1438
Minneapolis, MN 55455

Research pertaining to hypertension and stress disorders.
Jack Massry, Head

880 **University of Southern California Division of Nephrology & Hypertension**
1333 San Pablo St. 323-442-1040
Los Angeles, CA 90089 Fax: 323-442-2881
keck.usc.edu/nephrology-division
Research into hypertension and sleep disorders.
Kenneth R. Hallows, MD, Director
Gloria Yang-Kolodji, Operations Administrator; Research Lead

881 **University of Southern California: Division of Nephrology**
2025 Zonal Avenue 323-442-5100
Los Angeles, CA 90033-1034 www.usc.edu/health
Research into hypertension and sleep disorders.
Gbemisola A Adeseun, MD, MPH, Faculty
Vito M Campese, MD, Faculty

882 **University of Virginia: Hypertension and Atherosclerosis Unit**
Medical Center 804-924-8470
Charlottesville, VA 22908-0001
Dr Carlos DVM, Director

883 **Wake Forest University: Arteriosclerosis Research Center**
Department of Comparative Medicine
300 S Hawthorne Road 336-764-3600
Winston-Salem, NC 27103-2732
Hypertension research.
Thomas Clark

Support Groups & Hotlines

884 **National Health Information Center**
Office of Disease Prevention & Health Promotion
1101 Wootton Pkwy odphpinfo@hhs.gov
Rockville, MD 20852 www.health.gov/nhic
Supports public health education by maintaining a calendar of National Health Observances; helps connect consumers and health professionals to organizations that can best answer questions and provide up-to-date contact information from reliable sources; updates on a yearly basis toll-free numbers for health information, Federal health clearinghouses and info centers.
Don Wright, MD, MPH, Director

885 **Pulmonary Hypertension Association**
801 Roeder Road 301-565-3004
Silver Spring, MD 20910 800-748-7274
PHCR@PHAssociation.org
www.phassociation.org
A nonprofit organization funded and for pulmonary hypertension patients. Our mission is to seek a cure, provide hope, support, education and to promote awareness and advocate for the PH community.
Brad Wong, President & CEO
Kelly Williams, VP, Communications & Marketing

Journals

886 **American Journal of Hypertension**
American Society of Hypertension
45 Main Street 212-696-9099
New York, NY 11201 ash@ash-us.org
www.ash-us.org

887 **Ethnicity & Disease**
International Society on Hypertension in Blacks
2045 Manchester Street NE 404-875-6263
Atlanta, GA 30324-4110 member@ishib.org
www.ishib.org
International journal on ethnic minority population differences in disease patterns. Provides a comprehensive source of information on the causal relationships in the etiology of common illnesses through the study of ethnic patterns of disease.
John Willey, Publisher
Melanie T Cockfield, Director Administration

888 **Hypertension: Journal of the American Heart Association**
hyper.ahajournals.org
Lists current issues of journals about hypertension and the American Heart Association.

889 **Magazine of the National Institute of Hypertension Studies**
13217 Livernois Avenue 313-931-3427
Detroit, MI 48238-3162
Association news.

890 **News Report**
National Hypertension Association
324 E 30th Street 212-889-3557
New York, NY 10016-8329 nathypertension@aol.com
www.nathypertension.org
Offers information and medical updates regarding hypertension. Recent book publication: 100 Questions and Answers about Hypertension by WM Manger, MD, PhD, and RW Gifford, Jr, MT available throught National Hypertension Association.
W.M. Manger MD, PhD, Chairman

Digital Resources

891 **Stroke: Touching the Soul of Your Family**
National Stroke Association
9707 E Easter Lane 303-649-9299
Centennial, CO 80112-3747 800-787-6537
info@stroke.org
www.stroke.org
Fifteen minute video chronicling three stroke survivors and their courageous struggle to overcome daily challenges and educate others about stroke.
Colette Lafosse, Director Rehabilitation/Recovery Program

Web Sites

892 **American Society of Hypertension**
www.ash-us.org
To organize and conduct educational seminars, materials, and products in all aspects of hypertension and other cardiovascular diseases.

893 **Dietary Guidelines for Americans**
www.dietaryguidelines.gov
Publishes the Dietary Guidelines for Americans, a guide providing nutritional advice to promote health and prevent disease. Updated versions of the Dietary Guidelines are released by the US Departments of Agriculture (USDA) and Health & Human Services (HHS) every five years.

894 **Everyday Health**
www.everydayhealth.com
Aims to provide evidence-based health information from physicians and healthcare providers.

895 **FamilyDoctor.org**
www.familydoctor.org
Medical advice and information provided by the American Academy of Family Physicians. Resources include a medical dictionary, a symptom checker tool, a BMI calculator, and medication information.

896 **Healing Well**
www.healingwell.com
An online health resource guide to medical news, chat, information and articles, newsgroups and message boards, books, disease-related web sites, medical directories, and more for patients, friends, and family coping with disabling diseases, disorders, or chronic illnesses.

897 **Health Finder**
www.healthfinder.gov
Searchable, carefully developed web site offering information on over 1000 topics. Developed by the US Department of Health and Human Services, the site can be used in both English and Spanish.

898 **Healthline**
www.healthline.com

Provides medical and health articles and information.

899 **Healthlink USA**

www.healthlinkusa.com

Links to websites which may include treatment, cures, diagnosis, prevention, support groups, email lists, messageboards, personal stories, risk factors, statistics, research and more.

900 **Hormone Health Network**

www.hormone.org

Online support and resources for patients, with focus on hormone health, disease and treatment. Provided by the Endocrine Society.

901 **Inter-American Society of Hypertension**

www.iashonline.org

Website hosted by IASH, a non-profit professional organization devoted to the understanding, prevention and control of hypertension and vascular diseases in the American population. Members from 20 different countries in the Americas as well as Europe, Australia and Asia. Stimulates research and the exchange of ideas in hypertension and vascular diseases amoung physicians and scientists. Promotes the detection, control and prevention of hypertension and other cardiovascular risk factors.

902 **Lifeclinic.Com**

www.lifeclinic.com

Online information about blood pressure, hypertension, diabetes, cholesterol, stroke, heart failure and more. Maintains current, up-to-date and accurate information for patients to help them manage their conditions better and to improve communications between them and their doctors.

903 **Mayo Clinic**

www.mayoclinic.org

Mission is to empower people to manage their health by providing useful and up-to-date information and tools.

904 **MedicineNet**

www.medicinenet.com

An online resource for consumers providing easy-to-read, authoritative medical and health information.

905 **Medscape**

www.medscape.com

Medscape offers specialists, primary care physicians, and other health professionals the Web's most robust and integrated medical information and educational tools.

906 **MyPlate**

www.myplate.gov

Created and managed by the US Department of Agriculture's Center for Nutrition Policy & Promotion, MyPlate is a dietary guide providing resources and recipes to promote healthy eating for all Americans.

907 **National Heart, Lung & Blood Institute**

www.nhlbi.nih.gov

Information on the scientific investigation of heart, blood vessel, lung and blood disorders. Oversee research, demonstration, prevention, education and training activities in these fields and emphasizes the control of stroke.

908 **Nutrition.gov**

www.nutrition.gov

Sponsored by the United States Department of Agriculture (USDA), Nutrition.gov offers information on topics in food and nutrition, including healthy eating, physical activity, and food safety.

909 **Science Daily**

www.sciencedaily.com

Provides information on the latest news and research in science, health, the environment, and technology.

910 **The Nutrition Source**

hsph.harvard.edu/nutritionsource

From the Harvard T.H. Chan School of Public Health, The Nutrition Source provides news, information, and guidance for nutrition and healthy eating.

911 **UnlockFood**

www.unlockfood.ca

A website from Dietitians of Canada. Provides videos, recipes, and information on food and nutrition, as well as helps Canadians connect with a dietitian.

912 **Verywell**

www.verywellhealth.com

Offers health, medicine, and wellness information from health professionals.

913 **WebMD**

www.webmd.com

Provides credible information, supportive communities, and in-depth reference material about health subjects. A source for original and timely health information as well as material from well known content providers.

914 **World Health Organization**

www.who.int

An agency of the United Nations, World Health Organization (WHO) serves to promote global health. The WHO website provides fact sheets, publications, media, and other resources on various health topics.

KIDNEY DISEASE & LIVER DISEASE

The kidneys filter extra water and waste out of the body and create urine. Damaged kidneys can't efficiently filter waste from the blood, affecting digestion and nutrition. High blood pressure and diabetes put you at greater risk for kidney disease. Injury, cysts, stones, infections and cancer all cause kidney problems. A healthy eating plan, like the DASH diet, is essential for individuals with kidney and should be individualized in consultation with a physician and registered clinical dietician. The DASH diet is rich in vegetables, fruits, low-fat dairy products, whole grains, poultry, fish beans and nuts and low in sodium and salt. The liver aids in digesting food and processing and distributing nutrients. Liver diseases may be caused by viruses, drugs and alcohol, and other factors including cancer. A diet for those with liver disease is based on the underlying cause of disease. General recommendations include avoiding foods high in fat, sugar and salt, fried foods and fast foods.

Chronic kidney disease occurs when the kidneys are unable to filter excess water and waste out of the body during the process of making urine. The cause of the disease dictates the type of treatment. If diabetes is the cause, the first sign of associated kidney disease is protein in the urine from albumin, which should stay in the blood stream and not in the urine. Kidney disease caused by diabetes is diabetic kidney disease. Kidney disease caused by hypertension causes damage to the blood vessels in the kidneys causing improper filtration. Other causes of kidney disease include genetics, infection, drug toxicities, lupus, disorders of the immune system, and lead poisoning. If you have diabetes, high blood pressure, heart disease, or a family history of kidney disease, blood and urine testing is recommended to determine if the kidneys are functioning appropriately.

A low-sodium diet will assist in managing chronic kidney disease — less than 2,300 milligrams of sodium per day. To keep sodium low, choose fresh foods instead of processed foods, use spices, herbs and sodium-free seasonings, read labels to select lower sodium foods, and rinse canned vegetables, beans, meats and fish before cooking. Do not eat excess protein, as protein produces more waste, causing the kidneys to work harder. Choosing heart-healthy foods such as poultry without the skin, lean meat, fish, beans, vegetables and fruits, and low-fat or fat free dairy will prevent fat from building up in the blood vessels, heart and kidneys. Protecting kidneys by preventing or managing health conditions such as diabetes and heart disease and making healthy food choices may prevent chronic kidney disease.

The liver aids in digestion of food and processing and distributing nutrients throughout the body. There are many types and causes of liver diseases and conditions. Hepatitis is caused by viruses. Certain drugs (illegal, over the counter, or prescription) and alcohol overuse may cause liver disease. Liver cancer also causes interference with liver function. Injury or scar tissue in the liver can cause cirrhosis. An early sign of liver disease is jaundice, a yellowing of the skin.

Healthy eating to prevent or manage liver disease includes avoiding foods high in fat, sugar and salt, fried foods, and fast foods. Raw or undercooked shellfish should be avoided and alcohol should be limited to one drink a day for women and two for men. Eating a balanced diet — foods from all food groups — food high in fiber and drinking lots of water is important. Because diets vary according to condition, i.e. bile duct disease, cirrhosis, fatty liver disease, hepatitis C, hemochromatosis and Wilson disease, it is crucial to consult with a physician and dietician for the best diet for your specific condition. In addition to healthy eating, additional safety precautions may be necessary. With hepatitis C, limit foods with high iron levels and do not use iron pots. With hemochromatosis, avoid foods and pills with high iron, raw shellfish and do not use iron pots. With Wilson disease, limit foods with copper such as nuts, chocolate, mushrooms and shellfish and do not use copper pots.

Preventing disease through diet may not always be possible, but with kidney and liver disease, specific diets and nutrition interventions may help.

See page 251 for more information on kidney disease.

Agencies & Associations

916 **Agency for Toxic Substances and Disease Registry**
1200 Pennsylvania Avenue NW 800-232-4636
Washington, DC 20460 www.atsdr.cdc.gov
The Agency for Toxic Substances and Disease Registry (ATSDR), based in Atlanta, Georgia, is a federal public health agency of the U.S. Department of Health and Human Services. ATSDR serves the public by using the best science, taking responsive public health actions, and providing trusted health information to prevent harmful exposures and diseases related to toxic substances.
Patrick Breysse, Director

917 **American Association for the Study of Liver Diseases**
PO B Ox 25407 703-299-9766
Alexandria, VA 22314 aasld@aasld.org
www.aasld.org
Physicians, researchers, and allied hepatology health professionals dedicated to preventing and curing liver disease by fostering research on liver diseases.
Matthew D'Uva, Chief Executive Officer
Julie Deal, Deputy Chief Executive Officer

918 **American Association of Kidney Patients**
14440 Bruce B. Downs Boulevard 813-636-8100
Tampa, FL 33613 800-749-2257
info@aakp.org
www.aakp.org
Diana Clynes, Executive Director
Valerie Gonzalez, Director, Office Operations

919 **American Kidney Fund**
11921 Rockville Pike 800-638-8299
Rockville, MD 20852 866-300-2900
helpline@kidneyfund.org
www.kidneyfund.org
A non-profit national health organization providing direct financial assistance to thousands of Americans who suffer from kidney disease.
LaVarne A. Burton, President & CEO
Donald J. Roy, Jr., CPA, Executive Vice President & COO

920 **Association for Glycogen Storage Disease**
PO Box 896 info@agsdus.org
Durant, IA 52747 www.agsdus.org
Organization for parents of and individuals with glycogen storage disease (GSD) to communicate, share useful information, provide support, create awareness of GSD, and to foster research on glycogen storage diseases.
Iris Ferrecchia, President
Jessica Knepler, Vice President

921 **Centers for Medicare & Medicaid Services**
7500 Security Boulevard www.cms.gov
Baltimore, MD 21244
U.S. federal agency which administers Medicare, Medicaid, and the State Children's Health Insurance Program.
Chiquita Brooks-LaSure, Administrator
Jonathan Blum, COO

922 **Children's Liver Association For Support Services (CLASS)**
PO Box 186 724-581-5527
Monaca, PA 15061 classkidscares@gmail.com
www.classkids.org
An organization dedicated to addressing the emotional, educational and financial needs of families with children affected by liver disease and transplantation.
Stephan Circle, Co-President
Tamara Circle, Co-President

923 **Gastrointestinal Society - Canadian Society of Intestinal Research**
231 - 3665 Kingsway 604-873-4876
Vancouver, BC, V5R-5W2 866-600-4875
Fax: 855-875-4429
www.badgut.org
Aims to improve the lives of people with gastrointestinal and liver diseases and disorders by funding research, advocating for patient access to healthcare, and providing evidence-based information for patients.
Gail Attara, Chief Executive Officer
Kwynn Vodnak, Associate Director

924 **National Institute of Biomedical Imaging and Bioengineering**
9000 Rockville Pike 301-496-8859
Bethesda, MD 20892 info@nibib.nih.gov
www.nibib.nih.gov
The mission of the National Institute of Biomedical Imaging and Bioengineering (NIBIB) is to improve health by leading the development and accelerating the application of biomedical technologies.
Bruce J. Tromberg, PhD, Director
Jill Heemskerk, PhD, Deputy Director

925 **National Institute of Diabetes & Digestive & Kidney Diseases**
9000 Rockville Pike 800-860-8747
Bethesda, MD 20892 TTY: 866-569-1162
healthinfo@niddk.nih.gov
www.niddk.nih.gov
Research areas include diabetes, digestive diseases, endocrine and metabolic diseases, hematologic diseases, kidney disease, liver disease, urologic diseases, as well as matters relating to nutrition and obesity.
Griffin P. Rodgers, MD, MACP, Director
Gregory Germino, MD, Deputy Director

926 **National Institute of General Medical Sciences**
45 Center Drive 301-496-7301
Bethesda, MD 20892-6200 info@nigms.nih.gov
www.nigms.nih.gov
The National Institute of General Medical Sciences (NIGMS) supports basic research that increases understanding of biological processes and lays the foundation for advances in disease diagnosis, treatment and prevention.
Jon R. Lorsch, PhD, Director
Dorit Zuk, PhD, Acting Deputy Director

927 **National Institute on Alcohol Abuse and Alcoholism**
9000 Rockville Pike 301-443-3860
Bethesda, MD 20892 niaaaweb-r@exchange.nih.gov
www.niaaa.nih.gov
NIAAA supports and conducts research on the impact of alcohol use on human health and well-being. It is the largest funder of alcohol research in the world.
George F. Koob, Ph.D., Director
Patricia A. Powell, Ph.D., Deputy Director

928 **National Institute on Drug Abuse**
Office of Science Policy & Communications
301 North Stonestreet Avenue 301-443-1124
Bethesda, MD 20892 www.drugabuse.gov
NIDA's mission is to lead the Nation in bringing the power of science to bear on drug abuse and addiction.
Nora Volkow, MD, Director
Wilson Compton, MD, Deputy Director

929 **Nebraska Kidney Association**
11725 Arbor Street 402-932-7200
Omaha, NE 68144 www.kidneyne.org
Improve the lives of all Nebraskans through advocacy, education, early disease detection and patient services.

930 **Nurse Practitioners in Women's Health**
PO Box 15837 202-543-9693
Washington, DC 20003 info@npwh.org
www.npwh.org
Ensures the delivery and accessibility of primary and specialty healthcare to women of all ages by women's health and women's health focused nurse practitioners.
Heather L. Maurer, CEO
Donna Ruth, Director, Education

931 **Wilson Disease Association**
1732 First Avenue 414-961-0533
New York, NY 10128 866-961-0533
info@wilsonsdisease.org
www.wilsonsdisease.org

Serves as a communications support network for individuals affected by Wilson's disease; distributes information to professionals and the public; makes referrals; and holds meetings.
8 pages
Jean P. Perog, President
Rachel Albert, Vice President

Arizona

932 **Central Arizona Chapter of the American Association of Kidney Patients**
4401 W Hatcher Road 602-939-7248
Glendale, AZ 85302-3821
Dale A Ester, President

California

933 **Harbor-South Bay Orange County Chapter of the American Assoc. of Kidney Patients**
PO Box 8 714-527-8009
Seal Beach, CA 90740 delrita@aol.com
www.aakp.org
Rita McQuire, President

934 **Los Angeles Chapter of the American Association of Kidney Patients**
9854 National Boulevard 310-364-1807
Los Angeles, CA 90034 aakpla@yahoo.com
www.aakp.org
Robin Siegal, President

935 **Redding Chapter of the American Association of Kidney Patients**
790 Pioneer Drive 530-241-6451
Redding, CA 96001-0258 teamward@c-zone.net
www.aakp.org

936 **Sacramento Valley Chapter of the American Association of Kidney Patients**
565 Morrison Avenue 916-924-1996
Sacramento, CA 95838

Colorado

937 **Colorado Chapter of the American Association of Kidney Patients**
PO Box 8442 303-758-8610
Denver, CO 80201

938 **Western Slope Chapter of the American Association of Kidney Patients**
1539 Ptarmigan Ridge 970-244-9196
Grand Junction, CO 81056
Vicki Hathaway, CEO
Donna Sciacca, Director of Patient Programs/Services

Florida

939 **Kidney Association of South Florida**
6801 Lake Worth Road 561-434-4559
Lake Worth, FL 33467 jansym@bellsouth.net
www.aakp.org
Jan Symonette, President

940 **South Florida Chapter of the American Association of Kidney Patients**
5217 Northlake Boulevard 561-471-2588
Palm Beach Gardens, FL 33418 diazgray@aol.com
www.aakp.org
Robert Kirby, President

941 **Sunshine Chapter of the American Association of Kidney Patients**
PO Box 4716 305-821-4827
Hialeah, FL 33014-0716
Elaine Printup

Georgia

942 **Atlanta Georgia Chapter of the American Association of Kidney Patients**
6409 Lakeview Drive 404-932-1100
Buford, GA 30518
Pamela Sachs, Division President
Tracy Jenny, Division Program Director

943 **Rome Georgia Chapter of the American Association of Kidney Patients**
118 Woodcrest Drive 706-232-8989
Rome, GA 30161
Hazel Hayashida, Chief Executive Officer
Diana Pinard, Director of Organization Planning

Illinois

944 **Chicagoland Chapter of the American Association of Kidney Patients**
70 Lincoln Oaks Drive 708-325-3475
Chicago, IL 60514
Gloria Lang, Chief Executive Officer
Kate Grubbs O'Connor, Chief Operating Officer

Iowa

945 **Iowa Chapter of the Association of Kidney Patients**
2203 75th Place 319-391-1194
Davenport, IA 52806-1107
Dave Hagarty, Executive Director
Lori Donald, Accounting Coordinator

Louisiana

946 **Bayou Area Chapter of the American Association of Kidney Patients**
PO Box 400 504-532-3542
Lockport, LA 70374
Louisiana Kranze, Chief Executive Officer
Tracey Eldridge, Director of Special Events

New Jersey

947 **Garrett Mountain Chapter of the American Association of Kidney Patients**
PO Box 8496 973-523-3959
Haledon, NJ 07538
Hurwitz, President

948 **Meadowlands Chapter of the American Association of Kidney Patients**
PO Box 3032 201-471-5674
Clifton, NJ 07012-3032
Howard

949 **Northern New Jersey Chapter of the American Association of Kidney Patients**
1095 Stone Street 732-382-1092
Rahway, NJ 07065-1913
Burnett

New York

950 **Long Island Chapter of the American Association of Kidney Patients**
2 Maplewood Avenue 516-756-9126
Farmingdale, NY 11735
Margie Ng Makhuli, Chief Executive Officer
Laura Squadrito, Director of Programs and Services

951 **New York Chapter of the American Association of Kidney Patients**
450 Clarkson Avenue 718-270-1548
Brooklyn, NY 11203 linda.cohen@downstate.edu
www.aakp.org
Linda Welch, Kidney Early Evaluation Program Contact

Ohio

952 **Miami Valley Ohio Chapter of the American Association of Kidney Patients**
4511 W State Route 513-698-5847
W Milton, OH 45383
Bob B Gold, Division President
Danielle Estep, Division Program Director

Pennsylvania

953 **Lehigh Valley Chapter of the American Association of Kidney Patients**
1242 N 19th Street 610-776-1091
Allentown, PA 18104-3058 info@aakp.org
www.aakp.org
Jill Spink, Division President
Mary Reilly, Development Director

Texas

954 **American Association of Kidney Patients: Piney Woods Chapter**
PO Box 1012 903-537-7031
Mount Vernon, TX 75457 800-749-2257
Edwin Wager, President

955 **Lone Star Chapter of the American Association of Kidney Patients**
10042 Sugarloaf Drive 210-523-1605
San Antonio, TX 78245 www.aakp.org
Robert Eaton, CEO
Cameron Hernholm, Director of Development

Libraries & Resource Centers

956 **National Kidney and Urologic Diseases Information Clearinghouse**
3 Information Way 800-860-8747
Bethesda, MD 20892-3580 TTY: 866-569-1162
healthinfo@niddk.nih.gov
www.niddk.nih.gov
A service of the Federal Government's National Institute for Diabetes and Digestive and Kidney Diseases. Offers free information about benign prostate enlargement and other non-cancerous urinary tract problems.

Foundations & Research Centers

957 **Alabama Kidney Foundation**
PO BOX 12505 205-934-2111
Birmingham, AL 35202-2238 800-750-3331
www.alkidney.org
Gwen Deierhoi, President
E.W. Jackson III, Executive Director

958 **American Liver Foundation**
39 Broadway 212-668-1000
New York, NY 10006 800-465-4837
info@liverfoundation.org
www.liverfoundation.org
ALF raises awareness of liver disease through education, advocacy, and research for the prevention, treatment, and cure of liver disease, and provides support services to those affected.
Tom Nealon, President & CEO
Lynn Gardiner Seim, Executive Vice President & COO

959 **American Porphyria Foundation**
4900 Woodway 713-266-9617
Houston, TX 77056 866-APF-3635
www.porphyriafoundation.com
The APF is dedicated to improving the health and well-being of individuals and families affected by porphyria. Our mission is to enhance public awareness about porphyria, develop educational programs and distributing educational material for patients and physicians and support research to improve treatment and ultimately lead to a cure.
Desiree H Lyon, Executive Director
James Young, Chairman

960 **Clinical Research Center: Pediatrics Children's Hospital Research Foundation**
Children's Hospital Research Foundation
Elland & Bethesda Avenues 513-559-4412
Cincinnati, OH 45229
Studies of pediatric acquired diseases including liver disease and Reye's Syndrome.
Dr James G Redeker, Co-director

961 **Columbus Children's Research Institute**
700 Children's Drive 614-722-2000
Columbus, OH 43205 John.Barnard@NationwideChildrens.org
www.nationwidechildrens.org
Research institute dedicated to enhancing the health of children by engaging in the high quality cutting-edge research according to the highest scientific and ethical standards.
John A Barnard, Research Institute President
Steve Allen MD, CEO

962 **Division of Digestive & Liver Diseases of Cloumbia University**
630 W 168th Street 212-305-5960
New York, NY 10032-3784 hjw14@columbia.edu
www.cumc.columbia.edu
The Division's faculty members are devoted to research and the clinical care of patients with gastrointestinal, liver and nutritional disorders. The Division is also responsible for the Gastroenterology Training Program at the medical center and for teaching medical students, interns, residents, fellows and attending physicians aspects of gastrointestinal and liver diseases.
Howard J Worman MD, Division Director
Karen Wisdom, Director

963 **Georgetown University Center for Hypertension and Renal Disease Research**
3800 Reservoir Road NW 202-687-9183
Washington, DC 20007 www.georgetown.edu/research/hrdrc
International institute for basic and clinical investigation education and clinical practice in hypertension and renal disease.
Christopher Englert, Jr. CAE, President/CEO

964 **Kidney & Urology Foundation of America**
2 West 47th Street 212-629-9770
New York, NY 10036 800-633-6628
info@kidneyurology.org
www.kidneyurology.org
Sam Giarrusso, President
Kerri Shapiro, Director of Operations/Administration

965 **Kidney Disease Institute**
Wadsworth Center for Laboratories and Research
Empire State Plaza 518-474-7354
Albany, NY 12237 dohweb@health.state.ny.us
www.nyhealth.gov
An information and referral organization for polycystic kidney disease autoimmune kidney disease and transplantation.
Andrew M Cuomo, Governor
Nirav R Shah, Commissioner

966 **Lovelace Medical Foundation**
2425 Ridgecrest Drive SE 505-348-9400
Albuquerque, NM 87108-5127 info@lrri.org
www.lrri.org
Jackie Lovelace Johnson, Director
Frank Bond, Director

967 **Lovelace Respiratory Research Institute**
615 S Preston Street 502-852-7350
Louisville, KY 40202-0001 kdpnet.kdp.louisville.edu
Educates residents and patients regarding kidney diseases and offers a dialysis clinic for people afflicted with kidney disease.
George R Ottensmeyer, President

968 **Michigan Kidney Foundation**
1169 Oak Valley Drive 734-222-9800
Ann Arbor, MI 48108 800-482-1455
info@nkfm.org
www.nkfm.org
Andrew Boschma, Chairman
Daniel M Carney, President/CEO

969 **National Gaucher Foundation**
5410 Edson Lane
Rockville, MD 20852
800-504-3189
ngf@gaucherdisease.org
www.gaucherdisease.org
National foundation providing information and assistance for those affected by Gaucher disease, as well as education and outreach to increase public awareness.
Brian Berman, President & CEO
Amy Blum, Chief Operating Officer

970 **National Kidney Foundation**
30 E 33rd Street
New York, NY 10016
800-622-9010
855-653-2273
info@kidney.org
www.kidney.org
A health organization dedicated to preventing kidney and urinary tract diseases, improving the health and well-being of individuals and families affected and increasing the availability of all organs for transplantation.
Michael J. Choi, MD, President
Kevin Longino, CEO

971 **National Reye's Syndrome Foundation**
426 N Lewis Street
Bryan, OH 43506
419-636-2679
800-233-7393
www.reyessyndrome.org
Devoted to conquering Reye's syndrome, primarily a children's disease affecting the liver and brain, but can affect all ages. Provides support, information and referrals. Encourages research.
John Symonds, Executive Director

972 **Nevada Kidney Disease & Hypertension Centers**
210 S Desplaines Street
Chicago, IL 60661
312-654-2720
charlotte.chapple@ainmd.com
www.ainmd.com/
A medical group practicing nephrology in the Chicago metropolitan area and it suburbs. Includes 21 nephrologists with expertise in many areas in the field of nephrology including hypertension chronic and acute renal failure hemodialysis and peritoneal dialysis glomerulonephritis acid base disturbances fluid and electrolytes management. Provides personal high quality care to patients with kidney diseases.
Eduardo Kantor MD, Founder

973 **PKD Foundation Polycystic Kidney Disease Foundation**
Polycystic Kidney Disease Foundation
9221 Ward Parkway
Kansas City, MO 64114-3367
816-931-2600
800-PKD-CURE
pkdcure@pkdcure.org
www.pkdcure.org
The foundation exists to win the war with PKD. Their mission is to promote research into the treatment and cure of polycystic kidney disease by raising financial support for peer approved biomedical research projects and fostering public awareness among medical professionals patients and the general public.
Frank Condella, Jr, Chair
Michelle Davis, Interim CEO/Chief Development Officer

974 **Tennessee Kidney Foundation**
95 White Bridge Road
Nashville, TN 37205-2613
615-383-3887
800-380-3887
www.tennesseekidneyfoundation.org
Ron Carter, President
Bob Horton, First Vice President

975 **The C.H.I.L.D. Foundation**
2150 Western Parkway
Vancouver, BC, V6T-1V6
604-736-0645
Fax: 604-228-0066
www.child.ca
The C.H.I.L.D. Foundation supports research to help children with intestinal and liver disorders, including Crohn's disease and ulcerative colitis.
Mary Parsons, President & CEO

976 **University of California Liver Research Unit**
7601 E Imperial Highway
Downey, CA 90242
562-940-8961
Dr Allan Lee MD Facp, Professor InteRNal Medicine / Director

977 **University of Cincinnati Department of Pathology & Laboratory Medicine**
234 Goodman Street
Cincinnati, OH 45219-0533
513-584-7284
Fax: 513-584-3892
pathology@uc.edu
pathology.uc.edu
Research to understand the causes of disease and develop treatments for infectious diseases, diabete, obesity and lipid disorders, cancer and cardiovascular diseases.
Dani Zander, MD, Chair of Pathology
Michelle Cooper, Executive Director, Business & Admin

978 **University of Kansas Kidney and Urology Research Center**
3901 Rainbow Boulevard
Kansas City, KS 66160
913-588-5000
www.kumc.edu
Jared J Brosius, Chief
Joseph Messana, Professor/ Service Chief

979 **University of Michigan Nephrology Division**
University of Michigan Health System
1500 E Medical Center Drive
Ann Arbor, MI 48109
734-936-5645
www.med.umich.edu/intmed/nephrology
Focuses on kidney research.
Eric Mullen, Division Administrator
Susan Geisser, Financial Consultant

980 **University of Pittsburgh Medical Center**
200 Lothrop Street
Pittsburgh, PA 15213
412-647-8762
800-533-8762
upmc.com
The University of Pittsburgh Medical Center is a health care provider and insurer focused on developing new models of patient-centered care. Its mission is to engage in clinical research, education and innovation to ensure excellence in patient care.
G Nicholas Beckwith III, Chairperson
Jeffrey A Romoff, President and CEO

981 **University of Rochester: Nephrology Research Program**
601 Elmwood Avenue
Rochester, NY 14642-0001
585-275-3660
www.urmc.rochester.edu
Focuses on kidney disorders.
David A Bushinsky, MD, Division Chief

982 **University of Texas Southwestern Medical Center**
5323 Harry Hines Boulevard
Dallas, TX 75390-9151
214-645-8300
www.utsouthwestern.edu
Daniel K Podolsky, MD, President
J. Gregory Fitz, Executive Vice President

983 **Warren Grant Magnuson Clinical Center**
National Institute of Health
10 Center Drive MSC 1078
Bethesda, MD 20892
301-496-3311
800-411-1222
TTY: 866-411-1010
mmichael@cc.nih.gov
www.dnrc.nih.gov/reports/programs/ncc.as
Established in 1953 as the research hospital of the National Institutes of Health. Designed so that patient care facilities are close to research laboratories so new findings of basic and clinical scientists can be quickly applied to the treatment of patients. Upon referral by physicians, patients are admitted to NIH clinical studies.
John Slatopolsky, Director

984 **Washington University Chromalloy American Kidney Center**
One Barnes-Jewish Hospital Plaza
Saint Louis, MO 63110-1036
314-362-7209
renal.wustl.edu
Offers a dialysis unit for people afflicted with kidney disease.
Dr Eduardo Lanning RN/JD, President Board of Directors
Sean Tully, Vice President Board of Directors

985 **Yeshiva University Marion Bessin Liver Research Center**
Albert Einstein College of Medicine
1300 Morris Park Avenue
Bronx, NY 10461-1975
718-430-2000
www.einstein.yu.edu/centers/liver-resear
Liver disease research and therapy.
Allan W Wolkoff, MD, Director
David A Shafritz, MD, Associate Director

Arizona

986 **American Liver Foundation Arizona Chapter**
4545 E Shea Boulevard 602-953-1800
Phoenix, AZ 85028 866-953-1800
www.liverfoundation.org
Melissa McCracken, Executive Director
Ashley Drew, Events Manager

987 **National Kidney Foundation of Arizona**
4203 E Indian School Road 602-840-1644
Phoenix, AZ 85018 www.azkidney.org
Leonard J McDonald, Chair
Jeffrey D Neff, Chief Executive Officer

Arkansas

988 **National Kidney Foundation of Arkansas**
1818 N Taylor Street 501-664-4343
Little Rock, AR 72207 800-622-9010
nkfar@kidney.org
www.kidney.org
Nonprofit health organization. Our mission is to prevent kidney and urinary tract disease improve the health and well being of individuals and families affected by these diseases and increase the availability of all organs for transplantation.
R D Todd Baur, Member of the Board of Directors
Derek E Bruce, Member of the Board of Directors

California

989 **American Liver Foundation Greater Los Angeles Chapter**
5777 Century Boulevard 310-670-4624
Los Angeles, CA 90045 www.liverfoundation.org
Taly Fantini, Executive Director

990 **American Liver Foundation Northern CA Chapter**
870 Market Street 415-248-1060
San Francisco, CA 94102 800-292-9099
www.liverfoundation.org
Greg Martin, Executive Director

991 **American Liver Foundation San Diego Chapter**
2515 Camino del Rio S 619-291-5483
San Diego, CA 92108 800-749-2630
www.liverfoundation.org
Michele De Motto, Executive Director

992 **National Kidney Foundation of Northern California**
131 Steuart Street 415-543-3303
San Francisco, CA 94105 888-427-5653
infopacific@kidney.org
www.kidney.org/site/503/index.cfm
Work with kidney patients both pre ESRD dialysis and transplant. Financial assistance educational workshops scholarships children's and family camps transplant games information and referral.
Brad J Small, Division President
Connie M Nieri, Division Director of Finance/Operations

993 **National Kidney Foundation of Southern California**
15490 Ventura Boulevard 818-783-8153
Sherman Oaks, CA 91403 800-747-5527
nkfsca@kidney.org
www.kidney.org
Pier Merone, Division President
Natalie Kanooni, Division Program Manager

Colorado

994 **American Liver Foundation Rocky Mountain Division**
1660 S Albion Street 303-988-4388
Denver, CO 80222 www.liverfoundation.org
Joe McCormack, Executive Director

995 **National Kidney Foundation of Colorado/Idaho/Montana/Wyoming**
650 South Cherry Street 720-748-9991
Denver, CO 80246 800-596-7943
nkfcmw@kidney.org
www.kidney.org/site/505/
Brandi Krause, State Director
Stacey Lux, Development Director

996 **National Kidney Foundation of Colorado, Idaho, Montana, and Wyoming**
650 South Cherry Street 720-748-9991
Denver, CO 80246 800-596-7943
nkfcmw@kidney.org
www.kidney.org/site/505/
Brandi Krause, State Director
Stacey Lux, Development Director

Connecticut

997 **American Liver Foundation Connecticut Chapter**
127 Washington Avenue 203-234-2022
N Haven, CT 06473 www.liverfoundation.org
Offers support for patients and families provides educational meetings and conferences raising vital liver research dollars; encouraging the beautifully unselfish gift of organ donation and the medical miracle of organ transplantation.
12 pages
JoAnn Thompson, Executive Director

998 **National Kidney Foundation of Connecticut**
1463 Highland Avenue 203-439-7912
Cheshire, CT 06410 800-441-1280
nkfct@kidney.org
www.kidney.org/site/102/index.cfm
Marcia Hilditch, Program Manager
Deb Ramada, Development Coordinator

District of Columbia

999 **National Kidney Foundation of the National Capital Area**
5335 Wisconsin Avenue NW 202-244-7900
Washington, DC 20015-2030 infowdc@kidney.org
www.kidney.org/site/203/index.cfm
Pamela D Gatz, Division President
Sherrita Lancaster, Division Office Manager

Florida

1000 **American Liver Foundation Gulf Coast Chapter**
202 S 22nd Street 813-248-3337
Ybor City, FL 33605 www.liverfoundation.org
Jennifer Nillias, Executive Director

1001 **National Kidney Foundation of Florida**
1040 Woodcock Road 407-894-7325
Orlando, FL 32803 800-927-9659
nkf@kidneyfla.org
www.kidney.org/site/204/index.cfm
Andrew Helfan, President
Stephanie Hutchinson, CEO

Georgia

1002 **National Kidney Foundation of Georgia**
2951 Flowers Road S 770-452-1539
Atlanta, GA 30341 800-633-2339
nkfga@kidney.org
www.kidney.org
Barbara McDowell, President

Hawaii

1003 **National Kidney Foundation of Hawaii**
1314 S King Street 808-593-1515
Honolulu, HI 96814 800-488-2277
Glen@kidneyhi.org
www.kidneyhi.org

Hawaii's leading voluntary health agency to the education prevention and treatment of kidney and urinary tract diseases and increase the availability of all organs for transplantation in Hawaii.
Aileen Utterdyke, President
Glen Hayashida, CEO

Illinois

1004 **American Liver Foundation Illinois Chapter**
67 East Madison Street 312-377-9030
Chicago, IL 60603 www.illinois-liver.org
Kevin Sutton, Executive Director
Kristin Gray, Development Coordinator

1005 **National Kidney Foundation of Illinois**
215 W Illinois 312-321-1500
Chicago, IL 60654 kidney@nkfi.org
www.nkfi.org
Mark L Schwartz, President
Kate Grubbs O'Connor, Chief Executive Officer

Indiana

1006 **American Liver Foundation Indiana Chapter**
PO BOX 36085 317-635-5074
Indianapolis, IN 46236 877-548-3730
www.liverfoundation.org
Katrina Marshall, Executive Director

1007 **National Kidney Foundation of Indiana**
911 E 86th Street 317-722-5640
Indianapolis, IN 46240-1840 800-382-9971
nkfi@kidneyindiana.org
www.kidney.org/site/303/index.cfm
The mission of the NKFI is to prevent kidney and urinary tract disease improve the health and well-being of individuals and family affected by these disease and increase the availability of all organs for transplantation.
Margie Evans Fort, Chief Executive Officer
Heather Gallagher, Communications Director

Kansas

1008 **National Kidney Foundation of Kansas and Western Missouri**
6405 Metcalf Avenue 913-262-1551
Overland Park, KS 66202 800-596-7943
nkfkswmo@kidney.org
www.kidney.org/site/305/index.cfm
Sherri Denny, Regional Administrative Assistant
Alexandra Wilson, Special Events Manager

Kentucky

1009 **National Kidney Foundation of Kentucky**
250 E Liberty Street 502-585-5433
Louisville, KY 40202 800-737-5433
infonkfk@kidney.org
www.nkfk.org
April Enix, Director of Development
Nital Desai, Community Outreach Manager

Louisiana

1010 **National Kidney Foundation of Louisiana**
8200 Hampson Street 504-861-4500
New Orleans, LA 70118 800-462-3694
info@kidneyla.org
www.kidneyla.org
Shawn Donelon, Chairman
Torie Kranze, Chief Executive Officer

Maine

1011 **National Kidney Foundation of Maine**
85 Astor Avenue 781-278-0222
Norwood, ME 02062 800-542-4001
nkfofmrnv@kidneyhealth.org
www.kidney.org/site/105/index.cfm
Andrea Savisky RN CNN, Division Program Director
Mark Daley, Division Donor Records Director/User Ser

Maryland

1012 **National Kidney Foundation of Maryland**
Heaver Plaza, 1301 York Road 410-494-8545
Lutherville, MD 21093-2136 800-671-5369
www.kidneymd.org
Also covers the Harrisburg area of Pennsylvania and portions of Virginia and West Virginia.
Cassie Shafer, President/CEO
Christie Vera, Vice President of Development and Market

Massachusetts

1013 **National Kidney Foundation of MA/RI/NH/VT**
85 Astor Avenue 781-278-0222
Norwood, MA 02062 800-542-4001
www.kidney.org/site/105/index.cfm
Andrea Savisky RN CNN, Division Program Director
Mark Daley, Division Donor Records Director/User Ser

Michigan

1014 **American Liver Foundation Michigan Chapter**
21886 Farmington Road 248-615-5768
Farmington, MI 48336 888-MYL-IVER
www.liverfoundation.org
Jennifer L Stibbe, Executive Director
Meghan Likes, Community Events Coordinator

Minnesota

1015 **American Liver Foundation Minnesota Chapter**
2626 E 82nd Street 952-854-6181
Bloomington, MN 55425 dgirard@liverfoundation.org
www.liverfoundation.org
Dee Girard, Executive Director

1016 **National Kidney Foundation Serving MN, Dakotas & IA Division Office**
1970 Oakcrest Avenue 651-636-7300
Saint Paul, MN 55113 800-596-7943
jille@kidney.org
www.kidney.org/site/313/index.cfm
Jill Evenocheck, Division President
Amy Busack, Regional Vice President

1017 **National Kidney Foundation of Minnesota**
1970 Oakcrest Avenue 651-636-7300
Saint Paul, MN 55113 800-596-7943
jille@kidney.org
www.kidney.org/site/313/index.cfm
Also covers North Dakota and South Dakota.
Jill Evenocheck, Division President
Amy Busack, Regional Vice-President

Mississippi

1018 **National Kidney Foundation of Mississippi**
3000 Old Canton Road 601-981-3611
Jackson, MS 39216 800-232-1592
gail@kidneyms.org
www.kidneyms.org
Paul Howell, President
Lee Parrott, Vice President

Missouri

1019 **American Liver Foundation Greater Kansas City Chapter**
16 Hampton Village Plaza 314-352-7377
St. Louis, MO 63109 866-455-4837
www.liverfoundation.org
Richard Mattler, Executive Director

1020 **National Kidney Foundation of Eastern Missouri and Metro East**
1001 Craig Road 314-961-2828
Creve Coeur, MO 63146 800-489-9585
nkfemo@kidney.org
www.kidney.org/site/308/index.cfm
Chad Iseman, State Director
Alayna Tatum, Special Events Manager

New Mexico

1021 **National Kidney Foundation of New Mexico**
3167 San Mateo Boulevard NE 505-830-3542
Albuquerque, NM 87110 800-282-0190
nkfnm@kidney.org
www.kidney.org
Connie Giarrusso, President
Shirley Baer, Executive Director

New York

1022 **American Liver Foundation Greater New York Chapter**
39 Broadway 212-943-1059
New York, NY 10006 877-307-7507
www.liverfoundation.org
Randa Adib, Director, Development
Stephanie Paul, Gala Director

1023 **American Liver Foundation Western New York Chapter**
25 Canterbury Road 585-271-2859
Rochester, NY 14607 www.liverfoundation.org
Nancy Rodwa MNO, Executive Director

1024 **National Kidney Foundation of Central New York**
731 James Street 315-476-0311
Syracuse, NY 13203 877-8KI-DNEY
www.kidney.org/site/110/index.cfm
Nannette Carbone, Chief Executive Officer
Susan Burns, Director of Administration

1025 **National Kidney Foundation of Northeast New York**
1971 Western Avenue 518-458-9697
Albany, NY 12203 800-622-9010
www.kidney.org/about/local_info.cfm?sear
Carol MS Ed CFRE, Executive Director
Mary Jones, Division Development Director

1026 **National Kidney Foundation of Western New York**
310 Packetts Landing 585-598-3963
Fairport, NY 14450 800-724-9421
infoupny@kidney.org
www.kidney.org/site/109/index.cfm
Nonprofit health organization.
Joanne Spink, Division President
Megan Alchowiak, Community Outreach Manager

North Carolina

1027 **National Kidney Foundation of North Carolina**
5950 Fairview Road 704-552-1351
Charlotte, NC 28210 800-356-5362
www.nkfnc.org
Kenya Welch, Kidney Early Evaluation Program Contact

Ohio

1028 **National Kidney Foundation of Ohio**
2800 Corporate Exchange Drive 614-882-6184
Columbus, OH 43231-2804 800-242-2133
nkfoh@kidney.org
www.nkfofohio.org
Patti V.B. Gold, Division President
Danielle Estep, Division Program Director

Oklahoma

1029 **National Kidney Foundation of Oklahoma**
10600 S Pennsylvania Avenue 816-221-9559
Oklahoma City, OK 73170 800-622-9010
nkfok@kidney.org
www.kidney.org/about/local_info.cfm?sear
Jeff Baumgardner, CEO
Glenda McClure, Operations Manager

Pennsylvania

1030 **American Liver Foundation Delaware Valley Chapter**
1341 North Delaware Avenue 215-425-8080
Philadelphia, PA 19125 www.liverfoundation.org
Ivory Allison, Executive Director

1031 **American Liver Foundation Western Pennsylvania**
100 W Station Square Drive 412-434-7044
Pittsburgh, PA 15219 www.liverfoundation.org
Suzanna Masartis, Executive Director

1032 **National Kidney Foundation of Delaware Valley**
111 S Independence Mall E 215-923-8611
Philadelphia, PA 19106 800-697-7007
nkfdv@kidney.org
www.kidney.org/site/112/index.cfm
Also covers Delaware and Southern New Jersey.
Joseph Mullen, Chairman
Joanne Spink, Division President

1033 **National Kidney Foundation of Western Pennsylvania**
3109 Forbes Avenue 412-261-4115
Pittsburgh, PA 15213 800-261-4115
info@kidneyall.org
www.kidney.org/site/113/index.cfm
Also covers Northern West Virginia.
James Sullivan, Chairman
David Vanella, Vice Chairman

South Carolina

1034 **National Kidney Foundation of South Carolina**
508 Hampton Street 803-798-3870
Columbia, SC 29201 800-488-2277
karen.bailey@kidney.org
www.kidney.org/site/209/index.cfm
Beth Irick, Division President
Karen Bailey, Division Senior Administrative Assistant

Tennessee

1035 **American Liver Foundation Midsouth Chapter**
PO BOX 486 901-766-7668
Ellendale, TN 38029 866-756-7668
www.liverfoundation.org
Winn Stephenson, Division Founder
Tina Sandoval, Board Chair

1036 **National Kidney Foundation of East Tennessee**
5201 Kingston Pike 865-688-5481
Knoxville, TN 37919-1523 800-242-2133
nkfetn@kidney.org
www.kidney.org/about/local_info.cfm?sear
The National Kidney Foundation of East Tennessee works to prevent kidney and urinary tract diseases improve the health and well-being of individuals and family members affected by these diseases and increase the availability of all organs for transplantation.
Helen

1037 **National Kidney Foundation of West Tennessee**
857 Mount Moriah Road 901-683-6185
Memphis, TN 38117 800-273-3869
info@nkfwtn.org
www.kidney.org/about/local_info.cfm?sear
Bruce Skyer, Chief Executive Officer
Joseph Vassalotti, MD, Chief Medical Officer

Texas

1038 **National Kidney Foundation of North Texas**
5429 Lyndon B Johnson Freeway 214-351-2393
Dallas, TX 75240 877-543-6397
texasinfo@kidney.org
www.kidney.org/site/406/index.cfm
Public and professional education about kidney and urinary tract diseases. Peer mentoring medical emergency identification jewelry kidney early evaluation program Camp Reynal transplant games.
Marrie Collins, President
Mark Edwards, Division Program Director

1039 **National Kidney Foundation of Southeast Texas**
5429 Lyndon B Johnson Freeway 214-351-2393
Dallas, TX 75240 877-543-6397
texasinfo@kidney.org
www.kidney.org/site/406/index.cfm
Provides services for people who suffer with kidney and urinary tract diseases.
Marrie Collins, President
Mark Edwards, Division Program Director

1040 **National Kidney Foundation of Texas**
5429 Lyndon B Johnson Fwy 214-351-2393
Dallas, TX 75240 877-543-6397
texasinfo@kidney.org
www.kidney.org/site/406/index.cfm
Marie Collins, Division President
Mark Edwards, Divisional Program Director

1041 **National Kidney Foundation of West Texas**
5429 Lyndon B Johnson Fwy 214-351-2393
Dallas, TX 75240 877-543-6397
texasinfo@kidney.org
www.kidney.org/site/406/index.cfm
Marrie Collins, President
Mark Edwards, Division Program Director

1042 **National Kidney Foundation of the Texas Coastal Bend**
PO Box 9172 361-884-5892
Corpus Christi, TX 78469 info@coastalbendkidneyfoundation.org
www.coastalbendkidneyfoundation.org
Bess Stone, President
Becky Gardner, Executive Director

Utah

1043 **National Kidney Foundation of Utah**
3707 N Canyon Road 801-226-5111
Provo, UT 84604-4585 800-869-5277
NKFU@KidneyUT.org
www.kidneyut.org
Serving kidney dialysis and transplant patients through out Utah providing patient service and support programs medical research and public and patient education regarding kidney disease and its treatment and prevention and the promotion of organ donations.
E.J. Garn, Chairman
Deen Vetterli, Chief Executive Officer

Virginia

1044 **National Kidney Foundation of Virginia**
1622 East Parham Road 804-288-8342
Richmond, VA 23228 800-543-6398
www.kidney.org/site/203/index.cfm
An affiliate of the National Kidney Foundation it serves kidney patients and their families in Virginia and portions of West Virginia. Mission includes professional and public education prevention and working to increase the availability of all organs for donation.
Eleanor Myers, Regional Program Director
Liz King, Community Outreach Manager

Washington

1045 **American Liver Foundation Pacific Northwest Chapter**
PO BOX 22108 212-668-1000
Seattle, WA 98122 800-465-4837
www.liverfoundation.org
Dr. Stephen Corrigan Rayhill, MD, Director
Dr. Andrew Precht, MD, Director

Wisconsin

1046 **American Liver Foundation Wisconsin Chapter**
1845 N Farwell Avenue 414-763-3435
Milwaukee, WI 53202 dgirard@liverfoundation.org
www.liverfoundation.org
Dee Girard, Executive Director

1047 **National Kidney Foundation of Wisconsin**
16655 W Bluemound Road 262-821-0705
Brookfield, WI 53005-5935 800-543-6393
nkfw@kidneywi.org
www.kidneywi.org
Offers prevention detection and education programs for those at risk for kidney disease. The National Kidney Foundation of Wisconsin is making life's better through its programs and services. Brochures are offered at no charge.
Mary Braband, Chair
Cindy Huber, Chief Executive Officer

Support Groups & Hotlines

1048 **Children's Liver Association for Support Services**
25379 Wayne Mills Place 661-263-9099
Valencia, CA 91355 877-679-8256
www.classkids.org
Dedicated to addressing the emotional, educational, and financial needs of families with children with liver disease or liver transplantation. Telephone hotline, newsletter, parent matching, literature and financial assistance. supports research and educates public about organ donations.
Mark Sumner, Co-Founder
Diane Sumner, Co-Founder

1049 **Kidneeds**
Greater Cedar Rapids Community Foundation
200 First Street Southwest 319-366-2862
Cedar Rapids, IA 52404 kidneedsmpgn@yahoo.com
www.medicine.uiowa.edu/kidneeds/
Primary mission of kidneeds is to fund research on membranoproliferative giomerulonephritis type 2 (MPON type 2, aka, dense deposit disease). Phone support and annual newsletter availiable. No computerized version availiable. No mailing list availble.
Lynne

1050 **National Health Information Center**
Office of Disease Prevention & Health Promotion
1101 Wootton Pkwy odphpinfo@hhs.gov
Rockville, MD 20852 www.health.gov/nhic
Supports public health education by maintaining a calendar of National Health Observances; helps connect consumers and health professionals to organizations that can best answer questions and provide up-to-date contact information from reliable sources; updates on a yearly basis toll-free numbers for health information, Federal health clearinghouses and info centers.
Don Wright, MD, MPH, Director

1051 **National Reye's Syndrome Foundation**
426 N Lewis Street 419-636-2679
Bryan, OH 43506 800-233-7393
www.reyessyndrome.org
Devoted to conquering Reye's syndrome, primarily a children's disease affecting the liver and brain, but can affect all ages. Provides support, information and referrals. Encourages research.
John Symonds, Executive Director

1052 **Wilson Disease Association**
5572 North Diversey Boulevard 414-961-0533
Milwaukee, WI 53217 866-961-0533
info@wilsonsdisease.org
www.wilsonsdisease.org
Serves as a communications support network for individuals affected by Wilson's disease; distributes information to professionals and the public; makes referrals; and holds meetings.
8 pages
Mary L Graper, President
Stefanie F Kaplan, Vice-President

Journals

1053 **American Association for the Study of Liver Diseases**
1729 King Street 703-299-9766
Alexandria, VA 22314 aasld@aasld.org
www.aasld.org
Information for professionals interested in disease of the liver and biliary tract.
Sherrie H Cathcart, Executive Director

1054 **Hepatology**
American Assoc. for the Study of Liver Disease
1729 King Street 703-299-9766
Alexandria, VA 22314 aasld@aasld.org
www.aasld.org
Information for professionals interested in disease of the liver and biliary tract.
Sherrie H Cathcart, Executive Director

1055 **Kidney Beginnings: The Magazine**
American Association of Kidney Patients
3505 E Frantage Road 813-636-8100
Tampa, FL 33607 800-749-2257
info@aakp.org
www.aakp.org
This quarterly member magazine provides articles, news items and information of interest to those at risk or recently diagnosed with kidney disease, their famliy, and healthcare professionals.
Kmi Buettner, Executive Director

1056 **PKD Progress**
PKD Foundation
4901 Main Street 816-931-2600
Kansas City, MO 64112-2634 800-753-2873
pkdcure@pkdcure.org
www.pkdcure.org
Offers information and updated medical news for persons and professionals with an interest in kidney disorders.
Dave Switzer, Marketing/Public Relations Director

1057 **Renal Recipes Quarterly**
R&D Laboratories
4204 Glencoe Avenue 800-338-9066
Marina Del Rey, CA 90292-5612
Features timely holiday and ethnic food menus and recipes, shopping and food tips, analysis of nutrients and calculation of food exchanges.

1058 **aakpRENALIFE**
American Association of Kidney Patients
35052 E Frantage Road 813-636-8100
Tampa, FL 33607 800-749-2257
info@aakp.org
www.aakp.org
The official publication for AAKP members, offering articles, news and health care information for kidney patients,and health care professionals.
Kim Buettner, Executive Director

Digital Resources

1059 **It's Just Part of My Life**
National Kidney Foundation
30 E 33rd Street 212-889-2210
New York, NY 10016-5337 800-622-9010
www.kidney.org
A 15-minute program for adolescent dialysis patients and their families.

1060 **People Like Us**
National Kidney Foundation
30 E 33rd Street 212-889-2210
New York, NY 10016-5337 800-622-9010
www.kidney.org
A seven-part video series targeted toward the newly-diagnosed chronic kidney disease patient.
Simon Greenall, Author

Web Sites

1061 **American Association for the Study of Liver Diseases**
www.aasld.org/
Conducts symposia and educational courses for professionals interested in disease of the liver and biliary tract. The leading organization for advancing the science and practice of hepatology.

1062 **American Association of Kidney Patients**
www.aakp.org
Serves the needs and interests of kidney patients, for kidney patients, the purpose of this Association is to help patients and their families cope with the emotional, physical and social impact of kidney disease.

1063 **American Kidney Fund**
www.akfinc.org/
A nonprofit, national health organization providing direct financial assistance to thousands of Americans who suffer from kidney disease.

1064 **American Porphyria Foundation**
www.porphyriafoundation.com
Advances awareness, research, and treatment of the porphyrias; provides self-help services for members; and provides referrals to porphyria treatment specialists.

1065 **Children's Liver Alliance**
www.liverkids.org.au/
Empowering the hearts and minds of children with liver disease, their families and the medical professionals who care for them.

1066 **Dietary Guidelines for Americans**
www.dietaryguidelines.gov
Publishes the Dietary Guidelines for Americans, a guide providing nutritional advice to promote health and prevent disease. Updated versions of the Dietary Guidelines are released by the US Departments of Agriculture (USDA) and Health & Human Services (HHS) every five years.

1067 **Everyday Health**
www.everydayhealth.com
Aims to provide evidence-based health information from physicians and healthcare providers.

1068 **FamilyDoctor.org**
www.familydoctor.org
Medical advice and information provided by the American Academy of Family Physicians. Resources include a medical dictionary, a symptom checker tool, a BMI calculator, and medication information.

1069 **Gastrointestinal Society - Canadian Society of Intestinal Research**
www.badgut.org
Aims to improve the lives of people with gastrointestinal and liver diseases and disorders by funding research, advocating for patient access to healthcare, and providing evidence-based information for patients.

1070 **Healing Well**
www.healingwell.com
An online health resource guide to medical news, chat, information and articles, newsgroups and message boards, books, disease-related web sites, medical directories, and more for patients, friends, and family coping with disabling diseases, disorders, or chronic illnesses.

1071 **Health Finder**
www.healthfinder.gov
Searchable, carefully developed web site offering information on over 1000 topics. Developed by the US Department of Health and Human Services, the site can be used in both English and Spanish.

1072 **Healthline**
www.healthline.com
Provides medical and health articles and information.

1073 **Healthlink USA**
www.healthlinkusa.com
Health information concerning treatment, cures, prevention, diagnosis, risk factors, research, support groups, email lists, personal stories and much more. Updated regularly.

1074 **Liver Support**
www.liversupport.com
Information about the world's safest, most powerful liver-protecting supplement, milk thistle. Specifically facts about the safe, yet highly potent, Phytosome form.

1075 **MedicineNet**
www.medicinenet.com
An online resource for consumers providing easy-to-read, authoritative medical and health information.

1076 **MedlinePlus**
www.medlineplus.gov
A service of the National Library of Medicine, MedlinePlus is an online resource providing health and wellness information in both English and Spanish.

1077 **Medscape**
www.medscape.com
Medscape offers specialists, primary care physicians, and other health professionals the Web's most robust and integrated medical information and educational tools.

1078 **MyPlate**
www.myplate.gov
Created and managed by the US Department of Agriculture's Center for Nutrition Policy & Promotion, MyPlate is a dietary guide providing resources and recipes to promote healthy eating for all Americans.

1079 **National Kidney and Urologic Diseases Information Clearinghouse**
www.niddk.nih.gov
A service of the Federal Government's National Institute for Diabetes and Digestive and Kidney Diseases. Offers free information about benign prostate enlargement and other non-cancerous urinary tract problems.

1080 **Nutrition.gov**
www.nutrition.gov
Sponsored by the United States Department of Agriculture (USDA), Nutrition.gov offers information on topics in food and nutrition, including healthy eating, physical activity, and food safety.

1081 **Polycystic Kidney Research Foundation**
www.pkdcure.org
Provide information on research into the cause, treatment, and cure of polycystic kidney disease by raising financial support for peer approved biomedical research projects and fostering public awareness among medical professionals, patients and the general public.

1082 **Science Daily**
www.sciencedaily.com
Provides information on the latest news and research in science, health, the environment, and technology.

1083 **The Nutrition Source**
hsph.harvard.edu/nutritionsource
From the Harvard T.H. Chan School of Public Health, The Nutrition Source provides news, information, and guidance for nutrition and healthy eating.

1084 **UnlockFood**
www.unlockfood.ca
A website from Dietitians of Canada. Provides videos, recipes, and information on food and nutrition, as well as helps Canadians connect with a dietitian.

1085 **Verywell**
www.verywellhealth.com
Offers health, medicine, and wellness information from health professionals.

1086 **WebMD**
www.webmd.com
Provides credible information, supportive communities, and in-depth reference material about health subjects. A source for original and timely health information as well as material from well known content providers.

1087 **World Health Organization**
www.who.int
An agency of the United Nations, World Health Organization (WHO) serves to promote global health. The WHO website provides fact sheets, publications, media, and other resources on various health topics.

OBESITY

If your weight is 20 percent higher than what is considered healthy by medical professionals — or you have a 30 or higher BMI (body mass index is determined by the National Institutes of Health and relates body weight to height), you may be defined as overweight or obese. Obesity is a chronic health problem in the United States at over 40 percent. Severe obesity affects nearly 10 percent of the US population. Obesity is related to heart disease, type 2 diabetes, stroke and some cancers. These obesity-related diseases are considered the leading causes of preventable deaths. Managing the epidemic of obesity is complex, but developing a healthy lifestyle, including healthy eating habits, is critical. A healthy eating plan and regular physical activity are both prevention and treatment strategies.

Over 40 percent of the U.S. population is considered overweight or obese. According to the Centers for Disease Control (CDC) some groups are more impacted than others. Non-Hispanic black adults with a prevalence of almost 50 percent have the highest age-adjusted number of obese individuals. Hispanic adults (44.8 percent), non-Hispanic white adults (42.2 percent) and non-Hispanic Asian adults (17.4 percent) follow. Men and women with college educations have a lower prevalence of obesity than those with less education. In men, groups with both lower and higher incomes have a lower prevalence of obesity than those in middle-income groups. Obesity in women is lower in the highest income group than in both middle- and lower-income groups.

The causes of adult obesity are varied. While genetics does play a role, behavior is a significant contributing factor. Genes may contribute to obesity by increasing hunger and therefore, food intake. However, lack of physical activity, poor food choices, medication use, education and skills, and susceptibility to marketing images of food all play a much more significant role. Family history may be influential in how an adult makes food choices. Some diseases such as Cushing's Disease and polycystic ovary syndrome may lead to weight gain and some drugs such as steroids and antidepressants may also influence weight gain. Obesity is a serious disease that is directly associated with heart disease, diabetes, stroke and some cancers — leading causes of death worldwide.

The solution to the obesity epidemic is complex, and varies by individual based on gender, age, ethnicity, socioeconomic status, heredity and complicating physical conditions. Desire to achieve a healthy weight is crucial. A variety of resources provide information about healthy nutrition options that can help manage weight. Talking with your doctor about a healthy goal weight is the first step of a plan to manage obesity. Knowing your body mass index (BMI), your caloric needs and the best way to get them, and how to maintain regular physical activity are all personal actions that will help. Changing personal behaviors is crucial to overcoming obesity.

Healthy behaviors include healthy eating and regular physical activity. Calories in must be less than calories burned in order to lose weight. Physical activity can make you feel better, sleep better, reduces the risk of many chronic disease, and supports weight loss. The Physical Activity Guidelines for Americans, published by the U.S. Office of Disease Prevention and Health Promotion, recommends that adults get at least 150 minutes a week of moderate activity (like walking) and at least 2 hours a week of muscle-strengthening activities.

The Dietary Guidelines for Americans 2020-2025 (U.S. Department of Agriculture and the U.S. Department of Health and Human Services) says that the core elements of a healthy diet pattern throughout your lifespan should include nutrient-dense food and beverages that reflect personal taste, culture and budget; nutrient-dense foods provide vitamins, minerals and other nutrients with little or no added sugars, saturated fats and sodium, and includes vegetables, fruits, grains, dairy, protein and healthy oils, seafood and nuts. If you feel you need to lose weight, consider working with a registered dietician to devise a plan that meets your preferences and needs. The daily number of calories needed for weight loss depends on gender, activity level and other factors, and will usually range from 1,200 to 2,000. Consulting with your physician before beginning any weight loss program is recommended.

The health consequences of obesity may be significant. People who are obese are at an increased risk of serious diseases and health conditions including high blood pressure, unhealthy cholesterol levels, type 2 diabetes, heart disease, osteoarthritis, stroke, gallbladder disease and some forms of cancer. Obesity may also lower your quality of life, influence mental health, and have a significant impact on direct medical costs and job productivity. Achieving a healthy weight though physical activity and proper nutrition is a worthy goal.

See page 3 for more information on U.S. dietary guidelines.

Agencies & Associations

1089 **Academy of Nutrition & Dietetics**
120 South Riverside Plaza 312-899-0040
Chicago, IL 60606-6995 800-877-1600
media@eatright.org
www.eatright.org
Serves the public through the promotion of optimal nutrition, health, and well-being. Formerly the American Dietetic Association.
Patricia M. Babjak, Chief Executive Officer

1090 **Active Healthy Kids Global Alliance**
401 Smyth Road info@activehealthykids.org
Ottawa, Ontario, K1H-8L1 www.activehealthykids.org
Advocates the importance of quality, accessible, and enjoyable physical activity participation exercises for children and youth.
Mark Tremblay, President
Peter Katzmarzyk, Vice President

1091 **American College of Cardiology**
2400 N Street NW 202-375-6000
Washington, DC 20037 800-253-4636
Fax: 202-375-6842
membercare@acc.org
www.acc.org
The mission of the American College of Cardiology is to advocate for quality cardiovascular care, through education, research promotion, development and application of standards and guidelines, and to influence health care policy.
Cathleen C. Gates, Chief Executive Officer
Brendan Mullen, Senior Executive Vice President

1092 **American Obesity Treatment Association**
117 Anderson Court 334-403-4057
Dothan, AL 36303 info@americanobesity.org
americanobesity.org
Provides obesity awareness and prevention information.
Cesar Cuneo, Founder & President

1093 **Healthy Weight Network**
402 S 14th Street 701-567-2646
Hettinger, ND 58639 www.healthyweight.net
Promotes information and resources pertaining to the Health at Any Size paradigm.
Frances M. Berg, MS, Founder/Editor

1094 **National Association to Advance Fat Acceptance (NAAFA)**
PO Box 61586 916-558-6880
Las Vegas, NV 89160-1586 admin@naafa.org
www.naafa.org
Non-profit organization committed to improving the lives of fat individuals and reducing discrimination.
Tigress Osborn, Chair
Darliene Howell, Administrative Director

1095 **Nurse Practitioners in Women's Health**
PO Box 15837 202-543-9693
Washington, DC 20003 info@npwh.org
www.npwh.org
Ensures the delivery and accessibility of primary and specialty healthcare to women of all ages by women's health and women's health focused nurse practitioners.
Heather L. Maurer, CEO
Donna Ruth, Director, Education

1096 **Nutrition Science Initiative**
6020 Cornerstone Court W 858-914-5400
San Diego, CA 92121 www.nusi.org
Nutrition Science Initiative (NuSI) works to combat obesity, diabetes, and related metabolic diseases by supporting and improving the quality of nutrition research.
Gary Taubes, Chair

1097 **Obesity Canada**
8602 - 112th Street 780-492-8361
Edmonton, Alberta, T6G-2E1 info@obesitynetwork.ca
www.obesitycanada.ca
An organization of researchers, clinicians and other health professionals dedicated to reducing the mental, physical and economic burden of obesity in Canadians.
Dawn Hatanaka, Executive Director

1098 **Office of Women's Health**
200 Independence Avenue SW 202-690-7650
Washington, DC 20201 800-994-9662
womenshealth@hhs.gov
www.womenshealth.gov
Government agency under the Department of Health & Human Services, with free health information for women.
Dorothy Fink, MD, Deputy Asst. Secretary, Women's Health
Richelle West Marshall, Deputy Director

1099 **Overeaters Anonymous**
6075 Zenith Court NE 505-891-2664
Rio Rancho, NM 87174-4727 www.oa.org
A fellowship of individuals who meet in order to help solve their eating behaviors.

1100 **The Obesity Society**
1110 Bonifant Street 301-563-6526
Silver Spring, MD 20910 contact@obesity.org
www.obesity.org
The leading scientific society dedicated to the study of obesity. Committed to encouraging research on the causes and treatment of obesity, and to keeping the medical community and public informed of new advances.
Anthony Comuzzie, Chief Executive Officer
Christe A. Turner, Director, Finance & Operations

Libraries & Resource Centers

1101 **Weight-Control Information Network**
National Institutes of Health
31 Center Drive 800-860-8747
Bethesda, MD 20892-2560 TTY: 866-569-1162
healthinfo@niddk.nih.gov
www.win.niddk.nih.gov
WIN provides the general public, health professionals, and the media with up-to-date, science-based information on obesity, weight control, physical activity, and related nutritional issues. WIN provides tip sheets, fact sheets, and brochures for a range of audiences. Some of WIN's content is available in Spanish.

Foundations & Research Centers

1102 **Boston Obesity Nutrition Research Center (BONRC)**
www.bmc.org
Provides resources and support for studies in the area of obesity and nutrition. Comprised of four research cores located within the Boston area. In the areas of adipocytes, epidemiology and statistics, body composition, energy expenditure and genetic analyses, and transgenic animal models.

1103 **Center for Human Nutrition**
www.uchsc.edu/nutrition
A interdisciplinary team encompassing basic and clinical research, post-graduate training and career development of nutrition professionals, and commuity outreach. The research conducted at the CHN focuses on obesity prevention and treatment, nutrient metabolism, and micronutrient status in children. Activities conducted aim to improve the quallity of life by promoting physical activity and nutritional awareness.

1104 **Clinical Nutrition Research Unit (CNRU)**
depts.washington.edu/uwnorc
Promotes and enhances the interdisciplinary nutrition research and education at the Univeristy of Washington. By providing a number of Core Facilities, the CNRU attempts to integrate and coordinate the abundant ongoing activities with the goals of fostering new interdiscilinary research collaborations, stimulating new research activities, improving nutrition education at multiple levels, and facilitating the nutritional management of patients.

1105 **Harvard Clinical Nutrition Research Center**
Harvard Medical School 617-998-8803
Boston, MA 02215 allan_walker@hms.harvard.edu
nutrition.med.harvard.edu
Mission is to derive the benefit of continuity in assessing the effectiveness of the Center from year to year while still allowing flexibility for new insights as the Center's activities evolve.
W Allan Walker, Director
George Blackburn, Associate Director

1106 **Minnesota Obesity Center**
1334 Eckles Avenue 763-807-0559
St Paul, MN 55108 mnoc@tc.umn.edu
www.mnoc.umn.edu
Mission is to find ways to prevent weight gain obesity and its complications. The Center incorporates 46 Participating Investigators who are studying the causes and treatments of obesity. Provides the general public with a source of information on the happenings of the Center and on the current developments in the field of obesity.
Catherine C Welch, Program Coordinator

1107 **New York Obesity/Nutrition Research Center**
31 Center Drive MSC 2560 301-496-3583
Bethesda, MD 20892-2560 www2.niddk.nih.gov
Griffin P Rodgers, Director

1108 **Obesity Research Center St. Luke's-Roosevelt Hospital**
St. Luke's-Roosevelt Hospital
1090 Amsterdam Avenue 212-523-4196
New York, NY 10025 dg108@columbia.edu
www.nyorc.org
The mission of the New York Obesity Research Center is to help reduce the incidence of obesity and related diseases through leadership in basic research clinical research epidemiology and public health patient care and public education.
Dr Xavier Pi-Sunyer, Director
Janet Crane, Dietitians

1109 **Research Chair in Obesity Universit, Laval**
2725 Chemin Sainte-Foy 418-656-8711
Quebec, Canada, G1V-4G5 obesity.chair@crhl.ulaval.ca
www.obesity.ulaval.ca
Shares communication about nutrition, energy metabolism, obesity, lipid metabolism and cardiovascular research. Provides continuing education about obesity to health professionals, physicians and to the public regarding the causes, the complications and the treatment of obesity.
Denis Richard, PhD, Chair

1110 **University of Cincinnati Department of Pathology & Laboratory Medicine**
234 Goodman Street 513-584-7284
Cincinnati, OH 45219-0533 Fax: 513-584-3892
pathology@uc.edu
pathology.uc.edu
Research to understand the causes of disease and develop treatments for infectious diseases, diabete, obesity and lipid disorders, cancer and cardiovascular diseases.
Dani Zander, MD, Chair of Pathology
Michelle Cooper, Executive Director, Business & Admin

1111 **University of Pittsburgh Obesity/Nutrition Research Center**
www.pitt.edu/~mdm2/ONRCWeb
Goal is to develop more effective interventions for the prevention and treatment of obesity. Exists to support research functions for investigators studying the broad areas of obesity and nutrition. Focuses on behavioral aspects of obesity and behavioral treatment of this disease.

1112 **Vanderbilt Clinical Nutrition Research Unit (CNRU)**
www.vanderbilt.edu/nutrition/index.html
A core center grant funded by the National Institute of Diabetes and Digestive and Kidney Diseases (NIDDK). Nutrition research is carried out by faculty members i most academic departments and extends from basic laboratory research to clinical and applied research. Maintains service facilities to support both basic and clinical research. Supports research cores that bring nutrition investigators together to discuss their work.

Support Groups & Hotlines

1113 **Greater New York Metro Intergroup of Overeaters Anonymous**
Madison Square Station 212-946-4599
New York, NY 10159-1235 office@oanyc.org
www.oanyc.org
Tom M, Chairman
Raina M, Vice chairman

1114 **National Health Information Center**
Office of Disease Prevention & Health Promotion
1101 Wootton Pkwy odphpinfo@hhs.gov
Rockville, MD 20852 www.health.gov/nhic
Supports public health education by maintaining a calendar of National Health Observances; helps connect consumers and health professionals to organizations that can best answer questions and provide up-to-date contact information from reliable sources; updates on a yearly basis toll-free numbers for health information, Federal health clearinghouses and info centers.
Don Wright, MD, MPH, Director

Journals

1115 **CheckUp**
Medical University of South Carolina
67 President Street 843-792-2273
Charleston, SC 29425 800-424-6872
www.muschealth.com/weight
Provides health information about screenings, treatments, medical advances and services available through MUSC, as well as advice about nutrition and prevention.
Susan Kammeraad-Campbell, Managing Editor
Damon Simmons, Art Director

1116 **Official Journal of NAASO**
NAASO
8757 Georgia Avenue 301-563-6526
Silver Spring, MD 20910 www.obesity.org
Promotes research, education and advocacy to better understand, prevent and treat obesity and improve the lives of those affected.
Barbara E. Corkey, Editor-In-Chief
Deborah Moskowitz, Managing Editor

1117 **Trim & Fit**
Obesity Foundation
5600 S Quebec Street 303-850-0328
Englewood, CO 80111-2202
Offers nutrition facts and articles, low-fat recipes, medical information on heart disease and cancer relating to nutrition and more.
James F Merker CAE, Editor

Digital Resources

1118 **Obesity Online**
NAASO
301-563-6526
www.obesity-online.com
Educational resource for clinicians, researchers and educators with an interest in obesity and its related disorders.
Samuel Klein, Editor
Christie M. Ballantyne, Editor

1119 **Progress Notes**
Medical University of South Carolina
67 President Street 843-792-2273
Charleston, SC 29425 800-922-5250
www.muschealth.com/weight
Designed to inform the medical community developments at the Medical University of South Carolina and as a continuing medical education resource for practicing physicians and faculty.
Susan Kammeraad-Campbell, Managing Editor
Lynne Barber Associate Editor, Alex Sargent, Associate Editor

Web Sites

1120 Boston Obesity Nutrition Research Center (BONRC)
www.bmc.org
Provides resources and support for studies in the area of obesity and nutrition. Comprised of four research cores located within the Boston area. In the areas of adipocytes, epidemiology and statistics, body composition, energy expenditure and genetic analyses, and transgenic animal models.

1121 Center for Human Nutrition
www.uchsc.edu/nutrition
A interdisciplinary team encompassing basic and clinical research, post-graduate training and career development of nutrition professionals, and community outreach. The research conducted at the CHN focuses on obesity prevention and treatment, nutrient metabolism, and micronutrient status in children. Activities conducted aim to improve the quallity of life by promoting physical activity and nutritional awareness.

1122 Clinical Nutrition Research Unit (CNRU)
depts.washington.edu/uwnorc
Promotes and enhances the interdisciplinary nutrition research and education at the Univeristy of Washington. By providing a number of Core Facilities, the CNRU attempts to integrate and coordinate the abundant ongoing activities with the goals of fostering new interdisicilinary research collaborations, stimulating new research activities, improving nutrition education at multiple levels, and facilitating the nutritional management of patients.

1123 Dietary Guidelines for Americans
www.dietaryguidelines.gov
Publishes the Dietary Guidelines for Americans, a guide providing nutritional advice to promote health and prevent disease. Updated versions of the Dietary Guidelines are released by the US Departments of Agriculture (USDA) and Health & Human Services (HHS) every five years.

1124 EndocrineWeb
www.endocrineweb.com
A website of Remedy Health Media, EndocrineWeb provides information about endocrine disorders, including thyroid disorders, diabetes, obesity, Addison's disease, and more.

1125 Everyday Health
www.everydayhealth.com
Aims to provide evidence-based health information from physicians and healthcare providers.

1126 FamilyDoctor.org
www.familydoctor.org
Medical advice and information provided by the American Academy of Family Physicians. Resources include a medical dictionary, a symptom checker tool, a BMI calculator, and medication information.

1127 Healthline
www.healthline.com
Provides medical and health articles and information.

1128 MedicineNet
www.medicinenet.com
An online resource for consumers providing easy-to-read, authoritative medical and health information.

1129 Medscape
www.medscape.com
Medscape offers specialists, primary care physicians, and other health professionals the Web's most robust and integrated medical information and educational tools.

1130 MyPlate
www.myplate.gov
Created and managed by the US Department of Agriculture's Center for Nutrition Policy & Promotion, MyPlate is a dietary guide providing resources and recipes to promote healthy eating for all Americans.

1131 New York Obesity/Nutrition Research Center (ONRC)
www.niddk.nih.gov
Funded by the National Institute of Diabetes and Digestive and Kidney Diseases (NIDDK). A combined effort of Columbia anc Cornell Universities. Provides participating investigators of funded projects relevant to obesity research with valuable laboratory, technical, and educational services that otherwise would not be available to them, thereby improving the productivity an efficiency of their operations.

1132 North American Association for the Study of Obesity
www.obesity.org
The leading scientific society dedicated to the study of obesity. Committed to encouraging research on the causes and treatment of obesity, and to keeping the medical community and public informed of new advances.

1133 Nutrition.gov
www.nutrition.gov
Sponsored by the United States Department of Agriculture (USDA), Nutrition.gov offers information on topics in food and nutrition, including healthy eating, physical activity, and food safety.

1134 Research Chair on Obesity
obesity.chair.ulaval.ca
Ever since 1997, the Research Chair in Obesity is dedicated to support and launch initiatives leading to a better understanding of obesity through research on the mechanisms of body weight regulation, to facilitate communication between researchers, to promote the training of highly qualified personnel, to contribute to continuing education for health professionals, and to inform the public on the causes, consequences, treatments, and prevention of obesity.

1135 Science Daily
www.sciencedaily.com
Provides information on the latest news and research in science, health, the environment, and technology.

1136 The Nutrition Source
hsph.harvard.edu/nutritionsource
From the Harvard T.H. Chan School of Public Health, The Nutrition Source provides news, information, and guidance for nutrition and healthy eating.

1137 University of Pittsburgh Obesity/Nutrition Research Center
www.pitt.edu/~mdm2/ONRCWeb
Goal is to develop more effective interventions for the prevention and treatment of obesity. Exists to support research functions for investigators studying the broad areas of obesity and nutrition. Focuses on behavioral aspects of obesity and behavioral treatment of this disease.

1138 UnlockFood
www.unlockfood.ca
A website from Dietitians of Canada. Provides videos, recipes, and information on food and nutrition, as well as helps Canadians connect with a dietitian.

1139 Vanderbilt Clinical Nutrition Research Unit (CNRU)
www.vanderbilt.edu/nutrition/index.html
A core center grant funded by the National Institute of Diabetes and Digestive and Kidney Diseases (NIDDK). Nutrition research is carried out by faculty members i most academic departments and extends from basic laboratory research to clinical and applied research. Maintains service facilities to support both basic and clinical research. Supports research cores that bring nutrition investigators together to discuss their work.

1140 Verywell
www.verywellhealth.com
Offers health, medicine, and wellness information from health professionals.

1141 WebMD
www.webmd.com
Provides credible information, supportive communities, and in-depth reference material about health subjects. A source for original and timely health information as well as material from well known content providers.

1142 Weight-Control Information Network
www.win.niddk.nih.gov

The Weight-control Information Network (WIN) provides the general public, health professionals, and the media with up-to-date, science-based information on obesity, weight control, physical activity, and related nutritional issues. WIN provides tip sheets, fact sheets, and brochures for a range of audiences. Some of WIN's content is available in Spanish.

1143 **World Health Organization**

www.who.int

An agency of the United Nations, World Health Organization (WHO) serves to promote global health. The WHO website provides fact sheets, publications, media, and other resources on various health topics.

OSTEOARTHRITIS & NUTRITION

Osteoarthritis (OA), the most common form of arthritis, is a degenerative disease of the body's joints. It is often considered a disease of "wear and tear," most often affecting hands, hips and knees. As cartilage in a joint breaks down, bone changes occur causing pain, stiffness and swelling that may interfere with activities of daily living. The more body weight you carry, the more stress on joints and the highly likelihood of metabolic irregularities, both of which increase the risk of OA. Once you receive a diagnosis, there are some strategies that can help manage the condition. The Centers for Disease Control (CDC) recommends weight loss, being physically active through activities that protect your joints such as walking and swimming, and becoming educated about the disease. Since a healthy weight is important, understanding nutrition and its relationship to OA is a step in the right direction.

Osteoarthritis (OA) results in tissue breakdown in the joints over time. It is more common in older adults and more so in women over 50 years of age. Wear and tear on the joints from years of activities such as tennis, running and other sports may contribute to OA. Repetitive motion, being overweight, and family history are also contributing factors. Younger people may develop OA after an injury or with a joint that has formed incorrectly. Common symptoms of OA include joint pain, stiffness, swelling, inflammation and changes in how the joint moves and feels, usually loose or unstable. Over time, symptoms may get worse making it difficult to climb stairs, get in or out of a chair, make gripping motions or walk long distances. Depression and sleeping problems make occur as symptoms get worse.

If you suspect you may have arthritis, your doctor will discuss your medical history, perform a physical examination, review x-ray images of the joints, and run blood tests to rule out other causes. Joint fluid samples may indicate infection or gout. Once a diagnosis is made, a treatment plan will be developed.

Initial treatment may includes achieving a healthy weight, increasing daily exercise, using assistive devices if needed such as braces or canes, avoiding repetitive motions and taking medications if prescribed. The goals of treatment include reducing pain and other symptoms, maintaining quality of life and joint function and preventing the disease from getting worse. Educating yourself about the disease is an important way to help toward these ends.

One of the best ways to manage OA is achieving and maintaining a healthy weight and eating nutritious foods. Less weight means less stress on joints and, often, less pain. Exercise that doesn't put pressure on joints, like walking and swimming, is usually recommended to strengthen joints and increase the fluid that the joints need to function.

Certain foods can affect arthritis symptoms. Recent studies show that a Mediterranean diet with fruits and vegetables, healthy fats like olive oil and nuts, whole grains, fish, yogurt and red wine can reduce inflammation caused by OA. This diet also protects against weight gain and promotes bone health to decrease fracture risk. Avoiding red meat, sugar and most dairy will also contribute to less inflammation. Some patients have reported the Mediterranean diet has led to less use of non-steroidal anti-inflammatory drugs (NSAIDs) and less pain in as little as one week.

Certain foods and beverages should be avoided with OA, including sugar, processed foods and red meats, gluten, certain vegetable oils, salt, and alcohol. Foods that might alleviate symptoms include fatty fish such as salmon and tuna, dark leafy greens, nuts, olive oil, berries, garlic and onion and green tea. The Arthritis Foundation also recommends weighing yourself regularly to monitor your weight.

Just as important to making the right food choices is daily regular exercise. It not only helps with weight management, but often relieves achy joints. The Centers for Disease Control has partnered with the Y-USA, Arthritis Foundation, Osteoarthritis Action Alliance and the National Recreation and Parks Association to increase access to self-management programs and physical activity, especially walking programs. They encourage learning about OA management strategies, activity, maintaining or achieving a healthy weight, regular doctor visits and implementing strategies to protect your joints from further damage.

Through good nutrition and appropriate activity, the symptoms of OA may improve. Taking responsibility for self-management is important to managing this disease.

See page 191 for more information on the Mediterranean diet.

Agencies & Associations

1145 **American Academy of Pain Medicine**
1705 Edgewater Drive 800-917-1619
Orlando, FL 32804 Fax: 407-749-0714
info@painmed.org
www.painmed.org
The AAPM is a medical specialty society representing physicians and healthcare professionals practicing in the field of pain medicine. Its mission is to promote and advance pain care, education, training, advocacy, and research.
W. Michael Hooten, MD, President
Farshad M. Ahadian, MD, Treasurer

1146 **American Autoimmune Related Diseases Association**
19176 Hall Road 586-776-3900
Clinton Township, MI 48038 aarda@aarda.org
www.aarda.org
Awareness, education, referrals for patients with any type of autoimmune disease.
Molly Murray, President & CEO
Laura Simpson, Chief Operating Officer

1147 **American Chronic Pain Association**
11936 West 119th Street 913-991-4740
Overland Park, KS 66213-2216 acpa@theacpa.org
www.theacpa.org
The ACPA facilitates peer support and education for individuals with chronic pain in its many forms, in order to increase quality of life. Also raises awareness among the healthcare community, and with policy makers.
Kathy Sapp, Chief Executive Officer
Scott Farmer, Chief Operating Officer

1148 **American College of Gastroenterology**
6400 Goldsboro Road 301-263-9000
Bethesda, MD 20817 www.gi.org
ACG serves clinical and scientific information needs of member physicians and surgeons, who specialize in digestive and related disorders. Emphasis is on scholarly practice, teaching and research.
David A. Greenwald, MD, FACG, President
Amy S. Oxentenko, MD, FACG, Secretary

1149 **American Osteopathic Association**
142 E Ontario Street 312-202-8000
Chicago, IL 60611-2864 888-626-9262
info@osteopathic.org
www.osteopathic.org
Serving as the professional family for more than 145,000 osteopathic physicians (DOs) and osteopathic medical students, the American Osteopathic Association (AOA) promotes public health and encourages scientific research.
Joseph Giaimo, President
Kevin Klauer, Chief Executive Officer

1150 **American Physical Therapy Association**
3030 Potomac Avenue 703-684-2782
Alexandria, VA 22305-3085 800-999-2782
www.apta.org
The American Physical Therapy Association (APTA) is an individual membership professional organization representing more than 100,000 member physical therapists (PTs), physical therapist assistants (PTAs), and students of physical therapy.
Sharon L. Dunn, President
Matthew R. Hyland, Vice President

1151 **Arthritis Society**
393 University Avenue 416-979-7228
Toronto, Ontario, M5G-1E6 800-321-1433
info@arthritis.ca
www.arthritis.ca
Promotes, evaluates, and funds research in the areas of causes, prevention, treatment, and cures of arthritis.
Trish Barbato, President & CEO
Sian Bevan, Ph.D., Chief Science Officer

1152 **Centers for Medicare & Medicaid Services**
7500 Security Boulevard www.cms.gov
Baltimore, MD 21244
U.S. federal agency which administers Medicare, Medicaid, and the State Children's Health Insurance Program.
Chiquita Brooks-LaSure, Administrator
Jonathan Blum, COO

1153 **Myositis Association of America**
6950 Columbia Gateway Drive 800-821-7356
Columbia, MD 21046 tma@myositis.org
www.myositis.org
The MMA seeks to improve the lives of individuals affected by myositis, an inflammation of the muscles, through funding research and increasing public awareness.
Chrissy Thornton, Executive Director
Aisha Morrow, Senior Manager, Operations

1154 **National Association of Chronic Disease Directors**
325 Swanton Way info@chronicdisease.org
Decatur, GA 30030 www.chronicdisease.org
Non-profit public health organization committed to serving the chronic disease program directors of each state and jurisdiction in the United States.
John W. Robitscher, MPH, Chief Executive Officer
Marti Macchi, MEd, MPH, Senior Director, Programs

1155 **National Institute of Arthritis & Musculoskeletal & Skin Diseases**
National Institutes of Health
9000 Rockville Pike 301-495-4484
Bethesda, MD 20892 877-226-4267
TTY: 301-565-2966
niamsinfo@mail.nih.gov
www.niams.nih.gov
Supports research into the causes, treatment, and prevention of arthritis and musculoskeletal and skin diseases, the training of basic and clinical scientists to carry out this research, and the dissemination of information on research programs.
Lindsey A. Criswell, MD, MPH, DSc, Director
Robert H. Carter, MD, Deputy Director

1156 **National Institute on Aging**
31 Center Drive, MSC 2292 800-222-2225
Bethesda, MD 20892 TTY: 800-222-4225
niaic@nia.nih.gov
www.nia.nih.gov
Seeks to understand the nature of aging, and to extend healthy, active years of life. Free resources are available on topics such as Alzheimer's & dimentia, caregiving, cognitive heath, end of life care, and more.
Richard J. Hodes, MD, Director
Luigi Ferrucci, Scientific Director

1157 **Nurse Practitioners in Women's Health**
PO Box 15837 202-543-9693
Washington, DC 20003 info@npwh.org
www.npwh.org
Ensures the delivery and accessibility of primary and specialty healthcare to women of all ages by women's health and women's health focused nurse practitioners.
Heather L. Maurer, CEO
Donna Ruth, Director, Education

1158 **Osteoporosis Canada**
201 - 250 Ferrand Drive 416-696-2663
Toronto, Ontario, M3C-3G8 800-463-6842
www.osteoporosis.ca
National organization serving people who have, or are at risk for osteoporosis.
Famida Jiwa, President & CEO
Laurie Georges, Director, Finance & HR

1159 **Society For Post-Acute and Long-Term Care Medicine**
10500 Little Patuxent Parkway 410-740-9743
Columbia, MD 21044 800-876-2632
info@paltc.org
www.paltc.org
Provides education, advocacy, information and professional development to promote the delivery of standardized post-acute and long-term care medicine.
Karl Steinberg, MD, HMDC, CMD, President
Milta Little, DO, CMD, Vice President

1160 **St. Joseph's Medical Center**
7601 Osler Drive 410-337-1000
Towson, MD 21204 www.umms.org/sjmc
Thomas B. Smyth, MD, President & CEO

Libraries & Resource Centers

1161 **NIH Osteoporosis and Related Bone Diseases - National Resource Center**
2 AMS Circle 202-223-0344
Bethesda, MD 20892-3676 800-624-2663
TTY: 202-466-4315
www.osteo.org
Provides patients, health professionals and the public with an important link to resources and information on osteoporosis, Paget's disease of bone, osteogenesis imperfecta, and other metabolic bone diseases. The National Resource Center's mission is to expand awareness and enhance knowledge and understanding of the prevention, early detection, and treatment of these diseases.

Foundations & Research Centers

1162 **Affiliated Children's Arthritis Centers of New England**
New England Medical Center
750 Washington Street 617-636-7285
Boston, MA 02111-1533
Research organization comprised of a network of 15 territory pediatric centers throughout New England and based at the Floating Hospital of New England Medical Center.
Jane G Schaller MD, Coordinator

1163 **Arthritis & Autoimmunity Research Centre**
Canadian Blood Services Building
67 College Street 416-340-3843
Toronto, Ontario, M5G-2M1 tlockett@uhnres.utoronto.ca
www-old.uhnresearch.ca
The AARC is dedicated to researching the 100 chronic illnesses associated with arthritis and other autoimmune diseases.
Eleanor Fish, Executive Director
Theresa Lockett, Contact

1164 **Arthritis Foundation**
1355 Peachtree Street NE 800-283-7800
Atlanta, GA 30309 www.arthritis.org
A nonprofit organization that depends on volunteers to provide services to help people with arthritis. Supports research to find ways to cure and prevent arthritis and provides services to improve the quality of life for those affected by arthritis. Provides help through information, referrals, speakers bureaus, forums, self-help courses, and various support groups and programs nationwide.
Ann M. Palmer, President & CEO
Robin Kinard, Sr Vice President, Operations

1165 **Arthritis and Musculoskeletal Center: UAB Shelby Interdisciplinary Biomedical Rese**
Shelby Interdisciplinary Biomedical Research Bldg
1825 University Boulevard 205-934-0245
Birmingham, AL 35294-2182 rpk@uab.edu
www.main.uab.edu/amc
Arthritis and related rheumatic disorders are studied.
Robert Kimbe MD, Director
Jennifer A Croker, Executive Administrator

1166 **Boston University Arthritis Center**
580 Harrison Avenue 617-638-4590
Boston, MA 02118 mikyork@bu.edu
www.bumc.bu.edu
The research efforts of the Rheumatology Section relate to basic biologic mechanisms in the pathogenesis of scleroderma vasculitis amyloidosis osteoarthritis and systemic lupus erythematosus. There are concordant research efforts in clinical investigation of these disorders including testing of novel therapies.
Karen H Antman, Dean
Paul Monach, Associate Fellowship Program Director

1167 **Boston University Medical Campus General Clinical Research Center**
72 E Concord Street 617-638-4542
Boston, MA 02118 jkopp@bu.edu
www.ctsi.bu.edu
Integral unit of the University Hospital specializing in arthritis and connective tissue studies.
Courtney Alpert, Administrative Coordinator
Janice Kopp, Executive Director

1168 **Brigham and Women's Orthopedica and Arthritis Center**
Brigham and Women's Hospital
75 Francis Street 617-732-5500
Boston, MA 02115 800-BWH-9999
TTY: 617-732-6458
www.brighamandwomens.org
Research studies into arthritis and rheumatic diseases.
Matthew Lian MD, Director

1169 **Central Missouri Regional Arthritis Center Stephen's College Campus**
Stephen's College Campus
1205 University Ave 573-882-8097
Columbia, MO 65211 888-702-8818
TDD: 0
marrtc.missouri.edu
Research into arthritis and rheumatic diseases.
Liz Raine, MPH, CHES,, Health Educator
Beth Richards, BS, TRS, Director

1170 **Department of Pediatrics, Division of Rheumatology**
Duke University School of Medicine
T909 Children's Health Center 919-684-6575
Durham, NC 27710-1 rheum.pediatrics.duke.edu
Clinical and laboratory pediatric rheumatoid studies.
Laura Schanberg MD, Cochairman
Egla Rabinovich MD, Co-Chairman

1171 **Hahnemann University Hospital, Orthopedic Wellness Center**
Hahnemann University Hospital
230 N Broad St 215-762-7000
Philadelphia, PA 19102-1511 www.hahnemannhospital.com
Research activity at Hahnemann University into the areas of arthritis.
Dr. Arnold Berman, Director

1172 **Medical College of Pennsylvania Center for the Mature Woman**
3300 Henry Avenue 215-842-6000
Philadelphia, PA 19129
our purpose is to provide consumers information to help them get high quality services and products at the best possible prices.
Jon Schneider,MD, Director

1173 **Medical University of South Carolina**
96 Jonathan Lucas Street 843-792-1991
Charleston, SC 29403 800-424-MUSC
www.muschealth.com
Offers basic and clinical research on various types of arthritis.
Richard M Silver, Division Director/Professor
Gary S Gilkeson, Vice Chairman Research

1174 **Medical University of South Carolina: Division of Rheumatology & Immunology**
96 Jonathan Lucas Street 843-792-1991
Charleston, SC 29403 www.musc.edu
Offers basic and clinical research on various types of arthritis.
Richard M Silver, Division Director/Professor
Gary S Gilkeson, Vice Chairman Research

1175 **Multipurpose Arthritis and Musculoskeletal Disease Center**
School of Medicine Rheumatology Division
545 Barnhill Drive 317- 27- 843
Indianapolis, IN 46202 medicine.iupui.edu
The mission of this center is to pursue major biomedical research interests relevant to the rheumatic diseases. Current areas of emphasis include articular cartilage biology pathogenesis and treatment of various forms of amyloidosis the pathogenesis of

dermatomyositis and immunologic and biochemical markers of cartilage breakdown and repair.
Bernetta Hartman, Executive Assistant to the Chairman
Martin Friedman, VP Medicine Specialties Division, IUHP

1176 **National Institute of Arthritis & Musculoskeletal & Skin Diseases**
National Institutes of Health
9000 Rockville Pike 301-495-4484
Bethesda, MD 20892 877-226-4267
TTY: 301-565-2966
NIAMSinfo@mail.nih.gov
www.niams.nih.gov
Supports research into the causes, treatment, and prevention of arthritis and musculoskeletal and skin diseases, the training of basic and clinical scientists to carry out this research, and the dissemination of information on research programs.
Lindsey A. Criswell, MD, MPH, DSc, Director

1177 **National Osteoporosis Foundation**
251 18th Street S 800-231-4222
Arlington, VA 22202 info@nof.org
www.nof.org
The nation's leading resource for people seeking current and accurate medical information on the causes, prevention, detection and treatment of osteoporosis.
Elizabeth Thompson, CEO
Susan Greenspan, MD, President

1178 **Oklahoma Medical Research Foundation**
825 NE 13th Street 405-271-6673
Oklahoma City, OK 73104-5005 800-522-0211
contact@omrf.org
www.omrf.ouhsc.edu
Focuses on arthritis and muscoloskeletal disease research.
Dr Paul Kincade, Head of OMRF's Immunobiology
Philip M Silverman PhD, Member

1179 **Osteoporosis Center Memorial Hospital/Advanced Medical Diagn**
Memorial Hospital/Advanced Medical Diagnostic
1700 Coffee Road 209-526-4500
Modesto, CA 95355 www.memorialmedicalcenter.org
Memorial Medical Center is part of Memorial Hospitals Association a not-for-profit organization that exists to maintain and improve the health status of citizens in the greater Stanislaus County.
David Benn, Director
Bev Finley, Director

1180 **Regional Bone Center Helen Hayes Hospital**
Helen Hayes Hospital
51-55 Route 9W 845-786-4000
W Haverstraw, NY 10993 1 8-8 7- 734
TTY: 845-947-3187
info@helenhayeshospital.org
www.helenhayeshospital.org
The mission of the Regional Bone conduct a broad-based research program focused on the elucidation of cellular mechanisms underlying metabolic bone disease and the development of new treatments for bone disease.
David W Dempster PhD, Director
Adrienne Tewksbury, Grants Administrator

1181 **Rehabilitation Institute of Chicago**
345 E Superior Street 312-238-1000
Chicago, IL 60611 800-354-7342
TTY: 312-238-1059
www.ric.org
Expertise in treating a range of conditions from the most complex conditions including cerebral palsy spinal cord injury stroke and traumatic brain injury to the more common such as arthritis chronic pain and sports injuries.
Edward B Case, Executive Vice President and Chief Finan
Joanne C Smith, President and Chief Executive Officer

1182 **Rosalind Russell Medical Research Center for Arthritis at UCSF**
350 Parnassus Avenue 415-476-1141
San Francisco, CA 94117 rrac@medicine.ucsf.edu
www.rosalindrussellcenter.ucsf.edu
Arthritis research and its probable causes.
Ephraim P Engelman MD, Director
David Wofsy, Associate Director

1183 **University of Connecticut Osteoporosis Center**
263 Farmington Avenue 860-679-2000
Farmington, CT 06030 800-535-6232
www.uchc.edu
Jay R Lieberman, Director

1184 **University of Michigan: Orthopaedic Research Laboratories**
University of Michigan Mott Hospital
109 Zina Pitcher Place 734-936-7417
Ann Arbor, MI 48109-2200 www.orl.med.umich.edu
Develops and studies the causes and treatments for arthritis including new devices and assistive aids.
Dr SA Goldstein, Director

1185 **University of Pennsylvania Muscle Institute**
School of Medicine
700A Clinical Research Building 215-573-9758
Philadelphia, PA 19104-2646 www.med.upenn.edu/pmi/
Studies in tissue science.
E. Michael Ostap, PhD, Director

1186 **University of Vermont Medical Center**
111 Colchester Avenue 802-847-0000
Burlington, VT 05401 800-358-1144
www.uvmhealth.org/medcenter
Melinda L Estes, MD, President/CEO
Richarad Magnuson, CFO

1187 **Warren Grant Magnuson Clinical Center**
National Institute of Health
9000 Rockville Pike 301-496-2563
Bethesda, MD 20892 800-411-1222
TTY: 866-411-1010
prpl@mail.cc.nih.gov
www.clinicalcenter.nih.gov
Established in 1953 as the research hospital of the National Institutes of Health. Designed so that patient care facilities are close to research laboratories so new findings of basic and clinical scientists can be quickly applied to the treatment of patients. Upon referral by physicians, patients are admitted to NIH clinical studies.
John Gallin, Director
David Henderson, Deputy Director for Clinical Care

Alabama

1188 **Alabama Chapter of the Arthritis Foundation**
2700 Hwy 280 E 205-979-5700
Birmingham, AL 35223-3775 800-879-7896
info.al@arthritis.org
www.arthritis.org
Founded in 1948 this chapter affects thousands of lives through programs services information and referrals public and professional education and more for residents of Alabama. Research is a great priority of the chapter which supports the advancement
Kristin Whitehurst, Regional VP
Lisa Hemphill, Regional Development Director

Arizona

1189 **Arthritis Foundation: Central Arizona Chapter**
1313 E. Osborn Road 602-264-7679
Phoenix, AZ 85014 800-477-7679
info.caz@arthritis.org
www.arthritis.org
A nonprofit health agency serving the needs of Arizona residents with arthritis. This chapter provides arthritis self-help courses, aquatic programs, foundation clubs, a juvenile arthritis parent group, exercise programs and informational brochures.
Warren Rizzo, Chair
Robert Leslie, Vice Chair

1190 **Arthritis Foundation: Southern Arizona Chapter**
6464 E Grant Road 520-290-9090
Tucson, AZ 85715 800-444-5426
Richard M Brown EdD, CFRE, President

Arkansas

1191 **Arthritis Foundation: Arkansas Chapter**
6213 Father Tribou Street 501-664-7242
Little Rock, AR 72205-3002 800-482-8858
info.ar@arthritis.org
www.arthritis.org

Carla Davis, Secretary
Diane Denham, VP Finance/Administration

California

1192 **Arthritis Foundation: Northern California Chapter**
657 Mission Street 415-356-1230
San Francisco, CA 94105-4120 800-464-6240
info.nca@arthritis.org
www.arthritis.org

Offers research into the causes of arthritis and more effective treatments; serves people in California with arthritis through information and referral services, exercise programs, self-help courses, education and other activities.
PJ Handelhand, President
Deborah Jackson, Senior VP

1193 **Arthritis Foundation: San Diego Area Chapter**
9089 Clairemont Mesa Boulevard 858-492-1090
San Diego, CA 92123-1288 800-422-8885
info.sd@arthritis.org
www.arthritis.org

Offers various programs and services including professional seminars, a speakers bureau, public forums, exercise classes, patient and family support groups, arthritis self-help courses and medical research to the residents of the San Diego area living with arthritis.
Veronica Braun, President
Sandra Hayhurst, Director Health Promotion

1194 **Arthritis Foundation: Southern California Chapter**
800 W 6th Street 323-954-5750
Los Angeles, CA 90017-3775 800-954-2873
info.sac@arthritis.org
www.arthritis.org

Cynthia Callihan, Administrative Assistant
Christeen Amloian, Assistant Controller

Colorado

1195 **Arthritis Foundation: Rocky Mountain Chapter**
2280 S Albion Street 303-756-8622
Denver, CO 80222-4906 800-475-6447
info.rm@arthritis.org
www.arthritis.org

Serves Colorado, Montana, and Wyoming and is dedicated to finding solutions to over 100 forms of arthritis which affect 43 millions of people nationwide.
Kristie Archer, Programs Coordinator
Laura Rosseisen, President

Connecticut

1196 **Arthritis Foundation: Southern New England Chapter**
35 Cold Spring Road 860-563-1177
Rocky Hill, CT 06067 800-541-8350
info.sne@arthritis.org
www.arthritis.org

Offers programs and services for persons in the Rhode Island area who are living with arthritis.
Stephen Evangelista, CEO
Gail Campbell, CFO

District of Columbia

1197 **Arthritis Foundation: Metropolitan Washington Chapter**
2011 Pennsylvania Avenue NW 202-537-6800
Washington, DC 20006 info.mwa@arthritis.org
www.arthritis.org

The mission of the Arthritis Foundation is to improve lives through leadership in the prevention control and cure of arthritis and related conditions.
Calaneet Balas, President/CEO
Jacquelyn Hair, Director of Operations

Florida

1198 **Arthritis Foundation: Florida Chapter, Gulf Coast Branch**
3816 W Linebaugh Avenue 813-968-7000
Tampa, FL 33618 800-850-9455
info.fl.b4@arthritis.org
www.arthritis.org

Dedicated to improving the quality of life for those in the seven county area of Pinellas, Pasco, Citrus, Levy, Hillsborough, Hernando and Polk, who have one or more of over 100 conditions that comprise the disease known as arthritis. Provides patient education and referral services.
Alexa Simpkins, Events Coordinator
Alvi McConahay, Regional Executive Director

Georgia

1199 **Arthritis Foundation: Georgia Chapter**
2790 Peachtree Road 404-237-8771
Atlanta, GA 30305 800-933-7023
info.ga@arthritis.org
www.arthritis.org

A statewide health organization dedicated to reducing the devastating effects of arthritis by offering programs for people with arthritis and their families, information and educational services for people with arthritis, medical professionals and the general public.
Andrea Collins, Vice President Mission Delivery
Christina Lennon, VP Resource Development

Illinois

1200 **Arthritis Foundation: Greater Chicago Chapter**
35 E Wacker Drive 312-372-2080
Chicago, IL 60601 800-795-0096
info.gc@arthritis.org
www.arthritis.org

Offers self-help courses, wellness workshops, educational seminars, aquatic programs, brochures and publications for persons with arthritis in the state of Illinois.
Roxanne Bartol, Information Systems Coordinator
Tom Fite, President

1201 **Arthritis Foundation: Greater Illinois Chapter**
2621 N Knoxville Avenue 309-682-6600
Peoria, IL 61604-3623 greaterillinois@arthritis.org
www.arthritis.org

Craig Rogers, Area Director

Indiana

1202 **Arthritis Foundation: Indiana Chapter**
615 N Alabama 317-879-0321
Indianapolis, IN 46204 800-783-2342
info.in@arthritis.org
www.arthritis.org

Offers programs and services for the arthritis community of Indiana.
Jenny Conder, Area Vice President
BJ Farrell, Director of Development

Iowa

1203 **Arthritis Foundation: Iowa Chapter**
2600 72nd Street 515-278-0636
Des Moines, IA 50322-4724 866-378-0636
info.ia@arthritis.org
www.arthritis.org

Julie Dalrymple, Program Coordinator
Doyle Monsma CFRE, President/CEO

Kansas

1204 **Arthritis Foundation: Kansas Chapter**
1999 N Amidon Avenue 316-263-0116
Wichita, KS 67203-2122 800-362-1108
info.ks@arthritis.org
www.arthritis.org
Serves 103 counties and is governed by the Volunteer Board of Directors elected from throughout the state. Services offered include water exercise classes, arthritis support groups, children's summer camp, loan closet of hospital equipment and self-help programs.
Dennis Bender, Area VP
Valerie Fairchild, Program Director

1205 **Arthritis Foundation: Western Missouri, Greater Kansas City**
1900 W 75th Street 913-262-2233
Prairie Village, KS 66208 888-719-5670
info.wmo@arthritis.org
www.arthritis.org
The only organization in the area representing the National Office in support of its international research program and in providing services throughout the bi-state area. Offers a wide range of services and programs to deal with the needs of persons with arthritis.
Sherri Hayes, Director of Operations
Alyson Watkins, Special Events Coordinator

Kentucky

1206 **Arthritis Foundation: Kentucky Chapter**
2908 Brownsboro Road 502-585-1866
Louisville, KY 40206 800-633-5335
myoung@arthritis.org
www.arthritis.org
Serves residents of 117 counties in Kentucky and the counties of Floyd and Clark in Indiana. This chapter is a resource center for funding research education programs for health professionals, community education and support services for people with arthritis.
Barbara Perez, President/CEO
Annette Beach, Annual Giving Coordinator

Maryland

1207 **Arthritis Foundation: Maryland Chapter**
9505 Reisterstown Road 410-654-6570
Owings Mills, MD 21117 800-365-3811
info.md@arthritis.org
www.arthritis.org
This chapter supports research both locally and nationally to help find causes better treatments and ways to prevent the many forms of arthritis. Offers various educational booklets and brochures, a referral service for physician referrals, and other support services.
Barbara Newhouse, CEO
Gail Norman, COO

Massachusetts

1208 **Arthritis Foundation: Massachusetts Chapter**
29 Crafts Street 617-244-1800
Newton, MA 02458-1287 800-766-9449
info.ma@arthritis.org
www.arthritis.org
Offers essential information research programs and services for the close to one million Massachusetts residents with arthritis.
Suha Bekdash, Administrative Assistant
Carmen Quinonez, Finance Manager

Michigan

1209 **Arthritis Foundation: Michigan Chapter Chapter and Metro Detroit**
1050 Wilshire Drive 248-649-2891
Troy, MI 48084-1564 800-968-3030
info.mi@arthritis.org
www.arthritis.org
Supports research to prevent, control, and cure arthritis and related diseases. The Foundation also helps improve the lives of people with arthritis and their families by offering self-help classes, exercise programs, support groups, information and referrals.
Mary Sue Langen, Development Manager
Michelle Glazier, President/CEO

Minnesota

1210 **Arthritis Foundation: North Central Chapter**
1876 Minnehaha Avenue West 651-644-4108
Saint Paul, MN 55104 800-333-1380
info.mn@arthritis.org
www.arthritis.org
A nonprofit organization providing programs and services to anyone affected by arthritis in the Minnesota area. Offers aquatic programs support groups juvenile arthritis support groups, research, grants program and information and referrals.
Chris Davis, Community Development Coordinator
Deb Cassidy, Assistant to the President

Mississippi

1211 **Arthritis Foundation: Mississippi Chapter**
731 Avignon Drive 601-853-7556
Ridgeland, MS 39157 cbaker@arthritis.org
www.arthritis.org
Many Mississippians volunteer their services to help the chapter with fund raising and program support. Programs include land and water based exercise classes, and support groups, direct assistance to needy individuals to purchase arthritis medications and services.
Cynthia Baker, Development Specialist
Pamela Snow, Programs Director

Missouri

1212 **Arthritis Foundation: Eastern Missouri Chapter**
9433 Olive Boulevard 314-991-9333
Saint Louis, MO 63132 800-406-2491
info.emo@arthritis.org
www.arthritis.org
Jan Bignall, Director of Development
Karen Shoulders, Director of Programs

Nebraska

1213 **Arthritis Foundation: Nebraska Chapter**
600 N 93rd Street 402-330-6130
Omaha, NE 68114 800-642-5292
mpuccioni@arthritis.org
www.arthritis.org
For close to 40 years the Arthritis Foundation has been the source for help and hope to the 263,000 Nebraskans and residents of Pottawattamie County Iowa with arthritis. Provides a wide variety of services designed to help people better cope with arthritis.
Cindy Doerr, Program Director/Editor
Marzia Pucci Shields, Executive Director

New Hampshire

1214 **Arthritis Foundation: Northern New England Chapter**
6 Chenell Drive 603-224-9322
Concord, NH 03301 800-639-2113
info.sne@arthritis.org
www.arthritis.org
Stephen Evangelista, CEO
Margaret Duffy, Regional Program Director

New Jersey

1215 **Arthritis Foundation: New Jersey Chapter**
555 Route 1 South 732-283-4300
Iselin, NJ 08830 888-467-3112
info.nj@arthritis.org
www.arthritis.org
Offers various programs for the residents of New Jersey including support groups, self-help courses, water exercise and arthritis fitness classes and informational public forums.
Linda Gruskiewicz, President & CEO
Tanya Barbarics, Director

New York

1216 **Arthritis Foundation: Central New York Chapter**
3300 Monroe Avenue 585-264-1480
Rochester, NY 14618 www.arthritis.org
Melinda Merante, Executive Director
Nicole Mau, Director

1217 **Arthritis Foundation: Long Island Chapter**
501 Walt Whitman Road 631-427-8272
Melville, NY 11747-2189 into.li@arthritis.org
www.arthritis.org
The mission of the Arthritis Foundation is to fund research to find the cause and cures for arthritis and to improve the quality of life for those affected. There is a wide range of programs available for patients.
Patrick T McAsey, President
Roshane Gillespie, Program Secretary

1218 **Arthritis Foundation: New York Chapter**
122 E 42nd Street 212-984-8700
New York, NY 10168-1898 nfo.ny@arthritis.org
www.arthritis.org
Offers land exercise programs warm water resources and programs, self-help groups and courses, events and activities video clinics, peer support and a lending library to arthritis sufferers in the New York area.
Suzanne Bliss, President CEO

1219 **Arthritis Foundation: Rockland/Orange Unit**
Helen Hayes Hospital
Route 9W 845-947-3000
W Haverstraw, NY 10993 ameyerowitz@arthritis.org
www.arthritis.org
Aviva Meyerowitz, Community Outreach Coordinator
Beatrice Jasanya, Community Outreach Coordinator

1220 **New York Chapter of the Arthritis Foundation**
122 East 42nd Street 212-984-8700
New York, NY 10168-1898 info.ny@arthritis.org
www.arthritis.org
Offers people with arthritis, their families and all those with an interest in the rheumatic diseases, information on how to live every day to its fullest, even when affected by a chronic disease.

North Carolina

1221 **Arthritis Foundation: Carolinas Chapter**
4530 Park Road 704-529-5166
Charlotte, NC 28209 800-365-3811
info.car@arthritis.org
www.arthritis.org
Barbara Newhouse, President CEO
Candy Fuller, Community Development Coordinator

Ohio

1222 **Arthritis Foundation: Central Ohio Chapter**
3740 Ridge Mill Drive 614-876-8200
Hilliard, OH 43026 info.coh@arthritis.org
www.arthritis.org
Offers information and referral services, self-help courses, aquatics program equipment loans, clinics, home assessment and continuing education to help more than 350,000 people in Central Ohio, including over 5,000 children affected with the 100 types of arthritis
Stephanie Houck, Director of Special Events
David Painter, Director of Outreach

1223 **Arthritis Foundation: Northeastern Ohio Chapter**
4630 Richmond Road 216-831-7000
Cleveland, OH 44128-5525 800-245-2275
info.neoh@arthritis.org
www.arthritis.org
Barb Cvelbar, Director of Health Promotion
Cheryl Carter, Director of Development

1224 **Arthritis Foundation: Northwestern Ohio Chapter**
35 E Wacker Drive 31 -37 -208
Chicago, IL 60601 800-735-0096
info.gc@arthritis.org
www.arthritis.org
Tom Fite, CEO

1225 **Arthritis Foundation: Ohio River Valley Chapter**
7124 Miami Avenue 513-271-4545
Cincinnati, OH 45243 800-383-6843
info.orv@arthritis.org
www.arthritis.org
Barbara Perez, President/CEO
Edith Nixon, Chair

1226 **Arthritis Foundation; Great Lakes Region, Northeastern Ohio**
4630 Richmond Road 216-831-7000
Cleveland, OH 44128-5525 800-245-2275
info.neoh@arthritis.org
www.arthritis.org
Mary L Kudasick, Regional VP

Oklahoma

1227 **Arthritis Foundation: Oklahoma Chapter**
710 W. Wilshire Blvd 405-936-3366
Oklahoma City, OK 73116 800-627-5486
info.ok@arthritis.org
www.arthritis.org
Sherri O'Neil, Executive Director
Sherri Harris, Director Special Events

Pennsylvania

1228 **Arthritis Foundation: Central Pennsylvania Chapter**
3544 North Progress Avenue 717-763-0900
Harrisburg, PA 17110 800-776-0746
info.cpa@arthritis.org
www.arthritis.org
Serves 28 counties in the central Pennsylvania area. More than 441,233 persons in the chapter area are affected with one of the forms of arthritis seriously enough to require medical care. The chapter offers research services, professional education and training, parent and community services and public health education.
Douglas Knepp, Interim Executive Director

Tennessee

1229 **Arthritis Foundation: Southeast Region**
421 Great Circle Road 615-254-6795
Nashville, TN 37228 800-454-4662
info.tn@arthritis.org
www.arthritis.org
This chapter serves the residents of Tennessee by offering arthritis support through Life Improvement Series Classes, exercise programs, educational programs, free information, public forums and seminars.
David Popen Esq, CEO

Texas

1230 **Arthritis Foundation: North Texas Chapter**
4300 Macarthur 214-826-4361
Dallas, TX 75209-6524 800-442-6653
info.ntx@arthritis.org
www.arthritis.org
With over 1.5 million people in the North Texas Chapter area with arthritis, the chapter's mission is to improve lives through leadership in the prevention, control and cure of arthritis and related diseases.
Carla Brandt, CFO/COO
Jane Hynes, Director Administration/Info Systems

Utah

1231 **Arthritis Foundation: Utah/Idaho Chapter**
448 E 400 S 801-536-0990
Salt Lake City, UT 84111 800-444-4993
info.utid@arthritis.org
www.arthritis.org
A nonprofit organization serving individuals with arthritis and their families in Utah and Idaho by providing invaluable services, programs and activities.
Lisa B Fall, President
Leslie Nelson, Program Director

Virginia

1232 **Arthritis Foundation: Virginia Chapter**
3805 Cutshaw Avenue 804-359-1700
Richmond, VA 23230 800-456-4687
info.va@arthritis.org
www.arthritis.org
Founded in 1954 this chapter is a nonprofit voluntary health organization dedicated to finding the cause prevention and cure for the entire group of diseases called arthritis. Offered classes books and information to better manage arthritis.
Angela Courtney, Vice President Community Development
C Annie Magnant, President

Washington

1233 **Arthritis Foundation: Washington/Alaska Chapter**
3876 Bridge Way N 206-547-2707
Seattle, WA 98103 800-746-1821
tzuehl@arthritis.org
www.arthritis.org
Offers arthritis help lines and information lines for residents of Washington state. Provides self-help courses arthritis aquatic programs and resources for persons living with various forms of arthritis.
Barbara Osen, North Puget Sound Branch Director
Kim Mellen, Campaign Coordinator

Wisconsin

1234 **Arthritis Foundation: Wisconsin Chapter Foundation**
1650 S 108th Street 414-321-3933
W Allis, WI 53214-4021 800-242-9945
www.arthritis.org
Statewide programs offered. Including aquatics exercise programs, support groups, self-help courses, professional education, public education seminars, advocacy counsel, juvenile arthritis support programs and children's camp information and referral help.

Support Groups & Hotlines

1235 **Arthritis Foundation Information Helpline**
1355 Peachtree Street NE 800-283-7800
Atlanta, GA 30309-0669 www.arthritis.org
Offers information and referrals, counseling, physicians information and more to persons living with arthritis.
Ann M. Palmer, President & CEO

1236 **Kids on the Block Arthritis Programs**
Arthritis Foundation
PO Box 19000 404-872-7100
Atlanta, GA 31126-1000 800-283-7800
State and local programs that use puppetry to help children understand what it is like for children and adults who have arthritis.

1237 **National Health Information Center**
Office of Disease Prevention & Health Promotion
1101 Wootton Pkwy odphpinfo@hhs.gov
Rockville, MD 20852 www.health.gov/nhic
Supports public health education by maintaining a calendar of National Health Observances; helps connect consumers and health professionals to organizations that can best answer questions and provide up-to-date contact information from reliable sources; updates on a yearly basis toll-free numbers for health information, Federal health clearinghouses and info centers.
Don Wright, MD, MPH, Director

1238 **National Osteoporosis Foundation (NOF)**
1232 22nd Street NW 202-223-2226
Washington, DC 20037-1292 webmaster@nof.org
www.nof.org
Dedicated to reducing the widespread prevalence of osteoporosis through programs of research, education and advocacy. Provides referrals to existing support groups, as well as free resources, training and materials to assist people to start groups.
Amy Porter, Executive Director& CEO
Robert R Recker, Chairman of the Board

Journals

1239 **Arthritis Today**
Arthritis Foundation
1330 W Peachtree Strt NW 404-872-7100
Atlanta, GA 30309-2922 800-933-0032
www.arthritis.org
The authoritative and respected source of information for persons with arthritis, their families and health professionals who manage their care. As the official magazine of the Arthritis Foundation, it is backed by the Foundation's experience of 44 years and leadership in the fight against arthritis. This magazine gives its readers the advice, information and inspiration they need to live better with arthritis.

1240 **Osteoporosis Report**
National Osteoporosis Foundation
1150 17th Street, NW 202-223-2226
Washington, DC 20036-1292 800-221-4222
communications@nof.org
www.nof.org
A benefit to members of the National Osteoporosis Foundation (NOF), the Osteoporosis Report includes updates on recent research, strategies for bone health and other information. NOF is the only nonprofit, voluntary health organization dedicated to reducing the widespread prevalence of osteoporosis through programs of research, education and advocacy. Contact the foundation for membership information.

Digital Resources

1241 **Be BoneWise: Exercise**
National Osteoperosis Foundation
1150 17th Street, NW 202-223-2226
Washington, DC 20036-1292 800-221-4222
info@nof.org
www.nof.org
Take steps toward better bones, health, flexibility and balance with the offical weight bearing and strength training exercise video.

1242 **FIT Video**
Arthritis Foundation
550 Pharr Road 404-237-8771
Altlanta, GA 30023-6996 800-933-7023
info.ga@arthritis.org
www.arthritis.org

1243 **In Control**
Arthritis Foundation
1330 W Peachtree Strt NW 404-872-7100
Atlanta, GA 30309-2922 800-283-7800
An excellent at-home program which includes video, audio cassettes and the Arthritis Helpbook. Provides tools to help meet the challenges of arthritis.

1244 **Osteoperosis: The Silent Disease**
National Osteoperosis Foundation
1150 17th Street, NW 202-223-2226
Washington, DC 20036-1292 800-221-4222
info@nof.org
www.nof.org

A scripted, visual presentation covers basic bone biology, osteoperosis risk factors, diagnosis, prevention and treatment. Available as a slide presentation or power point CD Rom.

1245 **PACE I**
Arthritis Foundation
PO Box 6996
Alpharetta, GA 30023-6996
800-207-8633

1246 **PACE II**
Arthritis Foundation
PO Box 6996
Alpharetta, GA 30023-6996
800-207-8633
www.arthritis.com

1247 **Pathways to Better Living**
Arthritis Foundation
PO Box 6996
Alpharetta, GA 30023-6996
800-207-8633
www.arthritis.com

1248 **Patient Education Video**
National Osteoperosis Foundation
1150 17th Street, NW
Washington, DC 20036-1292
202-223-2226
800-221-4222
info@nof.org
www.nof.org

Discusses treatment, exercise, nutrition and coping strategies for those already diagnoses with osteoporosis.

1249 **Pool Exercise Program**
Arthritis Foundation Distribution Center
PO Box 6996
Alpharetta, GA 30023-6996
800-207-8633
www.arthritis.com

This video features water exercises that will help you increase and maintain joint flexibility, strengthen and tone muscles, and increase endurance. All exercises are performed in water at chest level. No swimming skills are necessary.

Web Sites

1250 **American Juvenile Arthritis Organization**
www.arthritis.com

Serves the special needs of young people with arthritis and their families. Provides information, inspiration and advocacy.

1251 **Arthritis Foundation**
www.arthritis.org

Provides services to help through information, referrals, speakers bureaus, forums, self-help courses, and various support groups and programs nationwide.

1252 **Dietary Guidelines for Americans**
www.dietaryguidelines.gov

Publishes the Dietary Guidelines for Americans, a guide providing nutritional advice to promote health and prevent disease. Updated versions of the Dietary Guidelines are released by the US Departments of Agriculture (USDA) and Health & Human Services (HHS) every five years.

1253 **Everyday Health**
www.everydayhealth.com

Aims to provide evidence-based health information from physicians and healthcare providers.

1254 **FamilyDoctor.org**
www.familydoctor.org

Medical advice and information provided by the American Academy of Family Physicians. Resources include a medical dictionary, a symptom checker tool, a BMI calculator, and medication information.

1255 **Healing Well**
www.healingwell.com

An online health resource guide to medical news, chat, information and articles, newsgroups and message boards, books, disease-related web sites, medical directories, and more for patients, friends, and family coping with disabling diseases, disorders, or chronic illnesses.

1256 **Health Finder**
www.healthfinder.gov

Searchable, carefully developed web site offering information on over 1000 topics. Developed by the US Department of Health and Human Services, the site can be used in both English and Spanish.

1257 **Healthline**
www.healthline.com

Provides medical and health articles and information.

1258 **Healthlink USA**
www.healthlinkusa.com

Health information concerning treatment, cures, prevention, diagnosis, risk factors, research, support groups, email lists, personal stories and much more. Updated regularly.

1259 **MedicineNet**
www.medicinenet.com

An online resource for consumers providing easy-to-read, authoritative medical and health information.

1260 **MedlinePlus**
www.medlineplus.gov

A service of the National Library of Medicine, MedlinePlus is an online resource providing health and wellness information in both English and Spanish.

1261 **Medscape**
www.medscape.com

Medscape offers specialists, primary care physicians, and other health professionals the Web's most robust and integrated medical information and educational tools.

1262 **MyPlate**
www.myplate.gov

Created and managed by the US Department of Agriculture's Center for Nutrition Policy & Promotion, MyPlate is a dietary guide providing resources and recipes to promote healthy eating for all Americans.

1263 **NIH Osteoporosis and Related Bone Disease**
www.niams.nih.gov/Health_Info/Bone

Provides patients, health professionals, and the public with an important link to resources and information on metabolic bone diseases. The center is dedicated to increasing the awareness, knowledge, and understanding of physicians, health professionals, patients, underserved and at-risk populations, and the general public about the prevention, early detection, and treatment of osteoporosis and related bone diseases.

1264 **National Arthritis & Musculoskeletal & Skin Diseases Information Clearinghouse**
www.niams.nih.gov

The mission of the National Institute of Arthritis and Musculoskeletal and Skin Diseases is to support research into the causes, treatment, and prevention of arthritis and musculoskeletal and skin diseases; the training of basic and clinical scientists to carry out this research; and the dissemination of information on research progress in these diseases.

1265 **National Osteoporosis Foundation**
www.nof.org

The National Osteoporosis Foundation is dedicated to preventing osteoporosis, promoting strong bones, and reducing human suffering through education, advocacy and research.

1266 **Nutrition.gov**
www.nutrition.gov

Sponsored by the United States Department of Agriculture (USDA), Nutrition.gov offers information on topics in food and nutrition, including healthy eating, physical activity, and food safety.

1267 **Science Daily**
www.sciencedaily.com

Provides information on the latest news and research in science, health, the environment, and technology.

1268 **The Nutrition Source**
hsph.harvard.edu/nutritionsource

From the Harvard T.H. Chan School of Public Health, The Nutrition Source provides news, information, and guidance for nutrition and healthy eating.

1269 **UnlockFood**

www.unlockfood.ca

A website from Dietitians of Canada. Provides videos, recipes, and information on food and nutrition, as well as helps Canadians connect with a dietitian.

1270 **Verywell**

www.verywellhealth.com

Offers health, medicine, and wellness information from health professionals.

1271 **WebMD**

www.webmd.com

Provides credible information, supportive communities, and in-depth reference material about health subjects. A source for original and timely health information as well as material from well known content providers.

SKIN DISORDERS & NUTRITION

The diagnosis of skin disorders requires consultation with a physician or dermatologist. Nutrition management may be a therapy strategy for skin conditions such as acne, psoriasis, rosacea, eczema and others. Some autoimmune disorders can cause skin conditions. Certain foods may trigger skin conditions while others may limit skin flare ups. For allergic skin reactions, food avoidance or elimination diets after testing may be helpful. Healthy eating of whole foods instead of highly processed foods may reduce skin reactions. Consultation with a registered dietician is often part of developing a specific diet approach to skin conditions.

As the largest organ of the body, the skin provides a protective barrier to injury, UV radiation and moisture loss, and aids in temperature regulation, and the production of vitamin D. The three layers of skin are the epidermis or outside layer, the dermis or inside layer, and the subcutaneous layer under the dermis comprised of connective tissue and fat. Skin can be damaged through exposure to irritants, or due to certain autoimmune diseases.

Acne is caused by pores that are clogged with an oily substance called sebum, or by bacteria and dead skin cells trapped in a hair follicle. Usually, the body's oil glands work to push out the offenders, but if the process is interrupted, acne may result. Treatment depends on the type of acne and is best managed by a physician or dermatologist if over-the-counter products are not effective. The American Academy of Dermatology Association reports that a low-glycemic diet may lead to less acne. Cow's milk has been reported to increase acne breakouts, but there is no evidence that yogurt or cheese are similar culprits. A person with acne may be able to identify specific foods or beverages that increase the number of pimples (clogged pores). Eliminating those foods or beverages for a few days to a month may reduce acne.

Psoriasis is an overproduction of skin cells causing visible clumps, patches or spots on the skin. It is not contagious but is a common, chronic condition in people of all ages and races, and requires physician management. Stress, injury to the skin such as an insect bite or sunburn, excess drinking, smoking and exposure to extreme temperature may all cause a flare up of the disease. There are no specific foods associated with the disease, but if a patient is able to correlate particular food with a flare up, elimination of the food is recommended. Eating a healthy, balanced diet is important to support whole body, including skin, health.

Rosacea is a common condition. Early symptoms include the tendency to blush or flush easily, which may then spread to become a more permanent redness on the nose, cheeks, forehead, ears, chin and other areas. There are four main types of rosacea: erythematotelangiectatic (visible blood vessels and redness); papulopustular (acne-like breakouts); phymatous (bumpy and thick skin texture); and ocular (swollen eyelids with a sty appearance). Treatments should be discussed with your physician or dermatologist. Foods associated with rosacea flare ups include alcohol and spicy foods. Other triggers include stress, exercise and certain skin and hair care products. Understanding what triggers rosacea leads to eliminating the causative factors.

Eczema is any condition that causes inflamed, itchy or irritated skin. It may result in contact dermatitis, atopic dermatitis or stasis dermatitis, none of which are contagious. Contact dermatitis occurs when an irritant touches the skin causing an itchy rash or blisters. Touching certain foods, such as fish, lemons, limes or nuts may trigger a skin reaction. When dermatitis erupts, it is important to remember any exposures that may be causative. If over-the-counter medications don't help, consulting with a physician or dermatologist is necessary. Atopic dermatitis, found in 1 in 10 Americans, causes dry, red skin with not one determinable cause. An elimination diet, under care of a physician or dermatologist, may help discover a cause. Stasis dermatitis, occurring in individuals with poor circulation, is often caused by an underlying condition such as heart or vein disease. A healthy diet specific to the patient is often recommended based on allergy testing, the underlying cause, and other factors.

Other skin diseases include skin cancer, athlete's foot and other fungal diseases, hives, changes in skin due to liver, kidney and other diseases, lupus, Lyme disease, and others. All skin related diseases have a nutritional component.

Maintaining a healthy diet and avoiding food or beverages that cause the skin condition to worsen are key to a comprehensive treatment plan. Keeping the skin healthy through diet is important. Salmon, avocados, walnuts and seeds, sweet potatoes, red or yellow bell peppers, tomatoes and broccoli are a few foods that are recommended for healthy skin. Green tea may protect the skin from aging and damage. Red grapes that contain resveratrol protect skin cells from damage. Eating a nutritious, balanced diet can improve skin health by providing the body with sufficient nutrients to maintain and repair the integrity of the largest organ in the body.

Agencies & Associations

1273 **American Academy of Dermatology**
PO Box 1968
Des Plaines, IL 60017
847-240-1280
888-462-3376
mrc@aad.org
www.aad.org
Largest dermatologic association in the world and represents all practicing dermatologists in the United States.
Kenneth J. Tomecki, MD, FAAD, President
Neal Bhatia, MD, FAAD, Vice President

1274 **American Autoimmune Related Diseases Association**
19176 Hall Road
Clinton Township, MI 48038
586-776-3900
aarda@aarda.org
www.aarda.org
Awareness, education, referrals for patients with any type of autoimmune disease.
Molly Murray, President & CEO
Laura Simpson, Chief Operating Officer

1275 **American Skin Association**
335 Madison Avenue
New York, NY 10017
212-889-4858
info@americanskin.org
www.americanskin.org
Organization whose membership includes patients, families, advocates, physicians and scientists working together to cure melanoma, skin cancer and disease.
Howard P. Milstein, Chair
David A. Norris, M.D., President

1276 **American Society for Dermatologic Surgery**
5550 Meadowbrook Drive
Rolling Meadows, IL 60008
847-956-0900
www.asds.net
Exclusively represents dermatologic surgeons to treat the health of skin.
Katherine J. Duerdoth, CAE, Executive Director
Tara Azzano, Director, Development

1277 **American Society of Plastic Surgeons**
444 E Algonquin Road
Arlington Heights, IL 60005
847-228-9900
memserv@plasticsurgery.org
www.plasticsurgery.org
Provides patients with free information about various surgical procedures and also provides the names of board certified plastic surgeons in the patient's area.
Joseph E. Losee, MD, President
Michael D. Costelloe, Executive Vice President

1278 **International Society of Dermatology**
85 High Street
Waldorf, MD 20602
386-437-4405
info@intsocderm.org
www.intsocderm.org
Promotes interest, education and research in dermatology.
George T. Reizner, MD, President
Marcia Ramos-e-Silva, Executive Vice President

1279 **National Eczema Association**
505 San Marin Drive
Novato, CA 94945
415-499-3474
800-818-7546
www.nationaleczema.org
Offers research and information to persons with eczema and other skin disorders.
Julie Block, President & CEO
Scott Sanford, COO

1280 **National Institute of Arthritis & Musculoskeletal & Skin Diseases**
National Institutes of Health
9000 Rockville Pike
Bethesda, MD 20892
301-495-4484
877-226-4267
TTY: 301-565-2966
niamsinfo@mail.nih.gov
www.niams.nih.gov
Supports research into the causes, treatment, and prevention of arthritis and musculoskeletal and skin diseases, the training of basic and clinical scientists to carry out this research, and the dissemination of information on research programs.
Lindsey A. Criswell, MD, MPH, DSc, Director
Robert H. Carter, MD, Deputy Director

1281 **National Institute of General Medical Sciences**
45 Center Drive
Bethesda, MD 20892-6200
301-496-7301
info@nigms.nih.gov
www.nigms.nih.gov
The National Institute of General Medical Sciences (NIGMS) supports basic research that increases understanding of biological processes and lays the foundation for advances in disease diagnosis, treatment and prevention.
Jon R. Lorsch, PhD, Director
Dorit Zuk, PhD, Acting Deputy Director

1282 **Nurse Practitioners in Women's Health**
PO Box 15837
Washington, DC 20003
202-543-9693
info@npwh.org
www.npwh.org
Ensures the delivery and accessibility of primary and specialty healthcare to women of all ages by women's health and women's health focused nurse practitioners.
Heather L. Maurer, CEO
Donna Ruth, Director, Education

Foundations & Research Centers

1283 **Agromedicine Program Medical University of South Carolina**
Medical University of South Carolina
171 Ashley Av.
Charleston, SC 29425-0100
843-792-1414
www.musc.edu
Does research into the effects of pesticides on humans including epidemiology and skin diseases.
Dr Stanley Schuman, Director
W Stuart Smith, Vice President for Clinical Operations a

1284 **American Porphyria Foundation**
4900 Woodway
Houston, TX 77056
713-266-9617
866-APF-3635
www.porphyriafoundation.com
The APF is dedicated to improving the health and well-being of individuals and families affected by porphyria. Our mission is to enhance public awareness about porphyria, develop educational programs and distributing educational material for patients and physicians and support research to improve treatment and ultimately lead to a cure.
Desiree H Lyon, Executive Director
James Young, Chairman

1285 **Dermatology Foundation**
1560 Sherman Avenue
Evanston, IL 60201-4808
847-328-2256
dfgen@dermatologyfoundation.org
www.dermatologyfoundation.org
Raises funds for the control of skin diseases through research, improved education and better patient care. Supports basic clinical investigations.
Janet A. Fairley, MD, President
Bruce U. Wintroub, MD, Chairman

1286 **Duke University Plastic Surgery Research Laboratories**
Medical Center
Box 3974
Durham, NC 27710-1
919-681-8555
elizabeth.yundt@duke.edu
plastic.surgery.duke.edu
Conducts studies on skin cancer and aging skin.
Gregory Georgiade, Chief Division of Plastic and Reconstru
Detlev Erdmann, Associate Professor of Surgery

1287 **Laboratory of Dermatology Research Memorial Sloane-Kettering Cancer Center**
Memorial Sloane-Kettering Cancer Center
1275 York Avenue
New York, NY 10065-6007
212-639-2000
www.mskcc.org/mskcc
Specific studies on the identification of skin disorders and dermatology.
Allan C Halpern, Chief Dermatology Service

1288 **Massachusetts General Hospital: Harvard Cutaneous Biology Research Center**
Massachusetts General Hospital
55 Fruit Street
Boston, MA 02114
617-726-5254
www.massgeneral.org

Dermatology research.
Peter L Flavin, President
John R Hinghman, Secretary

1289 **National Institute of Arthritis & Musculoskeletal & Skin Diseases**
National Institutes of Health
9000 Rockville Drive 301-495-4484
Bethesda, MD 20892 877-226-4267
TTY: 301-565-2966
NIAMSinfo@mail.nih.gov
www.niams.nih.gov
Supports research into the causes, treatment, and prevention of arthritis and musculoskeletal and skin diseases, the training of basic and clinical scientists to carry out this research, and the dissemination of information on research programs.
Lindsey A. Criswell, MD, MPH, DSc, Director

1290 **National Psoriasis Foundation**
6600 SW 92nd Avenue 503-244-7404
Portland, OR 97223-7195 800-723-9166
getinfo@psoriasis.org
www.psoriasis.org
Misson: To find a cure for psoriasis arthritis and to eliminate their devastating effects through research, advocacy, and education. Provides: patient services; public and professional education; community services; government affairs; research.
Randy Beranek, President/CEO
Bill Cardmon, Chief Field Operations

1291 **Orentreich Foundation for the Advancement of Science**
855 Route 301 212-606-0836
Cold Spring, NY 10516-4155 ofas@orentreich.org
http://www.orentreich.org/team
Conducts biomedical research on dermatology.
Norman Orentreich, Founder and Co-Director
David S Orentreich, Co-Director

1292 **Psoriasis Research Institute**
6600 SW 92nd Avenue 503-244-7404
Portland, OR 97223 800-723-9166
getinfo@psoriasis.org
www.psoriasis.org
Studies the causes symptoms and treatments of psoriasis.
Randy Beranek, President/CEO
Bill Cardmon, Chief Field Operations

1293 **Rockefeller University Laboratory for Investigative Dermatology**
Rockefeller University
1230 York Avenue 212-327-7458
New York, NY 10021-6399 www.rockefeller.edu
Research into skin disorders and the whole specialty of dermatology in general.
D Martin Carter MD, PhD, Head

1294 **Scripps Clinic and Research Foundation: Autoimmune Disease Center**
10550 N Torrey Pines Road 858-784-1000
La Jolla, CA 92037-1092 www.scripps.edu
Research into dermatomyostis and polymyositis.
Eng Tan, Professor Emeritus

1295 **Sulzberger Institute for Dermatologic Education**
PO Box 94020 847-330-0230
Palatine, IL 60094-4020 http://www.aad.org/
A nonprofit research center whose sole goal is to enhance patient care through the development and promotion of quality educational programs on the care and disorders of the skin, hair, nails and mucous membranes.
Dirk M. Elston, President
Lisa A. Garner, Vice president

1296 **University of California: San Francisco Dermatology Drug Research**
515 Spruce 415-476-2001
San Francisco, CA 94143-0001 www.ucsf.edu
Conducts clinical testing of new or existing pharmalogic agents used in the treatment of skin disorders.
John Koo MD, Director
Susan Desmond, Chancellor

1297 **University of Texas: Southwestern Medical Center at Dallas, Immunodermatology**
5323 Harry Hines Boulevard 214-648-3111
Dallas, TX 75390-7208 www.utsouthwestern.edu
Provides a focus for research into the causes prevention and management of diseases such as immune deficiencies and infections. Studies are aimed at increasing basic-level understanding of immunologic skin diseases.
Daniel K Podolsky MD, President
Diane Jeffries, Director

1298 **University of Vermont Medical Center**
111 Colchester Avenue 802-847-0000
Burlington, VT 05401 800-358-1144
www.uvmhealth.org/medcenter
Melinda L Estes, MD, President/CEO
Richarad Magnuson, CFO

Support Groups & Hotlines

1299 **National Health Information Center**
Office of Disease Prevention & Health Promotion
1101 Wootton Pkwy odphpinfo@hhs.gov
Rockville, MD 20852 www.health.gov/nhic
Supports public health education by maintaining a calendar of National Health Observances; helps connect consumers and health professionals to organizations that can best answer questions and provide up-to-date contact information from reliable sources; updates on a yearly basis toll-free numbers for health information, Federal health clearinghouses and info centers.
Don Wright, MD, MPH, Director

Journals

1300 **Dermatology Focus**
Dermatology Foundation
1560 Sherman Avenue 847-328-2256
Evanston, IL 60201-4808 dfgen@dermatologyfoundation.org
www.dermfnd.org
Designed to communicate to practitioners the latest advances in medical and surgical dermatology. The publication also serves as the Foundation's newsletter recognizing the accomplishments and activities of the many dermatologists who give not only their monetary support, but countless hours to develop the research and teaching careers of future leaders throughout the specialty.
Michael D. Tharp, President
Bruce U. Wintroub, Chairman

1301 **Dermatology World**
American Academy of Dermatology
P.O. Box 4014 847-240-1280
Schaumburg, IL 60168-4020 866-503-7546
www.aad.org
Offers Academy members information outside the clinical realm. It carries news of government actions, reports of socioeconomic issues, societal trends and other events which impinge on the practice of dermatology.

1302 **International Journal of Dermatology**
International Society of Dermatology
200 1st Street SW 507-284-3736
Rochester, MN 55905-0001 onlinelibrary.wiley.com
Focuses on information for dermatologists and the whole specialty of dermatology research and education.

1303 **Journal of Dermatologic Surgery and Oncology**
International Society for Dermatologic Surgery
930 N Meachan Road 847-240-1005
Schaumburg, IL 60173 www.aad.org
Focuses on medical updates and information on dermatology.
Terrie Duhadway, Executive Publisher

1304 **Journal of the Academy of Dermatology**
American Academy of Dermatology
930 E. Woodfield Road 847-240-1005
Schaumburg, IL 60173-4020 www.aad.org
A scientific publication serving the clinical needs of the specialty and provides a wide selection of articles on various topics impor-

tant to continuing medical education of Academy members and the international dermatologic community.
Terrie Duhadway, Executive Publisher

1305 **Progress in Dermatology**
Dermatology Foundation
1560 Sherman Avenue 847-328-2256
Evanston, IL 60201-4808 dfgen@dermatologyfoundation.org
www.dermfnd.org
The journal provides in-depth coverage of clinically relevant topics as well as basic scientific advances affecting all of dermatology. Distributed exclusively to members of the Foundation.
Michael D. Tharp, President
Bruce U. Wintroub, Chairman

1306 **Psoriasis Advance**
National Psoriasis Foundation
6600 SW 92nd Avenue 503-244-7404
Portland, OR 97223-7195 800-723-9166
getinfo@npfusa.org
www.psoriasis.org
Written especially for the psoriatis community four times a year. Provides current articles to keep you up to date with treatmetnt and research information, pave the way to empowerment, and connect you with others.
40 pages
Krista Kellogg, Chair
Pete Redding, Vice-Chair

1307 **Psoriasis Forum**
National Psoriasis Foundation
6600 SW 92nd Avenue 503-244-7404
Portland, OR 97223-7195 800-723-9166
getinfo@psoriasis.org
www.psoriasis.org
Dedicated to providing up-to-date and practical information to health care providers on the frontline of psoriasis treatment. Professional Members only.
Krista Kellogg, Chair
Pete Redding, Vice-Chair

Digital Resources

1308 **Allergic Skin Reactions**
American Academy of Allergy, Asthma and Immunology
555 East Wells Street 414-272-6071
Milwaukee, WI 53202-3889 800-822-2762
www.aaaai.org
In some people, allergy symptoms include itching redness, rashes, or hives. This video describes the symptoms, triggers, and treatment for common skin reactions such as dermatitis, hives and angioedema.

1309 **Basic Science Series**
American Academy of Dermatology
PO Box 4014 847-240-1280
Schaumburg, IL 60168-4014 866-503-7546
www.aad.org
Combines high-quality 35mm slides and accompanying narration on audiocassette and features topics that underline and support clinical dermatology. The series is useful for residents in training as well as practicing dermatologists.

1310 **CME Video Library**
American Academy of Dermatology
PO Box 4014 847-240-1280
Schaumburg, IL 60168-4014 866-503-7546
www.aad.org
A series of video programs developed by AAD experts recognized for their continued efforts in dermatologic advancement.

1311 **Facts About Acne**
American Academy of Dermatology
PO Box 4014 847-240-1280
Schaumburg, IL 60168-4014 866-503-7546
www.aad.org
The etiology of acne and treatment choices are explained by consultants, with patient encounters.

1312 **Mystery of Contact Dermatitis**
American Academy of Dermatology
PO Box 4014 847-240-1280
Schaumburg, IL 60168-4014 866-503-7546
www.aad.org
The causes and treatment of some common forms of contact dermatitis are shown with consultation and commentary.

1313 **National Library of Dermatologic Teaching Slides**
American Academy Of Dermatology
PO Box 94020 847-240-1280
Palatine, IL 60094-4020 866-503-7546
www.aad.org
A collection of dermatologic teaching slides offering the most comprehensive series ever assembled. Each set offers a realistic presentation of classic clinical skin conditions encountered by the dermatologist.

1314 **Skin Cancer: The Undeclared Epidemic**
American Academy of Dermatology
PO Box 4014 847-240-1280
Schaumburg, IL 60168-4014 866-503-7546
www.aad.org
Examples of skin cancer lesions, interviews with patients at screenings, and comments from Academy members.

1315 **Skin Care Under the Sun**
American Academy of Dermatology
PO Box 4014 847-240-1280
Schaumburg, IL 60168-4014 866-503-7546
www.aad.org
Dramatization of the dangers of overexposure to the sun, providing explanations of the effects of ultraviolet radiation on the skin.

Web Sites

1316 **American Academy of Dermatology**
www.aad.org
Promotes and advances the science and art of medicine and surgery related to the skin, promotes the highest possible standards in clinical practice, education and research.

1317 **American Porphyria Foundation**
www.porphyriafoundation.com
Advances awareness, research, and treatment of the porphyrias; provides self-help services for members; and provides referrals to porphyria treatment specialists.

1318 **American Society of Plastic and Reconstructive Surgeons**
www.plasticsurgery.org
The mission of ASPS is to advance quality care to plastic surgery patients by encouraging high standards of training, ethics, physician practice and research in plastic surgery. The Society is a strong advocate for patient safety and requires its members to operate in accredited surgical facilities that have passed rigorous external review of equipment and staffing.

1319 **Derma Doctor**
www.dermadoctor.com
The most informative skin care site on the Web. An extensive library of newsletters to help answer your questions.

1320 **Dermatology Foundation**
www.dermfnd.org
Raises funds for the control of skin diseases through research, improved education and better patient care. Supports basic clinical investigations.

1321 **Dietary Guidelines for Americans**
www.dietaryguidelines.gov
Publishes the Dietary Guidelines for Americans, a guide providing nutritional advice to promote health and prevent disease. Updated versions of the Dietary Guidelines are released by the US Departments of Agriculture (USDA) and Health & Human Services (HHS) every five years.

1322 **Everyday Health**
www.everydayhealth.com
Aims to provide evidence-based health information from physicians and healthcare providers.

1323 **FamilyDoctor.org**

www.familydoctor.org

Medical advice and information provided by the American Academy of Family Physicians. Resources include a medical dictionary, a symptom checker tool, a BMI calculator, and medication information.

1324 **Healing Well**

www.healingwell.com

An online health resource guide to medical news, chat, information and articles, newsgroups and message boards, books, disease-related web sites, medical directories, and more for patients, friends, and family coping with disabling diseases, disorders, or chronic illnesses.

1325 **Health Finder**

www.healthfinder.gov

Searchable, carefully developed web site offering information on over 1000 topics. Developed by the US Department of Health and Human Services, the site can be used in both English and Spanish.

1326 **Healthline**

www.healthline.com

Provides medical and health articles and information.

1327 **Healthlink USA**

www.healthlinkusa.com

Health information concerning treatment, cures, prevention, diagnosis, risk factors, research, support groups, email lists, personal stories and much more. Updated regularly.

1328 **MedicineNet**

www.medicinenet.com

An online resource for consumers providing easy-to-read, authoritative medical and health information.

1329 **MedlinePlus**

www.medlineplus.gov

A service of the National Library of Medicine, MedlinePlus is an online resource providing health and wellness information in both English and Spanish.

1330 **Medscape**

www.medscape.com

Medscape offers specialists, primary care physicians, and other health professionals the Web's most robust and integrated medical information and educational tools.

1331 **MyPlate**

www.myplate.gov

Created and managed by the US Department of Agriculture's Center for Nutrition Policy & Promotion, MyPlate is a dietary guide providing resources and recipes to promote healthy eating for all Americans.

1332 **National Psoriasis Foundation**

www.psoriasis.org

The National Psoriasis Foundation (NPF) is a non-profit, voluntary health agency dedicated to curing psoriatic disease and improving the lives of those affected.

1333 **Nutrition.gov**

www.nutrition.gov

Sponsored by the United States Department of Agriculture (USDA), Nutrition.gov offers information on topics in food and nutrition, including healthy eating, physical activity, and food safety.

1334 **Science Daily**

www.sciencedaily.com

Provides information on the latest news and research in science, health, the environment, and technology.

1335 **Skin Store**

www.skinstore.com

Carries over 500 of the finest skincare products, available at the lowest prices, delivered immediately to your home.

1336 **The Nutrition Source**

hsph.harvard.edu/nutritionsource

From the Harvard T.H. Chan School of Public Health, The Nutrition Source provides news, information, and guidance for nutrition and healthy eating.

1337 **UnlockFood**

www.unlockfood.ca

A website from Dietitians of Canada. Provides videos, recipes, and information on food and nutrition, as well as helps Canadians connect with a dietitian.

1338 **Verywell**

www.verywellhealth.com

Offers health, medicine, and wellness information from health professionals.

1339 **WebMD**

www.webmd.com

Provides credible information, supportive communities, and in-depth reference material about health subjects. A source for original and timely health information as well as material from well known content providers.

ULCERATIVE COLITIS

Ulcerative colitis (UC) is a type of inflammatory bowel disease (IBD), a group of diseases that affect the gastrointestinal tract. UC affects the large intestine (colon), rectum or both, causing tiny ulcers (sores) on the interior lining of the colon, usually spreading up from the rectum. Diarrhea is usually the first sign of UC, as the bowels move contents rapidly and empty frequently. UC also may cause pain and cramping, rectal bleeding, weight loss, fatigue and problems with defecation, and symptoms usually develop slowly rather than all of sudden. The disease can lead to life-threatening complications and has no known cure, but long-term remission is possible. Symptoms can usually be reduced through treatments such as anti-inflammatory drugs, immune system suppression, biologics, and medications to manage diarrhea. Diet and lifestyle changes can also help manage symptoms and decrease flare-ups of the disease.

Ulcerative colitis (UC) is a chronic inflammatory disease of the large intestine as a result of overreaction of your body's immune system. The sores or ulcers caused by UC cause abdominal pain and diarrhea. Studies have shown that UC could be triggered by the body's response to a viral or bacterial infection in the colon, whereas the body keeps sending infection-fighting white blood cells, long after the infection is cured, causing chronic inflammation and ulcers.

Most people are diagnosed with UC in their mid-thirties with men and women equally affected. Older men are more likely than older women to be diagnosed with the disease. The risk for developing UC increases by 30 percent in individuals with a parent or sibling with the disease. UC affects people of any ethnic or racial group. While UC and Crohn's disease share similar symptoms, Crohn's can affect the GI tract from mouth to the anus while UC affects only the colon and rectum. Different types of UC include ulcerative proctitis (limited to the rectum), left-sided colitis (from the rectum to the splenic flexure), and extensive colitis (affecting the entire colon).

Diagnosis must be made by a physician and includes a medical history, a physical examination, laboratory tests including blood and fecal (stool) testing, X-rays of the GI tract, endoscopy, and a biopsy of the lining of the colon. Medications may be prescribed to suppress inflammation, but diet and nutrition play an important role in managing symptoms. Some foods may aggravate symptoms, and individuals may react differently to foods. A healthy and soothing diet may reduce symptoms and promote healing by replacing nutrients lost to diarrhea. It is important to maintain a healthy diet as the disease often decreases your appetite at a time when you need extra energy to heal your body and maintain normal activities. Diarrhea can prevent your body from absorbing protein, carbohydrates, fat, water, vitamins and minerals, and some physicians may recommend dietary supplements in order to improve nutrition not gained through food.

Your physician will often recommend diet modifications that include soft bland foods rather than spicy foods. Dairy may be restricted if the patient is lactose intolerance. Fiber-rich foods such as fresh fruits, vegetables, whole grains and nuts may make symptoms worse. Some patients feel better eating five or six small meals per day rather than three larger meals. Meals should include a balance of healthy foods and ingredients. It is recommended that those with UC drink plenty of water, avoid alcohol, caffeine and carbonated beverages.

In addition to anti-inflammatory medications, combinations of biologics and immune-modulators may be used. In cases where medication and diet modifications do not work to control the disease, surgery may be considered, which may include removing the colon and rectum, and inserting a pouch (either external or internal) to collect waste. Surgery is a life changing treatment and should be approached carefully.

Managing a diagnosis of ulcerative colitis is physically and mentally stressful, and may limit social engagements due to food limitations or the constant threat of diarrhea. Asking for help from physicians, dieticians, organizations, family and friends is an important step in managing this chronic disease.

Agencies & Associations

1341 **American Academy of Pain Medicine**
1705 Edgewater Drive 800-917-1619
Orlando, FL 32804 Fax: 407-749-0714
info@painmed.org
www.painmed.org
The AAPM is a medical specialty society representing physicians and healthcare professionals practicing in the field of pain medicine. Its mission is to promote and advance pain care, education, training, advocacy, and research.
W. Michael Hooten, MD, President
Farshad M. Ahadian, MD, Treasurer

1342 **American Autoimmune Related Diseases Association**
19176 Hall Road 586-776-3900
Clinton Township, MI 48038 aarda@aarda.org
www.aarda.org
Awareness, education, referrals for patients with any type of autoimmune disease.
Molly Murray, President & CEO
Laura Simpson, Chief Operating Officer

1343 **American Chronic Pain Association**
11936 West 119th Street 913-991-4740
Overland Park, KS 66213-2216 acpa@theacpa.org
www.theacpa.org
The ACPA facilitates peer support and education for individuals with chronic pain in its many forms, in order to increase quality of life. Also raises awareness among the healthcare community, and with policy makers.
Kathy Sapp, Chief Executive Officer
Scott Farmer, Chief Operating Officer

1344 **American Gastroenterological Association**
4930 Del Ray Avenue 301-654-2055
Bethesda, MD 20814 Fax: 301-654-5920
member@gastro.org
www.gastro.org
AGA fosters the development and application of the science of gastroenterology by providing leadership and aid including patient care, research, teaching, continuing education, scientific communication and matters of national health policy.
Tom Serena, Chief Executive Officer
Nancy Chill, Vice President, Business Development

1345 **Centers for Medicare & Medicaid Services**
7500 Security Boulevard www.cms.gov
Baltimore, MD 21244
U.S. federal agency which administers Medicare, Medicaid, and the State Children's Health Insurance Program.
Chiquita Brooks-LaSure, Administrator
Jonathan Blum, COO

1346 **Connecting to Cure Crohn's & Colitis**
Los Angeles, CA www.connectingtocure.org
Raises awareness about Crohn's and colitis, funds research on these diseases, and provides support for patients and their families.
Stacy Dylan, Co-Founder & President
Dana Zatulove, Co-Founder & Vice President

1347 **Crohn's and Colitis Canada**
60 St. Clair Avenue E 416-920-5035
Toronto, Ontario, M4T-1N5 800-387-1479
Fax: 416-929-0364
support@crohnsandcolitis.ca
www.crohnsandcolitis.ca
The mission of Crohn's and Colitis Canada is to improve the lives of individuals affected by Crohn's disease and ulcerative colitis by raising public awareness, providing education, funding research, and advocating to governments and stakeholders.
Lori Radke, President & CEO
Brian Lim, VP, Development & Community Engagement

1348 **Gastrointestinal Society - Canadian Society of Intestinal Research**
231 - 3665 Kingsway 604-873-4876
Vancouver, BC, V5R-5W2 866-600-4875
Fax: 855-875-4429
www.badgut.org
Aims to improve the lives of people with gastrointestinal and liver diseases and disorders by funding research, advocating for patient access to healthcare, and providing evidence-based information for patients.
Gail Attara, Chief Executive Officer
Kwynn Vodnak, Associate Director

1349 **Girls with Guts**
6024 Ridge Avenue info@girlswithguts.org
Philadelphia, PA 19128 www.girlswithguts.org
Works to support and empower women with Crohn's disease and ulcerative colitis or ostomies.
Alicia Aiello, President
Manda Barger, Director, Development

1350 **ImproveCareNow**
Burlington, VT www.improvecarenow.org
ImproveCareNow is a network of patients, families, caregivers, researchers, and healthcare professionals advocating for the improvement of care received by children with Crohn's disease and ulcerative colitis.

1351 **National Institute of Diabetes & Digestive & Kidney Diseases**
9000 Rockville Pike 800-860-8747
Bethesda, MD 20892 TTY: 866-569-1162
healthinfo@niddk.nih.gov
www.niddk.nih.gov
Research areas include diabetes, digestive diseases, endocrine and metabolic diseases, hematologic diseases, kidney disease, liver disease, urologic diseases, as well as matters relating to nutrition and obesity.
Griffin P. Rodgers, MD, MACP, Director
Gregory Germino, MD, Deputy Director

1352 **North American Society for Pediatric Gastroenterology, Hepatology & Nutrition**
714 N. Bethlehem Pike 215-641-9800
Ambler, PA 19002 naspghan@naspghan.org
www.naspghan.org
Promotes research and provides a forum for professionals in the areas of pediatric GI liver disease, gastroenterology, and nutrition. Associated with fellow organizations in Europe and Australia (ESPGAN, AUSPGAN).
Margaret K. Stallings, Executive Director
Kim Rose, Associate Director

1353 **Nurse Practitioners in Women's Health**
PO Box 15837 202-543-9693
Washington, DC 20003 info@npwh.org
www.npwh.org
Ensures the delivery and accessibility of primary and specialty healthcare to women of all ages by women's health and women's health focused nurse practitioners.
Heather L. Maurer, CEO
Donna Ruth, Director, Education

1354 **United Ostomy Associations of America, Inc**
PO Box 525 800-826-0826
Kennebunk, ME 04043 www.ostomy.org
A national network for bowel and urinary diversion support groups in the United States. Its goal is to provide a non-profit association that will serve to unify and strengthen its member support groups, which are organized for the benefit of people who have, or will have intestinal or urinary diversions and their caregivers.
Christine Ryan, Executive Director
Jeanine Gleba, Advocacy Manager

Foundations & Research Centers

1355 **Crohn's & Colitis Foundation**
733 Third Avenue 800-932-2423
New York, NY 10017 info@crohnscolitisfoundation.org
www.crohnscolitisfoundation.org
CCF's mission is to cure and prevent Crohn's disease and ulcerative colitis through research, and to improve the quality of life of children and adults affected by the disease through education and support. The foundation offers patient and professional support.
Michael Osso, President & CEO
Allison Coffrey, Chief Development Officer

1356 **IBD Support Foundation**
8806 Horner Street 310-552-2033
Los Angeles, CA 90035 Fax: 310-552-2025
info@ibdsf.com
www.ibdsf.org
Focuses on providing support, education, and care to patients with Crohn's disease and ulcerative colitis.
Marci Reiss, DSW, LCSW, Founder & President
Adam Sadowsky, Vice President

1357 **NASPGHAN Foundation**
714 N. Bethlehem Pike 215-641-9800
Ambler, PA 19002 naspghan@naspghan.org
www.naspghan.org
The foundation's sole mission is to improve treatment and management of gastrointestinal, hepatobiliary, pancreatic, and nutritional disorders in children.

1358 **The C.H.I.L.D. Foundation**
2150 Western Parkway 604-736-0645
Vancouver, BC, V6T-1V6 Fax: 604-228-0066
www.child.ca
The C.H.I.L.D. Foundation supports research to help children with intestinal and liver disorders, including Crohn's disease and ulcerative colitis.
Mary Parsons, President & CEO

Support Groups & Hotlines

1359 **National Health Information Center**
Office of Disease Prevention & Health Promotion
1101 Wootton Pkwy odphpinfo@hhs.gov
Rockville, MD 20852 www.health.gov/nhic
Supports public health education by maintaining a calendar of National Health Observances; helps connect consumers and health professionals to organizations that can best answer questions and provide up-to-date contact information from reliable sources; updates on a yearly basis toll-free numbers for health information, Federal health clearinghouses and info centers.
Don Wright, MD, MPH, Director

Journals

1360 **Clinical Gastroenterology & Hepatology**
American Gastroenterological Association
4930 Del Ray Avenue 301-654-2055
Bethesda, MD 20814 member@gastro.org
www.gastro.org
Focuses on research, medical and professional developments in the science of gastroenterology.
John I. Allen, President
Michael Camilleri, President-Elect

1361 **Crohn's & Colitis 360**
Crohn's & Colitis Foundation
733 Third Avenue 800-932-2423
New York, NY 10017 info@crohnscolitisfoundation.org
www.crohnscolitisfoundation.org
A peer-reviewed, online, open access journal publishing articles on comprehensive care for patients with IBD, as well as research on prevention, treatment, and cures for IBD.
Miguel Regueiro, MD, Editor-in-Chief
Alan Moss, MD, Deputy Editor

1362 **Gastroenterology**
American Gastroenterological Association
4930 Del Ray Avenue 301-654-2055
Bethesda, MD 20814-3002 member@gastro.org
www.gastro.org
Focuses on research, medical and professional developments in the science of gastroenterology.
John I. Allen, President
Michael Camilleri, President-Elect

1363 **Inflammatory Bowel Diseases**
Crohn's & Colitis Foundation
733 Third Avenue 800-932-2423
New York, NY 10017 info@crohnscolitisfoundation.org
www.crohnscolitisfoundation.org
Peer-reviewed articles on issues and topics in the field of inflammatory bowel disease.
Fabio Cominelli, MD, Ph.D., Editor-in-Chief
Sonia Friedman, MD, Deputy Editor

1364 **Phoenix Magazine**
United Ostomy Association of America
PO Box 512 800-826-0826
Northfield, MN 55057 info@uoaa.org
www.uoa.org
America's leading ostomy patient magazine providing colostomy, ileostomy, urostomy and continent diversion information, management techniques, new products and much more.
Susan Burns, President

Web Sites

1365 **Crohn's & Colitis Foundation**
www.crohnscolitisfoundation.org
CCF's mission is to cure and prevent Crohn's disease and ulcerative colitis through research, and to improve the quality of life of children and adults affected by the disease through education and support. The foundation offers patient and professional support.

1366 **Dietary Guidelines for Americans**
www.dietaryguidelines.gov
Publishes the Dietary Guidelines for Americans, a guide providing nutritional advice to promote health and prevent disease. Updated versions of the Dietary Guidelines are released by the US Departments of Agriculture (USDA) and Health & Human Services (HHS) every five years.

1367 **Everyday Health**
www.everydayhealth.com
Aims to provide evidence-based health information from physicians and healthcare providers.

1368 **FamilyDoctor.org**
www.familydoctor.org
Medical advice and information provided by the American Academy of Family Physicians. Resources include a medical dictionary, a symptom checker tool, a BMI calculator, and medication information.

1369 **Gastrointestinal Society - Canadian Society of Intestinal Research**
www.badgut.org
Aims to improve the lives of people with gastrointestinal and liver diseases and disorders by funding research, advocating for patient access to healthcare, and providing evidence-based information for patients.

1370 **Healing Well**
www.healingwell.com
An online health resource guide to medical news, chat, information and articles, newsgroups and message boards, books, disease-related web sites, medical directories, and more for patients, friends, and family coping with disabling diseases, disorders, or chronic illnesses.

1371 **Health Finder**
www.healthfinder.gov
Searchable, carefully developed web site offering information on over 1000 topics. Developed by the US Department of Health and Human Services, the site can be used in both English and Spanish.

1372 **Healthline**
www.healthline.com
Provides medical and health articles and information.

1373 **Healthlink USA**
www.healthlinkusa.com
Health information concerning treatment, cures, prevention, diagnosis, risk factors, research, support groups, email lists, personal stories and much more. Updated regularly.

1374 **InflammatoryBowelDisease.net**
www.inflammatoryboweldisease.net

Serves to provide tools and resources to help patients, caregivers, and healthcare professionals better manage inflammatory bowel disease.

1375 **MedicineNet**

www.medicinenet.com

An online resource for consumers providing easy-to-read, authoritative medical and health information.

1376 **MedlinePlus**

www.medlineplus.gov

A service of the National Library of Medicine, MedlinePlus is an online resource providing health and wellness information in both English and Spanish.

1377 **Medscape**

www.medscape.com

Medscape offers specialists, primary care physicians, and other health professionals the Web's most robust and integrated medical information and educational tools.

1378 **MyPlate**

www.myplate.gov

Created and managed by the US Department of Agriculture's Center for Nutrition Policy & Promotion, MyPlate is a dietary guide providing resources and recipes to promote healthy eating for all Americans.

1379 **North American Society for Pediatric Gastroenterology, Hepatology & Nutrition**

www.naspghan.org

NASPGHAN strives to improve the care of infants, children and adolescents with digestive disorders by promoting advances in clinical care, research and education.

1380 **Nutrition.gov**

www.nutrition.gov

Sponsored by the United States Department of Agriculture (USDA), Nutrition.gov offers information on topics in food and nutrition, including healthy eating, physical activity, and food safety.

1381 **Science Daily**

www.sciencedaily.com

Provides information on the latest news and research in science, health, the environment, and technology.

1382 **The Nutrition Source**

hsph.harvard.edu/nutritionsource

From the Harvard T.H. Chan School of Public Health, The Nutrition Source provides news, information, and guidance for nutrition and healthy eating.

1383 **United Ostomy Associations of America, Inc**

www.ostomy.org

A national network for bowel and urinary diversion support groups in the United States. Its goal is to provide a non-profit association that will serve to unify and strengthen its member support groups, which are organized for the benefit of people who have, or will have intestinal or urinary diversions and their caregivers.

1384 **UnlockFood**

www.unlockfood.ca

A website from Dietitians of Canada. Provides videos, recipes, and information on food and nutrition, as well as helps Canadians connect with a dietitian.

1385 **Verywell**

www.verywellhealth.com

Offers health, medicine, and wellness information from health professionals.

1386 **WebMD**

www.webmd.com

Provides credible information, supportive communities, and in-depth reference material about health subjects. A source for original and timely health information as well as material from well known content providers.

SECTION THREE: CONDITIONS INDIRECTLY RELATED TO NUTRITION

CANCER

There are almost 200 types of cancer. It can affect almost any organ in the body, and is the second leading cause of death worldwide, with the most common cancers being lung, prostate, colorectal, stomach, liver, breast, cervical and thyroid. A cancer diagnosis places a burden on the individual, their caregivers, the health system and the economy. Up to 50 percent of cancer deaths can be prevented by avoiding or modifying key risk factors and implementing prevention strategies. Maintaining a healthy weight, eating a healthy diet with plenty of fruits and vegetables, avoiding tobacco use, limiting alcohol, practicing safe sex, getting vaccinated against hepatitis B and HPV, reducing sun exposure, avoiding air pollution, and managing chronic infections can all help prevent cancer. Once cancer has been diagnosed and treatments begin, getting adequate nutrition is critical. Many treatments such as chemotherapy and radiation may result in nausea, vomiting and weight loss. The National Cancer Institute's brochure Eating Hints: Before, during and after Cancer Treatment offers information on how to eat well before, during and after cancer treatment, how feelings affect appetite, and foods and drinks to help with eating problems. Consulting with a registered clinical dietician is always recommended. Maintaining appropriate nutrition during treatment for cancer is critical.

Agencies & Associations

1387 **ABCD: After Breast Cancer Diagnosis**
5775 N Glen Park Road 800-977-4121
Milwaukee, WI 53209 www.abcdbreastcancersupport.org
Provides free, personal support and resources to those affected by breast cancer.
Ellen Friebert Schupper, Executive Director
Judy Mindin, Director, Program Services

1388 **American Academy of Pain Medicine**
1705 Edgewater Drive 800-917-1619
Orlando, FL 32804 Fax: 407-749-0714
info@painmed.org
www.painmed.org
The AAPM is a medical specialty society representing physicians and healthcare professionals practicing in the field of pain medicine. Its mission is to promote and advance pain care, education, training, advocacy, and research.
W. Michael Hooten, MD, President
Farshad M. Ahadian, MD, Treasurer

1389 **American Cancer Society**
250 Williams Street NW 800-227-2345
Atlanta, GA 30303 www.cancer.org
A nationwide community based voluntary health organization dedicated to eliminating cancer as a major health problem, by preventing, saving lives, and diminishing suffering through research, education, advocacy, and services. Provides free printed materials.
Karen E. Knudsen, PhD, Chief Executive Officer
William G. Cance, MD, Chief Medical & Scientific Officer

1390 **American Childhood Cancer Organization**
PO Box 498 855-858-2226
Kensington, MD 20895-0498 staff@acco.org
www.acco.org
Founded by parents of children with cancer. The ACCO helps families of pediatric and adolescent cancer patients cope with the educational and emotional needs of the disease. The organization is the largest distributor of free childhood cancer books and other materials.
Ruth I. Hoffman, MPH, Chief Executive Officer
Aubrey Reichard-Eline, Director, Community Engagement

1391 **American Chronic Pain Association**
11936 West 119th Street 913-991-4740
Overland Park, KS 66213-2216 acpa@theacpa.org
www.theacpa.org
The ACPA facilitates peer support and education for individuals with chronic pain in its many forms, in order to increase quality of life. Also raises awareness among the healthcare community, and with policy makers.
Kathy Sapp, Chief Executive Officer
Scott Farmer, Chief Operating Officer

1392 **American Institute for Cancer Research**
1560 Wilson Boulevard 800-843-8114
Arlington, VA 22209 aicrweb@aicr.org
www.aicr.org
Not-for-profit research and educational organization. Provides grants for research into the causes, development, prevention and treatment of cancer through diet and nutrition. Offers publications, research results, conferences and various public services.

1393 **American Society of Colon and Rectal Surgeons**
2549 Waukegan Road 847-607-6410
Bannockburn, IL 60015 ascrs@fascrs.org
www.fascrs.org
ASCRS Represents more than 3,800 board certified colon and rectal surgeons, as well as other surgeons dedicated to advancing and promoting the science and practice of the treatment of patients with cancer, and other diseases affecting the colon and related areas.
Ronald Bleday, MD, President
Rocco Ricciardi, MD, Secretary

1394 **Americas Association for the Care of the Children**
PO Box 2154 303-527-2742
Boulder, CO 80306 aaccchildren.org
Carries out a variety of programs to promote the health of children. Publishes educational materials on child health of interest to parents, educators and health professionals.
Deborah Young, Founder & Executive Director
Judi Jackson, President

1395 **Bone Marrow & Cancer Foundation**
515 Madison Avenue 212-838-3029
New York, NY 10022 800-365-1336
bmcf@bonemarrow.org
bonemarrow.org
Goal is to improve the quality of life for bone marrow and stem cell transplant patients and their families by providing financial aid, education, and emotional support.
Robert Fishman, Chair
Christina Merrill, President & CEO

1396 **Breast Cancer Action**
548 Market Street 415-243-9301
San Francisco, CA 94104-5401 info@bcaction.org
www.bcaction.org
Seeks health justice for women at risk of and living with breast cancer.
Krystal Redman, Executive Director
Jayla Burton, Program Manager

1397 **Breast Cancer Society of Canada**
415 Exmouth Street 519-336-0746
Sarnia, Ontario, N7T-8A4 800-567-8767
bcsc@bcsc.ca
www.bcsc.ca
Funds Canadian research into improving detection, prevention, and treatment of breast cancer, as well as to find a cure, and creates awareness through education.
Antoine Abugaber, Chair

1398 **CanHelp**
PO Box 1678 800-364-2341
Livingston, NJ 07039 joan@canhelp.com
www.canhelp.com
Offers reports for cancer patients on orthodox and alternative therapies and coaching/counseling to help with treatment decision-making and coping.
Joan Runfola, Director

1399 **Canadian Breast Cancer Network (CBCN)**
331 Cooper Street 613-230-3044
Ottawa, Ontario, K2P-0G5 800-685-8820
cbcn@cbcn.ca
www.cbcn.ca
Survivor-directed, national network of organizations and individuals concerned about breast cancer, representing the concerns of all Canadians affected by breast cancer, and those at risk.
Jenn Gordon, Director, Operations
Niya Chari, Director, Public Affairs & Health Policy

1400 **Canadian Cancer Society**
55 St. Clair Avenue W 888-939-3333
Toronto, Ontario, M4V-2Y7 TTY: 866-786-3934
connect@cancer.ca
www.cancer.ca
A national community-based organization of volunteers whose mission is the eradication of cancer and the enhancement of the quality of life of people living with cancer.
Andrea Seale, Chief Executive Officer
Sandra Krueckl, EVP, Mission, Information & Servives

1401 **Cancer Bridges**
2816 Smallman Street 412-338-1919
Pittsburgh, PA 15222 cbteam@cancerbridges.org
www.cancerbridges.org
Provides a wide variety of support services to cancer patients, their families and friends including support groups, education classes, personal counseling and telephone help line.
Dani Wilson, Executive Director
Mia Tamburri, Program Director

1402 **Cancer Control Society**
PO Box 4651 323-663-7801
Modesto, CA 95352-4651 www.cancercontrolsociety.org
An informational organization offering books, films, videos, clinic tours and lists of patients with cancer.
Lorraine Rosenthal, Co-Founder
Frank Cousineau, President

1403 **CancerCare**
275 7th Avenue 212-712-8400
New York, NY 10001 800-813-4673
info@cancercare.org
www.cancercare.org
National non-profit organization that provides free, professional support services for anyone affected by a cancer diagnosis.
Patricia J. Goldsmith, Chief Executive Officer
Christine Verini, RPh, Chief Operating Officer

1404 **Center for Science in the Public Interest**
1220 L Street NW 202-332-9110
Washington, DC 20005 cspi@cspinet.org
www.cspinet.org
The nation's leading consumer group concerned with food and nutrition issues. Focuses on diseases that result from consuming too many calories, too much fat, sodium and sugar such as cancer and heart disease.
Peter Lurie, President
Sara Ghaith, Chief Operating Officer

1405 **Centers for Medicare & Medicaid Services**
7500 Security Boulevard www.cms.gov
Baltimore, MD 21244
U.S. federal agency which administers Medicare, Medicaid, and the State Children's Health Insurance Program.
Chiquita Brooks-LaSure, Administrator
Jonathan Blum, COO

1406 **Childhood Cancer Canada**
20 Queen Street W 416-489-6440
Toronto, Ontario, M5H-3R3 800-363-1062
info@childhoodcancer.ca
www.childhoodcancer.ca
Invests in national, collaborative research into childhood cancer, as well as supporting education and community programs.
Sandi Hancox, Executive Director, Interim
Asha Lewis-Isaacs, Development Officer

1407 **City of Hope**
1500 E Duarte Road 626-256-4673
Duarte, CA 91010 800-826-4673
www.cityofhope.org
City of Hope is an innovative biomedical research, treatment and educational institution dedicated to the prevention and cure of cancer and other life-threatening illness.
Robert Stone, President & CEO
Susan J. Brown, Ph.D., RN, Chief Nursing Officer

1408 **Colorectal Cancer Canada**
1350 Sherbrooke Street W 514-875-7745
Montreal, Quebec, H3G-1J1 877-502-6566
info@colorectalcancercanada.com
www.colorectalcancercanada.com
Seeks to raise public awareness of colorectal cancer, while supporting and advocating for patients. The Colorectal Cancer Association of Canada and Colon Cancer Canada amalgamated in 2017.
Barry D. Stein, President
Carole Brohman, Executive Director

1409 **Foundation for Advancement in Cancer Therapy**
PO Box 1242 info@rethinkingcancer.org
New York, NY 10113 rethinkingcancer.org
Distributes information on cancer prevention and nontoxic therapies for cancer.

1410 **International Association of Laryngectomees**
925B Peachtree Street NE 866-425-3678
Atlanta, GA 30309 office@theial.com
www.theial.com
Consists of local clubs worldwide that provide services and information to patients who have undergone laryngectomies, and their families. Members are given information on first aid, postoperative care, rehabilitation, esophageal speech and other speech alternatives. Directories of speech instructors and self-care supplies for the surgical site are distributed.
Helen Grathwohl, President
Jennifer Malkiewicz, Treasurer

1411 **Kidscope**
2045 Peachtree Road
Atlanta, GA 30309
www.kidscope.org
A nonprofit organization formed to help families and children better understand the effects from cancer in a parent. The name can also be read as Kids Cope - one of the goals being to improve the chances that a child will successfully cope with the diagnosis.

1412 **Leukemia and Lymphoma Society**
3 International Drive
Rye Brook, NY 10573
888-557-7177
www.lls.org
Dedicated to funding blood cancer research, education, and patient services.
Louis J. DeGennaro, Ph.D., President & CEO
Troy Dunmire, Chief Operating Officer

1413 **National Cancer Institute**
9609 Medical Center Drive
Bethesda, MD 20850
800-422-6237
nciinfo@nih.gov
www.cancer.gov
Offers educational information, public awareness, research grants, and more for patients, their families, and health care professionals. Information specialists answer cancer-related questions by phone, LiveHelp instant messaging, and e-mail.
Norman E. Sharpless, MD, Director
Douglas R. Lowy, MD, Principal Deputy Director

1414 **National Coalition for Cancer Survivorship**
8455 Colesville Road
Silver Spring, MD 20910
877-622-7937
info@canceradvocacy.org
www.canceradvocacy.org
Survivor-led advocacy organization working exclusively on behalf of people with all types of cancer and their families. Dedicated to assuring quality and care for all Americans.
Shelley Fuld Nasso, Chief Executive Officer
Woulita Seyoum, Senior Director, Finance & Operations

1415 **National Health Federation**
PO Box 688
Monrovia, CA 91017
626-357-2181
contact-us@thenhf.com
www.thenhf.com
A nonprofit consumer-oriented organization devoted to health matters. Dedicated to preserving freedom of choice in health care issues, prevention of diseases and the promotion of wellness.
Scott C. Tips, President
Gregory Kunin, Vice President

1416 **National Hospice & Palliative Care Organization (NHPCO)**
1731 King Street
Alexandria, VA 22314
703-837-1500
www.nhpco.org
The organization seeks to improve end-of-life care, widen access to hospice care, and improve quality of life for the dying and their loved ones.
Edo Banach, JD, President & CEO
Hannah Yang Moore, MPH, Chief Advocacy Officer

1417 **National Institute on Aging**
31 Center Drive, MSC 2292
Bethesda, MD 20892
800-222-2225
TTY: 800-222-4225
niaic@nia.nih.gov
www.nia.nih.gov
Seeks to understand the nature of aging, and to extend healthy, active years of life. Free resources are available on topics such as Alzheimer's & dimentia, caregiving, cognitive heath, end of life care, and more.
Richard J. Hodes, MD, Director
Luigi Ferrucci, Scientific Director

1418 **National Marrow Donor Program**
500 N 5th Street
Minneapolis, MN 55401-1206
800-627-7692
patientinfo@nmdp.org
bethematch.org
Created to improve the effectiveness of the search for bone marrow donors so that a greater number of bone marrow transplants can be carried out. Operates the Be The Match marrow registry.
Amy L. Ronneberg, Chief Executive Officer
Steven Devine, MD, Chief Medical Officer

1419 **National Ovarian Cancer Coalition**
12221 Merit Drive
Dallas, TX 75251
214-273-4200
888-682-7426
nocc@ovarian.org
www.ovarian.org
Aims to raise awareness about ovarian cancer and to promote education about the disease, while dispelling myths and misunderstandings. The coalition is committed to improving the overall survival rate and quality of life for women with ovarian cancer.
Melissa Aucoin, Chief Executive Officer

1420 **Office of Women's Health**
200 Independence Avenue SW
Washington, DC 20201
202-690-7650
800-994-9662
womenshealth@hhs.gov
www.womenshealth.gov
Government agency under the Department of Health & Human Services, with free health information for women.
Dorothy Fink, MD, Deputy Asst. Secretary, Women's Health
Richelle West Marshall, Deputy Director

1421 **People Against Cancer**
604 E Street
Otho, IA 50569-0010
515-972-4444
info@peopleagainstcancer.org
www.peopleagainstcancer.org
A nonprofit grassroots organization whose mission is to find the best cancer therapy for people with cancer worldwide.
Frank Wiewel, Founder

1422 **Rethink Breast Cancer**
50 Carroll Street
Toronto, Ontario, M4M-3G3
416-220-0700
hello@rethinkbreastcancer.com
www.rethinkbreastcancer.com
A charity helping young people who are concerned about and affected by breast cancer through innovative breast cancer education, research and support programs.
MJ DeCoteau, Founder & Executive Director
Alexandra Hourigan, Senior Events Manager

1423 **Rose Kushner Breast Cancer Advisory Center**
PO Box 757
Malaga Cove, CA 90274
lkkushner@yahoo.com
www.rkbcac.org
Provides a mail service offering referrals to health professionals as well as information about detection, diagnosis, treatment and physical and psychological rehabilitation for patients with breast cancer.

1424 **Support for People with Oral and Head and Neck Cancer (SPOHNC)**
PO Box 53
Locust Valley, NY 11560-0053
800-377-0928
info@spohnc.org
www.spohnc.org
Non-profit organization addressing the broad emotional, physical, and humanistic needs of oral and head and neck cancer patients.
James Sciubba, DMD, PhD, President
Mary Ann Caputo, Executive Director

Alabama

1425 **American Cancer Society: Alabama**
1100 Ireland Way
Birmingham, AL 35205
205-879-2242
www.cancer.org/docroot/com/com_0.asp
The American Cancer Society is the nationwide community-based voluntary health organization dedicated to eliminating cancer as a major health problem by preventing cancer, saving lives and diminishing suffering from cancer, through research and education.
Scarlet Thom (205-930-8889), Media/Public Relations Alabama

1426 **Leukemia and Lymphoma Society: Alabama Chapter**
Leukemia Society of America
100 Chase Park S
Birmingham, AL 35244
205-989-0098
888-560-9700
www.lls.org/aboutlls/chapters/al/
Dedicated to finding cures for leukemia and related cancers and to improving the quality of life for patients and their families.
Melanie Mooney, Executive Director
Kate McLean, Campaign Coordinator, Special Events

Alaska

1427 **American Cancer Society: Alaska**
3851 Piper Street
Anchorage, AK 99508
907-277-8696
leslie.jones@cancer.org
www.cancer.org
The American Cancer Society is the nationwide community-based voluntary health organization dedicated to eliminating cancer as a major health problem by preventing cancer saving lives and diminishing suffering from cancer through research and education.
Leslie Jones, Media/Public Relations Alaska

Arizona

1428 **American Cancer Society: Arizona**
4212 N 16th Street
Phoenix, AZ 85016
602-224-0524
800-227-2345
meg.kondrich@cancer.org
www.cancer.org
The American Cancer Society is the nationwide community-based voluntary health organization dedicated to eliminating cancer as a major health problem by preventing cancer saving lives, and diminishing suffering from cancer through research and education.
Meg Kondrich, Media/Public Relations Arizona

Arkansas

1429 **American Cancer Society: Arkansas**
901 N University
Little Rock, AR 72207
501-664-3480
jodie.spears@cancer.org
www.cancer.org
The American Cancer Society is the nationwide community-based voluntary health organization dedicated to eliminating cancer as a major health problem by preventing cancer, saving lives, and diminishing suffering from cancer, through research and education.
Jodie Spears, Media/Public Relations Arkansas

California

1430 **American Cancer Society Santa Clara County / Silicon Valley / Central Coast Region**
747 Camden Avenue
Campbell, CA 95008
408-871-1062
angie.carrillo@cancer.org
www.cancer.org
The American Cancer Society is the nationwide community-based voluntary health organization dedicated to eliminating cancer as a major health problem by preventing cancer, saving lives and diminishing suffering from cancer, through research and education.
Angie Carillo, Media/Public Relations Silicon Valley

1431 **American Cancer Society: Central Los Angeles**
3333 Wilshire Boulevard
Los Angeles, CA 90010
213-386-6102
katherine.spangle@cancer.org
www.cancer.org
The American Cancer Society is the nationwide community-based voluntary health organization dedicated to eliminating cancer as a major health problem by preventing cancer, saving lives, and diminishing suffering from cancer, through research and education.
Katie Spangle, Media/Public Relations Los Angeles Area

1432 **American Cancer Society: East Bay/Metro Region**
1700 Webster Street
Oakland, CA 94612
510-832-7012
patty.guinto@cancer.org
www.cancer.org
The American Cancer Society is the nationwide community-based voluntary health organization dedicated to eliminating cancer as a major health problem by preventing cancer, saving lives, and diminishing suffering from cancer, through research and education.
Patty Guinto, Media/Public Relations East Bay Area

1433 **American Cancer Society: Fresno/Madera Counties**
2222 W Shaw Avenue
Fresno, CA 93711
559-451-0722
www.cancer.org
The American Cancer Society is the nationwide community-based voluntary health organization dedicated to eliminating cancer as a major health problem by preventing cancer, saving lives, and diminishing suffering from cancer, through research and education.
Erica Jones, Media/Public Relations Fresno CA

1434 **American Cancer Society: Inland Empire**
6355 Riverside Ave
Riverside, CA 92506
951-683-6415
beckie.mooreflati@cancer.org
www.cancer.org
The American Cancer Society is the nationwide community-based voluntary health organization dedicated to eliminating cancer as a major health problem by preventing cancer, saving lives, and diminishing suffering from cancer, through research and education.
Beckie Moore, Media/Public Relations Riverside Region

1435 **American Cancer Society: Orange County**
1940 E Deere Avenue
Santa Ana, CA 92705-5718
949-261-9446
jennifer.horspool@cancer.org
www.cancer.org
The American Cancer Society is the nationwide community-based voluntary health organization dedicated to eliminating cancer as a major health problem by preventing cancer, saving lives, and diminishing suffering from cancer, through research and education.
Jennifer Horton, Media/Public Relations Orange County

1436 **American Cancer Society: Sacramento County**
1765 Challenge Way
Sacramento, CA 95815
916-446-7933
maria.robinson@cancer.org
www.cancer.org
The American Cancer Society is the nationwide community-based voluntary health organization dedicated to eliminating cancer as a major health problem by preventing cancer, saving lives, and diminishing suffering from cancer, through research and education.
Maria Robinson, Media/Public Relations Sacramento County

1437 **American Cancer Society: San Diego County**
2655 Camino Del Rio N
San Diego, CA 92108
619-299-4200
800-227-2345
robin.brown@cancer.org
www.cancer.org
The American Cancer Society is the nationwide community-based voluntary health organization dedicated to eliminating cancer as a major health problem by preventing cancer, saving lives, and diminishing suffering from cancer, through research and education.
Robin Brown, Media/Public Relations San Diego CA

1438 **American Cancer Society: San Francisco County**
201 Mission Street
San Francisco, CA 94105
415-394-7100
patty.guinto@cancer.org
www.cancer.org
The American Cancer Society is the nationwide community-based voluntary health organization dedicated to eliminating cancer as a major health problem by preventing cancer, saving lives and diminishing suffering from cancer, through research and education.
Patty Guinto, Media/Public Relations San Francisco

1439 **American Cancer Society: Santa Maria Valley**
426 E Barcellus
Santa Maria, CA 93454
805-922-2354
jeb.baird@cancer.org
www.cancer.org
The American Cancer Society is the nationwide community-based voluntary health organization dedicated to eliminating cancer as a major health problem by preventing cancer, saving lives and diminishing suffering from cancer, through research and education.
Jeb Baird, Media/Public Relations Santa Maria

1440 **American Cancer Society: Sonoma County**
1451 Guerneville Road
Santa Rosa, CA 95403
707-545-6720
www.cancer.org
The American Cancer Society is the nationwide community-based voluntary health organization dedicated to eliminating cancer as a major health problem by preventing cancer, saving lives and diminishing suffering from cancer, through research and education.
Angie Carillo, Media/Public Relations Central Coast

1441 **Leukemia & Lymphoma Society: Orange, Riverside, And San Bernadino Counties**
2020 E 1st Street
Santa Ana, CA 92705
714-881-0610
888-535-9300
www.leukemia-lymphoma.org
Dedicated to finding cures for leukemia and related cancers and to improving the quality of life for patients and their families.

1442 **Leukemia and Lymphoma Society: Greater Sacramento Area Chapter**
Leukemia Society of America
4604 Roseville Road 916-348-1793
North Highlands, CA 95660 www.leukemia.org
Dedicated to finding cures for leukemia and related cancers and to improving the quality of life for patients and their families.
Tracy Latino, Executive Director

1443 **Leukemia and Lymphoma Society: Greater Los Angeles Chapter**
Leukemia Society of America
6033 W Century Boulevard 310-342-5800
Los Angeles, CA 90045 www.leukemia-lymphoma.org
Dedicated to finding cures for leukemia and related cancers and to improving the quality of life for patients and their families.
Donna Lynch, Executive Director

1444 **Leukemia and Lymphoma Society: Orange, Riverside, And San Bernadino Counties**
2020 E 1st Street 714-881-0610
Santa Ana, CA 92705 888-535-9300
www.lls.org
Dedicated to finding cures for leukemia and related cancers and to improving the quality of life for patients and their families.

1445 **Leukemia and Lymphoma Society: Tri-County Chapter**
Leukemia Society of America
2020 E 1st Street 714-881-0610
Santa Ana, CA 92705 888-535-9300
www.leukemia-lymphoma.org
Dedicated to finding cures for leukemia and related cancers and to improving the quality of life for patients and their families.
John Walter, President & CEO
Louis J DeGennaro, Chief Mission Officer

Colorado

1446 **American Cancer Society: Colorado**
2255 S Oneida Street 303-758-2030
Denver, CO 80224 lynda.solomon@cancer.org
www.cancer.org
The American Cancer Society is the nationwide community-based voluntary health organization dedicated to eliminating cancer as a major health problem by preventing cancer, saving lives and diminishing suffering from cancer, through research and education.
Lynda Solomo, Media/Public Relations Colorado
Joel Quevill, Media/Public Relations Colorado

Connecticut

1447 **American Cancer Society: Connecticut**
Meriden Executive Park 203-379-4700
Meriden, CT 06450 www.cancer.org
The American Cancer Society is the nationwide community-based voluntary health organization dedicated to eliminating cancer as a major health problem by preventing cancer, saving lives and diminishing suffering from cancer, through research and education.
Simone Upsey, Media/Public Relations NH/MS/NL Counties
Christian Me, Media/Public Relations LF/FF Counties

1448 **Leukemia and Lymphoma Society: Connecticut Chapter**
Leukemia Society of America
321 Research Parkway 203-379-0445
Meriden, CT 06450 888-282-9465
www.lls.org/aboutlls/chapters/ct/
Founded in 1949 to help serve and educate the communities and residents who have been touched by leukemia, lymphoma, multiple myeloma and Hodgkin's disease.
Jean Montano, Executive Director
Dina Mariani, Deputy Executive Director

1449 **Leukemia and Lymphoma Society: Fairfield County Chapter**
Leukemia Society of America
25 Third Street 203-967-8326
Stamford, CT 06905 www.lls.org
Dedicated to finding cures for leukemia and related cancers and to improving the quality of life for patients and their families.

Delaware

1450 **American Cancer Society: Delaware**
92 Reads Way 302-324-4427
New Castle, DE 19720 dawn.ward@cancer.org
www.cancer.org
The American Cancer Society is the nationwide community-based voluntary health organization dedicated to eliminating cancer as a major health problem by preventing cancer, saving lives, and diminishing suffering from cancer, through research and education.
Dawn Ward, Media/Public Relations Delaware

1451 **Leukemia and Lymphoma Society: Delaware Chapter**
Leukemia Society of America
100 W 10th Street 302-661-7300
Wilmington, DE 19801 800-220-1617
www.leukemia-lymphoma.org
Our mission is to cure leukemia, lymphoma, Hodgkin's disease and myeloma and to improve the quality of life of patients and their families.
Timothy S Durst, Chairman
James Davis, Vice-Chair

District of Columbia

1452 **American Cancer Society: District of Columbia**
1875 Connecticut Avenue NW 202-483-2600
Washington, DC 20009 www.cancer.org
The American Cancer Society is the nationwide community-based voluntary health organization dedicated to eliminating cancer as a major health problem by preventing cancer, saving lives, and diminishing suffering from cancer, through research and education.
Angela Colli, Media/Public Relations Washington DC

Florida

1453 **American Cancer Society: Florida**
2006 W Kennedy Boulevard 813-254-3630
Tampa, FL 33606 www.cancer.org
The American Cancer Society is the nationwide community-based voluntary health organization dedicated to eliminating cancer as a major health problem by preventing cancer, saving lives, and diminishing suffering from cancer, through research and education.
C. Dunlap, Media/Public Relations Tampa Region
Kristen Redd, Media/Public Relations Tampa Region

1454 **Leukemia & Lymphoma Society: Suncoast Chapter**
3507 E Frontage Road 813-963-6461
Tampa, FL 33607 800-436-6889
www.lls.org
Serves patients with leukemia, lymphoma, multiple myeloma and Hodgkin's disease in Charlotte, Citrus, Collier, DeSoto, Hardee, Hernando, Hillsborough, Lee, Manatee, Pasco, Pinellas and Sarasota counties.

1455 **Leukemia and Lymphoma Society: Southern Florida Chapter**
Leukemia Society of America
3325 Hollywood Boulevard 954-961-3234
Hallandale, FL 33021 www.lls.org
Dedicated to finding cures for leukemia and related cancers and to improving the quality of life for patients and their families.

1456 **Leukemia and Lymphoma Society: Palm Beach Area Chapter**
Leukemia Society of America
4360 Northlake Boulevard 561-775-9954
Palm Beach Gardens, FL 33410 888-478-8550
www.lls.org
Dedicated to finding cures for leukemia and related cancers and to improving the quality of life for patients and their families.

Georgia

1457 **American Cancer Society: Georgia**
50 Williams Street 404-315-1123
Atlanta, GA 30303 elissa.mccrary@cancer.org
www.cancer.org
The American Cancer Society is the nationwide community-based voluntary health organization dedicated to eliminating cancer as a

major health problem by preventing cancer, saving lives, and diminishing suffering from cancer, through research and education.
E. McCrary, Media/Public Relations Georgia

1458 Leukemia and Lymphoma Society: Georgia Chapter
Leukemia Society of America
3715 Northside Parkway 404-720-7900
Atlanta, GA 30327 800-399-7312
dick.brown@lls.org
www.leukemia-lymphoma.org
Dedicated to finding cures for leukemia and related cancers and to improving the quality of life for patients and their families.
Dick Brown, Executive Director
Maureen Quin Davidson, Director TNT

Hawaii

1459 American Cancer Society: Hawaii
2370 Nuuanu Avenue 808-595-7544
Honolulu, HI 96817 800-ACS-2345
TTY: 866-228-4327
milton.hirata@cancer.org
www.cancer.org
The American Cancer Society is the nationwide community-based voluntary health organization dedicated to eliminating cancer as a major health problem by preventing cancer, saving lives, and diminishing suffering from cancer, through research and education.
Milton Hirata, Media Relations Contact - Hawaii

Idaho

1460 American Cancer Society: Idaho
2676 Vista Avenue 208-345-2184
Boise, ID 83705 800-ACS-2345
TTY: 866-228-4327
jim.ryan@cancer.org
www.cancer.org
The American Cancer Society is the nationwide community-based voluntary health organization dedicated to eliminating cancer as a major health problem by preventing cancer, saving lives, and diminishing suffering from cancer, through research and education.
Jim Ryan, Media Relations Contact - Idaho

Illinois

1461 American Cancer Society: Illinois
225 N Michigan Avenue 312-372-0471
Chicago, IL 60601 800-ACS-2345
TTY: 866-228-4327
melissa.leeb@cancer.org
www.cancer.org
The American Cancer Society is the nationwide community-based voluntary health organization dedicated to eliminating cancer as a major health problem by preventing cancer, saving lives, and diminishing suffering from cancer, through research and education.
Melissa Leeb, Media Relations Contact - Illinois

1462 Leukemia and Lymphoma Society: Illinois Chapter
Leukemia Society of America
651 W Washington Boulevard 312-651-7350
Chicago, IL 60661 800-742-6595
pam.swenk@lls.org
www.lls.org
Dedicated to finding cures for leukemia and related cancers and to improving the quality of life for patients and their families.
Pam Swenk, Executive Director
Jennifer Hufnagel, Director Donor Development

Indiana

1463 American Cancer Society: Indiana
5635 W 96th Street 317-344-7800
Indianapolis, IN 46278 800-ACS-2345
TTY: 866-228-4327
leslie.smith@cancer.org
www.cancer.org
The American Cancer Society is the nationwide community-based voluntary health organization dedicated to eliminating cancer as a major health problem by preventing cancer, saving lives, and diminishing suffering from cancer, through research and education.
Leslie Smith Babione, Media Relations Contact - Indianapolis
Katie Burton, Media/Public Relations Indiana

1464 Leukemia and Lymphoma Society: Indiana Chapter
Leukemia Society of America
941 E 86th Street 317-726-2270
Indianapolis, IN 46240 800-846-7764
amy.kwas@lls.org
www.lls.org
Dedicated to finding cures for leukemia and related cancers and to improving the quality of life for patients and their families.
Amy Kwas, Executive Director
Sarah Moore, Deputy Executive Director

Iowa

1465 American Cancer Society: Iowa
8364 Hickman Road 515-253-0147
Des Moines, IA 50325 800-ACS-2345
TTY: 866-228-4327
www.cancer.org
The American Cancer Society is the nationwide community-based voluntary health organization dedicated to eliminating cancer as a major health problem by preventing cancer, saving lives, and diminishing suffering from cancer, through research and education.
Chuck Reed, Media Relations Contact - Iowa

Kansas

1466 American Cancer Society: Kansas City
6700 Antioch 913-432-3277
Merriam, KS 66024 800-ACS-2345
TTY: 866-228-4327
christine.winter@cancer.org
www.cancer.org
The American Cancer Society is the nationwide community-based voluntary health organization dedicated to eliminating cancer as a major health problem by preventing cancer, saving lives, and diminishing suffering from cancer, through research and education.
Christine Winter, Media Relations Contact

1467 Leukemia and Lymphoma Society: Mid-America Chapter
Leukemia Society of America
6811 W 63rd Street 913-262-1515
Shawnee Mission, KS 66202 800-256-1075
janna.lacock@lls.org
www.lls.org
Dedicated to finding cures for leukemia and related cancers and to improving the quality of life for patients and their families.
Janna LaCock, Executive Director
Jill Ring, Development Director

1468 Leukemia and Lymphona Society: Kansas Chapter
Leukemia Society of America
300 N Main 316-266-4050
Wichita, KS 67202 800-779-2417
kelly.gerstenkorn@lls.org
www.lls.org/ks
Cure leukemia, lymphoma, Hodgkin's disease and myeloma and improve the quality of life for patients and their families.
Timothy S Durst, Chairman
James Davis, Vice-Chair

Kentucky

1469 American Cancer Society: Kentucky
701 W Muhammad Ali Boulevard 502-584-6782
Louisville, KY 40203 800-ACS-2345
TTY: 866-228-4327
www.cancer.org
The American Cancer Society is the nationwide community-based voluntary health organization dedicated to eliminating cancer as a major health problem by preventing cancer, saving lives, and diminishing suffering from cancer, through research and education.
Doug Dressman, Executive Director-Louisville

1470 Leukemia and Lymphoma Society: Kentucky Chapter
Leukemia Society of America

600 E Main Street 502-584-8490
Louisville, KY 40202-2661 800-955-2566
karyl.ferman@lls.org
www.lls.org

Founded in 1975 to serve Kentucky and Southern Indiana residents touched by leukemia and its related cancers. Goal is to find a cure for leukemia and its related cancers and to improve the quality of life for patients and their families.
Karyl D Ferman, Executive Director
Katie Anderson, Director Team in Training

Louisiana

1471 American Cancer Society: Louisiana
2605 River Road 504-469-0021
New Orleans, LA 70121 800-ACS-2345
TTY: 866-228-4327
jewel.m.bush@cancer.org
www.cancer.org

The American Cancer Society is the nationwide community-based voluntary health organization dedicated to eliminating cancer as a major health problem by preventing cancer, saving lives, and diminishing suffering from cancer, through research and education.
Jewel M Bush, Media Relations Contact

Maine

1472 American Cancer Society: Maine
1 Bowdoin Mill Island 207-373-3700
Topsham, ME 04086 800-ACS-2345
TTY: 866-228-4327
www.cancer.org

The American Cancer Society is the nationwide community-based voluntary health organization dedicated to eliminating cancer as a major health problem by preventing cancer, saving lives, and diminishing suffering from cancer, through research and education.
Susan Clifford, Media Relations Contact - Maine

Maryland

1473 American Cancer Society: Maryland
8219 Town Center Drive 410-931-6850
Baltimore, MD 21236 800-ACS-2345
TTY: 866-228-4327
www.cancer.org

The American Cancer Society is the nationwide community-based voluntary health organization dedicated to eliminating cancer as a major health problem by preventing cancer, saving lives, and diminishing suffering from cancer, through research and education.
Dawn Ward, Media Relations Contact - Baltimore Area

1474 Leukemia and Lymphoma Society: Maryland Chapter
Leukemia Society of America
11350 McCormick Road 410-527-0220
Hunt Valley, MD 21031-2001 800-242-4572
sharon.yateman@lls.org
www.lls.org

Dedicated to finding cures for leukemia and related cancers and to improving the quality of life for patients and their families.
Sharon E Yateman, Executive Director
Allyson Yospe, Deputy Executive Director

Massachusetts

1475 American Cancer Society: Boston
18 Tremont Street 617-556-7400
Boston, MA 02108 800-ACS-2345
TTY: 866-228-4327
kate.langstone@cancer.org
www.cancer.org

The American Cancer Society is the nationwide community-based voluntary health organization dedicated to eliminating cancer as a major health problem by preventing cancer, saving lives, and diminishing suffering from cancer, through research and education.
Kate Langstone, Media Relations Contact - Boston Area

1476 American Cancer Society: Central New England Region-Weston MA
9 Riverside Road 781-894-6633
Weston, MA 02493 800-ACS-2345
TTY: 866-228-4327
jessica.saporetti@cancer.org
www.cancer.org

The American Cancer Society is the nationwide community-based voluntary health organization dedicated to eliminating cancer as a major health problem by preventing cancer, saving lives, and diminishing suffering from cancer, through research and education.
Jessica Saporetti, Media Relations Contact

Michigan

1477 Leukemia and Lymphoma Society: Michigan Chapter
1421 E 12 Mile Road 248-581-3900
Madison Heights, MI 48071 800-456-5413
peggy.shriver@lls.org
www.lls.org

Peggy Shriver, Executive Director
Robin R Rhea, Director Operations

Minnesota

1478 American Cancer Society: Duluth
130 W Superior Street 218-727-7439
Duluth, MN 55802 800-ACS-2345
TTY: 866-228-4327
janis.rannow@cancer.org
www.cancer.org

The American Cancer Society is the nationwide community-based voluntary health organization dedicated to eliminating cancer as a major health problem by preventing cancer, saving lives, and diminishing suffering from cancer, through research and education.
Janis Rannow, Media Relations Contact

1479 American Cancer Society: Mendota Heights Mendota Heights
Mendota Heights
2520 Pilot Knob Road 651-255-8100
Mendota Heights, MN 55120 800-ACS-2345
TTY: 866-228-4327
lou.harvin@cancer.org
www.cancer.org

The American Cancer Society is the nationwide community-based voluntary health organization dedicated to eliminating cancer as a major health problem by preventing cancer, saving lives, and diminishing suffering from cancer, through research and education.
Lou Harvin, Media Relations Contact
Janis Rannow, Media Relations Contact

1480 American Cancer Society: Rochester
2900 43 Street NW 507-287-2044
Rochester, MN 55901 800-ACS-2345
TTY: 866-228-4327
janis.rannow@cancer.org
www.cancer.org

The American Cancer Society is the nationwide community-based voluntary health organization dedicated to eliminating cancer as a major health problem by preventing cancer, saving lives, and diminishing suffering from cancer, through research and education.
Janis Rannow, Media Relations Contact

1481 American Cancer Society: Saint Cloud
3721 23rd Street S 320-255-0220
Saint Cloud, MN 56301 800-239-7028
TTY: 866-228-4327
www.cancer.org

The American Cancer Society is the nationwide community-based voluntary health organization dedicated to eliminating cancer as a major health problem by preventing cancer, saving lives, and diminishing suffering from cancer, through research and education.
Janis Rannow, Media Relations Contact

1482 **Leukemia and Lymphoma Society: Minnesota Chapter**
5217 Wayzata Boulevard
Golden Valley, MN 55426
763-852-3000
888-220-4440
Murray.Schmidt@lls.org
www.lls.org

Murray Schmidt, Executive Director
Vickie Shaw, Deputy Executive Director

Mississippi

1483 **American Cancer Society: Jackson**
1380 Livingston Lane
Jackson, MS 39213
601-362-8874
800-ACS-2345
TTY: 866-228-4327
kelly.lindsay@cancer.org
www.cancer.org

The American Cancer Society is the nationwide community-based voluntary health organization dedicated to eliminating cancer as a major health problem by preventing cancer, saving lives, and diminishing suffering from cancer, through research and education.
Kelly Lindsay, Media Relations Contact

1484 **Leukemia and Lymphoma Society: Mississippi Chapter**
408 Fontaine Place
Ridgeland, MS 39157
601-956-7447
877-538-5364
Travis.Lee@lls.org
www.lls.org

Travis Lee, Campaign Director Team in Training
Natalie Michael, Campaign Director Team in Training

Missouri

1485 **American Cancer Society: Saint Louis**
4207 Lindell Boulevard
Saint Louis, MO 63108
314-286-8100
800-ACS-2345
TTY: 866-228-4327
christine.winter@cancer.org
www.cancer.org

The American Cancer Society is the nationwide community-based voluntary health organization dedicated to eliminating cancer as a major health problem by preventing cancer, saving lives, and diminishing suffering from cancer, through research and education.
Christine Winter, Media Relations Contact

Montana

1486 **American Cancer Society: Montana**
3550 Mullan Road
Missoula, MT 59808
406-542-2191
800-ACS-2345
TTY: 866-228-4327
jim.ryan@cancer.org
www.cancer.org

The American Cancer Society is the nationwide community-based voluntary health organization dedicated to eliminating cancer as a major health problem by preventing cancer, saving lives, and diminishing suffering from cancer, through research and education.
Jim Ryan, Media Relations Contact

Nebraska

1487 **American Cancer Society: Nebraska**
9850 Nicholas Street
Omaha, NE 68114
402-393-5800
800-ACS-2345
TTY: 866-228-4327
mike.lefler@cancer.org
www.cancer.org

The American Cancer Society is the nationwide community-based voluntary health organization dedicated to eliminating cancer as a major health problem by preventing cancer, saving lives, and diminishing suffering from cancer, through research and education.
Mike Lefler, Media Relations Contact

1488 **Leukemia and Lymphoma Society: Nebraska Chapter**
10832 Old Mill Road
Omaha, NE 68154
402-344-2242
888-847-4974
pattie.gorham@lls.org
www.lls.org

Pattie Gorham, Executive Director
Tonya Schroeder, Patient Services Manager - Portland Area

Nevada

1489 **American Cancer Society: Nevada**
6165 S Rainbow Boulevard
Las Vegas, NV 89118
702-798-6877
800-ACS-2345
TTY: 866-228-4327
paulette.anderson@cancer.org
www.cancer.org

The American Cancer Society is the nationwide community-based voluntary health organization dedicated to eliminating cancer as a major health problem by preventing cancer, saving lives, and diminishing suffering from cancer, through research and education.
Paulette Anderson, Media Relations Contact

New Hampshire

1490 **American Cancer Society: New Hampshire Gail Singer Memorial Building**
Gail Singer Memorial Building
2 Commerce Drive
Bedford, NH 03110
603-472-8899
800-ACS-2345
TTY: 866-228-4327
peter.davies@cancer.org
www.cancer.org

The American Cancer Society is the nationwide community-based voluntary health organization dedicated to eliminating cancer as a major health problem by preventing cancer, saving lives, and diminishing suffering from cancer, through research and education.
Peter Davies, Media Relations Contact

1491 **Leukemia and Lymphoma Society: Mountain States Chapter**
Leukemia Society of America
3411 Candelaria NE
Albuquerque, NM 87107
505-872-0141
888-286-7846
gina.panas@lls.org
www.lls.org

Dedicated to finding cures for leukemia and related cancers and to improving the quality of life for patients and their families. Serves New Mexico and the Greater El Paso, TX area.
Deborah Hoffman, Executive Director
Mikki Aronoff, Patient Services Manager - Portland Area

New Jersey

1492 **American Cancer Society: New Jersey**
2600 US Highway 1
N Brunswick, NJ 08902
732-297-8000
800-ACS-2345
TTY: 866-228-4327
marjorie.kaplan@cancer.org
www.cancer.org

The American Cancer Society is the nationwide community-based voluntary health organization dedicated to eliminating cancer as a major health problem by preventing cancer, saving lives, and diminishing suffering from cancer, through research and education.
Marjorie Kaplan, Media Relations Contact

New Mexico

1493 **American Cancer Society: New Mexico**
10501 Montgomery Boulevard NE
Albuquerque, NM 87111
505-260-2105
800-ACS-2345
TTY: 866-228-4327
john.weisgerber@cancer.org
www.cancer.org

The American Cancer Society is the nationwide community-based voluntary health organization dedicated to eliminating cancer as a major health problem by preventing cancer, saving lives, and diminishing suffering from cancer, through research and education.
John Weisgerber, Media Relations Contact

New York

1494 **American Cancer Society: Central New York Region/East Syracuse**
6725 Lyons Street
E Syracuse, NY 13057
315-437-7025
800-ACS-2345
TTY: 866-228-4327
kim.mcmahon@cancer.org
www.cancer.org

The American Cancer Society is the nationwide community-based voluntary health organization dedicated to eliminating cancer as a major health problem by preventing cancer, saving lives, and diminishing suffering from cancer, through research and education.
Kim McMahon, Media Relations Contact

1495 **American Cancer Society: Long Island**
75 Davids Drive 631-436-7070
Hauppauge, NY 11788 800-ACS-2345
TTY: 866-228-4327
jennifer.cucurullo@cancer.org
www.cancer.org
The American Cancer Society is the nationwide community-based voluntary health organization dedicated to eliminating cancer as a major health problem by preventing cancer, saving lives, and diminishing suffering from cancer, through research and education.
Jennifer Cucurullo, Media Relations Contact

1496 **American Cancer Society: New York City**
132 W 32nd Street 212-586-8700
New York, NY 10001-3983 800-ACS-2345
TTY: 866-228-4327
jennifer.cucurullo@cancer.org
www.cancer.org
The American Cancer Society is the nationwide community-based voluntary health organization dedicated to eliminating cancer as a major health problem by preventing cancer, saving lives, and diminishing suffering from cancer, through research and education.
Jennifer Cucurullo, Media Relations Contact

1497 **American Cancer Society: Queens Region / Rego Park**
97-99 Queens Boulevard 718-263-2224
Rego Park, NY 11374 800-ACS-2345
TTY: 866-228-4327
jennifer.cucurullo@cancer.org
www.cancer.org
The American Cancer Society is the nationwide community-based voluntary health organization dedicated to eliminating cancer as a major health problem by preventing cancer, saving lives, and diminishing suffering from cancer, through research and education.
Jennifer Cucurullo, Media Relations Contact

1498 **American Cancer Society: Westchester Region/White Plains**
2 Lyon Place 914-949-4800
White Plains, NY 10601 800-ACS-2345
TTY: 866-228-4327
jennifer.cucurullo@cancer.org
www.cancer.org
The American Cancer Society is the nationwide community-based voluntary health organization dedicated to eliminating cancer as a major health problem by preventing cancer, saving lives, and diminishing suffering from cancer, through research and education.
Jennifer Cucurullo, Media Relations Contact

1499 **Leukemia & Lymphoma Society Chapter: New York City**
475 Park Avenue S 212-376-7100
New York, NY 10016 800-955-4572
ossom@lls.org
www.leukemia-lymphoma.org
Dedicated to finding cures for leukemia and related cancers and to improving the quality of life for patients and their families. Educational materials, support services and financial aid available. Volunteer opportunities.
Michael Osso, Executive Director
Sara Lipsky, Deputy Executive Director

1500 **Leukemia & Lymphoma Society: Westchester/ Hudson Valley Chapter**
1311 Mamaroneck Avenue 914-949-0084
White Plains, NY 10605 www.lls.org/wch
Mission is to cure leukemia, lymphoma, Hodgkin's disease and myeloma, and to improve the quality of life of patients and their families.
Dennis P Chillemi, Executive Director
Diandra Kodl, Deputy Executive Director

1501 **Leukemia and Lymphoma Society Chapter: New York City**
475 Park Avenue S 212-376-7100
New York, NY 10016 800-955-4572
ossom@lls.org
www.leukemia-lymphoma.org
Dedicated to finding cures for leukemia and related cancers and to improving the quality of life for patients and their families. Educational materials, support services and financial aid available. Volunteer opportunities.
Michael Osso, Executive Director
Sara Lipsky, Deputy Executive Director

1502 **Leukemia and Lymphoma Society: Central New York Chapter**
Leukemia Society of America
401 N Salina Street 315-471-1050
Syracuse, NY 13203 800-690-8944
chip.lockwood@lls.org
www.lls.org
Dedicated to finding cures for leukemia and related cancers and to improving the quality of life for patients and their families.
Chip Lockwood, Executive Director
Kristen Duggleby, Campaign Director Donor Relations

1503 **Leukemia and Lymphoma Society: Long Island Chapter**
Leukemia Society of America
555 Broadhollow Road 631-752-8500
Melville, NY 11747 tammy.philie@lls.org
www.lls.org
Established to serve Long Islanders with leukemia, lymphoma, Hodgkin's disease and myeloma, their families and friends.
Tammy Philie, Executive Director
Nicole Kowaleski, Deputy Executive Director

1504 **Leukemia and Lymphoma Society: Upstate New York Chapter**
Leukemia Society of America
5 Computer Drive W 518-438-3583
Albany, NY 12205 866-255-3583
Maureen.Thornton@lls.org
www.lls.org
Dedicated to finding cures for leukemia and related cancers and to improving the quality of life for patients and their families.
Maureen O'Brien-Thor, Executive Director
Raechel Hunt, Patient Services Manager - Portland Area

1505 **Leukemia and Lymphoma Society: Western New York & Finger Lakes Chapter**
Leukemia Society of America
4053 Maple Road 716-834-2578
Amherst, NY 14226 800-784-2368
nancy.hails@lls.org
www.lls.org
Dedicated to finding cures for leukemia and related cancers and to improving the quality of life for patients and their families.
Nancy Hails, Executive Director
Luann Burgio, Deputy Executive Director

North Carolina

1506 **American Cancer Society: North Carolina**
8300 Health Park 919-334-5218
Raleigh, NC 27615 800-ACS-2345
TTY: 866-228-4327
www.cancer.org
The American Cancer Society is the nationwide community-based voluntary health organization dedicated to eliminating cancer as a major health problem by preventing cancer, saving lives, and diminishing suffering from cancer, through research and education.
Jeff Bright, Media Relations Contact

1507 **Leukemia and Lymphoma Society: North Carolina Chapter**
Leukemia Society of America
5950 Fairview Road 704-998-5012
Charlotte, NC 28210 800-888-9934
www.lls.org
Dedicated to finding cures for leukemia and related cancers and to improving the quality of life for patients and their families.
Tiffany Armstrong, Executive Director
Loreal Massiah, Patient Services Manager - Portland Area

North Dakota

1508 **American Cancer Society: North Dakota**
4646 Amber Valley Parkway
Fargo, ND 58104
701-232-1385
800-ACS-2345
TTY: 866-228-4327
jim.ryan@cancer.org
www.cancer.org

The American Cancer Society is the nationwide community-based voluntary health organization dedicated to eliminating cancer as a major health problem by preventing cancer, saving lives, and diminishing suffering from cancer, through research and education.
Jim Ryan, Media Relations Contact

Ohio

1509 **American Cancer Society: Ohio**
870 Michigan Avenue
Columbus, OH 43215
888-227-6446
TTY: 866-228-4327
www.cancer.org

The American Cancer Society is the nationwide community-based voluntary health organization dedicated to eliminating cancer as a major health problem by preventing cancer, saving lives, and diminishing suffering from cancer, through research and education.
Robert Paschen, Media Relations Contact

1510 **Leukemia and Lymphoma Society: Northern Ohio Chapter**
Leukemia Society of America
23297 Commerce Park
Cleveland, OH 44122
216-910-1200
800-589-5721
frank.canning@lls.org
www.lls.org

Dedicated to finding cures for leukemia and related cancers and to improving the quality of life for patients and their families.
Frank Canning, Field Director
Nancy Toghill, Office Manager

1511 **Leukemia and Lymphoma Society: Southern Ohio Chapter**
Leukemia Society of America
4370 Glendale Milford Rd
Cincinnati, OH 45242
513-698-2828
michelle.steed@lls.org
www.lls.org

Dedicated to finding cures for leukemia and related cancers and to improving the quality of life for patients and their families. This chapter serves a 22-county geographic area.
Michelle Steed, Executive Director
Gene Fisher, Operations Director

Oklahoma

1512 **American Cancer Society: Oklahoma**
6525 N Meridian
Oklahoma City, OK 73116
405-843-9888
800-ACS-2345
TTY: 866-228-4327
www.cancer.org

The American Cancer Society is the nationwide community-based voluntary health organization dedicated to eliminating cancer as a major health problem by preventing cancer, saving lives, and diminishing suffering from cancer, through research and education.
Christina Li, Media/Public Relations

1513 **Leukemia and Lymphoma Society: Oklahoma Chapter**
Leukemia Society of America
500 N Broadway
Oklahoma City, OK 73102
405-943-8888
888-828-4572
sherry.martin@lls.org
www.lls.org

Dedicated to finding cures for leukemia and related cancers and to improving the quality of life for patients and their families.
Sherry Marti MSW LCSW, Patient Services Manager - Portland Area
Jill Hull, Campaign Director Team in Training

Oregon

1514 **American Cancer Society: Oregon**
330 SW Curry Street
Portland, OR 97239
503-295-6422
800-ACS-2345
TTY: 866-228-4327
www.cancer.org

The American Cancer Society is the nationwide community-based voluntary health organization dedicated to eliminating cancer as a major health problem by preventing cancer, saving lives, and diminishing suffering from cancer, through research and education.
Gretchen Rosenberger, Media Relations Contact

1515 **Leukemia and Lymphoma Society: Oregon Chapter**
Leukemia Society of America
9320 SWBarbur Boulevard
Portland, OR 97219
503-245-9866
800-466-6572
Sarah.Varner@lls.org
www.lls.org

Dedicated to finding cures for leukemia and related cancers and to improving the quality of life for patients and their families.
Sarah Varner, Executive Director
Sue Sumpter, Patient Services Manager - Portland Area

Pennsylvania

1516 **American Cancer Society: Harrisburg Capital Area Unit**
Capital Area Unit
3211 N Front Street
Harrisburg, PA 17110
215-985-5336
888-227-5445
TTY: 866-228-4327
john.held@cancer.org
www.cancer.org

The American Cancer Society is the nationwide community-based voluntary health organization dedicated to eliminating cancer as a major health problem by preventing cancer, saving lives, and diminishing suffering from cancer, through research and education.
Colleen Fitz, Media Relations Contact
John Held, Media Relations Contact

1517 **American Cancer Society: Philadelphia**
1626 Locust Street
Philadelphia, PA 19103
215-985-5336
888-227-5445
TTY: 866-228-4327
john.held@cancer.org
www.cancer.org

The American Cancer Society is the nationwide community-based voluntary health organization dedicated to eliminating cancer as a major health problem by preventing cancer, saving lives, and diminishing suffering from cancer, through research and education.
John Held, Media Relations Contact
Colleen Fitz, Media/Public Relations

1518 **American Cancer Society: Pittsburgh**
320 Bilmar Drive
Pittsburgh, PA 15205
215-985-5336
888-227-5445
TTY: 866-228-4327
www.cancer.org

The American Cancer Society is the nationwide community-based voluntary health organization dedicated to eliminating cancer as a major health problem by preventing cancer, saving lives, and diminishing suffering from cancer, through research and education.
Dan Catena, Media Relations Contact

1519 **Leukemia and Lymphoma Society: Central Pennsylvania Chapter**
800 Corporate Circle
Harrisburg, PA 17110
717-652-6520
800-822-2873
beth.mihmet@lls.org
www.lls.org

Elizabeth Mihmet, Executive Director
Danielle Bubnis, Patient Services Manager

1520 **Leukemia and Lymphoma Society: Eastern Pennsylvania Chapter**
555 N Lane
Conshohocken, PA 19428
610-238-0360
800-482-CURE
ursula.raczak@lls.org
www.lls.org

Lydia Hernandez-Vele, Executive Director
Ursula Raczak, Deputy Executive Director

1521 **Leukemia and Lymphoma Society: Western Pennsylvania/West Virginia Chapter**
Leukemia Society of America

333 E Carson Street 412-395-2873
Pittsburgh, PA 15219-1439 800-726-2873
massaric@lls.org
www.lls.org

Tina Massari, Executive Director
Jeanne Caliguiri, Development Director

Rhode Island

1522 **American Cancer Society: Rhode Island**
931 Jefferson Boulevard 401-722-8480
Warwick, RI 02886 800-ACS-2345
TTY: 866-228-4327
jim.beardsworth@cancer.org
www.cancer.org
The American Cancer Society is the nationwide community-based voluntary health organization dedicated to eliminating cancer as a major health problem by preventing cancer, saving lives, and diminishing suffering from cancer, through research and education.
Jim Beardsworth, Media Relations Contact

1523 **Leukemia and Lymphoma Society: Rhode Island Chapter**
1210 Pontiac Avenue 401-943-8888
Cranston, RI 02920 koconisb@lls.org
www.lls.org

Bill Koconis, Executive Director
Gloria Hincapie, Patient Services Manager

South Carolina

1524 **American Cancer Society: South Carolina**
128 Stonemark Lane 803-750-1693
Columbia, SC 29210 800-ACS-2345
TTY: 866-228-4327
mjwardle@cancer.org
www.cancer.org
The American Cancer Society is the nationwide community-based voluntary health organization dedicated to eliminating cancer as a major health problem by preventing cancer, saving lives, and diminishing suffering from cancer, through research and education.
Mary Jane Wardle, Media Relations Contact

1525 **Leukemia and Lymphoma Society: South Carolina Chapter**
1247 Lake Murray Boulevard 803-749-4299
Irmo, SC 29063 www.lls.org

South Dakota

1526 **American Cancer Society: South Dakota**
4904 S Technopolis Drive 605-361-8277
Sioux Falls, SD 57106 800-ACS-2345
TTY: 866-228-4327
www.cancer.org
The American Cancer Society is the nationwide community-based voluntary health organization dedicated to eliminating cancer as a major health problem by preventing cancer, saving lives, and diminishing suffering from cancer, through research and education.
Charlotte Ho, Media Relations Contact

Tennessee

1527 **American Cancer Society: Tennessee**
2000 Charlotte Avenue 615-327-0991
Nashville, TN 37203 800-ACS-2345
TTY: 866-228-4327
www.cancer.org
The American Cancer Society is the nationwide community-based voluntary health organization dedicated to eliminating cancer as a major health problem by preventing cancer, saving lives, and diminishing suffering from cancer, through research and education.
Brian Gillespie, Media Relations Contact

1528 **Leukemia & Lymphoma Society: Tennessee Chapter**
404 BNA Drive 615-331-2980
Nashville, TN 37217 800-332-2980
winslowm@tn.leukemia-lymphoma.org
www.leukemia-lymphoma.org
Founded in 1982 to better serve the needs of Tennesseans. Offers contribution funded community services, family support groups, free educational materials and financial assistance for those affected by leukemia, Hodgkin's disease, myeloma and lymphomas.
Colleen Grady, Executive Director
Mary Winslow, Patient Services Manager

Texas

1529 **American Cancer Society: Texas**
2433 Ridgepoint Drive 512-919-1800
Austin, TX 78754 800-ACS-2345
TTY: 866-228-4327
justine.hall@cancer.org
www.cancer.org
The American Cancer Society is the nationwide community-based voluntary health organization dedicated to eliminating cancer as a major health problem by preventing cancer, saving lives, and diminishing suffering from cancer, through research and education.
Justin Hall, Media Relations Contact

1530 **Leukemia and Lymphoma Society: North Texas Chapter**
Leukemia Society of America
8111 LBJ Freeway 972-239-0959
Dallas, TX 75251 800-800-6702
Tina.Garcia@lls.org
www.lls.org
Dedicated to finding cures for leukemia and related cancers and to improving the quality of life for patients and their families.
Tina Garcia, Executive Director
Sarah Bayley, Donor Development Director

1531 **Leukemia and Lymphoma Society: South/West Texas Chapter**
Leukemia Society of America
431 Isom Road 210-377-1775
San Antonio, TX 78216-4170 800-683-2458
www.lls.org
Dedicated to finding cures for leukemia and related cancers and to improving the quality of life for patients and their families.
Jon Walter, President/CEO
Jimmy Nangle, CFO

1532 **Leukemia and Lymphoma Society: Texas Gulf Coast Chapter**
Leukemia Society of America
5005 Mitchelldale 713-680-8088
Houston, TX 77092 BillieSue.Parris@lls.org
www.lls.org
Dedicated to finding cures for leukemia and related cancers and to improving the quality of life for patients and their families.
Billie Sue Parris, Executive Director
Jane Thompson, Office Manager

Utah

1533 **American Cancer Society: Utah**
941 E 3300 S 801-483-1500
Salt Lake City, UT 84106 800-ACS-2345
TTY: 866-228-4327
patricia.monsoor@cancer.org
www.cancer.org
The American Cancer Society is the nationwide community-based voluntary health organization dedicated to eliminating cancer as a major health problem by preventing cancer, saving lives, and diminishing suffering from cancer, through research and education.
Patricia Monsoor, Media Relations Contact

Vermont

1534 **American Cancer Society: Vermont**
121 Connor Way 802-872-6300
Williston, VT 05495 800-ACS-2345
TTY: 866-228-4327
www.cancer.org
The American Cancer Society is the nationwide community-based voluntary health organization dedicated to eliminating cancer as a major health problem by preventing cancer, saving lives, and diminishing suffering from cancer, through research and education.
Chris Falk, Media Relations Contact

Virginia

1535 **American Cancer Society: Virginia**
4240 Park Place Court 804-527-3700
Glen Allen, VA 23060 800-ACS-2345
TTY: 866-228-4327
domenick.casuccio@cancer.org
www.cancer.org
The American Cancer Society is the nationwide community-based voluntary health organization dedicated to eliminating cancer as a major health problem by preventing cancer, saving lives, and diminishing suffering from cancer, through research and education.
Domenick Casuccio, Media Relations Contact

1536 **Leukemia and Lymophoma Society: National Capital Area Chapter**
Leukemia Society of America
5845 Richmond Highway 703-399-2900
Alexandria, VA 22303 donna.mckelvey@lls.org
www.lls.org
Serves the greater Washington DC metropolitan area including Northern Virginia Prince George's and Montgomery counties.
Gabrielle Urquhart, Executive Director
Beth Gorman, Deputy Director

Washington

1537 **American Cancer Society: Washington**
728 134th Street SW 425-741-8949
Everett, WA 98204 liz.lamb-ferro@cancer.org
www.cancer.org
The American Cancer Society is the nationwide community-based voluntary health organization dedicated to eliminating cancer as a major health problem by preventing cancer, saving lives, and diminishing suffering from cancer, through research and education.
Liz Lamb-Ferro, Media Relations Contact

1538 **Washington Leukemia and Lymphoma Society**
Leukemia Society of America
530 Dexter Avenue N 206-628-0777
Seattle, WA 98109 888-345-4572
wachapter@lls.org
www.leukemia-lymphoma.org
Dedicated to finding cures for leukemia and related cancers and to improving the quality of life for patients and their families.
Anne Gillingham, Executive Director
Kimberly Conn, Deputy Executive Director

West Virginia

1539 **American Cancer Society: West Virginia**
301 RHL Boulevard 304-746-9950
Charleston, WV 25309 800-ACS-2345
TTY: 866-228-4327
www.cancer.org
The American Cancer Society is the nationwide community-based voluntary health organization dedicated to eliminating cancer as a major health problem by preventing cancer, saving lives, and diminishing suffering from cancer, through research and education.
Amy Wentz Berner, Media Relations Contact

Wisconsin

1540 **American Cancer Society: Wisconsin**
N19 W24350 Riverwood Drive 262-523-5500
Waukesha, WI 53188 800-ACS-2345
TTY: 866-228-4327
peter.balistrieri@cancer.org
www.acscan.org/action/wi
The American Cancer Society is the nationwide community-based voluntary health organization dedicated to eliminating cancer as a major health problem by preventing cancer, saving lives, and diminishing suffering from cancer, through research and education.
Peter Balistrieri, Media Relations Contact
Christopher Hansen, President, ACS CAN

1541 **Leukemia and Lymphoma Society: Wisconsin Chapter**
Leukemia Society of America
200 S Executive Drive 262-790-4701
Brookfield, WI 53005 800-261-7399
bede.barthpotter@lls.org
www.lls.org
Founded in 1963 to serve Wisconsites touched by leukemia, lymphoma, Hodgkin's disease and myeloma.
Bede Barth Potter, Executive Director
Karen Ropel, Deputy Executive Director

Wyoming

1542 **American Cancer Society: Wyoming**
333 S Beech Street 307-577-4892
Casper, WY 82601 800-ACS-2345
TTY: 866-228-4327
joel.quevillon@cancer.org
www.acscan.org
The American Cancer Society is the nationwide community-based voluntary health organization dedicated to eliminating cancer as a major health problem by preventing cancer, saving lives, and diminishing suffering from cancer, through research and education.
John R Seffrin, CEO,ACS
Christopher Hansen, President, ACS CAN

Web Sites

1543 **American Academy of Dermatology**
www.aad.org
An organization of doctors who specialize in diagnosing and treating skin problems.

1544 **American Cancer Society**
www.cancer.org
Provides free printed materials, offers a range of services to patients and their families.

1545 **American Society of Colon and Rectal Surgeons**
www.fascrs.org
ASCRS Represents more than 3,800 board certified colon and rectal surgeons, as well as other surgeons dedicated to advancing and promoting the science and practice of the treatment of patients with cancer, and other diseases affecting the colon and related areas.

1546 **Association for the Cure of Cancer of the Prostate**
www.capcure.org

1547 **Bone Marrow & Cancer Foundation**
bonemarrow.org
Goal is to improve the quality of life for bone marrow and stem cell transplant patients and their families by providing financial aid, education, and emotional support.
Christina Merrill, President & CEO
Robert Fishman, Chair

1548 **Dietary Guidelines for Americans**
www.dietaryguidelines.gov
Publishes the Dietary Guidelines for Americans, a guide providing nutritional advice to promote health and prevent disease. Updated versions of the Dietary Guidelines are released by the US Departments of Agriculture (USDA) and Health & Human Services (HHS) every five years.

1549 **Everyday Health**
www.everydayhealth.com
Aims to provide evidence-based health information from physicians and healthcare providers.

1550 **FamilyDoctor.org**
www.familydoctor.org
Medical advice and information provided by the American Academy of Family Physicians. Resources include a medical dictionary, a symptom checker tool, a BMI calculator, and medication information.

1551 **Healing Well**
www.healingwell.com
An online health resource guide to medical news, chat, information and articles, newsgroups and message boards, books, disease-related web sites, medical directories, and more for patients,

friends, and family coping with disabling diseases, disorders, or chronic illnesses.

1552 **Health Finder**
www.healthfinder.gov
Searchable, carefully developed web site offering information on over 1000 topics. Developed by the US Department of Health and Human Services, the site can be used in both English and Spanish.

1553 **Healthline**
www.healthline.com
Provides medical and health articles and information.

1554 **Healthlink USA**
www.healthlinkusa.com
Health information concerning treatment, cures, prevention, diagnosis, risk factors, research, support groups, email lists, personal stories and much more. Updated regularly.

1555 **Hormone Health Network**
www.hormone.org
Online support and resources for patients, with focus on hormone health, disease and treatment. Provided by the Endocrine Society.

1556 **Leukemia and Lymphoma Society**
www.leukemia.org
A national voluntary health agency dedicated to curing leukemia, lymphoma, Hodgkin's disease and myeloma and to improving the quality of life of patients and their families.

1557 **MedicineNet**
www.medicinenet.com
An online resource for consumers providing easy-to-read, authoritative medical and health information.

1558 **MedlinePlus**
www.medlineplus.gov
A service of the National Library of Medicine, MedlinePlus is an online resource providing health and wellness information in both English and Spanish.

1559 **Medscape**
www.medscape.com
Medscape offers specialists, primary care physicians, and other health professionals the Web's most robust and integrated medical information and educational tools.

1560 **MyPlate**
www.myplate.gov
Created and managed by the US Department of Agriculture's Center for Nutrition Policy & Promotion, MyPlate is a dietary guide providing resources and recipes to promote healthy eating for all Americans.

1561 **National Hospice & Palliative Care Organization (NHPCO)**
www.nhpco.org
The organization seeks to improve end-of-life care, widen access to hospice care, and improve quality of life for the dying and their loved ones. NHPCO's website offers information on regulations, advocacy, quality and performance, education, and a variety of other resources.

1562 **National Ovarian Cancer Coalition**
www.ovarian.org
Aims to raise awareness about ovarian cancer and to promote education about the disease, while dispelling myths and misunderstandings. The coalition is committed to improving the overall survival rate and quality of life for women with ovarian cancer.

1563 **Nutrition.gov**
www.nutrition.gov
Sponsored by the United States Department of Agriculture (USDA), Nutrition.gov offers information on topics in food and nutrition, including healthy eating, physical activity, and food safety.

1564 **Science Daily**
www.sciencedaily.com
Provides information on the latest news and research in science, health, the environment, and technology.

1565 **Support for People with Oral and Head and Neck Cancer (SPOHNC)**
www.spohnc.org
Non-profit organization addressing the broad emotional, physical, and humanistic needs of oral and head and neck cancer patients.

1566 **The Nutrition Source**
hsph.harvard.edu/nutritionsource
From the Harvard T.H. Chan School of Public Health, The Nutrition Source provides news, information, and guidance for nutrition and healthy eating.

1567 **UnlockFood**
www.unlockfood.ca
A website from Dietitians of Canada. Provides videos, recipes, and information on food and nutrition, as well as helps Canadians connect with a dietitian.

1568 **Verywell**
www.verywellhealth.com
Offers health, medicine, and wellness information from health professionals.

1569 **WebMD**
www.webmd.com
Provides credible information, supportive communities, and in-depth reference material about health subjects. A source for original and timely health information as well as material from well known content providers.

1570 **Webhelp**
www.webhelp.com
Provides links to information, including research, treatment, prevention, support, and more.

1571 **World Health Organization**
www.who.int
An agency of the United Nations, World Health Organization (WHO) serves to promote global health. The WHO website provides fact sheets, publications, media, and other resources on various health topics.

CHRONIC PAIN

Dietary intake can influence the functions of the nervous system, the immune system and the endocrine system, which can directly influence pain. An optimal weight reduces the work load on joints and decreases overall inflammation. The musculoskeletal system is comprised of bones and muscles that support the body and nutrition plays an important role in the body's well-being. Dietary patterns and the foods we eat, and chronic musculoskeletal pain have an unclear link but a plant-based diet may offer pain relief, due to its anti-inflammatory characteristics. Proteins, fats and sugar may cause higher levels of pain. Patients with rheumatoid arthritis or fibromyalgia may show lower blood levels of important nutrients such as calcium, folate, zinc and vitamins A, E and K. Dietary intake and weight status impact the risk and severity of many chronic diseases including cardiovascular disease, diabetes and mental health. Appropriate diet may lead to less chronic pain. Discussing chronic pain with your healthcare provider, especially as it relates to non-medication interventions, is recommended. Consulting with a registered clinical dietician may also be advised.

Agencies & Associations

1572 **American Academy of Orofacial Pain**
174 S New York Avenue 609-504-1311
Oceanville, NJ 08231 Fax: 609-573-5064
aaopexec@aaop.org
www.aaop.org
The American Academy of Orofacial Pain is an organization of dentists and healthcare professionals dedicated to the management of orofacial pain through education, research, and patient care.
Jeffry R. Shaefer, President
Kenneth S. Cleveland, Executive Director

1573 **American Academy of Pain Medicine**
1705 Edgewater Drive 800-917-1619
Orlando, FL 32804 Fax: 407-749-0714
info@painmed.org
www.painmed.org
The AAPM is a medical specialty society representing physicians and healthcare professionals practicing in the field of pain medicine. Its mission is to promote and advance pain care, education, training, advocacy, and research.
W. Michael Hooten, MD, President
Farshad M. Ahadian, MD, Treasurer

1574 **American Chronic Pain Association**
11936 West 119th Street 913-991-4740
Overland Park, KS 66213-2216 acpa@theacpa.org
www.theacpa.org
The ACPA facilitates peer support and education for individuals with chronic pain in its many forms, in order to increase quality of life. Also raises awareness among the healthcare community, and with policy makers.
Kathy Sapp, Chief Executive Officer
Scott Farmer, Chief Operating Officer

1575 **American Headache Society**
19 Mantua Road 856-423-0043
Mount Royal, NJ 08061 Fax: 856-423-0082
ahshq@talley.com
www.americanheadachesociety.org
The American Headache Society is a professional society of health care providers committed to improving the care of people with headache disorders.
Peter J. Groadsby, MD, Ph.D., President
Todd J. Schwedt, MD, MSCI, Treasurer

1576 **American Migraine Foundation**
19 Mantua Road 856-423-0043
Mount Royal, NJ 08061 Fax: 856-423-0082
amf@talley.com
www.americanmigrainefoundation.org
Dedicated to increasing awareness and advancing research on migraine disorders and other diseases that cause severe head pain.
Nim Lalvani, MPH, Executive Director
Heather Phillips, MEd, Program Manager

1577 **American Osteopathic Association**
142 E Ontario Street 312-202-8000
Chicago, IL 60611-2864 888-626-9262
info@osteopathic.org
www.osteopathic.org
Serving as the professional family for more than 145,000 osteopathic physicians (DOs) and osteopathic medical students, the American Osteopathic Association (AOA) promotes public health and encourages scientific research.
Joseph Giaimo, President
Kevin Klauer, Chief Executive Officer

1578 **American Pain Association**
2 Bala Plaza 484-483-3131
Bala Cynwyd, PA 19004 Fax: 610-664-3003
info@painassociation.org
www.painassociation.org
The American Pain Association works to improve pain management through education, research, and product development.

1579 **American Physical Therapy Association**
3030 Potomac Avenue 703-684-2782
Alexandria, VA 22305-3085 800-999-2782
www.apta.org
The American Physical Therapy Association (APTA) is an individual membership professional organization representing more than 100,000 member physical therapists (PTs), physical therapist assistants (PTAs), and students of physical therapy.
Sharon L. Dunn, President
Matthew R. Hyland, Vice President

1580 **American Society for Pain Management Nurses**
4400 College Boulevard 913-222-8666
Overland Park, KS 66211 888-342-7766
Fax: 913-222-8606
aspmn@kellencompany.com
www.aspmn.org

Provides support for nurses in the field of pain management. Works to promote best nursing practices and ensure optimal nursing care for people affected by pain.
Maureen F. Cooney, DNP, FNP-BC, President
Ann M. Schreier, Ph.D., RN, Treasurer

1581 **Association of Migraine Disorders**
PO Box 870 www.migrainedisorders.org
North Kingstown, RI 02852
Dedicated to furthering knowledge and understanding of migraine disease.
Frederick Godley, MD, Founder & President
Michael Teixido, MD, Co-Founder & Vice President

1582 **Canadian Pain Society**
20 Crown Steel Drive 365-873-2320
Markham, Ontario, L3R-9X9 cps@secretariatcentral.com
www.canadianpainsociety.ca
Dedicated to healthcare professionals and lay persons with an interest in the field of pain.
Karen D. Davis, Ph.D., FCAHS, President
Hance Clarke, MD, Ph.D., FRCPC, Treasurer

1583 **Canadian Physiotherapy Association**
955 Green Valley Crescent 613-564-5454
Ottawa, Ontario, K2C-3V4 800-387-8679
information@physiotherapy.ca
www.physiotherapy.ca
The Canadian Physiotherapy Association is a professional organization representing physiotherapists, physiotherapist assistants, and physiotherapist students in Canada.
Amanda de Chastelain, President

1584 **Chronic Pain Association of Canada**
PO Box 66017 780-482-6727
Edmonton, Alberta, T6J-6T4 cpac@chronicpaincanada.com
chronicpaincanada.com
Seeks to prevent and alleviate chronic pain, and to improve patients' quality of life.
Terry Bremner, President
Barry Ulmer, Executive Director

1585 **Endometriosis Association**
8585 N 76th Place 414-355-2200
Milwaukee, WI 53223 800-992-3636
Fax: 414-355-6065
www.endometriosisassn.org
A self-help organization for women and persons affected by endometriosis. The Endometriosis Association's mission is to cure and prevent endometriosis, as well as to provide research, education, and support to those with the condition.
Mary Lou Ballweg, President
Sarah Whyte, Treasurer

1586 **International Association for the Study of Pain**
1510 H Street NW 202-856-7400
Washington, DC 20005-1020 iaspdesk@iasp-pain.org
www.iasp-pain.org
The International Association for the Study of Pain is the leading professional forum for science, practice, and education in the field of pain.
Colleen Eubanks, Chief Executive Officer

1587 **International Pain Foundation**
38556 N Dave Street 480-882-1342
San Tan Valley, AZ 85140 www.internationalpain.org
The International Pain Foundation (iPain) works to advance access and quality of care for people with conditions that cause chronic pain.
Barby Ingle, President
Ken Taylor, Vice President

1588 **International Pelvic Pain Society**
14306 Southcross Drive W 612-474-4140
Burnsville, MN 55306 info@pelvicpain.org
www.pelvicpain.org
Seeks to recruit, organize, and educate health care professionals actively involved with the treatment of patients who have chronic pelvic pain.
Georgine Lamvu, MD, MPH, FACOG, Chair
Mario Castellanos, MD, President

1589 **Interstitial Cystitis Association**
7918 Jones Branch Drive 703-442-2070
McLean, VA 22102 Fax: 703-506-3266
icamail@ichelp.org
www.ichelp.org
A nonprofit health association dedicated to improving the quality of care and lives for people with interstitial cystitis (also referred to as painful bladder syndrome, bladder pain syndrome, and chronic pelvic pain).
Michael Greenwell, Chair
Laura Santurri, Ph.D., MPH, Vice Chair

1590 **National Association of Chronic Disease Directors**
325 Swanton Way info@chronicdisease.org
Decatur, GA 30030 www.chronicdisease.org
Non-profit public health organization committed to serving the chronic disease program directors of each state and jurisdiction in the United States.
John W. Robitscher, MPH, Chief Executive Officer
Marti Macchi, MEd, MPH, Senior Director, Programs

1591 **National Association of Myofascial Trigger Point Therapists**
namtpt.president@gmail.com
www.myofascialtherapy.org
The NAMTPT is a professional organization dedicated to increasing public awareness of and access to myofascial pain treatment.
Kate Simmons, President
Heather Brown, Vice President

1592 **National Fibromyalgia & Chronic Pain Association**
www.fibroandpain.org
Seeks to unite patients, policy makers, and health and science communities to research fibromyalgia and chronic pain illnesses; also provides advocacy, support, and education.
Janet Favero Chambers, President

1593 **National Fibromyalgia Association**
3857 Birch Street nfa@fmaware.org
Newport Beach, CA 92660 www.fmaware.net
Offers resources, education, and support to improve the lives of individuals living with fibromyalgia.
Lynne Matallana, Founder & President

1594 **National Headache Foundation**
820 N Orleans 312-274-2650
Chicago, IL 60610-3131 888-643-5552
info@headaches.org
www.headaches.org
Seeks to raise awareness of migraine and headache disorders through education, research, and advocacy.
Vincent Martin, MD, AQH, President
Jill Dehlin, RN, CHES, Secretary

1595 **National Institute on Aging**
31 Center Drive, MSC 2292 800-222-2225
Bethesda, MD 20892 TTY: 800-222-4225
niaic@nia.nih.gov
www.nia.nih.gov
Seeks to understand the nature of aging, and to extend healthy, active years of life. Free resources are available on topics such as Alzheimer's & dimentia, caregiving, cognitive heath, end of life care, and more.
Richard J. Hodes, MD, Director
Luigi Ferrucci, Scientific Director

1596 **National Vulvodynia Association**
PO Box 4491 301-299-0775
Silver Spring, MD 20914-4491 Fax: 301-299-3999
www.nva.org
The National Vulvodynia Association (NVA) aims to improve the health and lives of women and persons affected by vulvodynia, a chronic vulvar pain condition.
Phyllis Mate, President
Lisa Goldstein, Executive Director

1597 **Peripheral Nerve Society**
1935 County Road B2 W 952-545-6284
Roseville, MN 55113 info@pnsociety.com
www.pnsociety.com
An international organization of physicians, scientists, and healthcare providers working to advance treatments for people with peripheral nerve disease.
Allison Kindseth, Executive Director
Jacquie Durant, Meetings & Strategic Partnership Manager

1598 **Reflex Sympathetic Dystrophy Syndrome Association (RSDSA)**
99 Cherry Street 203-877-3790
Milford, CT 06460 877-662-7737
info@rsds.org
www.rsds.org
Non-profit professional and consumer organization founded to support research into the cause, treatment, and cure of reflex sympathetic dystrophy syndrome. RSDSA also organizes support groups, promote awareness among health professionals and develop educational programs.
Jim Broatch, Executive VP & Director
Jeri Krassner, Special Events Coordinator

1599 **TMJ Association Ltd.**
PO Box 26770 262-432-0350
Milwaukee, WI 53226 info@tmj.org
www.tmj.org
A nonprofit advocacy organization for people with Temporomandibular Disorders (TMJ), which cause limited jaw movement and/or pain in the jaw joint area.
Terrie Cowley, President
Deanne Clare, Administrator

1600 **The Pain Community**
PO Box 1293 925-457-1759
Alamo, CA 94507-7293 www.paincommunity.org
The Pain Community (TPC) is a nonprofit organization advocating for quality pain care and improved access to effective pain management.
Karen Kiefer, Chair
Micke A. Brown, Vice Chair

1601 **U.S. Pain Foundation**
15 N Main Street 800-910-2462
West Hartford, CT 06107 contact@uspainfoundation.org
www.uspainfoundation.org
A nonprofit organization devoted to providing support, education, and advocacy for people living with chronic pain and their care providers.
Nicole Hemmenway, Chief Executive Officer
Pamela Lynch, Chief Financial Officer

1602 **Vulvar Pain Foundation**
PO Box 755 336-226-0704
Graham, NC 27253 www.thevpfoundation.org
A nonprofit organization supporting persons affected by vulvar pain and related disorders, including fibromyalgia, interstitial cystitis, and irritable bowel syndrome.

1603 **World Institute of Pain**
301 N Main Street 336-760-2933
Winston-Salem, NC 27101 wip@worldinstituteofpain.org
www.worldinstituteofpain.org
The World Institute of Pain is an organization of pain medicine professionals working to advance interventional pain practice and improve standards of care for pain patients.
D. Mark Tolliver, Executive Director

Web Sites

1604 **American Pain Society**
americanpainsociety.org
Multidisciplinary organization of basic and clinical scientists, practicing clinicians, policy analysts, and others.

1605 **Chronic Pain Research Alliance**
www.chronicpainresearch.org
An initiative of The TMJ Association, the Chronic Pain Research Alliance works to advance the diagnoses, treatment, and medical management of persons affected by Chronic Overlapping Pain Conditions (COPCs).

1606 **Dietary Guidelines for Americans**
www.dietaryguidelines.gov
Publishes the Dietary Guidelines for Americans, a guide providing nutritional advice to promote health and prevent disease. Updated versions of the Dietary Guidelines are released by the US Departments of Agriculture (USDA) and Health & Human Services (HHS) every five years.

1607 **Discovery Health**
www.discoverylife.com
A source of information on various health topics, including chronic pain and its symptoms and treatments.

1608 **Everyday Health**
www.everydayhealth.com
Aims to provide evidence-based health information from physicians and healthcare providers.

1609 **FamilyDoctor.org**
www.familydoctor.org
Medical advice and information provided by the American Academy of Family Physicians. Resources include a medical dictionary, a symptom checker tool, a BMI calculator, and medication information.

1610 **Fibromyalgia Network**
www.fmnetnews.com
Articles, news reports, resources, and general information about fibromyalgia and treatment.

1611 **Healing Well**
www.healingwell.com
An online health resource guide to medical news, chat, information and articles, newsgroups and message boards, books, disease-related web sites, medical directories, and more for patients, friends, and family coping with disabling diseases, disorders, or chronic illnesses.

1612 **Health Finder**
www.healthfinder.gov
Searchable, carefully developed web site offering information on over 1000 topics. Developed by the US Department of Health and Human Services, the site can be used in both English and Spanish.

1613 **Healthline**
www.healthline.com
Provides medical and health articles and information.

1614 **Healthlink USA**
www.healthlinkusa.com
Health information concerning treatment, cures, prevention, diagnosis, risk factors, research, support groups, email lists, personal stories and much more. Updated regularly.

1615 **Institute for Chronic Pain**
www.instituteforchronicpain.org
An educational and policy think tank focused on research, development, and promotion of scientific information in the field of chronic pain management.

1616 **International Pelvic Pain Society**
www.pelvicpain.org
Seeks to recruit, organize, and educate health care professionals actively involved with the treatment of patients who have chronic pelvic pain.

1617 **MedicineNet**
www.medicinenet.com
An online resource for consumers providing easy-to-read, authoritative medical and health information.

1618 **Medscape**
www.medscape.com
Medscape offers specialists, primary care physicians, and other health professionals the Web's most robust and integrated medical information and educational tools.

1619 **Nutrition.gov**
www.nutrition.gov

Sponsored by the United States Department of Agriculture (USDA), Nutrition.gov offers information on topics in food and nutrition, including healthy eating, physical activity, and food safety.

1620 Pain Points of View

www.paintpointsofview.com

Pain Points of View is an online resource center for people living with chronic pain, as well as their caregivers and healthcare professionals. It is an initiative of Collegium Pharmaceutical Inc.

1621 Science Daily

www.sciencedaily.com

Provides information on the latest news and research in science, health, the environment, and technology.

1622 The Nutrition Source

hsph.harvard.edu/nutritionsource

From the Harvard T.H. Chan School of Public Health, The Nutrition Source provides news, information, and guidance for nutrition and healthy eating.

1623 UnlockFood

www.unlockfood.ca

A website from Dietitians of Canada. Provides videos, recipes, and information on food and nutrition, as well as helps Canadians connect with a dietitian.

1624 Verywell

www.verywellhealth.com

Offers health, medicine, and wellness information from health professionals.

1625 WebMD

www.webmd.com

Provides credible information, supportive communities, and in-depth reference material about health subjects. A source for original and timely health information as well as material from well known content providers.

MENTAL ILLNESS

Food intake can influence both physical and mental health and wellbeing. Eating well, including a balanced diet of fruits, vegetables and nutrients can enhance a feeling of well-being and improve your mood. For example, a Mediterranean-style diet with lots of vegetables, seafood, garlic and fresh herbs, olive oil, cereal and grains is shown to reduce the symptoms of depression. To improve your mental health, you should avoid foods like caffeine and chocolate that trick the brain into releasing mood-altering chemicals, and foods that prevent conversion of certain foods into necessary nutrients like saturated fats and palm oil. Using food as a coping mechanism to deal with stressful and emotional situations should be addressed with a physician. Eating disorders such as anorexia nervosa have a significant mental health component. Nutrition and mental health are closely related and proper nutrition management is key.

Agencies & Associations

1626 A Common Voice
10402 Kline Street SW 253-537-2145
Lakewood, WA 98499 www.acommonvoice.org
A parent driven, nonprofit organization funded by Washington State Mental Health. Their goal is to provide support, technical assistance, and to bring Pierce County parents together who have experience raising children with complex needs, facilitaing partnership between communities, systems, familes, and schools.

1627 Action Autonomie
3958 rue Dandurand 514-525-5060
Montreal, Quebec, H1X-1P7 lecollectif@actionautonomie.qc.ca
www.actionautonomie.qc.ca
Community organization for individuals with mental illness who unite their efforts collectively in order to defend their rights. Action Autonomie educates others on their rights while navigating the mental health care system.

1628 Advocates for Children of New Jersey
35 Halsey Street 973-643-3876
Newark, NJ 07102 advocates@acnj.org
acnj.org
Advocates for Children of New Jersey is a statewide non-profit organization focused on advocating for the rights of children. ACNJ operates on behalf of children and families by collaborating with local, state and federal leaders to enact law and policy changes that will benefit the children of New Jersey. The mission of ACNJ is to raise awareness and to serve the needs of children through research, policy and strategic communications. ACNJ seeks to help children lead healthy, safe and educated
Cecilia Zalkind, President & CEO
Mary Coogan, Vice President

1629 Advocates for Human Potential (AHP)
490-B Boston Post Road 978-443-0055
Sudbury, MA 01776 ahpnet.com
Excels in research and evaluation; technical assistance and training; system and program development, including strategic planning and information management; and resource development and dissemination. Staff are experts in content areas critical to addressing the behavioral health needs of vulnerable populations.
Neal Shifman, President & CEO
Charles R. Galland, Chief Operating Officer

1630 African American Family Services
2616 Nicollet Avenue 612-813-5034
Minneapolis, MN 55408 contact@aafs.net
www.aafs.net
African American Family Services works with individuals, families and communities affected by addiction and mental illness. Provides culturally-specific mental health services.
Thomas Adams, Chief Executive Officer
Brianna Miller, Director, Advancement

1631 Alaska Association for Infant and Early Childhood Mental Health
PO Box 240331 alaska.aimh@gmail.com
Anchorage, AK 99524 akaimh.org
Nonprofit organization of parents and professionals dedicated to supporting the healthy mental, emotional and social development of infants and young children.
Gail Trujillo, President
Christopher Washko, Vice President

1632 Allendale Association
PO Box 1088 847-356-2351
Lake Villa, IL 60046 allendale4kids.org
The Allendale Association is a private, non-profit organization committed to providing quality care, education, treatment, support, and advocacy for troubled children in need of intervention and their families.
Jason Keeler, President & CEO
Chris Schrantz, Senior VP, Finance & Business Services

1633 Allwell Behavioral Health Services
2845 Bell Street 740-454-9766
Zanesville, OH 43701 info@allwell.org
www.allwell.org
A private not-for-profit community mental health service provider operating in Coshocton, Guernsey, Morgan, Muskingum, Noble and Perry counties. Provides traditional treatment services and specialized services. Counseling and support services include outpatient counseling services, medication management, 24-hour crisis intervention, employee assistance, residential services, and peer support.
James McDonald, President & CEO
Daniel Carpenetti, Chief Operating Officer

1634 American Academy of Child and Adolescent Psychiatry
3615 Wisconsin Avenue NW 202-966-7300
Washington, DC 20016-3007 communications@aacap.org
aacap.org
The AACAP is the leading national professional medical association dedicated to treating and improving the quality of life for children, adolescents, and families affected by these disorders. Members actively research, evaluate, diagnose, and treat psychiatric disorders and pride themselves on giving direction to and responding quickly to new developments in addressing the health care needs of children and their families.
Gabrielle A. Carlson, MD, President
Heidi B. Fordi, CAE, Executive Director

1635 **American Academy of Pediatrics**
345 Park Boulevard 800-433-9016
Itasca, IL 60143 aap.org
The mission of the AAP is to attain optimal physical, mental, and social health and well-being for all infants, children, adolescents, and young adults. A professional membership organization of 66,000 primary care pediatricians, pediatric medical sub-specialists, and pediatric surgical specialists.
Mark Del Monte, Chief Executive Officer
Christine Bork, Chief Development Officer

1636 **American Association for Geriatric Psychiatry**
6728 Old McLean Village Drive 703-718-6026
McLean, VA 22101 aagponline.org
The only national association that has products, activities, and publications which focus exclusively on the challenges of geriatric psychiatry. Practitioners, researchers, educations, students, and the public have relied on AAGP as the key driver for progress for elderly mental health care.
Rebecca Morgan, Executive Director
Victoria Cooper, Association Manager

1637 **American Association on Intellectual and Developmental Disabilities (AAIDD)**
8403 Colesville Road 202-387-1968
Silver Spring, MD 20910 aaidd.org
AAIDD provides worldwide leadership in the field of intellectual and developmental disabilities. The oldest and largest interdisciplinary organization of professionals and citizens concerned about intellectual and developmental disabilities. AAIDD promotes progressive policies, research, and universal human rights for people with intellectual and developmental diabilities.
Margaret A. Nygren, Executive Director & CEO
Paul D. Aitken, Director, Finance & Administration

1638 **American Holistic Health Association**
PO Box 17400 714-779-6152
Anaheim, CA 92817 mail@ahha.org
ahha.org
The leading national resource connecting people with vital solutions for reaching a higher level of wellness through a holistic approach to health and healthcare.
Suzan V. Walter, MBA, President
Gena E. Kadar, DC, CNS, Secretary

1639 **American Network of Community Options and Resources (ANCOR)**
1101 King Street 703-535-7850
Alexandria, VA 22314 ancor@ancor.org
ancor.org
A national trade association representing private providers of community living, employment supports, and services to individuals with disabilities. As a nonprofit organization, ANCOR continually advocates for the crucial role private providers play in enhancing and supporting the lives of people with disabilities and their families.
Barbara Merrill, Chief Executive Officer
Gabrielle Sedor, Chief Operations Officer

1640 **American Pediatric Society**
9303 New Trails Drive 346-980-9707
The Woodlands, TX 77381 info@aps1888.org
www.aps1888.org
Society of professionals working on pediatric health care issues, through research, advocacy, and education. The society offers conferences and a variety of publications.
Mary Leonard, President
Clifford W. Bogue, Secretary-Treasurer

1641 **American Psychiatric Association**
800 Maine Avenue SW 202-559-3900
Washington, DC 20024 apa@psych.org
psychiatry.org
The world's largest psychiatric organization. It is a medical specialty society representing more than 37,800 psychiatric physicians from the United States and around the world. Its member physicians work together to ensure humane care and effective treatment for all persons with mental disorders. Members are primarily medical specialists who are psychiatrists or in the process of becoming psychiatrists.
Saul Levin, MD, MPA, FRCP-E, CEO & Medical Director

1642 **American Psychological Association**
750 First Street NE 202-336-5500
Washington, DC 20002 800-374-2721
TTY: 202-336-6123
apa.org
The American Psychological Association seeks to advance psychology as a science, a profession, and as a means of promoting health, education, and human welfare. This organization of researchers, educators, clinicians, consultants, and students promotes research in psychology and the improvment of research methods; establishes high standards of ethics, conduct, and education; and disseminates psychological knowledge through professional and academic networks.
Jennifer F. Kelly, Ph.D., ABPP, President
Arthur C. Evans, Jr., Ph.D., Chief Executive Officer & EVP

1643 **American Speech-Language-Hearing Association**
2200 Research Boulevard 301-269-5700
Rockville, MD 20850 800-638-8255
TTY: 301-296-5650
asha.org
The professional, scientific, and credentialing association for members and affiliates who are audiologists, speech-language pathologists, and speech, language, and hearing scientists in the United States and internationally. Supports audiologists and speech-language scientists in their research and practices.
A. Lynn Williams, President

1644 **Ascension Borgess Hospital Behavioral Health Inpatient Care**
1521 Gull Road 269-226-4858
Kalamazoo, MI 49048 healthcare.ascension.org
Offers patients and families a wide array of services to address their mental health concerns.

1645 **AspireHope NY Inc.**
25 W Steuben Street 607-776-2164
Bath, NY 14810-1511 ahny@aspirehope.org
www.aspirehope.org
Provides independent peer services and support services for individuals and families.

1646 **Assistance League of Los Angeles**
6640 Sunset Boulevard 323-469-1973
Los Angeles, CA 90028 assistanceleaguela.org
Provides services to meet the physical and emotional needs of children and families. Focuses on helping children who live in poverty within Los Angeles communities through the development of programs designed to promote learning and improve self-esteem.
Melanie Merians, Chief Executive Officer
Rafe Pery, Chief Financial Officer

1647 **Association for Behavioral Health and Wellness**
1325 G Street NW 202-449-7660
Washington, DC 20005 info@abhw.org
www.abhw.org
An association of the nation's leading behavioral health and wellness companies that manage behavioral health insurance. These companies provide an array of services related to mental health, substance use, employee assistance, disease management, and other health and wellness programs to over 175 million people in both the public and private sectors.
Pamela Greenberg, President & CEO
Tiffany Huth, VP, Communications & Programs

1648 **Association for Behavioral Healthcare**
251 West Central Street 508-647-8385
Natick, MA 01760 www.abhmass.org
The Association for Behavioral Healthcare, formerly Mental Health and Substance Abuse Corporations of Massachusetts, is dedicated to promoting community-based mental health and substance abuse services, advocating for public policy changes, and addressing issues surrounding mental health and addiction treatment services.
Lydia Conley, President & CEO
Constance Peters, VP, Addiction Services

1649 **Association of Children's Residential Centers**
648 N Plankinton Avenue 877-332-2272
Milwaukee, WI 53203 info@togetherthevoice.org
www.togetherthevoice.org
Brings professionals together to advance the frontiers of knowledge regarding therapeutic living environments for adolescents with behavioral health disorders.
Dana K. Dorn, President
Kari Sisson, Executive Director

1650 **Association of Mental Health Librarians (AMHL)**
140 Old Orangeburg Road mhlib.org
Orangeburg, NY 10962
A professional organization of individuals working in the field of mental health information delivery. The organization is open to libraries, library assistants, and library associates. AMHL hosts an annual conference, and provides opportunities for networking and enhancing professional skills.
Len Levin, President
Stuart Moss, Treasurer

1651 **Attitudinal Healing International**
3001 Bridgeway 877-244-3392
Sausalito, CA 94965 info@ahinternational.org
ahinternational.org
Attitudinal Healing is based on the principle that it is not other people or situations that cause individuals distress. Rather, it is their own thoughts and attitudes that are responsible. AHInternational's mission is to create, develop, and support the official home portal for Attitudinal Healing and to help facilitate the organic creation and growth of independent centers, groups, and individuals worldwide.
Gerald G. Jampolsky, MD, Founder
Diane V. Cirincione-Jampolsky, Founder & Executive Director

1652 **Autism Society of North Carolina**
5121 Kingdom Way 800-442-2762
Raleigh, NC 27607 info@autismsociety-nc.org
autismsociety-nc.org
Committed to providing support for individuals within the autism spectrum and their families through advocacy, training and education, and residential, recreational, vocational, and community-based services.
Tracey Sheriff, Chief Executive Officer
Kristy White, Chief Development Officer

1653 **Baby Fold**
108 East Willow Street 309-452-1770
Normal, IL 61761 thebabyfold.org
The Baby Fold is an Illinois-based multi-service agency that provides residential, special education, child welfare, and family support services to children with emotional and behavioral disabilities and autism spectrum disorders, as well as at-risk children.
Dianne Schultz, President & CEO
Aimee Beam, VP, Development

1654 **Bazelon Center for Mental Health Law**
1090 Vermont Avenue NW 202-467-5730
Washington, DC 20005 communications@bazelon.org
www.bazelon.org
National legal advocate for people with mental disabilities. Through precedent-setting litigation and in the public policy arena, the Bazelon Center works to advance and preserve the rights of people with mental illnesses and development disabilities.
Holly O'Donnell, Chief Executive Officer
Kathy Chamberlain, Deputy Director, Development

1655 **Beacon Health Options**
200 State Street 888-204-5581
Boston, MA 02109 beaconhealthoptions.com
Beacon Health Options combines two behavioral health companies, Beacon Health Strategies and ValueOptions. Seeks to improve the quality and delivery of behavioral health care for regional health plans, employers, and federal, state and local governments. Provides behavioral health care services and programs in employee assistance and work and life support.
Glenn MacFarlane, President
Robert Flowe, Chief Financial Officer

1656 **Behavioral Health Clinics and Trauma Services - JRI**
Justice Resource Institute
160 Gould Street 781-559-4900
Needham, MA 02494 jri.org
Provides outpatient mental health services for children and families with developmental disabilities, behavioral and emotional problems, and medical complications. Services include in-home and outpatient therapies, mentoring services, in-home behavioral support, parent and caregiver support, and education, and mental health evaluation and consultation services to juvenile courts.
Andy Pond, MSW, MAT, President
Mia DeMarco, MPA, Chief Operating Officer

1657 **Bellefaire Jewish Children's Bureau**
One Pollock Circle 216-932-2800
Cleveland, OH 44118 800-879-2522
info@bellefairejcb.org
bellefairejcb.org
Bellefaire JCB provides a variety of behavioral health, education, and prevention services for children, adolescents, and their families. Serves children, families, and young adults throughout the United States through its residential and autism treatment programs. Bellefaire JCB also meets the needs of children internationally through its Hague-accredited international adoption program.
Adam G. Jacobs, Ph.D., President
Jeffrey Lox, LISW-S, ACSW, Executive Director

1658 **Best Buddies International (BBI)**
100 Southeast Second Street 305-374-2233
Miami, FL 33131 800-892-8339
info@bestbuddies.org
bestbuddies.org
An international organization that has grown from one original chapter to almost 1,500 middle school, high school, and college chapters worldwide. Best Buddies programs engage participants in each of the 50 United States, and in 50 countries around the world, to help enhance the lives of people with intellectual and developmental disabilities.
Anthony K. Shriver, Founder, Chair & CEO
Mark Lewis, Senior VP, Development & Marketing

1659 **Bethesda Lutheran Communities**
600 Hoffmann Drive 800-369-4636
Watertown, WI 53094 www.bethesdalc.org
A Christian organization whose mission is to provide homes, support, and awareness for people with intellectual and developmental disabilities.
Dave Sneddon, Interim President & CEO
Jeff Kaczmarski, Executive Vice President

1660 **Black Mental Health Alliance**
900 East Fayette Street 410-338-2642
Baltimore, MD 21203 info@blackmentalhealth.com
blackmentalhealth.com
BMHA promotes appropriate mental health care, service delivery, and theoretical understanding of all the mental health programs. An organization that provides training, education, consultation, public information, support groups, and resource referrals regarding mental health and related issues. The primary mission of BMHA is to provide a forum, training, and referral services for Black people and their communities.
Andrea Brown, Executive Director
Cheryl Maxwell, Program Manager

1661 **Brattleboro Retreat**
Anna Marsh Lane 802-258-3737
Brattleboro, VT 05302 www.brattleblororetreat.org
A not-for-profit hospital offering psychiatric and addiction treatment services for children, adolescents, and adults.
Louis Josephson, Ph.D., President & CEO
Gaurav Chawla, MD, CPE, Chief Medical Officer

1662 **Bridgewell**
10 Dearborn Road 781-593-1088
Peabody, MA 01960 info@bridgewell.org
bridgewell.org
Private, non-profit corporation that provides services and support for persons with developmental and psychiatric disabilities. Services offered include residential services, behavioral health ser-

vices, employment training, affordable housing, transitional homeless services, and substance abuse and addiction services.
Chris Tuttle, President & CEO
Elaine White, Chief Operating Officer

1663 Broadstep Behavioral Health
8521 Six Forks Road 919-589-1380
Raleigh, NC 27615 contact.broadstep@broadstep.com
www.broadstep.com
Provider of behavioral health and supportive living services.
C. Lynn Mason, President & CEO

1664 CAFCA
1176 Lincoln Street 720-240-9516
Denver, CO 80203 www.voiceforcokids.org
Provides agencies dedicated to helping Colorado's vulnerable children with research, education and training. The services provided by member agencies include: adoption, alcohol and drug treatment, day treatment, education, family support and preservation, foster care, group homes, independent living, kinship care, mental health treatment and counseling, pregnancy counseling, residential care at all levels.
Becky Miller Updike, Ph.D., Executive Director

1665 CASCAP
231 Somerville Avenue 617-492-5559
Somerville, MA 02143 info@cascap.org
cascap.org
Cascap Inc. seeks to assist underserved and disadvantaged members of the community and improve their quality of life. Provides a range of clinical, residential, and educational services for disabled, impoverished, or elderly individuals.
Michael Haran, Chief Executive Officer

1666 California Association of Marriage and Family Therapists
7901 Raytheon Road 858-292-2638
San Diego, CA 92111 infocenter@camft.org
camft.org
Independent professional organization representing the interests of licensed marriage and family therapists. Dedicated to advancing marriage and family therapy as a mental health profession. Seeks to maintain standards of quality and ethics for the profession and to raise awareness of the profession.
Nabil El-Ghoroury, Executive Director
Catherine Atkins, Deputy Executive Director

1667 California Association of Social Rehabilitation Agencies
3350 E 7th Street 562-343-2621
Long Beach, CA 90804 casra@casra.org
casra.org
Aims to improve the lives of people with psychiatric disabilities by developing mental health programs and services that promote growth and recovery, addressing legislative issues surrounding mental health services, and providing educational and training opportunities that address the importance of meeting mental health needs and social rehabilitation.
Chad Costello, MSW, CPRP, Executive Director
Joe Ruiz, Director, Training & Education

1668 California Health Information Association
5055 E McKinley Avenue 559-251-5038
Fresno, CA 93727 info@californiahia.org
californiahia.org
Nonprofit association that offers education, advocacy and resources for health information management professionals in California. Members contribute to the delivery of quality patient care through the management of personal health information.
Sharon Lewis, CEO & Executive Director
Debi Boynton, Operations & Finance Manager

1669 California Institute for Behavioral Health Solutions
2125 19th Street 916-556-3480
Sacramento, CA 95818 info@cibhs.org
cibhs.org
Nonprofit agency that assists professionals and agencies with improving the lives of individuals struggling with mental illness and substance use problems through training, technical assistance, research and policy development.
Percy Howard, III, LCSW, President & CEO
Rick Goscha, Ph.D., Senior VP, Programs

1670 California Psychological Association
1231 I Street 916-286-7979
Sacramento, CA 95814 cpa@cpapsych.org
cpapsych.org
A non-profit professional association for licensed psychologists in California. Provides support for psychologists by educating the public about psychological services, engaging in legislative advocacy, and promoting training, education and research in the field of psychology.
Jo Linder-Crow, Ph.D., Chief Executive Officer
Elizabeth Winkelman, JD, Ph.D., Director, Professional Affairs

1671 Calnet
3625 East Thousand Oaks Boulevard 805-660-8719
Westlake Village, CA 91362 calnetcare.com
A not-for-profit network serving to bring mental health and chemical dependency treatment providers together with managed care organizations for business opportunities.
Brent Lamb, President & CEO

1672 Canadian Art Therapy Association
PO Box 658 admin@canadianarttherapy.org
Parksville, BC, V9P-2G7 www.canadianarttherapy.org
A nonprofit organization promoting art therapy in Canada. Objectives are to encourage professional growth of art therapy through the exchange and collaboration of Art Therapists; to maintain national standards of training, practice, and professional registration; to foster research and publications in art therapy; and to increase awareness of art therapy as an important mental health discipline within the community Services.
Amanda Gee, President
Nicole Le Bihan, Vice President

1673 Canadian Federation of Mental Health Nurses
7270 Woodbine Avenue 905-415-2220
Markham, Ontario, L3R-4B9 www.cfmhn.ca
A national voice for psychiatric and mental health nurses in Canada, providing resources relevant to the field.
Tracy Thiele, President
Alison Toscano, General Manager

1674 Canadian Mental Health Association (CMHA)
250 Dundas Street W 416-646-5557
Toronto, Ontario, M5T-2Z5 info@cmha.ca
www.cmha.ca
Promotes the mental health of all and supports the recovery of people experiencing mental illness.
Margaret Eaton, National CEO
Kelly Puddister, National Executive Coordinator

1675 Center for Behavioral Health Statistics & Quality
Substance Abuse & Mental Health Services Admin.
5600 Fishers Lane 877-726-4727
Rockville, MD 20857 TTY: 800-487-4889
samhsa.gov
Federally funded agency providing statistics on behavioral health.
Michael King, Acting Director

1676 Center for Mental Health Services (CMHS)
Substance Abuse & Mental Health Services Admin.
5600 Fishers Lane 240-276-1310
Rockville, MD 20857 877-726-4727
TTY: 800-487-4889
www.samhsa.gov
Promotes the treatment of mental illness and emotional disorders by increasing accessibility to mental health programs; supporting outreach, treatment, rehabilitation, and support programs and networks; and encouraging the use of scientifically-based information when treating mental disorders. CMHS provides information about mental health via a toll-free number and numerous publications.
Anita Everett, MD, DFAPA, Director

1677 Center for Substance Abuse Prevention
Substance Abuse & Mental Health Services Admin.
5600 Fishers Lane 240-276-2420
Rockville, MD 20857 877-726-4727
TTY: 800-487-4889
www.samhsa.gov

Connects people and resources with strategies and programs designed to encourage efforts aimed at reducing and eliminating alcohol, tobacco and other drug problems in society. Works with federal, state, public and private organizations to develop prevention programs.
Jeffrey A. Coady, Acting Director

1678 **Centre for Addiction and Mental Health**
1001 Queen Street West 416-535-8501
Toronto, Ontario, M6J-1H4 800-463-2338
info@camh.ca
camh.ca
CAMH is Canada's leading addiction and mental health organization, integrating specialized clinical care with innovative research, education, health promotion and policy development. CAMH is fully affiliated with the University of Toronto, and is a Pan American Health Organization/World Health Organization Collaborating Centre. CAMH combines clinical care, research, education, policy and health promotion to transform the lives of people affected by mental health and addiction issues.
Tracey MacArthur, President & CEO
Bessy Leung, VP, Corporate Services & CFO

1679 **Chaddock**
205 South 24th Street 217-222-0034
Quincy, IL 62301 chaddock.org
A faith-based, not-for-profit organization dedicated to supporting children and families and providing hope and healing. Chaddock offers educational and treatment services for children who have experienced abuse, neglect, or trauma, including child and adolescent residential treatment, independent living and group home programs, special education school, in-home intensive program, and foster care and adoption services.
Debbie Reed, President & CEO
Kristen Patton, Director, Finance

1680 **Child & Parent Resource Institute (CPRI)**
600 Sanatorium Road 519-858-2774
London, Ontario, N6H-3W7 877-494-2774
TTY: 519-858-0257
cpri.ca
A tertiary centre that provides highly specialized voluntary services to children and youth with multi complex, severe behavioural disturbances and/or developmental challenges that impacts the child/youth in all areas i.e. home, school, and/or community. 100% funded by the Ontario Ministry of Children and Youth Services and services are offered at no charge.

1681 **Child Mind Institute**
101 East 56th Street 212-308-3118
New York, NY 10022 info@childmind.org
childmind.org
An independent, national nonprofpit organization that helps children and their families struggling with mental health disorders through free resources, access to effective treatments, and the advancement of pediatric research to improve diagnosis and treatment of mental health disorders in children.
Harold S. Koplewicz, MD, President & Medical Director
Maryana Geller, Chief Financial Officer

1682 **Children's Alliance**
100 S King Street 206-324-0340
Seattle, WA 98104-2885 action@childrensalliance.org
childrensalliance.org
Washington's statewide child advocacy organization. Champions public policies and practices that deliver the essentials that kids need to thrive — confidence, stability, health and safety.
Stephan Blanford, Executive Director
Adam Hyla E. Holdorf, Deputy Director

1683 **Children's Home Association of Illinois**
2130 North Knoxville Avenue 309-685-1047
Peoria, IL 61603 chail.org
Not-for-profit, multiple program and social service organization dedicated to providing community-based counseling, education and support programs for children and families in the Peoria area.
Matt George, Chief Executive Officer
Melissa Riddle, President & CFO

1684 **Coalition of Illinois Counselor Organizations**
myimhca@gmail.com
cico-il.org
The Coalition of Illinois Counselor Organizations represents and advocates for counselors and psychologists and their clients in Illinois, with focus on government branches and agencies, relevant segments of the private sector, and mental health organizations.
Rachel Banick, Director

1685 **Community Access, Inc.**
17 Battery Place 212-780-1400
New York, NY 10004 www.communityaccess.org
A non-profit agency providing housing and advocacy for people with disabilities.
Cal Hedigan, Chief Executive Officer
John Williams, Chief Development Officer

1686 **Community Behavioral Health Association of Maryland (CBH)**
18 Egges Lane 410-788-1865
Catonsville, MD 21228 info@mdcbh.org
mdcbh.org
Professional association representing the network of community behavioral health providers operating in the public and private sectors in Maryland. Strives to improve the quality of care for individuals and families with mental illness, addiction and substance use problems.
Shannon Hall, Executive Director
Lori Doyle, Public Policy Director

1687 **Community Health Partnership**
121 S Tejon Street 719-632-5094
Colorado Springs, CO 80903 info@ppchp.org
www.ppchp.org
Aims to improve the health of the Colorado Pikes Peak region. Areas of focus include homelessness, substance use, and suicide prevention.
Amber Ptak, Chief Executive Officer
Jennifer Mariano, Director, Programs

1688 **Community Partners Inc.**
401 N Bonita Avenue 520-721-1887
Tucson, AZ 85745 communitypartnersinc.org
Formerly Community Partnership of Southern Arizona, Community Partners Inc. is an organization that offers services in behavioral health care across Arizona.
Rose Lopez, President & CEO
Craig A. Norris, EVP & Chief Operating Officer

1689 **Compeer**
1179 Kenmore Avenue 800-836-0475
Buffalo, NY 14217 info@compeer.org
compeer.org
Nonprofit mental wellness organization. Develops a model program that matches volunteers and mentors with children and adults with mental health needs. Seeks to improve the quality of life for individuals and families with mental health challenges through support and inclusion.
Tim Boling, Chief Executive Officer
Cheri Alvarez, Chief Operating Officer

1690 **Council for Learning Disabilities**
11184 Antioch Road 913-491-1011
Overland Park, KS 66210 council-for-learning-disabilities.org
An international organization that promotes evidence-based teaching, collaboration, research, leadership, and advocacy. CLD is comprised of professionals who represent diverse disciplines and are committed to enhancing the education and quality of life for individuals with learning disabilities and others who experience challenges in learning.
Joseph Morgan, President
Margaret Flores, Vice President

1691 **Council on Quality and Leadership (CQL)**
100 West Road 410-275-0488
Towson, MD 21204 info@thecouncil.org
thecouncil.org
CQL offers consultation, accreditation, training, and certification services to organizations and systems that share the vision of dignity, opportunity, and community for all people. CQL provides

leadership to improve the quality of life for people with disabilities, people with mental illness, and older adults.
Mary Kay Rizzolo, President & CEO
Trina Meeth, VP, Finance & Administration

1692 Department of Health and Human Services/OA
200 Independence Avenue SW 877-696-6775
Washington, DC 20201 hhs.gov
The DHHS is the United States government's principal agency for protecting the health of all Americans, providing health and human services, and supporting initiatives in medicine, public health, and social services.
Xavier Becerra, Secretary
Andrea Palm, Deputy Secretary

1693 Depressive and Bipolar Support Alliance (DBSA)
55 E Jackson Boulevard 800-826-3632
Chicago, IL 60604 info@dbsalliance.org
dbsalliance.org
The Depression and Bipolar Support Alliance is the leading patient-directed national organization focusing on the most prevalent mental illnesses. The organization fosters an environment of understanding about the impact and management of these life threatening illnesses by providing up-to-date, scientifically based tools and information written in language the general public can understand.
Michael Pollock, Chief Executive Officer
John Quinn, Chief Financial Officer

1694 Devereux Arizona
2025 N 3rd Street 602-283-1573
Phoenix, AZ 85004 800-345-1292
devereuxaz.org
Nonprofit behavioral health organization providing clinical, educational and employment programs and services for individuals affected by learning, behavioral and emotional challenges.
Yvette Jackson, Executive Director
Janelle Westfall, Clinical Director

1695 Disability Rights New Jersey
210 S Broad Street 609-292-9742
Trenton, NJ 08608 800-922-7233
TTY: 609-633-7106
advocate@drnj.org
drnj.org
Legal and non legal advocacy, information and referral, technical assistance and training, outreach and education in support of the human, civil, and legal rights of people with disabilities in New Jersey.
Gwen Orlowski, Executive Director
Cathy Coryat, Chief Financial Officer

1696 Emotions Anonymous International Service Center
PO Box 4245 651-647-9712
St. Paul, MN 55104 info@emotionsanonymous.org
emotionsanonymous.org
A community-based organization to provide support managing mental health difficulties. Groups meet weekly to share experiences, strength, and hope.
Elaine Weber Nelson, Executive Director

1697 Eye Movement Desensitization and Reprocessing International Association
7000 N Mo Pac Expy 512-451-5200
Austin, TX 78731-3013 info@emdria.org
emdria.org
A professional association for EMDR practitioners seeking high standars of practice in EDMR therapy.
Wendy Byrd, President
Michael Bowers, Executive Director

1698 Families Anonymous, Inc.
701 Lee Street 847-294-5877
Des Plaines, IL 60016 800-736-9805
info@familiesanonymous.org
familiesanonymous.org
A 12 Step fellowship for families and friends of individuals who have dealt or are dealing with mental health issues, whether caused by drugs, alcohol, or related behavioral problems.

1699 Families Together in New York State
737 Madison Avenue 518-432-0333
Albany, NY 12208 info@ftnys.org
ftnys.org
Non-profit, parent-run organization that serves families of children and youth affected by social, emotional, and behavioral challenges through advocacy, information, referrals, public awareness, education, and training.
Paige Pierce, Chief Executive Officer
Daphne Brown, Director, Family Involvement & Outreach

1700 Family Focus
310 S Peoria Street 312-421-5200
Chicago, IL 60607 www.family-focus.org
Mission is to nurture children by strengthening family support.
Dara Munson, President & CEO
Sherneron Hilliard, Senior VP, Programs & Impact

1701 Family Network on Disabilities
26750 US Highway 19 N 727-523-1130
Clearwater, FL 33761 800-825-5736
fndusa.org
Family Network on Disabilities is a grassroots organization for individuals with disabilities or special needs and their families, as well as professionals and concerned citizens. FND seeks to assist families affected by disabilities through support services and the sharing of information. FND strives to eradicate systemic barriers and to work towards inclusion and equality of people with disabilities.
Richard La Belle, Chief Executive Officer
Joseph La Belle, Director, Programs

1702 Family Service Association of Greater Elgin
1140 North McLean Boulevard 847-695-3680
Elgin, IL 60123 fsaelgin.org
A private, non-profit agency, Family Service Association has served children, adolescents, and adults in the Greater Elgin area since 1931. The Family Service Association provides a range of counseling services and programs, including family support, outpatient therapy, school-based therapy and screening assessments.
Bernadette May, Executive Director
Janeth Barba, Director, Clinical Services

1703 Federation for Children with Special Needs (FCSN)
529 Main Street 617-236-7210
Boston, MA 02129 800-331-0688
info@fcsn.org
fcsn.org
The federation provides information, support, and assistance to parents of children with disabilities, their professional partners, and their communities. Promotes the active and informed participation of parents of children with disabilities in shaping, implementing, and evaluating public policy that affects them.
Pam Nourse, Executive Director
Chetna Putta, Director, IT & Administration

1704 Filipino American Service Group
135 North Park View Street 213-908-5050
Los Angeles, CA 90026 fasgi.org
Filipino American Service Group focuses on improving the physical and mental well-being of mentally ill, homeless, and/or low income individuals in Los Angeles. Provides independent health and social services. Aims to help enhance the quality of life for members of the community in Historic Filipinotown and the Greater Los Angeles area.
Yey Coronel, Executive Director
Reener Balingit, Program Coordinator

1705 Five Acres: Boys and Girls Aid Society of Los Angeles County
760 West Mountain View Street 626-798-6793
Altadena, CA 91001 800-696-6793
wecanhelp@5acres.org
5acres.org
Serves to prevent child abuse and neglect, and connect children to safe and loving families. Develops support services and outreach programs to help treat and educate abused and neglected children, conducts research and promotes evidence-based treatment, engages in advocacy, and provides educational resources to family, professionals and the community on the prevention of child abuse and neglect.

1706 **Florida Alcohol and Drug Abuse Association**
2868 Mahan Drive 850-878-2196
Tallahassee, FL 32308 fadaa@fadaa.org
fadaa.org
Statewide membership organization that represents more than 100 community-based substance abuse treatment and prevention agencies throughout Florida. FADAA supports providers and programs dedicated to the advancement of substance abuse treatment, prevention, and research, and has provided advocacy for substance abuse policies and related practice improvement.

1707 **Florida Health Care Association**
307 West Park Avenue 850-224-3907
Tallahassee, FL 32301 info@fhca.org
fhca.org
FHCA is dedicated to providing the highest quality care for elderly, chronically ill, and disabled individuals in Florida.
J. Emmett Reed, CAE, Chief Executive Officer
Dawn Segler, CPA, Chief Financial Officer

1708 **Frontier Behavioral Health**
107 S Division fbhwa.org
Spokane, WA 99202
Provider of behavioral healthcare services.
Jeff Thomas, Chief Executive Officer

1709 **Gam-Anon International Service Office Inc.**
PO Box 307 718-352-1671
Massapequa Park, NY 11762 gamanonoffice@gam-anon.org
gam-anon.org
A 12 step self-help organization for close friends and family of compulsive gamblers.

1710 **Georgia Parent Support Network**
1381 Metropolitan Parkway 404-758-4500
Atlanta, GA 30310 844-278-6945
info@gpsn.org
gpsn.org
The Georgia Parent Support Network assists children with mental, emotional, and behavioral challenges and their families through support, education, and advocacy.
Sue Smith, Ed.D., Chief Executive Officer
Brett Barton, LPC, Chief Operating Officer

1711 **Goodwill Industries International, Inc.**
15810 Indianola Drive contactus@goodwill.org
Rockville, MD 20855 www.goodwill.org
A nonprofit, community-based organization whose mission is to help people achieve self-sufficiency through the dignity and power of work, serving people who are disadvantaged, disabled or elderly. The mission is accomplished through providing independent living skills, affordable housing, and training and placement in community employment. The GoodWill Network includes 160 independent, local locations across the U.S. and Canada.
Ned Helms, Chair
Steven C. Preston, President & CEO

1712 **Grady Health Systems: Behavioral Health Center**
10 Park Place NE 404-616-4444
Atlanta, GA 30303 gradyhealth.org
Focuses on the treatment of individuals with chronic and mental illnesses and strives to offer quality, evidence-based mental health and substance abuse care for clients. Grady provides a full range of adult behavioral health services, including peer support, individual and group treatment, and medication clinics, and conducts research with the goal of advancing the treatment of clients with trauma and mental illness.
John M. Haupert, Chief Executive Officer
Robert Jansen, MD, Chief Medical Officer

1713 **Griffith Centers for Children**
10190 Bannock Street 303-237-6865
Northglenn, CO 80260 info@griffithcenters.org
griffithcenters.org
Serves Colorado Springs children and adolescents with emotional or behavioral problems, as well as children who were victims of abuse.
Christina Murphy, President & CEO
Tania Sossi, Chief Operations Officer

1714 **Hawaii Families As Allies**
PO Box 1971 808-682-1511
Aiea, HI 96701 hfaa@hfaa.net
hifamilies.org
Support and outreach group for parents with children who have mental disorders.
Shanelle Lum, Executive Director

1715 **Health Federation of Philadelphia**
123 S Broad Street 215-567-8001
Philadelphia, PA 19109 healthfederation@healthfederation.org
healthfederation.org
A non-profit membership organization of community health centers in Southeastern Pennsylvania. The Health Federation of Philadelphia seeks to improve the availability and quality of health care services for underserved families and people.
Natalie Levkovich, Chief Executive Officer
Robert Purdy, Senior Director, Finance & Operations

1716 **Health Services Agency: Behavioral Health Santa Cruz**
1400 Emeline Avenue 831-454-4170
Santa Cruz, CA 95060 santacruzhealth.org
Serves to improve and protect the public health of Santa Cruz County and to ensure access to quality health care and treatment for residents. The Health Services Agency develops programs and services in mental health, as well as environmental health, public health, medical care, and substance abuse prevention and treatment. The HSA advocates for public health policy and seeks to eliminate the stigma associated with mental illness and other diseases.

1717 **Healthcare Association of New York State**
1 Empire Drive 518-431-7600
Rensselaer, NY 12144 hanys.org
Statewide healthcare association serving as the primary advocate for more than 550 non-profit and public hospitals, health systems, long-term care, home care, hospice, and other health care organizations throughout New York State.
M. Beatrice Grause, RN, JD, President
Courtney Burke, Chief Operating & Innovation Officer

1718 **Holy Cross Services**
1030 N River Road 989-270-0252
Saginaw, MI 48609 customerservice@hccsnet.org
holycrossservices.org
Holy Cross Services is a private, not-for-profit child and family services provider based in Michigan. The mission of Holy Cross Children's Services is to assist children and adults in leading productive and healthy lives.
Sharon Berkobien, President & CEO
Steve Adamczyk, Chief Information Officer

1719 **Hong Fook Mental Health Association**
3320 Midland Avenue 416-493-4242
Toronto, Ontario, M1V-5E6 info@hongfook.ca
hongfook.ca
Hong Fook Mental Health Association aims to facilitate access to mental health services for people with linguistic and cultural barriers. Mental health services includes self-help programs; family initiatives; clinical services, including group psychotherapy, intake, and case management; youth programs; and prevention and promotion programs.
Ramon Tam, President
Eric Ngai, Treasurer

1720 **Human Resources Development Institute**
222 S Jefferson Street 312-441-9009
Chicago, IL 60661 info@hrdi.org
hrdi.org
Community-based behavioral healthcare organization. Human Resources Development Institute seeks to provide quality community and behavioral health care services and programs in the areas of mental health, disabilities, alcohol and substance abuse, family services, community health, and youth prevention.
Eugene Humphrey, Executive Director
Tammie Morris, Deputy Director

1721 **Human Services Research Institute**
2336 Massachusetts Avenue 617-876-0426
Cambridge, MA 02140 hsri.org

Assists state and federal government to enhance services and support people with mental illness and people with developmental disabilities.
David Hughes, President
John Agosta, Executive Vice President

1722 **Indiana Resource Center for Autism (IRCA)**
2810 E Discovery Parkway 812-855-6508
Bloomington, IN 47408 prattc@indiana.edu
iidc.indiana.edu/irca
The Indiana Resource Center for Autism focuses on providing communities, organizations, and families with the information and skills to support children and individuals with autism, Asperger's syndrome, and other pervasive developmental disorders. The IRCA conducts outreach training and research, disseminates information about autism spectrum disorders, and encourages communication among professionals and families concerned with autism.
Cathy Pratt, Ph.D., BCBA-D, Director
Pam Anderson, Community Outreach Coordinator

1723 **Institute of Living-Anxiety Disorders Center**
The Institute of Living
200 Retreat Avenue 860-545-7685
Hartford, CT 06106 instituteofliving.org
The Anxiety Disorders Center provides treatment, conducts research, and educates mental health professionals on anxiety disorders. Treatment options include group therapy, cognitive behavioral therapy, and virtual reality therapy, and are offered at no cost.
Michael Dewberry, MD, Medical Director

1724 **Institute on Violence, Abuse and Trauma**
10065 Old Grove Road 858-527-1860
San Diego, CA 92131 www.ivatcenters.org
IVAT strives to be a comprehensive resource, training, and research center dealing with all aspects of violence, abuse, and trauma. Through a focus on collaborations with various partnering organizations, IVAT desires to bridge gaps and help improve current systems of care on a local, national, and global level.
Sandi Capuano Morrison, Chief Executive Officer

1725 **International Society of Psychiatric- Mental Health Nurses**
2424 American Lane 608-443-2463
Madison, WI 53704-3102 info@ispn-psych.org
ispn-psych.org
The mission of ISPN is to unite and strengthen the presence and the voice of specialty psychiatric-mental health nursing while influencing health care policy to promote equitable, evidence-based and effective treatment and care for individuals, families, and communities.
Cheryl Woods Giscombe, President
Jessica Retzlaff, Executive Director

1726 **Jewish Family Service of Atlantic and Cape May Counties**
607 North Jerome Avenue 609-822-1108
Margate, NJ 08402 jfsatlantic.org
Multi-service family counseling agency committed to strengthening and preserving individual, family, and community well-being while following Jewish philosophy and values.
Andrea Steinberg, LCSW, Chief Executive Officer
Ann Thoresen, LCSW, Chief Operating Officer

1727 **Jewish Family Service of Dallas**
5402 Arapaho Road 972-437-9950
Dallas, TX 75248 info@jfsdallas.org
jfsdallas.org
Cathy Barker, Chief Executive Officer
Deizel Sarte, Chief Operations Officer

1728 **Jewish Family Service of San Antonio**
12500 NW Military Highway 210-302-6920
San Antonio, TX 78231 www.jfs-sa.org
Talli Goldman-Dolge, Chief Executive Officer
Kristy Dean, Chief Clinical Officer

1729 **Jewish Family and Children's Service**
1430 Main Street 781-647-5327
Waltham, MA 02451 info@jfcsboston.org
jfcsboston.org
The Jewish Family & Children's Service supports families and individuals through the provision of health care programs based upon Jewish traditions of social responsibility, compassion, and respect for all community members. JF&CS assists all persons in need of care, with particular focus on vulnerable populations such as children and adults with disabilities or mental illness, seniors, and people experiencing domestic abuse, hunger, or financial crisis.
Gail Schulman, Chief Executive Officer
Susan Lit, Chief Financial & Operations Officer

1730 **Joshua Center Programs**
Natchaug Hospital
189 Storrs Road 860-456-1311
Mansfield Center, CT 06250 800-426-7792
natchaug.org
The Joshua Center Programs at Natchaug Hospital provide a range of services designed to treat children and adolescents who are struggling with emotional and behavioral problems, including mental illness, emotional trauma, and substance abuse. Intensive, structured treatment programs include group therapy, psycho-education, individual and family treatment, and medication management. Programs utilize a positive approach with the goal of maintaining recovery. Treatment programs offered with Joshua
Deborah Weidner, MD, MBA, Medical Director

1731 **Judge Baker Children's Center**
53 Parker Hill Avenue 617-232-8390
Boston, MA 02120 info@jbcc.harvard.edu
jbcc.harvard.edu
A nonprofit organization dedicated to improving the lives of children whose emotional and behavioral problems threaten to limit their potential. Integrating education, service, research, and training, the Center is the oldest child mental health organization in New England and a national leader in the field of children's mental health. Promoting the best possible mental health of children through the integration of research, intervention, training, and advocacy.
Robert P. Franks, Ph.D., President & CEO
Gary R. Lyon, Ed.D, MPA, VP, Innovation & External Affairs

1732 **KY-SPIN (Kentucky Special Parent Involvement Network)**
10301-B Deering Road 502-937-6894
Louisville, KY 40272 800-525-7746
spininc@kyspin.com
kyspin.com
Non-profit organization dedicated to helping individuals with disabilities and their families improve their quality of life through information, resources, programs, training opportunities, and support networks.
Rhonda Logsdon, Executive Director
Kellie Smith, Assistant Director

1733 **Kentucky Partnership for Families and Children**
600 Teton Trail 502-875-1320
Frankfort, KY 40601 kpfc@kypartnership.org
kypartnership.org
Non-profit organization focused on the needs of children and youth with behavioral health challenges and their families. Works to enhance the quality of services, effect policy changes, and educate legislators about emotional disabilities in children.
Carol Cecil, Executive Director

1734 **Keys for Networking: Kansas Parent Information & Resource Center**
900 South Kansas Avenue 785-233-8732
Topeka, KS 66612 info@keys.org
www.keys.org
A non-profit organization offering assistance to families in Kansas whose children have behavioral, educational, emotional, and substance abuse challenges. Mission is to provide parents and youth in Kansas with services, information, resources, support, education, and training.

1735 **Learning Disabilities Association of America**
461 Cochran Road 412-341-1515
Pittsburgh, PA 15228 info@ldaamerica.org
ldaamerica.org
LDA's mission is to educate individuals with learning disabilities and their families through conferences, workshops, and sympo-

siums, as well as advocate for the rights of individuals with learning disabilities and provide support for parents.
Cindy Cipoletti, Executive Director
Nina DelPrato, Administrative Manager

1736 **Life Development Institute**
5940 W Union Hills Drive 623-773-1545
Glendale, AZ 85308 www.discoverldi.com
LDI is a special education school dedicated to motivating and inspiring its students to seek and experience success. Learning disability program staff and administrators are devoted to actively working with and supporting parents to help their child succeed and be independent for life.
Rob Crawford, MEd, Chief Executive Officer
Veronica Lieb Crawford, MA, President

1737 **Lifespire**
1 Whitehall Street 212-741-0100
New York, NY 10004 info@lifespire.org
lifespire.org
Lifespire seeks to provide support to individuals with disabilities and assist them with the development of the skills needed to become independent and contributing members of the community.
Thomas Lydon, President & CEO
Dave Henry, Chief Operating Officer

1738 **Little City Foundation (LCF)**
1760 W Algonquin Road 847-358-5510
Palatine, IL 60067 info@littlecity.org
littlecity.org
The mission of Little City Foundation is to provide quality services for children and adults with intellectual and developmental disabilities and to offer opportunities that will enable them to lead productive and fulfilling lives.
Shawn Jeffers, Executive Director
Jayne Drew, Chief Development Officer

1739 **Macomb County Community Mental Health**
22550 Hall Road 855-996-2264
Clint Township, MI 48036 mccmh.net
Offers a range of mental health treatment and support services for individuals affected by mental illness, developmental disabilities, and substance use disorders, and seeks to advance their recovery, independence, and self-sufficiency.

1740 **Maryland Psychiatric Research Center**
55 Wade Avenue mprc.umaryland.edu
Catonsville, MD 21228
The Maryland Psychiatric Research Center is a research center within the University of Maryland School of Medicine. The MPRC studies the causes and treatments of schizophrenia and related disorders, and provides treatments for patients with schizophrenia.
Robert W. Buchanan, MD, Director

1741 **Massachusetts Behavioral Health Partnership**
1000 Washington Street 617-790-4000
Boston, MA 02118 800-495-0086
TTY: 877-509-6981
masspartnership.com
The Massachusetts Behavioral Health Partnership provides medical and behavioral health care for MassHealth Members who select the Division's Primary Care Clinician Plan, as well as children in state custody.
Sharon Hanson, Chief Executive Officer
Nancy E. Norman, MD, MPH, Medical Director, Integration

1742 **Memphis Business Group on Health**
4728 Spottswood Avenue 901-767-9585
Memphis, TN 38117 memphisbusinessgroup.org
Memphis Business Group on Health is a coalition of member employers seeking to manage health benefits, implement wellness programs and promote a healthy workforce.
Cristie Upshaw Travis, Chief Executive Officer
Janis M. Slivinski, Administrative Assistant

1743 **Menninger Clinic**
12301 Main Street 713-275-5400
Houston, TX 77035 www.menningerclinic.org
Menninger is a leading psychiatric hospital dedicated to treating individuals with mood, personality, anxiety, and addictive disorders; teaching mental health professionals; and advancing mental healthcare through research.
Armando E. Colombo, President & CEO
Cory Walker, DO, Chief Medical Officer

1744 **Mental Health America**
500 Montgomery Street 703-684-7722
Alexandria, VA 22314 800-969-6642
www.mhanational.org
Mental Health America is a community-based nonprofit organization committed to enabling the mental wellness of all Americans and improving treatments and services for individuals with mental health needs. Provides information about a range of disorders; advocates for policies focused on advancing early intervention and prevention; and organizes education and outreach initiatives.
Schroeder Stribling, President & CEO
Theresa Nguyen, Chief Program Officer

1745 **Mental Health Center of North Central Alabama**
1316 Somerville Road SE 256-355-6105
Decatur, AL 35601 800-365-6008
mhcnca.org
Non-profit organization serving Lawrence, Limestone and Morgan counties. Provides treatment, education and assistance services and programs for people affected by mental health problems.
Henry White, President
Luke Slayton, Vice President

1746 **Mental Health Media**
25 West Street 617-562-1111
Westborough, MA 01581 www.mentalhealth-media.org
Mental Health Media, formerly The Mental Illness Education Project, is engaged in the production of video-based educational and support materials for the following specific populations: people with psychiatric disabilities, families, mental health professionals, special audiences, and the general public. The videos are designed to be used in hospital, clinical, and educational settings, and at home by individuals and families.

1747 **Mental Health and Aging Network (MHAN) - American Society on Aging (ASA)**
American Society on Aging
605 Market Street 800-537-9728
San Francisco, CA 94105 info@asaging.org
asaging.org
MHAN is dedicated to improving the supportive interventions for older adults with mental health problems and their caregivers by creating a network of professionals with expertise in geriatric mental health, improving systems of care for older adults with dementia, and advocating services and programs that help older adults with mental health issues.
Peter Kaldes, President & CEO
Robert R. Lowe, Chief Operating Officer

1748 **Mentally Ill Kids in Distress (MIKID)**
7816 North 19th Avenue 602-253-1240
Phoenix, AZ 85021 phoenix@mikid.org
mikid.org
Mentally Ill Kids in Distress provides support and assistance to families in Arizona with children and youth who are struggling with behavioral problems. MIKID seeks to improve the behavioral health and wellness of youth across Arizona. Offers information centers, assistance by phone, email or in person, support groups, educational meetings, referrals to resources, and direct support services.
Jeff Kazmierczak, RN, MSN, Chief Executive Officer
Bonnie Kolakowski, MBA, Chief Financial Officer

1749 **Metropolitan Family Services**
One North Dearborn 312-986-4000
Chicago, IL 60602 contactus@metrofamily.org
metrofamily.org
Metropolitan Family Services provides programs and services designed to help families across Chicago, DuPage County, Evanston/Skokie and the southwest suburbs achieve stability and self-sufficiency.
Ricardo Estrada, President & CEO
Theresa C. Nihill, Chief Operating Officer

1750 **Michigan Association for Children's Mental Health**
6017 W St. Joseph Highway 517-372-4016
Lansing, MI 48917 888-226-4543
acmh-mi.org
Michigan-based non-profit organization serving families of children and youth with emotional, behavioral, or mental health needs. Provides information, support, resources, referrals, advocacy, and networking and leadership opportunities for youth.
Jane Shank, Executive Director
Mary Porter, Business Manager

1751 **MindWise Innovations**
270 Bridge Street 781-239-0071
Dedham, MA 02026 info@mindwise.org
www.mindwise.org
Formerly known as Screening For Mental Health, MindWise Innovations provides resources to schools, workplaces, and communities to address mental health issues, eating disorders, substance abuse, and suicide.
Bryan Kohl, Executive Director
Marjie McDaniel, Vice President

1752 **Missouri Behavioral Health Council**
221 Metro Drive 573-634-4626
Jefferson City, MO 65109 mobhc.org
Seeks to improve access to mental health services for all residents of Missouri.
Brent McGinty, President & CEO
Rachelle Glavin, VP, Strategic Clinical Initiatives

1753 **Missouri Institute of Mental Health**
4633 World Parkway Circle 314-516-8400
Saint Louis, MO 63134 info@mimh.edu
mimh.edu
The Missouri Institute of Mental Health is a health services research organization providing professional training, research, program evaluation, policy development, and community outreach to the Missouri Department of Mental Health, as well as state agencies, service provider agencies, and other organizations and individuals pursuing information on mental health and related issues.
Robert Paul, Director
LaToshia Boyd-Lee, Program Director

1754 **Monadnock Family Services**
64 Main Street 603-357-4400
Keene, NH 03431 mfs.org
A nonprofit community mental health agency serving the mental health needs of children, youth and adults through counseling, support services, and programs in parent education, family support, youth development, and substance abuse prevention and treatment.
Brian Donovan, Chair
John Round, Treasurer

1755 **Mountain State Parent Child Adolescent Network**
1739 Saint Marys Avenue 304-428-0365
Parkersburg, WV 26101 800-244-5385
mspcan.org
A private non-profit, family-run organization that improves outcomes for children with serious emotional disorders and their families.
Donna Moss, Project Director
Laura Goodrich, Parent Coordinator

1756 **Nathan S. Kline Institute for Psychiatric Research**
140 Old Orangeburg Road 845-398-5500
Orangeburg, NY 10962 nki.rfmh.org
A facility of the New York State Office of Mental Health that has earned a national and international reputation for its pioneering contributions in psychiatric research, especially in the areas of psychopharmacological treatments for schizophrenia and major mood disorders, and in the application of computer technology to mental health services.
Donald C. Goff, MD, Director
Antonio Convit, MD, Deputy Director

1757 **National Alliance for Hispanic Health**
1501 16th Street NW 866-783-2645
Washington, DC 20036 www.healthyamericas.org
Members are Spanish-speaking mental health professionals and patients and those interested in services and decision-making that consider culture and community.
Jane L. Delgado, Ph.D., MS, President & CEO
Adolph P. Falcon, MPP, Executive Vice President

1758 **National Alliance on Mental Illness (NAMI)**
4301 Wilson Boulevard 703-524-7600
Arlington, VA 22203 888-999-6264
info@nami.org
www.nami.org
Committed to building better lives for the millions of Americans affected by mental illness by raising awareness and offering community support.
Daniel H. Gillison, Jr., Chief Executive Officer
Sherman Gillums, Jr., Chief Strategy & Operations Officer

1759 **National Association for Rural Mental Health**
660 North Capitol Street NW 202-942-4276
Washington, DC 20001 info@narmh.org
narmh.org
NARMH provides a forum for rural mental health professionals and advocates to identify and solve challenges, to work cooperatively toward improving the delivery of rural mental health services, and to promote the unique needs and concerns of rural mental health policy and practice issues. NARMH sponsors an annual conference where rural mental health professionals benefit from the sharing of knowledge and resources.
David Weden, President
Ron Manderscheid, Executive Director

1760 **National Association for the Dually Diagnosed (NADD)**
321 Wall Street 845-331-4336
Kingston, NY 12401 info@thenadd.org
thenadd.org
NADD is a nonprofit organization designed to increase awareness of, and provide services for, individuals with developmental disabilities and mental illness. NADD emphasizes the importance of quality mental healthcare for people with mental health needs and offers conferences, information resources, educational programs, and training materials to professionals, parents, and organizations.
Daniel Baker, President
Bruce Davis, Vice President

1761 **National Association of State Mental Health Program Directors**
66 Canal Center Plaza 703-739-9333
Alexandria, VA 22314 www.nasmhpd.org
Offers referrals to state mental health programs, services and physicians for persons with mental illness.
Brian Hepburn, MD, Executive Director
Jay Meek, CPA, MBA, Chief Financial Officer

1762 **National Center for Learning Disabilities**
1220 L Street NW 301-966-2234
Washington, DC 20005 ncld.org
The NCLD's mission is to ensure success for all individuals with learning disabilities in school, at work, and in life. They connect parents with resources, guidance, and support to advocate effectively for their children; deliver evidence-based tools, resources, and professional development to educators to improve student outcomes; and develop policies and engage advocates to strengthen educational rights and opportunities.
Lindsay E. Jones, President & CEO
Kena Mayberry, Chief Operating Officer

1763 **National Council for Behavioral Health**
1400 K Street NW 202-684-7457
Washington, DC 20005 communications@thenationalcouncil.org
thenationalcouncil.org
The unifying voice of America's behavioral health organizations. The National Council is committed to providing comprehensive, quality care that affords every opportunity for recovery and inclusion in all aspects of community life. The National Council advocates for public policies in mental and behavioral health that ensure that people who are ill can access comprehensive healthcare services, and also offer state-of-the-science education and practice improvement resources.
Charles Ingoglia, President & CEO
Jeannie Campbell, Executive Vice President & COO

1764 **National Disability Rights Network, Inc.**
820 1st Street NE
Washington, DC 20002
202-408-9514
TTY: 220-408-9521
info@ndrn.org
ndrn.org
NDRN is a nonprofit membership organization for the Protection and Advocacy Systems and the Client Assistance Programs. These programs work to guard against abuse, advocate for basic rights, and ensure acocunability throughout a variety of areas for people with disabilities and mental illnesses.
Curtis Decker, Executive Director
Eric Buehlmann, Deputy Executive Director, Public Policy

1765 **National Empowerment Center**
599 Canal Street
Lawrence, MA 01840
978-685-1494
800-769-3728
power2u.org
A consumer/survivor/expatient-run organization that is dedicated to helping people with mental health issues, trauma, and/or extreme states. Their central message revolves around recovery, empowerment, and healing.
Daniel B. Fisher, MD, Ph.D., Chief Executive Officer
Oryx Cohen, MPA, Chief Operating Officer

1766 **National Federation of Families**
15800 Crabbs Branch Way
Rockville, MD 20855
240-403-1901
ffcmh@ffcmh.org
ffcmh.org
A national organization focused on advocating for the rights of children affected by mental health challenges, assisting family-run organizations across the nation, and ensuring that children and families concerned with mental health have access to services.
Lynda Gargan, Ph.D., Executive Director
Kelly McNabb, Administrative Coordinator

1767 **National Health Foundation**
515 South Figueroa Street
Los Angeles, CA 90071
nationalhealthfoundation.org
Public charity whose mission is to improve the healthcare available to underserved groups through the development, support and provision of programs that address the systemic barriers in healthcare access and delivery.
Kelly Bruno, President & CEO
Mia Arias, Chief Operating Officer

1768 **National Institute of Mental Health**
6001 Executive Boulevard
Bethesda, MD 20892
866-615-6464
TTY: 301-443-8431
nimhinfo@nih.gov
www.nimh.nih.gov
One of 27 components of the National Institutes of Health, the Federal government's principal biomedical and behavioral research agency. The National Institute of Mental Health is an expert in mental disorders and aims to improve the treatment and recovery of mental illness through clinical research.
Joshua A. Gordon, MD, Ph.D., Director

1769 **National Institute on Drug Abuse (NIDA)**
Office of Science Policy & Communications
301 North Stonestreet Avenue
Bethesda, MD 20892
301-443-1124
www.drugabuse.gov
NIDA is part of the National Institute of Health, and aims to advance research on the causes and consequences of drug use and addiction in order to improve public health.
Nora Volkow, MD, Director
Wilson Compton, MD, Deputy Director

1770 **National Mental Health Consumers' Self-Help Clearinghouse**
selfhelpclearinghouse@gmail.com
mhselfhelp.org
The Clearinghouse is a peer-run national technical assistance center focused on achieving respect and equality of opportunity for those with mental illnesses. The Clearinghouse helps with the growth of the mental health consumer movement by evaluating mental health services, advocating for mental health reform, and providing consumers with news, information, publications, and consultation services.
Joseph Rogers, Founder & Executive Director
Susan Rogers, Director

1771 **National Network for Mental Health**
PO Box 1539
St. Catharines, Ontario, L2R-7J9
888-406-4663
info@nnmh.ca
nnmh.ca
The purpose of the NNMH is to advocate, educate, and provide expertise and resources that benefit the Canadian consumer/survivor community. The focus of the organization is to network with Candian consumer/survivors and family and friends of consumer/survivors to provide opportunities for resource sharing, information distribution, and education on issues impacting persons living with mental health issues/illness/disability.
Kathleen Thompson, Co-Chair
Walter Wai Tak Chan, Co-Chair

1772 **National Organization on Disability**
77 Water Street
New York, NY 10005
646-505-1191
info@nod.org
nod.org
NOD is a private, nonprofit organization that is dedicatd to helping people with disabilities live full, independent lives. NOD conducts research on disability employment issues, including the field's most widely used polls on employment trends and the quality of life for people with disabilities. They work in partnership with employers, schools, the military, service providers, researchers, and disability advocates.
Carol Glazer, President
Moeena Das, Chief of Staff

1773 **National Rehabilitation Association**
PO Box 150235
Alexandria, VA 22315
888-258-4295
info@nationalrehab.org
www.nationalrehab.org
The National Rehabilitation Association is concerned with the rights of people with disabilities. Their mission is to provide advocacy, awareness, and career advancement for professionals in the fields of rehabilitation. Members include rehab counselors; physical, speech, and occupational therapists; job trainers; consultants; independent living instructors; and other professionals involved in the advocacy of programs and services for people with disabilities.
Satinder Atwal, Chief Administrator Officer
James Liin, Membership Coordinator

1774 **Nebraska Family Support Network**
3568 Dodge Street
Omaha, NE 68131
402-345-0791
info@nefamilysupport.org
nefamilysupportnetwork.org

1775 **Nevada Principals' Executive Program**
7211 W Charleston Boulevard
Las Vegas, NV 89117
702-388-8899
800-216-5188
pepinfo@nvpep.org
nvpep.org
To strengthen and renew the knowledge, skills, and beliefs of public school leaders so that they might help improve the conditions for teaching and learning in schools and school districts.
Karen Taycher, Executive Director
Natalie Filipic, Director, Operations

1776 **New Hope Integrated Behavioral Healthcare**
80 Conover Road
Marlboro, NJ 07746
732-946-3030
800-705-4673
www.newhopeibhc.org
A nonprofit corporation serving those in need of treatment for alcoholism, drug addiction, and compulsive gambling. Over the years, New Hope has expanded its capacity and capabilities to include specialized programming for adolescents, women, and those with co-occuring disorders. New Hope constantly strives to advance the quality of addiction treatment through ongoing professional education and participation in select research projects.
Tony Comerford, Ph.D., President & CEO
David Roden, LCSW, LCADC, Vice President & COO

1777 **New Jersey Association of Mental Health & Addiction Agencies**
3635 Quakerbridge Road
Trenton, NJ 08619
609-838-5488
info@njamhaa.org
njamhaa.org
The New Jersey Association of Mental Health and Addiction Agencies represents mental healthcare and substance use treat-

ment providers serving New Jersey residents affected by mental illness or addictions and their families.
Debra L. Wentz, Ph.D., President & CEO
Julia Schneider, Chief Financial Officer

1778 **New York Association of Psychiatric Rehabilitation Services**
194 Washington Avenue 518-436-0008
Albany, NY 12210 nyaprs.org
New York Association of Psychiatric Rehabilitation Services (NYAPRS) is a statewide coalition of New Yorkers who receive or provide mental health services. NYAPRS is committed to improving the quality and availability of services for individuals with psychiatric disabilities. NYAPRS promotes mental health recovery and rehabilitation and works to fight the discrimination that persons with psychiatric disabilities face both within the mental health system and in the larger community.
Harvey Rosenthal, Chief Executive Officer
Len Statham, Chief Operating Officer

1779 **North American Training Institute**
314 West Superior Street 218-722-1503
Duluth, MN 55802 888-989-9234
info@nati.org
nati.org
The North American Training Institute is a not-for-profit organization based in Minnesota. NATI's mission is to promote research and professional training about gambling addiction. NATI provides resources and services for individuals at risk of developing a gambling addiction, particularly adolescents.
Elizabeth George, Chief Executive Officer

1780 **Northeast Business Group on Health**
80 Pine Street 212-252-7440
New York, NY 10005 nebgh@nebgh.org
nebgh.org
The Northeast Business Group on Health is a not-for-profit coalition of providers, insurers, and organizations in New York, New Jersey, Connecticut and Massachusetts. The mission of NEBGH is to promote a value-based health care system by improving health care delivery and contributing to health care decisions.
Candice Sherman, Chief Executive Officer
Amy Tippett-Stangler, Senior Vice President

1781 **Nueva Esperanza Counseling Center**
720 W Court Street 509-545-6506
Pasco, WA 99301

1782 **Office of Women's Health**
200 Independence Avenue SW 202-690-7650
Washington, DC 20201 800-994-9662
womenshealth@hhs.gov
www.womenshealth.gov
Government agency under the Department of Health & Human Services, with free health information for women.
Dorothy Fink, MD, Deputy Asst. Secretary, Women's Health
Richelle West Marshall, Deputy Director

1783 **Ohio Children's Alliance**
2600 Corporate Exchange Drive 614-461-0014
Columbus, OH 43231 www.ohiochildrensalliance.org
Ohio Children's Alliance is an association of child and family service providers in Ohio. The mission of the association is to strengthen the quality of services for children, young adults, and families in Ohio through efforts in policy advocacy, as well as support of member agencies.
Mark M. Mecum, Chief Executive Officer
Karen Hill, Chief Operating & Financial Officer

1784 **Ohio Council of Behavioral Health & Family Services Providers**
35 East Gay Street 614-228-0747
Columbus, OH 43215 theohiocouncil.org
A trade association representing Ohio-based organizations that provide alcohol and drug addiction treatment, mental health, behavioral healthcare and family services to their communities.
Teresa Lampl, Chief Executive Officer
Geoff Collver, Associate Director

1785 **Ohio Department of Mental Health & Addiction Services**
30 East Broad Street 614-466-2596
Columbus, OH 43215 877-275-6364
TTY: 614-752-9696
questions@mha.ohio.gov
mha.ohio.gov
State agency responsible for the oversight and funding of public mental health programs and services.
Lori Criss, Director
Justin Trevino, MD, Medical Director

1786 **Option Institute**
2080 S Undermountain Road 413-229-2100
Sheffield, MA 01257 800-714-2779
participantsupport@option.org
www.option.org
Self-defeating beliefs, along with attitudes and judgments, can lead to a host of physical and psychological challenges. The Option Institute offers programs designed to help people gain new perspectives on the attitudes and judgments that may be affecting their lives.
Barry Neil Kaufman, Co-Founder & CEO
Samahria Lyte Kaufman, Co-Founder

1787 **Oregon Family Support Network**
4275 Commercial Street SE 503-363-8068
Salem, OR 97302 info@ofsn.net
ofsn.org
A non-profit organization working to help families with children and youth affected by mental or behavioral disorders and to represent families and youth in local and state policy making. Provides advocacy, support, education and services.
Sandy Bumpus, Executive Director
Tammi Paul, Deputy Director

1788 **PACER Center**
8161 Normandale Boulevard 952-838-9000
Bloomington, MN 55437 pacer.org
PACER provides information, training, and assistance to parents of children and young adults with all disabilities (physical, learning, cognitive, emotional, and health). Its mission is to help improve the quality of life for young people with disabilities and their families.
Paula F. Goldberg, Executive Director

1789 **Parent Professional Advocacy League**
77 Rumford Avenue 866-815-8122
Waltham, MA 02453 info@ppal.net
ppal.net
Grassroots family organization providing support, education, publications, and advocacy for children with mental health needs and their families.
Lisa Lambert, Executive Director
Meri Viano, Associate Director

1790 **Parent Support Network of Rhode Island**
535 Centerville Road 401-467-6855
Warwick, RI 02886 psnri.org
Non-profit organization of families providing support for families with children and youth who have, or are at risk for, behavioral, emotional, or mental health problems. Parent Support Network promotes mental health and well-being with the goal of strengthening families. Parent Support Network provides advocacy, training, support services, and education, and works to raise public awareness on children and behavioral health.
Lisa Conlan Lewis, Executive Director, CPRS
Ragan Meriwether, Executive Manager

1791 **Parent to Parent of Omaha**
Ollie Webb Center
1941 South 42nd Street 402-346-5220
Omaha, NE 68105 olliewebbinc.org/parent-to-parent
Consists of parents, professionals, and others who are interested in providing emotional and peer support to parents of children with disabilities. Offers a parent-matching program which matches new parents wih parents who have had sufficient experience and training. Publications: The Gazette, newsletter, published 6 times a year. Also has chapters in Arizona and limited other states.
Laurie Ackermann, Executive Director
Robin McArthur, Operations Director

1792 **Parents Helping Parents**
Sobrato Center for Nonprofits
1400 Parkmoor Avenue 408-727-5775
San Jose, CA 95126 855-727-5775
info@php.com
php.com
PHP's mission is to help children and adults with special needs receive the support and services they need to reach their full potential by providing information, training, and resources to build strong families and improve systems of care.
Maria Daane, Executive Director
Mark Fishler, Director, Development

1793 **Planned Lifetime Assistance Network of Northeast Ohio**
29125 Cagrin Boulevard 216-504-2609
Pepper Pike, OH 44122 www.planofjfsa.org
PLAN is a membership organization that provides help and support for individuals living with mental illness, cognitive disabilities, and autism spectrum disorder and their families. PLAN seeks to help people achieve emotional and cognitive development through the provision of social and wellness programs, work and volunteer opportunities, and family advocacy.
Rebecca Rinaldi, Community Activities Administrator

1794 **Positive Education Program**
3100 Euclid Avenue 216-361-4400
Cleveland, OH 44115 info@pepcleve.org
pepcleve.org
The Positive Education Program (PEP) is a non-profit agency serving to help troubled children and youth develop skills to learn and grow successfully.
Habeebah R. Grimes, Chief Executive Officer
Michelle Breen, Chief Clinical Officer

1795 **Recovery International**
1415 W 22nd Street 312-337-5661
Oak Brook, IL 60523 866-221-0302
info@recoveryinternational.org
www.recoveryinternational.org
Recovery International is an organization that uses a peer-to-peer, self-help training system developed by Abraham Low in order to help individuals with mental health issues lead more productive lives.
Sandra K. Wilcoxon, Chief Executive Officer
Everlean Pelt, Office Administrator

1796 **Sheppard Pratt Health System**
6501 N Charles Street 410-938-3000
Baltimore, MD 21204 info@sheppardpratt.org
www.sheppardpratt.org
Provider of mental health, special education, substance use, and social services.
Harsh K. Trivedi, MD, MBA, President & CEO
Todd Peters, MD, VP & Chief Medical Officer

1797 **Sidran Institute**
7238 Muncaster Mill Road 410-825-8888
Derwood, MD 20855 admin@sidran.org
sidran.org
Sidran Institute provides useful, practical information for child and adult survivors of any type of trauma, for families/friends, and for the clinical and frontline service providers who assist in their recovery. Sidran's philosophy of education through collaboration brings together great minds (providers, survivors, and loved ones) to develop comprehensive programs to address the practical, emotional, spiritual, and medical needs of trauma survivors.
Esther Giller, President & Director

1798 **Southwest Solutions**
5716 Michigan Avenue 313-481-3102
Detroit, MI 48210 swsol.org
Southwest Solutions provides human development, economic development, and community engagement programs for individuals living with mental illness. Southwest seeks to help marginalized persons build meaningful futures.
Sean de Four, President & CEO
Michelle Sherman, Chief Operating Officer

1799 **Substance Abuse and Mental Health Services Administration (SAMHSA)**
5600 Fishers Lane 877-726-4727
Rockville, MD 20857 TTY: 800-487-4889
www.samhsa.gov
Part of the U.S. Department of Health and Human Services, SAMHSA promotes, monitors, evaluates and coordinates programs for the prevention and treatment of alcoholism and alcohol abuse.
Miriam Delphin-Rittmon, Ph.D., Assistant Secretary
Sonia Chessen, Chief of Staff

1800 **TN Voices**
500 Professional Park Drive 615-269-7751
Goodlettsville, TN 37072 800-670-9882
tnvoices.org
Speaks out as active advocates for the emotional and behavioral well-being of children and their families. A non-profit organization of families, professionals, business and community leaders, and government representatives committed to improving and expanding services related to the emotional and behavioral well-being of children.
Rikki Harris, Chief Executive Officer
Michelle Thomas, Chief Development Officer

1801 **Tennessee Association of Mental Health Organizations**
PO Box 1274 615-244-2220
Brentwood, TN 37024 800-568-2642
tamho@tamho.org
tamho.org
State-wide trade association representing primarily community mental health centers, community-owned corporations that have historically served the needs of the mentally ill and chemically dependent citizens of Tennessee regardless of their ability to pay.
Ellyn Wilbur, Executive Director
Alysia Smith Knight, Director, Policy & Advocacy

1802 **Tennessee Mental Health Consumers' Association**
3931 Gallatin Pike 615-250-1176
Nashville, TN 37216 888-539-0393
info@tmhca-tn.org
tmhca-tn.org
A not for profit organization whose members are mental health consumers and other individuals and groups who support our mission. TMHCA recognizes our members as individuals whose life experiences and dreams for the future are invaluable in the structuring of ourplans and policies.
Anthony Fox, President & CEO
Stacey Murphy, Chief Operating Officer

1803 **Texas Counseling Association (TCA)**
1210 San Antonio Street 512-472-3403
Austin, TX 78701 txca.org
The Texas Counseling Association is dedicated to providing leadership, advocacy and education to promote the growth and development of the counseling profession and those that are served.
Jan Friese, Executive Director
Chyenne Degelman, Office Administrator

1804 **The Arc New York**
29 British American Boulevard 518-439-8311
Latham, NY 12110 info@thearcny.org
www.thearcny.org
Formerly known as NYSARC, The Arc's goal is to improve the quality of life for people with intellectual and other developmental disabilities by providing support, information, direction, and services; to have one of the best service delivery systems in the nation, including family members, self-advocates, and professionals in all matters; and to continually build training and educational opportunities into all aspects of The Arc New York.
Erik Geizer, Chief Executive Officer
Kate Jerian, Chief Operating Officer

1805 **The Center for Family Support**
333 Seventh Avenue 212-629-7939
New York, NY 10001 www.cfsny.org
The Center for Family Support offers assistance to individuals with developmental and related disabilities, as well as their families, and provides support services and programs that are designed

to accommodate individual needs. Offers services throughout New York City, Westchester County, Long Island, and New Jersey.
Steven Vernikoff, Chief Executive Officer
Barbara Greenwald, Chief Operating Officer

1806 The Center for Workplace Mental Health
c/o American Psychiatric Foundation
800 Maine Avenue SW 202-559-3140
Washington, DC 20024 workplacementalhealth.org
The Center works with businesses to ensure that employees and their families living with mental illness, including substance use disorders, receive effective care. It does so in recognition that employers purchase healthcare for millions of American workers and their families.
Darcy Gruttadaro, JD, Director
Emma Jellen, Associate Director

1807 The Coalition for Behavioral Health
14 Penn Plaza 212-742-1600
New York, NY 10122 thecoalition@coalitionny.org
www.coalitionny.org
An advocacy organization of New York's mental health community representing over 100 non-profit community health agencies that serve clients in the five boroughs of New York City.
Amy Dorin, President & CEO
Nadia Chait, Director, Policy & Advocacy

1808 The SickKids Centre for Community Mental Health
440 Jarvis Street 416-924-1164
Toronto, Ontario, M4Y-2H4 855-944-4673
info@sickkidscmh.ca
www.sickkidscmh.ca
A nonprofit children's mental health centre providing mental health services to infants, children, youth, and families. Formerly known as The Hincks-Dellcrest Centre, the SickKids Center provides prevention, intervention, outpatient, and residential treatment programs; assists with the education and training of mental health clinicians and managers; conducts research and develops and evaluates new methods for treatment; and increases awareness of the issues surrounding children's mental health.
Christina Bartha, Executive Director
Neill Carson, Clinical Director

1809 The World Bank Group
1818 H Street NW 202-473-1000
Washington, DC 20433 www.worldbank.org
The World Bank helps develop low and middle income countries to improve peoples health and to guard against the poverty that can result from sudden illness, including mental disorders.
David Malpass, President
Anshula Kant, Chief Financial Officer

1810 Thresholds
4101 N Ravenswood Avenue 773-572-5500
Chicago, IL 60613 contact@thresholds.org
thresholds.org
Thresholds is an organization that serves people with severe and persistent mental illness with a range of programs designed with the individual's recovery as a goal. Their goal is to help those with mental illness reclaim their lives through care, employment, and advocacy.
Mark Ishaug, Chief Executive Officer
Debbie Pavick, Chief Clinical Officer

1811 Together Georgia
90-F Glendra Trace 404-572-6170
Newnan, GA 30265 office@togetherga.net
togetherga.net
Together Georgia, formerly the Georgia Association of Homes and Services for Children, is an organization consisting of child and family service providers dedicated to caring for children who have experienced risk and neglect. Together Georgia provides staff training and information, organizes regular meetings for members, and strives for a positive future for Georgia's children and families.
Juanita Stedman, Executive Director
Claire Wood, Deputy Director

1812 United Advocates for Children and Families
3133 Arden Way 916-692-8087
Sacramento, CA 95825 info@uacf4hope.org
uacf4hope.org
A nonprofit organization that works on behalf of children and youth with mental, emotional, and behavioral challenges and their families.
Earl Kelly, Chief Executive Officer

1813 Uplift
109 E 17th Street 307-432-4055
Cheyenne, WY 82001 800-492-3199
info@upliftwy.org
upliftwy.org
Providing support, education, advocacy, information and referral for parents and professionals focusing on emotional, behavioral and learning needs of children and youth.
Michelle C. Heinen, Executive Director

1814 Utah Parent Center
5296 S Commerce Drive 801-272-1051
Murray, UT 84107 800-468-1160
info@utahparentcenter.org
utahparentcenter.org
The Utah Parent Center is a statewide nonprofit organization founded in 1984 to provide training, information, referral and assistance to parents of children and youth with all disabilities: physical, mental, learning and emotional. Staff at the center are primarily parents of children and youth with disabilities who carry out the philosophy of Parents Helping Parents.
Joey Hanna, Executive Director
Esperanza Reyes, Associate Director

1815 VOR
836 S Arlington Heights Road 877-399-4867
Elk Grove Village, IL 60007 info@vor.net
vor.net
Through national programs, VOR achieves its mission to unite advocates, as well as educate and assist families, organizations, public officials, and individuals concerned with the quality of life and choice for persons with intellectual disabilities within a full array of residential options, including community and facility-based care.
Hugo Dwyer, Executive Director

1816 Vanderbilt Kennedy Center
110 Magnolia Circle 615-322-8240
Nashville, TN 37203 kc@vumc.org
vkc.vumc.org
Research and research training related to disorders of thinking, learning, perception, communication, mood and emotion caused by disruption of typical development. Available services include behavior analysis clinic, referrals, lectures and conferences, and a free quarterly newsletter.
Jeffrey Neul, MD, Ph.D., Director
Laurie Cutting, Ph.D., Associate Director

1817 Vermont Association for Mental Health & Addiction Recovery
100 State Street 802-223-6263
Montpelier, VT 05602 info@vamhar.org
vamhar.org
An advocacy organization seeking to promote mental wellness and recovery through education, training, and community support.
Peter Espenshade, President
Melissa Story, Chief Operating Officer

1818 Washington State Psychological Association
2525 E 29th Avenue 206-547-4220
Spokane, WA 99223 wspa@wapsych.org
wapsych.org
To support, promote and advance the science, education and practice of psychology in the public interest.
Marvo Reguindin, Executive Director
Samantha Slaughter, Director, Professional Affairs

1819 Wisconsin Association of Family and Child Agencies
16 N Carroll Street 608-257-5939
Madison, WI 53703 wafca.org
Kathy Markeland, Executive Director
Emily Coddington, Associate Director

1820 **Wisconsin Family Ties**
16 N Carroll Street 608-267-6800
Madison, WI 53703 800-422-7145
info@wifamilyties.org
wifamilyties.org
A parent-run organization working with families to improve children's mental health.
Hugh Davis, Executive Director
Jody Andruss, Development Director

1821 **Women's Support Services**
158 Gay Street 860-364-1080
Sharon, CT 06069 info@wssdv.org
wssdv.org
Support and advocacy for those affected by emotional, physical, psychological, or sexual trauma in the Northwest region of Connecticut and nearby areas in New York and Massachusetts. Raises awareness on domestic abuse and seeks to engage all members of the community in the movement to end domestic violence.
Alexandra Lange, Co-Chair
Barbara Kahn Moller, Co-Chair

1822 **Woodlands Behavioral Healthcare Network**
960 M60 E 800-323-0335
Cassopolis, MI 49031 TTY: 800-323-0335
woodlandsbhn.org
Provides community behavioral health services.
Tim Smith, Executive Director

1823 **World Federation for Mental Health**
6800 Park Ten Boulevard info@wfmh.global
San Antonio, TX 78213 wfmh.global
An international organization to advance the prevention of mental and emotional disorders, the proper treatment and care of those with such disorders, and the promotion of mental health. The Federation has responded to international mental health crises through its role as a worldwide grassroots advocacy and public education organization in the mental health field.
Gabriel Ivbijaro, Secretary General & CEO

1824 **Young Adult Institute and Workshop (YAI)**
220 E 42nd Street 212-273-6100
New York, NY 10017 communications@yai.org
yai.org
Serves more than 20,000 people of all ages and levels of mental, developmental, and learning disabilities. Provides a full range of early intervention, preschool, family supports, employment training and placement, clinical and residential services, as well as recreation and camping services.
George Contos, Chief Executive Officer
Ravi Dahiya, Chief Program Officer

1825 **Zero To Three**
1255 23rd Street NW 202-638-1144
Washington, DC 20037 800-899-4301
zerotothree.org
A national, nonprofit organization that provides information and resources on early development to parents, professionals, and policymakers. Zero to Three's mission is to improve the lives of infants and toddlers, and to promote their health and development.
Matthew Melmed, Executive Director
Janice Im, Chief Program Officer

Alabama

1826 **Mental Health America in Etowah County**
821 E Broad Street 256-547-6888
Gadsden, AL 35903
An affiliate of Mental Health America, which is a community-based non-profit organization committed to enabling the mental wellness of all Americans. MHA advocates for greater access to quality health services and seeks to educate individuals on identifying symptoms, as well as intervention and prevention.

1827 **Mental Health America in Montgomery**
1116 S Hull Street 334-262-5500
Montgomery, AL 36104 mha@mha-montgomery.org
mha-montgomery.org
An affiliate of Mental Health America, which is a community-based non-profit organization committed to enabling the mental wellness of all Americans. MHA advocates for greater access to quality health services and seeks to educate individuals on identifying symptoms, as well as intervention and prevention.

1828 **NAMI Alabama (National Alliance on Mental Illness)**
1401 I-85 Parkway 334-396-4797
Montgomery, AL 36106 800-626-4199
wlaird@namialabama.org
namialabama.org
NAMI Alabama is a non-profit organization of local support and advocacy groups committed to improving the treatment and care available to persons diagnosed with a mental illness in Alabama. NAMI Alabama aims to enhance the quality of life for Alabamians with mental health needs.
James Walsh, President
Joan Elder, First Vice President

1829 **National Alliance on Mental Illness: Alabama**
1401 I-85 Parkway 334-396-4797
Montgomery, AL 36106 www.namialabama.org
Local chapter of the National Alliance on Mental Illness, an organization dedicated to raising awareness on mental health and providing support and education for Americans affected by mental illness. Mission is to help consumers and families share information about services, care providers, and ways to cope with the challenges of mental illness.
Joan Elder, Chapter Co-President
Robin Demonia, Chapter Co-President

Alaska

1830 **National Alliance on Mental Illness: Alaska**
Anchorage, AK 907-277-0227
info@namianchorage.org
www.namianchorage.org
Local chapter of the National Alliance on Mental Illness, an organization dedicated to raising awareness on mental health and providing support and education for Americans affected by mental illness. Mission is to help consumers and families share information about services, care providers, and ways to cope with the challenges of mental illness.
Jason Lessard, Chapter Executive Director
Lily Werts, Education Program Administrator

Arizona

1831 **Mental Health America of Arizona**
5110 North 40th Street 602-576-4828
Phoenix, AZ 85018 mhaofarizona@gmail.com
mhaarizona.org
An affiliate of Mental Health America, the organization promotes care and treatment for people with mental illness, educates Arizonans about mental health and participates in advocacy efforts, and strives for better mental health for people in Arizona.
Josh Mozell, JD, Chair
Erin Callinan, MSW, Associate Director

1832 **National Alliance on Mental Illness: Arizona**
602-244-8166
jimdunnaz@msn.com
www.namiarizona.org
Local chapter of the National Alliance on Mental Illness, an organization dedicated to raising awareness on mental health and providing support and education for Americans affected by mental illness. Mission is to help consumers and families share information about services, care providers, and ways to cope with the challenges of mental illness.
Jim Dunn, Chapter Executive Director
Sherron Candelaria, Chapter President

California

1833 **Mental Health America of California**
2110 K Street 916-557-1167
Sacramento, CA 95816 mhac.org
An affiliate of Mental Health America, which is a community-based non-profit organization committed to enabling the mental wellness of all Americans. MHA advocates for greater ac-

cess to quality health services and seeks to educate individuals on identifying symptoms, as well as intervention and prevention.
Richard Van Horn, Chair
Carol Hood, Chair Elect

1834 **National Alliance on Mental Illness: Gold Country**
PO Box 1088 209-736-4264
Angels Camp, CA 95222 nami.org
Local chapter of the National Alliance on Mental Illness, an organization dedicated to raising awareness on mental health and providing support and education for Americans affected by mental illness. Mission is to help consumers and families share information about services, care providers, and ways to cope with the challenges of mental illness.
Marilyn Ricci, MS, RD, President

1835 **Orange County Psychiatric Society**
5000 Campus Drive 949-250-3157
Newport Beach, CA 92660 ocps.org
Works to promote public awareness of mental health and improve care for people affected by mental illness.
Robert Bota, MD, President
Karina Amaya, Executive Director

Colorado

1836 **Federation of Families for Children's Mental Health: Colorado**
7475 West Fifth Avenue 303-893-7984
Lakewood, CO 80226 844-252-8202
coloradofederation.org
Advocates for children, youth, and families affected by mental illness and aims to improve mental health programs, services, and policies in Colorado.
Sarah Davidon, President and Chair
Randy Garfield, Vice President

1837 **Mental Health America of Colorado**
1120 Lincoln Street 720-208-2220
Denver, CO 80203 800-456-3249
www.mentalhealthcolorado.org
An affiliate of Mental Health America, which is a community-based non-profit organization committed to enabling the mental wellness of all Americans. MHA advocates for greater access to quality health services and seeks to educate individuals on identifying symptoms, as well as intervention and prevention.
Vincent Atchity, President & CEO
Kay Greene, Development Director

Connecticut

1838 **Mental Health Connecticut (Mental Health America)**
61 S Main Street 860-529-1970
West Hartford, CT 06107 www.mhconn.org
An affiliate of Mental Health America, which is a community-based non-profit organization committed to enabling the mental wellness of all Americans. MHA advocates for greater access to quality health services and seeks to educate individuals on identifying symptoms, as well as intervention and prevention.
Kim Sirois Pita, Chair
Scott Brabant, Vice Chair

Delaware

1839 **Mental Health America in Delaware**
100 W 10th Street 302-654-6833
Wilmington, DE 19801 www.mhainde.org
An affiliate of Mental Health America, which is a community-based non-profit organization committed to enabling the mental wellness of all Americans. MHA advocates for greater access to quality health services and seeks to educate individuals on identifying symptoms, as well as intervention and prevention.
Larence Kirby, MA, LPCMH, President
Victoria Kim Chang, MSW, Vice President

1840 **Mental Health Association of Delaware**
100 West 10th Street 302-654-6833
Wilmington, DE 19801 800-287-6423
information@mhainde.org
mhainde.org/wp/
Nonprofit organization focused on improving mental health for people in Delaware through education, support, and advocacy for mental health issues.
Lawrence G Boyer, President
James Lafferty, Executive Director

Florida

1841 **Federation of Families of Central Florida**
National Federation of Families for Children's Men
237 Fernwood Boulevard 407-334-8049
Fern Park, FL 32730 info.ffcfl@gmail.com
ffcflinc.org
An affiliate of the National Federation of Families for Children's Mental Health, the Federation of Families of Central Florida serves children and youth with emotional, behavioral, and mental health challenges and their families through advocacy, support, and education.
Muriel Jones, Executive Director

1842 **Mental Health America in Southeast Florida**
7145 W Oakland Park Boulevard 954-746-2055
Lauderhill, FL 33313 www.mhasefl.org
An affiliate of Mental Health America, which is a community-based non-profit organization committed to enabling the mental wellness of all Americans. MHA advocates for greater access to quality health services and seeks to educate individuals on identifying symptoms, as well as intervention and prevention.
Diane Mittelstaedt, MS, Chair
Toni Powers, First Fice Chair

1843 **Mental Health America in Southwest Florida**
2335 9th Street N
Suite 404 239-261-5405
Naples, FL 34103 www.mhawfl.org
An affiliate of Mental Health America, which is a community-based non-profit organization committed to enabling the mental wellness of all Americans. MHA advocates for greater access to quality health services and seeks to educate individuals on identifying symptoms, as well as intervention and prevention.

1844 **Mental Health America of East Central Florida**
531 S Ridgewood Avenue 386-252-5785
Daytona Beach, FL 32114 info@mhavolusia.org
mhavolusia.org
An affiliate of Mental Health America, which is a community-based non-profit organization committed to enabling the mental wellness of all Americans. MHA advocates for greater access to quality health services and seeks to educate individuals on identifying symptoms, as well as intervention and prevention.

1845 **National Alliance on Mental Illness: Florida**
PO Box 961 850-671-4445
Tallahassee, FL 32302 info@namiflorida.org
namiflorida.org
Contains thirty-six affiliates in communities throughout Florida that provide education, advocacy, and support groups for individuals and families affected by mental illness. Seeks to help persons with mental health needs become productive members of the community.
April Lynn Chambers, Chapter President

Georgia

1846 **Mental Health America in Georgia**
2250 N Druid Hills Road NE
Suite 275 770-741-1481
Atlanta, GA 30329 mhageorgia.org
An affiliate of Mental Health America, which is a community-based non-profit organization committed to enabling the mental wellness of all Americans. MHA advocates for greater access to quality health services and seeks to educate individuals on identifying symptoms, as well as intervention and prevention.
Jewell Gooding, Executive Director
Taimere Wood, Director of Operations

1847 **National Alliance on Mental Illness: Georgia**
770-234-0855
programs@namiga.org
namiga.org

Local chapter of the National Alliance on Mental Illness, an organization dedicated to raising awareness on mental health and providing support and education for Americans affected by mental illness. Mission is to help consumers and families share information about services, care providers, and ways to cope with the challenges of mental illness.
Kim H. Jonesr, Chapter Executive Director

Hawaii

1848 **Mental Health America of Hawai'i**
1136 Union Mall
Honolulu, HI 96813
808-521-1846
800-753-6879
mentalhealthhawaii.org
An affiliate of Mental Health America, which is a community-based non-profit organization committed to enabling the mental wellness of all Americans. MHA advocates for greater access to quality health services and seeks to educate individuals on identifying symptoms, as well as intervention and prevention.
Kimberly Myoshi, President
Katherine Watanabe Bennett, JD, Vice President

1849 **National Alliance on Mental Illness: Hawaii**
770 Kapiolani Boulevard
Honolulu, HI 96813
808-591-1297
info@namihawaii.org
namihawaii.org
Local chapter of the National Alliance on Mental Illness, an organization dedicated to raising awareness on mental health and providing support and education for Americans affected by mental illness. Mission is to help consumers and families share information about services, care providers, and ways to cope with the challenges of mental illness.

Idaho

1850 **National Alliance on Mental Illness: Idaho**
1985 E 25th Street
Idaho Falls, ID 83404
208-242-7430
idahonami@gmail.com
idahonami.org
Local chapter of the National Alliance on Mental Illness, an organization dedicated to raising awareness on mental health and providing support and education for Americans affected by mental illness. Mission is to help consumers and families share information about services, care providers, and ways to cope with the challenges of mental illness.
Michael Sandvig, Chapter President

Illinois

1851 **Mental Health America of Illinois**
1103 Westgate Street
Oak Park, IL 60301
312-368-9070
becky@mhai.org
mhai.org
An affiliate of Mental Health America, which is a community-based non-profit organization committed to enabling the mental wellness of all Americans. MHA advocates for greater access to quality health services and seeks to educate individuals on identifying symptoms, as well as intervention and prevention.
Ray Connor, President & Executive Director
Joseph Troiani, PhD, CADC, Vice President

Indiana

1852 **Mental Health America in Indiana**
1431 N Delaware Street
Indianapolis, IN 46202
317-638-3501
800-555-6424
info@mhai.net
mhai.net
An affiliate of Mental Health America, which is a community-based non-profit organization committed to enabling the mental wellness of all Americans. MHA advocates for greater access to quality health services and seeks to educate individuals on identifying symptoms, as well as intervention and prevention.
Stephen C. McCaffrey, JD, President & CEO
David Berman, MPH, MPA, Vice President of Development

1853 **Mental Health America of Indiana**
1431 North Delaware Street
Indianapolis, IN 46202
317-638-3501
800-555-6424
mhai.net
A statewide organization focused on mental illness and addictive disorder recovery and prevention through education, advocacy, and public health reform.
Stephen C McCaffrey, JD, President and CEO
Lisa Hutcheson, MEd, VP, Policy and Programs

1854 **National Alliance on Mental Illness: Indiana**
921 E 86th Street
Indianapolis, IN 46240
317-925-9399
800-677-6442
info@namiindiana.org
namiindiana.org
Local chapter of the National Alliance on Mental Illness, an organization dedicated to raising awareness on mental health and providing support and education for Americans affected by mental illness. Mission is to help consumers and families share information about services, care providers, and ways to cope with the challenges of mental illness.
Barbara Thompson, Chapter Executive Director

Iowa

1855 **Iowa Federation of Families for Children's Mental Health**
106 South Booth
Anamosa, IA 52205
319-462-2187
888-400-6302
iffcmh.org
Iowa Federation of Families for Children's Mental Health provides support and assistance to parents of children who have emotional or behavioral disorders, are receiving mental health or special education services, or are in the juvenile justice system. Mission is to work towards a system that will allow families to live in safe and stable environments.
Lori Reynolds, Executive Director
Heidi Reynolds, Program Director

1856 **Mental Health America of Dubuque County**
PO Box 283
Dubuque, IA 52004
563-580-7718
info@mhadbq.org
mhadbq.org
An affiliate of Mental Health America, which is a community-based non-profit organization committed to enabling the mental wellness of all Americans. MHA advocates for greater access to quality health services and seeks to educate individuals on identifying symptoms, as well as intervention and prevention.
Sue Whitty, President
Heather Heins, Vice President

1857 **National Alliance on Mental Illness: Iowa**
3839 Merle Hay Road
Des Moines, IA 50310
515-254-0417
info@namiiowa.org
namiiowa.org
Local chapter of the National Alliance on Mental Illness, an organization dedicated to raising awareness on mental health and providing support and education for Americans affected by mental illness. Mission is to help consumers and families share information about services, care providers, and ways to cope with the challenges of mental illness.
Dawn Grittmann, Chapter President
Peggy Huppert, Chapter Executive Director

Kansas

1858 **Mental Health America of South Central Kansas, Inc.**
555 N Woodlawn Street
Suite 3105
Wichita, KS 67208
316-685-1821
www.mhasck.org
An affiliate of Mental Health America, which is a community-based non-profit organization committed to enabling the mental wellness of all Americans. MHA advocates for greater access to quality health services and seeks to educate individuals on identifying symptoms, as well as intervention and prevention.
Brendan O'Bryhim, Chairman
Arnold Hudspeth, Treasurer

1859 **National Alliance on Mental Illness: Kansas**
1801 SW Wanamaker Road
Topeka, KS 66604
785-233-0755
800-539-2660
info@namiKansas.org
namikansas.org
Local chapter of the National Alliance on Mental Illness, an organization dedicated to raising awareness on mental health and providing support and education for Americans affected by mental illness. Mission is to help consumers and families share information about services, care providers, and ways to cope with the challenges of mental illness.
David Schmitt, Chapter President
Dr. Sherrie Vaughn, Chapter Executive Director

Kentucky

1860 **Kentucky Psychiatric Medical Association**
PO Box 7246
Louisville, KY 40257
502-695-4843
kypsych.org
A non-profit association of physicians specializing in the treatment of mental illnesses and substance use disorders.
Marc Cruser, MD, President
Sajida Suleman, MD, Vice President

1861 **Mental Health America of Kentucky**
216e Reynolds Road
Suite F
Lexington, KY 40517
859-684-7778
mhaky@mhaky.org
www.mhaky.org
An affiliate of Mental Health America, which is a community-based non-profit organization committed to enabling the mental wellness of all Americans. MHA advocates for greater access to quality health services and seeks to educate individuals on identifying symptoms, as well as intervention and prevention.
Mary Malone, President
Sheila Schuster, PhD, Vice President

Louisiana

1862 **Louisiana Federation of Families for Children's Mental Health**
5627 Superior Drive
Baton Rouge, LA 70816
225-293-3508
800-224-4010
info@laffcmh.org
laffcmh.org
A parent-run organization focused on addressing the needs of children and youth with emotional, behavioral or mental challenges and their families. Works with parents to provide resources and advocate for improved mental health care for children in Louisiana.
Anthony D Beasley, President
Megan Harrison, Vice President

1863 **Mental Health America for Greater Baton Rouge**
544 Colonial Drive
Baton Rouge, LA 70806
225-929-7674
www.mhagbr.com
An affiliate of Mental Health America, which is a community-based non-profit organization committed to enabling the mental wellness of all Americans. MHA advocates for greater access to quality health services and seeks to educate individuals on identifying symptoms, as well as intervention and prevention.
Melissa Silva, Executive Director
Stephanie Francis, Development Director

Maine

1864 **National Alliance on Mental Illness: Maine**
52 Water Street
Hallowell, ME 04347
207-622-5767
800-464-5767
info@namimaine.org
namimaine.org
Local chapter of the National Alliance on Mental Illness, an organization dedicated to raising awareness on mental health and providing support and education for Americans affected by mental illness. Mission is to help consumers and families share information about services, care providers, and ways to cope with the challenges of mental illness.
Jenna Mehnert, MSW, Chapter Executive Director
Nicole Vera, Chapter Chief of Staff

Maryland

1865 **Mental Health America of Maryland**
1301 York Road
Suite 505
Lutherville, MD 21093
443-901-1550
info@mhamd.org
www.mhamd.com
An affiliate of Mental Health America, which is a community-based non-profit organization committed to enabling the mental wellness of all Americans. MHA advocates for greater access to quality health services and seeks to educate individuals on identifying symptoms, as well as intervention and prevention.
Tim Santoni, President
Beatrice Rodgers, Vice President

1866 **Mental Health Association of Maryland**
1301 York Road
Lutherville, MD 21093
443-901-1550
800-572-6426
info@mhamd.org
mhamd.org
The Mental Health Association of Maryland is a nonprofit organization committed to promoting mental health and preventing mental illness. MHAMD provides mental health research, education and training through outreach, advocacy, education and services oversight programs.
Oscar Morgan, President
Linda J Raines, Chief Executive Officer

Massachusetts

1867 **Depression and Bipolar Support Alliance of Boston**
115 Mill Street
Belmont, MA 02478
617-855-2795
info@dbsaboston.org
dbsaboston.netfirms.com
DBSA-BOSTON is a non-profit organization dedicated to helping people with psychiatric illnesses lead healthy lives.
Chuck Weinstein, LMHC, CPRP, President
Lillian Cravotta-Crouch, Vice President

1868 **Massachusetts Association for Mental Health (Mental Health America)**
50 Federal Street
6th Floor
Boston, MA 02110
617-742-7452
info@mhamd.org
www.mhamh.org
An affiliate of Mental Health America, which is a community-based non-profit organization committed to enabling the mental wellness of all Americans. MHA advocates for greater access to quality health services and seeks to educate individuals on identifying symptoms, as well as intervention and prevention.
Danna Mauch, PhD, President & CEO
Louise Povall, MHSM, Director of Finance & Admin

1869 **Massachusetts National Alliance on Mental Illness**
529 Main Street
Boston, MA 02129
617-580-8541
800-370-9085
namimass@aol.com
namimass.org
Nation's leading self-help organization for all those affected by severe brain disorders. Mission is to bring consumers and families with similar experiences together to share information about services, care providers, and ways to cope with the challenges of schizophrenia, manic depression, and other serious mental illnesses.
Steve Rosenfeld, President
Laurie Martinelli, Executive Director

Michigan

1870 **Mental Health America in Michigan**
2157 University Park Drive
Suite 1
Okemos, MI 48864
248-473-3143
www.mha.com
An affiliate of Mental Health America, which is a community-based non-profit organization committed to enabling the mental wellness of all Americans. MHA advocates for greater access to quality health services and seeks to educate individuals on identifying symptoms, as well as intervention and prevention.
John Fox, Chair
Brian Peters, CEO

Minnesota

1871 **Mental Health America Minnesota**
2233 University Avenue W
Suite 200 651-493-6634
St. Paul, MN 55114 www.mentalhealthmn.org
An affiliate of Mental Health America, which is a community-based non-profit organization committed to enabling the mental wellness of all Americans. MHA advocates for greater access to quality health services and seeks to educate individuals on identifying symptoms, as well as intervention and prevention.
Shannah Mulvihill, MA, Executive Director
Holly Raab, Program Manager

1872 **NASW Minnesota Chapter**
Iris Park Place, Suite 340 651-293-1935
Saint Paul, MN 55104 888-293-6279
nasw-heartland.org
NASW-MN is the state chapter of the National Association of Social Workers, a membership organization representing the interests of professional social workers. The mission of NASW-MN is to advance and promote the profession of social work, support the professional growth of its members, and advocate for clients through the promotion of social policies.
Deborah Tallen, MPA, MBA, Executive Director
Whitney Gladden, Program Coordinator

Mississippi

1873 **Mental Health Association of South Mississippi (Mental Health America)**
4803 Harrison Circle
Gulfport, MS 39507 228-864-6274
www.msmentalhealth.org
An affiliate of Mental Health America, which is a community-based non-profit organization committed to enabling the mental wellness of all Americans. MHA advocates for greater access to quality health services and seeks to educate individuals on identifying symptoms, as well as intervention and prevention.
Eric Oliver, President
Liz Hoop, Vice President

Missouri

1874 **Mental Health America of Eastern Missouri**
1905 S Grand Boulevard
St. Louis, MO 63104 314-773-1399
www.mha-em.org
An affiliate of Mental Health America, which is a community-based non-profit organization committed to enabling the mental wellness of all Americans. MHA advocates for greater access to quality health services and seeks to educate individuals on identifying symptoms, as well as intervention and prevention.
Suzanne King, President & CEO
Anne Shaw Heinrich, Vice President of Development

Montana

1875 **Mental Health America of Montana**
PO Box 88 406-587-7774
Bozeman, MT 59771 info@montanamentalhealth.org
montanamentalhealth.org
An affiliate of Mental Health America, which is a community-based non-profit organization committed to enabling the mental wellness of all Americans. MHA advocates for greater access to quality health services and seeks to educate individuals on identifying symptoms, as well as intervention and prevention.

1876 **National Alliance on Mental Illness: Montana**
555 Fuller Avenue 406-443-7871
Helena, MT 59624 info@namimt.org
namimt.org
Local chapter of the National Alliance on Mental Illness, an organization dedicated to raising awareness on mental health and providing support and education for Americans affected by mental illness. Mission is to help consumers and families share information about services, care providers, and ways to cope with the challenges of mental illness.
Gary Popiel, Chapter President
Matthew Kuntz, Chapter Executive Director

Nebraska

1877 **Mental Health America of Nebraska**
1645 N Street 402-441-4371
Lincoln, NE 68508 888-902-2822
info@montanamentalhealth.org
www.mha-ne.org
An affiliate of Mental Health America, which is a community-based non-profit organization committed to enabling the mental wellness of all Americans. MHA advocates for greater access to quality health services and seeks to educate individuals on identifying symptoms, as well as intervention and prevention.
Kent Mattson, Chair
Brittany Tran, Vice Chair

Nevada

1878 **National Alliance on Mental Illness: Western Nevada**
3100 Mill Street 775-440-5600
Reno, NV 89502 info@naminevada.org
naminevada.org
Local chapter of the National Alliance on Mental Illness, an organization dedicated to raising awareness on mental health and providing support and education for Americans affected by mental illness. Mission is to help consumers and families share information about services, care providers, and ways to cope with the challenges of mental illness.
Robin Reedy, Chapter Executive Director

New Jersey

1879 **Mental Health America in New Jersey**
673 Morris Avenue 973-571-4001
Springfield, NJ 07081 800-867-8850
www.mhanj.org
An affiliate of Mental Health America, which is a community-based non-profit organization committed to enabling the mental wellness of all Americans. MHA advocates for greater access to quality health services and seeks to educate individuals on identifying symptoms, as well as intervention and prevention.

1880 **Mental Health Association in New Jersey**
88 Pompton Avenue 800-367-8850
Verona, NJ 07044 njconnect@mhanj.org
mhanj.org
The Mental Health Association in New Jersey seeks to eliminate barriers to recovery and care and to improve mental health for all people through advocacy, education, training, and services.
Bill Waldman, MSW, Chairman
Victoria Brown, MSW, LCSW, Vice Chairman

1881 **New Jersey Psychiatric Association**
208 Lenox Avenue 908-588-3540
Westfield, NJ 07090 info@njpsychiatry.org
www.njpsychiatry.org
A professional organization of about 100 physicians qualified by training and experience in the treatment of mental illness.
Ramon Solhkhah, MD, President
Patricia DeCotiis, Executive Director

New Mexico

1882 **National Alliance on Mental Illness: New Mexico**
3900 Osuna Road NE 505-260-0154
Albuquerque, NM 87109 info@naminewmexico.org
naminewmexico.org
Local chapter of the National Alliance on Mental Illness, an organization dedicated to raising awareness on mental health and providing support and education for Americans affected by mental illness. Mission is to help consumers and families share information about services, care providers, and ways to cope with the challenges of mental illness.
Betty Whiton, Chapter President

New York

1883 **Mental Health America in New York State, Inc.**
194 Washington Avenue 518-434-0439
Albany, NY 12210 mhanys.org

An affiliate of Mental Health America, which is a community-based non-profit organization committed to enabling the mental wellness of all Americans. MHA advocates for greater access to quality health services and seeks to educate individuals on identifying symptoms, as well as intervention and prevention.
Glenn Liebman, CEO
Melissa Ramirez, Deputy Director

1884 **Mental Health Association in Orange County Inc**
73 James P Kelly Way 845-342-2400
Middletown, NY 10940 800-832-1200
mha@mhaorangeny.com
mhaorangeny.com
Seeks to promote the positive mental health and emotional well-being of Orange County residents, working towards reducing the stigma of mental illness, developmental disabilities, and providing support to victims of sexual assault and other crimes.
David Goggins, President of the Board
Nadia Allen, Executive Director

1885 **National Association of Social Workers New York State Chapter**
188 Washington Avenue 518-463-4741
Albany, NY 12210 800-724-6279
naswnys.org
The National Association of Social Workers is a membership association representing professional social workers. NASW New York State advocates for public policies that address health, welfare, and education issues involving individuals and families, continues the education of its members through workshops and seminars, and maintains professional standards within social work practice.
Peter Chernack, DSW, LCSW-R, President
Diane Bessel Matteson, PhD, Vice President

North Carolina

1886 **Mental Health America of Central Carolinas Inc.**
3701 Latrobe Drive 704-365-3454
Charlotte, NC 28211 mhacentralcarolinas.org
An affiliate of Mental Health America, which is a community-based non-profit organization committed to enabling the mental wellness of all Americans. MHA advocates for greater access to quality health services and seeks to educate individuals on identifying symptoms, as well as intervention and prevention.
Ashley Smith, President
Rob Jones, President-Elect

North Dakota

1887 **Mental Health America of North Dakota**
PO Box 4106 701-255-3692
Bismarck, ND 58502 mhand.org
An affiliate of Mental Health America, which is a community-based non-profit organization committed to enabling the mental wellness of all Americans. MHA advocates for greater access to quality health services and seeks to educate individuals on identifying symptoms, as well as intervention and prevention.
Carlotta McCleary, Executive Director
Tom Regan, President

1888 **National Alliance on Mental Illness: North Dakota**
naminorthdakota@gmail.com
namind.org
Local chapter of the National Alliance on Mental Illness, an organization dedicated to raising awareness on mental health and providing support and education for Americans affected by mental illness. Mission is to help consumers and families share information about services, care providers, and ways to cope with the challenges of mental illness. This organization is run soley by volunteers. Please allow for time for them to respond to emails.
Angela Hartman, Chapter President

1889 **National Association of Social Workers: North Dakota Chapter**
1120 College Drive, Suite 100 701-223-4161
Bismarck, ND 58503 nasw-heartland.org
NASW North Dakota is the state chapter of the National Association of Social Workers, an organization representing professional social workers. NASWND promotes the profession of social work and advocates for access to services for all.
Heidi Borstad, President

1890 **North Dakota Federation of Families for Children's Mental Health**
PO Box 3061 701-222-3310
Bismarck, ND 58502 877-822-6287
ndffcmh.org
The North Dakota Federation of Families for Children's Mental Health is an advocacy organization working to meet the needs of children and youth with emotional, behavioral and mental challenges and their families.
Carlotta McCleary, Executive Director
Jamie Becker, Executive Assistant

Ohio

1891 **Mental Health America of Ohio**
2323 W Fifth Avenue 614-221-1441
Columbus, OH 43204 info@mhaohio.org
mhaohio.org
An affiliate of Mental Health America, which is a community-based non-profit organization committed to enabling the mental wellness of all Americans. MHA advocates for greater access to quality health services and seeks to educate individuals on identifying symptoms, as well as intervention and prevention.
Kenton Beachy, MA, MPA, Executive Director
Tonya Fulwider, Associate Director

1892 **National Alliance on Mental Illness: Ohio**
614-224-2700
800-686-2646
namiohio@namiohio.org
namiohio.org
Local chapter of the National Alliance on Mental Illness, an organization dedicated to raising awareness on mental health and providing support and education for Americans affected by mental illness. Mission is to help consumers and families share information about services, care providers, and ways to cope with the challenges of mental illness.
Jack Sherman, Chapter President
Judge Joyce Campbell, Chapter First Vice President

1893 **National Association of Social Workers: Ohio Chapter**
400 West Wilson Bridge Road 614-461-4484
Worthington, OH 43085 info@naswoh.org
naswoh.org
NASW Ohio represents the interests of professional social workers in Ohio. The mission of NASW Ohio is to strengthen the profession of social work, maintain social work professional standards, and advocate for equitable social policies.
Danielle Smith, MSW, MA, LSW, Executive Director
Dorothy Martindale, BSSW, LSW, Membership Associate

Oklahoma

1894 **MHA (Mental Health America) of Oklahoma**
5330 E 31st Street 918-585-1213
Tulsa, OK 74135 info@mhaok.org
mhaok.org
An affiliate of Mental Health America, which is a community-based non-profit organization committed to enabling the mental wellness of all Americans. MHA advocates for greater access to quality health services and seeks to educate individuals on identifying symptoms, as well as intervention and prevention.

Oregon

1895 **National Alliance on Mental Illness: Oregon**
4701 Southeast 24th Avenue 503-230-8009
Portland, OR 97202 800-343-6264
namioregon@namior.org
namior.org
Local chapter of the National Alliance on Mental Illness, an organization dedicated to raising awareness on mental health and providing support and education for Americans affected by mental illness. Mission is to help consumers and families share information about services, care providers, and ways to cope with the challenges of mental illness.
Chris Bouneff, Chapter Executive Director
Michelle Madison, Chatper Outreach Manager

1896 **Oregon Psychiatric Physicians Association**
5434 River Road N info@oregonpsychiatricphysicians.org
Keizer, OR 97303 oregonpsychiatricphysicians.org
The Oregon Psychiatric Physicians Association is an organization of medical doctors in Oregon specializing in psychiatry. The OPPA works to ensure the effective treatment of individuals with mental disorders through public education, advocacy, and the provision of resources.
Patrick Sieng, Executive Director
Jennifer Boverman, Membership & Program Coordinator

Pennsylvania

1897 **Mental Health America in Pennsylvania**
4105 Derry Street 717-346-0549
Harrisburg, PA 17111 866-578-3659
info@mhapa.org
mhapa.org
An affiliate of Mental Health America, which is a community-based non-profit organization committed to enabling the mental wellness of all Americans. MHA advocates for greater access to quality health services and seeks to educate individuals on identifying symptoms, as well as intervention and prevention.
Tony Schweitzer, President
Carl Onufer, President-Elect

1898 **National Alliance on Mental Illness: Keystone Pennsylvania**
105 Braunlich Drive 412-366-3788
Pittsburgh, PA 15237 888-264-7972
info@namikeystonepa.org
namikeystonepa.org
The largest statewide non-profit organization dedicated to helping mental health consumers and their families rebuild their lives and conquer the challenges posed by severe and persistent mental illness.
Christine Michaels, Chief Executive Officer
Debbie Ference, Chief Operating Offcer

1899 **Pennsylvania Psychiatric Society**
400 Winding Creek Boulevard 800-422-2900
Mechanicsburg, PA 17050 papsych@pamedsoc.org
papsych.org
A district branch of the American Psychiatric Association, the PPS is a non-profit association comprising of 1,800 physicians who specialize in psychiatry. The Pennsylvania Psychiatric Society represents the interests of the psychiatric profession and their patients, and seeks to ensure the provision of high quality psychiatric services through education, advocacy, and the maintenance of ethical standards.
Dhanalakshmi Ramasamy, MD, DFAPA, President
Kavita K. Fischer, MD, FAPA, Vice President

Rhode Island

1900 **MHA (Mental Health America) of Rhode Island**
345 Blackstone Boulevard 401-726-2285
Providence, RI 02906 info@mhari.org
mhari.org
An affiliate of Mental Health America, which is a community-based non-profit organization committed to enabling the mental wellness of all Americans. MHA advocates for greater access to quality health services and seeks to educate individuals on identifying symptoms, as well as intervention and prevention.
Laurie-Marie Pisciotta, Executive Director
Clement Cicilline, MS, President

South Carolina

1901 **Federation of Families of South Carolina**
810 Dutch Square Boulevard 803-772-5210
Columbia, SC 29210 866-779-0402
fedfamsc.org
Nonprofit organization providing assistance and support for families of children with emotional, behavioral, or psychiatric disorders. The Federation offers support networks, educational materials, publications, conferences, workshops, and other activities. The goal of the Federation of Families of South Carolina is to meet the needs of children and youth with emotional, behavioral, and mental disorders and their families, and assist them in building productive lives.
Kathleen Scharer, President
Roxann McKinnon, Vice President

1902 **MHA (Mental Health America) South Carolina**
1823 Gadsden Street 803-779-5363
Columbia, SC 29201 nscott@mha-sc.org
mha-sc.org
Mental Health America of South Carolina is an affiliate of Mental Health America, a national mental health advocacy organization. MHASC focuses on educating the public about mental illness, advocating for adequate mental health care and sound mental health practices, and organizing conferences designed to address the issues surrounding mental health.
Joy Jay, Executive Director
Natasha M Scott, Director of Operations

South Dakota

1903 **National Alliance on Mental Illness: South Dakota**
PO Box 88808 605-271-1871
Sioux Falls, SD 57109 800-551-2531
namisd@midconetwork.com
namisouthdakota.org
Provides education and support for individuals and families impacted by mental illnesses and advocates for the development of a comprehensive mental health service system. Seeks to improve the lives of people affected by mental illness and to reduce the stigma of mental illness among the general public.
Wendy Giebink, Executive Director
John Williams, Fund Development Consultant

Tennessee

1904 **MHA (Mental Health America) of East Tennessee, Inc.**
9050 Executive Park Drive 865-584-9125
Knoxville, TN 37923 mhaet.com
An affiliate of Mental Health America, which is a community-based non-profit organization committed to enabling the mental wellness of all Americans. MHA advocates for greater access to quality health services and seeks to educate individuals on identifying symptoms, as well as intervention and prevention.

Texas

1905 **Depression and Bipolar Support Alliance Greater Houston**
3800 Buffalo Speedway 713-600-1131
Houston, TX 77098 dbsahouston@dbsahouston.org
www.dbsahouston.org
Depression and Bipolar Support Alliance Greater Houston provides free and confidential peer support groups for individuals living with, and family and friends affected by, depression and bipolar disorders.
Mary Collins, President & CEO
Jennifer Strich, LPC-S, NCC, Vice President of Programs

1906 **Mental Health America of Greater Dallas**
624 North Good-Latimer Expy 214-871-2420
Dallas, TX 75204 mhadallas.org
An affiliate of Mental Health America, which is a community-based non-profit organization committed to enabling the mental wellness of all Americans. MHA advocates for greater access to quality health services and seeks to educate individuals on identifying symptoms, as well as intervention and prevention.
Bonnie Cook, MAS, President & CEO
Mary Kate Kohl, Developmental Director

1907 **Mental Health America of Greater Houston, Inc.**
2211 Norfolk 713-523-8963
Austin, TX 78701 info@mhahouston.org
mhahouston.org
An affiliate of Mental Health America, which is a community-based non-profit organization committed to enabling the mental wellness of all Americans. MHA advocates for greater access to quality health services and seeks to educate individuals on identifying symptoms, as well as intervention and prevention.
Asim A. Shah, MD, Co-Chair
Katina D. Scott, Co-Chair

1908 **Mental Health America of Southeast Texas**
700 North Street 409-550-0134
Beaumont, TX 77701
An affiliate of Mental Health America, which is a community-based non-profit organization committed to enabling the mental wellness of all Americans. MHA advocates for greater access to quality health services and seeks to educate individuals on identifying symptoms, as well as intervention and prevention.

1909 **National Alliance on Mental Illness: Texas**
Austin State Hospital Campus 512-693-2000
Austin, TX 78703 800-950-6264
officemanager@namitexas.org
namitexas.org
Local chapter of the National Alliance on Mental Illness, an organization dedicated to raising awareness on mental health and providing support and education for Americans affected by mental illness. Mission is to help consumers and families share information about services, care providers, and ways to cope with the challenges of mental illness.
Yvonne Broach, Chapter President
Gregory Hansch, Chapter Executive Director

1910 **Texas Psychological Association**
PO Box 163236 512-528-8400
Austin, TX 78716 888-872-3435
admin@texaspsyc.org
texaspsyc.org
Jessica Magee, Executive Director
Dena Goldstein, Manager, Marketing & Communications

1911 **Texas Society of Psychiatric Physicians**
401 W 15th Street 512-478-0605
Austin, TX 78701 txpsychiatry@aol.com
www.txpsych.org
J. Clay Sawyer, MD, President
Lynda Parker, MD, Secretary-Treasurer

Utah

1912 **National Alliance on Mental Illness: Utah**
1600 West 2200 South 801-323-9900
West Valley City, UT 84119 education@namiut.org
namiut.org
Local chapter of the National Alliance on Mental Illness, an organization dedicated to raising awareness on mental health and providing support and education for Americans affected by mental illness. Mission is to help consumers and families share information about services, care providers, and ways to cope with the challenges of mental illness.
Annie Hanksr, Chapter President
Rob Wesemann, Chapter Executive Director

1913 **Utah Psychiatric Association**
310 E 4500 S 801-747-3500
Salt Lake City, UT 84107 utah.psychiatry.org
Paige DeMille, Executive Director

Vermont

1914 **National Alliance on Mental Illness: Vermont**
600 Blair Park 802-876-7949
Williston, VT 05495 800-639-6480
info@namivt.org
namivt.org
Local chapter of the National Alliance on Mental Illness, an organization dedicated to raising awareness on mental health and providing support and education for Americans affected by mental illness. Mission is to help consumers and families share information about services, care providers, and ways to cope with the challenges of mental illness.
Phil Blackburn, President and Chair
Laurie Emerson, Executive Director

1915 **Vermont Federation of Families for Children's Mental Health**
600 Blair Park Road 802-244-1955
Williston, VT 05495 800-639-6071
vffcmh@vffcmh.org
vffcmh.org
Supports families and children where a child or youth,age 0-22, is experiencing or at risk to experience emotional, behavioral, or mental health challenges.
Ted Tighe, President
Sherry Schoenberg, Vice President

Virginia

1916 **Mental Health America of Virginia**
2008 Bremo Road 804-257-5591
Richmond, VA 23226 info@mhav.org
mhav.org
An affiliate of Mental Health America, which is a community-based non-profit organization committed to enabling the mental wellness of all Americans. MHA advocates for greater access to quality health services and seeks to educate individuals on identifying symptoms, as well as intervention and prevention.
Bruce Cruser, Executive Director
Danielle Donaldson, Program Manager

Washington

1917 **NAMI (National Alliance on Mental Illness) Eastside**
16307 NE 83rd Street 425-885-6264
Redmond, WA 98052 info@nami-eastside.org
nami-eastside.org
Aims to improve mental health services and quality of life for those affected by mental health conditions through awareness, education, support, and advocacy.
Barbie Collins Young, Executive Director
Jennifer Curtis, Development Director

1918 **National Alliance on Mental Illness Washington Coast**
PO Box 153
Aberdeen, WA 98520 360-533-9888
nami-wacoast.org
Local chapter of the National Alliance on Mental Illness, an organization dedicated to raising awareness on mental health and providing support and education for Americans affected by mental illness. Mission is to help consumers and families share information about services, care providers, and ways to cope with the challenges of mental illness.

1919 **National Alliance on Mental Illness Pierce County**
PO Box 111923 253-677-6629
Tacoma, WA 98411 info@namipierce.org
namipierce.org
Local chapter of the National Alliance on Mental Illness, an organization dedicated to raising awareness on mental health and providing support and education for Americans affected by mental illness. Mission is to help consumers and families share information about services, care providers, and ways to cope with the challenges of mental illness.
Lovey Offerle, Chapter President
Daniel A. Sheehan, Chapter Vice President

1920 **National Alliance on Mental Illness: Seattle**
802 NW 70th Street 206-783-9264
Seattle, WA 98117 namiseattle.org
Works to improve mental health system delivery through education, referrals, and support.
Muguette Guenneguez, Executive Director
Katie Mahoney, Program Manager

1921 **National Alliance on Mental Illness: South King County**
515 West Harrison Street 253-854-6264
Kent, WA 98032-4403 namiskc.org
Mission is to bring consumers and families with similar experiences together to share information about services, care providers, and ways to cope with the challenges of schizophrenia, manic depression, and other serious mental illnesses.
Marsha Williams, President
Dan Hamilton, Vice President

West Virginia

1922 **National Alliance on Mental Illness: West Virginia**
The state organization of NAMI in West Virginia is currently being rebuilt. If you would like to help in this effort, contact

fieldcapacity@nami.org.There are local NAMI chapters within the state of West Virginial.

Wisconsin

1923 **Mental Health America of Wisconsin**
600 W Virginia Street 414-276-3122
Milwaukee, WI 53204 866-948-6483
info@mhawisconsin.org
mhawisconsin.org
An affiliate of Mental Health America, which is a community-based non-profit organization committed to enabling the mental wellness of all Americans. MHA advocates for greater access to quality health services and seeks to educate individuals on identifying symptoms, as well as intervention and prevention.
Jim Hill, Chair
Nathan Meier, Treasurer

1924 **National Alliance on Mental Illness: Wisconsin**
4233 West Beltline Highway 608-268-6000
Madison, WI 53711 800-236-2988
nami@namiwisconsin.org
namiwisconsin.org
Local chapter of the National Alliance on Mental Illness, an organization dedicated to raising awareness on mental health and providing support and education for Americans affected by mental illness. Mission is to help consumers and families share information about services, care providers, and ways to cope with the challenges of mental illness.
Kay Jewell, MD, President
Mary Kay Battaglia, Executive Director

Wyoming

1925 **National Alliance on Mental Illness: Wyoming**
137 West 6th Street 307-265-2573
Casper, WY 82601 888-882-4968
info@namiwyoming.org
namiwyoming.org
Local chapter of the National Alliance on Mental Illness, an organization dedicated to raising awareness on mental health and providing support and education for Americans affected by mental illness. Mission is to help consumers and families share information about services, care providers, and ways to cope with the challenges of mental illness.
Roy C Walworth, President
William Howell, Vice President

Web Sites

1926 **American Psychological Association**
www.apa.org
Mission is to advance psychology as a science and professional organization that represents psychology in the United States.

1927 **Coalition of Voluntary Mental Health Agencies**
www.cvmha.org/
An umbrella advocacy organization of New York's mental health community, representing over 100 non-profit community based mental health agencies that serve more than 300,000 clients in the five boroughs of New York City and its environs.

1928 **Community Access**
www.cairn.org/
A nonprofit agency providing housing and advocacy for people with psychiatric disabilities.

1929 **Dietary Guidelines for Americans**
www.dietaryguidelines.gov
Publishes the Dietary Guidelines for Americans, a guide providing nutritional advice to promote health and prevent disease. Updated versions of the Dietary Guidelines are released by the US Departments of Agriculture (USDA) and Health & Human Services (HHS) every five years.

1930 **Everyday Health**
www.everydayhealth.com
Aims to provide evidence-based health information from physicians and healthcare providers.

1931 **FamilyDoctor.org**
www.familydoctor.org
Medical advice and information provided by the American Academy of Family Physicians. Resources include a medical dictionary, a symptom checker tool, a BMI calculator, and medication information.

1932 **Federation of Families for Children's Mental Health**
www.ffcmh.org/
Providing leadership to develop and sustain a nationwide network of family-run organizations.

1933 **Healing Well**
www.healingwell.com
An online health resource guide to medical news, chat, information and articles, newsgroups and message boards, books, disease-related web sites, medical directories, and more for patients, friends, and family coping with disabling diseases, disorders, or chronic illnesses.

1934 **Health Finder**
www.healthfinder.gov
Searchable, carefully developed web site offering information on over 1000 topics. Developed by the US Department of Health and Human Services, the site can be used in both English and Spanish.

1935 **Healthline**
www.healthline.com
Provides medical and health articles and information.

1936 **Healthlink USA**
www.healthlinkusa.com
Health information concerning treatment, cures, prevention, diagnosis, risk factors, research, support groups, email lists, personal stories and much more. Updated regularly.

1937 **Internet Mental Health**
www.mentalhealth.com
A site whose goal is to improve understanding, diagnosis, and treatment of mental illness throughout the world. Includes information on specific disorders, medications, diagnosis, research, news, and other internet links.

1938 **MedicineNet**
www.medicinenet.com
An online resource for consumers providing easy-to-read, authoritative medical and health information.

1939 **MedlinePlus**
www.medlineplus.gov
A service of the National Library of Medicine, MedlinePlus is an online resource providing health and wellness information in both English and Spanish.

1940 **Medscape**
www.medscape.com
Medscape offers specialists, primary care physicians, and other health professionals the Web's most robust and integrated medical information and educational tools.

1941 **Mental Health America (formerly NMHA) Information Center**
www.mentalhealthamerica.net
Provides informational materials, lobbies for Federal mental health legislation, stimulates funding of research on the causes and treatment of mental illnesses.

1942 **National Alliance for the Mentally Ill**
www.nami.org
Over 900 affiliate groups nationwide offer support to members, advocate better lives for their loved ones, support research efforts and educate the public to reduce the stigma attached to serious mental illnesses.

1943 **National Mental Health Services Knowledge Exchange Network**
www.mentalhealth.org
Leading the national system that delivers mental health services. Provides the treatment and support services neede by adults with mental disorders and children with serious emotional problems.

1944 **Nutrition.gov**
www.nutrition.gov

Sponsored by the United States Department of Agriculture (USDA), Nutrition.gov offers information on topics in food and nutrition, including healthy eating, physical activity, and food safety.

1945 **Science Daily**

www.sciencedaily.com

Provides information on the latest news and research in science, health, the environment, and technology.

1946 **The Nutrition Source**

hsph.harvard.edu/nutritionsource

From the Harvard T.H. Chan School of Public Health, The Nutrition Source provides news, information, and guidance for nutrition and healthy eating.

1947 **UnlockFood**

www.unlockfood.ca

A website from Dietitians of Canada. Provides videos, recipes, and information on food and nutrition, as well as helps Canadians connect with a dietitian.

1948 **Verywell**

www.verywellhealth.com

Offers health, medicine, and wellness information from health professionals.

1949 **WebMD**

www.webmd.com

Provides credible information, supportive communities, and in-depth reference material about health subjects. A source for original and timely health information as well as material from well known content providers.

1950 **World Federation for Mental Health**

wfmh.global

Mission is to promote, among all people and nations, the highest possible level of mental health in its broadest biological, medical, educational, and social aspects.

1951 **World Health Organization**

www.who.int

An agency of the United Nations, World Health Organization (WHO) serves to promote global health. The WHO website provides fact sheets, publications, media, and other resources on various health topics.

SUBSTANCE ABUSE

Substance abuse is a complex condition to treat, and much depends on the substance that is being abused and the life style surrounding the person using it. Nutrition therapy requires coordination between physician, dietician, caregivers, and the patient. Good nutrition and hydration help the healing process by enhancing and ultimately restoring physical and mental health. Studies have shown that macro-and micronutrient deficiencies can cause depression, anxiety, and lack of energy, all of which may lead an individual seeking to manage their symptoms by abusing drugs. Many substances affect adequate nutrition by either suppressing the appetite, or stimulating the appetite, resulting in unhealthy weight loss or gain. Many substance abuse treatment programs emphasize nutrition intervention, as a healthy lifestyle may aid in recovery. Individualized counseling and comprehensive nutrition counseling are a vital part of freedom from substance abuse. The goals of counseling include healing and nourishing the body, stabilizing mood, reducing stress and cravings, addressing co-occurring medical issues such as diabetes or liver disease, and encouraging self-care and a healthy lifestyle.

Agencies & Associations

1952 **AAA Foundation for Traffic Safety**
607 14th Street NW — 202-638-5944
Washington, DC 20005 — info@aaafoundation.org
www.aaafoundation.org
A non-profit foundation conducting research with the goal of preventing traffic deaths. Raises awareness on road safety measures and driver education.
C.Y. David Yang, Executive Director

1953 **African American Family Services**
2616 Nicollet Avenue — 612-813-5034
Minneapolis, MN 55408 — contact@aafs.net
www.aafs.net
African American Family Services works with individuals, families and communities affected by addiction and mental illness. Provides culturally-specific mental health services.
Thomas Adams, Chief Executive Officer
Brianna Miller, Director, Advancement

1954 **Al-Anon Family Group Headquarters**
1600 Corporate Landing Parkway — 757-563-1600
Virginia Beach, VA 23454-5617 — 888-425-2666
wso@al-anon.org
www.al-anon.org
At Al-Anon Family Group meetings, family members and friends of problem drinkers share their experiences and learn how to apply the principles of the Al-Anon program to their individual situations.

1955 **Alcohol Justice**
24 Belvedere Street — 415-456-5692
San Rafael, CA 94901 — alcoholjustice.org
Promote evidence-based public health policies and organize campaigns with diverse communities and youth against the alcohol industry's harmful practices.
Cruz Avila, Executive Director
Keren Kuhn, Administrative Director

1956 **Alcoholics Anonymous**
475 Riverside Drive at W 120th St. — 212-870-3400
New York, NY 10115 — international@aa.org
www.aa.org
Alcoholics Anonymous is an international alliance of supportive individuals who have had a drinking problem. Membership is available to anyone wanting to improve their situation.

1957 **American Council on Addiction & Alcohol Problems**
2376 Lakeside Drive — 205-989-8177
Birmingham, AL 35244 — admin@acaap.us
acaap.us
The American Council on Addiction and Alcohol Problems is a non-profit organization whereby state organizations, national religious bodies, and other concerned groups unite to solve the issues caused by addiction.
Joseph C. Godfrey, President
Anita Bedell, Secretary-Treasurer

1958 **American Dental Association**
211 E Chicago Avenue — 312-440-2500
Chicago, IL 60611-2678 — www.ada.org
The nation's largest dental association, representing dentists. A leading source of oral health related information for dentists and their patients.

1959 **Brattleboro Retreat**
Anna Marsh Lane — 802-258-3737
Brattleboro, VT 05302 — www.brattlebororetreat.org
A not-for-profit hospital offering psychiatric and addiction treatment services for children, adolescents, and adults.
Louis Josephson, Ph.D., President & CEO
Gaurav Chawla, MD, CPE, Chief Medical Officer

1960 **Center for Substance Abuse Prevention**
Substance Abuse & Mental Health Services Admin.
5600 Fishers Lane — 240-276-2420
Rockville, MD 20857 — 877-726-4727
TTY: 800-487-4889
www.samhsa.gov
Connects people and resources with strategies and programs designed to encourage efforts aimed at reducing and eliminating alcohol, tobacco and other drug problems in society. Works with federal, state, public and private organizations to develop prevention programs.
Jeffrey A. Coady, Acting Director

1961 **Centre for Addiction and Mental Health**
1001 Queen Street West — 416-535-8501
Toronto, Ontario, M6J-1H4 — 800-463-2338
info@camh.ca
camh.ca
CAMH is Canada's leading addiction and mental health organization, integrating specialized clinical care with innovative research, education, health promotion and policy development. CAMH is fully affiliated with the University of Toronto, and is a

Pan American Health Organization/World Health Organization Collaborating Centre. CAMH combines clinical care, research, education, policy and health promotion to transform the lives of people affected by mental health and addiction issues.
Tracey MacArthur, President & CEO
Bessy Leung, VP, Corporate Services & CFO

1962 **Cocaine Anonymous World Services**
21720 S Wilmington Avenue 310-559-5833
Long Beach, CA 90810 cawso@ca.org
www.ca.org
Members are recovering from addiction, and offer support and maintain their sobriety by working together.

1963 **Dentists Concerned for Dentists**
651-275-0313
800-632-7643
dcdmn.com
A nonprofit organization for chemically dependent Minnesota dentists and concerned others.

1964 **Drug Abuse Resistance Education of America**
PO Box 512090 310-215-0575
Los Angeles, CA 90051 800-223-3273
Fax: 310-215-0180
www.dare.org
D.A.R.E. is a comprehensive K-12 education program taught in thousands of schools in America and 52 other countries. D.A.R.E. curricula address drugs, violence, bullying, internet safety, and other high risk circumstances that are too often a part of students' lives.
Francisco X. Pegueros, President & CEO
Thomas Hazelton, President, Development

1965 **Families Anonymous, Inc.**
701 Lee Street 847-294-5877
Des Plaines, IL 60016 800-736-9805
info@familiesanonymous.org
familiesanonymous.org
Addresses the needs of families who are concerned about a relative with a drug problem and with related behavioral problems. Offers informational packets, meetings and support networks for these families.

1966 **Florida Alcohol and Drug Abuse Association**
2868 Mahan Drive 850-878-2196
Tallahassee, FL 32308 fadaa@fadaa.org
fadaa.org
Statewide membership organization that represents more than 100 community-based substance abuse treatment and prevention agencies throughout Florida. FADAA supports providers and programs dedicated to the advancement of substance abuse treatment, prevention, and research, and has provided advocacy for substance abuse policies and related practice improvement.
Melanie Brown-Woofter, President & CEO
Jennifer Johnson, Senior Director, Public Policy

1967 **Hazelden Betty Ford Foundation**
PO Box 11 800-257-7810
Center City, MN 55012-0011 info@hazeldenbettyford.org
www.hazelden.org
Helps individuals, families, and communities struggling with alcohol abuse, substance abuse, and drug addiction by offering prevention and recovery solutions nationwide.
Joseph Lee, MD, President & CEO
Marvin D. Seppala, MD, Chief Medical Officer

1968 **Illinois Church Action on Alcohol and Addiction Problems**
1132 W Jefferson Street 217-546-6871
Springfield, IL 62702 866-940-6871
ilcaaap@sbcglobal.net
www.ilcaaap.org
An interdenominational Christian agency representing church groups in Illinois. Works to prevent alcohol and other drug-related problems through education, legislative action and public awareness.

1969 **Indian Health Service**
5600 Fishers Lane www.ihs.gov
Rockville, MD 20857
Provides a comprehensive program of alcoholism and substance abuse prevention and treatment for Native Americans and Alaskan natives.

1970 **Lawyers Concerned for Lawyers**
2550 University Avenue W 651-646-5590
Saint Paul, MN 55114 866-525-6466
help@mnlcl.org
www.mnlcl.org
A non-profit organization of recovering lawyers, judges, law students, and concerned others. Educates and arranges interventions and offers lawyer-only AA meetings.
Joan Bibelhausen, Executive Director
Bob Schuneman, Outreach Coordinator

1971 **Marijuana Anonymous World Services**
340 S Lemon Avenue 800-766-6779
Walnut, CA 91789-2706 support@marijuana-anonymous.org
www.marijuana-anonymous.org
Non-profit fellowship of individuals with marijuana addiction, seeking sobriety and support.

1972 **MindWise Innovations**
270 Bridge Street 781-239-0071
Dedham, MA 02026 info@mindwise.org
www.mindwise.org
Formerly known as Screening For Mental Health, MindWise Innovations provides resources to schools, workplaces, and communities to address mental health issues, substance abuse, and suicide.
Bryan Kohl, Executive Director
Marjie McDaniel, Vice President

1973 **Mothers Against Drunk Driving (MADD)**
511 E John Carpenter Freeway 877-275-6233
Irving, TX 75062 www.madd.org
Founded by a small group of mothers and currently one of the largest crime victims organizations in the world. Resources available online.
Ellen Willmott, Interim Chief Executive Officer
Vickie Bumgardner, Chief Financial Officer

1974 **Narcotics Anonymous World Services**
PO Box 9999 818-773-9999
Van Nuys, CA 91409 Fax: 818-700-0700
fsmail@na.org
www.na.org
A fellowship of men and women who meet to help one another with their drug dependency. Support and resources are available.

1975 **National Association for Children of Addiction (NACOA)**
10920 Connecticut Avenue 301-468-0985
Kensington, MD 20895 888-554-2627
nacoa@nacoa.org
www.nacoa.org
Advocates for all children and families affected by alcohol and other drug dependencies. Programs, training, and other resources are available.
Sis Wenger, President & CEO
Mary Beth Collins, Director, Programs

1976 **National Association of Addiction Treatment Providers (NAATP)**
1120 Lincoln Street 888-574-1008
Denver, CO 80203 info@naatp.org
www.naatp.org
Seeks to advance addiction services and support its membership of service providers.
Marvin Ventrell, JD, Chief Executive Officer
Katie Strand, MS, CMP, Chief Operating Officer

1977 **National Association of Alcoholism and Drug Abuse Counselors (NAADAC)**
44 Canal Center Plaza 703-741-7686
Alexandria, VA 22314 Fax: 703-741-7698
naadac@naadac.org
www.naadac.org
Largest membership organization serving addiction counselors, educators and other addiction-focused health care professionals who specialize in addiction prevention, treatment and education.
Cynthia Moreno Tuohy, Executive Director
Jessica Gleason, Deputy Director

1978 **National Association on Drug Abuse Problems**
355 Lexington Avenue 212-986-1170
New York, NY 10017 info@nadap.org
www.nadap.org
Private non-profit corporation providing skills, evaluation, job training and job placement to recovering drug addicts in the metropolitan New York area.
John A. Darin, President & CEO
Gary Stankowski, EVP & CCO

1979 **National Council on Alcoholism and Drug Dependence**
217 Broadway 212-269-7797
New York, NY 10007 info@ncadd.org
www.ncadd.org
Provides education, information, help and hope in the fight against addictions. Nationwide network of affiliates, advocates prevention, intervention and treatment, and is committed to ridding the disease of its stigma and its sufferers of their denial and shame.
Andrew N. Pucher, President & CEO
Jill Price, Director, Administration & Finance

1980 **National Crime Prevention Council**
2614 Chapel Lake Drive 443-292-4565
Gambrills, MD 21054 www.ncpc.org
Organization working to prevent crime and drug use by developing materials for parents and children, teaching strategies to communities, and raising awareness by coodinating with local agencies.
Paul Del Ponte, Executive Director

1981 **National Families in Action (NFIA)**
PO Box 133136 404-248-9676
Atlanta, GA 30333-3136 nfia@nationalfamilies.org
www.nationalfamilies.org
Non-profit organization that obtained the nation's first state laws banning the sale of drug paraphernalia. Leads a national effort to help parents replicate Georgia's laws in other states to prevent the marketing of drugs and drug use to children.
Sue Rusche, President & CEO

1982 **National Institute on Alcohol Abuse and Alcoholism (NIAAA)**
9000 Rockville Pike 301-443-3860
Bethesda, MD 20892 niaaaweb-r@exchange.nih.gov
www.niaaa.nih.gov
Leads the national effort to reduce alcohol-related problems through research, coordination, and collaboration.
George F. Koob, Ph.D., Director
Patricia A. Powell, Ph.D., Deputy Director

1983 **National Institute on Drug Abuse (NIDA)**
Office of Science Policy & Communications
301 North Stonestreet Avenue 301-443-1124
Bethesda, MD 20892 www.drugabuse.gov
NIDA's mission is to lead the Nation in bringing the power of science to bear on drug abuse and addiction.
Nora Volkow, MD, Director
Wilson Compton, MD, Deputy Director

1984 **National Organization on Fetal Alcohol Syndrome**
1200 Eton Court NW 202-785-4585
Washington, DC 20007 information@nofas.org
www.nofas.org
Dedicated to eliminating birth defects caused by alcohol consumption during pregnancy by raising awareness of safe pregnancy measures, and the consequences of drinking during pregnancy.
Tom Donaldson, President & CEO
Kathleen Tavenner Mitchell, Vice President

1985 **New Hope Integrated Behavioral Healthcare**
80 Conover Road 732-946-3030
Marlboro, NJ 07746 800-705-4673
www.newhopeibhc.org
A nonprofit corporation serving those in need of treatment for alcoholism, drug addiction, and compulsive gambling. Over the years, New Hope has expanded its capacity and capabilities to include specialized programming for adolescents, women, and those with co-occuring disorders. New Hope constantly strives to advance the quality of addiction treatment through ongoing professional education and participation in select research projects.
Tony Comerford, Ph.D., President & CEO
David Roden, LCSW, LCADC, Vice President & COO

1986 **Office on Smoking and Health: Centers for Disease Control & Prevention**
1600 Clifton Road 800-232-4636
Atlanta, GA 30329 TTY: 888-232-6348
tobaccoinfo@cdc.gov
www.cdc.gov/tobacco
Offers reference services to researchers through the Technical Information Center. Publishes and distributes a number of titles in the field of smoking and health.
Deirdre Lawrencer Kittner, Ph.D., Director
Brenna VanFrank, MD, MSPH, Medical Officer

1987 **Partnership to End Addiction**
711 Third Avenue 212-841-5200
New York, NY 10017 contact@toendaddiction.org
drugfree.org
Provides support and resources for families impacted by addiction, as well as engaging policymakers and researchers.
Creighton Drury, Chief Executive Officer
Emily Feinstein, Chief Operating Officer

1988 **Pennsylvania Association of County Drug and Alcohol Administrators**
PO Box 60769 717-526-1010
Harrisburg, PA 17106 Fax: 717-526-1020
www.pacdaa.org
The Pennsylvania Association of County Drug and Alcohol Administrators (PACDAA) is a professional association that represents the Single County Authorities (SCAs) across the Commonwealth. Its mission is to improve drug and alcohol prevention, intervention, and treatment services provided to Commonwealth residents.
Michele Denk, Executive Director
Brittney McCarthy, Management Associate

1989 **Remove Intoxicated Drivers (RID-USA)**
PO Box 520 888-283-5144
Schenectady, NY 12301 ridusa@verizon.net
rid-usa.org
Volunteers working to deter impaired driving, to help its victims obtain justice, restitution and peace of mind while navigating the criminal justice systems, and to curb the alcohol abuse which leads to drunk driving.

1990 **Research Society on Alcoholism**
7801 N Lamar Boulevard 512-454-0022
Austin, TX 78752-1038 Fax: 512-454-0812
www.rsoa.org
Assists and encourages the application of research to the solution of problems related to alcoholism.
Michael Miles, MD, Ph.D., President
Lara Ray, Ph.D., Vice President

1991 **SMART Recovery**
7304 Mentor Avenue 440-951-5357
Mentor, OH 44060 Fax: 440-951-5358
www.smartrecovery.org
Global coalition of support groups for people with addiction issues, specializing in a science-based 4-Point Program.
Mark Ruth, Executive Director

1992 **Sheppard Pratt Health System**
6501 N Charles Street 410-938-3000
Baltimore, MD 21204 info@sheppardpratt.org
www.sheppardpratt.org
Provider of mental health, special education, substance use, and social services.
Harsh K. Trivedi, MD, MBA, President & CEO
Todd Peters, MD, VP & Chief Medical Officer

1993 **Students Against Destructive Decisions**
655 15th Street NW 508-481-3568
Washington, DC 20005 info@sadd.org
www.sadd.org
Provides students with prevention tools to deal with the issues of underage drinking, drug use, risky and impaired driving, and other destructive decisions.
Rick Birt, President & CEO
Elizabeth Vermette, Vice President, Public Affairs

1994 **Substance Abuse and Mental Health Services Administration (SAMHSA)**
5600 Fishers Lane 877-726-4727
Rockville, MD 20857 TTY: 800-487-4889
www.samhsa.gov
Part of the U.S. Department of Health and Human Services, SAMHSA promotes, monitors, evaluates and coordinates programs for the prevention and treatment of alcoholism and alcohol abuse.
Miriam Delphin-Rittmon, Ph.D., Assistant Secretary
Sonia Chessen, Chief of Staff

Alabama

1995 **Division of Mental Illness and Substance Abuse Community Programs**
Department of Mental Health
11 N Union Street 334-242-3454
Montgomery, AL 36130 800-367-0955
Fax: 334-242-0725
Alabama.DMH@mh.alabama.gov
www.mh.alabama.gov
Nicole Walden, Director, Substance Abuse Treatment

Alaska

1996 **Office of Alcohol and Substance Abuse Department of Health and Social Services**
Department of Health and Social Services
350 Main Street 907-465-3030
Juneau, AK 99811 800-465-4828
Fax: 907-465-3068
Stacy.Toner@Alaska.gov
dhss.alaska.gov/Pages/default.aspx
William J. Streuss, Commissioner
Tara Horton, Special Assistant

Arizona

1997 **Alcoholism and Drug Abuse: Office of Community Behavioral Health**
Department of Health Services
150 N 18th Avenue 602-364-4558
Phoenix, AZ 85007-3228 Fax: 602-364-4570
cancerlr@azdhs.gov
www.azdhs.gov
The Arizona Department of Health Services promotes and protects the health of Arizona's children and adults. Its mission is to set the standard for personal and community health through direct care, science, public policy, and leadership.

1998 **Arizona Substance Abuse Task Force**
Arizona Governor's Office of Youth, Faith & Family
1700 W Washington Street 602-542-4043
Phoenix, AZ 85007 azsubstanceabusepartnership@gmail.com
substanceabuse.az.gov
The Arizona Substance Abuse Task Force is a coalition of leading substance abuse experts, providers and community members focused on addressing and reversing the growing epidemic of drug abuse and addiction in Arizona communities by finding the best treatments and reducing barriers to care.
Debbie Moak, Director

Arkansas

1999 **Arkansas Substance Abuse Prevention, Education and Early Intervention**
Arkansas Department of Human Services
305 South Palm Street 501-686-9164
Little Rock, AR 72205 Fax: 501-686-9182
TDD: 501-686-9176
jay.hill@dhs.arkansas.gov
humanservices.arkansas.gov
The Division of Behavioral Health Services is responsible for ensuring the provision of public behavioral health services, including mental health and substance abuse prevention, treatment, and recovery services throughout the State of Arkansas. The Division supports, certifies, licenses, and funds behavioral health providers throughout the state.
Jay Hill, Director
Kirk Lane, State Drug Director

2000 **Office of Alcohol and Drug Abuse Prevention**
305 South Palm Street 501-686-9866
Little Rock, AR 72205 877-726-4727
Fax: 501-686-9035
SAMHSA's mission is to reduce the impact of substance abuse and mental illness on America's communities.

California

2001 **Susbstance Use Disorder Program, Policy and Fiscal Division**
Department of Health Care Services
1501 Capitol Avenue, MS 4000 877-685-8333
Sacramento, CA 95899 www.dhcs.ca.gov
Directs prevention and treatment programs that address substance use disorders (SUD). Its core functions include developing and implementing SUD prevention strategies, reviewing and approving county SUD treatment program contracts, and granting applications submitted for state and federal funds for SUD services.
Jennifer Kent, Director

Colorado

2002 **Alcohol and Drug Abuse Division**
Department of Human Services
4055 S Lowell Boulevard 303-866-7480
Denver, CO 80236-3120 Fax: 303-866-7481
jaqueline.enriques@state.co.us
Janet Wood, Director
Mary McCann, Acting Manager

Connecticut

2003 **Connecticut Alcohol and Drug Policy Council (ADPC)**
410 Capitol Avenue 860-418-7000
Hartford, CT 06134 800-446-7348
Fax: 860-418-6780
TTY: 860-418-6707
portal.ct.gov/DMHAS
The mission of the Department of Mental Health and Addiction Services is to improve the quality of life of the people of Connecticut by providing an integrated network of comprehensive, effective and efficient mental health and addiction services that foster self-sufficiency, dignity and respect.
Miriam Delphin-Rittmon, PhD, Commissioner

Delaware

2004 **Delaware Division of Alcoholism, Drug Abuse & Mental Health**
State of Delaware
1901 N Du Pont Highway 302-255-9399
New Castle, DE 19720 800-652-2929
Fax: 302-255-4428
dhss.delaware.gov
The mission is to improve the quality of life for Delaware's citizens by promoting health and well-being, fostering self-sufficiency, and protecting vilnerable populations.

District of Columbia

2005 **Health Planning and Development**
825 N Capitol Street NE 202-727-8473
Washington, DC 20002 Fax: 202-727-8411
doh@dc.gov
dchealth.dc.gov/

Florida

2006 **Alcohol and Drug Abuse Program Department Of Children And Families**
Department Of Children And Families
1317 Winewood Boulevard 850-487-2920
Tallahassee, FL 32399-6570 Fax: 850-414-7474
www.dcf.state.fl.us/mentalhealth/sa

The Substance Abuse and Mental Health (SAMH) Program, within the Florida Department of Children and Families, is the single state authority on substance abuse and mental health as designated by the federal Substance Abuse and Mental Health Services Administration (SAMHSA). The Department's SAMH Program oversees a statewide system of care for the prevention, treatment, and recovery of children and adults with serious mental illnesses and/or substance abuse disorders.

Georgia

2007 **Alcohol and Drug Services Addictive Diseases Program**
Addictive Diseases Program
Two Peachtree Street NW 404-657-2331
Atlanta, GA 30303-3171 Fax: 404-657-2160
www.mhddad.dhr.georgia.gov
DBHDD contracts with providers in all 6 regions to provide outpatient and residential substance abuse treatment to men and women who are struggling with the disease of addiction

Hawaii

2008 **Alcohol and Drug Abuse Division**
Department of Health
601 Kamokila Boulevard 808-692-7506
Kapoleiu, HI 96707 Fax: 808-692-7521
ATRINFO@doh.hawaii.gov
www.hawaii.gov/health
The mission of the Department of Health is to protect and improve the health and environment for all people in Hawai'i

Idaho

2009 **Department of Health and Welfare**
1720 Westgate Drive 208-334-6747
Boise, ID 83704-0036 800-926-2588
Fax: 208-334-6738
www.healthandwelfare.idaho.gov

Illinois

2010 **Department of Alcoholism and Substance Abuse**
Department Of Human Services
100 W Randolph Street 312-814-3840
Chicago, IL 60601 800-843-6154
Fax: 312-814-2419
TTY: 800-447-6404
www.dhs.state.il.us

2011 **Illinois Division of Alcoholism and Substance Abuse**
Illinois Department of Human Services
401 South Clinton Street 800-843-6154
Chicago, IL 60607 TTY: 866-324-5553
www.dhs.state.il.us
The mission of the Division of Alcoholism and Substance Abuse is to provide a system of care along the continuum of prevention, intervention, treatment and recovery support where individuals with SUD, those in recovery and those at risk are valued and treated with dignity and where stigma, accompanying attitudes, discrimination, and other barriers to recovery are eliminated.

Indiana

2012 **Division of Addiction Services Department of Mental Health**
Department of Mental Health
402 W Washington Street 317-232-7800
Indianapolis, IN 46204-3614 800-662-4357
Fax: 317-233-3472
www.in.gov/fssa

Iowa

2013 **Department of Public Health: Division of Substance Abuse and Health**
Lucas State Office Building
321 E 12th Street 515-281-7689
Des Moines, IA 50319-0075 866-227-9878
Fax: 515-281-4535
www.idph.state.ia.us
The Iowa Department of Public Health (IDPH) partners with local public health, policymakers, health care providers, business and many others to fulfill our mission of promoting and protecting the health of Iowans.

2014 **Iowa Bureau of Substance Abuse**
Iowa Department of Public Health
Lucas State Office Building 515-281-7689
Des Moines, IA 50319 855-581-8111
idph.iowa.gov/substance-abuse
The Bureau of Substance Abuse is part of the Division of Behavioral Health, in the Iowa Department of Public Health. The Bureau focuses on and provides oversight for all aspects related to substance abuse prevention and treatment services in Iowa, in addition to injury prevention programs. The bureau actively works to address Prevention and Treatment needs by providing focus for training efforts, and identifying and securing available grant funding.
DeAnn Decker, Bureau Chief

Kansas

2015 **Substance Abuse Treatment Services**
Department for Aging and Disability Services
503 S Kansas Avenue 785-296-4986
Topeka, KS 66603-3404 866-645-8216
www.kdads.ks.gov
A division of the Community Services and Programs Commission, Alcohol and Drug Assessment and Referral Programs provide assessment and referral services for individuals with a current or past abuse pattern involving alcohol or other drug use.
Laura Howard, Secretary

Kentucky

2016 **Department For Behavioral Health, Developmental/Intellectual Disabilities**
275 E Main Street 4W-F 502-564-4527
Frankfort, KY 40621 Fax: 502-564-5478
chfs.ky.gov/agencies/dbhdid

Louisiana

2017 **Office of Human Services: Division of Alcohol and Drug Abuse**
628 N 4th Street 225-342-9500
Baton Rouge, LA 70802-2790 855-229-6848
Fax: 225-342-3875
TTY: 225-342-5568
dhhwebinfo@la.gov
www.dhh.louisiana.gov

Maine

2018 **Alliance for Addiction and Mental Health Services, Maine**
295 Water Street 207-621-8118
Augusta, ME 04330 Fax: 207-621-8362
mshaughnessy@masap.org
thealliancemaine.org
Statewide membership association for community behavioral health organizations that provide multi-level services, programming and coordinated leadership to ensure that Mainers have full access to the continuum of recovery-oriented systems of care for mental illness and substance use disorder - from prevention through treatment and into peer recovery support.
Malory Shaughnessy, Executive Director
Jennifer Christian, Project Manager

2019 **Office of Alcohol and Drug Abuse Prevention**
Ofice Of Substance Abuse
AMHI Complex, Marquardt Building 207-289-2595
Augusta, ME 04333-0159 Fax: 207-287-4334
www.maine.gov/dhhs/samhs/osa/

Maryland

2020 **Maryland State Alcohol and Drug Abuse Administration**
55 Wade Avenue 410-402-8600
Catonsville, MD 21228 Fax: 410-402-8601
adaainfo@dhmh.state.md.us
www.maryland-adaa.org

The Alcohol and Drug Abuse Administration is committed to providing access to a quality and effective substance abuse prevention, intervention and treatment service system for the citizens of Maryland.

Massachusetts

2021 **Bureau of Substance Addiction Services**
250 Washington Street
Boston, MA 02108
617-624-5111
mass.gov

Michigan

2022 **Office of Substance Abuse Services**
Department of Public Health
320 S Walnut Street
Lansing, MI 48913
517-373-4700
888-736-0253
Fax: 517-335-2121
TTY: 517-373-3573
www.michigan.gov/mdch

Minnesota

2023 **Chemical Dependency Program Division Department of Human Services**
Department of Human Services
Saint Paul, MN 55164-3899
651-431-2460
800-627-3529
Fax: 651-582-1865
dhs.info@state.mn.us
mn.gov/dhs/about-dhs/
The Minnesota Department of Human Services, working with many others, helps people meet their basic needs so they can live in dignity and achieve their highest potential.

Mississippi

2024 **Division of Alcohol & Drug Abuse: Mississippi**
Department of Mental Health
1101 Robert E Lee Building
Jackson, MS 39201
601-359-1288
877-210-8513
Fax: 601-359-6295
TTY: 601-359-6230
www.dmh.state.ms.us
Supporting a better tomorrow by making a difference in the lives of Mississippians with mental illness, substance abuse problems and intellectual/developmental disabilities one person at a time.

2025 **Mississippi Bureau of Alcohol and Drug Services**
Department of Mental Health
239 N Lamar Street
Jackson, MS 39201
601-359-1288
877-210-8513
Fax: 601-359-6295
TDD: 601-359-6230
dmh.ms.gov/alcohol-and-drug-services
The Bureau of Alcohol and Drug Services has the responsibility of administering fiscal resources (state and federal) to the public system of prevention, treatment, and recovery supports for persons with substance use disorders. The overall goal of the state's substance use disorder service system is to provide quality care within a continuum of accessible community-based services.

Missouri

2026 **Missouri Division of Alcohol and Drug Abuse**
Department of Mental Health
1706 E Elm Street
Jefferson City, MO 65102
573-751-4942
800-575-7480
Fax: 573-751-8224
TTY: 573-526-1201
dmhmail@dmh.mo.gov
dmh.mo.gov/ada/

Montana

2027 **Addictive and Mental Disorders Division**
Department of Public Health and Human Services
100 N Park
Helena, MT 59620-2905
406-444-3964
Fax: 406-444-4435
hhsamdemail@mt.gov
phhs.mt.gov/amdd/substanceabuse
Sheila Hogan, Director
Zoe Barnard, Administrator

Nebraska

2028 **Department of Public Instruction: Division of Alcoholism and Drug Abuse**
Division Of Behavioral Health
Lincoln, NE 68509-8925
402-471-7818
800-648-4444
Fax: 402-479-5162
www.hhs.state.ne.us

Nevada

2029 **Alcohol and Drug Abuse Bureau**
Department of Human Resources
4126 Technology Way
Carson City, NV 89706
775-684-5943
Fax: 775-684-5964
MHDS@MHDS.NV.GOV

New Hampshire

2030 **Office of Alcohol and Drug Abuse Prevention**
State Office Park South
129 Pleasant Street
Concord, NH 03301-3852
800-804-0909
Fax: 603-271-6105
www.dhhs.state.nh.us

New Jersey

2031 **Department of Health**
120 S Stockton Street
Trenton, NJ 08625-0362
609-292-7837
800-367-6543
Fax: 609-292-3816
georgene.rhodunda@dhs.state.nj.us
www.state.nj.us

2032 **Division of Narcotic and Drug Abuse Control**
120 S Stockton Street
Trenton, NJ 08625-0362
609-292-5760
800-238-2333
Fax: 609-292-3816
www.state.nj.us/humanservices

New Mexico

2033 **Substance Abuse Epidemiology Program**
Department of Health
1190 Saint Francis Drive
Santa Fe, NM 87502
505-827-0017
nmhealth.org/about/erd/ibeb/sap
Collects and analyzes data on substance abuse in New Mexico and shares the results with stakeholders.
Tony Rosenblatt, Contact

New York

2034 **Office of Addiction Services and Supports**
1450 Western Avenue
Albany, NY 12203-3526
518-473-3460
877-846-7369
Fax: 518-457-5474
communications@oasas.ny.gov
www.oasas.ny.gov
Arlene Gonz lez-S nchez, Commissioner
Sean M. Byrne, Executive Deputy Commissioner

North Carolina

2035 **Mental Health, Developmental Disabilities and Substance Abuse Services**
Department of Health and Human Services
2001 Mail Service Center
Raleigh, NC 27699-2000
984-236-5000
855-262-1946
contactdmh@dhhs.nc.gov
ncdhhs.gov/divisions/mhddsas
Victor Armstrong, Director

North Dakota

2036 **Division of Alcoholism & Drug Abuse: Department of Human Services**
1237 W Divide Avenue
Bismarck, ND 58501
701-328-8920
800-755-2719
Fax: 701-328-8969
www.nd.gov/dhs/services/mentalhealth/
The Mental Health and Substance Abuse Services Division provides leadership for the planning, development, and oversight of a system of care for children, adults, and families with severe emotional disorders, mental illness, and/or substance abuse issues.

Ohio

2037 **Bureau on Alcohol Abuse and Recovery**
Ohio Department of Health
30 East Broad Street
Columbus, OH 43215-2550
614-466-3445
Fax: 614-752-8645
info@ada.ohio.gov
www.odadas.state.oh.us
The mission of the Ohio Department of Mental Health and Addiction Services (OhioMHAS) is to provide statewide leadership of a high-quality mental health and addiction prevention, treatment and recovery system that is effective and valued by all Ohioans.

2038 **Bureau on Drug Abuse**
Ohio Department of Health
30 East Broad Street
Columbus, OH 43215
614-466-3445
Fax: 614-752-8645
info@ada.ohio.gov
The mission of the Ohio Department of Mental Health and Addiction Services (OhioMHAS) is to provide statewide leadership of a high-quality mental health and addiction prevention, treatment and recovery system that is effective and valued by all Ohioans.
Tracy J. Plouck, Director
Orman Hall, Director of the Governor's Cabinet Opiat

Oklahoma

2039 **Oklahoma Department of Mental Health and Substance Abuse Services**
2000 N Classen Boulevard
Oklahoma City, OK 73106
405-522-3908
800-985-5990
Fax: 405-548-9321
boardmembers@odmhsas.org
www.odmhsas.org
Provides information, assistant programs and other services to persons struggling with mental health and substance abuse in the state of Oklahoma.

Oregon

2040 **Behavioral Health Services**
Oregon Health Authority
500 Summer Street NE
Salem, OR 97301-1118
503-945-5772
oregon.gov/oha/HSD/AMH

2041 **Oregon Alcohol and Drug Policy Commission**
c/o OTIS
201 High Street SE
Salem, OR 97301
503-757-0989
adpc.or@dhsoha.state.or.us
www.oregon.gov/adpc
The Alcohol and Drug Policy Commission is an independent state government agency that was created by the Oregon Legislature to improve the effectiveness and efficiency of state and local alcohol and drug abuse prevention and treatment services.
Reginald Richardson Sr., Executive Director

Pennsylvania

2042 **Drug and Alcohol Programs**
Department Of Health
02 Kline Plaza
Harrisburg, PA 17104-0090
717-783-8200
877-724-3258
Fax: 717-787-6285
rkauffman@state.pa.us
www.ddap.pa.gov

Rhode Island

2043 **Division of Behavioral Healthcare Services**
BHDDH
14 Harrington Road
Cranston, RI 02920-0944
401-462-3201
Fax: 401-462-3204
TTY: 401-462-6087
bhddh.ri.gov/substance_use
The division oversees Mental Health Services and Substance Abuse Treatment and Prevention Services, and is a unit of the Department of Behavioral Healthcare, Developmental Disabilities and Hospitals.
Corina Roy, Director

South Carolina

2044 **South Carolina Commission on Alcohol and Drug Abuse**
Department Of Alcohol And Drug Abuse Services
2414 Bull Street
Columbia, SC 29201-9498
803-896-5555
Fax: 803-896-5557
www.daodas.sc.gov
The department's mission is to ensure the provision of quality services to prevent or reduce the negative consequences of substance use and addictions.

South Dakota

2045 **Division of Alcohol & Drug Abuse**
Department Of Human Services
3800 E Highway 34
Pierre, SD 57501-5070
605-773-5990
800-265-9684
Fax: 605-773-5483
TTY: 605-773-6412
infodhs@state.sd.us
www.dhs.sd.gov

Tennessee

2046 **Department of Mental Health and Substance Abuse Services**
Andrew Jackson Bldg.
Nashville, TN 37243
615-532-6500
800-560-5767
OCA.TDMHSAS@tn.gov
tn.gov/behavioral-health
Marie Williams, Commissioner

Texas

2047 **Texas Commission on Alcohol and Drug Abuse**
Department Of State Health
Austin, TX 78714
512-206-5000
866-378-8440
Fax: 512-458-7477
TTY: 800-735-2989
TDD: 800-735-2989
web.master@dshs.state.tx.us
www.dshs.state.tx.us/mhsa/
Mission is to improve health and well-being in Texas.

Utah

2048 **Division of Substance Abuse and Mental Health**
Department Of Human Services
195 North 1950 West
Salt Lake City, UT 84116
801-538-3939
Fax: 801-538-9892
dsamh@utah.gov
dsamh.utah.gov
The Utah Division of Substance Abuse and Mental Health is the State agency responsible for ensuring that prevention and treatment services for substance abuse and mental health are available statewide.

Vermont

2049 **Alcohol and Drug Abuse Programs of Vermont**
Department Of Health
108 Cherry Street
Burlington, VT 05402-1531
802-651-1550
Fax: 802-651-1573
www.healthvermont.gov

Virginia

2050 **Substance Abuse Services Office of Virginia**
Department of Behavioral Health & Development
1220 Bank Street
Richmond, VA 23218-1797
804-786-3921
800-451-5544
Fax: 804-371-6638
TTY: 804-371-8977
dbhds.virginia.gov
Available to citizens statewide, Virginia's public mental health, intellectual disability and substance abuse services system is comprised of 16 state-operated facilities and 40 locally-run community services boards (CSBs). The CSBs and facilities serve children and adults who have-or who are at risk of-mental illness, serious emotional disturbance, intellectual disabilities, or substance abuse disorders.

Washington

2051 **Washington Department of Social and Health Services, Alcohol and Drug Prog.**
Department Of Social And Health Services
Olympia, WA 98504-5330
877-301-4557
800-737-0617
Fax: 360-438-8078
TTY: 877-301-4557
starkkd@dshs.wa.gov
www1.dshs.wa.gov

West Virginia

2052 **West Virginia Division of Alcohol & Drug Abuse**
Department Of Health And Human Resources
350 Capitol Street
Charleston, WV 25304-3702
304-356-4811
Fax: 304-558-1008
www.dhhr.wv.gov
The Division on Alcoholism and Drug Abuse, an operating division of the Bureau for Behavioral Health and Health Facilities (BBHHF) within the West Virginia Division of Health and Human Services is charged in code with being the Single State Authority (SSA) primarily responsible for prevention, control, treatment, rehabilitation, educational research and planning for substance abuse related services
Craig A. Richards, Deputy Commissioner

Wisconsin

2053 **Office of Alcohol and Other Drug Abuse**
1 W Wilson Street
Madison, WI 53703-7851
608-266-1865
Fax: 608-266-1533
TTY: 608-267-7371
dhswebmaster@wisconsin.gov
John Easterday, Administrator
Susan Gadacz, Contact

Wyoming

2054 **Alcohol & Drug Abuse Programs of Wyoming**
Department Of Health
401 Hathaway Building
Cheyenne, WY 82002-0480
307-777-7656
866-571-0944
Fax: 307-777-7439
health.wyo.gov

Web Sites

2055 **AAA Foundation for Traffic Safety**
www.aaafoundation.org
The AAA Foundation for Traffic Safety was founded in 1947 by AAA to conduct research to address growing highway safety issues. The organization's mission is to identify traffic safety problems, foster research that seeks solutions and disseminate information and educational materials.

2056 **Al-Anon**
www.al-anon.alateen.org
The single purpose of this organization is to help families and friends of alcoholics, whether the alcoholic is still drinking or not.

2057 **Alateen**
www.al-anon.org/for-alateen
A part of the Al-Anon program, Alateen is for teenagers who have been affected by someone else's drinking, whether it be a family member or a friend.

2058 **American Council for Drug Education**
www.acde.org/
This organization provides information on drug use, publishes books and offers films and curriculum materials for prevention.

2059 **CSAP State Liason Program**
www.samhsa.gov
This program is designed to support alcohol and other drug abuse prevention efforts in the States.

2060 **Center for Substance Abuse Prevention**
www.samhsa.gov
The mission of the Center for Substance Abuse Prevention is to improve behavioral health through evidence-based prevention approaches.

2061 **Cocaine Anonymous**
www.ca.org
A support group based on the twelve steps of Alcoholics Anonymous that focuses specifically on problems of cocaine addiction.

2062 **Dentists Concerned for Dentists**
www.medhelp.org/amshc/amshc53.htm
A nonprofit organization for chemically dependent Minnesota dentists and concerned others.

2063 **Everyday Health**
www.everydayhealth.com
Aims to provide evidence-based health information from physicians and healthcare providers.

2064 **Families Anonymous**
www.familiesanonymous.org/
Addresses the needs of families who are concerned about a relative with a drug problem and with related behavioral problems.

2065 **FamilyDoctor.org**
www.familydoctor.org
Medical advice and information provided by the American Academy of Family Physicians. Resources include a medical dictionary, a symptom checker tool, a BMI calculator, and medication information.

2066 **Hazelden**
www.hazelden.com
Organization dedicated to providing quality rehabilitation, education and professional services for chemical dependency and related addictive behaviors.

2067 **Healing Well**
www.healingwell.com
An online health resource guide to medical news, chat, information and articles, newsgroups and message boards, books, disease-related web sites, medical directories, and more for patients, friends, and family coping with disabling diseases, disorders, or chronic illnesses.

2068 **Health Finder**
www.healthfinder.gov
Searchable, carefully developed web site offering information on over 1000 topics. Developed by the US Department of Health and Human Services, the site can be used in both English and Spanish.

2069 **Healthlink USA**
www.healthlinkusa.com
Health information concerning treatment, cures, prevention, diagnosis, risk factors, research, support groups, email lists, personal stories and much more. Updated regularly.

2070 **Indian Health Service**
www.ihs.gov
Charged with providing a comprehensive program of alcoholism and substance abuse prevention and treatment for Native Americans and Alaskan natives.

2071 **Lawyers Concerned for Lawyers**
www.mnlcl.org/
Lawyers Concerned for Lawyers provides free, confidential peer and professional assistance to Minnesota lawyers, judges, law students, and their immediate family members on any issue that causes stress or distress.

2072 **MedicineNet**
www.medicinenet.com
An online resource for consumers providing easy-to-read, authoritative medical and health information.

2073 **MedlinePlus**
www.medlineplus.gov
A service of the National Library of Medicine, MedlinePlus is an online resource providing health and wellness information in both English and Spanish.

2074 **Medscape**
www.medscape.com
Medscape offers specialists, primary care physicians, and other health professionals the Web's most robust and integrated medical information and educational tools.

2075 **MyPlate**
www.myplate.gov
Created and managed by the US Department of Agriculture's Center for Nutrition Policy & Promotion, MyPlate is a dietary guide providing resources and recipes to promote healthy eating for all Americans.

2076 **National Clearinghouse for Alcohol and Drug Information**
www.health.org

2077 **National Council on Alcoholism and Drug Dependence**
www.ncadd.org
Provides education, information, help and hope in the fight against addictions. Nationwide network of affiliates, advocates prevention, intervention and treatment, and is committed to ridding the disease of its stigma and its sufferers of their denial and shame.

2078 **National Crime Prevention Council**
www.ncpc.org
This organization works to prevent crime and drug use in many ways, including developing materials for parents and children.

2079 **Nutrition.gov**
www.nutrition.gov
Sponsored by the United States Department of Agriculture (USDA), Nutrition.gov offers information on topics in food and nutrition, including healthy eating, physical activity, and food safety.

2080 **Office on Smoking and Health**
www.cdc.gov/tobacco/
Offers reference services to researchers through the Technical Information Center. Publishes and distributes a number of titles in the field of smoking and health.

2081 **Safe Homes**
www.yescap.org/safehomes/safehomes.htm
This national organization encourages parents to sign a contract stipulating that when parties are held in one another's homes they will adhere to a strict no-alcohol/no-drug-use rule.

2082 **Science Daily**
www.sciencedaily.com
Provides information on the latest news and research in science, health, the environment, and technology.

2083 **Substance Abuse and Mental Health Services Administration**
www.samhsa.gov
The goal of this organization is to reduce incidence and prevalence of mental disorders and substance abuse and improve treatment outcomes for persons suffering from addictive and mental health problems and disorders.

2084 **The Nutrition Source**
hsph.harvard.edu/nutritionsource
From the Harvard T.H. Chan School of Public Health, The Nutrition Source provides news, information, and guidance for nutrition and healthy eating.

2085 **UnlockFood**
www.unlockfood.ca
A website from Dietitians of Canada. Provides videos, recipes, and information on food and nutrition, as well as helps Canadians connect with a dietitian.

2086 **Verywell**
www.verywellhealth.com
Offers health, medicine, and wellness information from health professionals.

2087 **WebMD**
www.webmd.com
Provides credible information, supportive communities, and in-depth reference material about health subjects. A source for original and timely health information as well as material from well known content providers.

2088 **World Health Organization**
www.who.int
An agency of the United Nations, World Health Organization (WHO) serves to promote global health. The WHO website provides fact sheets, publications, media, and other resources on various health topics.

SLEEP DISORDERS

The relationship between nutrition and sleep is critical. Your quality of sleep is influenced by certain foods and beverages that prevent you from getting the amount of sleep your body needs. A healthy body weight is also associated with getting enough sleep, and losing weight can be encouraged by good sleeping habits. Nutrition is the body's building block for health and proper body functioning. A balanced diet of vegetables, fruits and healthy foods that support all body systems and processes will also contribute to better sleep. For example, high-carbohydrate meals will make us feel sleepy, but will also interfere with a good night's sleep, proven to increase the times you wake up during the night, thus reducing the level of deep sleep. The DASH diet and the Mediterranean diet (see pages 167 and 191) and other well-balanced diets are known to help you sleep. Talking to a doctor or nutritionist will help to establish the best diet for you. Not getting enough, productive sleep is associated with obesity and a greater waist circumference, both precursors for cardiovascular disease and type 2 diabetes. Eating healthy foods, keeping a regular sleep schedule, relaxing before bed time, and not eating late at night will all support better sleep. Other strategies include keeping the bedroom dark, limiting screen time, getting lots of natural light and regular exercise.

Agencies & Associations

2089 **American Academy of Sleep Medicine**
2510 N Frontage Road 630-737-9700
Darien, IL 60561 Fax: 630-737-9790
contact@aasm.org
www.aasm.org

AASM is a professional society focused on advancing sleep medicine health care, education, and research.
Raman Malhotra, MD, President

2090 **American Autoimmune Related Diseases Association**
19176 Hall Road 586-776-3900
Clinton Township, MI 48038 aarda@aarda.org
www.aarda.org

Awareness, education, referrals for patients with any type of autoimmune disease.
Molly Murray, President & CEO
Laura Simpson, Chief Operating Officer

2091 **American Sleep Apnea Association**
1250 Connecticut Avenue NW 888-293-3650
Washington, DC 20036 asaa@sleepapnea.org
www.sleepapnea.org

Offers help and information to persons with sleep apnea and their families.
Gilles Frydman, Executive Director
Valerie Mead, Program Manager

2092 **American Sleep Association**
100 Cambridge Street contactasa@sleepassociation.org
Boston, MA 02114 www.sleepassociation.org

The mission of the American Sleep Association is to raise awareness of the importance of sleep, as well as the effects of sleep apnea, narcolepsy, insomnia, and other sleep disorders.

2093 **Canadian Sleep & Circadian Network**
5400 boulevard Gouin ouest 514-338-2222
Montreal, QC, H4J-1C5 Fax: 514-338-2531
www.cscnweb.ca

Works to improve knowledge about sleep and sleep disruption to foster healthier sleep for Canadians.
Julie Carrier, Ph.D., Scientific Director
Dominique Petit, Ph.D., Coordinator

2094 **Canadian Sleep Society**
2325 Allee des Bibliotheques info@css-scs.ca
Quebec, QC, G1V-0A6 www.css-scs.ca

A national organization devoted to improving sleep and health through education, advocacy, and support for research and high quality clinical care.
Celyne Bastien, Ph.D., President
Najib Ayas, MD, MPH, Secretary-Treasurer

2095 **Circadian Sleep Disorders Network**
4619 Woodfield Road csd-n@csd-n.org
Bethesda, MD 20814 www.circadiansleepdisorders.org

A nonprofit organization committed to supporting individuals with chronic circadian rhythm disorders through information, awareness, and advocacy.
Peter Mansbach, Ph.D., President
James Fadden, Vice President

2096 **International Pediatric Sleep Association**
3270 19th Street NW Fax: 612-465-5357
Rochester, MN 55901 info@pedsleep.org
www.pedsleep.org

Promotes pediatric sleep research, education, public policy, and clinical care worldwide.
Judy Owens, President
Patricia Franco, Vice President

2097 **Narcolepsy Network**
PO Box 2178 401-667-2523
Lynnwood, WA 98036 888-292-6522
info@narcolepsynetwork.org
narcolepsynetwork.org

Offers help and information to persons with narcolepsy and their families.
Keith Harper, President
Sharon O'Shaughnessy, MA, SLP, Vice President

2098 **National Heart, Lung, & Blood Institute**
31 Center Drive 877-645-2448
Bethesda, MD 20892 nhlbiinfo@nhlbi.nih.gov
www.nhlbi.nih.gov

The mission is to improve meaning of one American people by supporting and understanding research to prevent, detect, diagnose

and treat diseases of heart, lungs, blood vessels, and sleep disorders.
Gary H. Gibbons, Director

2099 **National Institute of Neurological Disorders and Stroke**
PO Box 5801 800-352-9424
Bethesda, MD 20824 www.ninds.nih.gov
Seeks to reduce the burden of neurological disease affecting individuals from all walks of life.
Walter J. Koroshetz, MD, Director
Nina Schor, MD, Ph.D., Deputy Director

2100 **National Sleep Foundation**
1010 N Glebe Road 703-243-1697
Arlington, VA 22201 nsf@thensf.org
www.thensf.org
Non-profit organization dedicated to improving public health and understanding of sleep disorders by supporting education and sleep-related research.
Lauren Hale, Ph.D., Chair
David Neubauer, MD, Secretary

2101 **Restless Legs Syndrome Foundation**
3006 Bee Caves Road 512-366-9109
Austin, TX 78746 info@rls.org
www.rls.org
A nonprofit agency dedicated to improving the lives of individuals with restless legs syndrome (RLS) by increasing awareness, improving treatments, supporting research, and offering science-based education and services.
Karla Dzienkowski, RN, BSN, Executive Director
Shamim Nabours, Membership Coordinator

2102 **Sleep Research Society**
2510 N Frontage Road 630-737-9702
Darien, IL 60561 coordinator@srsnet.org
www.sleepresearchsociety.org
Facilitates communication among research workers in the field of sleep medicine.
H. Craig Heller, Ph.D., President
John A. Noel, Executive Director

2103 **Society of Anesthesia and Sleep Medicine**
6737 W Washington Street 414-389-8608
Milwaukee, WI 53214 Fax: 414-276-7704
info@sasmhq.org
www.sasmhq.org
The Society of Anesthesia and Sleep Medicine (SASM) aims to advance education, research, communication, and standards of care for clinical problems common to anesthesia and sleep.
Marie Odden, Executive Director

2104 **Society of Behavioral Sleep Medicine**
1522 Player Drive 859-312-8880
Lexington, KY 40511 Fax: 859-303-6055
membership@behavioralsleep.org
www.behavioralsleep.org
The Society of Behavioral Sleep Medicine works to further research on the behavioral, psychological, and physiological factors affecting sleep and sleep disorders.
Kathryn Hansen, Executive Director

2105 **Wake Up Narcolepsy**
PO Box 60293 info@wakeupnarcolepsy.org
Worcester, MA 01606 www.wakeupnarcolepsy.org
A not-for-profit organization dedicated to increasing awareness of narcolepsy and supporting narcolepsy research and education.
Monica Gow, Co-Founder & Chair
David Gow, Co-Founder & Treasurer

2106 **World Sleep Society**
3270 19th Street NW 507-316-0084
Rochester, MN 55901 Fax: 612-465-5357
info@worldsleepsociety.org
www.worldsleepsociety.org
The mission of the World Sleep Society is to increase awareness on sleep, sleep health, and sleep disorders worldwide through education, research, and patient care.
Allan O'Bryan, Executive Director

Web Sites

2107 **American Sleep Apnea Association**
www.sleeppapnea.org
The American Sleep Apnea Association, founded in 1990, is a 501(c)(3) nonprofit organization that promotes awareness of sleep apnea, works for continuing improvements in treatments for this serious disorder, and advocates for the interests of sleep apnea patients.

2108 **American Sleep Association**
www.sleepassociation.org
The mission of the American Sleep Association is to raise awareness of the importance of sleep, as well as the effects of sleep apnea, narcolepsy, insomnia, and other sleep disorders.

2109 **American Sleep Disorders Association**
Provides full diagnostic and treatment services to improve the quality of care for patients with all types of sleep disorders.

2110 **Dietary Guidelines for Americans**
www.dietaryguidelines.gov
Publishes the Dietary Guidelines for Americans, a guide providing nutritional advice to promote health and prevent disease. Updated versions of the Dietary Guidelines are released by the US Departments of Agriculture (USDA) and Health & Human Services (HHS) every five years.

2111 **Everyday Health**
www.everydayhealth.com
Aims to provide evidence-based health information from physicians and healthcare providers.

2112 **FamilyDoctor.org**
www.familydoctor.org
Medical advice and information provided by the American Academy of Family Physicians. Resources include a medical dictionary, a symptom checker tool, a BMI calculator, and medication information.

2113 **Healing Well**
www.healingwell.com
An online health resource guide to medical news, chat, information and articles, newsgroups and message boards, books, disease-related web sites, medical directories, and more for patients, friends, and family coping with disabling diseases, disorders, or chronic illnesses.

2114 **Health Finder**
www.healthfinder.gov
Searchable, carefully developed web site offering information on over 1000 topics. Developed by the US Department of Health and Human Services, the site can be used in both English and Spanish.

2115 **Healthline**
www.healthline.com
Provides medical and health articles and information.

2116 **Healthlink USA**
www.healthlinkusa.com
Health information concerning treatment, cures, prevention, diagnosis, risk factors, research, support groups, email lists, personal stories and much more. Updated regularly.

2117 **Hormone Health Network**
www.hormone.org
Online support and resources for patients, with focus on hormone health, disease and treatment. Provided by the Endocrine Society.

2118 **MGH Neurology WebForums**
Online. Provides both unmoderated message boards and chat rooms for specific neurological disorders.

2119 **Mayo Clinic**
www.mayoclinic.org
Mission is to empower people to manage their health by providing useful and up-to-date information and tools.

2120 **MedicineNet**
www.medicinenet.com

An online resource for consumers providing easy-to-read, authoritative medical and health information.

2121 MedlinePlus
www.medlineplus.gov
A service of the National Library of Medicine, MedlinePlus is an online resource providing health and wellness information in both English and Spanish.

2122 Medscape
www.medscape.com
Medscape offers specialists, primary care physicians, and other health professionals the Web's most robust and integrated medical information and educational tools.

2123 National Heart, Lung & Blood Institute
www.nhlbi.nih.gov
Information on the scientific investigation of heart, blood vessel, lung, blood and sleep disorders.

2124 National Sleep Foundation
www.thensf.org
Information for millions of Americans who suffer from sleep disorders, and to prevent the catastrophic accidents that are related to poor or disordered sleep through research, education and the dissemination of information.

2125 Neurology Channel
www.healthcommunities.com
Find clearly explained, medically accurate information regarding conditions, including an overview, symptoms, causes, diagnostic procedures and treatment options. On this site it is possible to ask questions and get information from a neurologist and connect to people who have similar health interests.

2126 Nutrition.gov
www.nutrition.gov
Sponsored by the United States Department of Agriculture (USDA), Nutrition.gov offers information on topics in food and nutrition, including healthy eating, physical activity, and food safety.

2127 Science Daily
www.sciencedaily.com
Provides information on the latest news and research in science, health, the environment, and technology.

2128 Sleep Disorder Resource
www.sleepdisordersresource.com
A guide and directory offering information and resources for individuals living with sleep disorders, as well physicians, health care professionals, and educational professionals.

2129 Sleep Education
www.sleepeducation.org
A website from the American Academy of Sleep Medicine offering information on sleep, sleep disorders, and sleep treatment.

2130 Sleep Foundation
www.sleepfoundation.org
Owned by OneCare Media, Sleep Foundation provides information on sleep, health, and sleep science.

2131 Sleep Research Society
www.sleepresearchsociety.org
Facilitates communication among research workers in this field, but does not sponsor research investigations on its own.

2132 Sleepwell
www.mysleepwell.ca
Offers information designed to help people with insomnia to sleep without medications, with focus on cognitive behavioral therapy for insomnia (CBTi).

2133 The Nutrition Source
hsph.harvard.edu/nutritionsource
From the Harvard T.H. Chan School of Public Health, The Nutrition Source provides news, information, and guidance for nutrition and healthy eating.

2134 Verywell
www.verywellhealth.com
Offers health, medicine, and wellness information from health professionals.

2135 WebMD
www.webmd.com
Provides credible information, supportive communities, and in-depth reference material about health subjects. A source for original and timely health information as well as material from well known content providers.

STROKE

A healthy lifestyle can reduce the risk of stroke by almost 80 percent, and the lifestyle factor with the greatest influence is nutrition. A Mediterreanean diet (see page 191) can reduce stroke risk by 40 percent or more in high-risk patients. Considering your diet in regard to other diseases, such as diabetes, will also reduce risks. Patients at risk of stroke, in addition to following their healthcare providers recommendations, should all keep salt intake at 2-3 grams per day, limit intake of meat and avoid egg yolk. Studies also show stroke patients have a B12 deficiency. The risk of stroke can be greatly reduced with proper diet, moderate activity and stress reduction. Diet after stroke is also important. A person who has had a stroke may have problems using their hand or arm so eating may be difficult; problems with memory and thinking may cause a stroke victim to forget to eat or drink; swallowing problems (dysphagia) may make it difficult to eat. Talking with a physician and dietician is important to find a way to get adequate nutrition.

Agencies & Associations

2136 American Academy of Neurology
201 Chicago Avenue 612-928-6000
Minneapolis, MN 55415 800-879-1960
Fax: 612-454-2746
memberservices@aan.com
www.aan.com
A professional association representing more than 36,000 neurologists and neuroscientists dedicated to promoting and providing high quality neurologic care.
Mary E. Post, MBA, CAE, Chief Executive Officer
Angela Babb, MS, CAE, APR, Chief Communications Officer

2137 American Heart Association
7272 Greenville Avenue 800-242-8721
Dallas, TX 75231 www.heart.org
The American Heart Association is the nation's oldest, largest voluntary organization devoted to fighting cardiovascular diseases and stroke. Funds research and raises public awareness of heart diseases.
Nancy Brown, Chief Executive Officer
Suzie Upton, Chief Operating Officer

2138 American Speech-Language-Hearing Association
2200 Research Boulevard 301-269-5700
Rockville, MD 20850 800-638-8255
TTY: 301-296-5650
asha.org
The professional, scientific, and credentialing association for members and affiliates who are audiologists, speech-language pathologists, and speech, language, and hearing scientists in the United States and internationally. Supports audiologists and speech-language scientists in their research and practices.
A. Lynn Williams, President

2139 American Stroke Association
7272 Greenville Avenue 800-242-8721
Dallas, TX 75231 www.stroke.org
Dedicated to the prevention, diagnosis, and treatment of stroke. Funds research on stroke and advises the public on how to detect and avoid stroke.
Nancy Brown, Chief Executive Officer
Suzie Upton, Chief Operating Officer

2140 American Stroke Foundation
6405 Metcalf Avenue 913-649-1776
Overland Park, KS 66202 www.americanstroke.org
Provides support for stroke survivors and their caregivers.
Jane Savidge, Executive Director
Dory Sabata, Program Director

2141 Aphasia Access
405 N Stanwick Road 888-859-8832
Moorestown, NJ 08057 info@aphasiaaccess.org
www.aphasiaaccess.org
Assists healthcare professionals in communicating with people with communication disorders, including aphasia.
Elizabeth Hoover, Ph.D., President
Todd Von Deak, MBA, CAE, Executive Director

2142 Aphasia Institute
73 Scarsdale Road 416-226-3636
Toronto, Ontario, M3B-2R2 www.aphasia.ca
Dedicated to helping people with aphasia communicate through research, education, training, and service.
Aura Kagan, Executive Director
Rochelle Cohen-Schneider, Director, Clinical & Education Services

2143 Child Neurology Foundation
249 E Main Street 888-417-3435
Lexington, KY 40507 info@childneurologyfoundation.org
www.childneurologyfoundation.org
Offers education, resources, and support for children with neurologic conditions and their families.
Amy Brin, MSN, MA, PCNS-BC, Executive Director & CEO
Greta Pittard, Chief Operations Officer

2144 Children's Hemiplegia & Stroke Association
4101 W Green Oaks chasa.org
Arlington, TX 76016
Helps children who have survived an early brain injury that results in hemiplegia or hemiparesis. Also helpd adults who have been living with hemiplegia since childhood
Nancy Atwood, Executive Director

2145 Heart and Stroke Canada
1525 Carling Avenue 888-473-4636
Ottawa, Ontario, K1Z-8R9 www.heartandstroke.ca
Leading authority on cardiovascular disease, providing resources for individuals and funding scientific research on heart disease and stroke.
Doug Roth, Chief Executive Officer

2146 International Alliance for Pediatric Stroke
PO Box 77896 info@iapediatricstroke.org
Charlotte, NC 28271 www.iapediatricstroke.org
Raises awareness, promotes education and research, and shares medical information to advance the diagnosis, treatment, and prevention of pediatric stroke.
Mary Kay Ballasiotes, Executive Director

2147 National Aphasia Association
PO Box 87 naa@aphasia.org
Scarsdale, NY 10583 aphasia.org
Provides access to research, education, rehabilitation, therapeuticand advocacy services to individuals with aphasia and their caregivers
Darlene S. Williamson, President
Carol Kirshner, Secretary

2148 National Heart, Lung, & Blood Institute
31 Center Drive 877-645-2448
Bethesda, MD 20892 nhlbiinfo@nhlbi.nih.gov
www.nhlbi.nih.gov
The mission is to improve meaning of one American people by supporting and understanding research to prevent, detect, diagnose and treat diseases of heart, lungs, blood vessels, and sleep disorders.
Gary H. Gibbons, Director

2149 National Institute of Neurological Disorders and Stroke
PO Box 5801 800-352-9424
Bethesda, MD 20824 www.ninds.nih.gov
Seeks to reduce the burden of neurological disease affecting individuals from all walks of life.
Walter J. Koroshetz, MD, Director
Nina Schor, MD, Ph.D., Deputy Director

2150 National Institute on Deafness & Other Communication Disorders
31 Center Drive 800-241-1044
Bethesda, MD 20892-2320 TTY: 800-241-1055
nidcdinfo@nidcd.nih.gov
www.nidcd.nih.gov
Conducts and supports research and training with respect to disorders of hearing and other communication processes, including diseases affecting hearing, balance, voice, speech, language, touch, taste and smell through research performed in its own laboratories; a program of research grants; individual and institutional research training awards, career development awards, center grants, and contracts to public and private research institutions.
Debara L. Tucci, MD, MS, MBA, Director

2151 Office of Women's Health
200 Independence Avenue SW 202-690-7650
Washington, DC 20201 800-994-9662
womenshealth@hhs.gov
www.womenshealth.gov
Government agency under the Department of Health & Human Services, with free health information for women.
Dorothy Fink, MD, Deputy Asst. Secretary, Women's Health
Richelle West Marshall, Deputy Director

2152 Stroke Recovery Foundation
5621 Strand Boulevard 239-254-8266
Naples, FL 34110 www.strokerecoveryfoundation.org
Works to help stroke survivors maximize their recoveries, as well as reduce the negative effects of stroke for Americans.
Bob Mandell, Founder

2153 The Brain Attack Coalition
31 Center Drive 301-496-5751
Bethesda, MD 20892 www.brainattackcoalition.org
A group of professional, voluntary and governmental entities dedicated to reducing the occurrence, disabilities and death associated with stroke. the goal of the coalition is to strengthen and promote the relationships among its member organizations in order to help people who have had a stroke or are at risk for a stroke.
Mark Alberts, MD, Chair

2154 The Stroke Awareness Foundation
51 E Campbell Avenue 408-370-5282
Campbell, CA 95008 info@strokeinfo.org
strokeinfo.org
Supports hospital stroke center certification, training and redirection efforts, as well as promoting stroke awareness for the general public.
Pat Dando, Co-Founder & Chair
Noemi Conway, Executive Director

2155 World Pediatric Stroke Association
4716 Langwood Court 314-541-0603
Saint Louis, MO 63129 worldpsa@gmail.com
www.worldpediatricstrokeassociation.org
Formerly Brendon's Smile, the World Pediatric Stroke Association raises awareness and supports research relating to pediatric stroke and cerebrovascular disease.
Jessica J. Spear, Founder & President

Web Sites

2156 Dietary Guidelines for Americans
www.dietaryguidelines.gov
Publishes the Dietary Guidelines for Americans, a guide providing nutritional advice to promote health and prevent disease. Updated versions of the Dietary Guidelines are released by the US Departments of Agriculture (USDA) and Health & Human Services (HHS) every five years.

2157 Everyday Health
www.everydayhealth.com
Aims to provide evidence-based health information from physicians and healthcare providers.

2158 FamilyDoctor.org
www.familydoctor.org
Medical advice and information provided by the American Academy of Family Physicians. Resources include a medical dictionary, a symptom checker tool, a BMI calculator, and medication information.

2159 Health Finder
www.healthfinder.gov
Searchable, carefully developed web site offering information on over 1000 topics. Developed by the US Department of Health and Human Services, the site can be used in both English and Spanish.

2160 Healthline
www.healthline.com
Provides medical and health articles and information.

2161 Healthlink USA
www.healthlinkusa.com
Health information concerning treatment, cures, prevention, diagnosis, risk factors, research, support groups, email lists, personal stories and much more. Updated regularly.

2162 MedicineNet
www.medicinenet.com
An online resource for consumers providing easy-to-read, authoritative medical and health information.

2163 MedlinePlus
www.medlineplus.gov
A service of the National Library of Medicine, MedlinePlus is an online resource providing health and wellness information in both English and Spanish.

2164 Medscape
www.medscape.com
Medscape offers specialists, primary care physicians, and other health professionals the Web's most robust and integrated medical information and educational tools.

2165 MyPlate
www.myplate.gov
Created and managed by the US Department of Agriculture's Center for Nutrition Policy & Promotion, MyPlate is a dietary guide providing resources and recipes to promote healthy eating for all Americans.

2166 National Heart, Lung & Blood Institute
www.nhlbi.nih.gov
Information on the scientific investigation of heart, blood vessel, lung and blood disorders. Oversee research, demonstration, prevention, education and training activities in these fields and emphasizes the control of stroke.

2167 Nutrition.gov
www.nutrition.gov

Sponsored by the United States Department of Agriculture (USDA), Nutrition.gov offers information on topics in food and nutrition, including healthy eating, physical activity, and food safety.

2168 Science Daily

www.sciencedaily.com

Provides information on the latest news and research in science, health, the environment, and technology.

2169 Stroke Network

www.strokenetwork.org

Stroke support and resources for stroke survivors, caregivers, and health professionals.

2170 Stroke Survivor

www.strokesurvivor.com

Books and helpful products for stroke survivors with disabilities.

2171 Stroke Survivor Fitness

www.strokesurvivorfitness.com

Offers exercise and fitness information for stroke and brain trauma survivors.

2172 The Nutrition Source

hsph.harvard.edu/nutritionsource

From the Harvard T.H. Chan School of Public Health, The Nutrition Source provides news, information, and guidance for nutrition and healthy eating.

2173 UnlockFood

www.unlockfood.ca

A website from Dietitians of Canada. Provides videos, recipes, and information on food and nutrition, as well as helps Canadians connect with a dietitian.

2174 Verywell

www.verywellhealth.com

Offers health, medicine, and wellness information from health professionals.

2175 WebMD

www.webmd.com

Provides credible information, supportive communities, and in-depth reference material about health subjects. A source for original and timely health information as well as material from well known content providers.

THYROID DISEASE

Eating a well-balanced meal with sufficient nutrients is important with any disease. Because of the thyroid's role in the body, weight gain or loss may occur with medications taken for thyroid disease. Eating well is important: 5 servings of fruit and vegetables daily, high fiber foods such as potatoes and bread, dairy in moderation, protein including beans, meats, eggs and fish, and unsaturated oils and spreads. Six to eight glasses of water per day is also important. Supplements should be discussed with the physician before beginning any regimen and a clinical dietician may help plan a healthy meal plan. Vitamin D and calcium are important supplements. Iodine is essential for a properly functioning thyroid but if you are taking a synthetic thyroid medication such as levothyroxine for hypothyroidism, iodine supplements are not indicated, and if you are being treated for hyperthyroidism, taking an iodine supplement can worsen the condition. Generally, levothyroxine should be taken on an empty stomach first thing in the morning with a glass of water and waiting at least 30 minutes before eating or drinking. Iron tablets interfere with the absorption of thyroxine so wait at least two hours before taking any iron, including vitamins.

Agencies & Associations

2176 American Association of Clinical Endocrinology
904-353-7878
800-393-2223
www.aace.com
A professional community of physicians specializing in endocrinology, diabetes, and metabolism. Referrals and patient information available.
Paul Markowski, Chief Executive Officer
Tom Conway, Chief Financial Officer

2177 American Autoimmune Related Diseases Association
19176 Hall Road 586-776-3900
Clinton Township, MI 48038 aarda@aarda.org
www.aarda.org
Awareness, education, referrals for patients with any type of autoimmune disease.
Molly Murray, President & CEO
Laura Simpson, Chief Operating Officer

2178 American Head & Neck Society
11300 W Olympic Boulevard 310-437-0559
Los Angeles, CA 90064 Fax: 310-437-0585
admin@ahns.info
www.ahns.info
The American Head & Neck Society (AHNS) serves to improve research, education, and quality of care for head and neck oncology patients.
Christina Kasendorf, Executive Director
Colleen Elkins, Development Director

2179 American Thyroid Association
2000 Duke Street thyroid@thyroid.org
Alexandria, VA 22314 www.thyroid.org
Worldwide medical society and organization committed to the prevention, diagnosis, and treatment of thyroid disorders and thyroid cancer.
Amanda Perl, Executive Director
Kelly C. Hoff, Director, Development & Technology

2180 Endocrine Society
2055 L Street NW 202-971-3636
Washington, DC 20036 888-363-6274
info@endocrine.org
www.endocrine.org
Mission is to promote excellence in research, education, and the clinical practice endocrinology.
Kate Fryer, Chief Executive Officer
Paul Hedrick, Chief Financial Officer

2181 Graves' Disease & Thyroid Foundation
PO Box 2793 877-643-3123
Rancho Santa Fe, CA 92067 Fax: 877-643-3123
info@gdatf.org
www.gdatf.org
Provides education and support for people with Graves' disease and other thyroid related disorders.
Kimberly Dorris, Executive Director & CEO

2182 International Society of Endocrinology
625 N North Court www.isendo.org
Palatine, IL 60067
Serves to advance education, science, and patient care in endocrinology worldwide.
Margaret Wierman, Chair
Helen van Oers, Executive Director

2183 International Thyroid Oncology Group
5166 Commercial Drive 614-293-9779
Yorkville, NY 13495 www.itog.org
Focuses on developing new treatments for thyroid cancers.
Judy Dallas, Administrator

2184 Light of Life Foundation
PO Box 163 609-409-0900
Manalapan, NJ 07726 Fax: 609-409-0902
www.lightoflifefoundation.org
The Light of Life Foundation serves to improve the quality of life of thyroid cancer patients through education, awareness, patient support activities, and support of thyroid cancer care research.
Joan Shey, Founder & President

2185 MCT8-AHDS Foundation
13324 Highway 82 contact@mct8.info
Tahlequah, OK 74464 www.mct8.info
Aims to raise awareness and fund research on MCT8-AHDS Deficiency (Allan-Herndon-Dudley Syndrome), a genetic X-link disorder that only affects boys. MCT8-AHDS causes a genetic mutation of MCT8, which is responsible for the transport of thyroid hormones into the brain, resulting in improper brain development and mental delay.

2186 **Office of Women's Health**
200 Independence Avenue SW 202-690-7650
Washington, DC 20201 800-994-9662
womenshealth@hhs.gov
www.womenshealth.gov
Government agency under the Department of Health & Human Services, with free health information for women.
Dorothy Fink, MD, Deputy Asst. Secretary, Women's Health
Richelle West Marshall, Deputy Director

2187 **Pediatric Endocrine Society**
6728 Old McLean Village Drive 703-718-6023
McLean, VA 22101 Fax: 703-556-8729
info@pedsendo.org
www.pedsendo.org
Works to advance the endocrine health of children and adolescents.
Maureen Thompson, Executive Director
Jessica Widing, Associate Executive Director

2188 **Thyroid Cancer Canada**
308 Main Street 416-487-8267
Toronto, Ontario, M4C-4X7 Fax: 416-487-0601
info@thyroidcancercanada.org
www.thyroidcancercanada.org
A national nonprofit organization of thyroid cancer survivors dedicated to providing support and information to individuals impacted by the disease.
Sarah Eadie, President

2189 **Thyroid Cancer Survivors' Association Inc.**
PO Box 1102 877-588-7904
Olney, MD 20830-1102 Fax: 630-604-6078
thyca@thyca.org
www.thyca.org
A nonprofit organization devoted to providing current information and support services to thyroid cancer survivors, families, and health care professionals.
Howard Solomon, Chair
Gary Bloom, Executive Director

2190 **Thyroid Federation International**
PO Box 471 tfi@thyroid-fed.org
Bath, Ontario, K0H-1G0 www.thyroid-fed.org
A global network of organizations supporting individuals with thyroid disorders by providing resources and raising awareness.
Ashok Bhaseen, President
Peter Lakwijk, Treasurer

2191 **Thyroid Foundation of Canada**
PO Box 298 800-267-8822
Bath, Ontario, K0H-1G0 www.thyroid.ca
Established in 1980, the Thyroid Foundation of Canada was the first thyroid foundation in the world, and continues to provide resources and information for individuals affected by thyroid disease.
Laz Bouros, President
Kim McNally, Vice President

2192 **Thyroid Patients Canada**
28 Northgate Drive canadian.thyroid.patients@gmail.com
Bradford, Ontario, L3Z-2H5 www.thyroidpatients.ca
A patient-led nonprofit organization focused on providing support to people with thyroid disabilities and advocating for improvements to thyroid healthcare policy and research.
Tania S. Smith, Founder & President
Alexa Mahling Deskin, Vice President

2193 **Thyroid, Head and Neck Cancer Foundation**
PO Box 1021 info@thancfoundation.org
New York, NY 10276 www.thancfoundation.org
Develops research and education relating to thyroid, head and neck cancer.
Erika Rauscher, Executive Director
Jesse Fisher, Creative Director

Web Sites

2194 **American Thyroid Association**
www.thyroid.org
Promotes excellence and innovation in clinical care, research, education, and public policy.
David S Cooper MD, President
Gregory A Brent MD, Secretary

2195 **Dietary Guidelines for Americans**
www.dietaryguidelines.gov
Publishes the Dietary Guidelines for Americans, a guide providing nutritional advice to promote health and prevent disease. Updated versions of the Dietary Guidelines are released by the US Departments of Agriculture (USDA) and Health & Human Services (HHS) every five years.

2196 **EndocrineWeb**
www.endocrineweb.com
A website of Remedy Health Media, EndocrineWeb provides information about endocrine disorders, including thyroid disorders, diabetes, obesity, Addison's disease, and more.

2197 **Everyday Health**
www.everydayhealth.com
Aims to provide evidence-based health information from physicians and healthcare providers.

2198 **FamilyDoctor.org**
www.familydoctor.org
Medical advice and information provided by the American Academy of Family Physicians. Resources include a medical dictionary, a symptom checker tool, a BMI calculator, and medication information.

2199 **Healing Well**
www.healingwell.com
An online health resource guide to medical news, chat, information and articles, newsgroups and message boards, books, disease-related web sites, medical directories, and more for patients, friends, and family coping with disabling diseases, disorders, or chronic illnesses.

2200 **Health Finder**
www.healthfinder.gov
Searchable, carefully developed web site offering information on over 1000 topics. Developed by the US Department of Health and Human Services, the site can be used in both English and Spanish.

2201 **Healthline**
www.healthline.com
Provides medical and health articles and information.

2202 **Healthlink USA**
www.healthlinkusa.com
Health information concerning treatment, cures, prevention, diagnosis, risk factors, research, support groups, email lists, personal stories and much more. Updated regularly.

2203 **Hormone Health Network**
www.hormone.org
Online support and resources for patients, with focus on hormone health, disease and treatment. Provided by the Endocrine Society.

2204 **MedicineNet**
www.medicinenet.com
An online resource for consumers providing easy-to-read, authoritative medical and health information.

2205 **MedlinePlus**
www.medlineplus.gov
A service of the National Library of Medicine, MedlinePlus is an online resource providing health and wellness information in both English and Spanish.

2206 **Medscape**
www.medscape.com
Medscape offers specialists, primary care physicians, and other health professionals the Web's most robust and integrated medical information and educational tools.

2207 **MyPlate**

www.myplate.gov

Created and managed by the US Department of Agriculture's Center for Nutrition Policy & Promotion, MyPlate is a dietary guide providing resources and recipes to promote healthy eating for all Americans.

2208 **Nutrition.gov**

www.nutrition.gov

Sponsored by the United States Department of Agriculture (USDA), Nutrition.gov offers information on topics in food and nutrition, including healthy eating, physical activity, and food safety.

2209 **OneGRAVESVoice**

www.onegravesvoice.com

A website from the Graves' Disease & Thyroid Foundation providing news and resources on Graves' disease and thyroid eye disease.

2210 **Science Daily**

www.sciencedaily.com

Provides information on the latest news and research in science, health, the environment, and technology.

2211 **Thyroid Awareness**

www.thyroidawareness.com

An online resource from the American Association of Clinical Endocrinologists (AACE) offering information about thyroid conditions and treatment.

2212 **Thyroid Cancer Alliance**

www.thyroidcancerpatientinfo.org

An online resource providing information about different types of thyroid cancer for patients.

2213 **Thyroid Disease Manager**

www.thyroidmanager.org

Thyroid Disease Manager is a free source owned by Endocrine Education Inc., a not-for-profit corporation in Massachusetts. It offers up-to-date information and analyses on thyroid disease and thyroid physiology. Free registration is required.

2214 **Thyroid Eye Disease**

www.thyroideyes.com

Information about thyroid eye disease (TED) for people with Graves' disease and thyroid conditions.

2215 **Thyroid Federation International**

www.thyroid-fed.org

Aims to work for the benefit of those affected by thyroid disorders throughout the world.

2216 **Thyroid Foundation of Canada**

www.thyroid.ca

The Thyroid Foundation of Canada is a non-profit registered volunteer organization whose mission is to support thyroid patients across Canada through awareness, education, and research.

2217 **Thyroid International Recommendations Online (TIRO)**

tiro.expert

An online compilation of recognized international thyroid nodule and thyroid cancer data guidelines.

2218 **Thyroid Symptoms**

www.thyroidsymptoms.ca

Information on hypothyroidism symptoms, as well as resources for diagnosis and treatment.

2219 **Thyroid, Head & Neck Cancer (THANC) Guide**

www.thancguide.org

A website from the Thyroid, Head and Neck Cancer (THANC) Foundation. Provides information and resources for thyroid, head and neck cancer patients.

2220 **Verywell**

www.verywellhealth.com

Offers health, medicine, and wellness information from health professionals.

2221 **WebMD**

www.webmd.com

Provides credible information, supportive communities, and in-depth reference material about health subjects. A source for original and timely health information as well as material from well known content providers.

GENERAL RESOURCES

Agencies & Associations

2222 **Academy of Nutrition & Dietetics**
120 South Riverside Plaza 312-899-0040
Chicago, IL 60606-6995 800-877-1600
media@eatright.org
www.eatright.org
Serves the public through the promotion of optimal nutrition, health, and well-being. Formerly the American Dietetic Association.
Patricia M. Babjak, Chief Executive Officer

2223 **Administration for Children and Families**
330 C Street SW 202-401-9200
Washington, DC 20201 www.acf.hhs.gov
The Administration for Children & Families (ACF) is a division of the U.S. Department of Health & Human Services (HHS). ACF promotes the economic and social well-being of families, children, individuals and communities.
JooYeun Chang, Acting Assistant Secretary
Larry Handerhan, Chief of Staff

2224 **Agency for Healthcare Research and Quality**
5600 Fishers Lane 301-427-1104
Rockville, MD 20857 www.ahrq.gov
The Agency for Healthcare Research and Quality's (AHRQ) mission is to produce evidence to make health care safer, higher quality, more accessible, equitable, and affordable, and to work within the U.S. Department of Health and Human Services and with other partners to make sure that the evidence is understood and used.
David Meyers, MD, Acting Director
Jeffrey Toven, Executive Officer

2225 **Agency for Toxic Substances and Disease Registry**
1200 Pennsylvania Avenue NW 800-232-4636
Washington, DC 20460 www.atsdr.cdc.gov
The Agency for Toxic Substances and Disease Registry (ATSDR), based in Atlanta, Georgia, is a federal public health agency of the U.S. Department of Health and Human Services. ATSDR serves the public by using the best science, taking responsive public health actions, and providing trusted health information to prevent harmful exposures and diseases related to toxic substances.
Patrick Breysse, Director

2226 **American Academy of Environmental Medicine**
PO Box 195 316-684-5500
Ashland, MO 65010 www.aaemonline.org
The AAEM Promotes the education of healthcare professionals in the interaction between humans and the environment. Offers names of Clinical Ecologists and Allergy Specialists in the United States.
Lauren Grohs, Executive Director

2227 **American Autoimmune Related Diseases Association**
19176 Hall Road 586-776-3900
Clinton Township, MI 48038 aarda@aarda.org
www.aarda.org
Awareness, education, referrals for patients with any type of autoimmune disease.
Molly Murray, President & CEO
Laura Simpson, Chief Operating Officer

2228 **American Council on Science and Health**
New York, NY 212-362-7044
info@acsh.org
www.acsh.org
Serves to provide public support for evidence-based science and medicine.
Thom Golab, President
Josh Bloom, Ph.D., Senior Vice President

2229 **American Holistic Health Association**
PO Box 17400 714-779-6152
Anaheim, CA 92817 mail@ahha.org
ahha.org
The leading national resource connecting people with vital solutions for reaching a higher level of wellness through a holistic approach to health and healthcare.
Suzan V. Walter, MBA, President
Gena E. Kadar, DC, CNS, Secretary

2230 **American Nutrition Association**
211 West Chicago Avenue www.theana.org
Hinsdale, IL 60521
Works to advance health through personalized nutrition.
Michael Stroka, Chief Executive Officer

2231 **American Pediatric Society**
9303 New Trails Drive 346-980-9707
The Woodlands, TX 77381 info@aps1888.org
www.aps1888.org
Society of professionals working on pediatric health care issues, through research, advocacy, and education. The society offers conferences and a variety of publications.
Mary Leonard, President
Clifford W. Bogue, Secretary-Treasurer

2232 **American Public Health Association**
800 I Street NW 202-777-2742
Washington, DC 20001 www.apha.org
Aims to improve public health and advance the public health profession.
Georges C. Benjamin, Executive Director
James Carbo, Chief of Staff

2233 **American Society for Nutrition**
9211 Corporate Boulevard info@nutrition.org
Rockville, MD 20850 www.nutrition.org
Aims to advance nutrition through education, professional development, policy, advocacy, and science-based information.
Paul M. Coates, President
John E. Courtney, Chief Executive Officer

2234 **American Society for Parenteral and Enteral Nutrition (ASPEN)**
8401 Colesville Road 301-587-6315
Silver Spring, MD 20910 Fax: 301-587-2365
aspen@nutritioncare.org
www.nutritioncare.org
Offers information and continuing medical education to professionals involved in the care of parenterally and enterally fed patients. Membership includes complimentary subscriptions to two peer reviewed journals.
Wanda Johnson, Chief Executive Officer
Joanne Kieffer, Senior Director, Finance

2235 **Americas Association for the Care of the Children**
PO Box 2154 303-527-2742
Boulder, CO 80306 aaccchildren.org
Carries out a variety of programs to promote the health of children. Publishes educational materials on child health of interest to parents, educators and health professionals.
Deborah Young, Founder & Executive Director
Judi Jackson, President

2236 **Animal and Plant Health Inspection Service**
4700 River Road 844-820-2234
Riverdale, MD 20737 customerservicecallcenter@aphis.usda.gov
www.aphis.usda.gov
An agency of the US Department of Agriculture, APHIS works to protect the health of agriculture and natural resources in the US, as well as certify the health of agricultural exports.
Kevin Shea, Administrator

2237 **Association of Nutrition & Foodservice Professionals**
PO Box 3610 800-323-1908
St. Charles, IL 60174 info@anfponline.org
www.anfponline.org
A national nonprofit organization representing more than 15,000 nutrition and foodservice professionals. The association offers foodservice reference, resources, professional development, certification programs, and services for members.
Joyce Gilbert, Ph.D., RDN, President & CEO
Jay Carino, MBA, CAE, Vice President, Member Services

2238 **Canadian Nutrition Society**
Toronto, Ontario 888-414-7188
info@cns-scn.ca
www.cns-scn.ca
Promotes evidence-based nutrition science and education to optimize the health of all Canadians.
Andrea Grantham, Executive Director
Cara Curtis, Operations & Events Manager

2239 **Center for Nutrition Policy & Promotion**
USDA Food & Nutrition Service
1320 Braddock Place 703-305-2062
Alexandria, VA 22314 fns.usda.gov/cnpp
A part of the US Department of Agriculture's Food and Nutrition Service, the Center for Nutrition Policy & Promotion (CNPP) seeks to improve the health of Americans by developing and promoting science-based dietary guidance.

2240 **Center for Science in the Public Interest**
1220 L Street NW 202-332-9110
Washington, DC 20005 cspi@cspinet.org
www.cspinet.org
The nation's leading consumer group concerned with food and nutrition issues. Focuses on diseases that result from consuming too many calories, too much fat, sodium and sugar such as cancer and heart disease.
Peter Lurie, President
Sara Ghaith, Chief Operating Officer

2241 **Centers for Disease Control & Prevention**
1600 Clifton Road 800-232-4636
Atlanta, GA 30329-4027 TTY: 888-232-6348
www.cdc.gov
A part of the US Department of Health & Human Services, the CDC works to improve the health security of the nation and protect people from health, safety, and security threats.
Rochelle P. Walensky, MD, MPH, Director
Mitchell Wolfe, MD, MPH, Chief Medical Officer

2242 **Centers for Medicare & Medicaid Services**
7500 Security Boulevard www.cms.gov
Baltimore, MD 21244
U.S. federal agency which administers Medicare, Medicaid, and the State Children's Health Insurance Program.
Chiquita Brooks-LaSure, Administrator
Jonathan Blum, COO

2243 **Council for Responsible Nutrition**
1828 L Street NW 202-204-7700
Washington, DC 20036-5114 Fax: 202-204-7701
www.crnusa.org
CRN is a trade association dedicated to ensuring the responsible development and manufacture of dietary ingredients and supplements.
Steve Mister, President & CEO
Sandra Khouri, Senior VP, Finance & Administration

2244 **Department of Agriculture**
1400 Independence Avenue SW 202-720-2791
Washington, DC 20250 feedback@usda.gov
www.usda.gov
The United States government's principal agency for matters relating to food, agriculture, natural resources, rural development, and nutrition.
Thomas J. Vilsack, Secretary
Jewel H. Bronaugh, Deputy Secretary

2245 **Department of Health and Human Services**
200 Independence Avenue SW 877-696-6775
Washington, DC 20201 hhs.gov
The DHHS is the United States government's principal agency for protecting the health of all Americans, providing health and human services, and supporting initiatives in medicine, public health, and social services.
Xavier Becerra, Secretary
Andrea Palm, Deputy Secretary

2246 **Dietitians of Canada**
99 Yorkville Avenue 416-596-0857
Toronto, Ontario, M5R-1C1 contactus@dietitians.ca
www.dietitians.ca
A professional organization of dietitians in Canada. The association aims to maintain high professional standards, advocate for public policy that promotes health, and provide credible information on food and nutrition.
Leslie Beck, Chair

2247 **Environmental Working Group**
1436 U Street NW 202-667-6982
Washington, DC 20009 www.ewg.org
The mission of the Environmental Working Group (EWG) is to educate and inform the public of harmful agricultural and industry practices that pose a risk to human and environmental health.
Ken Cook, President
Scott Mallan, VP, Finance & Chief Operating Officer

2248 **Food Safety and Inspection Service**
U.S. Department of Agriculture
1400 Independence Avenue SW fsis.webmaster@usda.gov
Washington, DC 20250 www.fsis.usda.gov
The Food Safety and Inspection Service (FSIS) is the public health agency in the U.S. Department of Agriculture responsible for ensuring that the nation's commercial supply of meat, poultry, and egg products is safe, wholesome, and correctly labeled and packaged.
Paul Kiecher, Administrator
Terri Nintemann, Deputy Administrator

2249 **Food and Nutrition Service**
1320 Braddock Place 703-305-2062
Alexandria, VA 22314 fns.usda.gov
An agency of the US Department of Agriculture, Food & Nutrition Service works to end hunger and obesity through the development and administration of federal nutrition assistance programs.
Cindy Long, Administrator

2250 **Genetic Alliance**
26400 Woodfield Road 202-966-5557
Damascus, MD 20872 info@geneticalliance.org
geneticalliance.org
Genetic Alliance is a nonprofit health advocacy organization committed to transforming health through genetics and promoting an environment of openness centered on the health of individuals, families, and communities.
Sharon Terry, Chief Executive Officer
Natasha Bonhomme, Chief Strategy Officer

2251 **Health Canada**
Address Locator 0900C2 613-957-2991
Ottawa, Ontario, K1A-0K9 866-225-0709
Fax: 613-941-5366
TTY: 800-465-7735
hcinfo.infosc@canada.ca
www.canada.ca/health
A department of the Government of Canada, Health Canada helps Canadians improve their health. Health Canada provides services and evidence-based information on food and nutrition, healthy living, product safety, environmental health, and related health topics.

2252 **Health Resources & Services Administration**
5600 Fishers Lane 301-443-3376
Rockville, MD 20857 www.hrsa.gov
An agency of the US Department of Health & Human Services, the HRSA is responsible for providing and improving health care for

geographically isolated or economically or medically vulnerable people.
Diana Espinosa, Acting Administrator
Jordan Grossman, Chief of Staff

2253 **HealthyWomen**
PO Box 336 732-530-3425
Middletown, NJ 07748 877-986-9472
info@healthywomen.org
www.healthywomen.org
Independent, non-profit organization seeking to educate women in all areas of health, to allow them to make informed choices. The HealthyWomen website features numerous tools and health calculators, plus other media.
Beth Battaglino, RN-C, Chief Executive Officer
Phyllis Greenberger, MSW, SVP, Policy, Advocacy & Science

2254 **Indian Health Service**
5600 Fishers Lane www.ihs.gov
Rockville, MD 20857
An agency within the Department of Health and Human Services, Indian Health Service provides federal health services to Native Americans and Alaskan natives.

2255 **Institute for the Advancement of Food and Nutrition Sciences (IAFNS)**
740 15th Street NW 202-659-0184
Washington, DC 20005 iafns@iafns.org
www.iafns.org
The IAFNS is a nonprofit organization of scientists working to advance public health through food safety and nutrition research.
Wendelyn Jones, Ph.D., Executive Director
Marie Latulippe, MS, RDN, Director, Science Programs

2256 **International Food Information Council**
900 19th Street NW info@ific.org
Washington, DC 20006 www.ific.org
The International Food Information Council (IFIC) is a nonproft organization committed to promoting science-based information on health, nutrition, food safety, and agriculture.
Joseph Clayton, Chief Executive Officer
Silvia Dumitrescu, Vice President, Communications

2257 **International Life Sciences Institute**
740 15th Street NW 202-659-0074
Washington, DC 20005 Fax: 202-659-3859
info@ilsi.org
www.ilsi.org
A worldwide organization seeking to promote science that improves and protects human and environmental health.
Stephane Vidry, Ph.D., Global Executive Director
Helene Tournu, Ph.D., Senior Scientific Program Manager

2258 **National Association of Chronic Disease Directors**
325 Swanton Way info@chronicdisease.org
Decatur, GA 30030 www.chronicdisease.org
Non-profit public health organization committed to serving the chronic disease program directors of each state and jurisdiction in the United States.
John W. Robitscher, MPH, Chief Executive Officer
Marti Macchi, MEd, MPH, Senior Director, Programs

2259 **National Association of Nutrition Professionals**
PO Box 348028 209-224-0003
Sacramento, CA 95834 Fax: 510-580-9429
info@nanp.org
www.nanp.org
NANP is a professional association dedicated to advancing, supporting, and advocating for holistic nutrition professionals.
Nicole Hodson, Executive Director
Monica Nesbit, Development Manager

2260 **National Association of School Nurses**
1100 Wayne Avenue 240-821-1130
Silver Spring, MD 20910-5669 866-627-6767
Fax: 301-585-1791
nasn@nasn.org
www.nasn.org
Optimizing student health.
Donna J. Mazyck, Executive Director
Christopher Cephas, Chief Financial Officer

2261 **National Center for Complementary and Integrative Health**
9000 Rockville Pike 888-644-6226
Bethesda, MD 20892 TTY: 866-464-3615
info@nccih.nih.gov
nccih.nih.gov
The National Center for Complementary and Integrative Health (NCCIH) is the Federal Government's lead agency for scientific research on the diverse medical and health care systems, practices, and products that are not generally considered part of conventional medicine.
Helene Langevin, MD, Director
David Shurtleff, Ph.D., Deputy Director

2262 **National Health Federation**
PO Box 688 626-357-2181
Monrovia, CA 91017 contact-us@thenhf.com
www.thenhf.com
A nonprofit consumer-oriented organization devoted to health matters. Dedicated to preserving freedom of choice in health care issues, prevention of diseases and the promotion of wellness.
Scott C. Tips, President
Gregory Kunin, Vice President

2263 **National Heart, Lung, & Blood Institute**
31 Center Drive 877-645-2448
Bethesda, MD 20892 nhlbiinfo@nhlbi.nih.gov
www.nhlbi.nih.gov
The mission is to improve meaning of one American people by supporting and understanding research to prevent, detect, diagnose and treat diseases of heart, lungs, blood vessels, and sleep disorders.
Gary H. Gibbons, Director

2264 **National Institute for Occupational Safety and Health**
Patriots Plaza 1
395 E Street SW 800-232-4636
Washington, DC 20201 www.cdc.gov/niosh
The National Institute for Occupational Safety and Health (NIOSH) is the U.S. federal agency that conducts research and makes recommendations to prevent worker injury and illness.
John Howard, MD, Director

2265 **National Institute of Biomedical Imaging and Bioengineering**
9000 Rockville Pike 301-496-8859
Bethesda, MD 20892 info@nibib.nih.gov
www.nibib.nih.gov
The mission of the National Institute of Biomedical Imaging and Bioengineering (NIBIB) is to improve health by leading the development and accelerating the application of biomedical technologies.
Bruce J. Tromberg, PhD, Director
Jill Heemskerk, PhD, Deputy Director

2266 **National Institute of Environmental Health Sciences**
PO Box 12233 919-541-3345
Research Triangle Park, NC 27709 www.niehs.nih.gov
The mission of the NIEHS is to discover how the environment affects people in order to promote healthier lives.
Rick Woychik, PhD, Director
Gwen W. Collman, PhD, Acting Deputy Director

2267 **National Institute of Food and Agriculture**
1400 Independence Avenue SW nifa.usda.gov
Washington, DC 20250-2201
National Institute of Food and Agriculture (NIFA) provides leadership and funding for programs that advance agriculture-related sciences.
Carrie Castille, Director
William Hoffman, Chief of Staff

2268 **National Institute of General Medical Sciences**
45 Center Drive 301-496-7301
Bethesda, MD 20892-6200 info@nigms.nih.gov
www.nigms.nih.gov
The National Institute of General Medical Sciences (NIGMS) supports basic research that increases understanding of biological

processes and lays the foundation for advances in disease diagnosis, treatment and prevention.
Jon R. Lorsch, PhD, Director
Dorit Zuk, PhD, Acting Deputy Director

2269 **National Institute of Minority Health and Health Disparities**
6707 Democracy Boulevard 301-402-1366
Bethesda, MD 20892-5465 Fax: 301-480-4049
nimhdinfo@nimhd.nih.gov
www.nimhd.nih.gov
The mission of the NIMHD is to improve minority health and reduce health disparities through research, training, collaborations and partnerships, and information dissemination.
Eliseo J. Perez-Stable, MD, Director

2270 **National Institute of Nursing Research**
31 Center Drive 301-496-0207
Bethesda, MD 20892-2178 Fax: 301-480-4969
info@ninr.nih.gov
www.ninr.nih.gov
The NINR is committed to improving health by conducting research and research training on health and illness.
Shannon N. Zenk, Ph.D., MPH, RN, Director

2271 **National Institute on Aging**
31 Center Drive, MSC 2292 800-222-2225
Bethesda, MD 20892 TTY: 800-222-4225
niaic@nia.nih.gov
www.nia.nih.gov
Seeks to understand the nature of aging, and to extend healthy, active years of life. Free resources are available on topics such as Alzheimer's & dimentia, caregiving, cognitive heath, end of life care, and more.
Richard J. Hodes, MD, Director
Luigi Ferrucci, Scientific Director

2272 **Nurse Practitioners in Women's Health**
PO Box 15837 202-543-9693
Washington, DC 20003 info@npwh.org
www.npwh.org
Ensures the delivery and accessibility of primary and specialty healthcare to women of all ages by women's health and women's health focused nurse practitioners.
Heather L. Maurer, CEO
Donna Ruth, Director, Education

2273 **Nutrition Science Initiative**
6020 Cornerstone Court W 858-914-5400
San Diego, CA 92121 www.nusi.org
Nutrition Science Initiative (NuSI) works to combat obesity, diabetes, and related metabolic diseases by supporting and improving the quality of nutrition research.
Gary Taubes, Chair

2274 **Office of Dietary Supplements**
National Institutes of Health
6705 Rockledge Drive 301-435-2920
Bethesda, MD 20817 Fax: 301-480-1845
ods@nih.gov
ods.od.nih.gov
The mission of the Office of Dietary Supplements (ODS) is to enhance knowledge of dietary supplements through research and education. The ODS is part of the National Institutes of Health.
Joseph M. Betz, Ph.D., Acting Director

2275 **Office of Disease Prevention and Health Promotion**
Office of the Assistant Secretary for Health, HHS
1101 Wootton Parkway www.health.gov
Rockville, MD 20852
The ODPHP is responsible for leading disease prevention and health promotion initiatives to improve the nation's health. It is a part of the US Department of Health & Human Services.

2276 **Office of Women's Health**
200 Independence Avenue SW 202-690-7650
Washington, DC 20201 800-994-9662
womenshealth@hhs.gov
www.womenshealth.gov
Government agency under the Department of Health & Human Services, with free health information for women.
Dorothy Fink, MD, Deputy Asst. Secretary, Women's Health
Richelle West Marshall, Deputy Director

2277 **Partnership for Food Safety Education**
2345 Crystal Drive 202-220-0651
Arlington, VA 22202 info@fightbac.org
www.fightbac.org
Seeks to reduce the risk of foodborne illness for consumers by developing and promoting education programs and providing science-based health information and resources.
Britanny Saunier, Executive Director
Shawnte Loeri, Communications Associate

2278 **School Nutrition Association**
2900 S Quincy Street 703-824-3000
Arlington, VA 22206 Fax: 703-824-3015
servicecenter@schoolnutrition.org
www.schoolnutrition.org
A nonprofit professional association of school nutrition professionals dedicated to providing high-quality, low-cost meals for students nationwide.
Patricia Montague, Chief Executive Officer
Rhea Steele, Chief of Staff

2279 **Society For Post-Acute and Long-Term Care Medicine**
10500 Little Patuxent Parkway 410-740-9743
Columbia, MD 21044 800-876-2632
info@paltc.org
www.paltc.org
Provides education, advocacy, information and professional development to promote the delivery of standardized post-acute and long-term care medicine.
Karl Steinberg, MD, HMDC, CMD, President
Milta Little, DO, CMD, Vice President

2280 **Society for Nutrition Education and Behavior**
3502 Woodview Trace 317-328-4627
Indianapolis, IN 46268 800-235-6690
Fax: 317-280-8527
info@sneb.org
www.sneb.org
Aims to promote health and healthy behavior through the advancement of food and nutrition education.
Jasia Steinmetz, President
Yenory Hernandez-Garbanzo, Vice President

2281 **U.S. Food and Drug Administration**
10903 New Hampshire Avenue 888-463-6332
Silver Spring, MD 20993-0002 www.fda.gov
FDA is responsible for protecting the public health by assuring the safety, efficacy and security of human and veterinary drugs, biological products, medical devices, the nation's food supply, cosmetics, and products that emit radiation.
Janet Woodcock, MD, Acting Commissioner

Libraries & Resource Centers

2282 **Food Safety Research Information Office**
USDA ARS National Agricultural Library
10301 Baltimore Avenue 301-504-5022
Beltsville, MD 20705-2351 nal.usda.gov
Provides information on food safety and related research. A part of the National Agricultural Library.

2283 **Food and Nutrition Information Center**
USDA ARS National Agricultural Library
10301 Baltimore Avenue 301-504-5414
Beltsville, MD 20705-2351 fnic@ars.usda.gov
nal.usda.gov
Provides resources for nutrition and health professionals. A part of the National Agricultural Library.

2284 **National Agricultural Library**
10301 Baltimore Avenue 301-504-5755
Beltsville, MD 20705 800-633-7701
TDD: 301-504-6856
agref@usda.gov
nal.usda.gov
A national library of the United States, the National Agricultural Library carries a collection of resources on agriculture and its related sciences.
Paul Wester, Director
Scott Hanscom, Deputy Director

2285 **National Library of Medicine**
8600 Rockville Pike 301-594-5983
Bethesda, MD 20894 888-346-3656
nlmcommunications@nih.gov
nlm.nih.gov
A national library of the United States, the National Library of Medicine maintains and produces a collection of print and electronic medical resources, as well as conducts research on biomedical informatics and health information technology.
Patricia Flatley Brennan, Director
Jerry Sheehan, Deputy Director

Foundations & Research Centers

2286 **Agricultural Research Service**
US Department of Agriculture
1400 Independence Avenue SW 202-720-3656
Washington, DC 20250 Fax: 202-720-5427
ars.usda.gov
The research agency of the US Department of Agriculture, Agricultural Research Service works to develop solutions to agricultural challenges.
Chavonda Jacobs-Young, Administrator

2287 **Canadian Foundation for Dietetic Research**
c/o Dietitians of Canada
99 Yorkville Avenue 416-642-9309
Toronto, Ontario, M5R-1C1 Fax: 416-596-0603
info@cfdr.ca
www.cfdr.ca
Works to advance nutrition research and advance health in Canada by funding research projects in the areas of nutrition and dietetics.

2288 **Economic Research Service**
1400 Independence Avenue SW ers.usda.gov
Washington, DC 20250-0002
The US Department of Agriculture's Economic Research Service is responsible for conducting economic research to determine trends and emerging issues about American agriculture. Research topics include the agricultural economy, food and nutrition, food safety, and the environment.
Spiro Stefanou, Administrator
Jim Staiert, Associate Administrator

2289 **International Foundation for Nutrition and Health**
www.ifhn.org
The International Foundation for Nutrition and Health is a non-profit educational organization for healthcare practitioners who support the therapeutic use of whole food nutrition.

2290 **NIH Clinical Center**
National Institute of Health
10 Center Drive 301-496-4000
Bethesda, MD 20892 clinicalcenter.nih.gov
Established in 1953 as the research hospital of the National Institutes of Health. Designed so that patient care facilities are close to research laboratories so new findings of basic and clinical scientists can be quickly applied to the treatment of patients. Upon referral by physicians, patients are admitted to NIH clinical studies.
James K. Gilman, MD, Chief Executive Officer
John I. Gallin, MD, Chief Scientific Officer

2291 **National Agricultural Statistics Service**
1400 Independence Avenue NW 800-727-9540
Washington, DC 20250 nass.usda.gov
The National Agricultural Statistics Service (NASS) is an agency of the US Department of Agriculture. It is responsible for conducting surveys and preparing reports and statistics about American agriculture every year.
Hubert Hamer, Administrator
Kevin Barnes, Associate Administrator

2292 **National Health Foundation**
515 South Figueroa Street nationalhealthfoundation.org
Los Angeles, CA 90071
Public charity whose mission is to improve the healthcare available to underserved groups through the development, support and provision of programs that address the systemic barriers in healthcare access and delivery.
Kelly Bruno, President & CEO
Mia Arias, Chief Operating Officer

2293 **National Human Genome Research Institute**
Building 31, Room 4B09 301-402-0911
Bethesda, MD 20892-2152 www.genome.gov
The National Human Genome Research Institute began as the National Center for Human Genome Research (NCHGR), which was established in 1989 to carry out the role of the National Institutes of Health (NIH) in the International Human Genome Project (HGP).
Eric D. Green, M.D., Ph.D., Director
Lawrence Brody, Ph.D., Director, Division of Genomics & Society

2294 **National Science Foundation**
4201 Wilson Blvd 703-292-5111
Arlington, VA 22230 TDD: 703-292-5090
info@nsf.gov
www.nsf.gov
NSF is the only federal agency whose mission includes support for all fields of fundamental science and engineering, except for medical sciences.
France A. Cordova, Director
Joan Ferrini-Mundy, Chief Operating Officer

2295 **Nutritional Research Foundation**
4 Walter E Foran Boulevard 888-511-4443
Flemington, NJ 08822 info@nutritionalresearch.org
www.nutritionalresearch.org
A nonprofit organization dedicated to supporting nutritional research.
Joel Fuhrman, MD, President

Support Groups & Hotlines

2296 **National Health Information Center**
Office of Disease Prevention & Health Promotion
1101 Wootton Pkwy odphpinfo@hhs.gov
Rockville, MD 20852 www.health.gov/nhic
Supports public health education by maintaining a calendar of National Health Observances; helps connect consumers and health professionals to organizations that can best answer questions and provide up-to-date contact information from reliable sources; updates on a yearly basis toll-free numbers for health information, Federal health clearinghouses and info centers.
Don Wright, MD, MPH, Director

Journals

2297 **Advances in Nutrition**
American Society for Nutrition
9211 Corporate Boulevard info@nutrition.org
Rockville, MD 20850 www.nutrition.org
Publishes reviews of research on clinical nutrition, epidemiology, public health, nutrition education, and nutrition in biochemical, molecular, and genetic studies.
Katherine L. Tucker, Ph.D., Editor-in-Chief

2298 **American Journal of Clinical Nutrition**
American Society for Nutrition
9211 Corporate Boulevard info@nutrition.org
Rockville, MD 20850 www.nutrition.org
Publishes the latest research on human nutrition and dietetics.
Christopher Duggan, MD, MPH, Editor-in-Chief

2299 **Annual Review of Nutrition**
Annual Reviews
PO Box 10139
Palo Alto, CA 94303-0139
650-493-4400
800-523-8635
Fax: 650-424-0910
service@annualreviews.org
www.annualreviews.org/journal/nutr
Highlights significant developments in the field of nutrition.

2300 **Applied Physiology, Nutrition, and Metabolism**
Toronto, Ontario
888-414-7188
info@cns-scn.ca
www.cns-scn.ca
Publishes original research, reviews, and commentaries about the application of physiology, nutrition, and metabolism to the study of human health and fitness. Affiliated with the Canadian Nutrition Society, the Canadian Society for Exercise Physiology, and Exercise & Sports Science Australia.
Wendy E. Ward, Editor-in-Chief
Phil Chilibeck, Editor-in-Chief

2301 **Canadian Journal of Dietetic Practice and Research**
Dietitians of Canada
99 Yorkville Avenue
Toronto, Ontario, M5R-1C1
416-596-0857
contactus@dietitians.ca
www.dietitians.ca
A peer-reviewed journal of Dietitians of Canada. Publishes research and reviews relating to best practice in Canadian dietetics.

2302 **Current Developments in Nutrition**
American Society for Nutrition
9211 Corporate Boulevard
Rockville, MD 20850
info@nutrition.org
www.nutrition.org
An open-access journal that reviews, publishes, and disseminates nutrition research.
Jack Odle, Ph.D., Editor-in-Chief

2303 **Food & Nutrition**
120 South Riverside Plaza
Chicago, IL 60606-6995
312-899-0040
800-877-1600
foodandnutrition@eatright.org
www.eatright.org
Formerly the ADA Times, Food & Nutrition is the member and professional magazine of the Academy of Nutrition & Dietetics.

2304 **Journal of Human Nutrition & Food Science**
www.jscimedcentral.com/Nutrition
An international open access journal covering topics in nutrition, including food, nutrition therapy, dietary intake, nutritional status, and more.

2305 **Journal of Nutrition**
American Society for Nutrition
9211 Corporate Boulevard
Rockville, MD 20850
info@nutrition.org
www.nutrition.org
A scientific journal focusing on experimental nutrition. Offers research reports, reviews, commentaries, and more.
Teresa A. Davis, Ph.D., Editor-in-Chief

2306 **Journal of Nutrition Education and Behavior**
Society for Nutrition Education & Behavior
3502 Woodview Trace
Indianapolis, IN 46268
317-328-4627
800-235-6690
Fax: 317-280-8527
info@sneb.org
www.sneb.org
Publishes original research on nutrition education and behavior, as well as papers on related issues, policies, and practices.
Karen Chapman-Novakofski, Editor-in-Chief

2307 **Journal of Parenteral and Enteral Nutrition**
ASPEN
8630 Fenton Street
Silver Spring, MD 20910-3805
301-587-6315
aspen@nutr.org
www.nutritioncare.org
Offers information to professionals involved in the care of parenterally and enterally fed patients.
100 pages
Adrian Nickel, Director Communications/Marketing

2308 **Journal of the Academy of Nutrition and Dietetics**
120 South Riverside Plaza
Chicago, IL 60606-6995
312-899-4831
journal@eatright.org
www.eatright.org
Official research publication of the Academy of Nutrition and Dietetics.

2309 **Journal of the American College of Nutrition (JACN)**
American Nutrition Association
211 West Chicago Avenue
Hinsdale, IL 60521
www.theana.org
Publishes research on nutrition science.
Rachel Kopec, Editor-in-Chief

2310 **Nutrition Reviews**
International Life Sciences Institute
740 15th Street NW
Washington, DC 20005
202-659-0074
Fax: 202-659-3859
nutritionreviews@ilsi.org
www.ilsi.org
A peer-reviewed journal dedicated to publishing literature reviews in the areas of nutrition science, food science, clinical nutrition, and nutrition policy.
Douglas Taren, Ph.D., Editor-in-Chief

2311 **Nutrition in Clinical Practice**
ASPEN
8630 Fenton Street
Silver Spring, MD 20910-3805
301-587-6315
aspen@nutr.org
www.nutritioncare.org
Offers information to professionals involved in the care of parenterally and enterally fed patients.
100 pages
Adrian Nickel, Director Communications/Marketing

Web Sites

2312 **Academy of Nutrition & Dietetics**
www.eatright.org
Serves the public through the promotion of optimal nutrition, health, and well-being. Formerly the American Dietetic Association.

2313 **Cookspiration**
www.cookspiration.com
Cookspiration is a healthy eating planner developed by Dietitians of Canada. It is available online and via an app.

2314 **Dietary Guidelines for Americans**
www.dietaryguidelines.gov
Publishes the Dietary Guidelines for Americans, a guide providing nutritional advice to promote health and prevent disease. Updated versions of the Dietary Guidelines are released by the US Departments of Agriculture (USDA) and Health & Human Services (HHS) every five years.

2315 **Dietitians of Canada**
www.dietitians.ca
A professional organization of dietitians in Canada. The association aims to maintain high professional standards, advocate for public policy that promotes health, and provide credible information on food and nutrition.

2316 **Everyday Health**
www.everydayhealth.com
Aims to provide evidence-based health information from physicians and healthcare providers.

2317 **FamilyDoctor.org**
www.familydoctor.org
Medical advice and information provided by the American Academy of Family Physicians. Resources include a medical dictionary, a symptom checker tool, a BMI calculator, and medication information.

2318 **Food Insight**
www.foodinsight.org
Food Insight is an information hub providing resources about nutrition and food safety. It is maintained by the International Food Information Council (IFIC).

2319 **Food and Health Communications**
www.foodandhealth.com
Produces evidence-based food and nutrition education materials and resources for health educators.

2320 **FoodData Central**
fdc.nal.usda.gov
FoodData Central is an integrated data system that analyzes, compiles, and presents nutrient and food component data. It is managed by the Agricultural Research Service at the US Department of Agriculture.

2321 **FoodSafety.gov**
www.foodsafety.gov
A website of the US Department Health & Human Services providing food safety information from government agencies, including the Food Safety & Inspection Service (FSIS), the Food & Drug Administration (FDA), and Centers for Disease Control & Prevention (CDC).

2322 **Healing Well**
www.healingwell.com
An online health resource guide to medical news, chat, information and articles, newsgroups and message boards, books, disease-related web sites, medical directories, and more for patients, friends, and family coping with disabling diseases, disorders, or chronic illnesses.

2323 **Health Canada**
www.canada.ca/health
A department of the Government of Canada, Health Canada helps Canadians improve their health. Health Canada provides services and evidence-based information on food and nutrition, healthy living, product safety, environmental health, and related health topics.

2324 **Health Finder**
www.healthfinder.gov
Searchable, carefully developed web site offering information on over 1000 topics. Developed by the US Department of Health and Human Services, the site can be used in both English and Spanish.

2325 **Healthline**
www.healthline.com
Provides medical and health articles and information.

2326 **Healthlink USA**
www.healthlinkusa.com
Health information concerning treatment, cures, prevention, diagnosis, risk factors, research, support groups, email lists, personal stories and much more. Updated regularly.

2327 **HealthyWomen**
www.healthywomen.org
Independent, non-profit organization seeking to educate women in all areas of health, to allow them to make informed choices. The HealthyWomen website features numerous tools and health calculators, plus other media.

2328 **Hormone Health Network**
www.hormone.org
Online support and resources for patients, with focus on hormone health, disease and treatment. Provided by the Endocrine Society.

2329 **Mayo Clinic**
www.mayoclinic.org
Mission is to empower people to manage their health by providing useful and up-to-date information and tools.

2330 **MedicineNet**
www.medicinenet.com
An online resource for consumers providing easy-to-read, authoritative medical and health information.

2331 **MedlinePlus**
www.medlineplus.gov
A service of the National Library of Medicine, MedlinePlus is an online resource providing health and wellness information in both English and Spanish.

2332 **Medscape**
www.medscape.com
Medscape offers specialists, primary care physicians, and other health professionals the Web's most robust and integrated medical information and educational tools.

2333 **My Food Data**
www.myfooddata.com
Promotes healthy eating by providing nutrition data tools and articles. All nutrition information is sourced from the US Department of Agriculture's FoodData Central.

2334 **MyPlate**
www.myplate.gov
Created and managed by the US Department of Agriculture's Center for Nutrition Policy & Promotion, MyPlate is a dietary guide providing resources and recipes to promote healthy eating for all Americans.

2335 **Nutrition Connections**
www.nutritionconnections.ca
Nutrition Connections is a resource centre for nutrition information, education, training, and services. It is a program of the Ontario Public Health Association (OPHA).

2336 **Nutrition Value**
www.nutritionvalue.org
Online tool providing the nutrition information of common food products.

2337 **Nutrition.gov**
www.nutrition.gov
Sponsored by the United States Department of Agriculture (USDA), Nutrition.gov offers information on topics in food and nutrition, including healthy eating, physical activity, and food safety.

2338 **NutritionFacts.org**
www.nutritionfacts.org
An online resource providing free updates, videos, and information about healthy eating and nutrition research.

2339 **Office of Disease Prevention and Health Promotion**
www.health.gov
The ODPHP is responsible for leading disease prevention and health promotion initiatives to improve the nation's health. It is a part of the US Department of Health & Human Services.

2340 **RxList**
www.rxlist.com
RxList is an online medical resource providing pharmaceutical information on prescription drugs, as well as vitamins and dietary supplements.

2341 **Science Daily**
www.sciencedaily.com
Provides information on the latest news and research in science, health, the environment, and technology.

2342 **The Nutrition Source**
hsph.harvard.edu/nutritionsource
From the Harvard T.H. Chan School of Public Health, The Nutrition Source provides news, information, and guidance for nutrition and healthy eating.

2343 **UnlockFood**
www.unlockfood.ca
A website from Dietitians of Canada. Provides videos, recipes, and information on food and nutrition, as well as helps Canadians connect with a dietitian.

2344 **Verywell**
www.verywellhealth.com
Offers health, medicine, and wellness information from healthcare professionals.

2345 **WebMD**
www.webmd.com
Provides credible information, supportive communities, and in-depth reference material about health subjects. A source for original and timely health information as well as material from well known content providers.

2346 **World Health Organization**

www.who.int

An agency of the United Nations, World Health Organization (WHO) serves to promote global health. The WHO website provides fact sheets, publications, media, and other resources on various health topics.

SECTION FOUR:
APPENDIX & INDEXES

GLOSSARY OF TERMS

Acceptance and Commitment Therapy (ACT): Cognitive-behavioral therapy involving tolerating distress and sticking to one's values regardless of mental illness symptoms.

Anemia: A deficiency of red blood cells/hemoglobin that can lead to weakness and fatigue.

Amino Acids: The building blocks of proteins, which the body produces, and which also come from food.

Anorexia Nervosa: An eating disorder marked by self-starvation and the inability to keep a healthy body weight.

Atypical Anorexia: An eating disorder that meets some, but not all, of the diagnostic criteria for anorexia nervosa.

Atypical Bulimia: An eating disorder that meets some, but not all, of the diagnostic criteria for bulimia nervosa.

Avoidant and Restrictive Food Intake Disorder (ARFID): An eating disorder in which food consumed is limited by texture, taste, and/or past negative experiences.

Binge Eating: Eating an unusually large amount of food in a short space of time, while feeling unable to stop.

Binge Eating Disorder: Binge eating that occurs at least once a week for a period of three months, and an absence of purging behavior.

Body Checking: Obsessive, intrusive thoughts and behaviors involving repeatedly checking one's appearance and body parts in the mirror and/or frequently asking others whether they look fat.

Body Image: How a person thinks about and perceives their physical appearance.

Blood Glucose: The main sugar found in blood and the main source of energy for the body — also called blood sugar.

Bulimia Nervosa: An eating disorder involving binge eating and purging behaviors, and/or other behaviors that prevent weight gain, such as fasting and over-exercise.

Calories: A unit of energy in food.

Carbohydrates: Simple carbohydrates include natural and added sugars, while complex carbohydrates include whole grain breads and cereals, starchy vegetables and legumes.

Cognitive-Behavioral Therapy (CBT): A type of therapy that aims to change the way a person thinks and behaves.

Cholesterol: A waxy, fat-like substance that's found in all cells of the body, which is both made by the body makes and found in certain foods.

Compensatory Behavior: Certain eating disorder behaviors exhibited in an attempt to reverse the effects of eating or binge eating, such as exercise or purging.

Daily Value: The percentage of a certain nutrient in a food, based on a 2,000-calorie diet; 8% is generally considered to be good.

Dialectical Behavioral Therapy (DBT): A form of therapy used to treat eating disorders, which focuses on building skills relating to mindfulness, distress tolerance, interpersonal effectiveness, and emotion regulation.

Dehydration: A condition that occurs when not enough liquids are consumed to replace liquids lost through processes such as frequent urinating, sweating, diarrhea, or vomiting.

Diet: What a person eats and drinks; there are many specialized diets for various conditions and to achieve specific results.

Diabulimia: A condition describing an individual with type 1 diabetes who avoids or misuses insulin in order to purge calories.

Dietary Supplements: Consumed to supplement a diet, containing ingredients such as vitamins, minerals, herbs or other botanicals, amino acids, and other substances.

Digestion: The process of breaking down food into nutrients, which are used by the body for energy, growth, and cell repair.

Edema: A buildup of fluid in the body that leads to the swelling of extremities.

Egosyntonic: A mental condition compatible with one's own self-image, such as a person with anorexia nervosa appearing to enjoy the weight loss that accompanies the disorder.

Electrolytes: Minerals in body fluids, including sodium, potassium, magnesium, and chloride.

Enriched: Use to describe foods that have nutrients added to them to replace those lost during food-processing.

Enzymes: Substances that speed up chemical reactions in the body.

Evidence-Based Treatment: Treatments that have been shown to be effective through scientific evidence and research trials.

Fatty Acid: A major component of fats that is used by the body for energy and tissue development.

Family-Based Treatment (FBT): A therapy option for adolescents with anorexia and bulimia, in which caregivers take control of their food and eating until behaviors return to normal; psychological factors and co-occurring issues are also addressed.

Fear Foods: Foods that a person with an eating disorder believes will lead to rapid and significant weight gain.

Female Athlete Triad: A group of symptoms that includes irregular or absent menstrual periods, disordered eating, and low bone density.

Fiber: A type of carbohydrate found in plants that helps control weight, aid digestion, and prevent constipation.

Food Allergy: A reaction by the immune system caused by eating a certain food.

Food Restriction: When a person eats fewer calories than their body needs to maintain acceptable weight and/or adequate growth.

Food Rituals: Obsessive, rigid behaviors around food and eating; examples include chewing a specific number of times, cutting food into small pieces, or eating foods in a designated order.

Fortified: Describes foods that have nutrients added to them that weren't there originally.

Gastroparesis: Delayed emptying of the stomach that can lead to feeling prematurely full, as well as bloating, pain, and nausea.

Gluten: A protein found in wheat, rye, and barley, as well as in products such as vitamin and nutrient supplements, lip balms, and certain medicines.

Glycemic Index (GI): A measurement of how carbohydrate-containing food raises blood sugar.

Healthy Body Weight: A weight (usually a range) at which a person is considered to be physically and psychologically healthy.

High-Density Lipoproteins (HDL): Known as "good" cholesterol, HDL is one of the two types of lipoproteins that carry cholesterol throughout your body.

High-Fructose Corn Syrup (HFCS): A sweetener that is often used instead of sugar during the manufacturing of food.

Hydrogenated: Describes when a liquid fat such as vegetable oil is turned into a semi-solid, more shelf-stable fat, such as margarine.

Hypoglycemia: Low blood sugar.

Hypokalemia: Low potassium levels in the blood, which can lead to a heart attack.

Hyponatremia: Low sodium levels

Ketosis: A process where the body turns stored fat into energy to compensate for a lack of energy.

Lanugo: A fine, downy hair that grows on the body after prolonged, inadequate food intake, in an attempt to provide better insulation.

Lapse: An episode of eating disordered behavior after remission or recovery; also called relapse.

Low-Density Lipoproteins (LDL): Known as "bad" cholesterol, LDL is one of the two types of lipoproteins that carry cholesterol throughout your body.

Lecithin: Used as a thinner, a preservative, or an emulsifier, and often added to chocolates, baking products, and cosmetics.

Meal Plan: Certain foods in certain amounts to be eaten at certain times to ensure the proper balance of nutrients and to promote overall health and wellness.

Metabolism: The process the body uses to get or make energy from food.

Modified Food Starch: Used as a thickener, stabilizer, or fat replacer in foods like dessert mixes, dressings, and confections, and is extracted from corn, potato, wheat, and other starches.

Monosodium Glutamate (MSG): Used as a flavor enhancer, like salt, though some people experience a mild reaction after consuming it.

Monounsaturated Fat: Considered "healthy fat," found in avocados, canola oil, nuts, olives and olive oil, and seeds.

Nutrient: A chemical compound in food that is used by the body to function properly and maintain health.

Nutrition: A field of study focusing on foods and substances in foods that help animals (and plants) to grow and stay healthy, as well as behaviors and social factors related to food choices.

Orthorexia: A term used to describe a situation in which a person is obsessed with "eating healthy" or "clean eating."

Other Specified Feeding and Eating Disorder (OSFED): Grouping for serious eating disorders that don't meet the criteria for anorexia, bulimia, or binge eating disorder, but still impact a person's way of life.

Perfectionism: A drive for perfection that exists before the onset of, or alongside, an eating disorder, which may disappear during recovery.

Polyunsaturated Fat: A type of fat that is liquid at room temperature, of which there are two varieties: omega-6 fatty acids, found in liquid vegetable oils, such as corn oil, safflower oil, and soybean oil; and omega-3 fatty acids come from plant sources—including canola oil, flaxseed, soybean oil, and walnuts—and from fish and shellfish.

Potassium: Helps maintain normal blood pressure and keeps the heart and kidneys working normally.

Protein: Needed to build and maintain bones, muscles, and skin, proteins come from meat, dairy products, nuts, and certain grains and beans.

Psychodynamic Psychotherapy: A form of therapy aimed at understanding internal factors and motivations behind behaviors, with the goal of uncovering underlying issues and helping the behaviors cease.

Purging: Self-induced vomiting, and the use of laxatives or diuretics after eating to prevent weight gain and relieve anxiety.

Purging Disorder: An eating disorder in which a person regularly purges, with or without binge eating.

Refeeding Syndrome: A potentially fatal shift in fluids and electrolytes that may occur in malnourished patients receiving artificial refeeding, whether enterally or parenterally.

Restricting: Eating fewer calories than needed to maintain a healthy body weight and normal growth.

Safe Foods: Typically low-calorie foods that provoke less anxiety in a person with an eating disorder.

Saturated Fat: A type of fat that is solid at room temperature; found in full-fat dairy products (like butter, cheese, cream, regular ice cream, and whole milk), coconut oil, lard, palm oil, ready-to-eat meats, and the skin and fat of chicken and turkey, among other foods.

Sodium: Helps with the function of nerves and muscles, and also to keep the right balance of fluids in the body.

Subthreshold Disorder: An eating disorder that interferes with a person's normal life but does not meet formal diagnostic criteria.

Sugar: A type of simple carbohydrate found naturally in fruits, vegetables, milk, and milk products, and also added to many foods and drinks during preparation or processing.

Supportive Psychotherapy: A therapy that integrates approaches from psychodynamics, cognitive-behavioral therapy, and other methods.

Syncope: A temporary loss of consciousness and posture resulting from low blood sugar or low blood pressure, when the brain doesn't get enough oxygen.

Total Fat: A type of nutrient that gives the body energy and help absorb vitamins.

Trans Fat: A type of fat that is created when liquid oils are changed into solid fats, like shortening and some margarines, which makes them last longer without going bad.

Triglycerides: A type of fat found in the blood, too much of which may raise the risk of coronary artery heart disease, especially in women.

Vitamin: An organic compound found in food that the body can't produce on its own.

Whole Grain: Bran, nutrient-rich germ, and endosperm of grains such as wheat, oats, or rice, which have more fiber, vitamins, and minerals than processed white grains.

A

B

C

D

E

F

G

H

I

J

K

L

M

N

O

P

R

S

T

U

V

Alabama

Alaska

Arizona

Arkansas

California

Canada

Colorado

Connecticut

Delaware

District of Columbia

Florida

Georgia

Hawaii

Idaho

Illinois

Indiana

Iowa

Kansas

Kentucky

Louisiana

Maine

Maryland

Massachusetts

Michigan

Minnesota

Mississippi

Missouri

Montana

Nebraska

Nevada

New Hampshire

New Jersey

New Mexico

New York

North Carolina

North Dakota

Ohio

Oklahoma

Oregon

Pennsylvania

Rhode Island

South Carolina

South Dakota

Tennessee

Texas

Utah

Vermont

Virginia

Washington

West Virginia

Wisconsin

Wyoming

2021 Title List

Visit www.GreyHouse.com for Product Information, Table of Contents, and Sample Pages.

Opinions Throughout History

Opinions Throughout History: The Death Penalty
Opinions Throughout History: Diseases & Epidemics
Opinions Throughout History: Drug Use & Abuse
Opinions Throughout History: The Environment
Opinions Throughout History: Gender: Roles & Rights
Opinions Throughout History: Globalization
Opinions Throughout History: Guns in America
Opinions Throughout History: Immigration
Opinions Throughout History: Law Enforcement in America
Opinions Throughout History: National Security vs. Civil & Privacy Rights
Opinions Throughout History: Presidential Authority
Opinions Throughout History: Robotics & Artificial Intelligence
Opinions Throughout History: Social Media Issues
Opinions Throughout History: Sports & Games
Opinions Throughout History: Voters' Rights

This is Who We Were

This is Who We Were: Colonial America (1492-1775)
This is Who We Were: 1880-1899
This is Who We Were: In the 1900s
This is Who We Were: In the 1910s
This is Who We Were: In the 1920s
This is Who We Were: A Companion to the 1940 Census
This is Who We Were: In the 1940s (1940-1949)
This is Who We Were: In the 1950s
This is Who We Were: In the 1960s
This is Who We Were: In the 1970s
This is Who We Were: In the 1980s
This is Who We Were: In the 1990s
This is Who We Were: In the 2000s
This is Who We Were: In the 2010s

Working Americans

Working Americans—Vol. 1: The Working Class
Working Americans—Vol. 2: The Middle Class
Working Americans—Vol. 3: The Upper Class
Working Americans—Vol. 4: Children
Working Americans—Vol. 5: At War
Working Americans—Vol. 6: Working Women
Working Americans—Vol. 7: Social Movements
Working Americans—Vol. 8: Immigrants
Working Americans—Vol. 9: Revolutionary War to the Civil War
Working Americans—Vol. 10: Sports & Recreation
Working Americans—Vol. 11: Inventors & Entrepreneurs
Working Americans—Vol. 12: Our History through Music
Working Americans—Vol. 13: Education & Educators
Working Americans—Vol. 14: African Americans
Working Americans—Vol. 15: Politics & Politicians
Working Americans—Vol. 16: Farming & Ranching
Working Americans—Vol. 17: Teens in America

Education

Complete Learning Disabilities Resource Guide
Educators Resource Guide
The Comparative Guide to Elem. & Secondary Schools
Charter School Movement
Special Education: A Reference Book for Policy & Curriculum Development

Grey House Health & Wellness Guides

Autoimmune Disorders Handbook & Resource Guide
Cancer Handbook & Resource Guide
Cardiovascular Disease Handbook & Resource Guide
Dementia Handbook & Resource Guide

Consumer Health

Autoimmune Disorders Handbook & Resource Guide
Cancer Handbook & Resource Guide
Cardiovascular Disease Handbook & Resource Guide
Comparative Guide to American Hospitals
Complete Mental Health Resource Guide
Complete Resource Guide for Pediatric Disorders
Complete Resource Guide for People with Chronic Illness
Complete Resource Guide for People with Disabilities
Older Americans Information Resource

General Reference

African Biographical Dictionary
American Environmental Leaders
America's College Museums
Constitutional Amendments
Encyclopedia of African-American Writing
Encyclopedia of Invasions & Conquests
Encyclopedia of Prisoners of War & Internment
Encyclopedia of Rural America
Encyclopedia of the Continental Congresses
Encyclopedia of the United States Cabinet
Encyclopedia of War Journalism
The Environmental Debate
The Evolution Wars: A Guide to the Debates
Financial Literacy Starter Kit
From Suffrage to the Senate
The Gun Debate: Gun Rights & Gun Control in the U.S.
History of Canada
Historical Warrior Peoples & Modern Fighting Groups
Human Rights and the United States
Political Corruption in America
Privacy Rights in the Digital Age
The Religious Right and American Politics
Speakers of the House of Representatives, 1789-2021
US Land & Natural Resources Policy
The Value of a Dollar 1600-1865 Colonial to Civil War
The Value of a Dollar 1860-2019
World Cultural Leaders of the 20th Century

Business Information

Business Information Resources
The Complete Broadcasting Industry Guide: Television, Radio, Cable & Streaming
Directory of Mail Order Catalogs
Environmental Resource Handbook
Food & Beverage Market Place
The Grey House Guide to Homeland Security Resources
The Grey House Performing Arts Industry Guide
Guide to Healthcare Group Purchasing Organizations
Guide to U.S. HMOs and PPOs
Guide to Venture Capital & Private Equity Firms
Hudson's Washington News Media Contacts Guide
New York State Directory
Sports Market Place

2021 Title List

Visit www.GreyHouse.com for Product Information, Table of Contents, and Sample Pages.

Statistics & Demographics

America's Top-Rated Cities
America's Top-Rated Smaller Cities
The Comparative Guide to American Suburbs
Profiles of America
Profiles of California
Profiles of Florida
Profiles of Illinois
Profiles of Indiana
Profiles of Massachusetts
Profiles of Michigan
Profiles of New Jersey
Profiles of New York
Profiles of North Carolina & South Carolina
Profiles of Ohio
Profiles of Pennsylvania
Profiles of Texas
Profiles of Virginia
Profiles of Wisconsin

Canadian Resources

Associations Canada
Canadian Almanac & Directory
Canadian Environmental Resource Guide
Canadian Parliamentary Guide
Canadian Venture Capital & Private Equity Firms
Canadian Who's Who
Cannabis Canada
Careers & Employment Canada
Financial Post: Directory of Directors
Financial Services Canada
FP Bonds: Corporate
FP Bonds: Government
FP Equities: Preferreds & Derivatives
FP Survey: Industrials
FP Survey: Mines & Energy
FP Survey: Predecessor & Defunct
Health Guide Canada
Libraries Canada
Major Canadian Cities: Compared & Ranked, First Edition

Weiss Financial Ratings

Financial Literacy Basics
Financial Literacy: How to Become an Investor
Financial Literacy: Planning for the Future
Weiss Ratings Consumer Guides
Weiss Ratings Guide to Banks
Weiss Ratings Guide to Credit Unions
Weiss Ratings Guide to Health Insurers
Weiss Ratings Guide to Life & Annuity Insurers
Weiss Ratings Guide to Property & Casualty Insurers
Weiss Ratings Investment Research Guide to Bond & Money Market Mutual Funds
Weiss Ratings Investment Research Guide to Exchange-Traded Funds
Weiss Ratings Investment Research Guide to Stock Mutual Funds
Weiss Ratings Investment Research Guide to Stocks

Books in Print Series

American Book Publishing Record® Annual
American Book Publishing Record® Monthly
Books In Print®
Books In Print® Supplement
Books Out Loud™
Bowker's Complete Video Directory™
Children's Books In Print®
El-Hi Textbooks & Serials In Print®
Forthcoming Books®
Law Books & Serials In Print™
Medical & Health Care Books In Print™
Publishers, Distributors & Wholesalers of the US™
Subject Guide to Books In Print®
Subject Guide to Children's Books In Print®

2021 Title List

SALEM PRESS

Visit www.SalemPress.com for Product Information, Table of Contents, and Sample Pages.

LITERATURE

Critical Insights: Authors

Louisa May Alcott
Sherman Alexie
Isabel Allende
Maya Angelou
Isaac Asimov
Margaret Atwood
Jane Austen
James Baldwin
Saul Bellow
Roberto Bolano
Ray Bradbury
Gwendolyn Brooks
Albert Camus
Raymond Carver
Willa Cather
Geoffrey Chaucer
John Cheever
Joseph Conrad
Charles Dickens
Emily Dickinson
Frederick Douglass
T. S. Eliot
George Eliot
Harlan Ellison
Louise Erdrich
William Faulkner
F. Scott Fitzgerald
Gustave Flaubert
Horton Foote
Benjamin Franklin
Robert Frost
Neil Gaiman
Gabriel Garcia Marquez
Thomas Hardy
Nathaniel Hawthorne
Robert A. Heinlein
Lillian Hellman
Ernest Hemingway
Langston Hughes
Zora Neale Hurston
Henry James
Thomas Jefferson
James Joyce
Jamaica Kincaid
Stephen King
Martin Luther King, Jr.
Barbara Kingsolver
Abraham Lincoln
Mario Vargas Llosa
Jack London
James McBride
Cormac McCarthy
Herman Melville
Arthur Miller
Toni Morrison
Alice Munro
Tim O'Brien
Flannery O'Connor
Eugene O'Neill
George Orwell
Sylvia Plath
Philip Roth
Salman Rushdie
Mary Shelley
John Steinbeck
Amy Tan
Leo Tolstoy
Mark Twain
John Updike
Kurt Vonnegut
Alice Walker
David Foster Wallace
Edith Wharton
Walt Whitman
Oscar Wilde
Tennessee Williams
Richard Wright
Malcolm X

Critical Insights: Works

Absalom, Absalom!
Adventures of Huckleberry Finn
Aeneid
All Quiet on the Western Front
Animal Farm
Anna Karenina
The Awakening
The Bell Jar
Beloved
Billy Budd, Sailor
The Book Thief
Brave New World
The Canterbury Tales
Catch-22
The Catcher in the Rye
The Crucible
Death of a Salesman
The Diary of a Young Girl
Dracula
Fahrenheit 451
The Grapes of Wrath
Great Expectations
The Great Gatsby
Hamlet
The Handmaid's Tale
Harry Potter Series
Heart of Darkness
The Hobbit
The House on Mango Street
How the Garcia Girls Lost Their Accents
The Hunger Games Trilogy
I Know Why the Caged Bird Sings
In Cold Blood
The Inferno
Invisible Man
Jane Eyre
The Joy Luck Club
King Lear
The Kite Runner
Life of Pi
Little Women
Lolita
Lord of the Flies
Macbeth
The Metamorphosis
Midnight's Children
A Midsummer Night's Dream
Moby-Dick
Mrs. Dalloway
Nineteen Eighty-Four
The Odyssey
Of Mice and Men
One Flew Over the Cuckoo's Nest
One Hundred Years of Solitude
Othello
The Outsiders
Paradise Lost
The Pearl
The Poetry of Baudelaire
The Poetry of Edgar Allan Poe
A Portrait of the Artist as a Young Man
Pride and Prejudice
The Red Badge of Courage
Romeo and Juliet
The Scarlet Letter
Short Fiction of Flannery O'Connor
Slaughterhouse-Five
The Sound and the Fury
A Streetcar Named Desire
The Sun Also Rises
A Tale of Two Cities
The Tales of Edgar Allan Poe
Their Eyes Were Watching God
Things Fall Apart
To Kill a Mockingbird
War and Peace
The Woman Warrior

Critical Insights: Themes

The American Comic Book
American Creative Non-Fiction
The American Dream
American Multicultural Identity
American Road Literature
American Short Story
American Sports Fiction
The American Thriller
American Writers in Exile
Censored & Banned Literature
Civil Rights Literature, Past & Present
Coming of Age
Conspiracies
Contemporary Canadian Fiction
Contemporary Immigrant Short Fiction
Contemporary Latin American Fiction
Contemporary Speculative Fiction
Crime and Detective Fiction
Crisis of Faith
Cultural Encounters
Dystopia
Family
The Fantastic
Feminism

2021 Title List

SALEM PRESS

Visit www.SalemPress.com for Product Information, Table of Contents, and Sample Pages.

Flash Fiction
Gender, Sex and Sexuality
Good & Evil
The Graphic Novel
Greed
Harlem Renaissance
The Hero's Quest
Historical Fiction
Holocaust Literature
The Immigrant Experience
Inequality
LGBTQ Literature
Literature in Times of Crisis
Literature of Protest
Magical Realism
Midwestern Literature
Modern Japanese Literature
Nature & the Environment
Paranoia, Fear & Alienation
Patriotism
Political Fiction
Postcolonial Literature
Pulp Fiction of the '20s and '30s
Rebellion
Russia's Golden Age
Satire
The Slave Narrative
Social Justice and American Literature
Southern Gothic Literature
Southwestern Literature
Survival
Technology & Humanity
Violence in Literature
Virginia Woolf & 20th Century Women Writers
War

Critical Insights: Film

Bonnie & Clyde
Casablanca
Alfred Hitchcock
Stanley Kubrick

Critical Approaches to Literature

Critical Approaches to Literature: Feminist
Critical Approaches to Literature: Moral
Critical Approaches to Literature: Multicultural
Critical Approaches to Literature: Psychological

Critical Surveys of Literature

Critical Survey of American Literature
Critical Survey of Drama
Critical Survey of Graphic Novels: Heroes & Superheroes
Critical Survey of Graphic Novels: History, Theme, and Technique
Critical Survey of Graphic Novels: Independents and Underground Classics
Critical Survey of Graphic Novels: Manga
Critical Survey of Long Fiction
Critical Survey of Mystery and Detective Fiction
Critical Survey of Mythology & Folklore: Gods & Goddesses
Critical Survey of Mythology & Folklore: Heroes and Heroines
Critical Survey of Mythology & Folklore: Love, Sexuality, and Desire
Critical Survey of Mythology & Folklore: World Mythology
Critical Survey of Poetry
Critical Survey of Poetry: Contemporary Poets
Critical Survey of Science Fiction & Fantasy Literature
Critical Survey of Shakespeare's Plays
Critical Survey of Shakespeare's Sonnets
Critical Survey of Short Fiction
Critical Survey of World Literature
Critical Survey of Young Adult Literature

Cyclopedia of Literary Characters & Places

Cyclopedia of Literary Characters
Cyclopedia of Literary Places

Introduction to Literary Context

American Poetry of the 20th Century
American Post-Modernist Novels
American Short Fiction
English Literature
Plays
World Literature

Magill's Literary Annual

Magill's Literary Annual, 2021
Magill's Literary Annual, 2020
Magill's Literary Annual, 2019

Masterplots

Masterplots, Fourth Edition
Masterplots, 2010-2018 Supplement

Notable Writers

Notable African American Writers
Notable American Women Writers
Notable Mystery & Detective Fiction Writers
Notable Native American Writers & Writers of the American West
Novels into Film: Adaptations & Interpretation
Recommended Reading: 600 Classics Reviewed

2021 Title List

SALEM PRESS

Visit www.SalemPress.com for Product Information, Table of Contents, and Sample Pages.

HISTORY

The Decades

The 1910s in America
The Twenties in America
The Thirties in America
The Forties in America
The Fifties in America
The Sixties in America
The Seventies in America
The Eighties in America
The Nineties in America
The 2000s in America
The 2010s in America

Defining Documents in American History

Defining Documents: The 1900s
Defining Documents: The 1910s
Defining Documents: The 1920s
Defining Documents: The 1930s
Defining Documents: The 1950s
Defining Documents: The 1960s
Defining Documents: The 1970s
Defining Documents: American Citizenship
Defining Documents: The American Economy
Defining Documents: The American Revolution
Defining Documents: The American West
Defining Documents: Business Ethics
Defining Documents: Capital Punishment
Defining Documents: Civil Rights
Defining Documents: Civil War
Defining Documents: The Cold War
Defining Documents: Dissent & Protest
Defining Documents: Drug Policy
Defining Documents: The Emergence of Modern America
Defining Documents: Environment & Conservation
Defining Documents: Espionage & Intrigue
Defining Documents: Exploration and Colonial America
Defining Documents: The Formation of the States
Defining Documents: The Free Press
Defining Documents: The Gun Debate
Defining Documents: Immigration & Immigrant Communities
Defining Documents: The Legacy of 9/11
Defining Documents: LGBTQ+
Defining Documents: Manifest Destiny and the New Nation
Defining Documents: Native Americans
Defining Documents: Political Campaigns, Candidates & Discourse
Defining Documents: Postwar 1940s
Defining Documents: Prison Reform
Defining Documents: Secrets, Leaks & Scandals
Defining Documents: Slavery
Defining Documents: Supreme Court Decisions
Defining Documents: Reconstruction Era
Defining Documents: The Vietnam War
Defining Documents: U.S. Involvement in the Middle East
Defining Documents: World War I
Defining Documents: World War II

Defining Documents in World History

Defining Documents: The 17th Century
Defining Documents: The 18th Century
Defining Documents: The 19th Century
Defining Documents: The 20th Century (1900-1950)
Defining Documents: The Ancient World
Defining Documents: Asia
Defining Documents: Genocide & the Holocaust
Defining Documents: Nationalism & Populism
Defining Documents: Pandemics, Plagues & Public Health
Defining Documents: Renaissance & Early Modern Era
Defining Documents: The Middle Ages
Defining Documents: The Middle East
Defining Documents: Women's Rights

Great Events from History

Great Events from History: The Ancient World
Great Events from History: The Middle Ages
Great Events from History: The Renaissance & Early Modern Era
Great Events from History: The 17th Century
Great Events from History: The 18th Century
Great Events from History: The 19th Century
Great Events from History: The 20th Century, 1901-1940
Great Events from History: The 20th Century, 1941-1970
Great Events from History: The 20th Century, 1971-2000
Great Events from History: Modern Scandals
Great Events from History: African American History
Great Events from History: The 21st Century, 2000-2016
Great Events from History: LGBTQ Events
Great Events from History: Human Rights

Great Lives from History

Computer Technology Innovators
Fashion Innovators
Great Athletes
Great Athletes of the Twenty-First Century
Great Lives from History: African Americans
Great Lives from History: American Heroes
Great Lives from History: American Women
Great Lives from History: Asian and Pacific Islander Americans
Great Lives from History: Inventors & Inventions
Great Lives from History: Jewish Americans
Great Lives from History: Latinos
Great Lives from History: Scientists and Science
Great Lives from History: The 17th Century
Great Lives from History: The 18th Century
Great Lives from History: The 19th Century
Great Lives from History: The 20th Century
Great Lives from History: The 21st Century, 2000-2017
Great Lives from History: The Ancient World
Great Lives from History: The Incredibly Wealthy
Great Lives from History: The Middle Ages
Great Lives from History: The Renaissance & Early Modern Era
Human Rights Innovators
Internet Innovators
Music Innovators
Musicians and Composers of the 20th Century
World Political Innovators

2021 Title List

Visit www.SalemPress.com for Product Information, Table of Contents, and Sample Pages.

History & Government

American First Ladies
American Presidents
The 50 States
The Ancient World: Extraordinary People in Extraordinary Societies
The Bill of Rights
The Criminal Justice System
The U.S. Supreme Court

SOCIAL SCIENCES

Civil Rights Movements: Past & Present
Countries, Peoples and Cultures
Countries: Their Wars & Conflicts: A World Survey
Education Today: Issues, Policies & Practices
Encyclopedia of American Immigration
Ethics: Questions & Morality of Human Actions
Issues in U.S. Immigration
Principles of Sociology: Group Relationships & Behavior
Principles of Sociology: Personal Relationships & Behavior
Principles of Sociology: Societal Issues & Behavior
Racial & Ethnic Relations in America
World Geography

SCIENCE

Ancient Creatures
Applied Science
Applied Science: Engineering & Mathematics
Applied Science: Science & Medicine
Applied Science: Technology
Biomes and Ecosystems
Earth Science: Earth Materials and Resources
Earth Science: Earth's Surface and History
Earth Science: Earth's Weather, Water and Atmosphere
Earth Science: Physics and Chemistry of the Earth
Encyclopedia of Climate Change
Encyclopedia of Energy
Encyclopedia of Environmental Issues
Encyclopedia of Global Resources
Encyclopedia of Mathematics and Society
Forensic Science
Notable Natural Disasters
The Solar System
USA in Space

Principles of Science

Principles of Anatomy
Principles of Astronomy
Principles of Behavioral Science
Principles of Biology
Principles of Biotechnology
Principles of Botany
Principles of Chemistry
Principles of Climatology
Principles of Information Technology
Principles of Computer Science
Principles of Ecology
Principles of Energy
Principles of Geology
Principles of Marine Science
Principles of Mathematics
Principles of Modern Agriculture
Principles of Pharmacology
Principles of Physical Science
Principles of Physics
Principles of Programming & Coding
Principles of Robotics & Artificial Intelligence
Principles of Scientific Research
Principles of Sustainability
Principles of Zoology

HEALTH

Addictions, Substance Abuse & Alcoholism
Adolescent Health & Wellness
Aging
Cancer
Community & Family Health Issues
Integrative, Alternative & Complementary Medicine
Genetics and Inherited Conditions
Infectious Diseases and Conditions
Magill's Medical Guide
Nutrition
Psychology & Behavioral Health
Women's Health

Principles of Health

Principles of Health: Allergies & Immune Disorders
Principles of Health: Anxiety & Stress
Principles of Health: Depression
Principles of Health: Diabetes
Principles of Health: Nursing
Principles of Health: Obesity
Principles of Health: Pain Management
Principles of Health: Prescription Drug Abuse

2021 Title List

Visit www.SalemPress.com for Product Information, Table of Contents, and Sample Pages.

CAREERS

Careers: Paths to Entrepreneurship
Careers in the Arts: Fine, Performing & Visual
Careers in Building Construction
Careers in Business
Careers in Chemistry
Careers in Communications & Media
Careers in Education & Training
Careers in Environment & Conservation
Careers in Financial Services
Careers in Forensic Science
Careers in Gaming
Careers in Green Energy
Careers in Healthcare
Careers in Hospitality & Tourism
Careers in Human Services
Careers in Information Technology
Careers in Law, Criminal Justice & Emergency Services
Careers in the Music Industry
Careers in Manufacturing & Production
Careers in Nursing
Careers in Physics
Careers in Protective Services
Careers in Psychology & Behavioral Health
Careers in Public Administration
Careers in Sales, Insurance & Real Estate
Careers in Science & Engineering
Careers in Social Media
Careers in Sports & Fitness
Careers in Sports Medicine & Training
Careers in Technical Services & Equipment Repair
Careers in Transportation
Careers in Writing & Editing
Careers Outdoors
Careers Overseas
Careers Working with Infants & Children
Careers Working with Animals

BUSINESS

Principles of Business: Accounting
Principles of Business: Economics
Principles of Business: Entrepreneurship
Principles of Business: Finance
Principles of Business: Globalization
Principles of Business: Leadership
Principles of Business: Management
Principles of Business: Marketing

Grey House Publishing | Salem Press | H.W. Wilson | 4919 Route, 22 PO Box 56, Amenia NY 12501-0056

2021 Title List

Visit www.HWWilsonInPrint.com for Product Information, Table of Contents, and Sample Pages.

The Reference Shelf

Affordable Housing
Aging in America
Alternative Facts, Post-Truth and the Information War
The American Dream
American Military Presence Overseas
Arab Spring
Artificial Intelligence
The Business of Food
Campaign Trends & Election Law
College Sports
Conspiracy Theories
Democracy Evolving
The Digital Age
Dinosaurs
Embracing New Paradigms in Education
Faith & Science
Families - Traditional & New Structures
Food Insecurity & Hunger in the United States
Future of U.S. Economic Relations: Mexico, Cuba, & Venezuela
Global Climate Change
Graphic Novels and Comic Books
Guns in America
Hate Crimes
Immigration
Internet Abuses & Privacy Rights
Internet Law
LGBTQ in the 21st Century
Marijuana Reform
National Debate Topic 2014/2015: The Ocean
National Debate Topic 2015/2016: Surveillance
National Debate Topic 2016/2017: US/China Relations
National Debate Topic 2017/2018: Education Reform
National Debate Topic 2018/2019: Immigration
National Debate Topic 2019/2021: Arms Sales
National Debate Topic 2020/2021: Criminal Justice Reform
National Debate Topic 2021/2022
New Frontiers in Space
The News and its Future
Policing in 2020
Politics of the Oceans
Pollution
Prescription Drug Abuse
Propaganda and Misinformation
Racial Tension in a Postracial Age
Reality Television
Representative American Speeches, Annual Edition
Rethinking Work
Revisiting Gender
Robotics
Russia
Social Networking
The South China Sea Conflict
Space Exploration and Development
Sports in America
The Supreme Court
The Transformation of American Cities
The Two Koreas
U.S. Infrastructure
Vaccinations
Whistleblowers

Core Collections

Children's Core Collection
Fiction Core Collection
Graphic Novels Core Collection
Middle & Junior High School Core
Public Library Core Collection: Nonfiction
Senior High Core Collection
Young Adult Fiction Core Collection

Current Biography

Current Biography Cumulative Index 1946-2021
Current Biography Monthly Magazine
Current Biography Yearbook

Readers' Guide to Periodical Literature

Abridged Readers' Guide to Periodical Literature
Readers' Guide to Periodical Literature

Indexes

Index to Legal Periodicals & Books
Short Story Index
Book Review Digest

Sears List

Sears List of Subject Headings
Sears: Lista de Encabezamientos de Materia

History

American Game Changers: Invention, Innovation & Transformation
American Reformers
Speeches of the American Presidents

Facts About Series

Facts About the 20th Century
Facts About American Immigration
Facts About China
Facts About the Presidents
Facts About the World's Languages

Nobel Prize Winners

Nobel Prize Winners: 1901-1986
Nobel Prize Winners: 1987-1991
Nobel Prize Winners: 1992-1996
Nobel Prize Winners: 1997-2001
Nobel Prize Winners: 2002-2018

Famous First Facts

Famous First Facts
Famous First Facts About American Politics
Famous First Facts About Sports
Famous First Facts About the Environment
Famous First Facts: International Edition

American Book of Days

The American Book of Days
The International Book of Days